PELICAN BIOGRAPHIES

BAUDELAIRE

Enid Mary Starkie, who died in 1970, was Reader Emeritus in French Literature at the University of Oxford and Honorary Fellow of Somerville College, Oxford. She was educated and held scholarships at Alexandra College, Dublin, the Royal Irish Academy of Music, and Somerville College, Oxford, and also attended the Sorbonne in Paris. A leading English authority on French literature, she held many university appointments at Oxford and in America. A Doctor of the University of Paris, she was also an officer of the Légion d'Honneur, and in 1967 she received the C.B.E. Among her many publications the best known are her studies of the lives and works of writers such as Baudelaire, Rimbaud, Gide, Gautier, Eliot and Flaubert.

ENID STARKIE

Baudelaire

PENGUIN BOOKS

Penguin Books Ltd, Harmondsworth, Middlesex, England
Penguin Books Inc., 7110 Ambassador Road, Baltimore, Maryland 21207, U.S.A.
Penguin Books Australia Ltd, Ringwood, Victoria, Australia

—

First published by Faber & Faber 1957
Published in Pelican Books 1971

—

—

Made and printed in Great Britain
by Hazell Watson & Viney Ltd
Aylesbury, Bucks
Set in Linotype Georgian

Contents

INTRODUCTION

Mais si, sans se laisser charmer,
Ton œil sait plonger dans les gouffres,
Lis moi pour apprendre à m'aimer.

Introduction

A CENTURY has elapsed since *Les Fleurs du Mal* of Baudelaire was published. It was followed by the trial for obscenity, and the book was banned until certain poems – the 'pièces condamnées' – were deleted from the collection.

This trial in 1857 was the culmination of much abuse and slander which arose after the poet had begun to become well known. His writings had been described variously as putrid and scrofulous, poetry of the slaughter- and charnel-house. As a result the public was for long, not only unconscious of what Baudelaire stood for as a writer, but firmly rooted as well in prejudices much harder to eradicate than mere ignorance. When his name was mentioned, those who were not completely unaware of his existence, used to smile knowingly, conjuring up visions of Satanism, Black Masses, orgiastic revelry, and the unnatural practices of a decadent civilization. That was the Baudelaire whom legend fashioned in the fifties of the last century, who was handed down from father to son, and who persists, in many quarters, even today.

A hundred years ago, when Baudelaire's one collection of poems appeared for the first time, the main critics declared that his reputation would be shattered for he had dared, at last, to face his critics openly, and henceforth would be only one of the dead sea fruits of modern literature. Yet today, after a hundred years, he is probably the poet most widely read all over the world, though often on grounds having no bearing on literature. The reason is not hard to find as he is able to speak directly to modern man, conditioned by revolutions and upheavals. His mood harmonizes with our own, when the problems which confront us are those which preoccupied him, and many of the values which we are questioning are those he had long ago discarded.

In this hundred years Baudelaire's reputation has varied greatly. When he first reached fame, in the eighteen-eighties, France, after her defeat in the Franco-Prussian War, had turned to revulsion against all aspects of the Second Empire, and writers were seeking something new to replace the outworn fashion of *Le Parnasse*. Then they discovered the poet who had been so much misunderstood and abused during the previous period, and drew inspiration from his writings. They seized on his poem *Correspondances*, making of it the manifesto of the new movement, while his conception of '*Le symbole*' gave its name to their new school of poetry, *Le Symbolisme*. They admired in him chiefly the sensuous poet of rare sensations, who had wished, in his poetry, to emulate the evocative power of music, and, thinking they were following him, they tried to take over – often disastrously – the technical means of expression of music. But they appreciated most of all the poems of decay and horror, of the early years. They saw him chiefly as an aesthete and a dandy, a decadent, a man who blasphemed against accepted religion and morality, who smoked opium and hashish, who was alleged to dabble in Satanism, to attend Black Masses, and to practise all manner of vice and corruption. Des Esseintes, the hero of Huysmans' novel, *À Rebours*, was typical of the Baudelairian character of the day, and he was copied by many writers and men of fashion. In the 'eighties and 'nineties Baudelaire's influence came to be identified with everything morbid, decadent and immoral, although this entailed the neglect of many aspects of his work.

During the early years of the twentieth century his influence waned. Literary taste tended then towards internationalism, towards mass movements and the brotherhood of man, towards boundless energy and naïve effort. The First World War showed up these illusions, and, with the coming of peace, when Baudelaire's copyright expired and new editions of his works multiplied, he enjoyed a new vogue. It was the poet of sensual pleasures who was then extolled, the poet who was disillusioned with everything, and who was often cynical – whether this was true or not did not matter. He seemed then the poet who could best speak for modern man, the product of revolutions – political, social and industrial – and no other poet of the nineteenth century seemed to have been aware of these problems in so sensitive a manner. Later, as the years of peace progressed and changed, when the aridity of the search for happiness became apparent, many found in him an echo of their disgusts and disappointments. As dictatorships arose and individual human values were threatened, they found comfort in his revolt against the denial of the supreme importance of each individual human soul, against its enslavement to machine or state. The spiritual aspect of his work, hitherto unnoticed, began to be appreciated among those who saw that he was seeking what they too were anxious to find, a remedy for their despair and disillusionment.

Over twenty years ago I published a book on Baudelaire, in which I tried to demonstrate the spiritual nature of his personality, his inspiration and his writings. This was severely attacked in some quarters – indeed scoffed at – and I was accused of special pleading. I was young and inexperienced then, and that book, my first, was written from deep love of the poet and his works, but also from great ignorance. It has been out of print for many years, but I have not allowed it to be republished until I rewrote it. I do not now repent what I said when I was young, or repudiate it – indeed I believe even more passionately what I thought then, but I hope with sounder evidence and more authority.

During the past ten years I have noticed with much interest that many of the eminent Baudelaire scholars have come to share my views; the most notable being Marcel Ruff who, in his recent book, *L'Esprit du Mal et l'Esthétique Baudelairienne*, has produced the best work on the poet. His thesis is that, in his life and works, Baudelaire was an austere moralist preoccupied chiefly with the problem of sin and temptation. This is certainly true of him after he reached maturity. Baudelaire did not say that what he discovered, as he investigated the nature of human personality, was good, but only that it was necessary to analyse it, in order to understand the problem.

Baudelaire always claimed that there was an architecture, a plan, in his *Fleurs du Mal*, that it was not a haphazard collection, and that it was based on the Catholic theory of the sinfulness of man left to himself, without grace, and of his despairing efforts to reach a higher plane. It is the depiction of the struggle between man's aspiration towards goodness and his proclivity towards vice. Every man is made up of two beings, linked together, like Siamese twins, the highest and the lowest, side by side, the good gaining some intenser quality from the bad, from this proximity and interdependence. Acceptance of this, as Baudelaire accepted it, is not sophistry, as one critic has claimed. This plan existed already in the first edition of *Les Fleurs du Mal* published in 1857, but it was deepened in the second published in 1861.

Baudelaire did not, however, reach this point suddenly or immediately, and it is therefore important to realize the stages through which he passed. When he published the first edition he was thirty-six, and he had been writing poetry for fifteen years at least, much of which he incorporated in the collection. The question of the chronology of the poems is thus important, but difficult to establish. He himself is of little help, since he was interested chiefly in setting forth his conception of man's destiny.

In my first book I tried to establish some chronological order in the poems, and I have not abandoned or altered my theory. I do not intend to suggest that all the poems can be fitted into watertight compartments, for there is bound to be overlapping, and an occasional return to an earlier and successful inspiration. But such cases are not frequent enough to confuse, to any appreciable extent, the stages in his literary progression. The development of his genius becomes thus more comprehensible than if *Les Fleurs du Mal* is considered as a whole which sprang into existence in 1857, as the result of a single inspiration.

The difficulties in this chronological assessment occur chiefly in connection with the first edition since, in the second, with a few well-known exceptions, the new poems were those which were composed between 1857 and 1861. The same is true for the new poems in the third edition – at least for the last group which he himself published, in the final year of his creative life, under the title *Nouvelles Fleurs du Mal*, in the periodical *Le Parnasse Contemporain*, in 1866.

By the time he published the first edition of *Les Fleurs du Mal* in 1857, Baudelaire had reached maturity and he did not thereafter change in essentials.

Baudelaire's career as a poet seems to me to fall into four distinct periods, with a very marked change at the beginning of the third when, in 1852, under the influence of Poe and Swedenborg, he was completely altered, and evolved a new conception of aesthetics and life, which inspired him to take a new direction in his poetry.

The first period runs from his majority, when he began to consider seriously his future as a poet, to his twenty-fifth year, when his material circumstances were fundamentally altered. This was a period of apprenticeship, his experimental stage, when he was trying his hand at many things. It was a period of deliberate and conscious originality, when he set out to shock his contemporaries. Here are to be found the Lesbian poems, the Satanic poems, the poems of revolt and decay, and finally the great erotic poems.

The second period runs from the time when control of his financial affairs was taken from him, when his *conseil judiciaire* was appointed, when he was in money difficulties, and began to understand the harshness of life. Here occur the *spleen* poems, the first poems of depression, the first poems to show compassion for failures, and awareness of the beauty of city life. There is pessimism here, but it is that of youth and not as deep as that of his last years. This

was also the only period of his life when he was actively
connected with politics and social reform. It continues until
the *coup d'état* of 1851, when Louis Napoleon made himself
Emperor, when most writers turned away, in disgust, from
interest in political matters.

With the third period, after 1851, we reach the mature
Baudelaire, the highest point of his career as a poet. Here
spiritual preoccupation replaced interest in politics, when,
under the influence of Swedenborg, he formulated his
aesthetic doctrine, and composed his great spiritual poems
such as *Bénédiction*, *Les Phares* and *Correspondances*. It
was then too that he composed his spiritual love poems
which are in great contrast with the sensual love poems of
the first period. This was the moment of his greatest subtlety
in prosody. In this period also he wrote his greatest literary
and artistic criticism. It was a time of belief in himself, and
of confidence in the future.

The fourth, and last period, runs from his trial for obscenity in 1857 to his departure for Belgium in the spring
of 1864, which was the end of his career as a writer. This
was a time of deep dejection and depression, when he looked
back into the pit of the misspent years, and saw so few
ahead in which to redeem them. Then he composed the
poems which express horror of time fleeing past recall, the
poems describing failures. It is a far more bitter pessimism
than that of his youth. Towards the end, however, there is,
as compensation, the belief in something higher than mere
worldly success, a quest for moral victory, and the aim of
becoming a hero and a saint. Then he sang of 'la fertilisante
douleur', and expressed longing for death, peace and rest.
It is possible to believe that, after the publication of the
second *Fleurs du Mal*, he finally found a haven he had never
expected to find, and came to believe, what he had never
believed in before, the possibility of redemption, and the
forgiveness of sins, in the power of God's mercy and grace.
That is, I think, the meaning of his last poem *L'Imprévu*,
composed in 1863. If he had lived long enough to supervise

the third edition of *Les Fleurs du Mal*, which he was preparing when his final illness struck him down, he might, in the light of his final development, have altered the architecture of the work, and made it point a different moral.

After Baudelaire's death his friends and literary executors produced this third edition in 1868. They claimed that there existed a volume, partially, if not wholly, prepared for the press by himself. This volume cannot have existed with its plan complete; or, if it did, the editors did not follow it, for their aim seems to have been to include every line of his poetry which they could find, poems which had appeared in reviews, some of which he might himself have included in the 1861 edition if he had wished them to form part of it. They also added the largest part of *Les Épaves*, published in Belgium, which included the banned poems, although he had frequently declared that he did not intend to use any part of it for any future edition of *Les Fleurs du Mal*. There were early poems as well which they rescued. All these poems were forced into the plan of the 1861 edition, and put, higgledy-piggledy, into the section entitled *Spleen et Idéal*. With these additions the third edition does not make a homogeneous whole, and it is not the version which Baudelaire himself would have produced.

Since Baudelaire's own third edition does not exist it is difficult to produce the perfect complete edition. If the 1857 version is chosen, it contains the banned poems, but none of the great poems composed after 1857. If the 1861 version is taken, it does not include the banned poems, nor the *Nouvelles Fleurs du Mal* written after 1861.

Most editors have favoured the posthumous edition because it contains the largest number of poems, but it lacks the banned poems which are no longer banned, and it is based on a misunderstanding of the poet's intentions, or indifference to them and to the architecture of the work as a whole. Others have chosen the 1861 edition, printing the banned poems in a separate section, and chronologically, in a further section, the rest of the poems. But the banned poems by themselves lose their significance, for the emphasis is altered. One editor, while choosing the 1861 version, has placed the banned poems in the position which they occupied in the first edition, but in so doing has altered the structure of the second version. Another takes, as a basis, the 1857 edition, placing, in a further section, the thirty-five new poems of the second edition, and, in a further section still, the remaining poems. This possesses the disadvantage of giving the reader only the first edition in its entirety – not the one with which the poet was himself most pleased.

It is regrettable that we do not know what the third version of *Les Fleurs du Mal* would have been if Baudelaire had lived. It would probably have been as different from the second as this is from the first – but he too would have been hampered by the impossibility of publishing the banned poems in France – and it would probably have been finer than either.

The search for contributions which Baudelaire announced but of which the ultimate fate is unknown continues, but periodicals have now been so carefully sifted that it is becoming increasingly difficult to discover anything new. One of these, hitherto unmentioned by any other biographer or critic of Baudelaire, or by the poet himself in any list of projected works, is *Les Derniers Buveurs*, advertised in *La Presse* in December 1849 to be published shortly by *La Veillée Pittoresque*, a periodical due to appear for the first time at the end of December 1849. After much fruitless research I discovered that the paper did not come out until January 1850, and that it had only one number which does not include any contribution from Baudelaire.

In October 1852 *La Presse* advertised that the daily paper *Paris* was planning to publish shortly a set of unknown lithographs by Gavarni with the letterpress describing them by various authors, including Baudelaire. A search through the numbers of the paper for that year revealed nothing by him.

However I put forward a tentative claim for his authorship

of two articles in *Le Représentant de l'Indre* in February
1850, and one in *Le Socialiste de la Côte d'Or* in July 1850.
I do not mean to suggest that they can be claimed with any
certainty as definitely by him, but only that his authorship
would not be without verisimilitude, that it possesses as much
as that of the various contributions attributed to him by
other recent critics, on no sounder grounds. All the
ephemeral journalism of an author does not bear unmis-
takably his hall-mark – many articles unquestionably by
Baudelaire might just as easily have been written by
anyone else – and my arguments are not based solely
on considerations of style. None of these articles would
add anything to our knowledge of Baudelaire – except
biographically.

There exists a virtually unknown text by Baudelaire which
has not been mentioned or used by any other critic but
myself and which does not figure in any bibliography save
that of the edition of *La Nouvelle Revue Française* of 1933
– the only edition of the complete works to have collected it.
This is the document published in 1927, in a limited edition, by the *Éditions de la Grenade* under the title *Les
Années de Bruxelles* – the title is not by Baudelaire but
was given to it by its first editor, Georges Garonne. It consists of rough notes on loose sheets without page numbers,
containing reflections like those in *Les Journaux Intimes*,
interspersed with addresses in Belgium which might be useful, and has an unknown drawing by Baudelaire of an
elderly man with a beard, as a frontispiece – this has not
been reproduced in the edition of *La Nouvelle Revue
Française*. It is alleged to have come originally from a Belgian bookseller called Jean-Pierre Blanche, who knew Baudelaire when he was in Brussels, but at the moment of its
publication it belonged to a certain M. E. du Perron. I do
not know its present whereabouts and, as far as I know,
critics and commentators of Baudelaire are unaware of its
existence, since it is never mentioned – except by its first
editor, and in the edition of *La Nouvelle Revue Française*.

Its interest lies in the fact that it belongs to a period which possesses few texts by Baudelaire – his last years.

It is also difficult nowadays to find any new biographical material, but I discovered that, as late as 1846, for some unknown reason, Baudelaire signed on as a student at the École des Chartes although he does not seem to have proceeded with his studies. An empty folder, bearing his name and qualifications, exists in the archives of the school, and his name appears on a printed list of students for 1846.

It is frequently claimed that knowledge of a poet's life and understanding of his personality are no help in appreciating his writings, and these should be enjoyed for themselves alone. This, however, seems to me to be based on a misapprehension of the function and significance of biography. True, the intrinsic value of a work of art depends, from the artistic point of view, on itself alone, but those who enjoy it, responding to it sympathetically, will always be interested to discover all they can about the nature of the man who could produce it, and wish to come into contact deeply with his personality. Biography, rightly conceived and carried out, can be of help in this.

The biographer must realize that his subject, if he is an artist, is first and foremost an individual, the single example, after which the mould is broken; who will therefore be more interesting and significant to study where he is himself alone, and not where he can be used as a sample of a category or type. Poets have too often been used, as Baudelaire has been used, to illustrate a theory; or else as a specimen for the case-book of the pathologist or the psychoanalyst.

The study of an artist should then be a biography, not of his outward life alone, but essentially of his inner personality. It should also recognize that he will be most personally and individually alive in his creative work, and that he will often have only the husk of his personality left for mere living.

If an artist and his work have been successfully interpreted, it will become apparent how the work arises from his personality, and how his personality secreted it; how the soil produced the plant, and how that plant could have come only from that particular soil. Each explains the other. If this does not happen then there must have been some failure in interpretation. A work of art, even that of the most objective artist, must arise from something, from some seed, and have its roots in some soil. It cannot be a veneer which could be fixed indiscriminately to any under-wood. Artistic production is more like a skin which cannot be grafted on anyone else, for it must be of the same substance as that on which it grows.

Biography is an important literary art, in which interpretative and divining powers are most essential. Nothing can be invented, but the portrait must be built up from an infinite number of tiny particles, and the misplacing of one of these, the misdrawing of a single line, can falsify the whole picture. The brush must never falter or slip.

Biography partakes somewhat of the art of the novelist, and many a biographer has been a *novelist manqué* – but with a difference. The novelist deals not with actual truth but with verisimilitude, and he can never go beyond the probabilities of life. It is a truism that 'truth is stranger than fiction', and this 'strange truth' is not the domain of the novelist, although he must make verisimilitude seem 'strange' and 'true'. The biographer, on the other hand, has as his material the 'strangest' of 'truth', the personality and conduct of a unique artist, and he must interpret them so as to give them verisimilitude. A novelist *invents* his characters and situations so as to exemplify his personal philosophy of life and his conception of human nature. The biographer must invent nothing and he has as sole guide his intuition of the personality which he is trying to depict. He must therefore *find* in facts the evidence and raw materials which he needs for his portrait. If his intuition is correct, then the evidence to prove it must exist somewhere, even if it evades him. If the character is truly depicted then the circumstances which bring him to life must also be true. People do not act out of character, but only *seem* to do so when the interpretation is incomplete or faulty. Even the most complex personality is capable of interpretation. It is only a question of finding the solution, and the significant facts to develop this, and to give it concrete shape.

This biography of Baudelaire, blended with a study of his work, is a personal attempt to give 'verisimilitude' and centripetal form to the 'strange truth' of his character and life. It was undertaken also in the hope that perhaps, as a result, it might lead recalcitrant readers into deeper intimacy with the personality of a rare and noble being, into fuller understanding of him, and appreciation of the writings of a sublime poet. I have also tried to give a panorama of the world in which he moved and had his being.

Finally I would like to thank Mr W. T. Bandy for valuable help and advice in connection with Baudelaire and Poe, and for drawing my attention to the unsigned Obituary of Baudelaire, published in *La Chronique de Paris*, 15 September 1867, which was obviously written by a fellow-traveller on his trip to the East; Miss Joanna Richardson for indefatigable assistance in verifying material, especially in foreign periodicals difficult of access; and Mr Dan Davin for patient and sympathetic guidance in craftsmanship.

PART ONE

Ma jeunesse ne fut qu'un ténébreux orage,
Traversé çà et là par de brillants soleils;
Le tonnerre et la pluie ont fait un tel ravage
Qu'il reste en mon jardin bien peu de fruits vermeils.

[1]

The Early Years
1821 — 1839

THE accounts of Baudelaire's early life are singularly lacking in intimate details. It was not yet fashionable, in the
eighteen-thirties, to rhapsodize over babyhood and the first
glimmerings of human intelligence, so it happened that his
mother did not consider it of sufficient interest to tell her
son's biographers intimate details of his childhood. Yet she
knew, from his letters, what these early years had meant to
him, the one really happy period of his life, 'l'époque des
tendresses maternelles', as he called it. It was just that it
never occurred to her that anyone but herself would consider that phase of his development important.

Charles Baudelaire did not come as an unwanted child to
indifferent and unsympathetic parents. He was, on the contrary, a very precious treasure, his mother's one joy and
passion during the first seven years of his life. It was as if
Fate, in a moment of malicious levity, had played a trick on
him, allowing him at first to feel an important and indispensable being, and then had suddenly bereft him of this
security.

His mother was an ardent and passionate woman, with an
innate love of grandeur and luxury, which tended later to
become an obsession because her early life had been stunted
and starved of even the merest comforts. She, who longed
for security and a settled home life, was never destined to
enjoy them in full measure. She was born in exile, in England, in 1793 and died during the Commune in Paris, in
1871, scarcely richer than in her childhood. She kept, however, to the end of her life a love of finery, and always dressed
in elegant clothes, with beautiful lace and jewels. Her con-

temporaries have frequently described the charm of her manner and appearance, for nature had endowed her with the necessary gifts to grace the highest social positions. In his will, her second husband paid tribute to the sympathy and grace with which she fulfilled her duties as the wife of an ambassador and senator.

Caroline Dufays was the daughter of an officer in the army of Louis XVI who during the Revolution emigrated to England, where she was born in 1793 at Saint Pancras in London. She was left orphaned of both parents at an early age and was then brought up by an old friend of her father, a lawyer called Pierre Pérignon. He was a member of the rich middle class which had arisen under the First Empire, and he possessed a large house in Paris and a country mansion as well. He had sufficient room and means to provide for one more dependant, and so he took his old friend's orphan child to bring up with his own daughters.

In her guardian's house, Caroline Dufays formed habits of luxury which were to last the rest of her life. She was, however, in a dependent position, supported by his charity, and she suffered greatly as she contrasted the fate of his daughters with her own – the fine clothes they could buy without counting the cost, the attention they received from good-looking and elegant young men on account of their large *dot*, whereas she had nothing but her pretty face and her native charm. As a result of the fortunes which had vanished during the Revolution and the Napoleonic Wars, young Frenchmen did not think any more then than now of burdening themselves with a penniless girl, and they considered that marriage should help, and not hinder, them in the desperate struggle for existence. So no one had thought of asking for the hand of Caroline Dufays, and she had 'coiffé Sainte Cathérine' – that is to say, had passed her twenty-fifth birthday without having been sought in marriage – and soon she would no longer be able to hope for any suitor, however homely or humble. She could certainly not expect to find love and marriage at the same time, and would have to fly less high, being content with what she could find.

An elderly widower, François Baudelaire, a schoolmate of her guardian, was a frequent visitor at the house. He had been born in 1759 and now, in the early years of the Restoration, was a picturesque relic of the past, with his snow-white hair and his courtly old-world manners. Under Louis XVI he had been tutor to a noble family and was nearing middle age when the Revolution broke out.

Before Marcel Ruff's masterly doctoral thesis[1] very little was known about the early life of François Baudelaire, but he brought to light many significant details which do much to explain his son's spiritual development. He was brought up in the Jansenist tradition, pessimistic and austere, and very different from the Rousseau doctrine, based on belief in the natural goodness of man, which was current in educational practice at the end of the eighteenth century. He was trained for the priesthood and was eventually ordained. Thus, when Baudelaire used to claim to be the son of a priest, he was not, as hitherto believed, merely trying to shock. He taught at the Collège Sainte-Barbe, which had a Jansenist tradition, from 1783 to 1785, and the headmaster recommended him, while he was waiting to be ordained, to the Duc de Choiseul Praslin, who was a freemason, as tutor for his young sons. François Baudelaire was not without artistic gifts, for he possessed some talent for painting, and, like his son, won prizes for Latin verse at the Concours Général while at school.[2]

The Duc de Choiseul Praslin lived in a beautiful house in Paris – almost a palace – in the Rue de Bourbon – now Rue de Lille – across the Seine from the Tuileries Gardens. He had a fine collection of pictures by famous masters, and François Baudelaire used to copy them in his spare time.

At the end of the garden, near the river, was a little summerhouse which the Duke had filled with fine furniture and works of art, and there he installed the tutor and his pupils, allowing him to live his own life as if he were a man of

independent means, for he had his own carriage, his servants, and was richly provided for. He was granted, moreover, nearly two hundred pounds a year as pocket money,
which, in those days, was a good income. In that little house
he lived like a 'grand seigneur', giving his own dinner parties, which were frequently honoured by the presence of the
Duke and Duchess. Caroline Dufays was later to insist on
this lest it should be imagined that her husband had been in
a menial capacity in the household of the Duc de Choiseul
Praslin.[3] In these surroundings he, too, developed a taste
for grandeur and luxury which he handed on with interest
to his famous son. Nevertheless, whilst enjoying this life of
ease, he did not develop the vices of a parasite, as did many
others at the time in a similar position. He kept his independence of mind and did not consider that his political
opinions were bought along with his services. He had liberal
views and would have welcomed a moderate form of revolution, for he was an intelligent and cultivated man, the close
friend of Helvétius and Condorcet.

In the household of the Duc de Choiseul Praslin, François
Baudelaire lived the life of a fashionable priest in the
eighteenth century. He was offered a curacy in 1791 but he
refused it as he wished to remain with his pupils. The Revolution had broken out by then which changed many things,
for the old forms of the past were abandoned and many
priests gave up their vocations to marry. Later, when the
Church regained its power, they were allowed to regularize
their situation and remain in the world. It was thus that
François Baudelaire was not suspected afterwards of ever
having been a priest.

When the Revolution took a more serious turn, François
Baudelaire did not regret the past, although he had lost his
livelihood, but he hated violence in every form and took no
active part in events, living quietly on his savings to supplement what he could earn by giving drawing lessons. He
remained loyal to his former master and old pupils, and
used his influence with the party in power to spare them the

supreme hardships. He went to visit them in prison, and it
is alleged that he saved them from the guillotine in 1793.
When they were released, he paid for the education of his
younger pupil, out of his meagre earnings, and enabled him
to enter the École Polytechnique. The elder son, when he
became Duke, rallied to Napoleon whom he served as Court
Chamberlain and later as Senator. He was the father of the
Duc de Choiseul Praslin, who was convicted of brutally
murdering his wife and condemned to death, but he committed suicide in prison. Later, when writing of her son's
antecedents to his first biographer, his mother makes a
special point of this, so that it should not be believed that a
pupil of her husband could possibly have been connected
with a savage crime.

When the luck of the Duc de Choiseul Praslin turned, he
did not forget his former tutor who had helped the family
in their adversity, and he managed to secure a post for him
at the Senate, the duties of which were not clearly defined.
All that seems to have been expected was that he should
keep up a certain position, and live in a charming house at
the corner of the Luxembourg Gardens. These were the
days when Napoleon wished to dazzle the general public by
the magnificence of his civil servants. François Baudelaire
was allowed a carriage and pair, a footman and two secretaries. He remained at the Senate for fourteen years, until
the end of the Empire. His widow used later to describe
the elegant carriage, emblazoned with the imperial arms,
which she remembered, when he came to visit her guardian.

In 1797 his established position permitted him to marry.[4]
He chose a woman some years older than himself, Jeanne
Justine Rosalie Janin, who is usually claimed to have been
a woman of means. Marcel Ruff, however, proves that she
brought him only little more than one hundred pounds, and
that the land at Neuilly, which was hitherto alleged to be
part of her marriage portion, was in reality bought during
her married life, with her savings. She too had a taste for

painting and met her husband at a studio. A son, Alphonse, was born in 1805.

The uncertain nature of the political opinions of the Duc de Choiseul Praslin and his family finally ended François Baudelaire's career at the Senate. In 1814, when Louis XVIII returned to France, the Duke and his family went over, with seeming readiness, to his cause, returning however, with equal eagerness, to Napoleon during the Hundred Days. It was no wonder that Louis XVIII, when he finally and firmly became King, did not appreciate the loyalty of the Choiseul Praslin family and that he erased their names from his list of peers. François Baudelaire, whose fortunes had been linked with theirs for many years, was compulsorily retired, but since he was granted a substantial pension he did not greatly regret his position at the Senate. His wife had died the previous year, leaving him a comfortable capital, so that he did not need to look for further employment. He decided then to devote himself in peace and leisure to his passion for painting, and to the education of his young son. Soon however his solitude began to weigh heavily on him, and he needed, moreover, someone to look after his child, so he began to look round amongst his acquaintances for a suitable wife. His choice fell on the ward of his old friend, Caroline Dufays. She was well born, charming and pretty, she seemed to possess a good temper, she was elegant, ambitious, and best of all, with her lack of *dot*, she could not hope for a younger man. She, on her side, had been contemplating her future with increasing gloom, and, since there was no one more attractive or eligible on the horizon, she accepted him. They were married in September 1819 when he was fifty-nine and she twenty-six.

The couple settled in a comfortable apartment in a house in the Rue Hautefeuille, not very far from where he had lived with his first wife – the house was subsequently pulled down to make way for the Boulevard Saint Germain. The rooms were furnished with pieces he had managed to salvage from his days of splendour under Louis XVI – gilded tables and chairs, china and pictures. The catalogue of the sale after his death mentions pictures painted by himself and his first wife – there were seventeen in the drawing-room alone. Biographers have claimed that these were copies of what are usually called the 'galants petits maîtres' of the eighteenth century. However, Marcel Ruff has established[5] that this was not the case, that they were mostly large allegorical compositions, some of them nudes, and that there were some biblical subjects and bacchantes painted by his wife. He had a large library, comprising French classical authors – a complete Voltaire and the Encyclopaedia – also ten volumes of the occult philosopher and physiognomist, Lavater, whom Baudelaire was later to read with such interest. The *Antiquités d'Herculaneum* had the place of honour, for the copy had been inscribed to him by the Duchesse de Choiseul Praslin, from his devoted pupils. A sculptured hermaphrodite was said to stand in the centre of the drawing-room mantelpiece. In that apartment François Baudelaire's second son, Charles, was born on 9 April 1821.

Caroline, who hitherto had felt only the arid emotion of ambition, or the bitter emotion of envy, now felt passionate love for the first time, passionate and jealous first love, and this love, which should have gone to a man of her own age – husband or lover – she lavished on her baby son, being jealous of everyone who drew near him – even of his nurse-maid Mariette: 'la servante au grand cœur dont vous étiez jalouse' wrote Baudelaire later.[6] It is possible that she played, perhaps unconsciously, on the emotions of her little boy, expecting from him a precocity of feeling unwise to encourage in a small child, and it is likely that she herself enjoyed excessively his caresses, as he nestled in her arms, seeking love and protection against an unsympathetic world. Later he was to describe the pleasure he had experienced then at the touch of the silks and satins which she always wore, as he smelt the intoxicating scent of rich furs mingled with that of powder and perfume. It is unnecessary to look here for signs of precocious depravity, or to mention the Oedipus

complex. It is often through the richness of the clothes of
those whom he loves that a child receives his first emotional
thrill and experience of beauty. It is a similar sensation to
that which he feels when taken into a church for the first
time, before his religious sense has been awakened, as he
kneels by his nurse's side, in front of the altar dazzling with
flowers and candles, and smells, during Benediction, the
mysterious and elusive perfume of the incense rising through
the dim church to the darkened roof. It is unnecessary to
see abnormality in connection with such emotional experience. One must also not forget Baudelaire's sensuous precocity, and, from the little that we know of his early life, it
is clear that his mother encouraged the outward expressions
of love, and that she was confident of having no rival, except
perhaps the nursemaid.

In later life Baudelaire remembered his father with pious
affection, but he was only six years old when he died, and to
a child of six, a man of close on seventy must have seemed
more like a grandfather than a father, an old man with
white hair, leaning heavily on a stick, with whom he walked
in the Luxembourg Gardens.

His father meant little more to him than walks in the
parks on warm afternoons, when he used to point out the
beauties of the architecture and the sculpture. Thus it was
that Baudelaire, at the age of four or five, received his first
initiation into art, and began to notice form and line. He
declared later that his first education had been through
pictures.[7] François Baudelaire was possibly not a distinguished painter, and he followed chiefly the pseudo-classical
style of the eighteenth century, but even an indifferent artist
may possess artistic feeling and appreciation. It is partly
from him, and from his mother, also a painter, that
Baudelaire inherited the undoubted talent he showed for
drawing, and the sureness of his taste in artistic matters. He
had an intuition for the values which were permanent, and
the artists whom he singled out for praise are those who have
survived. If he had studied he might have become an original

artist, and the few drawings from him which have come down to us show some resemblance to the style of Degas and Toulouse-Lautrec.

When François Baudelaire died his pension ended with him, and the large apartment in the Rue Hautefeuille became too costly for his widow. An auction was held at which most of the furniture and pictures were sold, which realized between six and seven thousand francs, and there were, as well, eight thousand francs in investments, about six hundred pounds. A *conseil de famille* had been nominated to look after Baudelaire's interest during his minority – six members, amongst them the Duc de Choiseul Praslin, the sculptor Ramey, and the painter Naigeon who was also the curator of the Luxembourg Museum.

When all the affairs were settled, Baudelaire, his mother and his half-brother Alphonse, who was studying law, moved into an apartment in the Rue Saint André des Arts, and later in the Place Saint André des Arts, where they lived with Alphonse and his young wife after he married. This arrangement continued until Caroline's second marriage.

This change of home was almost the only difference which his father's death meant to Baudelaire, for he was more than ever his mother's companion and sole joy, especially during the first year of her widowhood, when mourning prevented her from going out into society. They used to go for long walks together in the old quarter of Paris where they now lived, round the Place Saint Michel, which had altered very little since the fifteenth century, for it was before the days of the wide boulevards on the left bank. They used to wander at evening along the silent and deserted banks of the river, waiting to see the sun sink slowly behind the hills to the west, and then, when the last rays had disappeared and the air began to grow chill, they would make for home, loitering as they went along the mysterious quays, very dimly lit since gas-lighting had not yet been introduced in that unfashionable quarter in the neighbourhood of Notre-Dame.

The summer months were spent at Neuilly, which, in those days, was a country village and a favourite resort for those who did not want to go further afield. The little house they occupied was part of Baudelaire's inheritance from his father, but he sold it later, when he reached his majority and needed ready money, though his father had advised that it should be kept, and in this he showed foresight for Neuilly was later to become part of Paris and the land appreciated accordingly. Alphonse, who had not sold his Neuilly property, later realized a substantial fortune from it. Baudelaire wrote of the little house at Neuilly in a poem from *Les Fleurs du Mal*.[8]

> *Je n'ai pas oublié, voisine de la ville,*
> *Notre blanche maison, petite mais tranquille;*
> *Sa Pomone de plâtre et sa vieille Vénus*
> *Dans un bosquet chétif cachant leurs membres nus,*
> *Et le soleil, le soir, ruisselant et superbe,*
> *Qui, derrière la vitre où se brisait sa gerbe,*
> *Semblait, grand œil ouvert dans le ciel curieux,*
> *Contempler nos dîners longs et silencieux,*
> *Répandant largement ses beaux reflets de cierge*
> *Sur la nappe frugale et les rideaux de serge.*

After a year, when his mother came out of mourning, Baudelaire found himself no longer treated as a little boy, but allowed to accompany her everywhere, even to receptions. There was one day which he recalled with particular vividness, when they visited a certain Madame Panckouke, in an old house in a silent street. Her drawing-room, to the little boy, seemed a veritable fairy palace, with its Chinese ornaments and rich Eastern hangings, and he stood spellbound with wonder. At last the lady of the house, dressed in velvet and furs, took him by the hand and led him to another room which, to his childish imagination, was like the magic cave which Sinbad the Sailor found on his wanderings, for it was piled to the ceiling with toys of every kind and description, and he was bidden choose what he liked best.⁹ It was thus, by indulging the children of others, that his childless hostess gave vent to her unexpended maternal love. Baudelaire, even at that early age, knew exactly what he wanted, the richest and most expensive toy, and he lifted his hand to seize it. But his mother, scandalized by his lack of social tact, obliged him to take a smaller and less dazzling toy. The memory was to remain with him for ever, and as somehow symbolical of his life.

In 1828, for some reason unexplained to Baudelaire, they moved to a small apartment in the Rue du Bac, and then he began to notice that a visitor used to come frequently to the house, almost daily, and stay for long hours. This was Captain Aupick, a brilliant, handsome young officer, with a fine record behind him and, in everyone's estimation, a distinguished future before him. He was the most attractive man that Caroline had ever met, with his regular features, his thick black curling hair, and his deep blue eyes which gazed at her with a steadfast and honest look. It was no wonder that she, whose senses hitherto had not been fully awakened, should fall deeply in love with him. Up to that moment, except in her love for her child, she had remained as cold as a virgin, and had never even imagined what real passion could be. Now this dazzling young officer placed everything at her feet, everything of which she had dreamt in her starved and romantic youth – luxury, gaiety, excitement, and the deep love of a passionate and honourable nature. Years later, when an old woman, writing to Asselineau, she was to talk of the 'golden life' which Aupick had given her, coupled with the deep affection and devotion which never wavered during the thirty years which they spent together.¹⁰ This was no idle boast, for it is borne out by his last will and testament.

Caroline was swept off her feet and transfigured by this first experience of overwhelming adult passion. Perhaps she may, temporarily, have forgotten her little boy and that, suffering from the change, he may have felt neglected. Yet

no one can blame her for attempting to make this final bid
for happiness, for life had been hard and niggardly to her
since the day of her birth, and she had never possessed any
of the things which youth feels are its birthright. She was
nearly thirty-five, close on the long evening of life, when the
time for enjoyment would have slipped away for ever. Biographers of Baudelaire have always been harsh and unsympathetic to her, and have not tried to understand her point
of view. She may have held a false idea of the value of the
material goods of this world, and of the importance of a
settled life, but this was a prejudice which she shared with
most of her contemporaries, and it should be remembered
that she had never enjoyed these things, while envying them
in others, and wanting them for herself, and especially for
her son. She desired his happiness and well-being above all
else in the world, but did not always realize the best way of
achieving them. Yet she was gifted with perception, and she
had something in her of the eighteenth-century breadth of
view which, although she was a deeply pious woman, made
her understand the effects of passion, and tolerant of them
in others. We see from her son's letters to her that he hid
nothing from her of the circumstances of his disordered
life, and confided in her more freely than children usually
do in their parents. She was also well-read and gifted with a
sound literary taste, so that he trusted her opinion on his
work as he trusted few people, and was anxious that it should
be favourable. She was, moreover, impossible to shock.
Biographers have been particularly severe on her on the
score of her second marriage, but she could never have
guessed how disastrous it was to *seem* to her son when he
grew up. The word 'seem' is deliberately used since it is
impossible to agree with all that has been said and written
about his attitude to his stepfather, nor can the things
which he said himself be credited, for they are obviously
the result of two strong and clashing personalities. It is
certain that, when she married for the second time, Caroline
Baudelaire felt that she could trust her husband to be good

to her son, and everything we know of him is worthy of admiration. She married him in November 1828, when Baudelaire was seven and a half years old.

Aupick was a self-made man in the best sense. The date of his birth is mysterious. There was no registration but a notary's act declared that he was born at Gravelines in February 1789 – he himself gives this date in the entry in *La Biographie Universelle* for 1855. Claude Pichois, who has made a thorough investigation into his life, declares [11] that he was the son of an Irishman in the Berwick-and-Irish regiment and of an Irishwoman called Amelia Talbot. His father was mortally wounded in September 1793 at the battle of Hondschoote, and his widow died soon afterwards. He was left penniless and was adopted by a certain Louis Baudard, a man of some means who always called him 'l'enfant de son âme'. He had been christened James, next called Jémis, and finally Jacques. He was educated at the military schools of La Flèche and Saint-Cyr, and gained most of his promotions on the battlefield. He reached the rank of sergeant while still at the military school, and, in 1809, he joined an infantry regiment as a second-lieutenant. He fought in the campaign of Austria, in Spain in 1812, where he was promoted to the rank of first-lieutenant; in Saxony in 1813, and became a captain in the Battle of France in 1814. Under the first Restoration he was decorated by the Duc d'Angoulême, but went over to Napoleon during the Hundred Days, and fought with great bravery at the Battle of Waterloo. He fought at the Battle of Fleurus where he was hit on the knee by a cannon-ball, which brought on caries from which he was to suffer for the rest of his life. He was first and foremost a soldier who did not bother much about change of régime, and he seems to have been able to accept the return of Louis XVIII. In 1817 he became a major, and in 1818 he was chosen by the Prince de Hohenlohe as Aide-de-Camp. He was recommended in the warmest terms by the Prince to the Minister of War, the Duc de Clermont-Tonnerre, and this meant that his future was assured. For a

penniless orphan of no birth this was most remarkable –
especially under the Restoration.

In October 1828 he asked permission to marry and, the
following month, he married the widow of François Baudelaire.

He was on the General Headquarters in Algeria from
March 1830 to June 1831, where he was promoted to
lieutenant-colonel. On his return to France he was sent to
Lyons to crush the risings and was made a colonel. He was
raised to the appointment of 'Général Commandant de la
Place de Paris' in 1839, and Head of the École Polytechnique
in 1847. Next he was nominated as Ambassador, to Turkey
in 1848 and to Spain in 1851. As ambassador he gained
the reputation of a kindly, intelligent, tactful and efficient
envoy, and was much regretted when he left. Finally he
was made a Senator in 1853. His career was a fine example
of disinterested public service – if lukewarm political
opinions are allowed – but he was proudest of his military
distinctions and, when he came to choose his motto, he
selected 'Tout par elle' – referring to his sword. A portrait,
painted when he was over sixty, shows him in his general's
uniform and wearing all his decorations, and it can be seen
that, although his hair is white, it is as thick as ever, and
that the hard years of service have not bowed him. In all
that we know of him he appears an upright and honourable
man, with a scrupulous, almost puritanical, standard of conduct. He was a Catholic in the same way as he was a soldier,
that is to say uncompromising and rigid, a stickler for duty.
But we can find no reference anywhere to his having been
anything but fair and kindly to his stepson. He was genuinely
fond of him as a child, also very proud of his intelligence,
and, according to his own lights, was an affectionate father,
prepared to give him the home and warm family life which
he himself had never enjoyed in his youth – he was never
to have any children of his own on whom to lavish his pater-
nal love which, after twenty years of camp and barrack life,
needed an outlet. He was, however, of the older pre-war

generation, brought up in a hard school which had tended to form character rather than personality. In his youth he had had no time for literature or the arts, and he now found it difficult to endure with patience the post-war youth of the Romantic movement, who had grown up without a firm hand over them, while their fathers had been fighting in far-flung wars, in the four quarters of Europe. The young men of the eighteen-thirties, on their side, no longer wanted to hear what their fathers had suffered on the battlefields of Europe, nor of the hardships which they had endured with fortitude when they had been young – their own problems were sufficient for them. They were weary also of hearing how badly the younger generation compared with their elders – the eternal tale, told with variations in every age since the world began, the jeremiad of the parents against the moral standards of the younger generation. As a result of his training he was inclined to be strict and martial in his educational methods – that was the way he had been brought up himself – and he saw his stepson as a rebellious recruit whose stubborn will and obstinacy must be broken, so that he could be properly disciplined. The words 'duty' and 'obligations' were those most frequently on his lips, and these were precisely the words which young men of Baudelaire's age least wanted to hear.

He disliked eccentricity and affectation in every form for he prided himself on being a plain, blunt man, and no father can be more irritating to a youth than the plain, blunt man. Gambling, borrowing, debts, and anything shady in money matters, were abhorrent to him, and indeed his scrupulousness in this respect seems to us exaggerated – indeed Irish! He considered that his salary as ambassador was not paid to him as a reward for services rendered, but to be spent on shedding lustre on the name of France, and so he never saved any portion of his income as ambassador, nor bought a life insurance for his wife, nor land to leave her when he died. When she became a widow everything had to be sold – horses, carriages, furniture – and her sole income then was the money left to her by her first husband and the pension she received as the widow of a general. All that her second husband left her was the tiny villa at Honfleur which he had built earlier in his career and had given her as a retreat for holidays. It was there she lived as a widow and later died.

Aupick had intended to act for the best with regard to his stepson, and to help him to become a God-fearing and useful citizen. Baudelaire, however, was to say later, 'To be a useful man has always seemed to me something very ugly'.[12] Aupick did not understand his stepson's tendency as a child, and also later as a young man, to romance about himself and to give himself airs, but considered this as merely conceited or deceitful. He also objected strongly to his blasphemous and immoral conversation, and did not realize that it was only the crudeness of a young man trying to assert his individuality and independence, and seeking to shock his elders. Even with the best will in the world, he failed with him completely, but Baudelaire was a very difficult youth, and any treatment, even that of the most sympathetic and lenient of fathers, would have been unsuccessful with him at eighteen, for he was going through the normal *Weltschmerz* of an artistic and self-centred young person, feeling, like most adolescents, out of tune with his surroundings and misunderstood by everyone. Most men and women, when they first grow up, feel that they are being misjudged by their elders, and often imagine, for a time, that they dislike their parents. This vague and somewhat shamefaced aversion, which they do not dare formulate even to themselves, might become chronic if they rationalize it and excuse it, attributing their discontent to the fact of being cursed with a stepfather.

Much nonsense has been written about the Oedipus complex in connection with Baudelaire, and of his sexual jealousy of his stepfather, while many foolish stories have been related to support this theory. It must be remembered that most of them were probably invented by the poet himself in later life, when his stepfather had become for him the symbol of the respectable middle class which he most abhorred, and when he wished to prove to himself that he had always hated him. Such a story is the one which relates how, though barely seven years old at the time, he had flung the key of the bedroom out of the window, on his mother's wedding night, so that her husband should not sleep with her.

It is true that Baudelaire's affection for his mother had an intensity unusual in so young a child, which she had encouraged, and it is probable that he felt jealousy when he found that the love, which hitherto he had enjoyed undivided, must now be shared with a stranger. There is, however, nothing abnormal and depraved in such feelings, and many a child who has been alone for a long time, and therefore much petted, is jealous of the new brother or sister and the baby must frequently be protected against him. Dogs are invariably jealous of the affection which their master bestows on any other new creature. There is no evidence anywhere that Baudelaire, as a child, felt any antipathy towards his stepfather, but, on the contrary, we see, in all his letters, how much he longed to please him and to be well thought of by him. 'Persuade him if you can', he wrote to his mother,[13] 'that I'm not a scoundrel, but a good boy.' This was written when he was eighteen.

According to all available evidence, friendly relations continued until Baudelaire left school, and shortly afterwards he wrote a letter, almost fulsome in its praise, when his stepfather was promoted to the rank of general. It is only after 1842 that definite signs of lack of sympathy, not merely of normal youthful revolt against restraint, appear, coupled with active dislike. In 1861, when he was forty, reviewing the events of his life, he mentions his stepfather's harshness and injustice to him as a child, but he was ill and despairing then, and did not see the past in true colours. He talks of the terrible unhappiness he had endured as a boarder at school in Lyons when he was ten, and yet the accounts of his schoolfellows show him, on the contrary, to

have been a happy little boy.[14] It is probable that he was in
awe of his stepfather, wishing to be well thought of by him,
but his constant regret was that he was never able to prove
to him that he was deserving of consideration. Aupick was
a soldier, and the soldier came high amongst those whom
Baudelaire thought worthy of admiration. Even as late as
1860, in *Mon Cœur mis à nu*, he places him in the same
rank as the priest and the poet.[15] His stepfather cannot have
realized this and, for his part, was always afraid that
Baudelaire would bankrupt his mother – who shall say that
his fears were unfounded, for, as long as he lived, and his
wife could enjoy the benefits of his large salary, her son used
to try, by every means in his power, to obtain money from
her. She had no secrets from her husband, and he could see
how much she suffered through her son, and was to continue to suffer through him for the whole of her life! When
she became a widow he tried to alter his behaviour, but the
habits of a lifetime cannot be changed overnight.

To return to the early years of Caroline's second marriage.
In November 1831 Lieutenant-Colonel Aupick, as he then
was, received orders to proceed to Lyons where a serious
strike had broken out which seemed to be assuming the
proportions of a minor revolution. It was soon quelled by
the Duke of Orleans and Marshal Soult, and Aupick, as a
reward for the part he had played, was made chief of staff
of the Division stationed in Lyons, and, as he was obliged
to remain there for some years, he sent for his wife and
stepson.

He probably thought that Baudelaire had been too much
with his mother, that there was the danger of his becoming
soft and sentimental, like so many of the youth of the day,
of whom he strongly disapproved, and the child, who was
now ten years old, did not seem to be developing into a
manly boy. It was time that his training began in real earnest,
and so he sent him as a boarder to the Collège Royal at
Lyons, where he remained from 1832 to 1835. This was the
time when schools were run on military lines – a relic of

Napoleonic days – the boys rose to the sound of a drum, and the drum announced the beginning and end of each lesson, and the hours of meals. It was the kind of life that one would have imagined most distasteful to a spoilt and sensitive little boy of Baudelaire's temperament. Yet Hignard, who was at school with him, tells us that he was happy there and that he was an enchanting little boy, keenly intelligent and eager, with a charming diffidence and shyness.[16] He seems to have worked well and to have won several minor prizes, amongst them one for drawing. His social gifts appear to have been highly developed at this early age, and his chief interests seem to have lain in acting and dancing. He was also beginning to show an instinct for language and the use of words, witness a letter written to his half-brother, when he was twelve, which is remarkable for so young a child, and at an age when other boys have difficulty in exteriorizing themselves, he had already developed a literary style and artistic pretensions. Although the theories of the Romantic Movement were only slowly beginning to break into the general consciousness, he had already adopted some of their mannerisms. Hignard tells us that he and Baudelaire used to read Lamartine and Hugo together and this, for the early eighteen-thirties, was very advanced, especially in the provinces.[17]

'Beaucoup de choses à dire, mais primo m'excuser. Dans ma paresse s'est un peu mêlé d'amour-propre; comme tu ne répondais pas, je croyais qu'il importait à mon honneur de ne pas écrire deux fois de suite. Mais j'ai reconnu que c'était du ridicule; d'ailleurs tu es mon aîné, je te respecte, tu es mon frère, je t'aime. Beaucoup de choses à te dire, je te le promets au commencement de ma lettre, eh bien, je vais m'acquitter de ma promesse. Je viens de me fouler le pied, de là emplâtre (ou amplâtre), et je déteste les amplâtres aussi bien que les médecins.

'On bâtit à Lyon sur la Saône un pont suspendu, tout en fil de fer. Toutes les boutiques vont être éclairées au gaze (*sic*); on creuse dans toutes les rues. Le Rhône, ce rapide

fleuve aux crues subites, vient encore de déborder. Car il
pleut beaucoup maintenant à Lyon. La verrerie qui est
située dans une presqu' île tout près de la ville (car nous y
allions en promenade, nous les collégiens) eh bien, le Rhône
empiète toujours sur l'istme (*sic*); il ronge, il mange. Cette
nuit enfin il a emporté l'istme. Ce sont des choses qui arri-
vent souvent dans le Rhône. Une irrégularité devient en-
foncement, la langue devient île; car le fleuve est très rapide.
Ma lettre est cochonnement griffonnée, mais ma plume est
très mauvaise, et puis je m'inquiète peu de cela. Il me tarde
de m'excuser de ma paresse par une longue lettre. Mais juge
donc quel cruel supplice, cette petite entorse m'empêche de
danser, moi qui ne manque pas une seule contre-
danse.

'Et puis! pendant mes vacances, eh bien, j'ai joué la
comédie, et puis je vais encore jouer un proverbe.

'Il y a bien des folies dans ma lettre; les idées sont peut-
être aussi irrégulières que l'écriture. Dieu merci, il y avait
si longtemps que notre correspondance était interrompue,
qu'il n'était pas difficile de trouver matière à cette conversation épistolaire. D'ailleurs il vaut mieux jacasser amicable-
ment que de faire du fatras et du patos (*sic*). "Mais comment
Théodore [18] a eu des prix! et Charles n'en a pas eu." Ventre
Saint Gris! j'en aurai. Dis à Théodore qu'il est cause que je
serai couronné. Un accessit d'excellence (le 4ième) et un de
thème (le 5ième). C'est vraiment pitoyable; mais je veux en
avoir et j'en aurai. Néanmoins mes compliments à Théodore,
pour moi honte, honte, honte! Dis-lui que de là-bas il me
fasse les cornes.

'Et ma sœur va-t-elle bien? Est-elle remise? Bien des
choses de la part de maman. Moi, je t'embrasse aussi. Parle-
moi, ou plutôt écris-moi tout de tous et de toi. "Carlos".' [19]

There is unusual maturity here from a boy of twelve,
who is already observing himself critically and objectively,
and one guesses that he is a little poking fun at himself, so
that one can almost hear the slight ironical laugh. Striking
also are the vitality and the feeling of intense excitement.

This was, however, the peaceful and innocent time of child-hood, before the troubled days of adolescence, when 'l'essaim des rêves malfaisants tord sur leurs oreillers les bruns adolescents.'[20]

Jules Mouquet tells us that Baudelaire's novel *La Fanfarlo* is the later reflection of a romantic adventure in which he was involved at the age of fifteen, while at Lyons, but his arguments are inconclusive and not persuasive.[21]

After some years at Lyons, the Aupicks returned to Paris in 1836 when the Colonel was appointed to the General Headquarters of his regiment. Baudelaire was then sent to the famous Lycée Louis-le-Grand, and his stepfather, proud of his scholastic successes at Lyons, introduced him to the headmaster in terms typical of the pomposity of his manner: 'Sir, I'm bringing you a valuable gift! Here's a pupil who'll bring honour to your establishment!'[22]

Baudelaire, however, as he grew out of childhood, lost much of his happiness and vivacity. He was becoming prone to those moods of deep melancholy, to that morbid *spleen* which was later to be a striking feature of his writings. He became more and more conscious of the intrinsic loneliness of his disposition, for he felt solitary even in the midst of his companions and friends. 'A feeling of solitude, even from my earliest childhood', he wrote later in some biographical notes, 'in spite of my family, and especially in the midst of friends. The conviction of an eternally solitary destiny.'[23]

His former school friend, Henri Hignard, who met him again three years after he had gone to the Lycée Louis-le-Grand, wrote that he found him much changed, embittered even, and he came to the conclusion that his present surroundings were less favourable to him. He was then eighteen, and Hignard tells us that he had already begun to write some of the poems which were later to be known, poems such as 'Tout à l'heure je viens d'entendre'. He was still a fervent Catholic and indeed was never to lose his interest in religion.[24] 'Dès mon enfance, tendance à la mysticité,' he wrote later in his *Journaux Intimes*,[25] 'Mes

conversations avec Dieu.' A poem written while he was at
school, reveals his pious inspiration.[26]

> *Vous avez, compagnon, dont le cœur est poète,*
> *Passé dans quelque bourg tout paré, tout vermeil.*
> *Quand le ciel et la terre ont un bel air de fête.*
> *Un dimanche éclairé par un joyeux soleil;*
>
> *Quand le clocher s'agite et qu'il chante à tue-tête,*
> *Et tient dès le matin le village en éveil,*
> *Quand tous pour entonner l'office qui s'apprête,*
> *S'en vont, jeunes et vieux, en pimpant appareil;*
>
> *Lors, s'élevant au fond de votre âme mondaine,*
> *Des sons d'orgue mourants et de cloche lointaine*
> *Vous ont-ils pas tiré malgré vous un soupir?*
>
> *Cette dévotion des champs, joyeuse et franche,*
> *Ne vous a-t-elle pas, triste et doux souvenir,*
> *Rappelé qu'autrefois vous aimiez le dimanche?*

Now that he had reached adolescence, the dreariness and
ugliness of school life became intolerable to him, and the
tedium of the curriculum unbearable.

> *Tous imberbes alors, sur les vieux bancs de chêne*
> *Plus polis et luisants que des anneaux de chaîne,*
> *Que, jour à jour, la peau des hommes a fourbis.*
> *Nous traînions tristement nos ennuis, accroupis*
> *Et voûtés sous le ciel carré des solitudes,*
> *Où l'enfant boit, dix ans, l'âpre lait des études.*[27]

He reached adolescence during the middle years of the
eighteen-thirties, and although the Romantic Movement
had finally won the day at the *Bataille d'Hernani* in 1830,
and with the entry of a Romantic poet, Lamartine, into
the stronghold of conservatism, the French Academy, the
next year, the new writers had not yet penetrated into the
school curriculum. Sainte-Beuve, Musset, and Gautier were
considered, by those entrusted with the training of the
young, unnecessary influences and positively dangerous.

But rumours and echoes from the outside world floated into the school, rich seeds on the wind, and the boys began to wonder what was this new literature about which people spoke with such warmth, or disapproval, hailing it as a new revelation. They began then to dream of more romantic food for their budding imaginations than what was offered to them by their teachers. In the hot summer days, particularly, as they sat in their musty classrooms, leaning their weary and bored heads on their hands, as they tried to fix their attention on the old classical text which their teacher was discussing and which seemed to them little more than a skeleton devoid of life, their bondage seemed more than ever irksome. They heard rumours of exciting events outside in which they had no part, and their monastic life of boarders seemed hard to bear. To a youth like Baudelaire, psychologically mature, the incarceration was especially harsh. He listened, with ears alert, for the sound of new books in which he could find nourishment for his developing mind and inquisitive imagination. In secret he read Romantic poets such as Byron and Shelley, and especially Sainte-Beuve, in whose *Poésies de Joseph Delorme* he discovered his own pessimism, his own doubts and the confused depth of his fast-growing personality. He read, with feverish interest, his one novel, *Volupté*, published in 1834, and this, more than any other single book, helped to crystallize what had been hitherto vague and undefined in him, and scarcely admitted even to himself. It was small wonder that teachers made efforts to prevent this novel from falling into the hands of their charges. He wrote of it himself some years later.[28]

> *Ce fut dans ce conflit de molles circonstances,*
> *Mûri par vos sonnets, préparé par vos stances,*
> *Qu'un soir, ayant flairé le livre et son esprit,*
> *J'emportai sur mon cœur l'histoire d'Amaury,*
> *Tout abîme mystique est à deux pas du doute,*
> *Le breuvage infiltré lentement, goutte à goutte, –*
> *En moi qui dès quinze ans, vers le gouffre entraîné,*
> *Déchiffrais couramment les soupirs de René,*

Et que de l'inconnu la soif bizarre altère,
– A travaillé le fond de la plus mince artère,
J'en ai tout absorbé, les miasmes, les parfums,
Le doux chuchotement des souvenirs défunts,
Les longs enlacements des phrases symboliques,
– Chapelets murmurant de madrigaux mystiques,
– Livre voluptueux, si jamais il en fut.

It is unfortunate that the school records for the years that
Baudelaire spent at Louis-le-Grand should have perished in
a fire at the end of the century. However, by good fortune,
the reports of some of the masters survive, and from these
we can form a picture of what he was like. He must have
been, from the teachers' point of view, troublesome and
undisciplined. He enjoyed the reputation amongst them
of not being 'assez sérieux', and they were shocked by his
bad taste, his 'faux goût', in literature, being totally incapable of appreciating the truly beautiful. This probably
only means that he expressed admiration for such works as
Sainte-Beuve's *Volupté*, or Gautier's *Comédie de la Mort*,
instead of extolling those by Casimir Delavigne. However,
what scandalized them most deeply was the open contempt
he expressed for history and historical method – this was
the greatest heresy in the nineteenth century. We realize
their innocent horror in the words: 'This pupil is convinced,
for he admits it openly himself, that history is completely
useless!'

Each term the masters reported very unfavourably on his
conduct and manners. In the second semester of 1838 a
report states that his character shows frivolity and levity,
that his conduct is undisciplined and affected, and his manners not always civil. 'Refuses to try!' appears again and
again in the reports. When he had enounced one of the out-
rageous paradoxes for which already at that early age he was
famous, the masters could only say that he was lying or
giving himself airs unsuited to his age. 'False and untrustworthy! He has several times lied to me! His manners are
sometimes too casual, and sometimes unpleasantly affected!'

– so runs a report when he was seventeen. The following term he was alleged to be 'disobedient, affected and frivolous in his conduct!'

At school Baudelaire was clearly a pupil whose unsatisfactory conduct was rendered chronic by the unimaginative lack of understanding of his teachers, and the foolish admiration of his schoolfellows. The masters made the mistake of taking seriously everything that he said, and of seeing in his all too successful attempts at baiting them, signs of precocious depravity. He realized very soon that he always had them at a loss, and he was not slow in making good use of his advantage. The flattery of his schoolfellows, who encouraged him to do what they themselves had not the spirit to do, obviously went to his head like the fumes of wine.

Nevertheless the masters were forced to admit that he had brains, as one report grudgingly states, and another that 'his work is good enough, but, in my opinion, could be still better!'

Intellectually he fulfilled his stepfather's promise to the school when he came to enrol him as a pupil, for he gained at first many prizes. When he was in the Third Division no one else had won as many as he. He was awarded prizes for Greek and Latin Prose and Translation, and a First Prize for Latin verse. In the Second Division he continued to excel in Latin, especially in verse, although he seems to have dropped behind in other subjects. While in the First Division the only prize he appears to have won was one for French Essay.[29]

Baudelaire was writing much poetry at this time, and Deschanel, who was in the same Division, tells us that they used both to spend the whole of the mathematics hour in writing and exchanging verse.[30] Some of these were the poems shown to Hignard. The most interesting and original poem of his schooldays is *Incompatibilité*, composed when he spent a holiday alone with his stepfather in the Pyrenees, and it contains many expressions which recall his mature

manner – such lines as 'Des échos plus morts que la cloche
lointaine' and 'Le silence qui fait qu'on voudrait se sauver'.

> *Tout là-haut, tout là-haut, loin de la route sûre,*
> *Des fermes, des vallons, par delà les côteaux,*
> *Par delà les forêts, les tapis de verdure,*
> *Loin des derniers gazons foulés par les troupeaux,*
>
> *On rencontre un lac sombre encaissé dans l'abîme*
> *Que forment quelques pics désolés et neigeux;*
> *L'eau, nuit et jour, y dort dans un repos sublime,*
> *Et n'interrompt jamais son silence orageux.*
>
> *Dans ce morne désert, à l'oreille incertaine,*
> *Arrivent par moments des bruits faibles et longs,*
> *Et des échos plus morts que la cloche lointaine*
> *D'une vache qui paît aux penchants des vallons.*
>
> *Sous mes pieds, sur ma tête, et partout le silence,*
> *Le silence qui fait qu'on voudrait se sauver,*
> *Le silence éternel de la montagne immense,*
> *Car l'air est immobile et tout semble rêver.*
>
> *On dirait que le ciel, en cette solitude,*
> *Se contemple dans l'onde, et que ces monts, là-bas,*
> *Écoutent recueillis, dans leur grave attitude,*
> *Un mystère divin que l'homme n'entend pas.*
>
> *Et lorsque par hasard une nuée errante*
> *Assombrit dans son vol le lac silencieux,*
> *On croirait voir la robe ou l'ombre transparente*
> *D'un esprit qui voyage et passe dans les cieux.*[31]

He was seventeen when he composed this poem, and it
may perhaps reflect already incompatibility between his
stepfather and himself. It may be the expression of the
irritation, which he had managed so far to conceal, against
the healthy and wholesome cheerfulness he had been obliged
to endure during the long days alone with Aupick, without
his mother's presence to relieve the strain. Perhaps the effort
to appear bright and normal was too much for the rebellious
and moody youth of seventeen, who had never learnt self-

restraint, nor to curb his impatience with what he would have called 'old fogeyism!'

Suddenly the following spring, in April 1839, before he had sat for his *baccalauréat* examination, a mysterious event occurred which resulted in his leaving school before the end of the term. The reason has not been stated anywhere and many guesses have been hazarded. Perhaps the school authorities discovered some escapade, or he boasted of it openly, almost daring them to take action – this would have been in character! Or perhaps, as has been suggested without any proof, it was a 'question de dortoir'. A letter from the headmaster of the *lycée* suggests that Baudelaire refused, when summoned, to give up a note which had been passed to him in class, even when told that he would suffer the utmost penalty, and he would not denounce the culprit.[32]

'This morning,' wrote the headmaster to Aupick, 'your son, when ordered by the assistant-headmaster to give up a note which one of his schoolfellows had just passed to him in class, refused to do so, but tore it into small pieces and swallowed them. On being summoned to my study he declared that he preferred any kind of punishment rather than give away the secret of his friend. When I begged him, for the sake of that friend whom he leaves exposed to the most unfortunate suspicions, to change his mind, he answered me with a sneer, the impertinence of which I feel I cannot tolerate. I am therefore sending you back the young man, who is certainly gifted with outstanding ability, but who has spoilt everything by his pig-headedness, from which the good conduct of the school has had to suffer on more than one occasion.'

Whatever the reason, it seems that Baudelaire was treated in a high-handed manner. The headmaster, however, may have honestly considered him an unhealthy influence in school and have thought that it would be better without him. He had always enjoyed a bad reputation with his teachers, and it is not likely that any of them would have spoken in his favour at whatever meeting decided his fate.

They probably all thought that, even if the charges were
unfounded, so dangerous and subversive a pupil was safer
out of the way. His conversation – and it was probably only
talk with him – often went beyond the bounds of what is
called decency. 'Charles was always a high-flier,' wrote one
of his schoolfriends,[33] 'sometimes full of the deepest mysticism, and sometimes of the grossest immorality – but in conversation only, which often went beyond the bounds of
moderation and good-sense.' All through his life Baudelaire's
conversation was more daring than his actions, but those
who heard him speak always took seriously what he said, and
believed him.

This time, however, he was genuinely upset by the result
of his actions, and his expulsion came to him as a surprise
and a great shock, so that it was in a chastened and morbid
state of mind that he returned home. We do not know how
he was received, nor what line of action his stepfather took,
but, reading between the lines of Baudelaire's letter to his
mother, we can guess that he did not hide his disappointment, and that his wife sided with him, leaving her son with
a feeling of loneliness and neglect. She seems to have fallen
ill as a result of the episode, and Baudelaire begs her to get
well quickly for his sake, so that his stepfather shall not
blame him for her state of health as well as for the rest.

When he was sent home in April 1839, Baudelaire had not
yet sat for his *baccalauréat*, and his stepfather, knowing
from the experience of years that he would not work regularly at home away from strict supervision, and with his
mother there to spoil him, sent him as a boarder to a Monsieur Lassègue who prepared boys for examinations. The
Lassègues, mother and son, were kindly middle-class folk,
especially chosen for their common sense and their rational
view of life, and it was hoped that they might influence
Baudelaire's unruly disposition. They were normal, prosaic
people, who had not much use for the arts, and he seems
to have grown tired very soon of their continual common
sense and the triviality of their conversation. The perpetual

cheerfulness of the household, he admits in his letters to his mother, gets on his nerves, and moreover, he felt lonely and in disgrace, sent, as a punishment, to a place where he had no friends with whom to talk and pass the time.

'My dearest, darling Mother,' he wrote to his mother,[34] 'I don't know what to say to you, and I've all kinds of things to say! First, I've a great longing to see you. How different it is to be with strangers; and it's not exactly our laughter and your kisses that I regret, but there's always something which makes our mother seem to us the best of all women. And here, with Monsieur and Madame Lassègue I never feel at ease. Certainly Monsieur Lassègue and his mother have all the virtues – wisdom, common sense, etc. – but all that's in a form that I don't care for. They are both happier, I know, than we are; at home I saw tears and trouble for Father, and worry for you. But, all the same, I think we're better like that!

'And now when I feel deep down in me something which lifts me up, something which I don't understand, a longing to embrace everything, a terror that perhaps I may never be able to acquire any education, an insane fear of life, or else merely when I gaze at a beautiful sunset out of my window, there is no one to whom I can talk of it, since you aren't here. And so what has happened is that I'm worse than before, than when I was at school. At school I always found something to do, not always lessons, I must admit, but still I worked at something. When I was expelled I must confess that it greatly upset me. At home then I also worked a little, but now nothing, nothing, absolutely nothing! And it's not a pleasant poetic idleness, not at all, I can tell you! It's a gloomy, depressing kind of stupid idleness. I didn't dare admit all this to Father, nor reveal myself to him in all the ugliness of my nature, he'd have found me too changed. He'd always seen me at my best. At school I worked now and again, I used to read, to weep sometimes, sometimes to fly into a rage, but at least I felt I was alive. Now not at all. I've sunk as low as I can, and I'm full of faults, not pleasant

faults. And if even this painful life at least induced me to
change for the better – but no – that energy which used to
drive me sometimes towards evil and sometimes towards
good, has completely left me, and there's nothing left but
idleness, boredom and sullen temper. I've gone down a lot
in my own estimation, I can tell you. If I'd been alone I'd
perhaps not have worked properly, but I'd have worked –
with you or with a good friend, I'd have kept straight –
amongst these strangers, I've been completely changed, upset, and put off the rails. I seem to be, don't I, using grand
words and subtleties to disguise very ordinary and commonplace faults....

   'Perhaps it's just as well that I should have seen all these
strangers, I'll love my mother all the more. Perhaps it's just
as well to have been stripped of all romance, I'll understand
all the better what I lacked. It's perhaps, as they say, only a
period of transition, a passing phase out of which I'll grow.
All these days your letters have hurt me, and made me feel
more distressed, but all the same, write to me. I love your
letters! In my distress I'm glad to feel the love of my mother
round me. I've at least got that. When you write to me, talk
to me of my own father at great length.'

   Although he considered himself then mature, at the age
of eighteen, he was, in many ways, young and helpless, and
in need of sympathy and comfort.

   Hignard who, being older than Baudelaire, was now at the
École Normale, spent one Sunday with him at this time, and
was much struck by the improvement in his state of mind.
Writing to his parents he said: [35] 'I spent the whole of last
Sunday with Baudelaire, who is a charming youth, a close
friend of mine. During the past year – for I saw him when
I first arrived in Paris – he has grown very handsome, but,
what pleases me even more, he has become very serious,
studious and pious.'

   Baudelaire succeeded in passing his *baccalauréat* at the
first attempt, without loss of time. The same week his stepfather was promoted to the rank of Major-General, and

Baudelaire wrote to congratulate him, also to try to win back his good opinion for himself by announcing his own success.[36]

'I've just read your good news in the paper,' he wrote to his stepfather, 'and I've good news of my own to tell you as well! I saw the news of your promotion this morning in the *Moniteur*, and I'm a *bachelier* since yesterday afternoon at four o'clock. My examination results were only middling, except in Latin and Greek, for these I got "very good" and that saved me! I'm indeed delighted to hear of your promotion! Coming from a son to his father, these aren't the conventional congratulations you'll receive from so many people! I'm glad because I've known you long enough to realize that you've deserved it this long time! Do I seem to be pretending to be a man, and congratulating you as if I were your equal, or even your superior? Well! I'll only add simply that I'm very, very glad!'

Baudelaire was later to state that his success in his examination had been due to influence, that he had been recommended to the examiners by a friend of his family, a lady who ran a *pension* for Catholic students and who was held in high esteem by the authorities.[37] This was, however, the kind of remark that he always made about himself.

Thus Baudelaire's schooldays came to an end without his having scored the notable successes which his parents had hoped from him when they had brought him at fifteen to the Lycée Louis-le-Grand. His greatest triumphs had been to have gained a Second Prize for Latin verse at the *Concours Général* in 1837, when he was sixteen, in open competition with all the *lycées* of France, and to have passed his *baccalauréat* with ease.

[2]

The Latin Quarter
1839 — 1842

Now that Baudelaire had passed his *baccalauréat* it was time for him to think of his future, and of qualifying for a career. He himself, however, was in no hurry to enslave himself in a new bondage, for all he craved for, after the prison years of the boarding-school, was liberty and leisure. His parents hoped for a brilliant future for him in the diplomatic service for which his quick intelligence and his good looks seemed to qualify him, and his stepfather was, moreover, a personal friend of the Heir Apparent, the Duke of Orleans, who could have supported him in any public career that he chose to adopt. Many young men of his age would have envied him the advantages which he possessed and which he himself, unfortunately, did not appreciate.

Thus, when, in the autumn of 1839, it was suggested that he should now set to work for the Foreign Office examinations, he categorically refused to consider any of the public services at all. His mother, who thought it of vital importance to make a success of life in the eyes of the world, was outraged at his decision for she failed to understand how anyone could be so foolish as to be reluctant to take advantage of influential connections. She herself, at his age, would have welcomed similar opportunities when her own future had looked very black. Baudelaire, however, had been dreaming in secret for some months of a literary life, for his interests at school had been mainly artistic, and he had followed with eagerness the glorious ascent of Victor Hugo, Vigny, Musset and Sainte-Beuve. It appeared to be a golden age for poets who made not only brilliant, but lucrative, careers, and Hugo, although only in his early thirties, was rumoured to have signed contracts with his publishers to the value of many thousands of pounds. Yet when Baudelaire made his decision known to his parents they were as horrified as if he had calmly informed them that he intended to join a circus as a clown. More than thirty years later, after his death, his mother still vividly remembered her outraged disappointment, and, writing to one of his friends, she said: 'What dismay we felt when Charles refused everything we offered to do for him! What a disappointment in our family life, hitherto so happy and united! What grief and sorrow! If Charles had only consented to be advised and guided by his stepfather how different his life would have been!'[1]

General Aupick acted, as usual, in a fair and just manner. He said that his stepson was still very young and undeveloped, that it would not harm him to be allowed to have his fling for a short time before beginning life in earnest, and that he himself was not averse from permitting young men to sow their wild oats, so long as the seed was not too fertile, that the sowing did not take too long, and especially so long as there was no harvest. The boy was only eighteen after all, so he could be granted a couple of years to finish his education in his own way, and, if he were kept short of money, no great harm could come to him. He thought that, after he had tasted the bitter fruit of liberty, he would soon grow weary of the irregular life, and become more amenable to reason.

In England Baudelaire, at this stage of his life, would have gone up to either Oxford or Cambridge, as an undergraduate, where, under proctorial and tutorial supervision, he would have done himself no permanent harm. He would probably have made a name for himself in undergraduate circles, in artistic and literary clubs, and this might have satisfied his need for eccentric self-expression. In this simple and adolescent manner he would have grown out of his 'green-sickness', and, under tutorial pressure, might even have learnt to work at set hours, in order to pass his examinations. It is, however, probable that he would have been a serious student, for, with his facility and felicity in Greek and Latin, he might have been a Balliol Scholar, and have read with distinction for Honour Moderations, while his taste for metaphysical and philosophical argument might have led him finally to Greats. But, in whatever manner he chose to spend his time, he would have been kept under kindly supervision during these critical years. Unfortunately the university system in France does not fulfil the same function as it does in England, and the life into which artistic and literary young men are plunged, on leaving school, is the Bohemian life of the Latin Quarter, the life of cafés, literary circles and student balls. At school Baudelaire had read of this exciting life, and had dreamt of it too, and now he was longing to taste the pleasures which were eventually to leave a bitter taste. From his study window, in the Rue Saint Jacques, he had often seen the merry bands of students, passing at carnival time – or indeed most evenings – in their noisy *monômes*, each with a pretty girl leaning on his arm, all shouting with joy and high spirits, and waving their velvet caps bright with multicoloured ribbons.[2]. Now he would himself be one of the gay throng, and not merely a spectator.

It has usually been said that Baudelaire was placed by his stepfather as a boarder in a student lodging-house, the Pension Bailly, at the corner of the Rue de l'Estrapade and the Place du Panthéon. Marcel Ruff[3] declares that there is no positive proof that he was ever there as a boarder. He may however have taken his midday meal there. It was a superior *pension* since it possessed a spacious garden with shady trees, opening on to the square in front of the École de Droit. The fees were high and the boarders were chiefly the sons of well-to-do provincial middle-class families, and had been sent to Paris to study at the Sorbonne, or at the Schools of Medicine or Law. The parents thought that their sons would be well cared for, but discipline and supervision were entirely lacking. Baudelaire, to give himself the status of a serious student amongst the others, was alleged to have signed on at the École des Chartes and to have followed intermittently its courses for almost ten years. But no record of his presence at this time is preserved in the archives of the school. Marcel Ruff has, however, discovered that he enrolled as a student at the École de Droit in November 1839, and that he remained there until July 1840.[4] It was usual for young men who were undecided about their future to read law, and many poets, later famous, started in this way.

This was an exciting time for literature, and it was in 1839 that *Madame Putiphar* by Petrus Borel was published, with its *Prologue* in verse which anticipates Baudelaire's later poetry.[5] It was in 1840 that the complete poems of Sainte-Beuve appeared which were to have more influence on the young poet's budding talent than those of any other contemporary.

It was while he was a student that Baudelaire began to take an interest in painting and to lay the foundations of his career as an art critic. At an exhibition at the Louvre in March 1840, he saw his first picture by Delacroix, *La Justice de Trajan*, and was immediately transported with enthusiasm. This was the beginning of his life-long interest in this painter to whom he was to devote, twenty years later, some of his most original articles.

With the young boarders of the Pension Bailly who were interested in art and literature, Baudelaire began to lead the gay and carefree life of the Latin Quarter – dancing, drinking, talking and making love. Each of them would have felt that he was not fully fledged if he did not flaunt a mistress, and Baudelaire's lady-love was the squint-eyed Louchette, of whom he later wrote with so little retrospective tenderness.[6] According to Prarond it was she who seduced him from his hitherto blameless life. He wrote, at this time, in a sonnet addressed to Baudelaire:

> *Vous aviez l'esprit tendre et le cœur vertueux,*
> *Tous les biens convoités d'une amitié naïve,*
> *Lorsqu'une femme belle et de naissance juive,*
> *Vous conduisit au fond d'un couloir tortueux.*

Elle vous fit couler, d'un doigt voluptueux,
La source des plaisirs aux égouts de Ninive;
Elle vous fit toucher, sur sa chair toute vive,
Du vice et de l'amour les secrets monstrueux.

Elle eût enivré Loth au fond d'une caverne,
Tenu comme Judith le sabre d'Holopherne
Et frappé du marteau le front de Sisara.

Et tétant au plaisir vos tristesses infimes,
De ce sein que le vice et l'amour déflora,
Vous avez fait couler vos funèbres maximes.[7]

It was probably at this time that Baudelaire contracted the venereal disease from which he was to die twenty-five years later, and it was then that he composed his own ghoulish epitaph:

Ci-gît qui, pour avoir par trop aimé les gaupes,
Descendit jeune encore au royaume des taupes.[8]

The names of the young men with whom Baudelaire associated as a student are now entirely forgotten, except for their recollections of him. They were Levavasseur, Dozon, Prarond, Philippe de Chennevières, Jules Buisson, all names unmentioned in histories of French literature, but all well known in free-lance journalism in the middle of the century. At this time they shared a common contempt for authority, for the opinions of their elders, and their ideal hero was Romantic and Byronic, a man who was a law unto himself.

With this gay and noisy band Baudelaire roamed about the Latin Quarter. It possessed, at this time, a character all its own which it was to lose later when the new boulevards were built, with their huge apartment-houses attracting the well-to-do classes. The Latin Quarter nowadays is inhabited by professors, lawyers, teachers, and even prosperous trades-people, but, in the early nineteenth century, it was almost entirely a student city, with a lower stratum of cut-throats and apaches. It had changed very little since the day of

Villon, and was still a maze of evil-smelling and dimly-lit narrow lanes, where one expected, at any moment, to see a desperate villain spring out from the depths of some foul-looking courtyard. The Rue Soufflot and the boulevards did not yet exist, and the widest streets were the Rue Saint-Jacques and the Rue Monsieur-le-Prince – now sadly fallen from their former glory, for they were then large avenues compared with the other alleys. The students used to act as if they owned the quarter, and would wander about the streets in their carpet slippers, just as if they were in their own homes, as they slouched along to the cafés and eating-houses. It was the most romantic period of the Latin Quarter. All the young men admired extravagance and eccentricity, and, for them, genius and disorder were synonymous terms. They prided themselves on their cyni-cism, their blasphemy, their heavy drinking, and, above all, on their prowess in love. Baudelaire was not an isolated example in these manners, for it was the fashion of the day for those who wished to appear modern and original.

Baudelaire was soon the centre of a noisy band of young men, with their thick black beards, their velvet caps pulled down rakishly over the right eye, with pipes in their mouths, and a smart little *grisette* in bonnet and shawl hanging on their left arm, next to their heart. They lounged about the Latin Quarter, whiling away the time, loafing in the cafés and drinking in the sordid underground bars, similar to those described by Eugène Sue in his *Mystères de Paris*. The smoking of opium and hashish was their newest and most daring vice. Little did Baudelaire realize at this time that, twenty years later, he would be bewailing his inability to break himself of the addiction. It is said that it was from Louis Ménard that the students learned the joys of the Artificial Paradises. He had been a contemporary of Baudelaire at the Lycée Louis-le-Grand, though they had not been intimate friends at the time – indeed they were never to become so – but both had distinguished themselves in Latin verse, and had won prizes at the same *Concours*

Général in 1837. In 1839 Louis Ménard had not yet become a distinguished Greek scholar, 'l'Helléniste du Parnasse' as he was later called, a figure of awe and reverence, but was merely a noisy young barbarian of eighteen or nineteen like the rest, who was studying for the competitive examination to enter the École Normale, to train as a teacher, and later, if he were fortunate, a university professor.

Undoubtedly the biggest influence on Baudelaire at this time was that of the fair, Norman giant, of magnificent health and prodigious strength, called Levavasseur. He was attracted chiefly by his amazing vitality and strength, and he recalls how, one morning, when he went to call on him he found him balancing on top of a complicated erection of tables and chairs, trying to emulate the exploits of some acrobats whom he had seen the previous evening, and he did not descend until he had performed the act with success.

Levavasseur was the founder of the École Normande at the Pension Bailly, composed of himself, Baudelaire, Prarond, Dozon and others similarly interested in the art of poetry. Their activities did not end with literature for they intended to have a good time as well, while they were young, and to live according to a philosophy of life which they had formulated, but which was not, it must be admitted, of great profundity. Baudelaire, as a late-comer, and, moreover, younger by several months than most of the others, played at first a very minor part in the association. Both Prarond and Levavasseur had already published literary works, though not of a very original nature. The former had written, under the pseudonym G. Delorme, a work modelled on the *Vie, Pensées et Poésies de Joseph Delorme* by Sainte-Beuve, while the latter had composed *Les Pensées d'Albert* which followed closely the same model. Nevertheless, in spite of their high achievements, they accepted him and did not make him feel unduly the inferiority of his state.

The three friends went everywhere together, and none of them would have contemplated doing anything without the others. It was to Levavasseur that Baudelaire entrusted his manuscripts when he was shipped abroad in 1841, feeling that he could not trust his own family with them.

One day Baudelaire dared to invite his new friends to his home – always a dangerous thing to do, since parents rarely think that their children choose their friends wisely, unless they happen to be people who may be able to advance them in their career. It was that day in December 1840 when the Prince de Joinville, the son of Louis-Philippe, returned in triumph to Paris with the ashes of Napoleon, and Baudelaire and his friends stood for several hours in the streets to watch the procession pass. Levavasseur later described how frozen they had become during the long hours of waiting, and how, afterwards, they had gone with Baudelaire to his home, where Madame Aupick had revived them with the warmth of her welcome and the charm of her manner, as well as with food and drink.

She herself viewed the visit in a very different light, for, when she saw the kind of companions her son now associated with, she was horrified at their roughness and the coarseness of their jests. She immediately grew anxious and began to think that he was sliding down the slippery slope to eternal damnation, as she listened to his blasphemous talk with his friends, and heard him ridiculing virtue and extolling vice. She had never heard him talk like this before, not even when he was at school, and she could only blame it on the company he was now keeping. She was so worried about the situation, that she did not dare to discuss it even with her husband, though she had no secrets from him. She realized that, however horrified she was herself, he would be even more so, and in favour of sterner methods. Had he not said one day, when he heard the kind of poems that Baudelaire was writing, 'Let him be a poet by all means, if he likes, but that is no reason for drawing his inspiration from the sewers!' In her anxiety she could only think of consulting her old friend and legal adviser, Ancelle, to ask for his advice. It was he who was administering her son's money, during his minority, and he had known him since his birth. Ancelle went to interview Baudelaire and tried to make him see sense, but the young man was at an age when advice and sermons are unpalatable food, and, besides, he suspected that the lawyer had been sent by his family to spy on him and to report on how he spent his time. Ancelle did not report favourably on what he had seen, and Madame Aupick wrote to him in greater distress than ever.

'I received a very painful impression from what you told me the other day about your conversation with Charles. That utter contempt which he expresses for humanity in general, and that total lack of belief in virtue, or in anything, all that is very disturbing, and I can't tell you how much the thought of it all frightens me. For it seems to me that when one does not believe in noble and honest sentiments, there is only one short step from committing evil, and the very thought of that makes me shudder! Up to now I'd been consoling myself with the illusion that, with my son, in spite of his wild and extravagant ideas, I need fear no real harm. I thought that, in spite of everything, he was pious and possessed a basis of firm beliefs, even if he no longer practised his religion. You see the tortures I'm in on Charles' account, and I can't disguise from myself that he's growing worse instead of better. His state is deteriorating because it isn't changing, and time is pressing! It isn't for lack of the most fervent prayers to God on my part for his improvement.'[9]

At last circumstances more grave than the rest brought the matter to the notice of General Aupick who, with his customary firmness, took the matter in hand immediately, and decided that something drastic must be done. His wife was now ready to see the gravity of the situation, and she agreed to his plan of a long sea journey to sever her son's connection with his friends, and to oblige him to live, for a few months at all events, a healthy open-air life, away from the temptations of a capital city.

'The time has come,' wrote General Aupick to Baudelaire's half-brother Alphonse,[10] 'to prevent the complete ruin of your brother. I am at last fully aware – or nearly so – of his position, his habits and customs. The danger is great! Perhaps there is still time for a remedy! But I must see you, and talk to you of what I'm doing, so that you should understand the depth of mental demoralization – not to mention physical – into which Charles has fallen!'

The General considered that the *conseil de famille*, which had looked after Baudelaire's affairs since he became an orphan, should be convened, but he did not want his stepson to hear of this until he was summoned before it – he obviously saw it as a kind of court-martial.

'Then,' went on Aupick, 'his faithful friends would point out to him the evil of his conduct, the errors into which he was slipping, and would gradually lead him on to what was being planned for him.

'There is, in my opinion, and in that of Paul and Labie,[11] an urgent need to remove him from the slippery pavement of Paris. They mentioned to me the plan of sending him on a long sea journey, to India, in the hope that, in a new atmosphere, torn away from his detestable connections, and faced with all the new things he would have to investigate, he might return to saner and truer views, and come back to us, a poet perhaps, but a poet who had drawn his inspiration from better springs than the sewers of Paris.'

Even at this stage Baudelaire's stepfather was in favour of nominating a *conseil judiciaire*,[12] for the young man, although he had not yet gained control of his own money, had already made a large number of debts.

In a subsequent letter Aupick set forth the plan for the journey, which was to cost four thousand francs and to be paid for from Baudelaire's capital. He added that he had already paid out of his own pocket three thousand francs to settle some of his stepson's debts, and that he could not himself afford to do any more.

Baudelaire had been enjoying his pleasant life of freedom and leisure for almost two years now and, with his disposition towards pleasure, he had found it absorbing. Like many people, before and since, he thought that life anywhere but in Paris was not to be contemplated, and he was furious when he discovered that decisions had been taken without consulting him, and that he was being treated as if he were still a schoolboy, he who had been living the life of an adult for two years. He tried, at first, to refuse to obey, but he was not yet twenty-one, his parents still held the purse-strings, and moreover he had not yet reached the stage of full realization of his strength, and awareness of the fact that, if he really did not intend to do a thing, and was willing to accept the consequences, his parents had no power to enforce their will. His stepfather seems to have succeeded in persuading him by peaceful arguments, and he was very proud of his success.

'I was especially worried,' he wrote to an unknown correspondent,[13] 'about some fresh escapades of my stepson, which had most bitterly distressed his unfortunate mother, and had made her all the more unhappy since she was trying to hide them from me. But, at last, with firmness and energy, I reached my objective, and Charles is no longer exposed to the dangers of Paris. He finally yielded to my arguments, and has left for Bordeaux, and, on the 10th of this month, he sails on a boat going to Calcutta. It is a journey of twelve or fifteen months. A fortunate, and quite unexpected, circumstance is that the captain, an ex-officer of the Imperial Navy, has very kindly offered to take charge of my young man, for whom he will, he assures me, do all that he would do for his own son, who, as a matter of fact, is travelling with them. Just as he was leaving, Charles wrote us a very nice letter. That is a good omen for all the good that we expect from this fairly severe ordeal to which we are submitting him.'

Baudelaire, having at last consented, began to boast to his friends of his trip to the East. In those days he knew Gérard de Nerval, and it is possible that he told Baudelaire that he was foolish to object to being sent, with no expense to himself, on such a glorious voyage of adventure. The very name of India would conjure up in Gérard de Nerval's mind scenes of magic beauty and enchantment beyond the dreams of man. He himself had just returned from his trip to Austria, more penniless than ever, but with his *wanderlust* in no way assuaged, and, at the very mention of Baudelaire's journey, he must have been seized with longing for far-off lands and fabulous cities, for to visit the East had always been his dearest wish. Hearing him discourse on its beauties, Baudelaire may have begun to imagine that there might, after all, be some pleasure to be gained from the trip, and that it need not be the dreary duty he had imagined. So he allowed himself to be shipped off without too much reluctance. He sailed from Bordeaux on a ship called *The Southern Skies*, on 9 June 1841, when he was twenty years old.

His good mood did not last long. Scarcely had they set sail when he began to regret his friends, and their literary discussions. Then, to take revenge on Captain Saliz, an old friend of his stepfather, he began to be extremely disagreeable to everyone on board, particularly to the captain's son, because it had been suggested that they might become friends and have interests in common, since they were of the same age. He resented the assumption that someone, merely because he happened to be the same age as himself, should prove sympathetic to him. Most of the passengers were comfortable middle-class families travelling with their children, and Baudelaire professed to despise them because they were unable to talk about literature, and did not know the latest books which had appeared in Paris. He took delight in scandalizing them, and in making fun of the virtues and social conventions which they had been taught to revere since childhood, and a wholesome respect for which they hoped to inculcate in their own children. They were especially horrified to hear such sentiments from the lips of a youth of the same age as their own boys, and so, afraid that he would corrupt them, they forbade them to have anything to do with him. This only hardened him into obstinacy. Captain Saliz certainly did all in his power to make the trip a pleasant one for him, and to keep him in good humour, but his efforts were in vain. It was not for Baudelaire's sake that he was anxious, but he probably hoped that General Aupick, who was a man of influence, would remember him when the occasion arose, and would then support him in high places.

Baudelaire began to grow lonely in his enforced solitude, and regretted his behaviour now that he saw its results, but it was then too late. Pride did not permit him to show that he realized that he had acted foolishly, but he retired into himself and became more melancholic and depressed. He was always susceptible to atmosphere and he felt very deeply the hostility of those around him. All this made him home-sick for Paris, and for the friends who admired him, loved him, and listened attentively when he spoke.

His depression reached its depths when, after a storm, the ship lost its mast and almost foundered. Then he decided that nothing would induce him to go any farther.

There exists a contemporary article describing Baudelaire's behaviour during his trip to the East, which was obviously written by a fellow-traveller, and rings true.[14] It describes his association with the ardent Negro nurse of a creole family returning home – his first experience of a coloured woman. However, he seems to have wearied of her passionate pursuit, and the captain was obliged to request her to remain in her cabin.

Baudelaire is said to have shown the utmost courage and resourcefulness during the storm round the Cape of Good Hope, when the ship almost foundered, and he was largely responsible for its safe arrival in port – though a wreck. As it berthed he behaved in a very characteristic manner. Landing was by a ladder plunging into the sea, and passengers were obliged to climb this whilst the wave was at its lowest and to reach the quay before it had risen again. He ascended the rungs, slowly and majestically, hampered by a bundle of books under his arm, so that the rising wave caught him and flung him into the sea. He was fished out by the sailors, his books were still under his arm – only his hat had gone to the sharks – and he continued his noble but dripping progress towards the centre of the town.

The ship docked at Mauritius for three weeks for repairs, and Captain Saliz, who was busy all day with contractors, had no time to look after Baudelaire. He booked a room for him at a hotel and then was obliged to leave him to his own devices. Baudelaire spent his time making friends with local literary people whom Saliz, as a man of action, obviously despised, for, in his letter to Aupick, he states that Baudelaire had dealings only with some literary people, in a country where they play a very small part indeed.[15] He spent his days chiefly at the house of a certain Autard de Bragard, talking literature to his heart's content, and this was a treat to him after the prosaic conversation of his travelling companions. Both de Bragard and his wife were glad to have news of what was happening in the literary world in France, and they made Baudelaire feel an important person, as if he himself had been one of the famous writers of the French capital. His hostess also was kind and motherly to him, for she was sorry to see a young man in so rebellious and pessimistic a frame of mind, with his hand against everyone. He could be charming when he liked, and with her he grew more gentle, and lost some of his violence and despair. He was able to talk to her of his dreams of becoming a poet, of the difficulties he was encountering, and he felt for her his first experience of pure love, the calf-love of a schoolboy. From his attitude towards her can be gauged how young and innocent at heart he had remained, in spite of his cynical talk, and his sordid experience.

He spent many happy days lying in the warm shade beneath the palm trees, and filling his mind and imagination with the store of dreams and images from which he would later draw some of his finest poems.

The three weeks passed too quickly. The ship was repaired and the captain in a hurry to be on his way to make up for lost time. Baudelaire however now declared, when he was

informed that everything was now ready to proceed to
Calcutta, that he would go no farther, and demanded to
be sent back to France by the next boat. Saliz, at first, refused to give way and to advance any of the money which
he had been given by Aupick for the entire journey.
Baudelaire retorted that this was of no consequence, that
he would remain at Mauritius and earn enough by his own
efforts to pay for his passage home. He added, to reassure
the captain, that his parents had merely wanted him to be
away temporarily from Paris, and that had been achieved
by the trip, even if it was curtailed. The captain was in a
quandary and did not know what to do, for he wanted, at
all costs, to avoid displeasing Aupick, and he did not know
which he would resent more, having his plans counteracted,
or his wife's son thwarted. At last, he made up his mind on
a compromise, and promised that if Baudelaire would come
with him as far as Réunion, he would there make arrangements for his return to France, if that was still his wish. He
hoped, however, once he had him on the high seas, to be
able to persuade him to continue the voyage to the end. He
felt nervous at the prospect of leaving him at Mauritius,
amongst people of whose influence he was uncertain, and of
whom the General might well disapprove. Later, one of the
complaints made by the *conseil de famille* was that Baudelaire had spent at Mauritius and Réunion the money voted
for the complete trip to India.

When they reached Réunion, realizing that nothing would
move Baudelaire, Saliz made arrangements with a friend,
captain of a ship bound for France, to take him as a passen-
ger and to look after him as if he were his own son.

While waiting for his ship at Réunion, Baudelaire wrote
a sonnet for Madame Autard de Bragard, but, through excessive delicacy, did not dare send it to her directly and enclosed it in a letter to her husband.

'When I was at Mauritius,' he wrote, 'you asked me for
verses for your wife, and I've not forgotten you both. Since
it's only decent and proper that verses written to a young

woman by a young man should pass through the hands of her husband before reaching her, I send them to you here to show her if that is your pleasure.

'Since I've left you I've often thought of you and your friends. I'll never, never, forget those wonderful mornings I spent with you, with Madame Autard and M.B. If I didn't love Paris so deeply and regret it so much, I'd stay as long as possible amongst you all, and I'd make you love me and think me less odd than I seem. It's very unlikely that I'll put in at Mauritius, unless the ship on which I sail calls for passengers.

'Here's my sonnet:

> *Au pays parfumé que le soleil caresse,*
> *J'ai vu dans un retrait de tamarins ambrés*
> *Et de palmiers d'où pleut sur les yeux la paresse,*
> *Une dame créole aux charmes ignorés.*
>
> *Son teint est pâle et chaud; la brune enchanteresse*
> *A dans le cou des airs noblement maniérés;*
> *Grande et svelte en marchant comme une chasseresse,*
> *Son sourire est tranquille et ses yeux assurés.*
>
> *Si vous alliez, Madame, au vrai pays de Gloire,*
> *Sur les bords de la Seine ou de la verte Loire,*
> *Belle, digne d'orner les antiques manoirs,*
>
> *Vous feriez, à l'abri des mousseuses retraites,*
> *Germer mille sonnets dans le cœur des poètes,*
> *Que vos regards rendraient plus soumis que des noirs.*[16]

'And so I'll expect you in France.

'My respectful wishes to Madame Autard.'[17]

It is a remarkable poem for a young man of twenty to write, and is markedly superior to any he had composed before his journey to the East.

According to his mother[18] and to Captain Saliz, and his own letter to Autard de Bragard gives the same impression, Baudelaire sailed for France from Réunion on 4 November 1841, on board *L'Alcide*, which did, in fact, leave that day.

However, after he returned to Paris, he always claimed to have gone to Calcutta, and he described to Asselineau how he had joined up with traders and had gone with them into the interior of India.[19] He also gave blood-curdling accounts of the cruel treatment he had suffered at the hands of the crew, and left his friends with the impression that he had been press-ganged, and taken by force on a pirate ship. He told the stories well and, as they improved with each telling, he had great success with his friends, and they never tired of hearing the tale of his adventures on the high seas with the buccaneers. In this way he was able to forget the cold reception he had received from his family on his speedy return, and the strained relations existing between him and them. He soon recovered his good spirits in Paris, and enjoyed once more sitting outside the cafés, adding new stories to his already large stock dealing with his adventures in the East. These tales were all believed by his friends, and many of them were repeated subsequently as true facts by biographers. These stories which he told were like those told by Sinbad the Sailor, or Ulysses when at last he came home to Ithaca. Simple and gullible young men like Banville believed every word that fell from his lips, and he has related some of them in his *Souvenirs* as authentic.

'Baudelaire had learnt,' he wrote, 'some extraordinary recipes in India, which he used to expound with great charm. Once, in some African kingdom, when he was staying as a paying-guest with a family where his mother had placed him, he grew bored with the conventional and narrow-minded ideas of his hosts, and went up into the mountains with a beautiful young Negro girl who did not know a word of French. In the wilds she had cooked for him mysterious spiced messes in a polished copper cauldron, round which a band of completely naked Negroes danced and shrieked.'

This is romantically described, with the local colour dear to the hearts of the French poets of the nineteenth century. The only objection to the story is that it is certainly untrue, that Baudelaire did not go to India, and went no nearer to

Africa than Mauritius and Réunion. He had, however, a talent for description, for evoking lands which he had only seen in imagination, and the fact that he found an audience ready to appreciate his gifts, only added to the zest of his excitement and spurred him on to further efforts. When he had told the story several times he could no longer separate what was true from what was fiction, and he later never remembered that he had not, in reality, gone to Calcutta.

It is only fair to add that Marcel Ruff believes that he did in fact go to India, and that he was telling the truth when he claimed to have visited Calcutta.[20] There are, however, many weighty arguments against his thesis. For one his mother's categoric statement that he was back in Paris by February – this would have been impossible if he had gone as far as India – and a mother would surely know when her son had returned home. Another is his own letter to her, in which he mentions writing to a shipping company to retrieve the papers addressed to him which Captain Saliz must have collected for him when he reached Calcutta – if he had gone to India himself he would have taken possession of them in person.[21] There is further the letter from his half-brother to General Aupick, while he was on the homeward journey, expressing sympathy with him and his wife in their anxiety on account of Baudelaire's future, because of his premature return to France.[22] If he had completed his journey there would have been no need for apprehension.

'I understand,' he wrote, 'all the anxiety which Charles' return must cause you, the anxiety which his future entails for you, and especially the grief of Madame Aupick.'

Alphonse Baudelaire considered, however, that they should wait for the young man's return before reaching any conclusions, and he himself thought that every reasonable person would yield to the advice of those who had sincere affection for him, and that the very fact that he had been persuaded to embark on this journey, in the first instance, was proof that his family still had influence on him, which would be able to prevail also after his return.

'It is, however, no small matter,' went on Alphonse Baudelaire,[23] 'to change ideas which have been distorted by many bad principles. We must not despair! You and I have seen many examples of what strength of will directed towards a definite object can achieve. Don't let's then lose hope. What is important to do first of all is to comfort Madame Aupick and persuade her maternal love that you and I desire only the future happiness of Charles.'

His main fear was that he and the General between them might cause a rift between her and her son, and he considered that the prodigal should be received warmly, as someone who had recognized the extent of his misdemeanours, but was prevented from writing to acknowledge them, through reluctance to admit them in words. He asked to be informed the moment he got back, and said that he would do everything in his power to bring him back to the fold, to united family life in which all the members are happy together.

'Griefs,' he added, 'are like storms, they can't last for ever! Good-bye, General! You can rely on my best wishes, on my help, and on my deep respect and friendship.'

There is, moreover, in *Le Voyage de Baudelaire aux Indes* by Charles d'Hévassi,[24] proof that the ship on which Baudelaire returned, *L'Alcide*, did not go to India but berthed in France on 16 February 1842.

And finally there are the statements in the interim order – the *Jugement d'avant faire part* – in August 1844, when the family council approached the Court with the view of applying for the appointment of a *conseil judiciaire* for Baudelaire. This document declared that the young man, even during his minority, had most extravagant tastes and habits, so that the family, in order to separate him from undesirable influences, decided to send him on a long sea journey, for the purpose of which five thousand five hundred francs were drawn from his capital, so that he should go to India, but that 'ledit Baudelaire, au lieu de se rendre à Calcutta, but de son voyage, s'arrêta à l'Île Bourbon, où il dépensa les fonds qui avaient été mis à sa disposition, sans tirer aucun profit de ce premier sacrifice.'

Whether his Eastern trip was completed or curtailed, Baudelaire gained immensely from it, and he returned with his imagination and sensibilities much enriched by the sights he had seen, and the dreams he had dreamt. The long months of inactivity on board the ship, when there was nothing else for him to gaze on, except the vast expanse of the open sea, deepened his inclination towards reverie. He was never to forget the lotus-eating life in the land of dazzling colours and luscious vegetation, where tropical plants, twisting and turning in the blue haze of heat, seemed to him, with their deliquescent shapes, only the ghost of his dreams. He was never to forget the languid afternoons, lying in the shade of the huts, beneath the burning sky, nor the drowsy hours later, in the twilight, thick with tropical scents. All this fertilized his imagination, giving him analogies, images and metaphors, from which he could draw in the coming years. He came back from the East with a romantic yearning for rich, warm countries, for exotic splendour, and beauty impossible to achieve in this world. This gave his poetry a quality peculiar to him alone.

This journey to the East was the turning-point in Baudelaire's life. He had set forth as a youth, still uncertain of himself, with vague longings towards the vocation of a poet; he returned with his imagination on fire, and determined more than ever to persevere in the career he had chosen.

[3]

The Dandy
1842 — 1844

BAUDELAIRE landed in France in February 1842,[1] and it is improbable that the fatted calf was killed in his honour by his family. He himself did nothing to make relations any less strained as, through some fatal nervousness, he had the knack of displeasing those whom he especially wished to please, and this was accentuated whenever he realized that he was out of favour. A kind of perversity led him to do the very things which he knew would most infuriate his elders and turn them against him, and then, when it was too late, he would regret his behaviour and the solitude he had created round himself through his own fault.

After his return to Paris his parents soon perceived that his trip abroad had worked no improvement in his state of mind, since he sank back immediately into the same kind of life which he had led before his departure, and from which they had wished to save him. He was still associating with the same disreputable friends, and was not taking life any more seriously, nor preparing himself for a regular profession. He was a year older but no wiser. General Aupick, whose temper had been rendered crotchety by an old wound which recently had begun to trouble him again, found it more than he could bear to suffer the cynicism of an idle youth of twenty, who did nothing all day but lounge about the house, smoking one pipe after the other, and holding forth on a subject about which the General considered he was not competent to speak – life and morals. When he was not at home he was frittering away his time in cafés with a band of wastrels like himself. He did not spare his stepson his caustic remarks. Baudelaire, who secretly went in awe of him, used to hide it under an air of bravado and answer him with insolence, making himself as unbearable as possible. His mother suffered greatly from the constant bickering and lack of harmony between the two beings whom she most loved, when all she asked was that they should live in peace and amity together. To avoid leaving her son alone with her husband, she used to make him accompany her to parties and receptions, but he, who saw through her plan, made no attempt to be pleasant to her friends, though he could be charming when he was so disposed. One afternoon, at a large reception at the house of influential friends of his stepfather, the conversation turned on the subject which is never far from a Frenchman's mind, women and love, and a distinguished old gentleman, bowing politely towards his hostess, remarked: 'Woman is the most charming and perfect of all God's creations!' Baudelaire, who had been listening, with an expression of contempt and disgust on his face, suddenly exclaimed, to the consternation of everybody, 'Do you really think so? I'm afraid I can't agree with you! I consider that women are only domestic animals, who should be kept locked up in captivity, where they should be fed and well cared for, but beaten periodically!' His outburst created a sensation in the conventional drawing-room, and his mother was covered in embarrassment and shame. He was never invited to the house again.

Two months after his return to Paris, Baudelaire reached his majority and, in spite of the objections of the *conseil de famille*, took over control of his inheritance under his father's will. He made up his mind that he would now take advantage of his independent means to leave his mother's house and strike out on his own, away from disapproval, far from the man who constantly made him feel inferior, for, in spite of his waywardness, he always suffered deeply from the adverse criticism of others, and this paralysed his power of action.

The capital sum which now came to him was somewhat over three thousand pounds which, in those days, was a large fortune for a young man of twenty-one. To Baudelaire, who had been kept short of money, it seemed the riches of an oriental monarch.

When he left home in June 1842, Baudelaire felt that life was good. He was twenty-one, he had a fortune at his disposal, and there was much for a young man to do in Paris. Now that he had escaped from his stepfather's coercive influence, he imagined that there would be nothing beyond his powers to achieve. At home he had felt that he was fighting for his very existence and this would have been the same even if the General had been his own father. It is only by constant struggle, or else by escape through flight, that the young can protect their still frail individualities from being swamped by the stronger personalities of authoritative parents. Often in such circumstances, the children feel that they hate their parents who, with the best will in the world, put obstacles in the way of their development.

Literary and artistic life was exciting in that summer when Baudelaire became free, and it seemed a lucky time for those who possessed talent. Banville, who was even younger than Baudelaire, for he was only nineteen, was already famous for a book of poems entitled *Les Cariatides*.

Paris was then the most enthralling city to live in provided one had money in one's pocket. It had been rapidly changing during the past ten years, and was beginning to assume the gay aspect which was to make it famous during the Second Empire, when it became the finest city in Europe, after Baron Haussmann had given it the appearance it still enjoys today. Since the Revolution of 1830 it had fast been growing rich, for the middle class had made large fortunes since the accession of Louis-Philippe, and comfortable life was beginning to be considered of the first importance. An English resident in Paris, writing in 1842, compared the comforts offered by London with those of Paris, in a manner unfavourable to England, for he considered the French, in every respect, more clean and civilized than the English.[2] Under Louis-Philippe the streets were being widened, better houses were being built, and the town was being embellished in many ways. L'Arc de Triomphe was finished in 1836, the Place de la Concorde the same year, while the church of La Madeleine was opened in 1842. With the rapid development of gas lighting Paris was fast becoming *'la ville lumière'* and the social life of the inhabitants – of one fraction at least – was undergoing a transformation. The hectic night life, for which it had long been famous, was increasing with rapid strides and attracting many foreigners. The improved lighting and the use of large plate-glass windows gave the cafés a splendour they had not hitherto possessed, while the use of wooden blocks for paving the streets and of macadam for the sidewalks, made it possible to place tables on the pavement itself, without exposing clients to the danger of being splashed with mud, or covered with dust, from passing vehicles. With the pleasure of sitting out of doors the large boulevard cafés reached the importance which they enjoy today. Under Louis-Philippe Paris attained a luxury which it had not known, even in the gayest days of the old world, before the Revolution.

Baudelaire, at twenty-one, with his independent means, suddenly came into the midst of this life of pleasure, and, with his inherited taste for luxury, his natural tendency for enjoyment, was an easy victim now that he had the means of gratifying his tastes.

His first concern was to find suitable surroundings which would express his personality. By nature he was far from being an untidy and slovenly bohemian, and had agreed with his friends of the Latin Quarter only in their desire for freedom and their contempt for useless and outworn conventions. His lot had been thrown in with theirs, when he left school and was still under age, only because he had not yet the means to shine in the society in which he felt at home, that of the *jeunesse dorée* of intelligent fops like Musset and Roger de Beauvoir. He did not care for the unshaven chins, the unwashed bodies and the dirty linen of the Latin Quarter heroes, and he disliked their squalor and their lack of civilized manners. There was little in common between him and bohemians like Aloysius Bertrand, who had literally died of hunger. Now that he had an income of his own, he no longer wanted to be identified with them, and the typical attic of the student no longer satisfied him. He settled first in a modest one-roomed flat on the Quai de Béthune in the Île-Saint-Louis, where he kept a manservant and was able to entertain his mother.[3] His former friends, Prarond and Levavasseur, when they came to see him, expressed surprise at his living so far from everything, everything being for them their old haunts round the Schools of the University. He did not listen to them for his ambitions were now set on higher things, and he was glad to make a break with his associates of the time before his majority. He was now seen less frequently at the cafés of the Latin Quarter, but had crossed the river, and used to haunt the new ones on the Boulevard de Gand – now Boulevard des Italiens – the Brasseries des Martyrs and the Divan Lepelletier, which opened its doors in 1837 and which had become the meeting-place of elegant writers such as Tattet, Arago and Roger de Beauvoir.

At the end of 1842, for some reason which is unknown, he left the Île-Saint-Louis and moved to the Rue Vaneau, where he seems to have remained for about six months, but his life at this juncture is mysterious and it is not known what he was doing. It appears, however, that his parents were already beginning to be seriously concerned at his spendthrift ways, and worried when they heard that he had been trying to realize his father's investments on the pretext of investing the proceeds in commercial stock, but in reality to procure ready money. In October 1842 his mother was trying to prevent him from obtaining complete control of his capital, and her struggles continued until June 1843, when, at her earnest request, and under threat of sterner measures, he consented to allow her to take charge of his financial affairs and to pay him the interest herself in monthly instalments.[4]

In the autumn of 1843 Baudelaire moved back to the Île-
Saint-Louis, this time to the Hôtel Lauzun, the beautiful
house built between 1650 and 1658 by the architect Le Vau
for Charles Gruyn, Sieur des Bordes. In 1682 it had passed
into the hands of the Duc de Lauzun, whose name it now
bears, and whose association with La Grande Mademoiselle,
the daughter of Gaston of Orleans, is known to history. This
house, one of the most perfect of its kind, with its painted
woodwork and its ceilings by Lesueur, gives a good picture
of the manner of living of a rich nobleman in the seventeenth
century. In the nineteenth century, however, the Hôtel
Lauzun had fallen from its former glory and, in 1844, it
was called L'Hôtel des Teinturiers because it had a dye
works in the ground-floor rooms at the end of the courtyard. Floods of coloured liquid used to flow over the cobbles
and columns of evil-smelling smoke rose from the basement
windows, as from some crematorium.[5] The show-rooms in the
front looking on to the river were unspoilt, and, in the
eighteen-forties, were inhabited by Fernand Boissard, a
young man of means who could afford to keep them as they
should be kept. He was gifted with many talents but came
to nothing because he squandered his gifts in passionate
admiration of too many arts, going from music to painting,
and from painting to poetry. Delacroix describes, in his
Journal,[6] his extraordinary virtuosity on the violin when
under the influence of hashish. And Gautier declared that
he wore himself out in a multiplicity of enthusiasms, but
that, if he had been obliged by necessity to canalize his
powers, he would have become an excellent painter.[7]
Another picturesque tenant at the Hôtel Lauzun at this
time was the well-known Dandy, Roger de Beauvoir, whose
name is met everywhere in the memoirs and letters of the
middle of the nineteenth century. He was endowed with
many gifts for he was handsome, rich and elegant, he was
the idol of all fashionable young men of the day who tried
to imitate him, and also the spoilt darling of the older
generation who never seemed to feel any inclination to

keep him in order. His apartment was one of the most
famous of his day and was even described in *La Mode*, which
is assuredly the height of fame. To a young man of twenty-
one he must have seemed very glamorous at the height of
his popularity and glory.[8] This was the Dandy whom
Baudelaire strove to emulate on an income of one tenth of
his, and it was no wonder that he entangled himself in
financial difficulties from which he was never to extricate
himself.

Baudelaire rented a small apartment composed of a suite
of rooms, with very high ceilings, leading one into the other.
Those who knew him at this time are not agreed about the
outlook of the apartment. Banville describes one large room,
with several small ones opening off it, all looking out on to
the river,[9] while Asselineau assures us that they were at the
back, up a service staircase.[10] Both enlarge on the luxury
of the fittings and mention that he kept a servant.

Baudelaire furnished his rooms richly and in so doing was
obliged to incur heavy debts. He bought the greater part of
his furniture and pictures from a dealer called Arondel,
whose shop was on the ground floor of the house, and who
took advantage of his youth to fleece him, and to make him
sign obligations the extent of which he did not understand.
He was still paying instalments and interest on these debts
when he died in 1867. It must be admitted that he often
behaved foolishly and when he grew tired of the pictures
and furniture he had ordered, but not paid for, he used to
persuade the dealer to take them back again at a discount,
and buy more on account. Banville says that it was a common sight to see furniture movers coming and going from
Baudelaire's apartment, bringing new furniture and bearing
the old away.

He papered his rooms in the broadest of black and red
stripes – this is common enough today in France but, in the
middle of the nineteenth century, was considered daring and
decadent. There were gilded mouldings on the panels, and
the curtains were of heavy antique damask. In the centre of

the sitting-room stood a beautiful walnut table of the eighteenth century, which served as a writing- as well as dining-table. There were large comfortable chairs and low divans, and the lights were dim and shaded, leaving the further depths of the room in mysterious shadow. No books were to be seen and when guests remarked on this with astonishment, Baudelaire, with a smile of pleasure at having surprised his friends, used to slide back the panels in one wall and point to rows of rare volumes within. He only possessed thirty or forty books in those days, but all were valuable and well chosen – old French poets, Latin poets of the late period, poets of the Renaissance – all bound in leather, tooled by hand and ornamented with gold, sixteenth-century bindings. On other shelves in the cupboards hidden within the walls, were tall bottles of Rhenish wine, and emerald green Hock glasses which looked like lovely flowers on their long, white, graceful stems.[11]

On the walls hung copies of Delacroix' pictures, a delightful portrait of Baudelaire by Émile Deroy,[12] which is valuable as the one record we have of the poet at this happy period of his life. Deroy showed great promise as a painter but he died at the early age of twenty-three. There was one original oil painting by Delacroix entitled *Sorrow*.

There were soft thick rugs everywhere to deaden the sound of footsteps, and a silent manservant appeared at intervals to bring food and drink, or to remove soiled plates, and Baudelaire himself would move noiselessly amongst his guests, sprinkling Eastern perfumes.

This was the kind of life made fashionable and notorious at the end of the century in the novel by Huysmans called *À Rebours*, in the Symbolist school in France, and in the aesthetic movement in England in the 'nineties.

The same care which Baudelaire devoted to his setting he also lavished on his appearance. Hignard tells us that he sometimes looked like a Titian portrait come to life, in his black velvet tunic, pinched in at the waist by a golden belt, with his dark waving hair and his pointed beard.[13] Some-

times again he wore plain black broadcloth, skin-tight trousers fastened under his shining patent-leather shoes, with
white silk socks, a coat with narrow tails, a fine white linen
shirt with broad turned-back cuffs, and a collar wide open
at the neck, tied loosely with a scarlet tie. Again, according
to Nadar,[14] he would wear pale pink gloves. Levavasseur
called him 'Byron dressed by Beau Brummell'. But, whatever
he wore, he designed it himself, and had it made with
meticulous care. At twenty-one he harried his tailor just as,
later in life, he was to drive his publisher to the verge of
madness by his insistence on accuracy of detail, and he demanded fitting after fitting until he was entirely satisfied.
There was always some detail which did not please him –
the tails were too short, or the collar did not fit, or else the
coat did not show a sufficient expanse of shirt front. At last,
when the result was completely to his satisfaction, and he
had strutted like a peacock before the mirror, admiring himself from all angles, he would turn to the tailor and say with
a lordly air: 'Make me a dozen suits like this!'[15]

    At this time one of Baudelaire's extravagances was the
smoking of hashish, and he was a member of the *Club des
Haschichins*, founded by Fernand Boissard, which used to
meet periodically in his apartment at the Hôtel Lauzun.
The Spoelberch de Lovenjoul Collection at Chantilly possesses several invitations from Boissard to Gautier to the
séances of the club, which usually took place in the evening
between five and six o'clock after a simple dinner. It did
not seem to be a very costly experience for Boissard informs
Gautier that the expenses will come to three or five francs
a-head, less than five shillings.[16] Typical meetings of the club
have been vividly described by Gautier.[17] He says that any
bourgeois philistine, if he could have penetrated into the
precincts, would have been terrified at the sight of the members, many of them famous men of letters, solemnly sitting
round a table, waving Renaissance daggers or oriental swords
round their heads, and bending over a bowl of astonishing-
looking green jam, the colour of which was made more lurid

and macabre by the flickering light of the lamps overhead.

It is usual to think of Baudelaire as he appears in his later portraits, with the grim and tragic expression. In the portrait by Deroy, however, he is young and happy and the painter has caught him in a gay and carefree mood. His face is long and oval, with delicate sensitive nostrils, and his complexion is almost that of a girl, while his hair hangs, after the fashion of the day, in loose ringlets over his shoulders, and he wears a little beard which, according to his friends, gave him the appearance of a 'Christ espiègle'. So fine and delicate are the arches of his eyebrows that today one would almost dare say that they were plucked. His hands are long and slender, full of expression, but most noticeable of all are his eyes, those astonishing eyes, 'two drops of black coffee' as Banville describes them, shining with intelligence and mischief. All his friends were agreed that, at twenty-one, Baudelaire had a charm which was irresistible, and a power of bewitching all those who came into contact with him. Banville who, as an already published author, was more important than he in the literary world, fell completely under his sway, as we realize from his account of their first meeting.[18]

'Night had fallen, clear, peaceful and magic,' wrote Banville. 'We had come out of the Luxembourg Gardens, we were walking on the boulevards, and in the streets, the mysterious movement and murmur of which the poet had always cherished with eagerness. In the course of that night, which has remained with me as the best memory of my youth, Baudelaire lavished on me alone the treasure and incalculable richness of his mind, and he was like the princess from the fairy tale who, from her half-open lips, pours out a flood of diamonds and precious stones. That magic night had fled on rapid wings while we were speaking.'

Baudelaire was certainly the most welcome companion for youthful days, and he did not need wine to become excited, for he seemed always to be intoxicated by his own conversation. Asselineau says that he was the only man with whom he had never felt a moment's boredom, for there were no awkward pauses when he was present, and he was one of the most brilliant conversationalists of his generation.[19] He was never at a loss for a topic, but could talk, with equal charm, on aesthetic, political or metaphysical matters. 'Conversation that great, that sole pleasure, of a spiritual human being, he wrote.[20] Wherever he happened to be sitting, people used to gather round him to hear what he was saying, and whenever he spoke he forgot everything – any urgent business or appointment – while his conversation would continue frequently from midday to midnight. As he spoke, it seemed to those who listened as if veils had been lifted from their eyes and that they could now see an infinity of images, of ideas, unfolding, and vistas of fairylands opening out before them.[21]

It was not only men who felt Baudelaire's charm. He had inherited from both his parents a polished and courtly manner which, in 1843, seemed almost an anachronism. Women especially appreciated his gentleness in contrast with the rougher contemporary manners, and he had enough of the feminine in him to be able to understand them. His attitude flattered them, and they were touched by his apparent respect, by the impression that he gave them of drawing near to a sacred shrine. At the same time he kept them constantly amused by his witty conversation and stimulated their imagination. He possessed, declared Banville, the personal gift of grace and charm, which used once to be the prerogative of kings and princes, but the secret of which has now been lost.[22]

But the women whom he met at this time were not solely those whom he treated with respect and deference. He also knew the girl whom he celebrated in a delightful poem, *À une Mendiante Rousse*, with its original rhythm – a verse of three seven-syllable lines, followed by one of four. Although we do not know her name, her face has come down to us in the magnificent portrait by Émile Deroy. Banville, to whom Deroy gave the portrait, has described it in *Mes Souvenirs*, and he has also celebrated its subject in a poem in *Les Stalac-*

tites entitled *À une Petite Chanteuse des Rues*. There is a further poem which she inspired, *À une Jeune Saltimban-que*, which appeared in *La Silhouette* in 1849, signed Privat d'Anglemont, and which a scholar seeks to attribute to Baudelaire,[23] but his arguments would not convince every-one. It is a poem that many contemporary poets might have written, and Privat d'Anglemont, who was a writer of some talent, could have composed it – it is in any case inferior to the one known to have been written by Baudelaire himself, and adds nothing to his reputation.

It was during the years when he was living at the Hôtel Lauzun that Baudelaire earned his reputation for eccen-tricity, affectation and immorality. Biographers, however, forget that he was only twenty-one, and that few men would care to retain in adult life the reputation they had enjoyed when they were little more than boys, or to hear reported, as their considered opinions, the paradoxical and blas-phemous sentiments they had expressed in their student days.

Baudelaire and his young friends, even when they con-sidered themselves hardened and mature men of the world, used often to behave like the youths they were in fact. Some-times, late at night, and overflowing with high spirits, they used to forget their pose of cynical dandies and revert to a state of primitive barbarism more suited to their years. They would then knock over the furniture in the apartment, and break the china and glass in some physical struggle. The neighbours, wishing to sleep, used to send for the concierge, who would arrive in person to remonstrate and to quell the disturbance. Baudelaire, to the amusement of a gallery of admiring friends, would answer, in tones of injured in-nocence: 'What row? There has been no row that I'm aware of! I was merely chopping wood in my sitting-room, and dragging my mistress round the floor by the hair of her head. But all that is nothing which is not done in any gentle-man's drawing-room!'[24] The neighbours, believing the stories which the concierge brought back, would shake their

heads and tell their friends, who, in turn, would pass the
stories on with interest, until they became part of the
Baudelaire legend.

Baudelaire soon realized his powers as a conversationalist,
and his faculty for shocking his elders – and even his contemporaries – for there were few things which he more
enjoyed than to see the amazement or horror reflected in
their faces. In the evenings, at the Café Procope or at the
Closerie des Lilas, he would sit for hours over his after-
dinner coffee, while people gathered round from the other
tables, to gain a vicarious thrill from overhearing the shocking opinions he would express. Knowing that they were
listening intently, he would lean back in his chair, then,
crossing his legs and watching the puffs of smoke rising up
from his cigar into the air, he would begin a story. 'I, who
am the son of an unfrocked priest, know what I'm talking
about!' Or else he would say: 'That was about the time that
I murdered my poor old father!' Next, slowly uncrossing
his legs, with a languid air, he would lean his elbows on the
table, and, staring at the cheese which the waiter had not yet
removed, would say in meditative tones: 'Don't you think
that the cheese they've given us this evening has a faint
taste of child's brain?' [25]

Philippe Audebrand used to say that Baudelaire told him
he was so spare and almost emaciated because he fed on a
diet of stewed frogs. [26]

Wherever Baudelaire sat all other conversation ceased
immediately and those who listened most intently were
those who spread the most unfavourable stories. It is true
that he himself was responsible with his desire to astound
his public, and he himself related the fantastic tales of his
love affairs, in which he claimed that he could never feel
love or desire for any normal woman, but felt attraction
only towards monsters. This was a pity, he concluded, as
these freaks of nature were always so delicate, and he had
already lost several giantesses through consumption, and
a couple of dwarfs through gastritis. 'One of them was only

seventy-two centimetres high,' he added regretfully, 'but one can't have everything in this world!'[27]

One evening, we are told,[28] as he sat amongst friends in a café, spinning as usual some incredible yarn, he noticed that a woman sitting at the next table was listening to him with great attention. Suddenly he paused in the middle of a sentence, and, turning to her, said with the utmost politeness: 'Mademoiselle, you who are crowned with sheaves of such golden corn, and who listen to me with such eager interest, do you know what I long to do? I long to bite into your white flesh, and, if you will permit me, I'll tell you how I'd like to make love to you! I'd like to take your two hands, bind them together, and then tie you up by your wrists to the ceiling of my room! When this was done I'd kneel before you in worship, and kiss your snow-white feet!'

The golden-haired woman did not wait to hear any more, for, struck with terror – as those who tell the story claim, but, what is more likely, in embarrassment, since no one likes to be the subject of public mockery – she departed, nervous of what he might say next, for he was known to stop at nothing. Now he merely shrugged his shoulders and said, as if regretfully: 'A pity! Silly little fool! It would have given me great pleasure!'

This is one of the stories frequently related by critics and biographers to exemplify the poet's sadistic tendencies and habits.

There were, however, occasions when his pose of cynicism misfired, as when he first met Leconte de Lisle, when he is alleged to have said to him,[29] 'If I had a son I'd teach him to pay no attention to the prejudices of morality, and I'd advise him to practise sodomy!' 'Naturally!' answered Leconte de Lisle coldly, 'sodomy is a generally accepted habit!'

Biographers and critics, who repeat these fantastic stories as if they were true facts, seeing in them the evidence of immorality, eccentricity or abnormality, forget – or do not know – that, in the middle of the nineteenth century, aspiring writers felt it necessary to develop some personal idiosyn-

crasy in order to distinguish themselves from the common
herd. Baudelaire reached manhood during the reign of
Louis-Philippe, an age universally considered vulgar and
prosaic, and devoid of refinement or prestige. The 'Bourgeois King', with his carefully rolled umbrella – the sign of
an economical and provident nature – was taken, by the
general public, as the symbol of the age. The domestic
virtues of the sovereigns, the simple and unaffected manners
of the whole royal family, pleased and flattered the middle
class which had become the most influential section of
French society. They were grateful to him for throwing open
the palace and gardens, on certain days, to the public, and
for giving them access even to the private apartments. Each
bourgeois couple was touched to see that the royal pair
shared the same room and the same conjugal bed, and they
were happy to notice everywhere evidence of a happy united
family life, very similar to their own. They were still more
pleased when the servant, who was showing them the royal
apartments, informed them that the King, just like any
father of a family, used to carve at table for everyone, even
if important guests were present, such as ambassadors or
kings. His sons, moreover, attended an ordinary *lycée*, just
like the simplest of his subjects, and there was much rejoic-
ing in the palace when one of them gained a prize. On half-
days they were allowed to invite their schoolmates to play
in the royal gardens, even if they were the grocer's sons from
round the corner.

Louis-Philippe's reign was a materialistic and unglamor-
ous age. Utility and profit were the only ideals which seemed
to move the masses of the public, and popular literature
suffered from the same defect. So it came about that certain
sections of the literary world, incapable of accepting this
prosaic middle-class ideal but, at the same time, out of
sympathy with the humanitarian doctrines of the political
reformers, banded themselves together into a little independent society, on the fringe of larger society, and prided
themselves on despising money and on living for Art alone,

art spelt with a very large capital letter. The artists and writers, who belonged to this society, reacted violently against all the conventions – in morality, in their manner of living and of dressing.

This was, however, no new manifestation in literature, and their elders, ten years before, after the Revolution of 1830, had been the notorious Bouzingos who were eventually crushed under the growing materialism of the age. Baudelaire's behaviour ceases to seem strange if it is compared with that of the writers of the previous decade. In the eighteen-thirties Gautier's usual dress was a frock-coat trimmed with black brandenburghs – not to mention his medieval red doublet of *Hernani* fame. Jehan du Seigneur always wore a black velvet tunic, with a taffeta tie, while Barbey d'Aurevilly's normal dress was a tight-fitting coat with wide pleated basques, opening on to a green silk waistcoat and a goffered lace jabot, and with these he wore skin-tight trousers of a white material with a pale blue stripe running down the side seams. The crowning touch was a wide-brimmed black hat lined underneath with crimson velvet. Théophile Dondey, who changed his name, by anagram, to Philothée O'Neddy, used to claim that he was obliged to keep his glasses on at night, as he was so short-sighted that otherwise he would be unable to see his dreams. Baudelaire never equalled Gérard de Nerval in eccentricity, who used to go on a visit to his friends, taking with him a large Renaissance bed, and then used to sleep on the floor beside it, out of respect for it. He used to bring a skull to parties with him as a drinking mug, claiming it was that of his father killed in the retreat from Russia, and he was also reputed to have gone walking in a public park in Paris, leading a live lobster on a pale blue leash.

The desire to astonish and to shock was common to all the rising poets and artists in the eighteen-thirties. A full understanding of the general trend of this period should inspire caution, and persuade critics not to take too seriously Baudelaire's extremely youthful eccentricities.[30]

[4]

The Black Venus
1842 — 1844

IT was at this time that Baudelaire formed what his friends
called his disastrous relationship with the mulatto woman,
Jeanne Duval, who was to bring him so much unhappiness.
It is not known precisely when they met but, by the autumn
of 1843, he was certainly deeply involved with her.[1] She was
an actress of no particular talent who played in a Latin
Quarter theatre called Le Théâtre du Panthéon, which was
eventually pulled down when that section of Paris was re-
built after the revolution of 1848. Descending the Rue Saint-
Jacques one came upon it suddenly, after passing under the
arch of Le Passage Saint-Benoit which led through the
buildings of an old abbey to a small courtyard, on one side
of which stood the remains of the chapel out of the walls of
which the theatre had been built.[2] The plays acted in it
were of mediocre quality, and the audience was chiefly
composed of students who used to wait in gangs every night
at the stage-door, to invite the actresses to a noisy supper of
beer and sausages in one of the bars near by. Baudelaire,
with his smart clothes and his polished manners, must have
struck a discordant note among the hirsute scholars.

Jeanne Duval had been chosen as a member of the cast
largely on account of her sex attraction. The part she was
given in one play consisted in saying, once every evening,
'Dinner is served, Madame!'[3]

Baudelaire differed from the common herd of students,
not only by his clothes, but also by the manner of his court-
ship. He did not try, as the average student would have
done, to burst into Jeanne Duval's dressing-room, nor even
to wait for her after the performance at the stage-door and

force his attentions on her. At first he sent her an expensive bouquet of hot-house flowers, just as if she had been a prima donna at the Royal Opera House, begging her respectfully for an audience at her pleasure. He was never less than courteous to every woman, and was said to have treated each servant-girl as if she were a noble lady, and he her most devoted suitor. For a few evenings, after he had been granted permission to speak with her, he came with a carriage to the stage-door and requested the honour of driving her home. It was only very gradually that he became more daring and exacting. She seems to have been mystified by this shy young man of a kind she had never yet encountered, who apparently had much money to squander in a foolish and extravagant manner, and who was said to belong to an important family. She finally, very graciously, granted him permission to establish her in an apartment of her own.

Was Baudelaire, when he started this relationship, merely trying once again to astonish and to impress? Did he perhaps derive pleasure from seeing people nudge each other as he entered a café accompanied by his mistress, and from imagining the whispered comments? 'I say! Have you seen Charles Baudelaire with his Negress?' Or was it genuine attraction that he felt? Did she perhaps awaken in him the memory of warm southern countries, of lazy afternoons spent lying beneath palm trees, the shade of which seemed deep purple against the brilliant skies, and from which fell a heavy blanket of drowsy languor, while a dark girl with velvet eyes, darker than her dusky skin, gently fanned his sleep, and kept from his couch the noxious buzzing insects?[4] Who can tell what was in his mind?

All we know is that Jeanne Duval played a decisive part in his life, greater than that played by any one individual – more important even than that of his mother. In spite of all the harsh things written against her, there must have been some quality in her which held him to the end, and in some queer way he must have been deeply attached to her. Certainly there must have been some good in her which neither his mother nor his friends were able to perceive. They saw only the quarrels, or heard his outbursts, in rare moments of expansion, after he had been exasperated beyond the pitch of endurance by some cruelty, treachery or arrant stupidity on her part. What he felt for her, at the end, must have been something deeper than mere passion, something warmer than human pity, which is all that outside observers saw in his later attitude to her. But he had to experience suffering, hatred and disgust before he reached that final stage. In their private life together, she must have been less cruel than she has been painted. Once, when he was obliged to leave her, he described her as his only companion and sole joy, and declared that several times she had sold her furniture and jewels for him.[5] It was true that it was he who had given them to her, but if she had been as evil as all critics claim, she would not have consented to sacrifice them.

From the scanty evidence we possess – in Baudelaire's letters to his mother, where he unburdened himself of his distress – it would seem that the suffering which she caused him came chiefly through ignorance, weakness and through her addiction to drugs and drink – things she did not care what means she used to get, for, after she lost her beauty through excess, he was the only person from whom she could obtain enough money to buy them.

Now she gave up her undistinguished stage career, and settled in the little apartment which he gave her, and which she furnished in oriental style, with Eastern rugs and hangings, as a suitable setting for her dusky beauty. This information we obtain from Nadar, who knew her before he realized that she was Baudelaire's mistress.[6] It is difficult to discover anything precise about Baudelaire's relationship with her, or about her appearance or personality. Accounts vary so much that we are not even certain whether she was beautiful. But whether she was or not is of no account; what is important is that she was beautiful in the poet's eyes. Of that there can be no doubt. Whenever he mentions her in his letters, or in his private journals, even after he had ceased to love her with passion, he talks of her extraordinary beauty, and expresses surprise that everyone should not have realized this.[7] The drawings he made of her show clearly how he saw her. There is no doubt that his conception of her inspired him, uplifted him and made him feel alive. 'Que m'importe la réalité placée hors de moi si elle m'a aidé à vivre, à sentir que je suis et ce que je suis.'[8]

There is only one known authentic portrait of Jeanne Duval, painted by Manet, when she was in middle age, and it was found in his studio after his death, with a note in his handwriting, which stated that it is of Jeanne Duval, the mistress of Baudelaire.[9] She is reclining on a couch, with the upper part of her body leaning against the back, and she is dressed in a full crinoline. Her face is angular, and somewhat haggard, but shows good bones. Most remarkable are the extraordinary length of her hand which rests over the back of the sofa and the long slimness of her foot. Her hair is not as it has been described by those who knew her in her youth, black and curly, it looks straight as it hangs down on each side of her face, and it is dark red in colour. Perhaps it was that, as she was painted in her forties, her hair was going grey and she had tinted it with henna, which often has the effect of making it straight. There is something tragic in the face which possesses nevertheless the memory, the blurred impression, of beauty, as the broken, excavated statue recalls its former perfection. Her dark eyes, sunken deep, still burn with a bright fire.

Nadar tells us that she was a dark girl with eyes as large as saucers, that her nose and mouth were perfect and would not have seemed out of place in an Egyptian queen, while her hair fell in waves and curls, in a dark foaming cascade, over her shoulders. She glided in and out of the room, he said, with feline grace, with the tortuous and sinuous movements of a Javanese dancer. With her shining, silken dresses, billowing round her, she seemed, even when she walked, as if she danced.

Banville said that there was something divine in her as well as bestial.

Baudelaire has described her in his poems, as she was during these early years, and one feels in every line that he wrote his passion and his adoration for her beauty. But what she herself thought of him and of his worship is not clear, for she spoke very little. When we catch glimpses of her, she is always sitting alone in silence, reclining half dressed on a couch, and gazing into the distance with languid, half-seeing eyes. No one could have guessed what thoughts floated behind the dark eyes or what the disdainful curl of the lips meant. Baudelaire said:[10]

> *Tes yeux, où rien ne se révèle*
> *De doux ni d'amer,*
> *Sont deux bijoux froids où se mêle*
> *L'or avec le fer.*

She only knew that Baudelaire was spending money lavishly on her, and it is clear that she was dazzled by the munificence of his gifts, and the luxury of his rooms at the Hôtel Lauzun. She thought, as indeed did all his friends, that he was a person of immense wealth. She knew that his mother was the wife of a personal friend of the Heir Apparent, a man destined to reach the highest honours in the land. She used to talk to Nadar, before he knew it was Baudelaire, of the great wealth and old-world manners of her lover. It is clear, from Nadar's account, that she considered him a generous, kind-hearted lunatic, rather than a satisfactory lover or companion. He is very insistent on this point and tells us that she used to go into paroxysms of laughter whenever Baudelaire was mentioned in the character of a lover, as if this were indeed the best joke in the world. She did not understand his sensitivity, his shyness, his love of beauty and his longing for perfection; that he gave to everything that he undertook the same meticulous care: the writing of a sonnet, or the making of a suit. He did not however ask her to understand, or to be intelligent, for it was not what

she was that concerned him most, but what she made him
feel, the emotion she awakened in him. He asked her only
to be beautiful, and to permit him to gaze at her with worship, to his heart's content.

> *La très-chère était nue, et, connaissant mon cœur,*
> *Elle n'avait gardé que ses bijoux sonores,*
> *Dont le riche attirail lui donnait l'air vainqueur*
> *Qu'ont dans leurs jours heureux les esclaves des Mores.*
>
>   .   .   .   .
>
> *Elle était donc couchée et se laissait aimer,*
> *Et du haut du divan elle souriait d'aise*
> *À mon amour profond et doux comme la mer,*
> *Qui vers elle montait comme vers sa falaise.*
>
> *Les yeux fixés sur moi, comme un tigre dompté,*
> *D'un air vague et rêveur elle essayait des poses,*
> *Et la candeur unie à la lubricité*
> *Donnait un charme neuf à ses métamorphoses;*
>
> *Et son bras et sa jambe, et sa cuisse et ses reins,*
> *Polis comme de l'huile, onduleux comme un cygne,*
> *Passaient devant mes yeux clairvoyants et sereins;*
> *Et son ventre et ses seins, ces grappes de ma vigne,*
>
> *S'avançaient, plus câlins que les Anges du mal,*
> *Pour troubler le repos où mon âme était mise,*
> *Et pour la déranger du rocher de cristal*
> *Où, calme et solitaire, elle s'était assise.*
>
>   .   .   .   .
>
> *– Et la lampe s'étant résignée à mourir,*
> *Comme le foyer seul illuminait la chambre,*
> *Chaque fois qu'il poussait un flamboyant soupir,*
> *Il inondait de sang cette peau couleur d'ambre!* [11]

When Jeanne Duval came to the Hôtel Lauzun, Baudelaire used to make her sit in an armchair opposite the
window, so that the light streamed in on her.[12] He would
then gaze at her with admiration, kneel before her in worship and kiss her feet. Sometimes he would read poems to

her which he had composed, or else poems in a language which she did not understand. She used to remain, placidly reclining in her armchair, with scarcely a movement on her imperturbable face, dreaming perhaps of the distant lands where she was born, but, every now and then, she yawned and stretched herself like a Persian cat, and her body rippled like the surface of the sea ruffled by a light breeze. It was not surprising if sometimes she became bored, and thought her lover odd and unbalanced, it was no wonder that she often felt dissatisfied at being worshipped like an image in a shrine.

Baudelaire has analysed his attitude towards love with clearsightedness in a tale which he wrote at this time, *La Fanfarlo*, in which he studied himself in the person of the hero, Samuel Cramer. For Cramer, as for Baudelaire, passion seemed to be less an affair of the senses than of the higher faculties, especially of the imagination. Love for him was first a longing for perfect beauty, and he loved the human body because it seemed to him to be the concrete and material expression of divine harmony, as a beautiful piece of architecture mysteriously inspired with movement. 'Tantôt il lui demandait la permission de lui baiser la jambe, et il profitait de la circonstance pour baiser cette belle jambe dans telle position qu'elle dessinât nettement son contour sur le soleil couchant.' [13]

Was this all that there was between Baudelaire and Jeanne Duval, this aesthetic worship? Did he prefer, as so many of his biographers have thought, to smell the flower of passion, but not to pluck it? Some of the friends who knew him best in these early years, seem to have thought so. Sentimental Banville did not ask himself the question, though his remarks imply this opinion. But Nadar was definite on the point and stated categorically that Baudelaire never possessed Jeanne Duval, nor any other woman.[14] It is impossible for us now to be certain of the truth, since even his contemporaries were ignorant of it. One thing appears clearly from a study of the poet's letters and writings, and that is,

if he never possessed a woman it was not through indifference
or lack of desire, but must have been on account of some
physical infirmity. Little is known about his experiences
with women since he never fully confided in anyone, not
even in those who knew him at an age when young men keep
nothing from each other. Perhaps his sensitivity did not
permit him to acknowledge to others a physical disability,
and to imagine his case being discussed among his friends.
On the contrary, although he never mentioned details, he
gave them the impression that he was sexually promiscuous,
even while expressing in every line he wrote the profoundest
contempt for women. In truth this contempt did not exist,
for intimate friendship with intelligent and cultivated
women was a necessity to him, and he had, all through his
life, many devoted women friends. It is permissible to read
into his diatribes against women his feeling of inferiority
before them, his despair at his incapacity to give them complete satisfaction. With them, or thinking of them, he seems
to have been to an exaggerated extent conscious of their
physical appetites and desires. 'La Femme est naturelle, c'est
à dire abominable.' [15] Or again, 'La jeune fille est une petite
sotte et une petite salope; la plus grande imbécillité unie à
la plus grande dépravation.' [16] Then, to give himself confidence, and to keep his self-respect, he used to pretend to
despise them, and to consider them as belonging to the lower
creatures. 'J'ai toujours été étonné qu'on laissât les femmes
entrer dans les églises. Quelle conversation peuvent-elles
avoir avec Dieu? La femme ne sait pas séparer l'âme du
corps. Elle est simpliste comme les animaux. – Un satirique
dirait que c'est parce qu'elle n'a que le corps!' [17]

His close women friends, however, were not deceived by
this pretence, for they seem to have understood him, and to
have done their utmost to put him at his ease with them.
Madame Meurice wrote to him, when he was on his lecture
tour in Belgium, to make him feel that there are some people
at least who still remember him and love him. 'Ah! if only
you were in Paris you would come and smoke a cigarette in

my window-box, for my garden is so small as not to deserve
any more ambitious name. I often sit in it in the evening, just
as I was sitting the first time you came to see me – do you
remember? My husband is often out to dinner and I dine
alone or in *tête-à-tête* with imaginary friends. You've been
my guest on several occasions, though you yourself may not
have been aware of it. Do come back, and turn these imaginary dinners into real ones! And we'll talk together afterwards. You're the only person in the world who has made
me believe that one needn't necessarily be bored if one talks
of other things but politics.' [18]

Baudelaire was indeed far from being the sexually de-
bauched young man he wished it to be believed. Hignard
tells us that the poet gave him the poem which begins 'Hélas!
qui n'a gémi sur autrui, sur soi-même?' at this time, which
reflects a very much more innocent and naïve state of mind. [19]

> Hélas! qui n'a gémi sur autrui, sur soi-même?
> Et qui n'a dit à Dieu: 'Pardonnez-moi, Seigneur,
> Si personne ne m'aime et si nul n'a mon cœur?
> Ils m'ont tous corrompu; personne ne vous aime!'
>
> Alors, lassé du monde et de ses vains discours,
> Il faut lever les yeux aux voûtes sans nuages
> Et ne plus s'adresser qu'aux muettes images,
> De ceux qui n'aiment rien consolantes amours.
>
> Alors, alors, il faut s'entourer de mystère,
> Se fermer aux regards, et sans morgue et sans fiel,
> Sans dire à vos voisins: 'Je n'aime que le ciel';
> Dire à Dieu: 'Consolez mon âme de la terre!'
>
> Tel, fermé par son prêtre, un pieux monument,
> Quand sur nos sombres toits la nuit est descendue,
> Quand la foule a laissé le pavé de la rue,
> Se remplit de silence et de recueillement. [20]

Whenever we have evidence of his relations with women he
appears as timid and as shy as any schoolboy. We know
what his attitude was towards Madame Autard de Bragard

when he was twenty, and what his behaviour to Madame
Sabatier was when he was thirty. Both Nadar, and the painter
Rops, state that he died a virgin. It is true that Rops only
knew him at the end of his life when it is quite possible that
he might have become impotent, or have ceased to have
physical relationships with women. Nadar's statement would
be more difficult to refute, since he knew Baudelaire at
twenty-one and was a close friend of his. He also knew Jeanne
Duval and he affirms that she told him that there had never
been anything between them, but platonic worship on
Baudelaire's side, who expected nothing more from her than
to be allowed to read his poems to her. He was, she said, 'a
gentle inoffensive lunatic, whose passion spent itself in ver-
sifying'.[21] Perhaps she found him unsatisfactory as a lover
and these words express disappointment and disillusionment. Such a state of mind might be the inspiration of his
poem, *Sed non Satiata*, inspired by her.

> *Bizarre déité, brune comme les nuits,*
> *Au parfum mélangé de musc et de havane,*
> *Œuvre de quelque obi, le Faust de la savane,*
> *Sorcière au flanc d'ébène, enfant des noirs minuits,*
>
> *Je préfère au constance, à l'opium, au nuits,*[22]
> *L'élixir de ta bouche où l'amour se pavane;*
> *Quand vers toi mes désirs partent en caravane,*
> *Tes yeux sont la citerne où boivent mes ennuis.*
>
> *Par ces deux grands yeux noirs, soupiraux de ton âme,*
> *O démon sans pitié! verse-moi moins de flamme;*
> *Je ne suis pas le Styx pour t'embrasser neuf fois,*
>
> *Hélas! et je ne puis, Mégère libertine,*
> *Pour briser ton courage et te mettre aux abois,*
> *Dans l'enfer de ton lit devenir Proserpine!*[23]

With regard to Nadar's assertion, it must be remembered
that he was a coarse-grained man who respected nothing,
and it is probable that it was he himself, though he says it
was a friend, who desired Jeanne Duval as a lover, and, very

possibly, he made her his mistress without Baudelaire's knowledge. If this were so he would prefer to think that his friend had not wished, or had been unable, to have physical relations with her. Nadar does not contemplate the possibility of his having had earlier relationships with women, with squint-eyed Louchette, or the red-haired beggar-girl, of whom both Prarond and Levavasseur tell us. There is no positive proof of the poet ever having had physical relationship with any woman, except for the undisputed fact of his having suffered from syphilis. In a letter to his mother, he tells her that he contracted the disease when very young, presumably at the age of twenty or twenty-one, when he composed the epitaph mentioned in an earlier chapter. He was certainly treated for the disease and died of it. As far as can be judged from his own amateur diagnosis in his correspondence, since there was no post-mortem, and no report from any doctor exists, the disease appears, according to modern medical opinion, to have been contracted and not inherited, though this can no longer be proved with complete certainty. Nadar does not definitely state that Baudelaire remained a virgin on account of impotence, though that is the only possible conclusion to reach from his remarks. On the other hand, the fact of his having died of syphilis cannot be advanced, as has so frequently been done, as irrefutable proof of his not having been impotent, since there are various ways of contracting the disease, and varying degrees and forms of impotence which need not preclude the contracting of it in the normal fashion.

A study of the erotic poems of Baudelaire suggests the view that the most intense physical sensations he ever received were through the organ of sight, sensations amounting almost to orgasm. This may conceivably have been the result of incapacity to reach full satisfaction in a normal manner. A passage from the *Journaux Intimes* might lead to the conclusion that he had the inclinations of a *voyeur*:

'Je crois que j'ai déjà écrit dans mes notes que l'amour ressemblait fort à une opération chirurgicale. ... Entendez ces soupirs, prélude d'une tragédie de déshonneur, ces gémissements, ces cris, ces râles, qui ne les a proférés, qui ne les a irrésistiblement extorqués? … Ces yeux de somnambule révulsés, ces membres dont les muscles jaillissent et se roidissent comme sous l'action d'une pile galvanique; l'ivresse, le délire, l'opium, dans leurs furieux résultats, ne vous donneront certes pas d'aussi curieux exemples.' [24]

It is evident that Baudelaire's sensuality was cerebral rather than physical. In *La Fanfarlo* he writes: 'La jouissance avait engendré chez lui ce contentement savoureux qui vaut peut-être mieux que l'amour comme l'entend le vulgaire.' [25]

There is no certainty that he ever enjoyed complete satisfaction in physical love, and a sensual erotic poem such as *Le Léthé* might suggest the exasperation of desire rather than its fulfilment. Whenever he has written of love it was always in terror or in disgust: 'Épouvantable jeu où il faut que l'un des joueurs perde le gouvernement de soi-même.'[26]

Nevertheless, when all these arguments have been weighed, the conviction remains that there was more in Baudelaire's feelings for Jeanne Duval than merely cerebral orgasm. It is impossible not to feel that it was with her that he experienced the most intense, perhaps the only intense, physical sensations of his life. The emotional mood expressed in the poems inspired by her bears this out if they are compared with any of his other love poems, even those written for the actress Marie Daubrun.

When the available evidence has been sifted, one surmises – and it can be no more than surmise – that a likely explanation is that in his youth Baudelaire was not completely impotent, though he may have become so later, either through venereal disease, or through some other cause, but merely pathologically timid, and that he found it impossible to have intercourse with a woman whom he respected. It may have been that Jeanne Duval, either through physical or merely psychological means, succeeded in stimulating him and making him virile. He does not seem to have been

timid or afraid before her, of whom he never made a friend,
nor seemed, in his youth at all events, to have regarded as a
human being. In different ways they were both dependent
on each other, there was between them so much bitterness,
humiliation, degradation and shame, that he did not need
to feel inferior in front of her, and he thus enjoyed an
intimacy with her he was to enjoy with no other woman.

However, although she was ready to do his will in everything, she had her revenge in her own way. The most intense feelings of ecstasy he ever experienced may have been
those she roused in him, but also some of his greatest suffering came through her. She was cruel and made him feel, as
no one else could, the degradation of his bondage. Even that
he could have endured, if she had only shown him sometimes that she cared or had given him some sympathy, but
nothing ever seemed to move her.

> *Car j'eusse avec ferveur baisé ton noble corps,*
> *Et depuis tes pieds frais jusqu'à tes noires tresses*
> *Déroulé le trésor des profondes caresses,*
>
> *Si, quelque soir, d'un pleur obtenu sans effort*
> *Tu pouvais seulement, ô reine des cruelles!*
> *Obscurcir la splendeur de tes froides prunelles.*[27]

Her hardness and cruelty did not, however, extinguish his
love for her, indeed her very coldness and indifference only
seemed to inflame his passion. She seemed then more unattainable and more worthy of conquest than ever. He longed
to discover what dark thoughts floated behind those steely
eyes which were as expressionless as pools of cold black
water.

> *Je t'adore à l'égal de la voûte nocturne,*
> *O vase de tristesse, ô grande taciturne,*
> *Et t'aime d'autant plus, belle, que tu me fuis,*
> *Et que tu me parais, ornement de mes nuits,*
> *Plus ironiquement accumuler les lieues*
> *Qui séparent mes bras des immensités bleues.*

Je m'avance à l'attaque et je grimpe aux assauts,
Comme après un cadavre un chœur de vermisseaux,
Et je chéris, ô bête implacable et cruelle!
Jusqu'à cette froideur par où tu m'es plus belle! [28]

When he lay with his head pillowed in the hollow of her breasts, he would willingly have let the world go by, and would have accepted eternal damnation on her account. At other times, when passion was stilled, and he paused to reflect on their relationship, he felt diminished in his own eyes. He saw her then, in these moments of bitter clearsightedness, as the woman in *Les Métamorphoses du Vampire*,[29] one of the banned poems. Sometimes he tried to escape from her obsession, to break the spell that bound him to her, and to forget her with other bought women, but, as he lay beside them, he would only think of her, of her grace and beauty, and especially of the wonder of her thick black hair.[30] He knew then that no escape was possible for him and that, even if he broke free, he would find his way back once more into captivity. To keep in her good graces he was obliged to suffer every humiliation, for she was unfaithful to him even with his friends, or with the tradespeople who came to the house. He could refuse her nothing since his need for her was so great. As he wrote in *La Fanfarlo*:[31]

'Il avait singé la passion; il fut contraint de la connaître, mais ce ne fut pas l'amour tranquille; ce fut l'amour terrible, désolant, honteux, l'amour maladif des courtisanes. Il connut toutes les tortures de la jalousie, et l'abaissement et la tristesse où nous jette la conscience d'un mal incurable et constitutionnel.'

Some of the poems inspired by Jeanne Duval reveal the greatest intensity of his joy, some also show the greatest depths of his humiliation, as *Le Vampire*.[32]

Toi qui, comme un coup de couteau,
Dans mon cœur plaintif es entrée;
Toi qui, forte comme un troupeau
De démons, vins, folle et parée,

De mon esprit humilié
Faire ton lit et ton domaine;
– Infâme à qui je suis lié
Comme le forçat à la chaîne,

Comme au jeu le joueur têtu,
Comme à la bouteille l'ivrogne,
Comme aux vermines la charogne
– Maudite, maudite sois-tu!

J'ai prié le glaive rapide
De conquérir ma liberté
Et j'ai dit au poison perfide
De secourir ma lâcheté.

Hélas! le poison et le glaive
M'ont pris en dédain et m'ont dit:
'Tu n'es pas digne qu'on t'enlève
À ton esclavage maudit,

Imbécile! – de son empire
Si nos efforts te délivraient,
Tes baisers ressusciteraient
Le cadavre de ton vampire.'

Passionate love for Jeanne Duval seems to have been over by 1845.[33] After that date, as the result of his limited income, he was no longer able to provide her with the same luxury, and consequently their life together became a torture to both of them. Nevertheless, for the rest of his life, he remained bound to her by ties of loyalty, sympathy, and even of affection. He was never unmindful of what he owed to others, and he never forgot the fire of rapture she had once kindled in him. She had given him a sensation of power and fulfilment which no other woman was ever to give him, and for that he would remain for ever in her debt. He continued to feel affection for her, even when passion was spent, and he no longer desired it. That is the explanation of his behaviour towards her which many biographers have considered despicable weakness or lack of resolution. It was of her surely that he thought when he composed *Le Cheval de Race*, a prose poem from *Spleen de Paris*, when she was old and had lost her beauty.[34]

'Elle est bien laide. Elle est délicieuse pourtant!

'Le Temps et l'Amour l'ont marquée de leurs griffes et lui ont cruellement enseigné ce que chaque minute et chaque baiser emportent de jeunesse et de fraîcheur.

'Elle est vraiment laide; elle est fourmi, araignée, si vous voulez, squelette même; mais aussi elle est breuvage, magistère, sorcellerie! en somme, elle est exquise.

'Le Temps n'a pu rompre l'harmonie pétillante de sa démarche ni l'élégance indestructible de son armature. L'Amour n'a pas altéré la suavité de son haleine d'enfant; et le Temps n'a rien arraché de son abondante crinière d'où s'exhale en fauves parfums toute la vitalité endiablée du Midi français: Nîmes, Aix, Avignon, Narbonne, Toulouse, villes bénies du soleil, amoureuses et charmantes.

'Le Temps et l'Amour l'ont vainement mordue à belles dents; ils n'ont rien diminué du charme vague, mais éternel, de sa poitrine garçonnière.

'Usée peut-être, mais non fatiguée, et toujours héroïque, elle fait penser à ces chevaux de grande race que l'œil du véritable amateur reconnaît, même attelés à un carrosse de louage ou à un lourd chariot.

'Et puis elle est si douce et si fervente! Elle aime comme on aime en automne; on dirait que les approches de l'hiver allument dans son cœur un feu nouveau, et la servilité de sa tendresse n'a jamais rien de fatigant.'

This prose poem was written almost twenty years after the beginning of their relationship, but he had to go through much suffering and humiliation before he reached this compassionate and tender sympathy.

[5]

The Fruits of the Tree
1842 — 1844

FROM a superficial examination of Baudelaire's life at this time, it would seem that he was frittering it away in luxury, frivolity and dissipation. This was, however, far from being true, and his days cannot have been spent only in pleasure and debauch, in flitting from café to bar, and from bar to dance-hall. We are told by many of his friends that he spent long hours in libraries, museums and picture galleries, developing and training his artistic sense, acquiring the knowledge and experience which, in later years, was to surprise his critics, and to astonish posterity. Although he had no regular profession, he must have been working steadily, if intermittently, and he was certainly far from being the idle waster that his parents imagined. He did not like to work at stated hours, and needed long periods of leisure in which to mature any problem which interested him, and to bring to fruition any poem on which he was working. It was his temperament to be as recklessly spendthrift with his time as he was with his money, and he did not care to be obliged to account for every moment. His family might not have considered his activities very valuable or profitable, yet it was precisely this leisure which was an important and fertilizing element in his development. 'C'est par le loisir que j'ai en partie grandi,' he wrote.[1] 'À mon grand détriment, car le loisir sans fortune augmente les dettes et les avanies résultant des dettes. Mais à mon grand profit relativement à la sensibilité et à la méditation.'

His leisure permitted him to develop his talents, without external constraint, in the fruitful years of his youth, allowing him to accumulate his intellectual, spiritual, and also more frivolous, capital, a store from which he was to draw the inspiration and subject-matter of his poems of maturity.

From the accounts of his contemporaries it appears that he was writing in a more concentrated manner during these two years of luxury and leisure than ever again in his life, and his close friends all speak of the many and varied poems and articles which he used to read to admiring audiences almost every evening as he sat in a café, and they add that he had not yet considered the possibility of publishing anything. This may have been because he could not find a publisher or editor prepared to take the risk of printing him, and in his *Journaux Intimes* he mentions his difficulties, for many years, in finding a publisher.[2] It may also have been that, even at that age, he was already suffering from that contradiction in his character which, in later life, was to cause him so much distress, his desire for work coupled with intensity of vision, and, at the same time, his inability to force himself to undertake the ungrateful task of giving adequate shape to his dreams. A fragment of a play written in 1843, which is autobiographical in intent, shows this clearly.[3]

> *Allons! Toujours des mots! Un travail de manœuvre!*
> *Rien de ce que rêva l'écrivain de son œuvre!*
> *Des mots! Des sons! Du vent! Et rien de ce qui fait*
> *Notre esprit glorieux, notre cœur satisfait!*
> *Sentir toujours en soi, luttes intérieures,*
> *Deux hommes, sans repos, se disputant les heures.*

Prarond, who knew Baudelaire from 1839, when they were at the Pension Bailly together, and saw him daily, except for the months of his trip to Mauritius, until the end of 1843, declares that the largest number of *Les Fleurs du Mal* were composed by 1844, that copies of the poems were circulating round the literary cafés of the day, and he adds that, as early as 1843, Baudelaire was already being claimed as the most promising of the coming poets, destined to make a glorious name for himself. There is no reason to doubt this opinion since it is borne out by many other contemporary writers. It is, however, important to realize that, even if the poems written at this time are numerically the largest, they are not the highest in artistic achievement, nor the most profound, and they certainly do not include his great spiritual poems. It is true that the reputation which he enjoyed until comparatively recently was the result of the kind of poetry written in his youth, the reputation of an erotic, satanic and blasphemous poet. Although this is an important aspect of his work, it is only one phase in his spiritual and literary development.

Caussy refuses to accept the testimony of Prarond,[4] saying, in support of his scepticism, that he was mistaken over *Les Yeux de Berthe*, of which a manuscript exists in Baudelaire's handwriting, dated Brussels 1864 and dedicated to a girl whom he met at that time, and he declares that if Prarond was mistaken in attributing this poem to the period of youth, then he may well be mistaken in other cases as well. However, Caussy himself is wrong in believing that this poem was written in Belgium, for it was published in France in March 1864 in *La Revue Nouvelle*, before Baudelaire left the country at all, and it is not certain that Prarond was in fact wrong. He does not call the poem *Les Yeux de Berthe* but *Les Yeux de mon Enfant*, and it is possible that a poem of that title did at one time exist which has not come down to us in its first form, and that in 1864 he remodelled and used it. Then, a little later in Brussels, having no other poem available, he may have copied it out and dedicated it to his new friend, knowing that she would not be likely to discover its publication in the obscure French periodical. He had, in any case, no objection to using again the same material if the mood was similar. In a letter addressed to Madame Sabatier, he used some of the same expressions which he had previously used in writing to Madame Marie, since the emotion which he wished to convey was identical. The drawing of Berthe, which he made in Brussels in 1864, on the manuscript, resembles those he had made of Jeanne Duval when he was young. It is possible that he composed *Les Yeux de mon Enfant*, inspired by Jeanne Duval, in 1842 or 1843, but did not publish it amongst his earliest poems – many of the poems written at this time did in fact remain unpublished for twenty years – as, for instance, *L'Albatros* – and that, in 1864, being short of copy, he used it in a review. Also, when he met the young woman called Berthe, her beauty, so like that of his dark mistress in her youth, awakened in him the memory of that early passion so that the poem once more seemed apposite and he dedicated it to her. He certainly cannot have met her in Brussels since the poem appeared before he went there, and since she is supposed to be the inspirer also of two prose poems, one entitled *Les Bienfaits de la Lune*, dedicated to Mademoiselle B. and published in 1863, and the other *La Soupe et les Nuages*, alleged as well to have been composed earlier.

It is reasonable to accept the testimony of Prarond since it corresponds with that of Du Camp, Asselineau, Banville, Champfleury, and many others. Indeed, Champfleury even claims that, when he got to know Baudelaire in 1845, he saw a complete volume of poems by him, professionally transcribed, bound and ready for publication. This was, he claimed, the nucleus of the future *Les Fleurs du Mal*.

It is not, however, certain that the poems written before 1845 were then exactly in the same form as when they appeared in 1857. It is conceivable – indeed probable – that the poet improved them technically, in versification and imagery, but the initial inspiration would have been that of the earlier years. *À une Dame Créole*, sent in October 1841 to Monsieur Autard de Bragard in Mauritius, was greatly improved in the version which appeared in *L'Artiste* in 1845, and again in the first version of *Les Fleurs du Mal* in 1857.

It is not possible to ascribe an exact date to each of the poems, but we can date a certain number and thus form a general impression of his literary development, which would

probably not be vastly altered by certainty of the date of
each individual poem.

After correlating the isolated facts and grouping the
poems we know to have been at this time in various categories, we can form an opinion of the general trend of his
inspiration during the youthful years of leisure, which run
from the spring of 1842 to the autumn of 1844. The conclusions suggested by the available evidence, lead to a
deeper understanding of the personality and talent of the
poet.

Several poems which we are in the position to date accurately were written before he settled in L'Hôtel Lauzun. They
were *L'Albatros*, which appeared for the first time in *La
Revue Française* in 1859; *A une Malabaraise* which, although
it was published in *L'Artiste* in 1846, was only included in
the posthumous edition of *Les Fleurs du Mal* in 1868; and
finally *A une Dame Créole*, published in *L'Artiste* in 1845,
but which was composed in Réunion in October 1841.

L'Albatros, according to Prarond, was composed immediately after Baudelaire's return from Mauritius, and was
inspired by an episode which occurred on the journey, when
an albatross fell wounded on the deck of the ship, and was
tortured by the crew. The poet's school-friend, Hignard,
declared that he heard him read it when he was living at the
Hôtel Lauzun.[5] His account should be accepted with caution,
for he thought that he heard it in its final form, including
the fourth verse which, we are told, was added, just before
publication in 1859, on the advice of Asselineau, to make
the symbolical image stand out more clearly.[6] This would
seem the true version of the genesis of the poem, since a
manuscript has come to light consisting of three verses
only.[7] Hignard's memory may have been conditioned
through help from the published version. This poem has
been usually much admired, and it figures in most antholo-
gies of French poetry. The present author does not share
this general consensus of opinion, and finds its symbolism
more conventional than is usual with Baudelaire, and would,

on this account alone, even if it were not for the testimony
of the poet's friends, place it amongst his earlier compositions.

The two other poems which are undoubtedly of the same
period are *À une Dame Créole*, sent to Monsieur Autard
de Bragard in October 1841, and *À une Malabaraise* which
is of the same inspiration.

There are as well a certain number of poems not contained in *Les Fleurs du Mal*, two of which were written at
this time. The one which starts: 'Hélas! qui n'a gémi' was
given by Baudelaire to Hignard, when he met him again
after an absence of some years,[8] and it expresses an immaturity and adolescent optimism strange in a sophisticated young
man of twenty-one, which is very much less mature than *À
une Dame Créole*, and which may well have been composed
before he went abroad, but which he gave to his friend, in
memory of their schooldays together. The other poem,
which begins: 'Tous imberbes alors', inspired by Sainte-
Beuve's writings, was sent to the critic in 1844, and is chiefly
interesting as revealing Baudelaire's taste in literature in his
formative period.

Other poems alleged by certain critics to have been composed in the spring of 1843 are still a matter for conjecture.
It will be remembered that Baudelaire had belonged to a
literary society when he was at the Pension Bailly, before his
trip abroad, composed of Prarond, Levavasseur and Dozon
who wrote under the name of d'Argonne. He renewed his
acquaintance with them on his return to Paris. Both Prarond
and Levavasseur, on account of their earlier writings, mentioned in a previous chapter, were anxious now to see their
names in print, and, knowing that their friend Baudelaire
had poems ready, they invited him, with the condescension
which befitted their state as established authors, to collabor-
ate with them and also to share expenses of bringing out a
joint volume. He accepted but suggested that they should
invite a fourth contributor to make the expenses lighter
still, and Dozon was then asked to join them.

Baudelaire submitted his manuscript to the self-consti-
tuted selection committee in February 1843, with a covering
note to Prarond.[9]

'On Monday you'll receive the rest of scribbling,' he
wrote. 'You must teach me how to put it into pages, and how
to arrange the sheets. I rely on you to correct them, and I
beg you to be very severe with any sign of childishness of
style.'

Prarond and Levavasseur took him at his word and
adopted a critical, and even patronizing, attitude to his
contributions, not realizing that he was the most original
poet amongst them. Their final verdict was that his poems
were not suitable for publication in the form in which he
had submitted them, and they proceeded to alter them in
accordance with their own taste. Levavasseur, in a poem
addressed to Prarond, later referred to their joint association.[10]

> *Ce fut dans ce temps-là que d'une amour fervente*
> *Nous aimâmes aussi la Muse sa servante,*
> *Nous nous mîmes à quatre à hanter la maison,*
>
> *Vous et moi, mon ami Baudelaire, et Dozon,*
> *Nous aimions follement la rime. Baudelaire*
> *Cherchait à l'étonner plus encor qu'à lui plaire.*

In later years, when Baudelaire had become famous, he
was ashamed of their conduct and admitted that his poetry
was of a vastly different weave from their *calicot*, adding
that he had submitted for inclusion in their joint volume,
many of the poems which afterwards appeared in *Les Fleurs
du Mal* in 1857.[11]

Baudelaire did not accept their ruling nor their corrections. He was no longer the uncertain youth he had been
in the days at the Pension Bailly, but had much developed
and matured since he had been abroad, and he now knew
what he wanted. He did not get angry, nor argue, but, with
great dignity, removed his copy, and the book went to press

without his contributions. It was privately printed and appeared in May or June 1843. That is the account given by Levavasseur.

This volume of verse did not awaken much interest and a critic, writing in *L'Artiste* in 1844, said: 'There is nothing new or original in this collection of poems. In form they are mere Hugo, and, as far as the ideas are concerned, Musset should, by rights, claim his share of the royalties.'[12] This means that the book was inspired by the conventional tendencies of the day, and was a work which any author, trying his wings, might have produced.

Since 1844 the collection has remained buried beneath the dust of oblivion in a library. In 1929, however, Jules Mouquet, a French scholar, discovered the little book and made a close study of its poems. He came to the conclusion that most of Prarond's were written by Baudelaire, and that those of Levavasseur, if not actually composed by him, show strong evidence of his style. In spite of the testimony of Baudelaire's friends, he became convinced that the poet wished his poems to appear with those of his friends, but that, for some obscure reason, he was reluctant to face the public under his own name.[13] Mouquet's analysis of *Jour de Pluie* is his trump card, where he compares some lines of it with a passage from Baudelaire's story entitled *La Fanfarlo*, published in 1847.[14] It is true that, as he claims, the poet would have been unlikely, as late as 1847, to have borrowed from a work by Prarond and Levavasseur written in 1843, though he might have quoted from himself. He forgets, however, that *La Fanfarlo* has always been thought to have been written at the time when the poet was living at the Hôtel Lauzun, though only published some years later.

When the passage from Baudelaire's story is examined in the light of Mouquet's assertions, they prove to be unconvincing. In the excerpt in question, the hero, Samuel Cramer, is described as reciting a prose version of what he calls a few verses in his first manner – 'quelques mauvaises stances

composées dans sa première manière'. After quoting this
passage Mouquet bids us turn over the pages; then we shall
find, he states, a description of a storm borrowed from a
poem in his friends' collection, *Jour de Pluie*, a few lines of
which have been incorporated in the prose without alteration.
This is very misleading for Mouquet gives the false impression that it is in the prose version of 'quelques mauvaises
stances composées dans sa première manière' that the similarities with *Jour de Pluie* occur. It is not so, and Baudelaire
does not give the substance of the prose version recited by
Samuel Cramer. The two passages which Mouquet links together have no connection with each other, and the storm
described by Baudelaire in the person of the author, has
nothing whatsoever to do with the passage which Cramer
recited, the nature of which we are left to imagine. To reach
the second passage we have to turn over, not a few pages as
Mouquet claims, but twenty-two, a considerable number
considering that the whole story has only forty-two.[15] Moreover, only two lines from Prarond's poem bear any resemblance to the description of the storm in *La Fanfarlo*, for it
cannot be considered a striking similarity that Baudelaire
should say 'le temps était noir' and Prarond 'les nuages
étaient noirs' since it would be difficult to compose a description of a storm in which similar expressions did not
occur.

On the other hand the two lines in question express a
mood which is generally called Baudelairian. Prarond had
said:[16]

> Le ruisseau lit funèbre où s'en vont les dégoûts,
> Charrie en bouillonnant les secrets des égouts.

Whereas Baudelaire wrote in *La Fanfarlo*:[17]
'Le ruisseau, lit funèbre, où s'en vont les billets doux et les
orgies de la veille, charriait en bouillonnant les mille secrets
aux égouts.'

Two lines out of fifty are a very small proportion, and the
attributing of the rest to Baudelaire can be only on arbitrary

grounds. It is possible that he may have suggested the lines, but it may also be that they were inspired by Petrus Borel, or Philothée O'Neddy, or others of that school.[18]

The explanation may be that Baudelaire's influence had impressed itself on his friends, without their realizing it, and that it was they who, in 1843, had been imitating his early manner as expressed in the poems they had heard him recite. They had all been close friends for so many years, and had discussed aesthetic problems so much together, that no one could any longer exactly remember to whom the pearls had originally belonged – they may even have been joint productions – and, in any case, the similarities occur only in isolated phrases.

It is also noticeable that of the poems which Mouquet wishes to ascribe almost entirely to Baudelaire, some are dated June, July, August, October and December 1841, a time when he was away from Paris on his sea voyage. In June and July he was at sea; in September he was at Mauritius; in October at Réunion; and in December on the way home. The poems, however, reveal no trace of his new surroundings which we know, from *À une Dame Créole*, written at the time, to have greatly moved him.

These so-called *Juvenilia* might possibly have been written and discarded by Baudelaire, but they might as easily have been composed by anyone else – by any member of the Bouzingo group ten years before. Since they have echoes of Hugo and Musset, why should they not also be reminiscent of an earlier Baudelaire, who had been the constant companion of the budding poets, and had shared their literary activities? Banville was, as we know, much influenced by Baudelaire in his early days and, since he published his work first, this might as well tempt critics to claim, inaccurately, that it was he who influenced his fellow-poet.

If Mouquet's claim is true it is difficult to explain the accounts of Prarond and Levavasseur, and there is no adequate reason to doubt their testimony since, in other respects, it is trustworthy and consistent. That Baudelaire should wish to

discard these poems, if indeed he ever wrote them, would be
comprehensible, but that honest men like Prarond, Levavasseur and Dozon should claim as their own what they
had not composed is difficult to credit. For consider their
subsequent careers.

Levavasseur, who was a man of means, went back to his
home in Normandy, Le Château de la Lande de Longé, when
he had finished his studies. He became Mayor of his home
town in 1849 and held that office for thirty-six years. From
1852 to 1879 he represented the Canton of Briouze at the
Conseil Général of L'Orne. He contributed to various literary
papers – such as *Le Corsaire-Satan*, and became the
accredited poet of Normandy. He published five collections
of poetry – besides this early joint effort – and also wrote a
life of Corneille. He died in 1896 at the age of seventy-six
greatly honoured and respected. A monument was erected
in his memory in the public square of his native town.

Prarond was renowned as the poet of Abbeville, as Levavasseur was of Normandy. He was well known in the free-
lance journalism in the middle of the century. He too eventually had his monument in his native town, and was decorated
with the cross of *Chevalier de la Légion d'Honneur* in 1890.
He died in 1909, at the age of eighty-eight, full of honours
and years.

Dozon did not become so well known as either Prarond or
Levavasseur. He gave up poetry and would certainly never
have wanted to claim the works of another. He became a
specialist in Slavonic languages and was for many years
French Consul in the Danube provinces.

In 1852, in a work dealing with modern writers, Prarond
mentions the old friends of his youth – Levavasseur, Champfleury, Murger, Banville and others – but cites Baudelaire
only as a writer who 'amongst others we hope not to have
lost for ever'. He goes on to say that Baudelaire had enjoyed
the rare fortune of having made a name without publishing
a single line of verse, merely by reading his poems to his
friends. Prarond would hardly have written in such terms

if he himself had appropriated the only poems of his friend which had ever appeared in print.

Mouquet's second theory refers to a somewhat later period but it can appropriately be discussed here. It is that Baudelaire wrote all the poems which Privat d'Anglemont published under his own name between 1844 and 1847. It is difficult to see why Privat d'Anglemont, who was far better known as a writer than Baudelaire in 1844, should need to borrow poems from anyone to pass off as his own.

Privat d'Anglemont was born in Guadeloupe in 1815 and came from a rich and highly respected family. He was sent to Paris for his education and was a pupil at the Lycée Henri Quatre. After he passed his *baccalauréat*, he signed on as a student at the École de Médecine. At the age of twenty-one he was very handsome and a popular figure in the literary world. When he reached his majority he went back to Guadeloupe to take possession of his inheritance. He spent only twenty-four hours in his native land, and returned immediately to France, although the journey, at that time, took forty-five days each way. After his arrival in Paris he proceeded to live the bohemian life of his contemporaries, the *Bouzingos*, and, in a few years, he had squandered the whole of his capital. He became a well-known journalist, contributing to *Le Magasin Pittoresque, Le Magasin des Familles, La Gazette de Paris, Le Figaro, Le Siècle* and *Le Corsaire-Satan* – he was indeed one of the two contributors to be given a free copy of this last paper – and Baudelaire, at his most popular, was never to be in as great demand with editors as he.

Alfred Delvau declared [19] that if one wanted to characterize the bohemian one would choose Privat d'Anglemont as the typical example. After he had spent all his money he used to live almost entirely in cafés, going from one to the other as long as any were open, and sleeping wherever he could find hospitality, but often in the open. In his life of extreme want he developed tuberculosis, and moved from the public ward of one hospital to the other in search of rest and cure, until finally, with his health permanently broken, he was received as incurable by the Hospice Dubois which looked after impoverished men of letters. He died there in 1859 at the age of forty-four. Devoted and grief-stricken crowds followed his coffin to the cemetery.

He wrote two monographs on the popular dance-halls of the day, *Le Prado* in 1846 and *La Closerie des Lilas* in 1848, also sketches about the various little trades carried on in the capital, which were published in book form in 1854 under the title *Paris-Anecdotes*. His best work, *Paris Inconnu*, appeared posthumously in 1861, and gives a vivid picture of the years of his youth in Paris during the eighteen-thirties.

He also published five sonnets in *L'Artiste* between November 1844 and January 1846, two poems in his *Closerie des Lilas* in 1848 and one in *Le Corsaire-Satan* in July 1846.[20] These are the poems which Mouquet wishes to attribute to Baudelaire. His theory is that Baudelaire felt nervous of publishing his poems under his own name and tried them out under the names of Levavasseur, Prarond and especially Privat d'Anglemont. His arguments are based largely on the ineptitude for verse of these writers. But these poems are not for the most part such that Baudelaire would be the poorer for being deprived of them, nor would they make great poets of those who claimed them. It must also be remembered that in 1845 Baudelaire was beginning to print poems under his own name, for *À une Dame Créole* came out in *L'Artiste* in May that year, indeed in the same month as one of the sonnets signed by Privat d'Anglemont, and only a few months after another poem, *À Yvonne Pen-Moor*, on the same theme as his own. The following year he published, in the same paper, *L'Impénitent* and *À une Malabaraise*, poems vastly superior to those signed by Privat d'Anglemont.

It might be that Baudelaire gave Privat d'Anglemont the poems which he no longer considered good enough to sign himself, and he might conceivably only have revised the work of his friend. But there are no adequate grounds for believing that Privat d'Anglemont could not himself have

composed *À Madame Du Barry* since it resembles a poem
undoubtedly by him, *Madame Joséphine de Fer*, while his
coloured blood and tropical background could have given
him the inspiration for *À Yvonne Pen-Moor* just as readily
as his stay in Mauritius gave Baudelaire the subject matter
for *À une Malabaraise* which is similar in theme.

It is true that one of the sonnets published in *La Closerie
des Lilas* could have been composed by Baudelaire, the one
which opens, 'J'aime ses grands yeux bleus, sa chevelure
ardente',[21] but Privat d'Anglemont did not, in fact, claim
that it was by himself, only that it was given to him by a
girl to whom a poet 'now well known' gave it in 1843 – this
may well have been Baudelaire. It does seem as if, later,
Baudelaire did intend to claim it as his own, for, when Poulet
Malassis republished it in *Nouveau Parnasse Satyrique du
Dix-Neuvième Siècle*, Baudelaire corrected the proofs.[22]

> J'aime ses grands yeux bleus, sa chevelure ardente
>   Aux étranges senteurs,
> Son beau corps blanc et rose, et sa santé puissante
>   Digne des vieux jouteurs.
>
> J'aime son air superbe et sa robe indécente
>   Laissant voir les rondeurs
> De sa gorge charnue à la forme abondante
>   Qu'admirent les sculpteurs.
>
> J'aime son mauvais goût, sa jupe bigarrée,
> Son grand châle boiteux, sa parole égarée,
>   Et son front rétréci.
>
> Je l'aime ainsi! Tant pis ... Cette fille des rues
> M'enivre et me fascine avec ses beautés crues.
>   Tant pis! Je l'aime ainsi!

All the other poems, hitherto attributed to Privat d'Anglemont, might have been written by him, or by someone else,
but they are not very significant since they are not equal to
those which we know Baudelaire to have composed even as
early as 1842.

If we believe with Mouquet that Baudelaire was trying to play one of his practical jokes, then it was strange that, in a society where everything was known, the secret was so well kept, especially as Baudelaire's works were widely known through his habit of reading what he had written to his friends. It is true that Arsène Houssaye, who was editor of *L'Artiste* in 1844, declared that he had seen through his disguise, but this was nearly half a century later, in 1892, when Baudelaire had become famous, and Privat d'Anglemont was forgotten.[23]

Even if we accept these very questionable *Juvenilia*, now attributed to Baudelaire by Mouquet and other critics, we do not find that they throw much new light on the poet's personality or talent, or on his development, since we have other poems, undoubtedly of the same period, which are compositions of a far higher order. *Incompatibilité*, written when he was seventeen, *À une Dame Créole*, *À une Malabaraise* and *L'Albatros*, the most recent of which was composed at least a year before the joint production of Prarond, Levavasseur and Dozon, and several years before the appearance of the poems signed by Privat d'Anglemont.

Although his view of the authorship of the *Juvenilia* is not absolutely convincing, Mouquet provides us with a valuable piece of information which permits us to date two poems in *Les Fleurs du Mal*. Levavasseur had included in one of his poems a line which he claimed he had borrowed from a friend. This was taken from *Les Deux Bonnes Sœurs*, which must therefore have been composed before 1843.[24] He also proves that Levavasseur must have known *La Lune Offensée*.[25] And it seems probable that Dozon knew *Le Rêve d'un Curieux*.[26] Baudelaire did not publish this poem until 1860, and critics have laboured in vain to harmonize it with what he was writing at the time when it appeared.

Baudelaire reached maturity early, maturity not only of sensation and experience, but also of expression. There is no objection, on that score, to the theory that he had composed the greatest number of *Les Fleurs du Mal* before the end of

1844, when he was twenty-three, but postponed publication for thirteen years, first because he was too sensitive to adverse criticism and did not consider that he had reached the perfection which he thought essential in a poet, and later because he could find no publisher prepared to take the risk of bringing out an edition of his poems.

After correlating the evidence to be obtained from Crépet, Champfleury, Asselineau, Prarond, Levavasseur, Banville, Du Camp, and now from Mouquet, it is possible to make a list of the poems from *Les Fleurs du Mal* which were probably composed during the period of Baudelaire's youth and leisure. This list would include the following: *L'Albatros, À une Malabaraise, À une Dame Créole, Don Juan aux Enfers* – this is a rendering in verse of a contemporary picture by Delacroix – *Le Rebelle,*[27] *Le Reniement de Saint Pierre, Les Yeux de mon Enfant, L'Âme du Vin, Le Vin de l'Assassin, Le Vin des Chiffonniers, Allégorie, Le Crépuscule du Matin, Je t'adore à l'egal de la voûte nocturne, Une Nuit que j'étais près d'une affreuse juive, La Servante au grand Cœur, Je n'ai pas oublié voisine de la Ville, Sur le Tasse en Prison, À Théodore de Banville, À une Mendiante Rousse, Le Rêve d'un Curieux, La Lune Offensée, Les Deux Bonnes Sœurs,* and *Une Charogne.*

In this list only two of the erotic love poems figure but the present author, for reasons presently to be discussed, would add all the love poems written under the influence of Jeanne Duval; also the Lesbian poems, *Femmes Damnées, Delphine et Hippolyte* and *Lesbos.* These poems must have been written before the end of 1845, since they were advertised on the cover of Baudelaire's *Salon* early in 1846, and since they belong, in character, to the period of experimentation, when the poet was trying new and varied inspirations, and had not yet reached certainty of where his real talent lay. They belong to a phase of a youthful interest in abnormality, when he was nearest to the inspiration of the wild poets of the Bouzingo movement.

There are several other poems, not included in the above

list, which it would be reasonable to consider as early since
they do not show any particular originality, nor any of the
qualities typical even of Baudelaire's early talent. One of
these, *J'aime le Souvenir de ces Époques Nues*, reveals a
strong influence of André Chénier, whom the poet had admired at school, but in whom he soon afterwards lost interest. Another is *Les Bohémiens en Voyage* which reveals
traces of romantic sentimentality very alien to the poet's
inspiration even as a young man. And finally *Le Soleil* and
L'Élévation which expresses a youthfulness and immaturity,
a healthy, normal mood, which he must have considered
trite and commonplace in his sophisticated phase. In these
four poems he had not yet broken away from early influences, and was trying to write verse on the model of remembered masters, not seeking to give expression to what he
found in himself.

From an analysis of this list it should be possible to form
an opinion of the general characteristics of Baudelaire's
literary development and production before 1845. Three
poems are autobiographical: *Je n'ai pas oublié voisine de la
Ville*, *La Servante au grand Cœur*, and *La Lune Offensée*.
These were probably composed just after the poet left home,
in that period of estrangement from his mother, when he
imagined that she was siding with his stepfather against
him, and betraying him to his enemies, at the time when his
parents were considering removing from him the management of his financial affairs. The first two express regret and
longing for the past, for the days of childhood, when there
was no one to come between his mother and himself. The
third reveals a bitterness of which he must have felt
ashamed, even at the time, for he did not print it until
1862, and then only in a periodical, when he was short of
copy, and he never considered including it in his complete
works – probably out of respect for his mother. Although
he sent her a copy of all that he wrote, he did not send her
the review in which the poem appeared. It ends:[28]

Je vois ta mère, enfant de ce siècle appauvri,
Qui vers son miroir penche un lourd amas d'années,
Et plâtre artistement le sein qui t'a nourri.

Of the erotic poems, already mentioned, written under the influence of Jeanne Duval, only two can definitely be dated as having been written before 1845. It is not unreasonable however to include all those of the same inspiration. It tallies with what we know of Baudelaire's methods that all the poems expressing the burning intensity of his passionate love for his mulatto mistress should have been composed when it was at its height. Passionate love for her seems to have been over by 1845 when, in straitened means, he was no longer able to keep her in luxury, and, when forced into close proximity, their life became an endless wrangle so that he found her a hindrance rather than an inspiration. Writing in 1848 he said, 'You have ill-treated me solely on account of an unfortunate woman whom, for a long time now, I have only cared for out of a sense of duty.'[29] Baudelaire almost always wrote at the moment of intense emotion even if, on reflection, he altered the composition in technical details, and it is thus hard to believe that these poems celebrating his passion could have been composed at any other moment than when it was a living experience in him. Moreover, after 1850 he was writing love poems for Marie Daubrun, also spiritual poems in honour of Madame Sabatier, and certainly no longer felt passion for Jeanne Duval, but only exasperation mingled with compassion.

Baudelaire's eroticism was not unusual in a young man of his age, but what was new and original was his manner of expression. It was surely from the *Champavert* of Petrus Borel or the *Feu et Flamme* of Philothée O'Neddy that he conceived the idea of rendering in the highest form of poetry an emotion which was not the sublimated love of which Lamartine, Hugo or Musset sang, but was a reaction against romantic love, being physical love or lust which hitherto had found expression only in lewd little poems in the style of Béranger. Baudelaire's eroticism reaches the magnificence of the *Song of Solomon*. This eroticism, of which much has been written, was only one phase of his development and was not the final or only expression of his genius.

In this period Baudelaire expressed not only sensual joys but also the pleasure to be found in wine. Prarond declares that *L'Âme du Vin*, *Le Vin de l'Assassin* and *Le Vin des Chiffonniers* were composed before 1843, and there is nothing in their style which indicates that they should be attributed to a later date. Moreover, Banville took a line from *L'Âme du Vin* for a heading to his own poem entitled, *La Chanson du Vin*, which was published in 1843. The other poems, on the same theme, belong in style and inspiration to the same period.

To this stage also belong, according to the available evidence, the poems of rebellion and revolt against God, the poems expressing admiration for Satan, and the wish that the powers of darkness should prevail rather than those of light. Naturally those poems which merely reflect a belief in the powers of the devil as a tempter of mankind should not be considered satanic, since this is a belief shared by all sections of the Christian religion. Critics have laboured in vain to harmonize the poems of revolt and blasphemy with the spiritual poems of the middle and later years, and some have advanced the view that it was only in the realms of theory that Baudelaire toyed with Satanism and with mysticism, that they did not express fundamental beliefs. These critics speak as if all the poems published in the collection of 1857, and composed over a period of sixteen years, had been written at the same time. A simpler explanation is that there is in fact no connection of inspiration between such poems as *Le Reniement de Saint Pierre*, and *Les Phares* and *Bénédiction*, that they refer to vastly different stages in his development. It is possible then to believe that all the blasphemous poems were composed in the first period of Baudelaire's literary career, before he was twenty-five, at an age when it was considered daring and amusing to blaspheme, and to defy the power which had formerly been cited by the elders to quell youthful independence, God Almighty. It was considered more bold in the eighteen-forties than it would be today, to express agnostic sentiments and contempt for Christian ideals, especially in a society in which Catholicism was symbolic of respectability.

It is evident that, at this time, Baudelaire had not yet shaken off current literary influences and conventions. His manner of life at the Hôtel Lauzun is proof that he had not yet discarded Byronic arrogance, pride and artificiality. Satanism, in the middle of the nineteenth century, was the usual form which revolt took, and Satanism, rather than atheism, represented rebellion against accepted religious ideas and ideals.

Satanism, which had disappeared during the Empire and the Restoration, broke out once more after 1830, with many excesses. This is evident in the literature at the beginning of the reign of Louis-Philippe, right up to the end of the Second Empire, and many writers show traces of it.[30] They professed to consider that Lucifer was a gentleman compared to Christ, and to believe that he alone had left humanity any dignity and pride. Even such a realistic and prosaic writer as Proudhon, in his *De la Justice dans la Révolution et dans l'Église*, wrote a paean of praise in honour of Satan, which he ends by swearing that he will dedicate his pen to his service, to him who is the symbol and spirit of liberty. This Satanism was often no more than a mild affectation, or an expression of the aestheticism of the age. Baudelaire's poems, in this vein, belong to a young and derivative stage. There is no proof that he was ever involved in active Satanism, and no evidence that he was present at any of the Black Masses in Paris, let alone at the notorious and scandalous one in 1855.[31] If he had been the Satanist which most critics are willing to believe, it is unlikely that he would not have been present, and, if he had been present, it is inconceivable that there would have been no trace of it in his work, and no mention in his correspondence or in his Journals.

The only two poems in this vein for which we have no evidence of date are *Abel et Cain* and *Les Litanies de Satan*, but there is no adequate reason for attributing them to a later period, when they would only strike a discordant note, since we know that others similar were composed when he was young. These blasphemous poems are, in any case, only a very small proportion of his work as a whole, even at this time, *Les Litanies de Satan* may possibly have been composed in 1845, when Brierre de Boismont published his *Hallucinations* which we know that Baudelaire studied from the very beginning. Marie de Sens, one of the cases studied in this work, confesses that she used to recite a litany to Satan: [32]

> *Lucifer, miserere nobis.*
> *Belzébuth, miserere nobis.*

This may have been the starting-point of Baudelaire's poem, especially of the line: 'O Satan, prends pitié de ma longue misère.' [33] Or else he may have been inspired by the story entitled *Monsieur de l'Argentière* from *Champavert* by Petrus Borel. [34]

Prarond tells us that *Don Juan aux Enfers*, first known as *L'Impénitent*, when it appeared in *L'Artiste* in 1846, and *Le Rebelle* published only in the second version of *Les Fleurs du Mal* in 1861, were well known by 1844. While Mouquet shows that *Le Rêve d'un Curieux* must have been familiar to Dozon in 1843. [35] Though this last poem can hardly be described as Satanic, or even blasphemous, it is inspired by the same attitude towards religious matters which Baudelaire shows elsewhere in the arrogant years of his youth. It describes the experiences of a man who dreams that he is dying, as he watches the sands of time flow gradually to the bottom of the hour-glass. He longs for death, as a child, in a theatre, longs for the play to begin. Then suddenly, the horrible truth dawns on him, and he realizes that he has died but did not know it, that he has been dead for some time, that the curtain had gone up but the stage was empty.

> *J'étais mort sans surprise et la terrible aurore*
> *M'enveloppait – Eh! quoi! N'est-ce donc que cela?*
> *La toile était levée et j'attendais encore.*[36]

The rebel, in the poem of that name, refuses to bow down before God and to accept salvation: 'Mais le damné répond toujours "Je ne veux pas!"'[37]

The most powerful example of Baudelaire's blasphemous poetry is *Le Reniement de Saint-Pierre*. This poem was responsible for much of his disfavour with the Church, and his mother disapproved of it so violently that, after his death, she tried to have it excluded from the third edition of *Les Fleurs du Mal*. 'As a sincere Christian,' she wrote to Asselineau, who was supervising its publication,[38] 'I can't allow this poem to appear, and certainly if my son were alive today he wouldn't write such a work, since, in his last years, he showed deep religious conviction and feeling!' It was only when Asselineau threatened to give up his part in the editing of the work, that, at last, reluctantly, she gave her consent. The poet himself was fully aware, at the time of first publication, of the sensation which this poem would cause, and he tried to soften its effect by adding a footnote which stated that it was the expression of youthful ignorance and pride, which nevertheless had its place in the plan and architecture of his work as a whole. In 1857 the critics saw this as an effort on his part to avoid censure, and did not realize that it was the truth.

'Amongst the following poems,' wrote Baudelaire, 'the one which perhaps possesses the most individual character is one which has already appeared in one of the main reviews of France,[39] where it was considered for what it really is, an expression of the arguments of rebellion and ignorance. The author of *Les Fleurs du Mal*, in order to be faithful to his tragic plan, has been obliged to assume a part, just as an

actor might, in order to give expression to the false arguments of sophistry and corruption.'[40]

It was a part that he himself had once played in one phase
of his development and out of which he had grown. But, on
publishing *Les Fleurs du Mal*, he arranged and grouped
the poems according to a plan he conceived at that time, as
he looked back on his past, showing how each stage of his
development had its important place. The Satanic poems
reveal an arrogant spirit which would not have been possible to him in his mature life.

> Qu'est-ce que Dieu fait donc de ce flot d'anathèmes
> Qui monte tous les jours vers ses chers Séraphins?
> Comme un tyran gorgé de viande et de vins,
> Il s'endort au doux bruit de nos affreux blasphèmes.
>
> Les sanglots des martyrs et des suppliciés
> Sont une symphonie enivrante sans doute.
> Puisque, malgré le sang que leur volupté coûte,
> Les cieux ne s'en sont point encor rassasiés!
>
> – Ah! Jésus! souviens-toi du jardin des Olives!
> Dans ta simplicité tu priais à genoux
> Celui qui dans son ciel riait au bruit de clous
> Que d'ignobles bourreaux plantaient dans tes chairs vives.
>
> Lorsque tu vis cracher sur ta divinité
> La crapule du corps de gardes et des cuisines,
> Et lorsque tu sentis s'enfoncer les épines
> Dans ton crâne où vivait l'immense Humanité;
>
> Quand de ton corps brisé la pesanteur horrible
> Allongeait tes deux bras distendus, que ton sang
> Et la sueur coulaient de ton front pâlissant,
> Quand tu fus devant tous posé comme une cible,
>
> Rêvais-tu de ces jours si brillants et si beaux
> Où tu vins pour remplir l'éternelle promesse,
> Où tu foulais, monté sur une douce ânesse,
> Des chemins tout jonchés de fleurs et de rameaux,

Où, le cœur tout gonflé d'espoir et de vaillance,
Tu fouettais tous ces vils marchands à tour de bras,
Où tu fus maître enfin? Le remords n'a-t-il pas
Pénétré dans ton flanc plus avant que la lance?

– Certes, je sortirai, quant à moi, satisfait
D'un monde où l'action n'est pas la sœur du rêve;
Puissé-je user du glaive et périr par le glaive.
Saint-Pierre a renié Jésus ... il a bien fait! [41]

This is a magnificent outburst from the vulnerable sensitivity of youth, an expression of its revulsion in front of the suffering which it cannot understand, nor reconcile with its own idealism, and of its subsequent revolt. It has in it something of the violence of Petrus Borel in the *Preface* to *Champavert*, of the pride of Alfred de Vigny in *Le Mont des Oliviers*, and the despair of Gérard de Nerval in *Le Christ aux Oliviers*.[42]

Le Reniement de Saint-Pierre, *Le Crépuscule du Matin* and *Une Charogne* are the most mature poems in this period, and the most finished in form.

Since his adolescence the poet had been prone to periodic moods of depression and pessimism. He thought at first that the life of pleasure and frivolity would bring him satisfaction and joy, but he soon discovered that licence and indulgence did not procure him the happiness he had expected, and he was too clear-sighted and too self-critical not to rate at its true value the life he was leading, even if he had chosen it himself. This self-analysis was making him grow deeper, and he was gradually freeing himself from the conventional influences of the day. Often, as he sat working into the early hours of the morning, to make up for the time he had frittered away during the day, or else when he came at dawn, through the sleeping town, from his mistress's apartment to his own in the Île-Saint-Louis, he used suddenly to be moved by the strange beauty of the city, which the other poets of the day considered unaesthetic, the deep meaning of which they did not understand, and which he himself had hitherto

been too frivolous to notice. It was probably after such a
mood that he composed *Le Crépuscule du Matin*, in the vein
which, in later years, was to be one of his most original and
successful, inspired by the modern city, in which the different elements of its teeming life were raised to the heights
of great lyrical and spiritual poetry. In this form he struck
out on his own and imitated no one, and no other poet who
followed him in this style was to scale such heights as he.
François Coppée only succeeded in being trite and commonplace, but Baudelaire, even at twenty-two, was profoundly
moving.

> *La diane chantait dans les cours des casernes,*
> *Et le vent du matin soufflait sur les lanternes.*
>
> *C'était l'heure où l'essaim des rêves malfaisants*
> *Tord sur leurs oreillers les bruns adolescents;*
> *Où, comme un œil sanglant qui palpite et qui bouge,*
> *La lampe sur le jour fait une tache rouge;*
> *Où l'âme, sous le poids du corps revêche et lourd,*
> *Imite les combats de la lampe et du jour.*
> *Comme un visage en pleurs que les brises essuient,*
> *L'air est plein du frisson des choses qui s'enfuient,*
> *Et l'homme est las d'écrire et la femme d'aimer.*
>
> *Les maisons çà et là commençaient à fumer,*
> *Les femmes de plaisir, la paupière livide,*
> *Bouche ouverte, dormaient de leur sommeil stupide;*
> *Les pauvresses, traînant leurs seins maigres et froids,*
> *Soufflaient sur leurs tisons et soufflaient sur leurs doigts.*
> *C'était l'heure où parmi le froid et la lésine*
> *S'aggravaient les douleurs des femmes en gésine;*
> *Comme un sanglot coupé par un sang écumeux*
> *Le chant du coq au loin déchirait l'air brumeux;*
> *Une mer de brouillards baignait les édifices,*
> *Et les agonisants dans le fond des hospices*
> *Poussaient leur dernier râle en hoquets inégaux.*
> *Les débauchés rentraient, brisés par leurs travaux.*
>
> *L'aurore grelottante en robe rose et verte*
> *S'avançait lentement sur la Seine déserte,*

> *Et le sombre Paris, en se frottant les yeux,*
> *Empoignait ses outils, vieillard laborieux.*[43]

Une Charogne is the poem, in this period of his youth, which reveals more than any other Baudelaire's increasing depth and powers of reflection. He was beginning to weigh up the life he was leading and to judge its vanity, the vanity of pleasure and excess, the vanity of passion. In 1842, when composing *Les Deux Bonnes Sœurs*, he had written:

> *Au poète sinistre, ennemi des familles,*
> *Favori de l'enfer, courtisan mal renté,*
> *Tombeaux et lupanars montrent sous leurs charmilles*
> *Un lit que le remords n'a jamais fréquenté.*[44]

Now, in *Une Charogne*, he expresses revolt against the tyranny of the flesh and the vanity of becoming attached to what will not endure. *Une Charogne*, in spite of the adverse criticism it has endured, could be used as the text for an orthodox sermon on the theme that everything here below is vanity and will inevitably return to dust and ashes. After a description, in almost biblical style, of a carcass lying decaying and forgotten by the side of the road, the poet says to the beautiful woman leaning on his arm, that she, the light of his life, young and radiant as she is, will one day also come to that, and be no more than rotting flesh and bone, like the carrion they have just seen by the wayside. For him, however, as a poet, there remains the consolation that, when they have both returned to dust, he will have fixed for eternity, in a form which decay will not be able to attack, the divine essence of her whom he had loved with such adoring passion.

> *Et pourtant vous serez semblable à cette ordure,*
> *À cette horrible infection,*
> *Étoile de mes yeux, soleil de ma nature,*
> *Vous, mon ange et ma passion!*
>
> *Oui! telle vous serez, ô la reine des grâces*
> *Après les derniers sacrements,*

Quand vous irez, sous l'herbe et les floraisons grasses,
  Moisir parmi les ossements.

Alors, ô ma beauté! dites à la vermine
  Qui vous mangera de baisers,
Que j'ai gardé la forme et l'essence divine
  De mes amours décomposés.[45]

Many readers have misunderstood this poem, and the feeling which inspires it, seeing in it merely a morbid interest in putrefaction and decay. They have not seen that the poet, in the midst of his life of pleasure, suddenly realized that all must end one day, and that the woman at his side, who meant everything to him – joy, beauty, and inspiration – might one day die and leave him, and, since it was her body that he worshipped, he could not contemplate, without deep pain, its final dissolution.

The significance of such contemplation of death and decay must nevertheless not be exaggerated. To youth, in the fullness of its health and strength, death seems far more terrible than it does to age already leaning towards the embrace of the earth, and longing almost for the rest which the grave will bring. It is youth, and not age, that terrifies itself with visions of ultimate decay and annihilation. It must also not be forgotten that ten years before it had been fashionable amongst poets to use similar material as new subjects for poetic composition. It inspired the writings of Petrus Borel and Philothée O'Neddy, while Gautier, in 1838, had composed a whole collection of poems entitled *La Comédie de la Mort* with death as its central theme.

If Baudelaire's literary production in this first period of his career is briefly reviewed, it will appear that at first he had written poems on the model of those which he had admired as a schoolboy; next those expressing nostalgic longing for the past, for the happy days of childhood; then came the sensual poems of pleasure, women and wine, the erotic poems which rank amongst his highest achievement; next follow poems of blasphemy and revolt; and finally those expressing disillusionment and suffering, recoil from the pleasures of the senses. Here is found the beginning of deeper thought, and aspiration towards something higher. The erotic and Satanic poems were blind alleys, incapable of further exploration, but *Le Crépuscule du Matin* and *Une Charogne* give promise of a new and greater Baudelaire.

It is significant that it is the poems we can ascribe, with little hesitation, to this first period which aroused most horror and disgust, poems of youthful inspiration, *Les Femmes Damnées*, *Le Léthé*, *Le Reniement de Saint-Pierre* and *Une Charogne*.

At this time Baudelaire was not merely writing poetry. He, who all his life was attracted by the stage, was also trying his hand at dramatic composition, and we know that he was working at one play at least. Whether this play should be called *Idéolus* or *Manoel* – they are the same in substance – has been diversely argued by Mouquet, who discovered the manuscript, by Jean Pommier and Jacques Crépet.[46] Pommier and Crépet are of the opinion that it is *Idéolus* which should largely be attributed to Baudelaire, although he wrote it in collaboration with Prarond, and that *Manoel* is by the latter with some suggestions from the former. Wherever the truth may lie, Baudelaire must have abandoned the effort of collaboration, for fragments only exist of either work, both of which have some autobiographical interest as far as he is concerned, but neither of which is artistically finished.

Baudelaire was not only composing original creative works in solitude, with a view to later publication, but was trying, at the same time, to earn money by becoming a contributor to some literary paper. He obtained an introduction to Victor Hugo, in the hope that, through him, he might achieve his ambition, but the older poet did not understand him nor care for him, and thought that he needed to go into retreat in the country to work in solitude.[47] After Baudelaire's death, he said of him in 1869: 'I met rather than knew Baudelaire.

He frequently shocked me, and I dare say that I must often have also irritated him.'

When his fortunes deteriorated in 1843 Baudelaire strove harder than ever to obtain journalistic contracts. He applied to a new periodical entitled *Le Tintamarre, The Racket*, which was founded in March 1843 by Commerson. It was a Sunday paper which Audebrand alleged was one of the most original and most typically Parisian of all the little satirical papers which flourished under Louis-Philippe.[48] In its second number, dated 29 April 1843, it defined its meaning and its aims. '*The Racket* is,' it declared, 'every kind of noise – industrial racket, musical din, literary hub-bub, theatrical uproar, commotion of every sort, clamour of every kind. Our aim! to nose out self-advertisement, to unmask charlatanism, to track down quack PUFF in all its treacherous disguises, under its philanthropical masks, that is the main thought which has inspired the creation of this paper! However, let us hasten to add that our principal aim, when we founded *The Racket*, was to become the impartial and resounding echo of all discoveries and improvements in industry, in literature, in music, in fashion and in the theatre; to encourage useful inventions and the honourable men who propagate them.' The paper also prided itself on not employing among its contributors, any of the well-known writers. It declared: 'From January the readers of *The Racket* will be able, as in the past, to count on the non-contribution of Victor Hugo, Lamartine, Chateaubriand, Alexandre Dumas, Eugène Sue and so forth!'

It was the kind of paper that one would expect an irreverent and rebellious young man like Baudelaire to be attracted by, and he did in fact apply for employment as a contributor. In the Correspondence Column for the week from 31 August to 6 September we can read 'To Mr Ch. B. There would be, as a result of his article, a fine of 500 francs and a sentence of three months' imprisonment!' For the week of 17 to 24 September, we find, in the same column: 'To Mr Ch. B. His article on Madame L. Co. will not be published. It contains details which concern the private life of its subject, and which do not fall within the scope of this paper.' This was Louise Colet, who had just been awarded a prize by the Academy, and whose person and work Baudelaire could not endure. Again, later in the year, in the week of 3 to 9 December, the Correspondence Column announced: 'To Mr Ch. B. His article would entail a fine of 500 francs and three months' imprisonment. We would like to pay less dearly for our contributions!'

For Baudelaire, as for many young men, satire was synonymous with libel.

In November 1843, in a letter to his mother, Baudelaire mentions that he has just had an interview with the editor of *Le Bulletin de l'Ami des Arts* and that a story by him was shortly to appear in the paper.[49] This may have been *La Fanfarlo*, the only story we know him to have written, but it may also be something else that has not survived, for he was certainly writing a great deal at this time. He informs her also that he is about to be appointed to the permanent staff but, in this statement, he was, as usual, too optimistic. He also alleges that he is going to be taken on to the staff of *L'Artiste*. At the end of 1843 that paper changed hands and was taken over by Arsène Houssaye, who became its editor in January 1844. It is possible that he promised Baudelaire some work, and it is certainly there that his first poem to be printed appeared, but this was nearly a year and a half later, when *À une Dame Créole* was published, in May 1845.

At the end of 1843 an article by Baudelaire was refused by *La Démocratie Pacifique* on the grounds of its immortality.[50] Crépet alleges that this was one of the articles which had previously been turned down by *Le Tintamarre*.[51]

This was, however, not the end of the poet's attempts at slanderous journalism, for Crépet believes that a large part of the book published in March 1844 under the title *Les Mystères Galans des Théâtres de Paris* (*Actrices Galantes*) should be attributed to him.[52] It was certainly believed at the time that he had a hand in it, and that he – or he and Privat d'Anglemont together – was responsible for the libellous passage in the chapter entitled *Coulisses* against his landlord Jérôme Pichon, with whom he was often in arrears for his rent, and the dealer Arondel who had fleeced him, leaving him with debts which were to last the rest of his life, where reflections were made on their meanness and avarice even in the matter of their debauch. 'On ne fait aujourd'hui que la débauche pot au feu.'[53] The pseudonyms under which they figure are not difficult to solve – 'Hieronyme Pichon' and 'Lord Arundell'. Pichon took exception to this personal attack, and Arondel, whose skin seems to have been tougher, does not appear to have taken offence for himself, but only to have wished to reconcile Baudelaire with his landlord and to oblige him, by force if necessary, to apologize to him.

'I hasten to let you know,' he wrote to Pichon, 'that I shall invite Baudelaire to lunch and that you'll probably find him at my house at half past eleven. As for Privat he's much more difficult to catch, because he is homeless, and the most disagreeable man that I know, for all his wit and talent are expended in slandering and calumniating the friends of his friends. As for Baudelaire I'm more than sure that he had no intention of insulting you, or me either. I'll help you to the best of my ability to force him to apologize and to take back publicly the calumnies that they've published about us. So tomorrow you can count on me. If I can't persuade him willingly, I'll force him with my stick, or my fists if necessary.'[54]

He must have succeeded in persuading Baudelaire to yield with good grace, for he wrote Pichon a clever letter which is not a denial of authorship, but only of the truth of the alleged facts. It is, however, conceivable that the damaging paragraph was by Privat d'Anglemont alone, and this would explain why Baudelaire was not more explicit, since he did not wish to betray his friend. Here, as in the sonnets previously discussed, it is difficult to distinguish between the style and matter of two authors so similar at this time.

'I learned yesterday,' wrote Baudelaire, 'that several people attributed to me, on the assertion of the bookseller Legallois, a few lines in an article contained in a book published by him, and in which your name, or a homonym of it, was printed. I declare that the accusations linked with this name are, to my knowledge, completely false. I would consider it unnecessary, in any other circumstances, to protest against these absurd imputations from which your character and the respect you enjoy should sufficiently protect you.'[55]

The Legallois mentioned here was a bookseller and publisher who had advertised, in October 1843, that he was about to bring out a series of portraits entitled *Actrices Galantes de Paris*, the first of which would portray Mademoiselle Plessis and Rachel. The synopsis of the chapters dealing with the latter indicated that the subject matter would be slanderous.[56] She took an action against the publisher on the score of the advertisement and demanded 20,000 francs damages. Legallois wrote an abject letter of apology which was read in the courts, and Rachel was persuaded to withdraw her case, but he was forbidden to publish the book.[57]

It was then that Legallois conceived the plan of getting his book published in another way. Crépet discovered that *Les Mystères Galans des Théâtres de Paris* was produced by a group of young men whose names were: Nadar, Privat d'Anglemont, Matthieu-Dairnvaell, Mesuré, Baudelaire and a priest called Constant, who was later to write under the name Éliphas Lévi. Much of the substance of the book was the same as that first planned by Legallois, except that the names of the victims were now disguised. Hère-Mignonne, for instance, was intended for Rachel, an allusion to her part of Hermione in Racine's play *Andromaque*, while *Histoire d'une Guitare* is the same as the previous *Histoire d'une Guitare de Mademoiselle Rachel*.[58] We have no information of the actress having raised any difficulties, and if this is so then the young men were lucky for she is very harshly treated in the work.

Crépet believes that Baudelaire was responsible for the

largest part of the book, and he makes out a very good case for his point of view. However, he only publishes one of the articles, the one on Ponsard, in the *Juvenilia*.[59]

If he is right then these are Baudelaire's first writings to appear in print, unless one accepts that he did in fact compose the poems published by Prarond and Levavasseur.

Later in that year, 1844, Baudelaire mentions, in a letter to his mother, that he has almost completed three books.[60] These may have been *De la Peinture Moderne, De la Caricature* and *La Fanfarlo*.

It is clear that he was working consistently during his time at the Hôtel Lauzun, but that he did not have much luck with editors and publishers, for he was considered violent, blasphemous and slanderous. He was, however, fully alive to literature and to what was happening in it, and he was doing his utmost to earn a living through journalism. He showed a vivid and a lively mind for there was much variety in what he was attempting, and he would have been right to feel confidence in his future as a writer. He had, however, not yet published anything – not under his own name at all events.

Although there was some sadness and pessimism in this period, especially at the end, one should not exaggerate their depth or intensity, nor their effect on him, for nothing dims the feeling of excitement one finds in all his projects.

The years at the Hôtel Lauzun were for him, on the whole, years of pleasure and fulfilment, with confidence in himself, and the enjoyment of close friendships, leisure and study. They were the only truly happy years of his adult life.

[6]

The Day of Reckoning
1844

THE glittering life of luxury and extravagance could not however last for ever. Baudelaire was squandering large sums of money in his attempt to outshine the *jeunesse dorée* as they were called, the gilded youth, wealthy men like Roger de Beauvoir and Fernand Boissard. He was not only living in splendour himself, but he was keeping Jeanne Duval in a separate establishment as well, in a style that befitted the mistress of one whose ambition it was to shine amongst the richest dandies of the day.

By the end of 1842 his mother was already beginning to grow anxious, but by the middle of 1843 matters had become far more serious, and he was often in grave financial difficulties.[1] The tradespeople, Arondel especially, from whom he had bought most of his pictures and furniture on credit, began to show uneasiness when they saw that he was making no attempt to settle his accounts. Hitherto they had readily agreed to give him credit because they had imagined that he was a wealthy young man, with great expectations, the stepson of a famous general with higher office still to come. Now bills began to pour in by every post, and his creditors used to wait for him on his doorstep, to catch him as he came or went. To evade them he was obliged sometimes to flee from home, to spend the night in some low hotel, hiding away like a criminal.

Next Ancelle, who had administered his inheritance during his minority with exemplary skill, also began to grow anxious at seeing, not only income, but capital as well, being frittered away, and this was more than a middle-aged Frenchman could be expected to bear with equanimity. As a careful businessman, he could not reconcile himself to the idea of spendthrift youth being allowed to dissipate at will money it had not earned. It also offended his sound bourgeois traditions that a mere boy, seemingly incapable of sense, should be allowed to control his capital and to squander it in emulating a man like Roger de Beauvoir, whose way of life was the scandal of middle-class homes, who was always to be seen hanging round the dressing-rooms of the boulevard theatres, and whose mistresses were numerous and of ill-repute.

Baudelaire had been accustomed, whenever he was in trouble, to turn to his mother for help, and now, even in his pride of independence, he sought her out once more, like a child in search of protection against a harsh world. At the end of 1842 when, at his request, she had temporarily taken charge of his financial affairs, she had sanctioned the sale of nearly four hundred pounds of capital to settle some pressing debts, and had persuaded him to try to live on an allowance of ten pounds a month, which he would receive out of his income from her hands. On several occasions after this, against her husband's wishes, and indeed probably without his knowledge, she had advanced further large sums to him from her private purse as loans, which he was making no attempt at repaying – once nearly four hundred pounds and another time over two hundred. But she was very much troubled in her mind. On the one hand she could not bear to see her son looking unhappy and, on the other, she was unable to hide her anxiety from her husband, nor the truth about the money she had lent. Her son became a subject of dissension between them, and her life very unhappy and distressed. Her husband used to tell her that she was acting in a foolish maner, like most sentimental women, that moreover she was ruining her son's character and making him incapable of taking life seriously and of earning his living. Torn between her love for her only child and her belief in the essential rightness of her husband's views, she made unceasing efforts to encourage her son to work and to settle down. He, on his side, was making valiant, if unavailing attempts to obtain journalistic work. In every letter he told her of his labours and his successes, counting chickens long before they were hatched – indeed often before the eggs were even laid – and, pathetically, tried to impress her with the sense of his importance, knowing that this would reach his stepfather. He mentioned many short stories which he alleged were about to be published in the course of 1844. What happened to them ultimately is not known since they never appeared in print, and were not found amongst his papers after his death. Perhaps they were written but could not be published on account of their libellous and blasphemous nature, and then he lost them on his frequent moves from one hotel to another, leaving his papers behind because he could not settle his account. Or perhaps they were never written at all, and he was only trying to impress his mother with his diligence and success as a writer. It is, however, probable that they did in fact exist, at least in a rudimentary state, since they were mentioned to others as well.[2] He always imagined that any editor who had shown an interest in his work, would inevitably publish it, and he saw himself in advance as a permanent member of the staff. No amount of disappointment ever cured him of his trust in his luck, nor of his belief, each time, that at last he was near the end of his tribulations. This was to continue to the day of his death. In the meantime he felt very strongly the disapproval of his stepfather and could not bear to go to see his mother in his house, but expected her to meet him outside.

'I couldn't describe to you,' he wrote to her,[3] 'the depressing and harsh effect that cold and cheerless house has on me. I enter it only with the greatest precautions, and I slink out of it furtively, as soon as possible, like a criminal.'

Those tempted to judge Baudelaire severely for his frequent borrowings from his mother should remember in his favour that he was genuinely convinced that it was only a temporary measure until he could make a start. He had confidence not only in his talent but in his future and in his ability to make a successful career as a writer. Those whose opinion he trusted and valued were constantly assuring him that he had a golden future before him, and compliments were showered on him whenever he read his poems. He was sincere in believing that it was only a difficult moment to get through until he would be able to command the large sums of money which other writers, such as Hugo, were able to extract from their publishers. He gambled on the future, but all those who have ever achieved anything have always acted likewise, and his instinct was a sound one, but fate treated him in a niggardly manner – he was later to call it 'le guignon' – and his difficult moment was to last the whole of his life.

To his mother, with her love of an ordered life and a good bank balance, the time of waiting seemed long. She did not know what to believe moreover, and she was buffeted hither and thither like a rubber ball in a rough sea, by her husband and Ancelle, telling her that she must make a firm stand before it was too late and before her son had become an utter wastrel. She herself was deeply distressed by his extravagance, for she was by nature thrifty, and her youth, filled with envy of the wealth of others, had given her an exaggerated view of the value of money, so that she imagined that happiness was not possible without it, and she could not bear to see good money, so difficult to procure, melting away so easily. Besides, as a devout Catholic, though unusually broadminded in such matters, she was outraged at the sight of her son living openly with a low actress, who was moreover a coloured woman with no beauty or distinction. All things considered, she would have welcomed anything which would have obliged him to mend his way of life. Yet she did not wish to be unjust to her child in whose gifts she believed, for her first husband had inspired in her belief in the value of art and literature, and she thought it only fair that his son should be allowed to develop any talents he possessed. She was, however, not strong enough to withstand public opinion, and she did not know which way to turn – the only person to whom she could unburden her heart was Baudelaire himself, and he was the culprit. Like most young people he had never really believed that his elders cared for him or worried about his escapades, except to disapprove because they were old-fashioned, and to impose arbitrarily their tyrannical rule, but he was now very much upset, when he discovered the state to which he had reduced his mother.

'I didn't know,' he wrote to her,[4] 'since the kind of life I'm leading, and all my worries, prevent me from thinking of anything else, that you, who've always had the kindness to forgive so many things, were so deeply distressed. You can't imagine how pained I felt, and how ashamed, when I discovered how much I'd hurt you, the harm I'd done you without realizing its consequences. I wish I could mend all that, but will that ever be possible now? Soon, perhaps, when I've extricated myself from my first difficulties, and my mind is less worried, I'll be able to be for you what I'd like to be at all times and for ever.'

Ancelle, who thought that he could read Baudelaire like a book – not that he ever read one worth reading – since he had known him from infancy, used all his influence to prevent her from seeing her son, fearing he would succeed in wheedling more money and delays out of her. He also realized that she was a woman who lived on her emotions and could never resist an appeal to her heart.

The atmosphere of suspicion and tension was beginning to affect Baudelaire, making him unsure of himself, and incapable of decisive action. He realized, from unconscious hints dropped by his mother, that the *conseil de famille* had met, but that she was afraid to tell him anything about it. He was in no doubt concerning the nature of their deliberations, and realized that, when any two members of the family were gathered together, it was himself and his misdeeds that they discussed. What they discovered was that half of his capital was now gone past recall. There was consternation and scandal in the ranks of the family but they could not get away from the figures, and it was agreed that a halt must now be called.

In July 1844 an application was made to the court to empower the *conseil de famille* to investigate Baudelaire's extravagances, and to take measures to put a stop to them. On 10 August the *Première Chambre du Tribunal de la Seine* made an order that the *conseil de famille* of the 'sieur Baudelaire' was to be convened to discuss the application. It met on 24 August and investigated the poet's conduct since he left school in 1839. It established his extravagance, even during his minority, and that, when money was advanced from capital to enable him to take the sea trip to India, he did not in fact go there, but spent the money in Mauritius. It went through his debts and discovered that he owed a restaurant nearly forty pounds, twenty to a tailor; that two pictures, for which he had paid twenty pounds, had been sold for less than a pound – and many similar facts. Since his majority he had spent half his capital, and this did not include all the outstanding debts which, according to subsequent calculations, must have amounted to over another thousand pounds. 'Monsieur Baudelaire,' the *conseil de famille* declared,[5] 'when he reached his majority came into possession of his entire fortune, and then gave himself up to the wildest extravagance, so that, in the space of eighteen months, he squandered half his inheritance.'

It was then decided that a *conseil judiciaire* must be appointed to administer what was left, just as if the poet had been a minor, or a certified lunatic, and to pay him the interest on his remaining capital in monthly instalments. On 27 August the *Tribunal de la Seine* brought in a verdict against him and finally on 21 September, he was provided, by law, with a *conseil judiciaire* in the person of Ancelle, who was an old friend of the family. It was decided that it should be anyone except his mother, 'par suite de sa santé, et de la faiblesse d'une mère pour ses enfants.'

The members of the *conseil de famille* realized that Baudelaire, with his sense of personal independence and violent temper, would not receive this information gladly, and they entrusted his mother with the unpleasant task of breaking the news to him.[6] She tried to sugar the pill by assuring him that there was no disgrace in such an arrangement, nothing that need wound his pride, that it was something which might happen to anyone, since everyone could not be expected to have a head for business – especially not a poet whose thoughts must be centred on higher matters. Baudelaire, however, would not have the blow softened, and much preferred to receive it squarely in the face. He refused to look on the bright side, and would only see, what was in fact the truth, that he had been declared incapable by law of managing his own financial affairs. He had been living now for more than two years without any outside restrictions, spending his money as he liked, and the mere thought of the *conseil judiciaire* dictating his standard of expenditure was more than he could bear. His friends had been accustomed to listen to him when he spoke, to look up to him with respect as an important person, and his reputation was the equal of that of any man about town. What would they now think when they heard that he, who was twenty-three, had been declared incapable of running his own affairs, and that a mere lawyer was empowered to dole him out his pittance each month, like a schoolboy's pocket money? He had often laughed at others himself, and had poked fun at them, and he knew well what wits like Roger de Beauvoir would say – de Beauvoir who never in his life let the opportunity slip of making an amusing story or a witty poem at someone else's expense. What verses would he now be circulating amongst his friends at the Divan Lepelletier? Baudelaire felt that he would never again dare pass through the doors of that café which was the meeting-place of the most interesting people of the day.

When he tried to explain his fears to his mother, he was infuriated because she refused to believe that they were legitimate, and persisted in assuring him that his despair was only a passing phase. 'But, will you never realize,' he answered,[7] 'that, for my sins, I'm not as other men!'

Each time that they met everything used immediately to turn to bitterness, and, when she would not listen to him, he flew into one of the rages for which he had always been notorious, and further argument was impossible.

At last, one day, weary of incessant bickering and mis-understanding, he decided to control himself, to sit down quietly for one whole afternoon, and to write as calmly and collectedly as he could, to explain everything to her, right from the very beginning. His letter started quietly but, as he wrote, his anger rose while he worked himself into a state of righteous indignation, contemplating the preposterous, un-fair and unbearable plan.

'I implore you,' he wrote,[8] 'to read this with great atten-tion because it's very serious, and because it's a last and final appeal to your good sense, and to the deep love which you profess to have for me. First let me say that I'm sending you this letter in the strictest confidence and beg you not to show it to anyone.

'Next I beg you most sincerely not to see, in this letter, any attempt at being pathetic, or at moving you, except by the soundness of my reasoning. The curious habit which all our discussions have taken lately of turning immediately into bitter wrangling – which, as a matter of fact, I don't at all feel – the state of agitation I'm in perpetually, your obstinate and fixed resolve never to listen to what I've got to say – all this forces me to use the letter form, in order to persuade you how wrong you are, in spite of your love for me.

'I'm writing this after deep and mature reflection, and when I consider the state in which I've been for the last few days, caused by anger and amazement, I ask myself inces-santly how and by what means I could endure the thing if it ever became an accomplished fact! You continue to repeat, to get me to swallow the pill, that's it's all quite natural and not at all degrading. That's quite possible and all very well! But what on earth does it matter what it would be for anyone else, for the majority of people, if it's quite another matter for me? – You say that you consider my rage and grief are only temporary, you're convinced that you're merely causing me a childish hurt for my own good. But can't you get one thing into your head, one thing which you seem always to forget, that, unfortunately, for my sins, I'm not as other men – and what you consider only a passing grief and a temporary necessity, I can't, I can't bear it! When we're alone together, the two of us, you may treat me as you like, but I refuse absolutely and most emphatically, everything which is prejudicial to my personal liberty! And, don't you think there's something horribly cruel in handing me over to the jurisdiction of a pack of men who'll only be bored with the whole thing, and who don't know me? And indeed who can boast of really knowing me, and of guessing where I want to get, and what patience I'm capable of? I think you're making a very grave mistake. I tell you all this calmly, because I consider myself as already condemned by you without a hearing, and I'm convinced that you'll not listen to me now. But remember one thing, you're wilfully and knowingly causing me the greatest pain of which you can't possibly guess all the anguish.

'You've broken your promise in two ways. When you very kindly lent me the four hundred pounds, it was agreed between us that, at the end of a given time, you'd have the right to take a certain percentage of all that I earned. After that I made a few more debts, but when I told you that they were only for tiny sums, you promised to wait a little longer. Indeed a few trifling advances of money, coupled with what I could earn, would easily have wiped them out quickly. But now you've made up your mind, in the wildest and most hectic manner possible, and you've acted with such suddenness that I don't know myself what to do, and I've had to abandon all my plans. I'd imagined that my first literary work, which was almost a work of erudition, could come to the notice of some people, that you'd be complimented on my achievement, and then, seeing money coming in regularly, you'd not have refused to wait a little longer, and would have made a few more advances, so that at the end of a few months, I'd have been completely freed, that is to say at the same point as I was when you lent me the four hundred pounds. But not at all, you wouldn't wait – you wouldn't wait even a fortnight. Just look at your illogical mind and the falseness of your reasoning. You hurt me very deeply, and take steps wounding to my pride, just when success is perhaps beginning, just when the day I've promised you for so long is about to dawn, that's precisely the time you choose to cut the ground from under my feet – for, as I've told you already, I refuse to consider the *conseil judiciaire* as something harmless and innocuous. I feel its effects already, and here you've fallen into still greater error, when you believe that it will act as a tonic, but you couldn't ever imagine what I felt yesterday, what a feeling of discouragement overwhelmed me when I realized that things were getting serious. I felt a sudden inclination to send everything to the devil, not to bother about anything any more, and merely to say to myself, "There's nothing left to do now, but to be satisfied and to spend like an idiot anything she'll give me."

'It's a proof of how wrong you are that Ancelle could say to me, "I told your mother that if squandering the whole of your capital forced you afterwards to work and to take up a profession then I'd be in favour of letting you go your own way, but that I didn't believe this would ever happen." I don't think it's possible to say anything more insulting and stupid than that. I'd never have dared go as far as that, to have contemplated calmly squandering the whole of my capital.

'And now, although I'm only your son, you must have enough respect for my person not to wish to hand me over to the jurisdiction of strangers, when you realize what pain this will cause me. I assure you that this is no threat to force you to yield, but only what I feel – the result will be exactly the opposite of what you expect, that is to say utter depression of the spirit.

'And now I come to something else, which will probably mean more to you than all sorts of promises and hopes. You say that you're only acting through anxiety and love, on my behalf, that you wish to save my capital, at all costs, in spite of myself. Well! I agree and I propose to give you all facilities for saving it. Why should you care about the means so long as you reach the same result? Why do you want to insist on using the one way that hurts me so much, the one against which my whole being revolts? What's the good of it all? You'll never make me believe that with all the jobbery and trickery of lawyers there's no other way out which can satisfy you, except the one which you've chosen. And why, oh why? One can't be more frank or honest than I've been with you, how could I give you better proof of my good faith and of my agreement with you? I infinitely prefer to have no money at all and to depend entirely on you, than to endure the jurisdiction of anyone else – the former is an act of liberty, the second an infringement of my liberty.

'Now to conclude I beg and implore you, in the most humble manner possible, to save yourself all this worry, and me a still greater humiliation. For God's sake, no supervisors or strangers in our life! No confidences with outside people! I wish all plans to be suspended until I've had a long conversation with Ancelle and with you. I'll go and see him this very evening, and I hope I'll be able to bring him along with me to see you. I'm certain, dead certain, that after a first bit of success, it'll be easy for me, provided you help me a little, to reach shortly a good position.

'I can only repeat my request again and again most insistently – I know you're wrong – and after that if I haven't succeeded in explaining to you most clearly how much nicer and more reasonable it would be to arrange everything in a friendly manner between ourselves alone, then do your damnedest and the devil take the hindermost. For the last time I beg you to remember that I'm not asking you for any favours, only a change in the means of reaching your objective.'

He waited anxiously, wondering what the result of his letter would be, hoping that he had not upset her, for she was nervously disposed and worries always made her take to her bed. He was longing to see her and to hear what his fate was to be. Then, receiving no answer, he wrote again: 'Once more I beg you to weigh your intentions very carefully, before you remove my last resource from me, which is yourself!'

Through July and August 1844 the pleas continued and, at the end, he felt that she had cast him off, turning traitor, and had delivered him bound hand and foot to his enemies, who neither understood nor loved him. He had assured her that he would accept any conditions she might choose, so long as no strangers were brought into his life, and the disgrace made public; he promised her to leave his money to her to administer, to allow her to hand him whatever sum she liked every month, so long as everything remained between the two of them alone. The *conseil de famille*, however, would not allow her to agree to his request, for they were afraid that if control were left to her, Baudelaire would be able to wheedle extra money out of her, and that the last stage would then be worse than the first. Even if his long letter moved her, it remained without result. Perhaps, contrary to his request, she showed it to her husband, and to Ancelle, to prove to them that he had become reasonable. Perhaps they made her feel that it was childish hysteria, only impressive words and play-acting. Aupick and Ancelle had always mistrusted those who spoke rather than acted, and moreover they both considered that there were no grounds, judging from past experience, for believing that Baudelaire was a reformed character. He had been highly strung from childhood, had always taken everything in a melodramatic manner, and was incapable of seeing things in their just proportion. Ancelle's opinion particularly carried much weight, and he firmly believed that his ward would not settle down for a long time yet.

Matters followed their preordained course, just as if the

arguments and heartache had never existed. In September 1844 Ancelle came weightily into Baudelaire's life, never to leave it again. Ancelle, the scourge, the 'fléau', was always there, wherever he turned, like the skeleton at an Egyptian feast. It was he who handed him his meagre pittance every month, it was before him that he was obliged to bow and scrape to obtain the smallest advance to pay the most pressing bills, and he had to call on him in person to receive even what was due to him. He used to say later that he knew every stone on the road to Neuilly, where Ancelle lived.

It must be admitted that Ancelle's position was neither pleasant nor easy with a man of Baudelaire's temperament who bore him a grudge and who, with his gift for cold and biting irony, which he had once used with good effect on his teachers at school, could make those who displeased him feel like the dust beneath his feet.

Ancelle, though limited and narrow-minded, was generous and kind, and never bore his ward any malice for the insulting things he wrote to him, and Baudelaire often addressed him in a way no young man should a man of Ancelle's age and position.[9] He was a hard-working, middle-class lawyer, not gifted with over-much imagination or sense of humour, and his profession had increased his love of law and order, and of a well-regulated life. Nevertheless, in his own way, he was an important person, a magistrate, a town councillor, and he was mayor of Neuilly for twenty years in the important stage of its history, when it was developing from a village into a town which eventually became part of Paris. He was remembered as an active and public-spirited man, and there is today a Rue Ancelle in Neuilly – posthumous fame can rise no further since the victor of a world war is accorded no more. He was genuinely fond of Baudelaire in his gruff, disapproving way, for he had dandled him on his knee as a baby, but he could not be expected to approve of his way of life, and he considered him a good fellow, with a deplorably weak character whom a doting mother had spoilt. He was always mistrustful when he came to beg for advances, and was convinced that he would squander his entire capital without even acquiring habits of work. So he always kept him waiting, even for the money which was due to him – that was his policy – hoping that the need would pass, or that he had not really been in such straits as he had represented, or else that he would find the money elsewhere on his own initiative. But Baudelaire, who was incapable of taking anything calmly, used to fly into a rage at all the delays, and, when his letters remained unanswered – which was generally the case – he used to write the insolent and insulting things which we read in his correspondence, intending to wound.

On the other hand Ancelle's slowness and his reluctance to discuss anything openly made their relations more strained than they need have been. After the poet's death, when his friends were making arrangements for the publishing of his complete works, Asselineau wrote to Poulet Malassis that the lawyer, whom they were obliged to consult, was a man who could never be found when he was needed, who was always unpunctual in appointments, and who put so many difficulties in the way of meeting him that it protracted excessively any business in which he was involved.[10] To have refused outright, giving reasons for this refusal, would have irritated and annoyed Baudelaire less than Ancelle's infuriating habit of completely ignoring requests and suggestions. He also made the mistake, often made by sensible people in such circumstances, of minimizing the gravity of his ward's financial distress, and later, of his physical condition. He could never refrain from thinking that he was romancing or play-acting in order to gain sympathy, but in this he was mistaken. Nevertheless by degrees he grew very fond and proud of his ward – this must be remembered to the credit of both men. He preserved all his letters, methodically filed, even those in which he himself was described in unflattering terms. When he began to suspect that the poet was a more important person than he had hitherto imagined, he was filled with a desire to know everything about him – all his friends and his activities. Baudelaire could not realize that his behaviour was prompted by affection and was, in fact, the highest form of flattery, but could only see, as he thought, that the lawyer was poking his nose into what did not concern him, in order to spy on him, and to report adversely to his stepfather. Ancelle, when Baudelaire became known, or notorious, used frequently to visit the cafés where he knew he would find him, and would, uninvited, go to sit at his table, insisting on being introduced to his friends. The poet would then endure an agony of self-conscious torture, imagining that people were nudging one another and saying behind his back: 'I say! do you see Charles Baudelaire with his *conseil judiciaire*?' – when most people probably knew nothing about his private affairs and cared little about them.[11]

Ancelle's behaviour was due partly to the curiosity of a quiet and ageing man, who had never in his life done anything daring, about the gay and exciting life of which he had heard but of which he knew very little. Secretly, in spite of his righteous disapproval, he admired his ward as a man about town, who was all the things which he could never hope to be himself. In a pathetic effort to understand his writings, he even began to read modern literature and ventured on criticism, but he does not seem to have been very successful as a judge of aesthetics, not, at least, in the eyes of Baudelaire, who wrote to his mother,[12] 'Ancelle knows as much about literature as an elephant about dancing the bolero!'

Asselineau said to Poulet Malassis: 'Old Ancelle is a worthy man. He commits the strangest errors with regard to our friend, but he loves him sincerely, and talks of him daily with great warmth.'[13] Indeed, after the funeral, he even declared that he was the only person who had really been moved, and that he had been unable to stop weeping. While Madame Aupick said that when the third edition of *Les Fleurs du Mal* was about to appear posthumously, he used to go every day to stand outside Michel Lévy's shop, with his nose glued to the window-pane, to see whether the book was yet on view.[14]

Baudelaire himself, towards the end of his life, came to realize the affection that Ancelle bore him, and to appreciate his friendship, when he felt himself abandoned by everyone else. It was to him that most of his letters from Belgium were written, in his tragic years of exile and increasing ill-health. 'I thank you from the bottom of my heart,' he once wrote,[15] 'for all the affection which you have shown me, and which I have so often repaid with harshness!' Twenty years however were to elapse before he reached a just appreciation of his guardian's devotion, and, during all these years, he was obliged, every month – and often more frequently – to tramp out to Neuilly to receive his allowance, and to hear Ancelle chatter interminably, platitude after platitude, until he could willingly have murdered him. He was a garrulous old man who liked to hear himself speak, and, since he was insensitive to atmosphere, he never realized the impatience of his enforced audience. He was all the more garrulous – perhaps deliberately – when he did not intend to grant his ward's desperate plea for an advance, or for permission to sell out capital to pay some pressing debts. It is, however, thanks to him that Baudelaire died still owning a substantial part of his capital.[16] Whether this was a desirable result is open to question, for it is thanks to him also that at no period of his life was he ever able to free himself from his debts.

In the meantime, he not only ignored completely what Baudelaire was saying, but would insist on carrying on his own platitudinous conversation. 'You've the best of mothers, haven't you? I suppose you do love your mother, don't you?' Or another time: 'You do believe in God, don't you? You can't deny that there is a God who governs everything!' Or more irritating still to Baudelaire: 'There's no doubt that Louis-Philippe was a great king who has never yet been given his due! But he'll come into his own one day, and be enshrined in the hearts of his people!'[17] Each of these remarks was diluted in an endless flow of wishy-washy chatter, while he fumbled in his pocket for the keys of the safe, or stood, with his hand on the lock, and paused before opening it, as if he had the whole day for the operation. In the meantime Baudelaire was beside himself with impatience, since all he wanted was to obtain his money and be off, for several appointments were awaiting him at different ends of Paris and, according to his usual practice, he had allowed no time for transit.

What he found most humiliating of all was the knowledge that Ancelle, his mother, and his stepfather were discussing him and his intimate affairs, encroaching on his spiritual privacy, and forcing their way into his personal sanctuary as a human being. He was, moreover, furious that anyone should presume to manage his affairs for him, since he considered himself very business-like with his complicated methods of borrowing and repayment, with his subtle schemes which obviated the embarrassment of any two bills falling due the same day. On paper it was an ingenious and skilfully worked out plan which must have entailed intelligence, energy and care which could have been more profitably employed in another direction.

It was no wonder that his mother was anxious and full of fears whenever she considered his future, and, on the advice of those whom she trusted and respected, she had finally allowed herself to be persuaded into agreeing to the appointment of a *conseil judiciaire*, thinking it wiser to do all business through her legal adviser rather than directly with her son himself.

When the events of the summer of 1844 are considered from the distance of a century, it is difficult not to come to the conclusion that between them all – the General, Ancelle, the *conseil de famille* and even his own mother – they sadly mismanaged Baudelaire's financial affairs, in a narrow desire to save his capital at all costs. What was essential in his interest at that moment was to clear him completely of debt, and thus permit him to start afresh, with no encumbrances, so that he could try to live on what he might earn with his pen. But they left him owing more than a thousand pounds, with only a diminished income of seventy-five pounds a year to live on and from which to pay his debts. He was only twenty-three, entirely devoid of knowledge of business or of practical life, for his kind of experience since his majority had taught him nothing in these respects. Now, in order merely to pay the interest on his debts, he was obliged to borrow, on an ever-increasing scale, for the remaining twenty-three years of his life. All things considered, it would have been wiser to have left him with no income at all, but clear of debts, and he could then have lived a modest life on what he earned, supplemented by an allowance from his family, if they could ever have contemplated granting one to a man not training himself for a respectable career. Certainly his stepfather could have afforded to support him, since he had no children of his own, and was earning a large salary, with the prospects of higher promotion. The allowance could have been paid to him in such a way as not to wound his pride – it could have come, as far as he need know, from his mother alone. During the last twelve or fifteen years of his life, he was earning through literature sufficient money to support himself, and he used to say that, if it were not for his crippling debts, he would then have been a rich man, but that everything that he earned, unfortunately, melted away in paying the interest on debts of twenty years' standing, incurred when he was little more than a youth. It is also possible that he might have been able to earn more if he had not been obliged to spend so much time, energy and thought, on merely saving himself from bankruptcy.

It may well have been that his family had been unable to obtain a full statement of his debts from him, and he may have feared, at the time, to make matters worse by revealing the true state of his disastrous affairs.

After the appointment of the *conseil judiciaire* it became impossible for Baudelaire ever again to obtain substantial sums of money at any one moment. All he could count on were gifts from his mother or advances from Ancelle, and these were always too small to be of any serious use in settling his debts. These windfalls, as he considered them, only tended to increase his improvidence, for they were useless to offer to any of his creditors, and he used to spend them immediately in treating the friends who had come to his aid when he had been short of ready money. In this way his family were left with the impression that he was being constantly helped with advances and gifts, while he, on his side, always felt that they had been very stingy to him. In his letters he frequently points out to his mother that every time he tries to obtain from Ancelle a sum sufficient to settle his debts, the lawyer persists in granting him sums so small that they are useless for the purpose, and yet they nibble away his capital with no profit to anyone.

With the appointment of his *conseil judiciaire* Baudelaire's life was completely changed. Gone were the days of glorious youth! He was, however, a poet whom wealth and leisure would not have spoilt, for he would have been able to profit from both. This is amply shown by the works which he composed during the so-called period of idleness at the Hôtel Lauzun. His life would have been fuller and richer if the material cares could have been lifted from his shoulders; for too much of his energy and imagination were to be spent henceforth in planning how to keep creditors at bay, and to wrest from his art the means of carrying on his daily life. It is certain that the pointless struggle did him some damage as an artist.

The appointment of the *conseil judiciaire* made relations more bitter than ever before between Baudelaire and his stepfather, for he blamed him entirely for what had happened, and for turning his mother against him. Intercourse between the two men became very strained and the break evident. Nothing was ever to heal the breach which now opened between them.

PART TWO

Comme vous êtes loin, paradis parfumé
Où sous un clair azur tout n'est qu'amour et joie,
Où tout ce que l'on aime est digne d'être aimé!
Où dans la volupté pure le cœur se noie!
Comme vous êtes loin, paradis parfumé.

[1]

The Apprentice to Literature
1845 — 1847

AFTER the appointment of his *conseil judiciaire* it was not merely Baudelaire's life which underwent transformation, but his appearance as well. It was then that he changed his manner of dressing, and adopted the plain and severe black which he was to wear for the rest of his life. The bright blue coats with the golden buttons disappeared, also the velvet tunics with the jewelled belts, the gaudy silk waistcoats, and the goffered *jabots*. He was never again to be seen in anything but black broadcloth, though still of an original cut and designed by himself. His shirt was now always plain white linen, with a loose collar open at the throat, and broad turned-back cuffs. With this he wore a soft silk tie, sometimes coloured, but more often black. He had shaved off his little beard, and his long wavy locks were cropped close to his head, like a prisoner ready for execution, his friends said. His light-hearted and carefree expression soon disappeared, and his face gradually assumed the hard and bitter lines which we know from the later photographs and portraits. With an expression of ironical disdain, he tried to pretend indifference to the sarcastic jokes and jibes, of which he felt convinced he was the victim, since it had become known that he had been checked, like a naughty, wilful child, in his reckless extravagance. Bitterness seized hold of him every time he thought of his predicament. If only his mother had listened to him, and had not inflicted on him the disgrace of the *conseil judiciaire*, he might have fabricated some romantic story to account for his altered circumstances, but she had left him humiliated, with no opportunity of disguising his shame. He knew well that he had enemies amongst those who were jealous of his ascendancy, also amongst those who disapproved of his way of living, and now all these would rejoice to see his pride brought low. And so he hid his sensitivity and wound beneath assumed indifference lest anyone should approach him to pity or to patronize. This *noli me tangere* attitude, behind which he safeguarded his spiritual privacy, which was to become later, in spite of himself, his inviolate solitude, is a striking feature of his personality.

The alteration of his circumstances had come too suddenly; and he was unable to adapt himself quickly to his new conditions, and he suffered greatly from his lack of success. He was making valiant efforts at earning a living, but he had been taken by surprise and was entirely unprepared for the change, since his years at the Hôtel Lauzun had left him unsuited for dealing with life in a practical way. Now he was pitchforked into a rough and vulgar world, where everyone was obliged to fight for what he wanted, with any weapons he could find, or else go under and be trampled underfoot by those who came after him. He was experiencing the unsympathetic rigours of life, which the young encounter when they leave the shelter of home or university for the first time, where everything had aimed at their interest and delight, and to rock them gently in their self-esteem. For Baudelaire the change was especially harsh as he was obliged to continue to live amongst those who had known him in the days of his splendour, and he had no settled employment. He had lavish tastes, was surrounded by extravagant friends whose circumstances remained unaltered, and who moreover expected certain things from him. Furthermore the criticism to which he was subjected at home made him self-conscious and unsure of himself, so that he was dogged by constant fear of failure, the particular terror of vulnerable youth, which poisons the best years of its life. He was haunted by the suspicion that perhaps his family was right after all in discouraging him from a literary career, that perhaps his aspirations were vain, and he did not possess the ability to achieve anything valuable. Amongst the middle-aged, ecstatic rhapsodizing is common about the happiness of youth, its bright hopes and powers of illusion. But discouragement, deep unhappiness, self-mistrust and self-disgust, are far more characteristic of it. Youth has its ideals and dreams, but it has not yet learnt the comfortable philosophy of compromise, and experiences deep distress in trying to harmonize these ideal aspirations with the tribulations which beset them and are liable to destroy them.

It was during the years which followed the appointment of his *conseil judiciaire* that Baudelaire's *spleen* began to appear. Hitherto it had been vague melancholy that he had expressed, or youthful horror of death and final dissolution, or else the temporary bitterness and despair from his suffering at the hands of his mistress. Now it seemed as if the vital spark had been dimmed, and he had no strength or desire for any effort. This was not an entirely new or original literary development for it is to be found in the works of the Bouzingo movement, ten years before, in the writings of Petrus Borel and Philothée O'Neddy.[1]

In his mood of *spleen* the poet imagines himself sitting in his lonely room, waiting for the work which does not come, and he fancies that he hears within himself all the dead memories of a thousand years, the dead hopes which are as many in number as the corpses piled up in a charnel-house, or those lying buried in a churchyard. Nothing, he thinks, can equal the dreariness of the long and empty days, falling fast round him like heavy, leaden snowflakes, with each moment the weight of eternity. This is the inspiration of one of the *spleen* poems.[2]

> Quand le ciel bas et lourd pèse comme un couvercle
> Sur l'esprit gémissant en proie aux longs ennuis,
> Et que de l'horizon embrassant tout le cercle
> Il nous verse un jour noir plus triste que les nuits;

Quand la terre est changée en un cachot humide,
Où l'Espérance, comme une chauve-souris,
S'en va battant les murs de son aile timide
Et se cognant la tête à des plafonds pourris;

Quand la pluie étalant ses immenses traînées
D'une vaste prison imite les barreaux,
Et qu'un peuple muet d'infâmes araignées
Vient tendre ses filets au fond de nos cerveaux.

Des cloches tout à coup sautent avec furie
Et lancent vers le ciel un affreux hurlement,
Ainsi que des esprits errants et sans patrie
Qui se mettent à geindre opiniâtrement.

Et de longs corbillards, sans tambours et musique,
Défilent lentement dans mon âme; l'Espoir,
Vaincu, pleure, et l'Angoisse atroce, despotique,
Sur mon crâne incliné plante son drapeau noir.

He felt that he must tear himself away from this barren
state of contemplation of his own depression. Time was
flying fast, and the mountain of his debts was rising. It is
easier to compel oneself to start a work of criticism or translation than one of imaginative creation. Thus the first work
that Baudelaire advertised as appearing shortly was one on
painting, which *La Presse* announced on 10 April as 'printing,
to be published in the near future, *Modern Painting* by
Baudelaire Dufayis.'[3] This is probably the work which he
mentioned to his mother in his letter the previous July,[4]
but which never appeared, and which may never have been
finished.

In *Mon Cœur mis à nu* and in his *Note Biographique*
Baudelaire says that, since childhood, his chief passion had
been for painting.[5] At the Hôtel Lauzun, the painters, Boissard and Deroy, had been his constant companions and,
with them, he used to visit museums and exhibitions, listening to long and professional discussions on the art and

practice of painting. Prarond tells us that, between 1842 and 1844, he had been more engrossed in art than in poetry, and that he had considered verse composition as a pastime which he did not yet take seriously. Later, in 1852, Prarond was to consider him as purely an art critic, and to express the hope that he would, one day, return to poetry.[6]

It was not then an accident that Baudelaire's first published work was one of art criticism, the *Salon* of 1845, which appeared in April that year. Asselineau says that it was at this *Salon* that he first met Baudelaire, in company with Deroy, that afterwards they went to a café together where the painter discussed the exhibition with Baudelaire, telling him which artists should be noticed, and what were their main characteristics. In spite of this apparent lack of personal views, it is a penetrating work for a young man of twenty-four to produce. He was especially clear-sighted about Delacroix whose work he knew well, and he was one of the few critics at the time to consider him apart from the Romantic movement, apart from the tendencies expressed by Victor Hugo. He also dared to question the influence exercised by Hugo on the painting of the age, particularly on Boulanger, on whom he considered that it had been disastrous.

Baudelaire himself never made any claims for this first work, and he never cared to hear it praised — probably because he felt that it was not entirely his. He realized that it was only a beginning, a preface, so to speak, to his future literary and critical production.

In this *Salon* Baudelaire had naturally not found himself as a critic, and he had not yet evolved any definite theory of art. It is an interpretative piece of criticism by one who possesses an intuitive judgement of values, and who is not entirely ignorant of the technical aspects of his subject. Sometimes, however, he merely contents himself with giving the subject of the pictures — the plot one might say — and this would only interest the ignorant general public, and not professional artists. When Baudelaire had

become a practised critic, his criticism possessed the rare
quality of appealing not only to the uninitiated, but to the
professional as well.

The *Salon* ends with a passage of criticism which reveals
Baudelaire's conception of modern art, even if he had not
yet formulated a doctrine. He advises the painters of the
day to look for their inspiration in their own age, and not
to consider prosaic the manifestations of modern life. He
realized, even then, that nobility and poetry could be discovered in the struggles of contemporary man. He perceived, as few Realists, and none of the Naturalists did,
that such a doctrine did not necessarily entail materialism
in art or literature. He was later to appreciate the application of his views in the works of Courbet, Degas, and Guys.

'Du reste constatons,' he wrote,[7] 'que tout le monde peint
de mieux en mieux, ce qui nous paraît désolant; – mais
d'invention, d'idées, de tempérament, pas d'avantage
qu'avant. – Au vent qui soufflera demain nul ne tend
l'oreille; et pourtant l'héroïsme *de la vie moderne* nous
entoure et nous presse. – Nos sentiments vrais nous étouf-
fent assez pour que nous les connaissions. – Ce ne sont ni les
sujets ni les couleurs qui manquent aux épopées. Celui-là
sera le *peintre*, le vrai peintre, qui saura arracher à la vie
actuelle son côté épique, et nous faire voir et comprendre,
avec de la couleur ou du dessin, combien nous sommes
grands et poétiques dans nos cravates et nos bottes vernies. –
Puissent les vrais chercheurs nous donner l'année prochaine
cette joie singulière de célébrer l'avènement du *neuf*!'

Baudelaire hoped that the success of his pamphlet would
bring him offers of regular work, for it was favourably
noticed in several quarters. However, all that he succeeded
in placing was an early poem, *À une Dame Créole*, composed in 1841, which was published in May 1845 in *L'Artiste*.
He discovered that earning his living at the point of his
pen, was a discouraging and unremunerative occupation,
unless he was willing to prostitute his art. He gave expression to this conviction in *La Muse Vénale*.[8]

O muse de mon cœur, amante des palais,
Auras-tu, quand Janvier lâchera des Borées,
Durant les noirs ennuis des neigeuses soirées,
Un tison pour chauffer tes deux pieds violets?

Ranimeras-tu donc tes épaules marbrées
Aux nocturnes rayons qui percent les volets?
Sentant ta bourse à sec autant que ton palais,
Récolteras-tu l'or des voûtes azurées?

Il te faut, pour gagner ton pain de chaque soir,
Comme un enfant de chœur, jouer de l'encensoir,
Chanter des Te Deum *auxquels tu ne crois guère,*

Ou, Saltimbanque à jeun, étaler tes appas
Et ton rire trempé de pleurs qu'on ne voit pas,
Pour faire épanouir la rate du vulgaire.

He was much disappointed and discouraged at his lack
of financial success, when he had imagined that his tribulations were at an end, and that he would be able soon
to please his mother, so that she could speak of him with
pride to her husband.

Suddenly it must have seemed to him that life was too
difficult and complicated, and that there was no point in
striving, since everything would always be against him. At
the end of June 1845 occurred his mysterious suicide
attempt which the critics who are unfavourably disposed
towards him, consider a melodramatic piece of play-acting,
or else an unpardonable essay at softening his mother's
heart to persuade her to give him money. They justify this
opinion by showing that afterwards he made fun of the
episode. It was, however, his habit to pretend that he was
not serious lest anyone should suspect he possessed a heart,
and tried to discover its secret. The state of mind which
had inspired the *spleen* poems, could have led to the violent
act of suicide with a man of his temperament who was at
the end of courage and endurance. The letter which he
wrote to Ancelle to entrust his mistress to his care, if theatri-

cal in parts, seems based on sincere feeling. He would always have dramatized his actions, even when they were genuine.

'When Jeanne Lemer[9] has given you this letter I shall be dead!' he wrote.[10] 'She doesn't know this. You know my last will and testament! Except for the part reserved for my mother Mademoiselle *Lemer* is to inherit everything I leave, after you have paid my debts, a list of which I enclose in this letter.

'I'm dying in a horrible state of anxiety. Remember our conversation yesterday. I wish, I insist, that my last wishes shall be strictly carried out. Only two people can contest my will: my mother and my brother – and they can only contest it on the grounds of insanity. My suicide, added to the general confusion of my life, can only give them the pretext for defrauding Mademoiselle Lemer of what I wish to leave her. I must therefore explain to you my *suicide* and my conduct towards Mademoiselle *Lemer*, – so that this letter, addressed to you, the contents of which you will impart to her, may help her in her defence, in the event of my will being contested by the persons mentioned above.

'I am *killing* myself – without *grief*. I don't feel any of that agitation of mind which men call *grief*. – My debts have never been a source of *grief* to me. Nothing is easier than to control such matters. I'm killing myself because I can't live any longer, because the fatigue of going to sleep and of waking up again is unbearable to me. I'm killing myself because I'm useless to others – *and dangerous to myself*. I'm *killing* myself because I believe I am immortal and because I *hope*. – As I write these lines my mind is so clear that I'm collecting notes for Monsieur *Théodore de Banville*, and that I possess sufficient strength to look after my manuscripts.

'I give and leave everything that I possess to Mademoiselle Lemer, even my small stock of furniture, and my portrait – because she is the only being in whom I've found some rest and peace. Can I be blamed for wishing to repay the few pleasures that I've found on this horrible earth?

'I don't know my brother well – he has never lived *in me nor with me* – and he doesn't need me.

'My mother, who so frequently and always involuntarily, has poisoned my life, doesn't need this money either. She has her *husband*, and possesses a *human being*, affection, *friendship*. I've got no one but *Jeanne Lemer*. I've found peace only in her, and I don't wish, I can't bear the thought, that they might deprive her of what I'm giving her, on the plea that my mind is deranged. You've heard me speak to you, in the last few days. – Was I mad?

'If I knew that by begging my mother herself, and showing her the deep humiliation of my mind, I could obtain from her a promise not to contest my last wishes, I would do it immediately, – I'm so sure that, being a woman, she'd understand me better than anyone else – and could, by herself, dissuade my brother from stupid opposition.

'Jeanne Lemer is the only woman that I've loved – and she has nothing. And it's to you, Monsieur Ancelle, one of the few men I've known possessing a noble and gentle mind, that I entrust my last wishes with regard to her.

'Read her this so that she'll know the reasons for the bequest, and her defence, in the event of my last arrangements being thwarted. Make her understand, you who are a careful man, the value and the importance of any sum of money. Try to find some reasonable plea from which she can profit, and which will make my last wishes useful to her. Advise her and guide her and, dare I say it, love her – for my sake at least. Point out to her my terrifying example – and how disorderliness of mind and life inevitably lead to dark despair or to total destruction. – *Reason and utility! I beg you!*

'And do you really think that my will and testament can be contested, and can they remove from me the right to perform a really good and reasonable action before I die?

'You see now that this will isn't a piece of brag, nor an

act of defiance against social and family sentiment, but only the expression of what is left in me of humanity — of love, and the sincere wish to help a creature who has been some-times my joy and my peace.

'Goodbye!

'Read her this. — *I have faith in your loyalty, and know that you won't destroy it.*

'Give her some money *immediately*. She doesn't know my *last wishes*, — and expects to see me come to extricate her from some difficulties.

'In the event of his last wishes being contested, a dead man has surely the right to be generous!

'The other letter which she will give you, is for you alone, and it contains a list of all the debts that must be paid for me, to safeguard my memory.'

The current account of his attempted suicide does not tally with this letter. It alleges that on a certain evening, as he was sitting in a café with Jeanne Duval, he seized a knife and ran it into his breast. He remembered nothing after that until he recovered consciousness, and found him-self at a police station. The constable in charge would not hear of his returning to his own lodgings, but insisted on letting his family know what had happened, and he was taken to his stepfather's house in the Place Vendôme.

His attempt at suicide certainly startled his parents, making them wonder whether they might not have been too harsh to him, and driven him too far. His mother must have been aghast at the thought that she had nearly lost her child in this senseless manner. There was a family reconciliation, after which Baudelaire gave up his apart-ment at the Hôtel Lauzun, and went to live at home, where his mother looked after him, and even helped him in his literary work by acting as his secretary, copying out his poems to have them ready for publication. She may have cherished the hope that he would now, like any normal son, live regularly at home, and keep his small income as pocket-money.

Soon, however, the clash of strong opposing personalities began again, and life returned to its former wrangling and bickering. It is possible that the General made his stepson feel that, having been forgiven his trespasses, he should, in gratitude for the leniency shown him, make efforts at reformation and at earning a respectable living. At last one day, being unable to endure the life any longer, Baudelaire slunk out of the house, when no one was in, leaving a letter for his mother on the table in the hall, or in her room. From what he says, the disputes which led up to this sudden departure can be readily imagined. He speaks very differently now of his stepfather, no longer calling him 'mon ami' but 'your husband'.[11]

'I'm leaving and I'll only return when I'm in a more stable mental and financial state,' he wrote. 'I'm leaving for several reasons. First because I've sunk into such a terrible state of depression and apathy, that I feel I need a lot of solitude to recover and to regain my moral strength. Secondly because it is absolutely impossible for me to make myself into what your husband would like me to be; and so I feel that it would be only robbing him to live any longer under his roof. And finally because I don't think it right or seemly that I should be treated by him as he now seems determined to treat me. – I'll probably have to live a very hard life, but I know I'll be happier that way. –

'Today or tomorrow I'll send you a letter to tell you which of my things I need, and where to send them. My mind is finally and irrevocably made up, after mature reflection; and so it's no use your complaining, but you should try to understand it.'

When he had found lodgings, he sent for his belongings, and he had no longer an apartment of his own, but only a hotel room. For the rest of his life, except for the few months when he lived in his mother's house at Honfleur in 1859, he was to live in hotel rooms or casual lodgings.

'You must send me immediately,' he wrote to his mother,[12] 'to the Hôtel Dunkerque, the little trunk which contains

my underclothes – also my shoes and slippers – and the two
black ties – *also all my books*. I need them badly and immediately! You mustn't send me any letter of complaint,
nor ask me to come back – for I won't come back! All that
I can assure is that you'll be pleased in a short time.'

He firmly kept to that decision, and never again, as long
as his stepfather was alive, did he sleep under his mother's
roof.

He told his friends, to account for his sudden departure,
that he had left his mother's house because claret only was
drunk at her table, and he could drink nothing but bur-
gundy. This was the kind of remark that his friends
expected from him, and they would have been disappointed
if he had failed to give it to them.

His attempted suicide, however, had one good result for
him; it seemed, for a time, at all events, to purge his nature
of depression and despair, so that he was able to begin work
again, and the year and a half which followed it was a fruitful period during which he succeeded in publishing in
different periodicals various contributions, for which he was
paid. It looked as if he was on the road to success, and as
if he could earn a living with his pen.

The success of his first *Salon* opened for him the doors
of the *Corsaire-Satan* and there, for the next year and a
half, he published contributions regularly, beginning in
November 1845, with a review of *Les Contes Normands* of
Jean de la Falaise, and followed, three weeks later, by the
fragment of a play entitled *Sapho* which, at the time, was
attributed to Arsène Houssaye but which is now known to
have been the joint production of Baudelaire, Banville,
Dupont and Vitu.[13] In the same number appeared an
original article, under the title *Comment on paie ses Dettes
quand on a du Génie*.[14] This is an attack on Balzac's way
of commissioning hacks to write articles which he then
signed, in order to make money to pay his debts. Baudelaire
who, in other respects, was one of Balzac's most fervent
admirers, and who, himself, was also crushed by debts, did

not approve of this way of solving a difficulty and never, even in his most penurious days, resorted to it himself. In January 1846, in the same paper, he published his second piece of original art criticism, *Le Musée Classique du Bazar Bonne-Nouvelle*, which has some acute remarks on Ingres' art and which, although no pictures by Delacroix were shown at the exhibition, seized the pretext of this to speak of him with the young critic's usual admiration. The following month he published a notice on the *Prométhée Délivré* by his former schoolmate at the Lycée Louis-le-Grand, Louis Ménard, who wrote under the name N. De Senneville. This is a play in verse, which its author published at his own expense, and which shows a strong influence of Alfred de Vigny, but also of the new classical revival. It was, on the whole, favourably reviewed, except by Baudelaire, the severity of whose notice was largely the result of inexperience, and antipathy to the false Hellenic influence current at the time, and who, six years later in *L'École Païenne*, was to be still more severe on this inspiration which he was to call 'un pastiche inutile et dégoûtant'. However, Louis Ménard never forgave him for his comments, and their relations became very strained. Nor were they improved when the author found, in a second-hand book-box on the quays, the inscribed copy of the work he had presented to Baudelaire.[15] He took his revenge ten years later by composing a parody of Baudelaire's style entitled *Incompatibilité* and sending it to the *Revue des Deux Mondes* where the first large batch of *Les Fleurs du Mal* had appeared in 1855, under the pseudonym of Courbet.[16] It reflects the current conventional view of the poet's inspiration, the last verses of which are typical of the whole poem:

> *J'aime avec passion les choses dégoûtantes;*
> *Et mon cœur faisandé, livide et purulent,*
> *Sous l'ondulation des vermines mangeantes,*
> *N'est qu'un lambeau de chair, fétide et pantelant.*

Or donc, vierge aux doux yeux, aimes-tu les ivrognes?
– J'ai vidé plus d'un broc loin du regard de Dieu,
Et j'ai cuvé mon vin sur un tas de charognes
Dans quelque cul-de-sac, n'ayant ni feu ni lieu.

L'imprescriptible amour des plaisirs déshonnêtes
A ratissé mon front lépreux, ridé, pelé.
Mais qu'importe, sorcière adorable, ange ailé,
Tous les péchés n'ont pas de cheveux sur leurs têtes.

In the same month Baudelaire published in *L'Esprit Public* a tale entitled *Le Jeune Enchanteur*, in the prevailing classical style, in a desire perhaps to make a bid for popularity. Later he would not consider including this in editions of his works. In this he was well advised as it is not a successful work, and very different from his usual inspiration; and especially as it has now been proved to be merely the translation of a tale which had appeared in an English Keepsake in 1836, called *Forget-me-not*, under the title *The Young Enchanter*, alleged to have been taken from a papyrus of Herculaneum by a poet called George Croly, who was writing between 1780 and 1860 and was a friend of Byron.[17]

In March 1846 came two works: *Choix de Maximes Consolantes sur l'Amour*, published in *Le Corsaire-Satan*, and an anonymous pamphlet entitled *Le Salon Caricatural* which is a satire on the real *Salon*, and which Poulet Malassis declared in 1864 had been composed by Banville, Baudelaire and Vitu.[18] The *Prologue* certainly would appear to have been written by Baudelaire.[19]

Choix de Maximes Consolantes sur l'Amour is an interesting and original work coming from the pen of a young man not yet twenty-five, even if it can be said to have been influenced by Stendhal's work *De l'Amour*. It shows an unusual understanding of the complicated and subtle moods of passion, which would not seem out of place in a modern psycho-analytical treatise.

'Je suppose votre idole malade. Sa beauté a disparu sous

l'affreuse croûte de la petite vérole, comme la verdure sous les lourdes glacés de l'hiver. Encore ému par les longues angoisses et les alternatives de la maladie, vous contemplez avec tristesse le stigmate ineffaçable sur le corps de la chère convalescente; vous entendez subitement résonner à vos oreilles un air mourant exécuté par l'archet délirant de Paganini, et cet air sympathique vous parle de vous-même, et semble vous raconter tout votre poème intérieur d'espérances perdues. – Dès lors, les traces de petite vérole feront partie de votre bonheur et chanteront toujours à votre regard attendri l'air mystérieux de Paganini. Elles seront désormais non seulement un objet de douce sympathie, mais encore de volupté physique, si toutefois vous êtes un de ces esprits sensibles pour qui la beauté est surtout la promesse du bonheur. C'est donc surtout l'association des idées qui fait aimer les laides; car vous risquez fort, si votre maîtresse grêlée vous trahit, de ne pouvoir vous consoler qu'avec une femme grêlée.' [20]

Baudelaire seems to have been proud of this essay, and pleased with it, for he sent it to his sister-in-law, the wife of his half-brother Alphonse, with a strange letter, coming from a brother-in-law to a woman whom he had known for almost twenty years, and who was the sister of a close school-friend. This somewhat precious and artificial letter is, as it were, the rough sketch of the letters he will write six years later to Madame Sabatier, and the one to Marie Daubrun.

'Madame,' he wrote, in a tone of distant respect,[21] 'you may be curious to know how Baudelaire-Dufays treats a subject as difficult, and, at the same time, as natural, as love. I am sending you here this pamphlet which has just appeared from my pen. I could not choose a better judge than you, and I become your justiciable with entire confidence.[22] How I wish that my brother could hear me plead my cause – or rather that of the whole of the human race – before the tribunal of love, as I say in the article I am sending you, he would appreciate the vocation which drives me towards the Muses as I, for my part, appreciate the enthusiasm with which he devotes himself to the arduous labours of Themis. To each of us our lot in the world, mine to instruct my fellowmen in the conduct they should observe in order to find happiness. And so I shall have the honour, dear Madame, to send you shortly my catechism of the loved woman, in the hope of being read and criticized by you.[23] My beginnings in the profession proclaim me a partisan of the love of Antony.[24] But you will see that it is a love far from being worthy of contempt. What will you say, I wonder, of the principles and advice which I give to the members of the fickle sex, who only feign love? I wish the lover who really loves to be constant, and you have proof of this in this one sentence, "Love sincerely, and may your love not be a torment to the love of others". This one passage will, doubtless, inspire you with the desire to read the whole article, and also the catechism which is about to appear.

'Will you deign, Madame, to act as Providence to me in the career which is opening before me, through the channel of love – I had almost said, through the influence of woman.

'Please accept my respectful greetings, offered with the enthusiasm of a poet who wishes to walk in the footsteps of Parny.[25]

> Your most humble servant,
> BAUDELAIRE-DUFAYS.'

It is hard to believe that this letter was written by a man of twenty-three, who for four years had been the lover of Jeanne Duval, and who, by the age of twenty, had known squint-eyed Louchette.

The following month, in April 1846, he published in *L'Esprit Public* a further article entitled *Conseils aux Jeunes Littérateurs*, inspired by wise and grave advice which unfortunately he himself certainly did not follow. At this time he believed that, with effort and strength of will, all obstacles could be surmounted, that there was no such thing as ill-luck, and that those who complained of 'le guignon' were only those who had not succeeded. He said:[26]

'C'est pourquoi il n'y a pas de guignon. Si vous avez du guignon, c'est qu'il vous manque quelquechose. Ce quelquechose, connaissez-le, et étudiez le jeu des volontés voisines pour déplacer plus facilement la circonférence.'

He was to write very differently ten years later when he attributed his lack of success to 'le guignon'.

At this time Baudelaire was in a reasonable and diligent frame of mind, preparing with energy and hard work to be a well-informed critic. It was in 1846 that, for some reason which is not clear, he signed on as a student at the École des Chartes, as a printed list for February proves, studying history and palaeography.[27] It is strange that he should have done this as late as this, when he was twenty-five.

With so much work published and promised, Baudelaire felt that he could apply to his mother for help, now that his feet were firmly planted on the ladder of success, and could turn to her with pride in his achievement, not merely as an unsuccessful suppliant.

She was pleased with the signs of so much diligence, and must have written with encouragement, since he thanked her for her kind and sympathetic letter, and then dared ask her for a loan to tide him over until he was paid for the work which he had been commissioned to write. He thought that there could be no humiliation in asking for an advance, since the money was virtually earned, and he had now only to write the articles which were already planned.

'I thank you for the kind and sweet letter you left at my place,' he wrote,[28] 'I'd love you to come and see me *tomorrow morning*. I want to speak to you about *money*. But don't be afraid! I don't exactly want to borrow from you – it's only a question of a special arrangement which is easier to explain than to write.

'I find myself, as the result of a series of lucky, and at the same time, unlucky, transactions, in a position to earn a lot of money in a short time – and at the same time I'm *crushed*

by the debts that you know and which become each day
more shameful – I've five articles commissioned by *L'Esprit
Public* – two by *L'Époque*, two more for *La Presse* – one for
La Revue Nouvelle – All this means an enormous sum of
money – I've never felt such high hopes – But, at the same
time, I've got my *Salon* on my hands, that is to say one
whole volume to write in a week.

'You see how busy I am, and you can readily forgive me
for not going to explain all this to you in person. I've even
been obliged, for the last few days, to send one of my friends
to do my shopping.'

Few of these articles were ever published, certainly not
in the periodicals which he mentions, nor under the titles
he quotes. It is not known what arrangements his mother
made with him when they met, but it is very probable that
she granted his request, for she was always ready to be
impressed and pleased with any signs of improvement in
him, and to encourage him to further efforts.

One work mentioned in the letter did, however, appear,
and that was his *Salon* of 1846, which came out in May,
and which was his first really important work of criticism,
a marked advance on the *Salon* of the previous year, and
ranking amongst his most subtle and illuminating aesthetic
writings. This time he was no longer satisfied, as previously,
with giving a mere account of the exhibition, but wished,
as well, to formulate independent and original theories.
Even if, as Pommier suggests,[29] he has obviously read
Stendhal's work on painting, and owes something to it, he
has read it wisely and to some profit, and there is enough
original material to make the reputation of a brilliant critic.
The best criticism, he claims, is the one which opens up new
horizons to its readers, and a picture is nature reflected in
the temperament of the artist; this criticism, in its turn, is
the same picture reflected in an intelligent, sensitive and
well-informed mind. This is the first hint of his later theory
of *correspondances* in nature and art. He elaborates this
further when he discusses Hoffmann's view that colours

produce certain vibrations, or direct impressions on the mind, not to be distinguished from those created by sound. Baudelaire claimed that painting, like music, had its own harmony, the harmony of light and shade. Then follows a magnificent passage – a prose poem it might be called – describing the melody of colour in nature. This passage, by itself, would be sufficient to refute the view frequently held, that he was insensible to the beauties of nature.

'La sève monte et, mélange de principes, elle s'épanouit en *tons mélangés*; les arbres, les rochers, les granits se mirent dans les eaux et y déposent leurs *reflets*; tous les objets transparents accrochent au passage lumières et couleurs voisines et lointaines. À mesure que l'astre du jour se dérange, les tons changent de valeur, mais respectant toujours leurs sympathies et leurs haines naturelles, continuent à vivre en harmonie par des concessions réciproques. Les ombres se déplacent lentement, et font fuir devant elles ou éteignent les tons à mesure que la lumière, déplacée elle-même, en veut faire résonner de nouveaux. Ceux-ci se renvoient leurs reflets, et, modifiant leurs qualités en les glaçant de qualités transparentes et empruntées, multiplient à l'infini leurs mariages mélodieux et les rendent plus faciles. Quand le grand foyer descend dans les eaux, les rouges fanfares s'élancent de tous côtés; une sanglante harmonie éclate à l'horizon, et le vert s'empourpre richement. Mais bientôt de vastes ombres bleues chassent en cadences devant elles la foule des tons orangés et rose tendre qui sont comme l'écho lointain et affaibli de la lumière. Cette grande symphonie du jour, qui est l'éternelle variation de la symphonie d'hier, cette succession de mélodies, où la variété sort toujours de l'infini, cet hymne compliqué s'appelle la couleur.

'On trouve dans la couleur l'harmonie, la mélodie et le contrepoint.' [30]

The *Salon* ends on the same note as that of the previous year, with a chapter entitled *De l'Héroïsme de la Vie*

Moderne, voicing the hope that artists will soon arise who will perceive the beauty in contemporary life, 'la beauté moderne'.

'Il ya donc une beauté et un héroïsme modernes!

'La vie parisienne est féconde en sujets poétiques et mer-veilleux. Le merveilleux nous enveloppe et nous abreuve comme l'atmosphère; mais nous ne le voyons pas. ... Les moyens et les motifs de la peinture sont également abon-dants et variés; mail il y a un élément nouveau, qui est la beauté moderne.' [31]

The *Salon* of 1846 laid the foundations of Baudelaire's reputation as a critic in a glorious manner. It was favour-ably noticed in many quarters. Henri Murger was one of the first to draw attention to it in the *Post-Scriptum* to his own *Salon* of the same year, in the *Moniteur de la Mode* in May, and he drew the obvious comparison between Baudelaire and Diderot, Stendhal and Hoffmann – not that Murger himself had much knowledge of any of them – and he ended by declaring: 'In a word Monsieur Baudelaire has written an original work, strange and full of youthful and noble daring. What is more, it is a work which will last!' In this he spoke more truly than he can have realized at the time, for, although it is not as mature as some of his later works, it remains one of his most original and attrac-tive, and it has been considered one of the finest studies of painting of the period. [32]

Baudelaire continued his contributions to *Le Corsaire-Satan* with a review of Houssaye's *Romans, Contes et Nouvelles* in September 1846, and this enabled him to pub-lish two further poems in his paper, *L'Artiste: Don Juan* in September and *À une Malabaraise* in December. He also managed to appear in *Le Tintamarre*, where, with Vitu and Banville, he contributed *Les Causeries du Tintamarre* under the pseudonyms, François Lambert, Marc Aurèle, and Joseph d'Estienne. It is not known whether these names hid separate personalities or whether the articles were joint efforts. Mouquet does not commit himself, [33] but Crépet claims to find the hand of Baudelaire in most of the articles.[34] The subject is now of academic interest only, since none of the articles are as original or interesting as those which Baudelaire had already signed himself.

In January 1847 he published his only novel, a long short story, entitled *La Fanfarlo*, which he had begun many years previously, and hoped to bring out very much sooner, for it is constantly mentioned in his correspondence as about to appear.[35] It reveals traces of the influence of Balzac, especially of *La Fille aux Yeux d'Or*, while the character of La Fanfarlo herself owes something to Beatrix from *Le Lys dans la Vallée*, and the poems of the hero, Samuel Cramer, are like those of Lucien de Rubempré, *Les Marguerites*, in *La Muse du Département*. Though the story may not be the highest form of fiction, it remains nevertheless a subtle and penetrating study, written in a style which would not have seemed out of place in the aesthetic movement of the 'nineties. Its chief interest today lies in its self-analysis, and Baudelaire has, in it, analysed with rare insight, his own personality at the time of his extravagant life at the Hôtel Lauzun, in the person of the hero, Samuel Cramer.

This work marked the last burst of energy in Baudelaire for a long time, and his zest for work faded as suddenly as it had begun. After its publication in January 1847, his output slowed down and he fell into one of these moods of lethargy, idleness and incapacity for work which were to recur with such frequency throughout his life, especially after a bout of creative activity. Was he idle because he could find no editor prepared to take his work; or was it that he could not force himself to bring any composition to the pitch of perfection which he thought necessary; or was it that he was going through a period of sterility and felt that he had nothing to say? A poem of this period, *La Cloche Fêlée*, would lend colour to the view that depression, boredom and lack of success had induced in him a state of intellectual aridity.[36]

Il est amer et doux, pendant les nuits d'hiver,
D'écouter, près du feu qui palpite et qui fume,
Les souvenirs lointains lentement s'élever
Au bruit des carillons qui chantent dans la brume.

Bienheureuse la cloche au gosier vigoureux
Qui, malgré sa vieillesse, alerte et bien portante,
Jette fidèlement son cri religieux,
Ainsi qu'un vieux soldat qui veille sous la tente!

Moi, mon âme est fêlée, et lorsqu'en ses ennuis
Elle veut de ses chants peupler l'air froid des nuits,
Il arrive souvent que sa voix affaiblie

Semble le râle épais d'un blessé qu'on oublie
Au bord d'un lac de sang, sous un grand tas de morts,
Et qui meurt, sans bouger, dans d'immenses efforts.

We have no information of his activities during 1847
since no correspondence exists to enlighten us. Letters were
obviously written to his mother for later he asks her to
return them so that he can destroy them because they were
bitter and cruel.[37] In spite of these letters – or because of
them – there was a period of estrangement between himself
and his mother. Since his zeal for work had flagged, and he
continued to borrow money from her which he did not
attempt to repay, she was growing increasingly exasperated
with him, and frequently did not answer his letters. Once
he even sent her his pawn tickets, asking her to redeem the
pledged articles and to pay the arrears of interest.[38] When
she wrote to him in reproach, he answered by the insulting
letters which he later retrieved from her, but which had
bitterly hurt her and offended her. To Ancelle, who was
trying to put in a good word for his ward, she answered:[39]

'I can't hear you say that my son has no clothes and no
food without my heart bleeding. But I don't intend to make
up my differences with him, for I can't, and won't, forgive
so quickly the wounding things he dared to write to me, his
mother, and I shall give him back my affection only when
he's proved himself worthy of it. So he needn't write to me

henceforth. However, if he ever shows the slightest disappointment in his career, I undertake, through the General,
to get him some kind of job.'

He too was hurt by what he called her cruel answers to
his requests, and he did not write to her for a long time, nor
see her. It was only when he was at the end of all hope, in
December 1847, that he approached her once more. Then,
looking back on the achievements of the year, he saw that
it was one of the most ill-spent of his life. So discouraged
was he then that he contemplated leaving France, abandoning his dreams and his ambitions, and going out East again,
where he knew that work of a kind could be obtained, and
existence could be calm and peaceful, provided one was
willing to forgo ambition and to consider the absence of
desires as the highest bliss.

When he had made up his mind to leave his country,
since there was nothing left for him to do, his whole nature
recoiled from the contemplation of such a future, and he
felt that he could not renounce his hopes for literary fame
without a struggle, for in spite of continued lack of success,
he still had confidence that he would make a name. At this
critical point he thought once more of his mother, who had
never failed to answer his appeals when he had been in
distress, and he resolved, before taking a final and irrevoc-
able step, to play his final card, and to beg her to help him
for the last time, promising to return to the habits of hard
work which he had practised all through 1846. He felt confident that, if she would only help him, he would be able to
recover his energy and his zest for work.

He spent three days in nerving himself for the ordeal of
writing to her, for it was unbearable to him to admit total
defeat. At last, seizing his courage in both hands, he sat
down to compose one of the long letters of explanation
and justification which came so frequently from his
pen.[40]

'In spite of the cruel letter with which you answered my
last request, I thought it was permissible to approach you

again, not that I don't fully realize the anger this will cause
you, and the trouble I'll have in making you understand
the justice of this request, but because I feel convinced that
it will be infinitely and definitely useful, and that I hope
to make you share this conviction too. Please note that
when I say "once more" I mean very sincerely: one last
time. I know that I owe you thanks for your kindness in
providing me with things necessary for a more reasonable
life than I've been living for a long time, that is to say,
some furniture. But, after the furniture was bought, I found
myself without a penny, and also without some of the things
no less essential, such as a lamp and so forth. All you need
know is that I was obliged to have a long discussion with
Monsieur Ancelle to buy wood and coal. If you only knew
what an effort I had to make to take up my pen and write
to you again, since I despair of ever making you realize,
you whose life is always so easy and ordered, how it happens that I can find myself in such straits. Just imagine one
moment my everlasting inability to work, my hatred of this
idleness, my inability to get out of it on account of my perpetual need of money. Certainly, in such a case, it is better
to turn to you once more, however much it humiliates me,
than to indifferent people with whom I wouldn't find the
same sympathy. ... My idleness is rusting me, devouring
me, killing me. I don't know how I find the strength to
conquer the disastrous effect of this idleness, to keep my
clarity of mind, and the hope, which never leaves me, of
success, happiness and peace. Now here is what I entreat
you on my bended knees, because I feel that I've reached
not only the limits of other people's patience, but of my
own as well. Do please send me, *even if it costs you terrible
trouble, and even if you don't see the imperative necessity
of this last favour, not only the sum mentioned, but also
sufficient to live on for three weeks.* You fix the sum as you
think best. I've got such perfect confidence in the use I'll
make of my time, and in my strength of will, that I *know
positively* that if I could live a regular life for a fortnight

or three weeks, my *brain would be saved*. It is one last try, a gamble. Gamble on the unknown, Mother, I implore you! The explanation of these last six years so strangely and so disastrously spent, if I hadn't enjoyed health of mind and body which nothing has been able to destroy – is very simple – it comes to one thing, and one thing only. Carelessness and the postponing to the morrow of the most reasonable plans of conduct, and consequently poverty and still more poverty. I'll give you one example: it has happened sometimes that I've been obliged to remain for three days in bed, because I had no shirt to put on, or no wood. Frankly, laudanum and wine are bad aids against sorrow. They pass the time but they don't improve life. And even to make oneself sodden one needs money. The last time you had the kindness to give me fifteen francs I'd not eaten anything for two whole days, forty-eight hours – I spent all my time coming and going on the road to Neuilly, and I didn't dare admit my plight to Ancelle, that I was bearing up only thanks to the brandy I'd been given, I who loathe liqueurs, for they give me a pain. May such admissions – for your sake and for mine – never be known by living men or by posterity, for I still believe that I'm the concern of posterity. No one could believe that it could be possible for a sensible human being, with a good and sympathetic mother, to have sunk to such a state. And so you mustn't allow this letter, written for you alone, the first person to whom I've ever made such confidences, to leave your possession. You'll be able to find in your heart reasons for understanding that such expressions of distress can only be addressed to you, and can go no further. Besides, before I wrote to you, I considered everything, and I've firmly resolved not to see Ancelle again, with whom, by the way, I've had several disagreeable interviews – and if you should make the mistake of considering this final attempt as ordinary and similar to the others, and show him this letter, or even give him advice. I've just reread these two pages and they seem to me odd, even to myself. I've never before dared to complain out loud. I hope that you'll put down this state of excitement to the *suffering which I endure and which you can't guess*. The apparent inactivity of my life, contrasting with the ceaseless activity of my brain, throws me into the most astounding rages. I'm angry with myself on account of my faults, and with you because you doubt the sincerity of my intentions. ... One last time, wishing to put an end to this impossible situation and believing in my will-power, I've dared to implore you again, to make a final attempt, one last gamble, as I said to you before, even if it should seem to you excessive, and even if it should cause you inconvenience. For I guess, and understand very well, how any irregular expenditure must be unbearable and the source of worry to a housewife, especially to you whom I know so well from having lived with you. But I'm in an unusual state of mind, and I wanted to discover, one last time, if my mother's money can help me – and I think this is sure and certain. I'm suffering too much not to wish to put an end to the present situation one *last time*. I've said all this several times before, I think.

'In spite of the terrible grief I'd feel to leave Paris and to say farewell to so many fine dreams, I've made the sincere and firm resolve to do it, if I can't guarantee to live and work hard on the money I'm asking from you. And it would be to go far away. People whom I knew at Réunion have been kind enough to remember me, and I'd find a post easy to fill, and a salary ample for a country where living is cheap once one is established there. *But oh! the fearful boredom, and intellectual deterioration of the warm and deep blue lands*. Nevertheless I'll do that in punishment and expiation of my pride, if I fail in my final resolve. Don't look for this post amongst official positions. It is almost a domestic situation, and means only teaching everything, except chemistry and mathematics, to the children of friends. But don't let's speak of it any more, for the necessity of such a resolve makes me shudder. Only I'll add that if I thought it necessary to punish myself for having failed in

my dreams, I'd insist, since a secure and easy life was waiting for me, that all the debts I left behind me should be
paid. The very thought of such abdication and decay makes
me shudder, and so I implore you not to show this letter,
even in confidence, to Ancelle, for I think it shameful for
a man to doubt his own success. I've got until the month
of February to accept or to refuse and I intend to give you
by New Year's Day the proof that your money has been
well spent.

'Well! here is my plan, and it is very simple. About eight
months ago I was asked to write two important articles
which are not yet finished, one a history of caricature and
the other a history of sculpture. That would mean six
hundred francs. This would only serve for my most pressing
needs. Those articles are child's play for me. . . .

'Well, I've calculated that the extreme weariness of my
creditors, who consider their debts fairly bad ones, and their
consciousness, for the most part, of having scandalously
cheated me, would permit me to reduce the total amount of
my debts to six or eight thousand francs at the outside.
That sum would be easy enough to find, with diligence and
persistence; believe me, I know what I'm talking about,
with the experience I've acquired in the bustle of newspaper
offices and publishing houses. Whom should I entrust with
the painful job of coming to an agreement with them:
Ancelle or myself, or someone else? I don't yet know. But
I insist that you promise me that once this task is accomplished, and when, moreover, I've allowed a few months to
elapse to prove to you that I'm able not only to pay my
debts, but also to avoid making fresh ones, I'll insist that
you help me with your support, to persuade them to give
me back the free disposal of my own money. Then, too,
you'll give me back those cruel letters which you mentioned, and which you judge so harshly. If you only knew
what a complicated mass of big and small worries makes up
my usual and continuous suffering. I've tried, at least this
once, to write you a decent letter. The unfortunate thing

is that I need your help and thus can't take any steps with you which won't seem interested.

'I'm most terribly tired and I've got a kind of wheel turning round and round in my head. – One last time, dearest Mother, I beg you, for the sake of my future salvation – This is the first time, I think, that I've taken you into my confidence at such length about plans which are important and precious to me. Perhaps this will persuade you that, from time to time, I do consider humbling my pride in front of my mother! Time is flying and a few more days of this idleness could destroy me entirely. As I've already told you, I've so miscalculated my powers of endurance, that I've reached the limits of my own patience, and I'm incapable of further effort unless I'm helped a little. If by any chance it occurred to you to ask Monsieur Ancelle for money, don't tell him what it's for, and since it's you I've asked for help, give me the pleasure of receiving this favour from you alone. Please answer me at once. For three days now I've been trying to nerve myself to write to you, but I didn't dare.

'You can trust the messenger.

'And just one more word: for a long time now you've been trying to shut me out from your presence. You hope, I suppose, by this to hasten the end of my difficulties. I've made mistakes I know, but that isn't criminal, and do you think I'm strong enough to stand this perpetual solitude? I promise faithfully to come to see you only when I've good news to give you. But from that moment I'll insist on seeing you, and on being properly received, in such a way that, by your manner, expression, and your words, you'll protect me in your home against everyone.

'Goodbye. I'm glad I've written to you.'

His mother sent money back by the messenger the same day. She was moved, as she always was, by signs of distress in him, and she consented to see him again. He wrote the following day to thank her.[41]

'I thank you from the bottom of my heart. Never did help arrive more opportunely! Believe me, I realize perfectly

the value of this money. Your letter caused me no less pain
than mine must have done you. I know that well! I guessed
everything!

'However I hope one day to repay you in everything and
don't imagine by that I'm speaking only of the money, *I
want to repay you more than your money.* If you'll write
to me – as I understand you want to – my address, which
you don't know, is 36 Rue de Babylone – What you send me
must – *of necessity* – suffice. I know the value of that sum,
and I'll have to make it do.

'Don't give my address to anyone!

CHARLES BAUDELAIRE DEFAYIS.'

Madame Aupick helped her son to some temporary alleviation of his difficulties. But, as was her usual practice, she
was unable – or did not dare – trust him sufficiently to
advance a sum large enough to clear him of debt. Who shall
say that she was unjustified, for his conduct had never given
her any grounds to hope for reform in him. He himself
always thought that his chief worries lay in the debts which
he had incurred before the appointment of his *conseil judiciaire*, and that he added to his insolvency by borrowing
in order to pay the interest on them. In this manner, he
used to say, without living extravagantly, the total sum
which he owed had grown to alarming proportions. It must
be admitted, however, that he never resorted to the harshest
methods with himself, in order to clear himself, and, not
even in the days of his greatest distress, did he ever consider
selling his pictures and books – indeed he was always adding to them. On the other hand it must also be acknowledged that he never thought of disowning his obligations
and going bankrupt, though he was often assured by his
friends that, by doing so, he would have led a more peaceful
life.

Sometimes he could not refrain from feeling that his
mother could have been more generous to him now that her
husband's position was so brilliant and secure. He con-

trasted then the luxury of her present life with the poverty
of his. Like a queen, she moved, richly dressed and covered
with jewels, among kings and diplomats, while he lacked
even the bare necessities of life. So shabby had he become,
he said, that he was ashamed to go to her house, to face
the mocking glances of her servants who had known him
in the days of his splendour.[42] He could not bear the thought
that people might be pointing to him as a failure, *raté*, the
wastrel stepson of the General. He used then, in order to
see his mother, ask her to meet him at a picture gallery,
and he suffered to think that, with a little generosity and
trust on her part, he might once more know a life free from
anxiety, in which he could work in peace.

On the other hand he did not always realize her point of
view nor her personal difficulties. At her back she had a
stern husband who, while loving her deeply, continued to
disapprove of the life her son was leading, and who did not
consider that he had yet given proof that he had reformed,
or was making any strenuous efforts at leading the life of a
respectable Frenchman. He would never have sanctioned
any large measure of generosity since he saw no grounds
for believing that such measures would be efficacious or
final. His wife admired him, considering him right in all
his views, for she herself had often been uncertain of the
stability of the character of her son. Thus, torn between
her love and admiration of her husband, and her love and
mistrust of her son, she continued, unknown to the former,
to give or to lend Baudelaire, when his need was great, small
sums of money which were frittered away in current expenditure and profited no one.

[2]

The Revolutionary
1847 — 1848

His mother and stepfather would have been still more anxious about his future if they had realized the company which their son was now keeping, and who were his most recent close friends. Since the change in his circumstances he had been consorting largely with those whom his parents would have called the riff-raff of Bohemia, many of whom were later to be implicated in the revolution of 1848.

Paris was becoming increasingly restive. The Louis-Philippe régime was proving unpopular with most sections of the public, since it was generally considered to exist only for the benefit of a minority who, devoid of conscience, and unmindful of their responsibilities, were filling their pockets at the expense of the majority. The young in particular were in a state of revolt and inclined towards advanced socialism. These hot-headed youths were, for the most part, members of La Bohème. This Bohemia, which came into existence in the middle years of the eighteen-forties, was very different in character from the light-hearted Bouzingos ten years before, who had come from the middle class and who, though they never possessed sufficient means to gratify all their extravagant tastes, had never suffered from the extremes of want – all except the ill-fated Petrus Borel. This new Bohemia was also different from the groups of youths of the Latin Quarter, the students from the Sorbonne, and the Law and Medical Schools. This was a grimmer Bohème, a world of frequent failures who, perhaps through no fault of their own, had not succeeded in the battle of life. Many came to a tragic end, and some literally died of hunger, as Aloysius Bertrand did, in the public ward of a hospital, through illness brought on by lack of food. There was also

Joseph Débrosses, nicknamed *Le Christ*, a painter who died of consumption in his early twenties and who had never, in his short life, sated his hunger. Lassailly died insane, in great poverty; and Barbara committed suicide. It was one of them, Charles Bataille, who wrote:[1]

> *Joyeux enfants de la Bohème*
> *Rions du sort et de ses coups.*
> *La Société qui nous aime,*
> *Nous garde pour l'heure suprême,*
> *Quand même,*
> *À tous,*
> *Un lit à l'hôpital des fous.*

It was no wonder that these young men were inclined towards socialism and would have welcomed a revolution which would change the social order as they knew it, and perhaps put them in the way of earning some money. They imagined that a new scheme of life might be more favourable to artists and to poets – in their opinion, it certainly could be no worse.

Among these new Bohemians popular imagination has seized upon the name of Murger for special fame, because he wrote the book which, for the uninitiated, evoked most vividly their eccentric and picturesque life. Yet it was not personal inspiration which urged Murger to compose *La Vie de Bohème*, for his own taste was more sentimental. He began his career as a writer of love poems in the debased Romantic tradition, and it was his friend Champfleury who, in 1846, showed him where his true talent lay, in describing what he had seen himself and knew from personal experience. Thus *La Vie de Bohème* was originally intended to be not a Romantic work but one of realism.

Henri Murger was the son of a Paris concierge of the poorest class, and he spent his youth in reading Romantic poetry and in dreaming of becoming a famous poet, the follower of Musset. In 1841 he founded the *Cercle des Buveurs d'Eau*, so called because its members were as poor as he and could afford no stronger drink than water. It used to meet in a sordid little hotel in the Rue des Canettes, called L'Hôtel Merciol, not far from the church of Saint Sulpice. It was there that Murger lodged when he had the money to pay for his room, for, otherwise, he was obliged to rely on the hospitality of friends. To this low hotel there came to see him – amongst others – Champfleury, Banville, and Baudelaire. The feminine members were Musette and Mimi, who are immortalized in *La Vie de Bohème*, under their own names and undisguised. There was also Louise, Clésinger's model, a country girl who, though not exactly beautiful, possessed the proportions which in those days were considered aesthetic, and so always found as much professional work as she wanted in the principal studios of Paris. She made a good living as a model but, as she was generous and warm-hearted, she was always prepared to offer the hospitality of her table and of her bed to any impecunious youth, so long as he was an artist of some sort – painter, sculptor or poet. She was an inveterate artistic snob and would make no exceptions. When one lover left her, as in the course of time all were bound to, lest the bed should grow cold – as she used to say – she quickly chose another to occupy his place, but she never had to look far, for the Bohemians all loved her and called her 'la bonne Louise!'

L'Hôtel Merciol was not the only meeting-place of La Bohème, for there was as well the Café Tabourey, near the Théâtre de l'Odéon, and also the Café Momus in the Rue des Prêtres Saint-Germain l'Auxerrois – its proprietor had artistic ambitions and was therefore kind in the controversial matter of credit. Champfleury tells us that one member of La Bohème, Fauchery, drew up the regulations for the society under three headings. The first stipulated that no rent must ever be paid; the second that all furniture must be removed through the window; and the third that tailors, shoemakers, restaurant-keepers, and all tradespeople belong to the family of Mr Credit.[2] Murger, Champfleury, Dupont, Gérard de Nerval and Baudelaire came to consider this

café as their own private club for which they paid no sub-
scription and for which they had their own system of
'black-balling' those whom they did not consider suitable
as clients, whilst the landlord was helpless before their disapproval, for they had it in their power to ruin his trade
and his reputation, even though they might, themselves,
not be profitable financially.

Sometimes elegant Arsène Houssaye, the Dandy of the
earlier period, now the editor of the important literary
periodical called *L'Artiste*, would even be seen threading
his way through the room dim with smoke, and spreading
alarm as he passed, for he usually came to discover why his
contributors, few of whom could ever finish an article on
time, had not delivered their copy, and expecting, if possible, to extract it on the spot.[3]

Although Murger was the most famous of the writers
whom Baudelaire met at this time, the most influential was
unquestionably Champfleury, whose real name was Jules
Fleury-Husson. He was only loosely connected with the
Bohemians and was not at all typical of them, for he had
the knack of success. He was one of them because, in that
life, he could most easily find the realistic material which
he needed for his novels, and he exploited it for gain. If
he is mentioned at all today in a history of French literature it is because he marks a stage in the development of
the realist novel from Balzac to Flaubert. He is generally
considered as the chief exponent of realism. There is, however, a great difference between what has been called his
'réalisme étriqué' and the imaginative realism of Flaubert
or Baudelaire. Champfleury's doctrine – if indeed it can
be honoured by that title – forced him to describe only
what he had seen with his own eyes, but unfortunately the
kind of life he led condemned him to see almost nothing.
He held the doubtful theory that realism meant pedestrian
triviality, and that is why his novels are today unread. A
journalist once said of him that he imitated Balzac just
as a valet might imitate a master in whose services he had

been for many years.[4] He imagined that Balzac's chief merit lay in the external description of the vulgar details of everyday life. Perhaps the most witty, yet perspicacious, thing ever said of him was by Véron in the *Panthéon de Poche*: 'When I was a little boy,' wrote Véron, 'I used to stand spellbound gazing in at the window of a pork-butcher's shop, where one of the assistants, who had artistic leanings, used to model every day some new artistic conception in the white lard. Champfleury's literature is precisely that: he shapes and models triviality.'[5]

Champfleury was six months younger than Baudelaire. He had been an indifferent scholar at school and, when he arrived in Paris, with no intellectual achievements behind him, he was obliged to earn his living as a messenger to a bookseller, and fetch goods from the publishing houses. He had, however, a keen and versatile mind, was interested not only in literature, but in music and painting and, by hard work, made himself a connoisseur in all three. He was ambitious and from his early youth was determined to succeed. From 1843, when he was not yet twenty-two, he was a regular contributor to *Le Corsaire-Satan* and he and Privat d'Anglemont were the only contributors who had the privilege of receiving the paper without charge – Baudelaire was never to achieve such eminence. It was in 1844 that Champfleury met Murger and became a member of the club at the Hôtel Merciol, and, shortly afterwards, in an attempt at artistic communism, set up house with him. This did not prove successful as Champfleury, a hard-working and ambitious man, with solid bourgeois traditions in his blood, was well aware of the differences between 'mine and thine', and although he lived amongst the Bohemians, never really became one of them. He soon began to realize that Murger was getting the best of the bargain without contributing anything, except his pleasant personality, to the communal venture, and he parted company with him after a few months.

Champfleury became famous overnight when he published, in 1847, his *Chien Caillou* which Victor Hugo hailed, in exaggerated terms, as a masterpiece. He had the gift, completely wanting in Baudelaire, of finding patrons prepared to risk large sums to provide him with the means of publishing his works.

It is not known precisely at what moment Baudelaire became associated with La Bohème but it must have been, at latest, in the early months of 1845 since in May that year he asked Champfleury to review his *Salon* in *Le Corsaire-Satan*.[6] He may have met him – and also the others – at the offices of the paper which prided itself on employing young, and hitherto unknown, talent. There were, however, many opportunities otherwise for them to have met; for Baudelaire, after the appointment of his *conseil judiciaire*, when he could no longer shine amongst the *jeunesse dorée*, nor dazzle by the luxury of his entertainment, began to consort with men as poor as himself, while still keeping something of his former dandyism. Toubin, a medical student who knew him at this time, says that, contrary to the custom of the usual Bohemian, he used to wash, and wear clean linen, though his clothes were of a cut some years behind the prevailing fashion.[7] He claims that it was he who brought him to the Café de la Rotonde, where the revolutionaries used to meet in order to hear Courbet discourse, as he sat there every evening, smoking his long pipe and expressing violently socialistic sentiments. It was there, adds Toubin, that Baudelaire met Murger, Champfleury and the working-man poet, Dupont.

Baudelaire has been frequently, but incorrectly, identified with La Bohème, when it was only that he consorted with them because his means no longer permitted him to live in the society for which he felt that his talents and personality suited him. It appears, from all accounts, that the Bohemians themselves considered him somewhat affected and precious, and that they despised him a little.

The leader amongst these revolutionary Bohemians, who were in fact the nucleus of the realist school in literature, was not a writer but a painter, Courbet. Before the revolution of 1848 he was unknown to the general public, and he was only to begin to show his true talent as a painter in his *Après-Midi d'Ornans* of 1848 and his *L'Homme à la Ceinture de Cuir* of 1849. His most characteristic and famous pictures were painted between 1850 and 1855. Amongst these are *L'Enterrement à Ornans*, *Le Casseur de Pierres* and *L'Atelier* which was refused at the *Salon* of 1855. This last picture, painted in 1848 or 1849, represented the artist himself, seated in his studio and painting one of his opulent landscapes, whilst, at his back, stands the model, a naked woman, very different from the sexless classical nudes of the period – those of Ingres for instance. In the left of the picture can be seen the romantic bric-à-brac of academic art, and, in the right, are the painter's personal friends, Proudhon and Baudelaire, the latter characteristically sitting apart from the others and absorbed in his own pursuits, deep in the study of some manuscript. Courbet, according to Champfleury, once said of him: [8] 'I don't know how to finish this portrait of Baudelaire, as his face changes from day to day!' The portrait of the poet in *L'Atelier* is interesting as one of the few records of his appearance at this time, and it was said to be a very good likeness.

Courbet opens the third period of French painting in the nineteenth century, and he seemed to have arisen in answer to Baudelaire's prayer at the end of his *Salon* of 1845 that an artist would come forward to give lasting expression to modern man, dressed in his dark contemporary clothes, in his middle-class setting, and thus give poetry to modern realism and truth.

Critics have claimed that Courbet, like Rubens, possessed the natural gifts of a painter, and that few artists have been able to render as perfectly as he, the feeling of solid substances such as rock and wood, the texture of rich materials and flesh. At a moment when the general public was weary of Romanticism and the imitations of classicism, he taught a new lesson of truth and realism, not the commonplace

realism of a Champfleury, but broad human realism based
on the intuitive conviction of the greatness and beauty of
life itself. He possessed great energy and vitality, and was
more proud of his physical prowess than of his painting.
He was handsome in a primitive way, though some thought
him coarse and unrefined, for he was a simple peasant from
Franche Comté who enjoyed his food and drink. He had
a hearty contempt for the bourgeoisie, especially the money-
grubbing bourgeois which the reign of Louis-Philippe had
exalted, and he also despised honours, decorations and every
kind of sinecure. He was later to suffer poverty and imprisonment on account of his principles, and was destined
to die in great poverty, in exile, with all his goods confiscated.

In the years leading up to the revolution of 1848 Courbet
had, however, not yet become an important figure, and this
was to happen only after his one-man show in 1855, which
was held in protest against the exclusion of his pictures
from the *Salon* of that year. Although two of his pictures
– *Le Hamac* and *L'Homme à la Pipe* of 1847 – were considered promising, he was known chiefly as a hard-drinking
and hard-living Bohemian, the friend of advanced socialists.

Courbet is interesting for French literature because it was
with him that Baudelaire spent the turbulent years before
the revolution. It is strange therefore that he, who had
written so much about the painters of his day, should have
written no article on Courbet. According to the painter he
had planned to write one on him, and for this purpose
accompanied him back to his studio. Courbet was much
flattered and installed the poet behind a screen so that he
could work at peace while he himself slept, and prepared
for him, as aids to inspiration, liqueurs, wine and cigars. During the night the painter woke periodically and cried out
to the poet: 'Well, how is your article getting on?' and
Baudelaire always answered: 'I'm studying my documents!'
When day came Courbet arose and went to see what he
had written, but found him asleep, having finished his work

on his 'documents' – the wine, liqueurs and cigars. The article was never written. 'What matter!' Courbet used to say afterwards, whenever he told the story, 'It was my best article, the only one I can remember!'[9]

It was through Courbet that Baudelaire met Proudhon who had some influence on him, but only for a short time, through his economic theories. The poet never became intimate with him as he was disgusted by his uncivilized manner, his coarseness and lack of refinement.[10] He felt more sympathy for Pierre Dupont whom he also met at this time, the patriotic workman poet, who was to be exiled in 1851 on account of his revolutionary songs. Dupont was the son of a Lyons working man and, from his earliest childhood, had known want and had suffered bitterly in the struggle for existence. Baudelaire learned much from him about the kind of life he had hitherto not known. He admired him for the same reasons which drew him towards Courbet, because, without slavishly following the prevailing fashion of the day, he saw artistic possibilities in the only life which he had personally known, and understood how literature could draw fresh strength and inspiration from the deep stream of the working masses.

Baudelaire was deeply moved the first time that he heard the *Chant des Ouvriers*, 'that wonderful cry of melancholy and sorrow' he called it.[11] Though the poem is clumsy at times, and inexperienced in expression, it may be considered as the starting point of one vein of inspiration in Baudelaire, and it confirmed him in his belief in the possibilities of a change from Romanticism which was not the prevailing classicism of the eighteen-forties.

Baudelaire's intimacy with the Bohemians and the socialists had brought him into touch with a kind of life which he hitherto had been unaware of. Now he knew of the hardships of those who struggled to extricate themselves from the direst poverty. His new friends had all risen from the lowest classes, for Courbet was a peasant, Dupont the son of a workman in a manufacturing town, and Murger the son of a poor Paris concierge. From intimacy with them he began to conceive of another ideal than that of sensual pleasure, which was all he had considered during the days of his social glory. In the last years he had seen around him so many failures, and he understood how small a thing it is that makes for success or failure. In his youth he had been proud and arrogant, but now he had grown gentle, with a deeper understanding, since he had known want himself, and he understood what these things meant, and the deep depression and feeling of humiliation that comes from need. We find in his poetry a new vein, one which he is going to exploit with so much success, a note dimly sounded in the *Crépuscule du Matin* a few years before. One of the most characteristic poems in this period is the sister poem, *Crépuscule du Soir*, which ends:

> *Recueille-toi, mon âme, en ce grave moment,*
> *Et ferme ton oreille à ce rugissement.*
> *C'est l'heure où les douleurs des malades s'aigrissent!*
> *La sombre Nuit les prend à la gorge; ils finissent*
> *Leur destinée et vont vers le gouffre commun;*
> *L'hôpital se remplit de leurs soupirs. – Plus d'un*
> *Ne viendra plus chercher la soupe parfumée,*
> *Au coin du feu, le soir, auprès d'une âme aimée.*
> *Encore la plupart n'ont-ils jamais connu*
> *La douceur du foyer et n'ont jamais vécu.*[12]

Baudelaire, more than any other French poet, understood and appreciated sympathetically the poorer masses of the city, and he expressed their sufferings without any doctrinaire aim, without any desire to teach a lesson in social administration. He possessed the qualities to make such a poet, not only as a result of the life he was now leading, but also by reason of his insatiable curiosity into the manner of life of other men, into their various ways of making bearable 'the painful operation of living'. He used to wander at night through the streets of Paris, when the queer little people, who fear the glaring light of day, come creeping out of their burrows to go about their self-imposed tasks. He had often talked with them, and followed them to try to penetrate their secret. His own life seemed to him at times hard to bear, and their lives were not seemingly more endurable. What was it then that made them wish to continue to exist? What was the secret of the pleasure they took in life? At evening, when night was beginning to fall, when the dark curtains of the skies were drawn, shutting out the night, he used to wander through the streets taking what he called his 'bain de multitude', letting the atmosphere seep into him through every pore. He expressed in his poems all the life of a modern city, the vice, the misery, the barren dreams and the despair, for with him sin and excess are never without their inevitable companions, self-disgust and remorse. He would have liked to have given them something better than death to long for, which he describes in *La Mort des Pauvres*.[13]

> C'est la Mort qui console, hélas! et qui fait vivre;
> C'est le but de la vie, et c'est le seul espoir
> Qui, comme un elixir, nous monte et nous enivre,
> Et nous donne le cœur de marcher jusqu'au soir;
>
> À travers la tempête, et la neige, et le givre,
> C'est la clarté vibrante à notre horizon noir;
> C'est l'auberge fameuse inscrite sur le livre,
> Où l'on pourra manger, et dormir, et s'asseoir;
>
> C'est un Ange qui tient dans ses doigts magnétiques
> Le sommeil et le don des rêves extatiques,
> Et qui refait le lit des gens pauvres et nus;
>
> C'est la gloire des Dieux, c'est le grenier mystique,
> C'est la bourse du pauvre et sa patrie antique,
> C'est le portique ouvert sur les Cieux inconnus!

The best examples in this vein were to be written ten years later when Baudelaire felt himself to be a member of the band of 'déshérités', the brotherhood of failures, when he had almost abandoned hope of personal success,

of being one of those who rode the waves to the shore, and
were not merely flotsam and jetsam thrown up on a bank,
when he looked back into the pit of the misspent years,
and saw so few ahead.

In these years leading up to the revolution of 1848
Baudelaire also formed the two closest friendships of his
life – his relationship with Courbet, Champfleury, and Dupont, was artistic and literary rather than intimate – and
these were with Asselineau, faithful and kind Asselineau,
the staunchest of all his friends, and Poulet Malassis, his
future publisher.

Asselineau tells us that he met Baudelaire for the first
time at the *Salon* of 1845 with the young painter Deroy.[14]
He was the gentlest of men, with none of the ruthless egoism
necessary for success. He had large brown eyes, gentle like
those of a heifer; thick fair hair and, later, a shaggy beard
which gave him the appearance of a Russian *moujik*. His
hair and beard were to turn white while he was still young,
and this was to give him a patriarchal air. It used to be suggested that his surname derived from the Latin *aselinus*,
which meant 'a little ass'. He might indeed have been the
little brother ass of Saint Francis. He was also not without
the foolishness ascribed to the donkey, and Baudelaire used
occasionally to make fun of him, as in a letter to Poulet
Malassis.[15] 'You'll laugh, but please keep it a secret, but our
good Asselineau said to me, when I reproached him, with
his love of music, for not going to the Wagner concerts,
that firstly it was too far from where he lived and secondly
that he'd heard that Wagner was a republican!'

Kindness, rather than foolishness, was his main characteristic, and Banville, in a poem, describes him as he sits beside Baudelaire in a café:[16]

> *On voit le doux Asselineau*
> *Près du farouche Baudelaire.*

Asselineau's great passion in life was poetry. Banville used
to say that few men have understood the art as well as he,

nor known as thoroughly all the intricate and complicated
rules of prosody. Yet he published no original works himself, since, in his modesty, he did not consider that he had
been gifted with the flame of creative genius.[17] Such humility was rare in the society in which he moved. He once
composed a *pantoum*, probably the first in the French
language, then, instead of showing it to his friends, he hid
it away in an obscure Belgian periodical where Banville
came across it by chance, and let it serve as a model for his
own poetry. Asselineau loved poetry with the intensity of
a devouring passion, and he considered that God had created
no higher being than the poet. It was therefore his pride
that he had lived in the intimacy of the greatest poets of his
time, and especially with Baudelaire. He was undoubtedly
his most devoted friend, because, unlike his other friends, he
never felt jealousy or envy. Du Camp, Champfleury, and
even Gautier, were somewhat afraid of the eminence which
Baudelaire might attain. Asselineau offered him the gift
of deep sympathy, and also intelligent criticism, asking
nothing in return for himself, but considered it his privilege to be allowed to admire in his own way, and to work
quietly in obscurity himself, with no desire for personal
glory. The love which he accorded to the poets themselves,
he gave also to their printed works, and he had one of the
finest collections of books of the nineteenth century, for he
bought first and rare editions, whatever their price, editions
of fine paper, with rich bindings, editions with illustrations.
He spent a fortune on books and soon possessed every first
edition, every limited edition, of all the great writers of his
day. As a young man he had lived in a rich apartment,
artistically furnished, where he used to entertain his friends
for he had, as well as what he earned, a private income. As
his passion for books increased, he sought ways and means
to obtain more money to indulge his craving. He then gave
up his private home and went as a paying guest to his sister
spending what he saved thereby on further books. At one
point in his life, another love came to distract his mind from

his main passion, for he fell disastrously in love, and sold
his books – it was as if he were tearing out his vitals – and
followed the woman to Italy. She proved heartless and disappointing, and he returned broken-hearted to Paris, less
at the thought of the loss of love than at the vain sacrifice
of his beloved books. He started once more to build up his
library, and soon possessed as fine a collection as the
first.

Towards the end of his life Asselineau reached his heaven
on earth, when he was appointed librarian at the *Bibliothèque Mazarine*, where the duties were slight, and where
his books were housed in dignity and comfort. According to
Banville, the Mazarine library is the fairyland of libraries,
where the librarian is king. He is housed in a spacious apartment looking over the Tuileries Gardens and the banks of
the Seine, and he may wander at will, at any hour of the day
or night, through the library in the palace, with its rich
carved panelling, and tables and chairs with their finely
moulded bronze feet. There Asselineau dreamed away his
days until the Franco-Prussian War broke out, followed by
the Commune. When everyone left Paris for Bordeaux he
remained behind to look after the library entrusted to his
care, packing the rare editions in cases, and hiding them
away in the cellars, so that no harm should come their way.
At great personal risk he prevented the Communards from
using priceless folios to build up their barricades in the
streets.[18] His conduct was, however, misinterpreted later, and
it was alleged that he was a Communard because he had
not fled from Paris like his chiefs. This, says Banville, broke
his heart, and he died soon afterwards.

After 1845 he was Baudelaire's closest and dearest friend
who shared his passion for work well done.

Poulet Malassis was, temperamentally, very different from
Baudelaire, and it was their intellectual interests and their
shared hatred for convention, which drew them together.
He would not have understood, nor appreciated, the deeper
aspect of his friend's nature, his deep-rooted piety, and his

need for spiritual values. What Baudelaire liked in him was his independent spirit, his loyalty to his friends, and his rare generosity. Poulet Malassis, like Baudelaire, was a brilliant conversationalist, and he attracted many friends through his wit and humour, which had something of the biting irony of a Voltaire. Yet, beneath the sarcastic mask, he hid warm and loyal affection for his friends. His good humour never failed him, even after illness, bankruptcy and exile, for he kept, right to the end, his faculty for seeing the amusing side of everything – even of his own failure. It is true that he sometimes hurt his more sensitive friends, like Baudelaire, by his inability to appreciate their visions, for he had little use himself for the life of the spirit, and nothing was sacred for him, since he took nothing seriously – not even his own business.

Poulet Malassis, who was four years younger than Baudelaire, was the last descendant of a firm of printers, and his father owned one of the oldest presses in the country, which dated back to the sixteenth century. At school he had been a brilliant pupil and, at the early age of sixteen, he had begun publishing little historical articles in the local periodical, articles which showed a considerable talent for research. When he was seventeen he published, from his father's press, a remarkable production for a youth, a reprint of the first edition of a book which he discovered in the library at Alençon, a work by Guillaume de Rouillé entitled *Épistre des Rossignols du Parc d'Alençon* (*À la très illustre Royne de Navarre, Duchesse d'Alençon et de Berry*). The book was produced in an edition limited to thirty copies printed on fine paper. Even an experienced publisher could have been proud of such an achievement.

His interest in printing, however, distracted Poulet Malassis from his studies and he passed his *baccalauréat* only at the age of twenty-one. Then, in order to make use of his talent for research, he entered the École des Chartes in Paris in 1847. Perhaps it was then that he met Baudelaire who was a student there at all events in 1846. But he could also have met him at one of the cafés where the revolutionaries used to meet.

We do not know what part Poulet Malassis played in the February revolution of 1848, but, during the June incidents, he published a subversive paper entitled *L'Aimable Faubourien, Journal de Canaille*.[19] It had five issues between the fifth and eighteenth of June. He was arrested with a gun in his hands, and would have been executed if it had not been for the intervention of an influential friend of his father, Oudinot de la Favrerie. He was first imprisoned in the fort of Ivry and then sent to Brest, but he was soon released through the help of the Deputy from his home town, Drouet de Vaux, and permitted to return to his studies in 1849. He was obliged to start again from the very beginning, as he had lost a year through his revolutionary activities.[20] He, who had left the provinces as a hard-working young man, determined to finish his studies in the shortest possible time, became demoralized through friendship with Baudelaire, Toubin, Nadar and Murger – Bohemians who worked only when dire necessity drove them to this unpleasant way of passing the time. When he entered the École des Chartres he was placed fourth of his year, but, at the examinations in 1850, he was only tenth out of thirteen students, while, in the following year, he had sunk to twelfth place. After that he was heard of no more in the records of the school – it is true that his father died in 1852 and he was then obliged to return to Alençon to take over the family business. He played an important part in Baudelaire's life.

The revolution of 1848 seized on the imagination of intellectual and artistic youth in France, and most of the young writers – Leconte de Lisle, Baudelaire, Ménard, Dupont, Murger, Champfleury and many others – were implicated in it in some manner. It was partly that it was in some measure a revolt against romanticism and false values, a form of belief in the future, an expression of the new realistic doctrine in the practical sphere. Later, when pre-

paring notes for an autobiography, and analysing his state
of mind in 1848, Baudelaire wrote: 'Mon ivresse de '48, de
quelle nature était cette ivresse? Goût de la vengeance;
plaisir naturel de la démolition. Ivresse littéraire, souvenirs
de lectures.' [21] But, at the time, his reforming zeal, though
short-lived, was more sincere than he would later admit.
Nevertheless he certainly had a desire for vengeance against
the society which was treating him harshly, a fierce longing to destroy that society, and he was also influenced by
the hot-headed speeches of those who were now his daily
companions – Proudhon, Courbet, Dupont and Toubin. He
personally had little to lose by change, and it might bring
some improvement in his financial state – it certainly could
not make it worse. He may also have been moved by a
malicious desire to make his stepfather's bourgeois friends
lose their smug security, and tremble for their future. His
views had been changing during the previous year, since
he had known men at the bottom of the social scale who
had never, at any moment, known comfort, and, in some
cases, even absence of want. Bourgeois ideals and traditions
were becoming abhorrent to him. Yet, as late as 1846, he
had opened his *Salon* of that year with a call to arms to
the bourgeoisie, asking them to come forward to help in
the cause of civilization and culture, telling them that they
had in their hands justice and power, that they were the
most important section of the community, in numbers and
intelligence, and he ended by dedicating his work to them.
Since that day, however, he had suffered a revulsion of
feeling, and had come to dislike the qualities which were
exemplified by his parents, and especially their attitude
towards his mistress, Jeanne Duval, which he found more
despicable than their early disapproval. They had always
professed to be people of scrupulous honesty and honour,
believing themselves sincere in this, and now they were
preaching the necessity of making a final break with a
woman who had become a hindrance and an encumbrance,
since he no longer loved her. He, for his part, was pro-

foundly shocked at such an attitude, and did not consider that there should be two standards of conduct, one towards a girl of his own class, had he married one, and one towards the woman with whom he shared his life, even if he had not given her his name. He did not consider that her treatment of him lessened his obligations towards her. He tried, in a letter to his mother, to put his point of view. No parent, however, would have been capable of appreciating such an attitude.[22]

'With that irritable obstinacy,' he wrote, 'and that vehemence which are characteristic of you, you've browbeaten me solely on the score of a woman whom, for a long time now, I've cared for only out of a sense of duty and obligation. That's all! It's indeed strange that you, who so often, and at such length, have argued with me about spiritual matters and a sense of duty, shouldn't have understood this relationship, in which I've nothing to gain, and in which a desire for atonement and a wish to reward devotion are the only deciding factors. However frequently a woman may have been unfaithful, however cruel she may be, if she has shown some particle of devotion and good will, that is sufficient to make an honourable man – a poet especially – feel obliged to reward her. I ask your pardon for dwelling on this, but it has always been a sore point with me that you didn't seem to understand, from the first, the simple meaning of my request.... However, to return to the point. I feel I must give you these explanations. Whom does it harm, now that I'm twenty-eight, all but four months, and cut off by my tastes and principles from respectable society, yet cherishing unbounded poetic ambitions, whom does it harm, I ask you, if, while I dream my literary dreams, I fulfil, at the same time, an obligation – or what I consider such – detrimental to the ordinary accepted ideas of honour, wealth and position? Please note that it isn't your consent that I'm seeking, but only the admission that I may perhaps be right!'

As 1848 opened Guizot was still Prime Minister, after

many years of office, but he was meeting with increasing opposition, as most of the evils of the régime were attributed to him. Opposition came from several quarters. There were firstly the socialists, as was natural; secondly the young men from the universities and professional schools; thirdly the bulk of the working class whose situation had been worsened by two very severe winters; and finally certain journalists, amongst them Armand Marrast, editor of *Le National*, and Louis Blanc of *La Réforme*. The situation was rendered more complicated by the attitude of the National Guard. This was a body of men which had been founded especially to establish the régime of Louis-Philippe, after the revolution of 1830, and they had been, at first, a very privileged section of the community. This had changed in the course of the reign of Louis-Philippe, who no longer thought it necessary to flatter them, and they had the additional grievance of being without votes for they did not fulfil the income qualification for franchise. They were very antagonistic to Guizot who had answered, when the electorate clamoured for wider representation: 'The remedy is in your own hands! Get rich! Enrichissez-vous!'

Most of the famous writers of the day, such as Lamartine, Vigny and Hugo, were in favour of reform. A banquet was therefore planned to take place on 22 February in order to protest against the policy of Louis-Philippe. Guizot, at the last moment, banned it and this led to minor disturbances in Paris. The signal for these was given by an article from the pen of Armand Marrast in *Le National*, on 20 February, in which he published the programme of the prohibited banquet. He demanded that the populace of Paris should stage a demonstration in protest against the action of the government. This they did in an orderly manner and, at this stage, all that was demanded was a moderate measure of reform.

Matters, however, became more serious when on 22 February a body of students marched in demonstration

from the Latin Quarter to the Chambre des Députés to
lay their petition before the Assemblée. On the same day
a large number of workers, who had stayed away from
work, poured down from their quarters, on the heights
round the city, and mingled with the bourgeoisie in the
Champs Elysées and the Place de la Concorde, when they
crossed the bridge with the object of blockading the
Chambre des Députés, shouting, 'Down with Guizot!
Death to Guizot!'

It is then that we hear of Baudelaire. On the afternoon
of 22 February, in company with Courbet and Toubin, he
followed the crowd surging into the Place de la Concorde,
only meaning to be onlookers, not thinking of participa-
tion. Suddenly a detachment of troops came on foot, from
the Champs Elysées, with fixed bayonets, to prevent the
crowd from gathering. Baudelaire and his friends were
forced back against the Tuileries Gardens, where they took
refuge on the parapet separating them from the Place.
The mob began to throw stones at the troops, who moved
forward in serried ranks, threatening with their fixed
bayonets. One of the crowd, pursued by a couple of soldiers,
tried to hide behind a tree, but he slipped and fell, and a
soldier ran him through the body with his bayonet, as he
lay on the ground. This was just beside where Baudelaire
and his companions were standing. They were horrified at
this act of barbarity and, as soon as they could escape from
the crowd, they went to the offices of *La Presse* to denounce
the crime to the editor.[23]

The King still hoped that the rising might be put down
without serious bloodshed. But the following day, 23 February, the National Guard refused, when ordered, to defend
the government. They gathered in the Champs Elysées
and cried 'Down with the ministers!' The same day there
was fighting round the Palais Royal and even the troops
now were beginning to express sympathy for the rioters,
and antipathy for the government. The mob of Paris was
beginning to feel its strength. The King was afraid to call

out the army against the National Guard for fear that they should join forces, and that afternoon he forced Guizot to resign in the hope of appeasing the masses. The middle class now thought that the revolution was over, and put away their arms.

That night, towards ten o'clock, the army began to fraternize with the crowds in the streets, but the officers tried to prevent this. A musket accidentally went off, which led to general firing, as a result of which almost a hundred people were killed. This was a match to the powder magazine, for the crowd thought that it had been intentional. By midnight the barricades were raised in the streets, with cries of 'Down with the King! Long live the Republic!' The bodies of the dead were carried in procession by the crowd asking for vengeance. The National Guard joined the rebels and handed over their barracks to them.

Early the next morning, 24 February, the King appointed Bugeaud, the victor of Algeria, to restore order by the most energetic measures. If these had been carried out there would have been great bloodshed for the populace were prepared for action, having the arms which they had looted from shops or armouries or had obtained from the National Guard. Proclamations were drawn up and Proudhon told the workers to resist, assuring them that they were the masters. The Tuileries Palace was attacked by a hundred thousand insurgents, helped by the National Guard, and pillaged.

Then Louis-Philippe, who had retired to his palace at Saint-Cloud, decided to dismiss Bugeaud, and offered to appoint Ledru-Rollin as Prime Minister; but the temper of the mob had by now grown violent, and the King then abdicated in favour of his grandson, the infant orphan of the dead Duke of Orleans. But this did not placate the extremists. The socialists were the most powerful party and they swept away the Regent and the boy King, demanding a Republic. There was not a representative of law and order left in Paris, not an armed soldier. Only the mob had arms, and the National Guard had gone over completely to their side.

It is on the afternoon of that day, 24 February, that we hear of Baudelaire again. An eye-witness caught sight of him, and was struck by his hysterical air, and his appearance of playing a part in a melodrama, or a vaudeville. He suddenly saw him at the corner of the Rue de Buci, in the middle of a crowd of vociferating and gesticulating students. Buisson, the eye-witness, called to him, since he was the only person in the crowd whom he knew by sight, and Baudelaire came running to him, brandishing a bright new rifle and cartridge case, and shouting with excitement, 'I've just fired my first shot!' Buisson could not restrain a smile as he beheld the rifle which was obviously new and had been looted from a store. Baudelaire, however, was far too excited to notice his incredulity, and he kept on shouting almost hysterically: 'We must go and shoot General Aupick! Down with General Aupick!'[24] His stepfather was, at this time, head of the École Polytechnique.

There was now no King and no government, only the Assemblée Nationale, a legally elected body of representatives of the people, whose functions were, for the time being, in suspense, and who were more anxious for order than for any wild measures of reform, for peace rather than for any great social change. With them Lamartine proclaimed a Provisional Government, a moderate republican government. But the same day, in the offices of *La Réforme*, Louis Blanc and a workman called Albert formed a socialist government, and the question then arose which of the two governments was going to take charge of the affairs of the country. The Hôtel de Ville was still held by the mob, but Lamartine and his colleagues had the courage to go to demand the confirmation of their office by the sovereign right of the people, and Lamartine went, in person, to the Hôtel de Ville to induce the rioters to ratify the newly proclaimed government. The members of the government were received with acclamation by some, and by others with hostility. It was touch-and-go, but Lamartine won by courage and personality. The mob had the power but they had no programme and no policy, and they did not know how to proceed. Proudhon was to declare the following day: 'On 24 February, there were neither purpose nor ideas!' The insurgents did not possess the disciplined authority necessary to take the place of power which they had destroyed. There was anarchy under the name of Republic.

The government party of Lamartine grew in strength when the men from *Le National*, under Armand Marrast, joined them – they too now wanted law and order quite as much as reform. Lamartine's party was supported by the Assemblée and the authority of France, and Louis Blanc by the Paris mob.

Here again we encounter Baudelaire. Blanqui, who had returned that day from long political exile, tried to create the *Société Républicaine Centrale* and it came into being on 26 February. It had three hundred and twenty-five members amongst whom Éliphas Lévi, Toussenel and Baudelaire figure. Baudelaire attended the first two meetings, and then he seems to have lost interest, or to have grown disgusted, for he was not present at the third meeting, and never became a regular member.

His lack of interest may have been because, with Champfleury and Toubin, he had founded a revolutionary paper called *Le Salut Public*, the first number of which appeared on 27 February. The trio started with a working capital of eighty francs, belonging to Toubin – little more than three pounds – and no further money was forthcoming, even though every number of the first issue was sold out, as the newsvendors had absconded with the proceeds.[25] There was a second number which, according to Crépet,[26] appeared on first or second March, though it was generally thought to have been published on 28 February. This second number had a vignette by Courbet. This time it was

not entrusted to newsvendors, and Baudelaire, clad in a
white smock, sold it himself in the streets.

The three editors were each responsible for a third of
the paper, and the articles were all written at the Café
de la Rotonde, in the Rue de l'École de Médecine, but each
issue was hurriedly put together in an hour. Since the contributions are unsigned, and are not distinguished or distinct in character, it is difficult to be certain which pen
was responsible for each.[27] There was not sufficient money
left for a third number, and that was the end of *Le Salut
Public*.

The revolution was now over, and it was time to set the
country in order once more. Lamartine agreed on a compromise with the advanced socialists, and accepted two of
them, Louis Blanc and Albert, as members of the Provisional Government.

Louis Blanc accepted office because he thought that he
might, by the force of his personality, be able to dominate
the ministry, and introduce immediately advanced socialist
measures. In order to pacify him, his colleagues, at first,
accepted his dictation, but, by the beginning of April, signs
of deep dissatisfaction began to appear. The new government had accepted the principle of the right of everybody
to work, and the Ateliers Nationaux were opened to provide work where none existed. However, when taxes were
raised by forty-five per cent in order to pay for the new
measures, and when the socialists were suggesting seizing
and nationalizing the factories and the land, the peasants
and the bourgeoisie united to oppose the too progressive
government. After two months of a more or less socialist
régime the country, as a whole, had enough of it.

When the elections were to be held in April we hear of
Baudelaire again. He and Toubin followed them with great
interest, but his politics had greatly changed since February, and he seemed no longer to believe in socialism, but
to think that his friend had gone too far. He thought this
especially of Esquiros, who was a candidate in his ward

and who, in his election speech, talked of 'l'infâme Guizot'
and 'l'infâme Louis-Philippe!' He painted a sombre picture
of the state of the working class during his reign, and
reduced some of his audience to tears. Baudelaire, who
hated the public show of emotion, began to heckle him,
and, rising to his feet, asked him with icy courtesy, whether
the interests of the lower middle class were not as sacred
as those of the workers.[28] Esquiros answered that he had
not forgotten that section of the public so worthy of sympathy and interest, but then returned immediately to his
favourite topic, the condition of the working classes under
the July Monarchy. Baudelaire did not leave him in peace
but interrupted him, saying, 'Since we are talking about
commerce, what is your opinion of free trade, which is,
you'll agree, the coping-stone of the socialist edifice?'
Esquiros was forced to admit that he had not yet investigated this important topic, but assured his heckler that he
would, in the event of his being elected as a member of the
Assemblée, give it his full attention. He was, however, by
now unnerved by these interruptions, and retired from the
platform to sit beside his wife.

He was followed by Arsène Houssaye, whom Baudelaire
did not really like, and he began, as Esquiros had done, to
attack the policy of Louis-Philippe, especially his weakness
towards England. When he paused in his speech, Baudelaire arose again and asked him for his opinion on the
treaties of 1815. In confused stammering and stuttering,
Houssaye was forced to admit that he had not yet had the
time to master that subject, but he promised the electorate
that he would do so at the earliest opportunity.

In the meantime Baudelaire had not lost interest in
political journalism and, in April 1848, he obtained work
on another paper, *La Tribune Nationale*.[29]

La Tribune Nationale had been founded in February
1848 and, before April, had published only two numbers,
on 26 February and on 12 March. The paper was founded
by Jules Scmeltz and the chief contributors were Lamen-

nais and Esquiros. It was then of socialist inspiration. It does not seem to have been successful, and later it changed hands, being bought by Combarel de Leyval, who financed it and made its policy conservative. He appointed Baudelaire as *Secrétaire de la Rédaction*. The first number of the new series appeared on 10 April, the next on 26 May, and thereafter it became a daily paper until 6 June, when it disappeared as Combarel seems, by then, to have given up financing it.

There were twelve numbers of *La Tribune Nationale* with which Baudelaire was concerned. The part he played in the paper was not a very important one, for he was only the *Secrétaire de Rédaction*, that is to say that he was responsible for arranging the material for publication, but not necessarily for composing it, and there is no proof that he wrote any contributions published in the paper. Bandy and Mouquet, however, believe that they see his hand in some of the articles.[30] They have not sufficient evidence to be convincing in their arguments, which are largely based on verbal similarities between the articles and the poet's own style.

The evolution of Baudelaire's political opinions was very marked between February and June 1848. The *Salut Public*, with which he was connected in February, had been republican and socialist. The first two issues of *La Tribune Nationale*, with which he was not concerned, had been democratic and socialist, but the final issues, in which he had responsibility, had become conservative.

In the elections of April 1848 the socialists were badly defeated and only obtained a quarter of the votes. The popular agitators, afraid of being completely extinguished, made the new government's policy towards Poland the excuse for an attempt at rising to take command of the situation in May, on the pretext of forcing France into war with Russia on behalf of Poland. The bourgeoisie did not want war, but they wanted still less the continuance of the socialist régime, and they came to the rescue of the government. The attempted rising was quickly subdued, and Barbès and Louis Blanc were deported. It was then thought that the Ateliers Nationaux were a hot-bed of socialism, and it was decided, in June, to close them. The younger men without work were to be compelled to enlist in the army, and the older men were to be drafted to the provinces where they were needed to build railway embankments.

As a result of the closing of the Ateliers one of the most bloody revolts Paris had ever known broke out on 23 June. Fifty thousand workmen came into conflict with the combined forces of the army and the bourgeoisie. The following day the government created a military dictatorship under General Cavaignac. During the fighting on the three subsequent days it is said that the workmen lost ten thousand dead and wounded, and that the number of officers killed exceeded the number lost during the Napoleonic wars. Two generals lost their lives, as well as the Archbishop of Paris. It took three whole days to subdue the slum quarters of the Faubourg Saint-Antoine. Those who were taken prisoner with arms in their hands were shot at sight, and eleven thousand were deported to Algeria.

We hear from Levavasseur that Baudelaire was implicated in the fighting in June. His friends Poulet Malassis and Louis Ménard were certainly concerned in it, and it is possible that they dragged him in as well. Levavasseur was walking in the gardens of the Palais Royal when he suddenly caught sight of Baudelaire and Dupont. The latter was calm and dignified, but his companion was in a state of extreme excitement. Levavasseur was afraid that, by his recklessness, he might get himself arrested, and perhaps even executed, for they were shooting people at the slightest provocation, and he was shouting revolutionary slogans, expressing a desire to see the end of the social order, and saying that he wished to be the first martyr. This certainly does not tally with the cautious sentiments expressed by *La Tribune Nationale*, which had been in opposition to socialism. Levavasseur and Dupont managed to drag Baudelaire into a neighbouring café where they were known, and the proprietor friendly. After they had succeeded in calming him, they took him home out of harm's way. This is all that is known of the part he played in the June revolution in 1848. It is possible that Levavasseur, who was no longer seeing Baudelaire frequently, imagined that he was still a socialist, and it is not clear, from his account, what his friend was opposing.[31] There was now no question of doing violence to his stepfather for he and his wife had left France in May for Turkey, where the General had been appointed ambassador in Constantinople.[32]

After three days of bitter fighting the revolution was over and the principal leaders were either in prison or in exile. Poulet Malassis was incarcerated in Brest uncertain of his fate; while Ménard, the author of *L'Ode aux Fusillés de Juin* and of revolutionary articles under the title *Prologue d'une Révolution*, being doubtful of what the government's attitude might be towards him, had fled to Belgium.

The Assemblée then set to work to restore order and to form a strong government, and, in October, the new constitution was passed. Although, theoretically at all events, the people were granted full powers, all the executive power was to be in the hands of a president elected for a term of four years, whose powers were immense for he had the right of choosing his own ministers, officers and officials. Since it was too soon to attempt to bring back a Bourbon or an Orleanist, the majority of moderate men decided to support Louis Napoleon, the nephew of the late Emperor, for the presidency. It was said that many illiterate peasants voted for him thinking that Napoleon the Great had returned.

With the advent of the new republican constitution of October 1848, the artists and men of letters ceased to take an interest in politics, and to have any desire to share in the government of the country. In spite of all the blood-shed and suffering of the past nine months, the same selfish interests and intrigues had formed once more, and there was no change in the condition of the masses – only added misery and poverty. Leconte de Lisle, Baudelaire and Ménard, for the rest of their lives, were to devote all their energies to a quest for beauty, instead of an endeavour to create a political and social Utopia here below. Baudelaire was later to talk of the 'effet foudroyant' which the *coup d'état* of 2 December 1851, by which Louis Napoleon made himself Emperor, had had on him;[33] he declared that he was completely purged of an interest in politics, and he wrote to Ancelle that, if he had voted for anyone, he could only have voted for himself.[34]

[3]

The Slough of Despond
1848 – 1852

WHAT became of Baudelaire between the June revolution in 1848 and December 1849 is not known as there are no letters extant to any of his friends, and none of his contemporaries mention his activities. It was a time of estrangement from his mother, when she was communicating with him solely through Ancelle, and one letter only from Baudelaire to her has come down to us, that of December 1848. His movements are next known in December 1849, when he was at Dijon on the mysterious visit recorded in his letters to Ancelle, which ended abruptly early in 1850. Some critics allege that he had gone to Châteauroux in October 1848 to edit a paper but, for reasons to be discussed later, the present author does not share this opinion.[1]

Some biographers claim that he went to Dijon only to evade his creditors in Paris, but Asselineau tells us that he went there to edit a government paper.[2] It would be characteristic of him that, since he had become conservative, he should be a supporter of the new republican government which was reactionary. In a letter to Ancelle, written from Dijon, he expressed disgust with the socialism of the rabble.[3]

'You know that Madier de Montjau is reputed to have tremendous talent – he's one of the democratic eagles! Well! I thought him pitiable! He was posing as an enthusiastic revolutionary, and then I pointed out to him the inevitable consequences – peasant socialism, fierce, stupid and bestial socialism, of torches, picks and scythes!

He took fright and that cooled his ardour a bit! He's either a fool or else merely a vulgar self-seeker!'

According to Asselineau, Baudelaire soon turned the government paper into one of opposition, but this does not seem likely in view of the above letter – Asselineau was writing very much later, when he only remembered the part that Baudelaire had played in the revolution of 1848, and, in any case, he was not seeing him at this time. Baudelaire had clearly intended a long stay at Dijon for he contemplated taking an apartment and had tried to obtain an advance from Ancelle to furnish it. Ancelle was, however, adamant in his refusal, for he had received strict injunctions from the Aupicks in Constantinople to give him no more than his bare allowance. In the absence of the parents he permitted himself as well to offer advice to Baudelaire on his behaviour to his mother. His ward, who had already been angered at the way Ancelle had received Jeanne Duval when he had sent her to obtain the necessary advance for his move to Dijon, was not prepared to accept his advice. It seems that the lawyer had hurt her pride, making her feel her dubious position, and that she had complained to her lover who had seen it as a personal affront to himself. And now, as an added insult, Ancelle was preaching to him on filial duty. His mother had left him in coolness and had not written to him since she had gone to Turkey. He was suffering from the estrangement and, like most people in a similar predicament, did not feel that the blame was entirely his, thinking that those whose hardships were behind them were being cruel and unsympathetic, and unappreciative of his difficulties. He would certainly not tolerate dictation from his mother's legal adviser, and he wrote one of the most insolent letters he ever wrote, telling him that he had only made himself a figure of fun in front of Jeanne Duval, with his pomposity which impressed no one. He advised him henceforth to talk less, to be more restrained in his manner, and to keep his advice for those whom, as mayor of Neuilly, he united in matrimony, as they would probably appreciate it more. It was the kind of letter which no young man should write to a man of Ancelle's age and position.[4]

Nothing is known of the paper on which Baudelaire was said to be working while at Dijon. An examination of the papers published locally during the Second Republic – *Le Spectateur* which was conservative, *L'Ordre* which was anti-socialist, *Le Citoyen* and its successor *Le Peuple*, which each lasted only a few weeks before being banned by the government – reveals nothing remotely like Baudelaire's in style, though this is not necessarily proof that he did not publish anything since all the ephemeral journalism of a writer does not necessarily carry his hallmark. Only one paper suggested any relevance to him, *Le Socialiste de la Côte d'Or*, which came out three times a week and which lasted from the beginning of February 1850 until the middle of August, when it was seized by the government on account of its opposition to and criticism of the President, Louis Napoleon. If Baudelaire was on its staff its advanced opinions may have been the reason for his leaving Dijon earlier than he had intended. The paper was directed by Victor Meunier whom Baudelaire had known while he was working in Paris on *La Démocratie Pacifique*. He was the husband of Isabelle Meunier, the translator of Poe whose version of some of the tales when they had appeared in 1847 in *La Démocratie Pacifique* had been his first encounter with the works of the American author. Some of her translations were also to appear in *Le Socialiste de la Côte d'Or*, reprinted from *La Démocratie Pacifique*.

Baudelaire may have gone to Dijon to discuss Poe with her, but, as he had planned a long stay, it may have been that her husband had promised him work on the paper, the first number of which appeared on 8 February 1850. It is possible that he went to Dijon at the end of 1849 to prepare for the birth of the paper five weeks later.

In that paper there appeared an article which is vastly

superior in conception and style to any others in the local press and it stands out in isolation from them. It might conceivably be by Baudelaire. It appeared on 26 July 1850, after he had certainly left Dijon, but he might have submitted it before his departure and, in any case, at that time, he was sending many articles to various papers, few of which are known to have appeared. It would naturally not be possible to prove that it was written by Baudelaire, but it came undoubtedly from the pen of someone gifted with some talent for, and experience of, writing, someone cultivated and well-read, who knew how to use his material well. It was signed 'Un Passant' and was contributed by someone newly arrived in Dijon – Baudelaire intended at first to sign his *Spleen de Paris* 'Le Promeneur Solitaire' or 'Le Rôdeur Parisien' which are somewhat similar pseudonyms. The writer has a feeling for style, and for a telling phrase as, for instance, that the municipal subsidy was 'un Gâteau de Roi pétri à l'aide des sueurs du peuple qu'on nomme l'impôt'. He uses much of Baudelaire's stock-in-trade – his demons, skeletons, graveyards and ghosts. 'Des éclats de rire diabolique', 'sombre et silencieux comme un tombeau', and so forth. Many of his ideas are those which Baudelaire held at this time – notably in his *Salon* of 1846 – concerning the importance of the proletariat and bourgeoisie in art, and the belief that hitherto they had been starved in this respect. 'Un Passant' declares that 'le prolétaire est un sol vierge sur lequel les arts doivent prendre un nouvel et prodigieux accroissement; le devoir des artistes est de marcher vaillamment à la conquête de ce nouveau monde'; and that 'le peuple se lasse de pourvoir à tout et de ne jouir de rien' and that 'chaque être dans la création porte en lui l'instinct sacré des arts. Ce qui lui manque c'est la faculté de développer cet instinct sublime toujours refoulé'. His treatment of his subject also resembles that of Baudelaire in his prose works, his manner of using the first person singular and of making a personal experience of an abstract idea. He uses also certain tricks of style

which are Baudelaire's, expressions such as 'la vile multitude', and his obsession with the gaze from the eyes of the
poor, especially of the children. He describes the children
'aux yeux émerveillés et brillants comme des escarboucles'
in the same way as Baudelaire does in *Le Gâteau*, *Le Joujou du Pauvre* and in *Les Yeux des Pauvres*. There are also
some trifling details which, by themselves, would certainly
not constitute proof of anything. The fact that Baudelaire's
mother was now in Turkey might have suggested to him
the metaphors of 'le Bosphore', 'le Grand Turc' and 'le
Sultan'; while his recent review of *Le Gâteau du Roi* by
Janin might have made him think of that simile. 'Un Passant' also makes a mistake frequently made by Baudelaire
in his correspondence: 'ayions' – though naturally this
could be made by others as well.

None of these taken separately constitutes a vestige of
proof but, taken together, and in conjunction with the fact
that this article stands out amongst the others in the Dijon
papers at this time, might permit the hypothesis with some
verisimilitude. It is not more unlike his style than that of
the articles which certain editors now attribute to Baudelaire on no sounder grounds.[5]

Baudelaire was not happy at Dijon. His financial situation was very strained since he probably found it difficult
to obtain credit in a town where he was not well known. His
mistress had to bear with patience his black moods, his
irritability and his fits of temper as well as lack of money
and amusement in a dull provincial town. She was expected
to behave like any middle-class wife, to keep house for him,
to see that meals were served when he came in at any hour
that he liked, and all on a miserable pittance.[6] He no longer
had the money to buy jewels and fine clothes for her, and
she, who in her life of idleness had formed habits of self-
indulgence, could not now obtain the means to satisfy her
extravagant tastes. Nadar says that she frequently took
lovers,[7] while Baudelaire himself told his mother that she
had often been unfaithful to him,[8] and he hints to Ancelle[9]

that boredom, coupled with lack of money, might induce her to prostitute herself for gain at Dijon.

To add to his other worries Baudelaire fell ill with a recurrence of the syphilis which he had thought permanently cured.[10] It was therefore in a mood of deep depression and disgust that he composed *Un Voyage à Cythère*, either at Dijon, or soon after his return to Paris – certainly before 1852.[11]

This is in a more profound vein than all his previous poems, and reveals a depth of suffering and experience uncommon in a man of his age. It was inspired by the memory of a passage from Gérard de Nerval's article, *Voyage à Cythère*. This appeared in *L'Artiste* in 1844, but it is clear that Baudelaire did not have it with him when he composed the poem, and that he had not known it when it had appeared. Indeed he may never have read it in the original, and may have known it only through Champfleury, who had summarized it in an article dealing with de Nerval's work, published in *Le Messager des Théâtres et des Arts* in March 1849. He had been a close friend of Champfleury since 1845 and he may well have read his article on publication – it is certain that he must have known it – and the subject was one that would strike his imagination forcibly, and with special significance, when he fell ill at Dijon. This makes it probable that the poem was not written in 1844 as has often been suggested because of the appearance of de Nerval's article in June that year.

The passage which had inspired Baudelaire was the following:

'While we were sailing along the coast, before sheltering in Port Saint Nicolo, I suddenly caught sight of a small erection dimly outlined against the clear blue sky, and, seen from the summit of its rock, it seemed to me, from a distance, to be the statue of some protecting deity. However, as we drew nearer, I saw clearly that it was a gibbet composed of three branches of which only the middle one was occupied. It was the first gibbet I had ever seen in my life. ... Thus it was that I discovered that Venus had left no trace behind her in the capital of her island.'

That is the point of departure for Baudelaire's poem. The first part is merely an amplification of de Nerval's opening, a description of the beauties of Cythera. Then comes suddenly, as a brutal antithesis, the vision of the corrupting corpse devoured by vultures. The poet has, however, given more to the theme than this conventional contrast, for he has drawn a deep lesson from it so that his poem reaches the noble heights of a symbol. No one knew better than he how passion can destroy a human being. He had deeply suffered in his relationship with women, there was little more for him to learn in this respect, and he bore, moreover, in his own flesh and blood the indelible imprints of passion, and would bear them to the grave.

> *Habitant de Cythère, enfant d'un ciel si beau,*
> *Silencieusement tu souffrais ces insultes*
> *En expiation de tes infâmes cultes*
> *Et des péchés qui t'ont interdit le tombeau.*
>
> *Ridicule pendu, tes douleurs sont les miennes!*
> *Je sentis à l'aspect de tes membres flottants,*
> *Comme un vomissement, remonter vers mes dents,*
> *Le long fleuve de fiel des douleurs anciennes;*
>
> *Devant toi, pauvre diable au souvenir si cher,*
> *J'ai senti tous les becs et toutes les mâchoires*
> *Des corbeaux lancinants et des panthères noires*
> *Qui jadis aimaient tant à triturer ma chair.*
>
> *— Le ciel était charmant, la mer était unie;*
> *Pour moi tout était noir et sanglant désormais,*
> *Hélas! et j'avais, comme en un suaire épais,*
> *Le cœur enseveli dans cette allégorie.*
>
> *Dans ton île, ô Vénus, je n'ai trouvé debout*
> *Qu'un gibet symbolique où pendait mon image . . .*
> *— Ah! Seigneur! donnez-moi la force et le courage*
> *De contempler mon cœur et mon corps sans dégoût.*[12]

Baudelaire left Dijon some time early in 1850 for he was back in Paris in May.[13] It is possible that, before returning there, he went to Châteauroux, where he was alleged to have gone that year to edit a paper founded by the father of his friend Arthur Ponroy. This is the visit about which there is so much controversy.

In 1887 Firmin Boissin, under the pseudonym of Simon Brugal, published an article in *Le Figaro* according to which he had learnt from Arthur Ponroy that Baudelaire had gone to Châteauroux in 1850 to edit a daily paper entitled *Le Journal de Châteauroux*. Ponroy had said that the paper was founded by his father, that the place of editor was vacant and that it was offered to Baudelaire.[14]

'C'était en 1850,' wrote Simon Brugal. 'Baudelaire encore ignoré comme poète, menait une vie luxueuse que lui permettait, comme jadis à Trapadoux, l'héritage paternel. Mais sa fortune fut bientôt dissipée. Dans la gêne, il cherchait de quoi gagner sa vie avec sa plume. Le père d'Arthur Ponroy, avoué dans l'Indre, venait avec ses amis de fonder à Châteauroux un journal quotidien pour défendre les principes conservateurs. La place de rédacteur en chef était à prendre; Ponroy la proposa à Baudelaire qui accepta et partit.

The writer of the article obtained his information from Arthur Ponroy. He is writing more than thirty-five years after the events concerned, and he makes some mistakes. Arthur Ponroy's father did in fact found a paper but it was not a daily paper and it was not called *Le Journal de Châteauroux*. Investigation of all the papers published in Châteauroux during the Second Republic: *Le Conciliateur de l'Indre*, which lasted from 1851 to 1852; *L'Indre* which ran only for a year, 1849; *Le Moniteur de l'Indre* in 1852; *Le Journal de l'Indre* which ran from 1848 to 1851; *Le Représentant de l'Indre*, from 1848 to 1852; *Le Républicain de l'Indre* from 1848 to 1852; and finally *Le Travailleur de l'Indre* from 1849 to 1850; proved that it was *Le Représentant de l'Indre* which was founded by the father of Arthur Ponroy in October 1848, that it came out twice a week and that

Arthur Ponroy was its 'rédacteur' from February 1850 until
October 1851. It is possible that Baudelaire went to Châteauroux, on leaving Dijon, when his friend was editing the
paper. *Le Figaro* did not say that it was his father who had
offered Baudelaire the position but he himself. It was also
alleged that Baudelaire had turned the paper into an ultra-
conservative one. The title of the paper was in fact altered
in March 1850 from *Le Représentant de l'Indre* to *Le Représentant de l'Indre, Journal des Principes d'Ordre et de Con-
servation*, and, in a signed editorial, Arthur Ponroy wrote:

'Le Socialisme, au contraire, est le premier malaise qui
monte au cœur d'une civilisation en pleine puissance d'elle
même. Le Socialisme c'est la vanité des petits par le cœur
et l'esprit, contre le travail sérieux des gens capables et
honnêtes. Le Socialisme c'est l'entrave dont on essaie
d'embarrasser leurs pieds et le brutal niveau que l'on impose
à leur tête.'

On 5 and 12 February 1850 there appeared in the paper
two articles obviously by the hand of a practised writer,
which show a gift for irony and invective not common in
provincial journalism, and which could have come from
the hand of Baudelaire. They are those in which *Le Représentant de l'Indre* attacked *Le Travailleur de l'Indre* on
the grounds of its arrogant socialism, and drew an unfavourable comparison between the bourgeois of the 'parti
de l'ordre' and the revolutionary socialist in the person of
Armand Marrast. The sentiments expressed again recall
those of Baudelaire in his *Salon* of 1846. *Le Figaro* alleged
that he had written in his first article 'Lorsque Marat, cet
homme doux, et Robespierre, cet homme propre, de-
mandaient celui-là trois cent mille têtes, et celui-ci la per-
manence de la guillotine, ils obéissaient à l'inéluctable
logique de leur système.' These words are found in no
article in *Le Représentant de l'Indre*, but in an editorial
of 5 February the name 'Marrast' occurs which has the same
sound as 'Marat'. Baudelaire was violently opposed to Armand Marrast who had risen to power as a result of the

1848 revolution. The article of 12 February expresses his well-known contempt for Proudhon.

Most biographers accept the testimony of *Le Figaro*, for Simon Brugal stated categorically that Baudelaire went to Châteauroux in 1850 – 'C'était en 1850' – and he obtained the facts from Arthur Ponroy who was concerned in the events himself, and was a friend and contemporary of Baudelaire.

René Johannot, however, because *Le Représentant de l'Indre* was founded in October 1848, claims that Baudelaire went there at that time, and that he collaborated in the first number of the paper.[15] Porché, Bandy and Mouquet accept this view, and the last two are convinced that several of the articles in that number are by him.[16] One of these, entitled *Actuellement*, has now been placed amongst his collected works in the edition published by *Le Club du Meilleur Livre* in 1955.

Johannot has one powerful argument difficult to refute, based on a sentence in a letter from Baudelaire to his mother in December 1848, in which he said: 'The day before yesterday Ancelle told me that my trip "dans l'Inde [or l'Indre] que j'ai fait il y a quelque temps" was, without my knowledge, paid for by you.'

When this letter was first published the word in question was read as 'Inde', as this was the only journey that Baudelaire was known to have made. Johannot suggests that it should be interpreted as 'Indre', and that it refers to the visit to Châteauroux. He points out, logically, that the five hundred francs mentioned in the letter, would not have sufficed for a journey to India – indeed we know that five thousand francs were borrowed from his estate for this purpose – and that one would not say 'il y a quelque temps' for an event which had occurred seven years before.

There are objections to this view. It is not very likely that a staid and middle-aged lawyer would appoint a young scatterbrained man like Baudelaire as editor of his conservative paper, or give him a responsible position on it.

But his son, Baudelaire's friend and contemporary, might
have done so when he took charge of it. On going to a big
town like Châteauroux Baudelaire would surely have said
'mon voyage à Châteauroux' and not 'dans l'Indre'. One
does not normally say, if one is going to Toulon, that one
is going 'dans le Var'; or to Rouen 'dans l'Île-et-Vilaine';
or to Marseilles 'dans les Bouches du Rhône'; or to Dijon
'dans la Côte d'Or' – especially not a century ago when the
names of the departments were still a comparative novelty.
Also would he say of an event which had happened as
recently as six weeks before 'il y a quelque temps'?

It seems clear that Baudelaire made a trip somewhere in
1848 which was paid for by his mother, but it is not proved
that it was in fact to Châteauroux nor in October. In an
undated letter to his mother, which must have been written
before May 1848, at latest, he tells her that he may have to
leave before her. Her husband was appointed to Turkey
in the middle of April that year, and they left France before the middle of May. Baudelaire would not, as early as
that, have been thinking of going to Châteauroux to edit
a paper which was not to appear until 20 October.

The letter in question has not been seen by those who
suggest the emendation, and its whereabouts are unknown.
It is possible that, in the actual letter, the word bears no
resemblance to either word, and that the first editor jumped
to the conclusion that it was 'Inde' because it was known
that Baudelaire had once intended to go there. The problem cannot be solved until the letter turns up in the original,
but the passage now appears as 'dans l'Indre' in the *Correspondance Générale*.

It is conceivable that Baudelaire went to Châteauroux in
February 1850, on leaving Dijon, and that he wrote the
articles published on 5 and 12 February.[17]

This second journalistic venture, whenever it occurred,
remains as mysterious as the first, and we do not know
what Baudelaire was doing, or the nature of his duties.
Legend has it that he scandalized the subscribers by the

violence of his articles, and especially by the manner of his life. The subscribers were, for the most part, respectable fathers of families who took exception to the irregularity of his life, and considered his living openly with a coloured mistress a bad example for young people, and a danger to the public morality of the town. One of the chief share-holders of the paper was asked to speak to him on the matter. Very nervously he broached the subject. 'It has come to the notice of the directors of the paper, Monsieur Bau-delaire,' he began in great embarrassment, 'that – ahem – Madame Baudelaire is not your lawful wife, but only – ahem – your mistress!' [18]

Then Baudelaire, who always lost control of himself at the first signs of interference in his private affairs, is said to have replied in a rage, but with a show of dignity. 'Sir! the mistress of a poet is often better than the wife of an attorney!' The remark was not even original – or not en-tirely so – for it was the emendation of one taken from *Madame Putiphar* by Petrus Borel, who had borrowed it from Rousseau.

The rejoinder appears to have finished Baudelaire's jour-nalistic career at Châteauroux, for this shareholder was a lawyer in a small way, and very self-conscious and jealous of his personal dignity and prestige.

In May 1850 Baudelaire was back in Paris. He was des-titute and as unhappy as ever. One of the causes of his unhappiness was his estrangement from his mother. She was still adopting the course of action which her husband had advised so often, sternness and severity, for she was beginning to believe that he and Ancelle were right when they said that Baudelaire would never become self-support-ing as long as she allowed her heart to be softened at the sight of his need. Now she had stopped writing to him and was determined not to show him any affection until he had given proof of having reformed. She helped him from time to time by sending him money through Ancelle, just enough to prevent him from suffering the greatest privations, but she sent no letter, and no affectionate messages. This was what he minded most, and thought harshest, that she should express no concern or interest in his actions, but sent him charity through her lawyer, as if to some pauper organization.

'For the last few months,' he wrote to her in December 1850, 'I've been planning to write to you. Several times I've tried, but I've had to abandon the attempt! My endless worries, and my solitude, have made me a little bitter and hard, and also, doubtless, a little clumsy! I'd like to be able to make my style more gentle, but even if your pride finds it offensive, I hope you'll be able to appreciate the sincerity of my intentions, and the credit I deserve for taking such a step which formerly would have been so pleasant to me, but which, in the present state, which you've created between us, must be my very last attempt!

'The fact that you've deprived me of your friendship, and of all the intercourse which a man has a right to expect with his mother, that concerns your conscience, or perhaps also your husband, but I'll investigate that some other day!

'But a certain inherent delicacy should warn you that one can't presume to oblige those whom one insults, or at least those who are indifferent to one – for that is a fresh insult! You can guess that I'm referring to the money which Ancelle has received for me! What? He receives money without a letter to tell me how to spend it, or to advise me on its use! But, think for a moment. You've lost all right to be charitable and philanthropic towards me, for I needn't speak of maternal feelings! Are you sorry then? But I'll not accept the expression of your remorse if it doesn't take another form. Or, to put it still more clearly, if you don't become at once, and completely, a mother. Otherwise I'll feel obliged to get a solicitor to send a refusal to Ancelle on my behalf, to accept any money coming from you, and I'll take all necessary steps to see that my wishes are respected!

'I don't think it necessary for me to point out to you the importance of this letter, nor that your answer must be addressed to me, to myself alone, do you understand? My future conduct towards you, and also towards myself, will depend on your answer, or on your silence. I'll be thirty years old in three months exactly, and this fact arouses in me the thoughts which you may easily guess! And so, morally, a part of my future life is in your hands! I hope you'll be able to answer what I long to hear!

'And, if you deign to understand the importance of this letter, you'll add, in your answer, exact information on the state of your health. And furthermore, since you've got such an influence on Monsieur Ancelle, you ought to tell him, when you write to him, not to make my life such a burden to me! I wish and insist that he takes no part whatsoever in the question I'm discussing with you today! I'll accept no answer through him.' [19]

Her indifference was more apparent than real. A month earlier, in November 1850, Maxime Du Camp and Flaubert visited Constantinople and were received at the embassy. During the conversation Aupick asked them what new authors had appeared on the horizon, since he had left France two years before. Du Camp, knowing nothing of Baudelaire's family circumstances, nor that he was the stepson of the ambassador, mentioned him as the young poet most frequently talked of, and most notorious in advanced literary circles, saying that a great future was prophesied for him. Since he knew him chiefly by hearsay and not personally, and wanted to seem knowledgeable about literary matters in the capital, he painted a lurid picture of his reputation, in accordance with the legend rather than the facts. He noticed the embarrassment of both the ambassador and his wife, and did not pursue the subject. Later one of the secretaries told him who Baudelaire was, and that he was a source of much anxiety to his parents, so that his name was never mentioned in the presence of the ambassador. [20] Du Camp, when telling the story in 1882,

makes it reflect discredit on Aupick, explaining that his
hatred of his stepson inspired him to behave like this towards him in order to separate him from his mother. The
General, however, had valid grounds for misgiving: it was
seven years since the appointment of the *conseil judiciaire*,
and Baudelaire had not yet proved by deeds that he had
begun to take life seriously. On the contrary, he had been
implicated in the revolution of 1848, on the side of the
socialists, who were well-known antagonists of law and
order, and accepted morality. Aupick knew that he had
taken an active part in the riots, and it may possibly have
been his protection in high places which had saved him
from the penalties which his friends, Poulet Malassis, Leconte de Lisle and Louis Ménard, had suffered.

His mother, however, was delighted with what she had
heard from Du Camp and later, when she could leave her
duties as hostess, she drew him aside and said to him:
'You do think, don't you, that he's got talent, the young
poet of whom you were speaking?'

At the end of April 1851 General and Madame Aupick
left Constantinople and arrived back in Paris early in May.
Aupick had first been appointed to the embassy in London, but asked to be relieved of the appointment, since he
did not wish it to be said he was spying on the family of
Louis-Philippe who had gone there as exiles. He exchanged
appointments with Comte Colonna-Walewski, who had
been nominated to Madrid. Through Ancelle Madame Aupick arranged to meet her son. The lawyer, who could never
realize how great were the difficulties involved, had promised her that Baudelaire would go to see her at her hotel
and dine with her and her husband. Baudelaire refused,
for he felt that he could not face his stepfather, who disapproved of him, and before whom he always felt at a
disadvantage. He would only meet his mother in some
neutral spot, away from her home. When at last they did
meet, she was startled at the change in his appearance
which had taken place during her three years' absence, for

he seemed to have aged, and she saw a look of súffering on his face which she did not remember seeing there before. She did not then know that he had been ill while at Dijon, but she was shocked at his shabbiness and he looked as if he had not had enough to eat. Almost twenty years later she had not forgotten this first impression of him, after an absence of three years, when she wrote to Asselineau.[21] Now her heart was once more tortured by doubt, and she wondered whether her husband and she were needlessly harsh. Might she not drive him to the same temptation as on that terrible, and never to be forgotten, day in June 1845 when he had attempted suicide?

There was an attempt at reconciliation, but her son could not help disappointing her again. By August he was once more in difficulties, and was trying to borrow money from her to settle the most pressing of his debts, or the interest on them. Once more she tried sternness, and severed all relations.

Firmness, however, instead of goading him to work, only depressed him. His lack of success, coupled with this estrangement, affected him deeply and made him incapable of regular work. All his close friends describe his incapacity for concentrated effort. Du Camp writes:[22]

'He dreamed of working, but could never make up his mind to start, for the slightest pretext would take him out of the house. However, he used to calculate that, by working so many hours a day, he would produce a specified number of pages, which would bring him in a certain sum of money. He deduced from this that he would need only two or three months to settle his debts, and reach peace. That was all very well in theory, but he never got any further than the calculations, and put off the practice until the morrow.'

This resembles Courbet's experience over the unwritten article.[23]

Asselineau, in his *Baudelairiana*,[24] describes the same state of affairs, and shows how any trifle was enough to prevent him from sitting down to the work which it was imperative for him to produce. Time and again the poet had come to him at four or five in the afternoon saying:

'My dear fellow, I want you to do something to oblige me. I know you won't like it, and that it will be a nuisance to you, but it's absolutely essential! I've promised to hand in by midday tomorrow a whole page of copy. It's not naturally the quantity that bothers me, for you know the rapidity with which I normally work! A page of print to produce in sixteen hours, that's mere child's play for me! However, on account of my worries, it's impossible for me to work at home, so you must lend me the hospitality of your room until tomorrow midday! I shan't disturb you in any way, you can put me where you like, and I'll make no noise whatsoever!'

Asselineau always answered that he would do all he could to oblige him, and that in any case he was out for the day, and would be away until bedtime.

'Oh! when you return,' Baudelaire would invariably answer, 'the work will be finished! Let me see, what time is it now? Five o'clock! Now which is the better plan, to dine first, or only when the work is finished?'

He always decided that dinner would inspire him, and that he would work all the more rapidly afterwards. At first Asselineau used to expect, when he returned home late that night, to find his friend hard at work, but he usually discovered only an empty room and on the table the roll of paper still unopened, and the new pens still virgin. Towards one or two in the morning there would be a ring at the door and Baudelaire would appear, shamefacedly trying to explain what had happened.

'Sacré Saint-Ciboire! I went out to dine as I told you I would, and, when I'd finished I took a little stroll on the boulevard, and whom should I meet but that idle chatterbox S. who never has anything to do, and he made me have a pint with him, and blathered on until after midnight, so that I couldn't stop him long enough to get away! But it doesn't matter, for I was thinking out my article all the time he was chattering, and all I need now is the actual time necessary to write it down!'

Then, looking at his watch, he would add: 'I see that it's now one o'clock, and I've still eleven hours before I need hand in my manuscript. At four sheets an hour, that should amply suffice! So I'll take forty winks to get S.'s chatter out of my head!'

Next morning Asselineau used to awake at eight o'clock, and see Baudelaire still lying in bed, his face to the wall. 'I'm not asleep!' he used to cry out, 'I've been awake this long time, and I'm just getting up!'

On the table the roll of paper was still unopened, and the pens untouched. Naturally the poet did not finish the article, and did not hand in the review! He lunched with Asselineau, and discoursed with him on literature for the whole of the afternoon, and the article joined the heap of those which he had not finished, and had brought no nearer completion than their original conception. This happened frequently and infuriated those who tried to obtain work for him, alienating the good will of many editors of reviews and papers, and, worst of all, more often than not, whenever he could extract an advance, he had spent the money before he had earned it, money which he was sometimes never to earn. He would then have to consider ways and means of repaying the sums which he had spent in anticipation, and this added to his ever-growing mountain of debts.

There were many articles in these years which were announced, but never afterwards came to light, and it is impossible nowadays to decide whether they were ever written. We know from Asselineau that some contributions were in fact refused by the *Revue Politique* edited by Amail: the two *Crépuscules*, which have already been mentioned, *Le Vin de l'Assassin*, *Le Reniement de Saint-Pierre*, *L'Âme du Vin* and *Le Vin des Chiffonniers* – all poems. Amail was apparently a Saint-Simonien and a virtuous republican, and he said to the poet, as he handed him back his manuscript: 'Our paper doesn't print that kind of fanciful stuff!' [25]

To judge from the variety of titles announced at this time, it would seem to have been a fertile period in his life – at least in ideas.

On the back page of *La Presse* of Monday, 10 December 1849, there appeared the advertisement of a new weekly entitled *La Veillée Pittoresque, Musée Encyclopédique Illustré*, the first number of which was to appear on 20 December, and thereafter every Saturday, enriched with six full-page illustrations. The notice states that the publication will be non-political, that it will be based on the highest morality, and that all the contributions will be new, and hitherto unpublished. It announces, amongst others, a work by Gérard de Nerval called *Les Kalifes de Bagdad*, and one by Baudelaire entitled *Les Derniers Buveurs*. There is no further information about these, nor whether they are in prose or verse. There is no mention of *Les Derniers Buveurs* anywhere in Baudelaire's correspondence, nor in any notes for future works, nor in the testimony of his friends. Judging from the nature of the periodical, it can be surmised that it was probably a short story.

The *Bibliothèque Nationale* in Paris possesses only one number of the paper, which is not dated, and it would seem to be the only number to have been issued. According to its Editorial it had had many unforeseen and unfortunate delays. It excuses itself on the grounds that it needed time to be able to offer its readers the most perfect production possible, and declares that, if they will only have patience, it will become one of the finest papers of all time.

The number must have appeared early in 1850 as one of the contributions, entitled *Revue de Paris*, begins, 'The year 1849 is dead! Long live 1850, provided it behaves better than its predecessor did!' It goes on to say that there appears to be a new rebirth in the country, that business is improving, the workmen working, the theatres opening once more, and the artists, like nightingales in springtime, are buoyed up with the feeling that their distress is a thing of the past. The chief fault of the wretched year 1849, says the article, was that it lasted too long, but it hopes that *La Veillée* will be at the fireside of every family, and that it will win many friends and much sympathy. It ends: 'La *Veillée Pittoresque* vivra!' Nevertheless, in spite of this gallant assertion this is the only number, and it is not known whether *Les Derniers Buveurs* ever saw the light.

Later in the year, on 3 June 1850, *La Presse* printed on its back page an advertisement which said that the greatest authors of the day had promised to contribute to *Le Magasin des Familles*, amongst them, Hugo, Gautier, Banville, Dumas fils and Murger; and it announced in its coming numbers various articles by Gautier, and one entitled *L'Influence des Images sur les Esprits* par Baudelaire (*sic*)'. Nothing further is known about this article and it appears nowhere else.

In the same month, however, the paper did print two poems of his, *Châtiment de l'Orgueil* and *Le Vin des Honnêtes Gens*, saying that they came from a collection entitled *Limbes* which was to appear shortly.

On 4 June 1850 *La Presse* advertised that *La Semaine* was going to publish in the near future, amongst other works, *Werther* by Goethe, *Adolphe* by Constant, and 'La Fanfarlo par Chasles (*sic*) Beaudelaire (*sic*),' and on 19 June this work is called *La Fanfario*. This would be a reprint since it had already been published in 1847.

After this there was a falling off in contributions advertised or published, and nothing appeared until his *Du Vin et du Haschisch* came out in *Le Messager de l'Assemblée* between 7 and 11 March 1851. This is a first draft of *Les Paradis Artificiels* which he was to publish ten years later, and in which he made use of parts of the hashish section for *Le Poème du Haschisch*. Although Baudelaire professes in the first work to believe that the effect of wine is beneficent and hashish dangerous – 'Le vin est utile, il produit des résultats fructifiants. Le haschisch est inutile et dangereux'[26]

– it is not by wine that he is best inspired, and only when speaking of the effects of hashish does he approach in a small measure the magic of *Les Paradis Artificiels*. In this last work he dropped the section dealing with wine, as being too vulgar and clumsy a key to unlock the doors of paradise.

Du Vin et du Haschisch was a success with the public and this permitted him to publish, in the same paper, a selection of his poems, eleven in number, the largest number he had ever yet printed together. They include *Le Spleen* (*Pluviose Irrité*), *Le Mauvais Moine*, *L'Idéal*, *Le Spleen* (*Le Mort Joyeux*), *Les Chats*, *La Mort des Amants*, *La Mort des Artistes*, *Le Tonneau de la Haine*, *La Béatrix* (*De Profundis Clamavi*), *Le Spleen* (*La Cloche Fêlée*), *Les Hiboux*.

The note which accompanied these poems stated that they came from a collection entitled *Limbes* which was shortly to be published by Michel Lévy, and which was intended to trace the history of the spiritual unrest of modern youth. They are indeed mostly of *spleen* inspiration, but they contain, nevertheless, the exquisite *La Mort des Amants*, a poem which he alone could have composed, giving a promise already of the voluptuous nostalgia of the later *Invitation au Voyage*.

> *Nous aurons des lits pleins d'odeurs légères,*
> *Des divans profonds comme des tombeaux,*
> *Et d'étranges fleurs sur des étagères,*
> *Écloses pour nous sous des cieux plus beaux.*
>
> *Usant à l'envi leurs chaleurs dernières,*
> *Nos deux cœurs seront deux vastes flambeaux,*
> *Qui réfléchiront leurs doubles lumières*
> *Dans nos deux esprits, ces miroirs jumeaux.*
>
> *Un soir fait de rose et de bleu mystique,*
> *Nous échangerons un éclair unique,*
> *Comme un long sanglot, tout chargé d'adieux;*
>
> *Et plus tard un Ange, entr'ouvrant les portes,*
> *Viendra ranimer, fidèle et joyeux,*
> *Les miroirs ternis et les flammes mortes.*[27]

Baudelaire had now reached his thirtieth birthday and he had covered much ground during the past ten years. He had experienced and suffered much, but his spiritual nature had been thereby enriched. He was ripe now for the great works of maturity. An entry which he made in a lady's autograph album in August 1851 throws a bright light on his state of mind. The album belonged to the grandmother of Paul Fuchs, who inherited it from her, and it had been presented to her by a group of friends in 1837. It was a charming little book, bound in Morocco leather, tooled in gold, which evoked, says Fuchs,[28] the picture of a whole age. It contained drawings of women in the eighteen-thirties, poems by Musset, Banville, Champfleury, and Dupont; drawings by Maurice Sand; and finally, most precious of all, the page by Baudelaire, dated 26 August 1851.

'As man advances through life, and begins to see things from a higher angle, then everything which the world has agreed to call beauty loses much of its importance for him, as well as carnal pleasure, and other trifles of that sort. In the eyes of a clear-sighted and disillusioned man each season has its beauty, and it is not spring which is the most enchanting, nor winter the most evil. Henceforth beauty will not mean for him the promise of physical pleasure and happiness. It is Stendhal who says that beauty will henceforth be the form which seems to promise most kindliness, most loyalty in fulfilling one's share of the bargain, most honesty in keeping trust, most delicacy in intellectual perception. Ugliness will mean cruelty, avarice, falseness and stupidity.

'Many men do not know these things, and only learn them later to their own cost. Just a few of us know them now, but each one of us knows them for himself alone. By what means could I ever make it clear to a young flibbertigibbet that the great attraction and sympathy which I feel for ageing women, for those poor unfortunate creatures who have suffered much through their lovers, their husbands, through their children, and most of all through their own fault, are coupled with no sensual desire?

'If the notion of virtue and love is not mingled with all our pleasures, then these pleasures will only become anguish and the source of remorse.'

There is something here of the mood which inspired him later when he composed *Les Petites Vieilles* or *Le Cheval de Race*.

The owner of this document, writing in 1925, expresses surprise at the spiritual state of mind which it reveals and which, he declares, is very different from that exemplified in *Les Fleurs du Mal*. Thirty years ago readers of the poet had not yet learnt to appreciate that Satanism was not his most characteristic mood, but that on the contrary he was, at his highest, a man moved by deep spiritual preoccupations. He said later, in an article on Marceline Desbordes-Valmore,[29] 'Je me suis toujours plu à chercher dans la nature extérieure et visible, des exemples et des métaphores qui me servissent à caractériser les jouissances et les impressions d'un ordre spirituel.'

It was this stage that he was now reaching, as he embarked on the fourth decade of his life.

[4]

The Revelation of Poe
1852—1854

BAUDELAIRE was roused from his disgust and depression at the *coup d'état* of 2 December 1851, by which the President made himself Emperor, and which purged him of any further interest in politics – 'I've decided,' he wrote, 'to remain henceforth aloof from all human polemics'[1] – by his passion for the writings of Edgar Allan Poe. Although he had known his works for five years by then, it was not until early in 1852 that he showed any real interest in them, or thought of translating them extensively. Then suddenly he mentions them frequently in his correspondence,[2] and set to work on his notices and translations. His first article appeared in March and April 1852, and the first translation in April the same year.

Baudelaire had probably first read extracts from the writings of Poe when Isabelle Meunier began to publish translations of the tales in *La Démocratie Pacifique*, starting with *The Black Cat* in January 1847, which was accompanied by a note stating that:

'The extract which we are publishing today is translated from an author well known beyond the Atlantic Ocean, and beginning to be read in France. We offer this tale in order to show to what strange arguments the extreme partisans of the dogma of natural perversity are reduced. Here is a story intending to support this dogma in which the author, although moving at full sail in the midst of fantasy, only dares make this so-called natural perversity intervene, after making his characters go through several years of drunkenness.'

Asselineau declares that Baudelaire first knew of Poe through the translation of *The Black Cat* by Isabelle Meunier – whom he calls Adèle Meunier – when it was published in *Le Journal du Loiret*, and that a friend of Baudelaire's, Barbara, who worked on the paper in Orleans, sent him the cuttings.[3] W. T. Bandy is inclined to agree with this opinion, although it is not the usual one.[4] An examination of the *Journal du Loiret* reveals that the first translation of Poe by Isabelle Meunier to be published there appeared only on 17 June 1848, reprinted from *La Démocratic Pacifique*, and it was not *The Black Cat* but *The Gold Bug*. By June 1848 Baudelaire must already have known the works of Poe since his own first translation, *Mesmeric Revelation*, appeared the following month in *La Liberté de Penser*. He is much more likely to have first read Poe in *La Démocratie Pacifique* than in *Le Journal du Loiret*, for he knew it well, and Victor Meunier who worked on it, the husband of the translator. *The Black Cat* was in effect the first story to be translated by Isabelle Meunier and published in *La Démocratie Pacifique*.

Very soon Baudelaire could think and talk of nothing else but Poe, and, writing to his mother, he said,[5] 'I've found an American author who has aroused in me the most astonishing sympathy. I've written a couple of articles on him, his life and works, which are written with great passion.'

He would have liked to have become for Poe what Loève-Weimars had been for Hoffmann earlier in the century, when he translated his tales into French, and thus exercised a deep influence on the macabre side of Romanticism. Asselineau said that Baudelaire drove his friends almost mad with his incessant questions about Poe. Everywhere he went he used to ask people whether they had ever heard of him, and, if they expressed ignorance or indifference, he would manifest horror and disgust. Once, hearing that a famous American writer had arrived at a hotel in Paris, he forced his way into his presence and found him trying on a new suit of clothes. In spite of this, he insisted on asking him, as he stood there, an incongruous figure in vest and pants, whether he had ever known Poe personally, and how his reputation now stood in the United States. The American, a best-seller himself, obviously thought that Poe was very small fry indeed, since he had not reached fame and wealth, never having earned a respectable living, and having finally died of drink. He gave Baudelaire to understand that he was scarcely worthy of consideration.[6]

Baudelaire's mother had been born in England, and he himself had spoken the language as a child, though he had largely forgotten it, except for reading purposes. Now he set to work to learn it again, not merely standard English, which he could acquire in literary texts with the aid of a dictionary and grammar, but colloquial and everyday speech. He used to go to a wineshop in the Rue de Rivoli where the grooms and servants of the English visitors at the rich hotels in the quarter congregated to drink whisky. Baudelaire used to sit amongst them, chattering with them, and making valiant efforts to appreciate the British humour of *Punch*.[7]

The weariness which normally overtook him as he strove to give adequate expression to his vision, when he was creating original works, was absent when he was translating, for here was something that he could force himself to do, and not feel short of inspiration, or unsure of what he intended to express. While he was at work on Poe he astounded his friends by his diligence, and by devoting to his translations the time he had never yet managed to give to anything else, sacrificing even his most precious habits – his long hours of idleness as he sat chatting with his friends in some café; his aimless wandering at night round the town; his endless discussions on aesthetics and philosophy, into the small hours of the morning. All this he was able to sacrifice now. While he was working on Poe he scarcely went anywhere, Asselineau says, and, to save himself the time needed to rise from his table to admit his friends, he used to leave the key in the lock outside, so that they could come in if they wanted to. Then, seeing him completely engrossed in what he was doing, they used to leave again, while he had not even been aware of their interruption.[8]

He was for a time so absorbed in this work that one of his less reverent friends once asked him flippantly: 'Is it true that you are still on the Poe?'[9]

Baudelaire's article on Poe, which appeared in 1852, was the first in any foreign language to be published on the American and it marks an important date in comparative literature studies.

W. T. Bandy, who has made many remarkable discoveries concerning Baudelaire, established that the Mann, whom the poet mentions in his correspondence,[10] was an American of the name of William Wilberforce Mann who, for ten years from 1846 to 1856, was Paris correspondent to *The Southern Literary Messenger* on which Poe had once worked, and that he gave Baudelaire information about it – indeed lending him back numbers of the review,[11] and discussing Poe with him. Bandy also discovered two articles in *The Southern Literary Messenger* which must have provided Baudelaire with the material for his own first article. These are the obituary by J. R. Thompson, which was published in November 1849; and a long review of the first two volumes of the Redfield edition of Poe's complete works by John M. Daniel, which appeared in March 1850, and from which Baudelaire borrowed extensively. Bandy even declares that the greatest part of his article is merely a translation, without attribution, of the substance of Daniel's article in *The Southern Literary Messenger*. In this he is not completely fair, though he tries to find excuses and justification for Baudelaire. He calls his action a 'hoax' that he has been playing on the public, and sees it as similar to what he had done in the case of *The Young Enchanter*, but the circumstances are very different. In *The Young Enchanter* he had passed off as his own a work he had not written and nothing but need could justify such appropriation. When he set out to write about Poe, he had not known him personally, and was obliged to obtain his material from some source, so that the biographical details and the description of the American poet could not be original. In the first two sections of his article, dealing with these, Baudelaire has used remarkably well, with talent, discrimination and subtlety, the facts which he has obtained second-hand, and which he could not invent. His account is very much better written than that of his American predecessor, told with irony, and subtlety of style, which are his alone. As a Frenchman, and a psychologist, he speculates on the facts which are at his disposal, trying to fit them into a pattern which has verisimilitude – as when he reflects on the sudden transformation which took place in Poe's appearance at one moment of his life, concluding that some woman was involved, an older woman. He has also cleverly combined the facts he obtained from *The Southern Literary Messenger* with details he himself discovered in Paris from those who had known Poe personally. What is interesting, and moving also, is the way he has been able to see the destiny of Poe in terms of his own, either in what has happened to him, or in what he dreams – as when, perhaps unconsciously, he compares the attitude of Poe's mother-in-law to him, with the behaviour of his own mother. There are many passages in his article which have no counterpart in the English, as for instance his opening discussion on ill-fated destinies, those pursued by 'le guignon'; on 'l'ivrognerie littéraire' which he describes as 'un des phénomènes les plus communs et les plus lamentables de la vie moderne' and which he explains as the price charged by Fate for spiritual gifts and awareness – 'Tout mystique a un vice caché'. They deserve our love and our pity, Baudelaire thinks, for they have 'beaucoup souffert pour nous'. And he ends his article with the prayer:

'Vous tous qui avez ardemment cherché à découvrir les lois de votre être, qui avez aspiré à l'infini, et dont les senti-

ments refoulés ont dû chercher un affreux soulagement
dans le vin de la débauche, priez pour lui. Maintenant son
être corporel purifié nage au milieu des êtres dont il entre-
voyait l'existence, priez pour lui qui voit et qui sait, il inter-
cédera pour vous.'

Ten years later, in his *Journaux Intimes*, Baudelaire still
asked Poe to intercede for him.

Section Three of the article is devoted to a study of Poe's
works and here, declares Bandy, 'except for an elaborate
discussion of seven of the short stories, and a few inept comments on "To Helen" there is substantially not one line of
original criticism, the section being based, fundamentally,
like the first two, on judgements expressed by Daniel and
Thompson.'

But the discussion on the seven tales is the largest part
of this section – ten pages to half a page on the poetry –
and, even if Baudelaire has largely given their substance, he
does convey an impression of what are their distinctive
characteristics. But the value of the article does not lie in
the literary criticism it contains. It is important because of
the picture which it evokes of the personality and nature of
Poe, painted with the raw materials obtained in the articles
published in *The Southern Literary Messenger*, and this
picture is more vivid and more moving than the one by
which it is inspired.

A significant fact emerges from Bandy's discovery that,
at the time of writing his first article, Baudelaire had seen
very little of Poe's works, did not know the poetry or the
critical works, except from the passages quoted in review,
and had not yet read *Arthur Gordon Pym*. For these he
was therefore obliged to depend on the opinions of others.
At that time he knew only the Wiley and Patmore edition
of the tales of 1845, and had not seen the Redfield edition,
nor the Griswold Memoir. He was only to know all these
when he revised his article to serve as an Introduction to
the first volume of his translations, *Histoires Extraordinaires*,
published in 1856. Considering how little material he had

at his disposal in 1852, his achievement was remarkable, and deserving of praise rather than blame.

It therefore follows that the influence of Poe on Baudelaire is very much less significant than has hitherto been suggested. By 1856, when he had seen the whole of the American author's writings, the bulk of his own poetry was already written, a large number of poems even before 1843, when he had not yet seen a line of Poe, and some of these poems figure amongst those in which a particular influence of Poe is alleged to occur.[12]

The coincidence of the similarity between Baudelaire and Poe is one of the most curious in the history of literature, where such coincidences are not rare, two authors writing at the same time and producing, unknown to each other, works of similar inspiration. Such a phenomenon should teach caution in placing too much reliance on academic studies of influences and imitations.

Baudelaire drew nothing from Poe which was not already in himself, and his most valuable gain was confidence in his own aesthetic principles, and the courage to continue to cultivate the vein in which he felt that his real genius lay. He found in Poe, for the first time, someone of his own spiritual family, who had, independently, reached the conclusions towards which he had been himself groping in the dark, scorned by his contemporaries. Writing later to a friend about Manet, who had been accused of imitating Goya, even though he had not yet seen his pictures, Baudelaire said:[13]

'You don't believe what I'm telling you? You're sceptical about the possibility of such mathematical parallelism in nature? Well! don't they accuse me of imitating Edgar Allan Poe? And do you know why, with such infinite patience, I translated Poe? It was because he was like me! The first time I ever opened a book by him I discovered, with rapture and awe, not only subjects which I had dreamt, but whole phrases which I'd conceived, written by him twenty years before.'

He wrote, in the same vein, to another friend.[14]

'I can tell you something most peculiar and scarcely credible! It was in 1846 or 1847 that I first came across a few fragments of Poe, and I was most strangely moved! His complete works were only collected after his death, in a single edition, but I had the patience to get to know some Americans residing in Paris in order to borrow from them old copies of the newspapers and periodicals to which Poe had contributed. Then I found, believe it or not, poems and stories which I'd already conceived, but only in a vague and formless manner, which Poe had planned and brought to perfection.'

Baudelaire is here being too modest since his own fame as a poet and a critic outshines that of Poe. However, as far as he was concerned, Poe was important because this new interest roused him from the state of depression into which he had fallen, and gave him the courage to take up his creative burden once more. Finding in Poe what he had already found in himself gave him the confidence in his own powers which he needed. As has been so aptly stated by André Gide: 'L'influence ne crée pas, elle éveille!'

Baudelaire's new energy is also seen in his independent attempts at journalism at this time. Now he dreamed of founding a literary paper which would express his new aesthetic and philosophic theories. From the end of 1851 until the end of February 1852, with Champfleury and some other literary friends, he was directing a magazine entitled *La Semaine Théâtrale*, in which in November he published his article, *Les Drames et Romans Honnêtes*; in January another article, *L'École Païenne*, an attack against the classical revival; and finally in February his two *Crépuscules* – *Crépuscule du Matin* and *Crépuscule du Soir*. This was the last number of the paper to appear, for it then went bankrupt.[15] A few days later, nothing daunted, he was planning to found another review, with Champfleury, Albert Thomas and Armand Baschet.[16] The paper was to be entitled *Le Hibou Philosophe* and, judging by the notes referring to it which have been published,[17] it was to be inspired by high literary and philosophic conceptions. Champfleury, a realist in business matters, who probably only wanted some paper where he could find a regular outlet for his work, must have smiled somewhat sceptically when Baudelaire declared that they would grow rich and famous together. He would not indeed have been wrong to express doubt concerning the fate of this periodical which in fact was stillborn; for the public, and even the collaborators, cared very little about profundity of aims, and no funds were forthcoming to pay even the initial cost of paper and printing. The man who had promised to provide the capital at the last moment withdrew, as he was afraid that the paper would be a failure on account of the loftiness of Baudelaire's plans.[18]

Baudelaire did not even then lose heart, but determined to obtain publication of a large selection of his poems, most of them written many years before and copied out, ready for printing in two volumes, as early as the end of 1849.[19] Writing to his mother, the previous August, he mentions his 'book' of poetry, but expresses misgiving over its success.[20] It is true that, although he was becoming well known as an art critic, he was finding it difficult to make his way as a poet. Yet some of his early admirers considered that he was squandering his talents by not being primarily a poet. His old friend of Latin Quarter days, Ernest Prarond, writing an introduction to a collection of modern poets, said in 1852:[21]

'Amongst others whom we hope not to have lost for ever, there is one particularly, who enjoyed the strange fate of having made a name for himself without publishing a single line of verse, merely by reciting the noblest poetry to a small gathering of friends. This poet, who once, on the occasion of an exhibition at the *Louvre*, wrote a complete treatise on modern painting,[22] is Monsieur Baudelaire. We sincerely hope that, having become a poet once more, and remaining one, he may occupy the attention of the critic who next undertakes what I am attempting today.'

Prarond must, however, have lost sight of Baudelaire not to realize that he did in fact still compose poetry, and he seems not to have been aware of the batch which had appeared in a magazine the previous year, *Le Messager de l'Assemblée*, in April.

It was certainly not lack of material which was preventing Baudelaire from occupying the attention of the critics, but lack of confidence on the part of publishers and editors. Now, however, he hoped that with friends directing the *Revue de Paris*, he would be able to print some of his poems there. In October 1851 Gautier, Louis Cormenin, Arsène Houssaye and Maxime Du Camp bought up the goodwill of the periodical which, when it was founded by Doctor Véron in 1829, had become immediately popular, and had known great success, but had subsequently been overshadowed by the *Revue des Deux Mondes* of Buloz. Gautier and his friends wished to make it more up-to-date, after they became part owners, and their first number appeared in October 1851.[23]

Baudelaire hoped particularly that Gautier, being himself a poet, might open the review to his poetry and, in February or March 1852, he sent him two batches of poems so that he could choose those he considered most suitable for inclusion. The two batches make up the twelve poems which were published in facsimile in 1917 by Van Bever.[24] The poems of the first batch were the following: *Crépuscule du Matin, Crépuscule du Soir, La Robe Trouée de la Mendiante Rousse, La Rançon, Le Vin des Chiffonniers, Le Reniement de Saint-Pierre, La Caravane des Bohémiens,* and *La Mort des Pauvres*. It was accompanied by a note which stated that they were taken from the book which was to be published shortly by Michel Lévy under the title *Limbes*. The second batch consisted of: *L'Outre de la Volupté (Les Métamorphoses du Vampire), La Fontaine de*

Sang, L'Artiste Inconnu and *Un Voyage à Cythère*. This batch was accompanied by a letter to Gautier.[25]

'Here's my second little lot. I hope you'll be able to make a choice amongst them! These are my personal preferences: The two *Crépuscules, La Caravane, Le Reniement de Saint-Pierre, L'Artiste Inconnu, L'Outre de la Volupté, La Fontaine de Sang* and *Un Voyage à Cythère*. Support me for all you're worth! And if they don't complain too much about this type of poetry, I'll give them some more soon, and even more startling!'

Only two of the poems were published in *La Revue de Paris*, both very much later in the year, in October – *Le Reniement de Saint-Pierre* and a poem which he had not submitted, *L'Homme et la Mer*, one of his more easily appreciated compositions.

Perhaps Gautier's co-directors overruled his judgement and did not allow him to include his friend's verses. But perhaps it was only that he was personally timid, and he may not have really believed in Baudelaire. According to Du Camp, he said at this time:[26]

'I'm afraid that the same thing will happen with Baudelaire that happened with Petrus Borel. In the days of our youth, when the Romantic School still had its first fiery ardour, and I used to wear a crimson doublet, we used to say "Hugo had better look to his laurels, for as soon as Petrus Borel begins to publish his works then he'll disappear!" Well! Petrus Borel has published *Champavert, Madame Putiphar* and *Les Rhapsodies,* and old Hugo hasn't disappeared! – far from it! Nowadays they threaten us with Baudelaire, and they say to us that when he has published his poetry, Musset, Laprade, and I, we'll all go up in smoke! I don't believe it. Baudelaire will miss fire as Petrus Borel did.'

Du Camp, writing in 1883, at the height of Baudelaire's popularity, condescendingly remarks that he did not miss fire, but on the contrary took his place honourably in the second rank of poets, and that it would not be possible to

write a history of poetry in the middle of the century without giving him some place in it.

The *Revue de Paris* took Baudelaire's article on Poe, which
appeared in March and April 1852; but it accepted only
one of his translations, which it published in October. His
first translation came out in *L'Illustration* in April 1852,
and there were two more that year, besides the one printed
in *La Revue de Paris* – in *Le Magasin des Familles* in October, and again in *L'Illustration* in December. He was not
finding it easy to place his translations. All through 1852
and 1853 he had hawked them round to different reviews,
and he managed to publish some, at irregular intervals
in *L'Illustration*, in *Le Magasin des Familles*, in *Le Journal d'Alençon*, in *Paris Journal* and in *Le Monde Littéraire*.
His only translation from the poems, *The Raven*, accompanied by the essay on *The Philosophy of Composition*,
appeared in *L'Artiste* in March 1853. During the first half
of 1854 he was trying to obtain a contract from one of the
government papers, either *Le Moniteur* or *Le Constitutionnel*. Sainte-Beuve was a regular contributor to the
former and Baudelaire tried to secure his support but the
critic did nothing for him, claiming that he was on bad
terms with the editor, Turgan.[27] The *Constitutionnel* would
not publish any extracts until they had the completed
manuscript of the first book of tales, but Baudelaire had
not yet finished the translation. *Le Pays* kept him hanging
fire for six months before they gave him their decision,
and it was only in June 1854 that, thanks to the support
of Barbey d'Aurevilly, they granted him a contract. He
remained with them until April 1855. Although they interrupted his translations in October and November 1854,
while they serialized popular novels, he had completed with
them the publication of *Les Histoires Extraordinaires* by
April 1855. Whether his inability to find a permanent berth
on a paper for so long was due to his own fault or to circumstances is not clear. It was certainly his fault, aggravated
by poverty, which was responsible for the failure of the book

of translations to be published in January 1853 – it appeared finally only in 1856. He had found a publisher prepared to take the risk of launching the volume, but he lost the contract because he was unable to deliver the manuscript ready for press at the agreed time. Perhaps he had allowed himself to be diverted from translation by other work the previous year. On 21 October 1852 an advertisement in *La Presse* stated that the daily paper *Paris* was going to bring out the unpublished works of Gavarni, with a letterpress by various authors, amongst whom were Banville, Roger de Beauvoir, Dumas fils, the Goncourt brothers, and Baudelaire. Nothing further was ever heard about this text of Baudelaire.

Thus Baudelaire was not the first to bring out a volume of translations of Poe's tales but was anticipated by Alphonse Borghers, one of the contributors to *La Revue Britannique*, who published one in Hachette's collection, *La Bibliothèque des Chemins de Fer*, which was sold at railway stations, and which contained two of the tales. This volume was described and favourably reviewed by Gautier in *La Presse* on 5 September 1853.

For almost a year, when he was writing for *Le Pays*, Baudelaire worked with a diligence and energy which surprised all those who were used to his ways, and not only at translation but also at criticism which will be discussed later. The security of his contract as a regular contributor gave him the confidence which is reflected in his creative work.

This bout of energy did not last. In 1855 he could again have secured the publication of the book of tales, which was now ready, since all had been serialized, for Dutacq, who was on the board of directors of *Le Pays* and was at the same time a publisher, was anxious to obtain an option. Unfortunately Baudelaire quarrelled with the paper before the contract was signed, and this put an end to his association with the prospective publisher. He had been commissioned by the paper to write a series of articles describing the *Exposition des Beaux Arts* which was held that year,

and he had devoted an entire article to praise of Delacroix. This was a time when Delacroix was not in favour with
the public. The editor, claiming that Baudelaire had violated the terms of his contract, broke it, and engaged
someone else to finish the series. Incensed by this treatment,
Baudelaire left the paper and was once more without an
outlet for his writings. This was in 1855.

When Baudelaire's translations of Poe began to appear
in book form, they came out at close intervals. *Les Histoires Extraordinaires* was published in 1856, with his first
article revised and improved for Introduction. *Les Nouvelles
Histoires Extraordinaires* came out in 1857, with a new
notice on Poe entitled *Notes Nouvelles sur Poe*. *Les Aventures de Gordon Pym* was published in 1858, *Eureka* in 1863,
and *Histoires Grotesques et Sérieuses* in 1865. He had intended to write a further study on Poe, as a preface to one
of these last works, and to call it *Dernières Notes sur Poe*,
but this was never composed – or at all events never discovered, although later, when offering it to his publisher
along with the other articles on Poe, to make a substantial
contribution, he stated that he had left it with other papers
at his mother's house at Honfleur.[28]

It was through his translations of Poe that Baudelaire
earned whatever substantial sums of money he ever made,
and it is certain that during his lifetime his reputation with
the public rested chiefly, if not entirely, on this achievement. He himself always described himself proudly as the
translator of Edgar Allan Poe,[29] as if he considered this his
greatest claim to fame, and it was always urged in demands
for recognition for him. When the volumes of translations
began to appear, they sold more copies than any of his
other works, and they represented a steady, if small, source
of income until, during a time of great poverty in 1863, he
sold the rights to Michel Lévy for the sum of two thousand
francs – only eighty pounds. Before 1869, when the complete
edition of his works was published and the translations took
their place amongst his collected writings, the *Histoires*

Extraordinaires had run through six editions, the *Nouvelles Histoires Extraordinaires* four, and *Les Aventures de Gordon Pym* had reached its third printing.

Baudelaire made his own selection amongst Poe's tales, and established the order in which they were to be published. In a letter to Sainte-Beuve he explained the considerations which weighed with him. In the first volume he intended to attract the reader, to arouse his interest, to hand him a bait, and so it would contain what he called tricks, hoaxes and conjecture, and the only piece here which was morally linked with the second volume was *Ligeia*. The second volume would consist of material that was fantastic in the extreme – 'hallucinations, mental disease, the supernatural, and pure grotesque'.

To discuss the talent and achievement of Baudelaire as a translator would lead too far. At their best his translations are a classic of French prose. But he did not reach this standard from the outset. At first he made some blunders and mistranslations, but he improved in accuracy and knowledge of the language as he proceeded – this is noticeable if the earlier portions are compared with the latest – and also in fluency and ease of style.

As for his commentaries, the ideas they contain will be discussed in a later chapter when his aesthetic theories are analysed.

Baudelaire was not the first to translate Poe, but he achieved an excellence not reached hitherto, and his point of view towards his author was new and original. He placed Poe amongst the mystical writers and not amongst those who were the producers of literary tricks. In this he was different from poets who followed him, also devotees of Poe – Mallarmé and Valéry – who were not interested in this aspect of his work and genius.

Towards a New Aesthetic
1852 – 1854

BAUDELAIRE's attitude to Poe, and his conception of him, are symptomatic of his development at this time, as a thinker and an artist. His mind was increasingly turning towards philosophy and mysticism, and his interest in the American writer came to hasten his maturity at a critical stage in his psychological evolution. Poe became, as it were, the lay figure on which he draped his own aesthetic and spiritual conceptions, and much of what he imagined he discovered in Poe he found in reality in himself. It is at this time that philosophy became his chief preoccupation – or what he considered philosophy: a search for the explanation of the mystery of life, and particularly of the spiritual life hereafter. When he abandoned his interest in social reform and political causes, he turned towards religious thought, and the individual contemplation of eternity. 'There is nothing as interesting as religion,' he wrote.[1] He confessed to Poulet Malassis [2] that he cherished the ambition to write a metaphysical novel and that philosophy seemed to him now the only thing in life worthy of the attention of a poet and a spiritual being. We now see his philosophic – and later his aesthetic – beliefs being coloured by the theories of Swedenborg. Indeed the influence of Swedenborg affected even his interpretation of Poe, whom he saw as a solitary figure wandering and lost in a world of mystery and supernatural problems which he was trying to solve. This view is apparent in his first article on Poe, where he describes him as a man whose sole aim was to interpret the life to come. The article ends with a peroration, in the Swedenborgian manner, affirming that the poet's now purified and spiritual essence had soared amongst the beings whose existence he had perceived only dimly so long as he was bound by earthly fetters, but that he had now become an intercessor for the rest of struggling humanity. This interpretation of the writings of Poe, coupled with his view of the philosophy of Swedenborg, becomes the basis of Baudelaire's spiritual poems after 1852.

It is not known precisely when Baudelaire became acquainted with the philosophy of Swedenborg, but his works were translated and were well known to most writers from the beginning of the reign of Louis-Philippe.[3] Balzac especially was influenced by him, and Baudelaire greatly admired Balzac, saying that he had always been astonished that he passed for an observer when, on the contrary, he had always seemed to him a passionate visionary.[4]

Baudelaire's knowledge of the works of Swedenborg does not seem to have been deep, and it is likely that it was largely obtained from the three books which make up the *Livre Mystique* of Balzac – *Louis Lambert*, *Séraphita* and *Les Proscrits* – published together in one book in 1835. However, it is very probable that he also knew *Du Ciel et de l'Enfer* and the *Doctrine de la Nouvelle Jérusalem* by Swedenborg, since his ideas are very similar.

The first mention of the name of Swedenborg in Baudelaire's writings occurs in *La Fanfarlo*, published in January 1847, in which the hero is said to keep a volume of the Swedish philosopher as a bedside book. The name is barely mentioned and there is no attempt to suggest the nature of the philosophy and its effect on the hero.

La Fanfarlo came out the same year as Baudelaire first encountered the work of Poe. It is probable that the influence of the two writers worked on him in a subterranean way for some years, perhaps even without his realizing its full extent, until it finally came to fruition when, after the end of 1851, he turned to literature and religious preoccupations, disillusioned with politics and public life. He pro-

duced no critical works showing any influence of
Swedenborg, before the article on Poe, published in 1852.
There is no mention of any of the spiritual poems before
the publication of the article – not in the names of the
poems rumoured to have been composed before 1843; not
in the letter to Ancelle in January 1850; not in the letter to
Gautier in February or March 1852; not in the autograph
manuscript of that year, published in facsimile by Van
Bever; and not in the batch of poems published by *Le Messager de l'Assemblée* in April 1851. On this account, and
not for arbitrary reasons, the spiritual poems are here ascribed to this period, beginning with the Second Empire
and ending with the publication of *Les Fleurs du Mal* in
1857. Since most of the poems appeared for the first time
in that collection, it is not possible to give them unchal-
lengeable dates. Jean Pommier believes that *Correspondances*, because of the similarity between some of its ideas
and Baudelaire's *Salon* of 1846 and because Éliphas Lévi
had written a poem of the same title, must have been composed in 1846.[5] The poem is, however, not mentioned before
its publication, it was one of which the poet was particularly
fond and proud, and it seems, therefore, inconceivable that,
if it had been composed so early, he would not have sent it
to Gautier amongst the poems which he submitted for
publication in the *Revue de Paris*. In style it is very different from any poems which we know to have been written
before 1851, although its mood resembles that of poems
which were certainly composed later, such as *La Vie Antérieure*, or those inspired by Madame Sabatier, sent to her
between 1852 and 1854, such as *Harmonie du Soir*, for
instance.

Pommier, then, believes that the influence of Swedenborg
was profound in Baudelaire from the time of his *Salon* of
1846, but most of the texts of the poet which he uses as
proof – except the poem of doubtful date, *Correspondances*
– were written after 1851 : the article on Poe and the notice
on *L'Exposition Universelle* of 1855, the letter to Toussenel

1856, the *Notes Nouvelles sur Poe* 1857, and the *Paradis Artificiels* 1860, and so forth.

The period which opens in 1852, under the influence of Poe and Swedenborg, is the most actively productive in Baudelaire's life, and it continues, after the publication of his collection of poems, until his departure for Belgium in the spring of 1864, when his disease was reaching its acute and final stage, and when he wrote no new works.

The poems of this period express the essential and highest Baudelaire, the Baudelaire who had broken with both the realist and 'Art for Art's Sake' movements, and become a spiritual and philosophic poet, occupied with mysticism and the problem of sin. The poems which he composed then are the culmination of all that has preceded them, the highest point of his achievement, and his later work will only flow in the same channel, deepening it, but not altering its course.

Under the influence of Swedenborgian philosophy Baudelaire came to contemplate the world around him with new eyes. Swedenborgians are convinced that material objects exist in this world only because they have their origin in the world of the spirit, and the hidden relation between things here below and in the invisible world they call 'correspondences'. We cannot see the objects in the world of the spirit except indirectly through their worldly 'correspondences', through their symbols. Everything in this world is merely a symbol, and these symbols are the language of nature, a hieroglyphic language in which every material form expresses an idea, and this language existed long before the languages which human beings now speak were evolved. The philosopher is the man who can see beyond the concrete images, beyond the mere shell, into the heart of things. The true thinker will be the man who can decipher the hidden writings of nature, and interpret the mysterious book of the universe. Swedenborg said in *Divine Love* that hitherto the world had not known what 'correspondences' were because it was ignorant of the meaning of the spiritual.

When things which have their origin in the spiritual world
become perceptible to the senses, then there must be 'correspondence' between the spiritual and the natural, and the
same 'correspondence' exists between spiritual creatures and
man.

Swedenborg thought that the whole of the natural world
corresponded exactly to the spiritual world, not only conceived collectively, but in all its parts. Everything here
below is a hieroglyphic which it needs only a trained and
learned mind to decipher, though no man has yet existed
possessing the full wisdom to solve the riddle entirely. For
those who have learnt to interpret them, but to them alone,
telegraphic symbols are intelligible and they put the receiver of the message into direct and immediate contact
with an unseen personality, who can convey his message
only because the receiver has learnt to interpret the symbols by means of which he has transmitted his message. In
the same way the Swedenborgians believed that if we could
read the symbols before us we could come into direct contact with the deity, so that the meaning of the universe
would suddenly become clear to us, and we would recognize
the unity in its design, since we had come into intimate
relationship with the unseen mind behind it.

That, briefly put, is the spiritual doctrine which inspired
Baudelaire in the period beginning in 1852, when he became convinced that the first step towards direct contact
with the unseen mind was aspiration towards spiritual perfection, and the conscious development of spirituality. The
possibility of this spiritual aspiration in man was proof to
him of the divine spirit working through him.

Baudelaire at thirty appeared as a man whom no one had
yet suspected to exist, who had at last found himself after
wandering through many arid deserts, and trying many
ways of escape. Now, as he approaches middle age and
human passions begin to weaken, he wonders whether the
spiritual flowers of which he dreams will be able to take
root and blossom in the burnt-up soil which life has ravaged.

In a poem entitled *L'Ennemi,* published in June 1855, he writes: [6]

> *Ma jeunesse ne fut qu'un ténébreux orage,*
> *Traversé çà et là par de brillants soleils;*
> *Le tonnerre et la pluie ont fait un tel ravage,*
> *Qu'il reste en mon jardin bien peu de fruits vermeils.*
>
> *Voilà que j'ai touché à l'automne des idées,*
> *Et qu'il faut employer la pelle et les râteaux*
> *Pour rassembler à neuf les terres inondées,*
> *Où l'eau creuse des trous grands comme des tombeaux.*
>
> *Et qui sait si les fleurs nouvelles que je rêve*
> *Trouveront dans ce sol lavé comme une grève*
> *Le mystique aliment qui ferait leur vigueur?*
>
> *– O douleur! ô douleur! Le Temps mange la vie,*
> *Et l'obscur Ennemi qui nous ronge le cœur*
> *Du sang que nous perdons croît et se fortifie!*

If this spiritual aspiration were merely religious belief in Baudelaire, it would not deserve to be treated at length, since a poet's *ideas* are irrelevant, but it becomes one of his aesthetic beliefs and colours his view of the place and function of the poet in the scheme of things. God was a reality for the poet, and poetry, which he calls

'une aspiration vers une beauté supérieure, manifestée dans un enthousiasme et dans un soulèvement de l'âme',[7]

can only be the symbol, the imperfect image of eternal beauty, and the value of this imperfect image will depend on the degree of spiritual development of the poet. Genius for him was not the power of production, but the power of reception, and this receptive power was only possible in total forgetfulness of self, in the sacrifice of self. When the poet has thus become the channel for the voice of the Eternal, he can in some measure continue the work of the Creator; he can reveal, in visible signs, the beauty which he was permitted to behold. Great poets do not imitate slavishly what they have seen – indeed this would not be possible, from the very nature of their spiritual experience – but they transpose their vision into their own native idiom. This work of transposition is artistic composition. Baudelaire thought that only poets who had attained a high degree of spiritual awareness would be successful in finding the images, the analogies, and the metaphors, to render their vision. Poetry then becomes the living expression of the analogy existing between the world of the spirit and the world of matter.

'Tout est hiéroglyphique, et nous savons que les symboles ne sont obscurs que d'une manière relative, c'est à dire selon la pureté, la bonne volonté ou la clairvoyance native des âmes. Or qu'est-ce qu'un poète (je prends le mot dans son acception la plus large) si ce n'est un traducteur, un déchiffreur? Chez les excellents poètes il n'y a pas de métaphore, de comparaison ou d'épithète qui ne soit pas d'une adaptation mathématiquement exacte dans la circonstance actuelle, parce que ces comparaisons, ces métaphores et ces épithètes sont puisées dans l'inépuisable fonds de l'universelle analogie, et qu'elles ne peuvent être puisées ailleurs.'[8]

The spiritual aspect of Baudelaire's theory of poetry separates him from the other poets of the Art for Art's Sake movement, whose aesthetic ideas he had previously shared. They, on account of their lack of spiritual vision, their neglect of it at all events, tended to consider their ideal as not art for art's sake, but art for technique's sake.[9] In an article written at this time Baudelaire declared:[10]

'La puérile utopie de l'école de *l'art pour l'art*, en excluant la morale, et souvent même la passion, était nécessairement stérile. Elle se mettait en flagrante contravention avec le génie de l'humanité. Au nom des principes supérieurs qui constituent la vie universelle, nous avons le droit de la déclarer coupable d'hétérodoxie. Sans doute des littérateurs très-ingénieux, des antiquaires très-érudits, des versificateurs qui, il faut l'avouer, élevèrent la prosodie presque à la hauteur d'une création, furent mêlés à ce mouvement, et tirèrent des moyens qu'ils avaient mis en commun des effets très-surprenants.'

Baudelaire believed that artists, of whatever kind they might be, were links in a chain that united humanity with God. Artists, each in his different way, render the aspirations of humanity which – since man can rarely master inarticulateness – would otherwise remain unexpressed. They are also the interpreters of man to the Almighty, for they have learnt, often only dimly, to read the mysterious symbols of the world. They express man's despairing cry as he feels lost in the enveloping darkness, they are the 'appels de chasseurs perdus dans les grands bois'.[11] They are the beacons which light up humanity on its path through the darkness, kindled to help it with sympathy and comfort on its weary way towards eternity, and also to indicate to God that man is here, still waiting and suffering. All artists, in their various ways, give proof to Him of their struggles and longings to rise superior to the evil which drags their steps, and of their aspirations towards the beauty which they dimly perceive.

> *Ces malédictions, ces blasphèmes, ces plaintes,*
> *Ces extases, ces cris, ces pleurs, ces 'Te Deum',*
> *Sont un écho redit par mille labyrinthes;*
> *C'est pour les cœurs mortels un divin opium!*
>
> *C'est un cri répété par mille sentinelles,*
> *Un ordre renvoyé par mille porte-voix;*
> *C'est un phare allumé sur mille citadelles,*
> *Un appel de chasseurs perdus dans les grands bois!* [12]

Baudelaire thought that his part as intercessor for mankind gave the artist a privileged position, the highest in the scheme of things. In a poem, *Bénédiction*, he expresses the hope that, in Heaven, there will be a special place set apart for artists, to recompense them for the suffering which they endured in the world, since they saw clearly what others failed to see, the indignity and ugliness in the state of sin, because of their vision of spiritual beauty. He realized all this from his own experience, yet when he spoke of it no one listened to him, not even his own mother, for she failed to understand his dreams, but only saw her disappointment at his inability to become the worldly success which she could have admired. Earlier her misunderstanding had wounded him, but he now realized the function of the poet, and this belief gave him the courage to bear the sordid conditions of his life.

Suffering was a new lyric theme in nineteenth-century French poetry. Earlier Alfred de Vigny had exclaimed, 'J'aime la majesté des souffrances humaines', and had seen them as an injustice laid on man by a jealous God. Alfred de Musset had said, 'Rien ne nous rend si grands qu'une grande douleur'; while Éliphas Lévi, Baudelaire's friend, wrote a treatise on the value of suffering as a moral force, *Le Livre des Larmes*, published in 1845, which the poet must have known, and from which he drew some inspiration. Éliphas Lévi said, 'La douleur n'est donc pas un mal, mais un remède amer à tous nos maux' – Baudelaire calls it, in *Bénédiction*, 'un divin remède'. And again, 'Toute douleur morale est un pas vers la sagesse, toute douleur physique est un pas vers la mort et un avertissement des vanités de la vie. La misère et la maladie sont des remèdes à notre paresse sensuelle qui s'endort dans le bien-être matériel.' Further, 'À la tête de toutes les souffrances intérieures il faut placer cet horrible néant de l'âme qui, n'ayant rien, ne désire et ne regrette plus rien' and 'la douleur est le grand avertisseur des erreurs humaines.'

Baudelaire knew that suffering was the taskmaster who had ploughed up his nature to enrich it, to turn his thoughts towards spiritual truths which would have remained outside his experience otherwise. Suffering is the only coin which man possesses with which to pay for sin and vice, and he should be grateful that these means have been granted to him of settling his account.

> *– Soyez béni, mon Dieu, qui donnez la souffrance*
> *Comme un divin remède à nos impuretés*

> *Et comme la meilleure et la plus pure essence*
> *Qui prépare les forts aux saintes voluptés!*
>
> *Je sais que vous gardez une place au Poète*
> *Dans les rangs bienheureux des saintes Légions,*
> *Et que vous l'invitez à l'éternelle fête*
> *Des Trônes, des Vertus, des Dominations.*
>
> *Je sais que la douleur est la noblesse unique*
> *Où ne mordront jamais la terre et les enfers,*
> *Et qu'il faut pour tresser ma couronne mystique*
> *Imposer tous les temps et tous les univers.*[13]

He saw suffering also as the tribute which man pays to virtue, his awareness of his spiritual degradation, the surest proof of his human dignity.

> *Car c'est vraiment, Seigneur, le meilleur témoignage*
> *Que nous puissions donner de notre dignité*
> *Que cet ardent sanglot qui roule d' âge en âge*
> *Et vient mourir au bord de votre éternité.*[14]

Baudelaire did not merely draw on the doctrines of Swedenborg for inspiration and the subject matter for his poetry; he perceived, as well, the use which could be made of them in the realms even of technique, and this is one of the most original aspects of his art, destined to alter French poetry radically at the end of the century. In realizing the deep-lying connection which exists between all the arts, he guessed also the application which could be made of the doctrine of 'correspondences' in the technical aspect of poetic composition. Since art, in its totality, expresses experience of a spiritual nature – a vision – man's aspiration towards beauty; since art is merely the language in which this vision becomes concrete, then each of the arts renders, in its own particular language, using its own symbols, what it has perceived in the domain where there are no boundaries, or separation into individual arts, in the realm of truth and beauty. It follows, therefore, that it matters little in which of the arts the vision finally takes shape. This

theory of unity of Art was to become one of the main tenets
of the Symbolist Movement, and one of its most fruitful
aesthetic principles, though dangerous in inexperienced
hands. Symbolist art, whether it be music, painting, or
poetry, seeks to enter into contact with the beauty lying
behind the material objects 'behind the trembling of the
veil of the Temple' as Yeats says, believing that it is only
through the *Symbole* that it can give adequate expression
to the beauty it has perceived, which vanishes when one
tries to fix it in the material form of art, just as a dream
fades when one seeks to recall it on waking. The *Symbolistes*
believed, following Baudelaire, that it was vouchsafed to the
artist, when in a state of inspiration, to enjoy a complete
vision of beauty – that he entered into the *Inner Castle* of
Saint Teresa of Avila – but that the poem, symphony, or
picture, which was its outcome, could never be this reality
which their eyes had beheld, when the Heavens had parted
before their gaze, but only its imperfect image, its symbol.
André Gide has expressed this conviction very forcibly in
his *Traité du Narcisse*.[15]

'Les apparences sont imparfaites, elles balbutient les
vérités qu'elles recèlent; le poète, à demi-mot, doit comprendre, puis redire ces vérités…. Le poète qui sait qu'il
crée, devine à travers chaque chose, et une seule lui suffit,
symbole, pour révéler son archétype; il sait que l'apparence
n'en est que le prétexte, un vêtement qui le dérobe, et où
s'arrête l'œil profane, mais qui nous montre qu'elle est là.
Le poète pieux contemple; il se penche sur les symboles, et
silencieux descend profondément au cœur des choses. Et
quand il a perçu, visionnaire, l'Idée, l'intime Nombre har-
monieux de son Être, qui soutient la forme imparfaite, il
la saisit, puis, insoucieux de cette forme transitoire qui la
revêtait dans le temps, il sait lui donner une forme éternelle,
sa forme véritable enfin, fatale … paradisiaque et cristal-
line.'

As early as 1846, when he was composing his second
Salon, Baudelaire, after reading the translation of the

Kreisleriana of Hoffmann, had been struck by an ambition
to enrich art with the theories of the German writer. Hoffmann had declared that it was not only in a state of dreaming, or in that phase fraught with illusions which precedes
deep sleep, but also when fully awake, that whenever he
heard music he had often been struck by the existence of
the hidden and deep connection existing between colours,
sounds and perfumes. He was convinced that all these things
have been brought into existence by one and the same ray
of light, and that somewhere in infinity they all fused together to form the perfect harmony. The smell of deep red
carnations, he said, always had on him a strange effect;
whenever their perfume reached his nostrils, he would fall
into a state of reverie, and imagine he heard, coming out
of the distance, the low sound of a horn. He went on to
say – Baudelaire does not quote the passage, but he must
have known it – that it was no empty figure of speech when
a musician says that colours and scents reach his inner
consciousness in the form of sound. Physicists claim that
hearing is only inward seeing, and thus, for the musician,
hearing is only an inner, and to him more perfect, form of
seeing, a musical seeing. Thus a musician cannot fully perceive the sense of what he has seen until he has translated
it into his own idiom, the language of sound, until his ear
has transformed into a comprehensible thing for him what
his eye had registered in merely a mechanical way.

As well as the *Kreisleriana* of Hoffmann Baudelaire knew
other examples of early attempts at the use of 'correspondences'. He knew Sainte-Beuve's poem, *Les Rayons
Jaunes* from the collection *Les Poésies de Joseph Delorme*,
published in 1829, which is pure impressionism. He must
also have known Gautier's articles in *La Presse* in 1840, on
2 March, where he talked of dancing being 'de la mélodie
visible, et, si l'on peut parler ainsi, les jambes chantent très
harmonieusement pour les yeux', and on 7 November, where
he describes the opera *Lucrèce Borgia* as being 'vert poison';
and a further article in the same paper, on 10 July 1843,

where, describing the effects which hashish had on him, he
says that his hearing had become so acute that he was able
to hear the sounds of colours. Earlier, in 1836, Thoré, whom
Baudelaire was later to know, published his *Art des Parfums*, in which he claimed that 'avec les parfums on peut
exprimer toute la création aussi bien qu'avec des lignes
ou la couleur. Seulement la peinture et la sculpture repré-
sentent directement les objets ... tandis que les parfums,
comme la musique, réveillent l'intuition des choses.' And
later. 'Il s'agit de faire pour les odeurs ce qu'on a fait pour
les sons, de les hiérarchiser suivant une certaine gamme, de
les classer en tons et demi-tons, et quand vous aurez déter-
miné les parfums en notes, vous écrirez des *lettres en parfums*, comme M. Urham des lettres en *musique*, et vous
jouerez des drames, des comédies et même des vaudevilles
en parfums.' [16]

Thoré's ideas were later to be put into practice in November 1952, when perfume concerts, with the audience sitting
round a machine producing 'silent smell tunes', were
planned in Paris.[17] Étienne Souriau, a professor of aesthetics
at the Sorbonne and a Monsieur Fraenkel, a technical assis-
tant, invented the machine, and it was alleged that 'there is
no reason why smell-art lovers should not meet like music
lovers at a concert or art lovers at a picture gallery'. At
the meeting in Paris, Professor Souriau explained to a couple
of hundred perfume-makers that 'there is no reason why
hearing and seeing should be the only centres capable of
receiving great art, since a trained nose can detect several
thousand different perfumes'. He admitted that 'so far our
researches have not been able to produce a great perfume
symphony, but we can produce concert rhythms'. The
scent-makers were not convinced and Edmund Roudnicke,
'the perfume industries' chief philosopher', is alleged to
have said: 'The art of perfume is complete in itself; it has
its own melody. Professor Souriau's ideas are heretical.'

In 1845, before Baudelaire, another writer, Alphonse
Karr, made 'correspondences' between colours and abstract

qualities, between colours and musical instruments, between colours and perfumes, the subject of one of the letters of *Roger*.[18]

'Il y a pour moi, attachée aux odeurs, aux couleurs, une foule d'idées mystérieuses qu'il me serait à peu près impossible de définir, ou dont la définition me donnerait aux yeux de bien des gens tout l'art d'un rêveur à cervelle creuse. ... Les couleurs sont la musique des yeux : elles se combinent comme les notes, il y a sept couleurs comme il y a sept notes de musique, il y a des nuances comme il y a des demi-tons.'

He went on to give the impression he received from each colour, the sound he associated with it and the smell.

In his *Salon* of 1846 Baudelaire had seen only in a limited manner the use which could be made of Hoffmann's theory, but had not realized its full implications, for he only thought of a kind of 'audition colorée', and was merely concerned with the connection between colours and sounds. He had not yet conceived of the unity of all the arts. The idea had probably been working secretly within him, however, and linked on to the influence of Swedenborg and Poe, deepening it, so that, after what was in effect a spiritual revelation, he was able to apply it to his own creative works in the period when he gave expression to this new form of symbolism. It was only in 1855, when writing of the *Exposition Universelle*, that he finally elaborated the doctrine. At the same time he exemplified the theory in his poem entitled *Correspondances*, mentioned earlier in this chapter, which was to become the manifesto of the Symbolist Movement.

> *La nature est un temple où de vivants piliers*
> *Laissent parfois sortir de confuses paroles;*
> *L'homme y passe à travers des forêts de symboles*
> *Qui l'observent avec des regards familiers.*
>
> *Comme de longs échos qui de loin se confondent*
> *Dans une ténébreuse et profonde unité,*
> *Vaste comme la nuit et comme la clarté,*
> *Les parfums, les couleurs et les sons se répondent.*

Il est des parfums frais comme des chairs d'enfants,
Doux comme les hautbois, verts comme les prairies,
– Et d'autres, corrompus, riches et triomphants,

Ayant l'expansion des choses infinies,
Comme l'ambre, le musc, le benjoin, et l'encens,
Qui chantent les transports de l'esprit et des sens.[19]

To reach the total aspect of beauty Baudelaire drew on
the idioms of all the arts, and rendered what his eye had
seen, not solely in line and colour, and what his ear had
perceived, not merely in harmony, but glided imperceptibly
from one mode of expression to the other. Since 'les parfums, les couleurs et les sons se répondent', he could render
all the hues of the rainbow by means of harmony, all the
sounds of the scale by means of colour and line. This is one
of his great poetic triumphs and reveals the maturity of his
technique. By the finest gradations he could render infinite
shades of emotion which defy analysis. His highest achievement lay in conveying a spiritual and emotional state, rather
than in describing it – 'un état d'âme' the *Symbolistes* were
to say. It is this quality which gives his poems their musical
effect, which is independent from the mere harmony of the
actual words, for they are evocative in the same way as
music is. Pure description can suit one case only, but emotion
suggested may awaken other evocations, not connected with
the subject of the poem. What is seen is of little importance,
Baudelaire would say, since what we see has existence for us
only to the extent to which we feel it, and so it is the emotion
which he seeks to arouse in us, which will continue to extend
outwards, in ever increasing and widening circles.

His power of suggesting an emotional state, by varying
modes of expression, is seen at its most perfect in the *pantoum*, *Harmonie du Soir*, which he wrote inspired by
Madame Sabatier, and which does succeed in emulating the
evocative power of music. This poem, probably more than
any other of Baudelaire's, fulfils the ideals of the Symbolists
to 'décrire non la chose mais l'effet qu'elle produit' and 'le

suggérer, voilà le rêve', though few of them were able to reach such noble heights.

> *Voici venir les temps où, vibrant sur sa tige,*
> *Chaque fleur s'évapore ainsi qu'un encensoir;*
> *Les sons et les parfums tournent dans l'air du soir;*
> *Valse mélancolique et langoureux vertige!*
>
> *Chaque fleur s'évapore ainsi qu'un encensoir;*
> *Le violon frémit comme un cœur qu'on afflige;*
> *Valse mélancolique et langoureux vertige!*
> *Le ciel est triste et beau comme un grand reposoir.*
>
> *Le violon frémit comme un cœur qu'on afflige,*
> *Un cœur tendre qui hait le néant vaste et noir,*
> *Le ciel est triste et beau comme un grand reposoir;*
> *Le soleil s'est noyé dans son sang qui se fige . . .*
>
> *Un cœur tendre qui hait le néant vaste et noir,*
> *Du passé lumineux recueille tout vestige!*
> *Le soleil s'est noyé dans son sang qui se fige . . .*
> *Ton souvenir en moi luit comme un ostensoir* [20]

The spiritual poems of Baudelaire were not appreciated, and he was unable to publish them before they appeared in the complete volume of *Les Fleurs du Mal* in 1857. Even friends like Gautier and Sainte-Beuve, who professed to admire him, did not realize or understand the new quality which they contained. In the middle of the nineteenth century Baudelaire was considered by most poets, and the general public, as an erotic and satanic poet, attracted by the macabre elements in Poe. Gautier said condescendingly that he was a good fellow, but that he had a crack in him – 'une lésure' – while Sainte-Beuve spoke of him as 'mon petit ami libertin'.[21] They might enjoy his pessimistic poems, in the *spleen* mood, but what they most admired was his subversive attitude towards the Romantic School, and also towards the *École du Bon Sens*; and when they spoke of him with praise – which was not very often – it was chiefly to use his name as a weapon with which to batter down the self-satisfaction of the bourgeoisie. There were few to understand his new vein since there was nothing in it to startle or to shock, and the age was too deeply sunk in materialism and frivolity, or else too eager to 'épater le bourgeois', to appreciate at its true value the spiritual aspect of Baudelaire's art.

[6]

Solitude

1852

BAUDELAIRE was so completely changed in his new phase that his disordered life with Jeanne Duval became unendurable. She, for her part, was doing all in her power to irritate and exasperate him. During the early years of their relationship, in a foolish attempt to treat her as an equal, he had tried to educate her in order to make her a more interesting and stimulating companion, and also to fill her empty days with occupation, to save her from the accompaniments of boredom – drugs and drink. She had proved stupid and incapable of education, and had always expressed contempt for his interests and activities. This was especially painful to him during the time of his enthusiasm for Poe, when he could think and talk of nothing else, and needed sympathetic listeners. Jeanne Duval would show no sympathy, and was incapable of listening intelligently. Since he was so busy at that time he could not look after her, and she, having little to do, used to occupy herself with reading his correspondence, and going through his pockets and the drawers of his bureau, in search of material which she could use against him. She suspected him of lying when he told her that he had no money, for she could not believe it possible that the stepson of an ambassador, the intimate of kings, could be left in such penury. She recognized the writing of those who wrote to him, and opened his letters, especially if they were from his mother, to see if there was any money enclosed. If she found unfavourable references to herself – and these were frequent – she used to rail against him, saying that he did nothing to defend her, but allowed her to be insulted by everyone. To escape her vigilance and nagging, he was obliged to have his correspondence addressed care of his friends or else sent *poste restante* to the post office, for there was no place at his lodgings under lock and key where he could keep his property safe from her prying eyes. To him all this was a torture for, like most artists, he valued personal and spiritual privacy.

She was also cruel to him in trivial ways, sending away his cat, which was his greatest joy, and bringing dogs to the house because she knew that he hated them. She seemed totally uninterested in him and, as Baudelaire himself said naïvely, she did not admire him.[1]

He found it impossible to work regularly at home, and so, to obtain peace, he was obliged to seek the shelter of a café or a public library, and there he worked as long as it was open. Sometimes also he slept in the daytime in order to use the night for writing, while she was asleep, and he used to flee from the house as soon as she awoke.

They could not meet without quarrelling, and there was one terrible day, which he could not recall without terror, when, his endurance taxed beyond breaking point, the fierce anger of his youth had flared up, and he had struck her so that she fell, splitting her head open on the leg of a table. In a sudden flash he had realized with horror how small a thing can turn a man into a murderer, and he had fled from the room in terror of himself.

Sometimes, when home became unbearable, he used to take up his bag and escape to some hotel to evade, if only for a night, her glowering countenance and her angry voice. He lived in a constant state of exasperation, which made work an impossibility, and this induced a sensation of frustration at a moment when he needed all his energy for his new activities.

At last he came to the conclusion that he would never be able to achieve anything as long as he was tied to her, and that he must have peace at all costs. After weeks of torture and self-examination he decided to make the final break. He had not written to his mother for some months, always hoping that his situation would improve, and that he would be able to write to her with pride of achievement. That day had, however, not yet dawned!

Now that he had determined on the parting, he realized that she and her husband, who had never approved of his relationship with Jeanne Duval, would not be displeased at the final cutting of the knot, and the thought of this humiliated him.

Finally he decided to write to his mother, to tell her of his decision, and his letter, written in rage and disappointment, is a pathetic document voicing the disillusionment and broken hopes of a noble nature. Only someone like Baudelaire would have persevered in hoping for ten years, in spite of frequent proofs to the contrary, that he would ever make of Jeanne Duval an intelligent companion. He composed his letter, sitting at a table in a café, while hearing the rhythmical tap of billiard balls near him, and the sound of the merriment of all those around him.[2]

'It's two o'clock in the afternoon, and if I want my letter to leave today I've only two and a half hours left, and I've masses of things to say. I'm writing in a café near the G.P.O., in the midst of the noise of billiards and cards, in order to have peace, and the possibility of undisturbed thought. You'll understand all this when I've finished writing.

'How could it happen that in nine months I couldn't find the time to write to my mother? It's truly astounding! Yet every day I think of it, and every day I say to myself: I'll write today! And the days get frittered away in a mass of fruitless expeditions, or in the composing of a lot of morbid articles, hurriedly put together, in order to earn a little money.

'My letter will be confused – that's the inevitable consequence of the state of mind I'm in, and also of the short time at my disposal. I'll divide it into sections according as I remember some of the more important things I've got to tell you, and which I've been turning over in my mind for a long time.

'Jeanne has become an obstacle, not only to my personal happiness, which would be a trifle – I too am capable of sacrificing my pleasures, as I've frequently proved – but also to the cultivation of my mind. These last nine months have been a decisive experiment. The great duties I've got to accomplish – payment of my debts, making a fortune, winning fame, amends for all the pain I've caused you – all these can never be achieved in such conditions. Once upon a time she possessed some qualities, but she's lost them all, or else I've become more clear-sighted. I ask you is it possible to live with a creature who has no kind of gratitude for all your efforts, who hinders them through endless malice or stupidity, who considers you only as her servant or her slave, her property, with whom it's impossible to exchange a single word on politics or literature, a creature who refuses to learn anything even though you've offered to teach her yourself, a creature who doesn't even think anything of me, and isn't interested in my work, who would fling my manuscripts into the fire if that would bring her more money than allowing them to be published, who sends away my cat which was my only joy at home, and brings in a dog just because the very sight of dogs displeases me. Who can't, or won't, understand that to be able to be mean, even for one month, would permit me to finish a long book thanks to this temporary respite. I ask you is it possible, is it possible, to endure all that? I've tears of rage and shame in my eyes as I write all this to you. And indeed I'm very glad that I've no fire-arms at home, for I often think of what would happen if I became suddenly unable to control myself, and I remember the awful night when I split her head open against the leg of a table.

'This is all I've found where, ten years ago, I imagined I'd find peace and rest. ... But I had to come to a decision! I've been pondering on it for four months! but what was I to do? My pride was even stronger than my suffering, and I didn't want to leave this woman without giving her a substantial sum of money. But where was I to find it? The money I was earning was being frittered away in current expenses from day to day. I'd have had to save up for that. My mother, to whom I didn't even dare write since I'd nothing good to tell her, couldn't lend me this sum of money, since she hadn't got it herself. You see I've thought out everything carefully, and yet I must leave her. I *must* leave her for ever!'

He then explained to her what he intended to do, the plan he had been hatching for several months. His main concern was that he must leave Jeanne Duval immediately and for ever. And, since he was unable to give her a substantial sum of money with which to provide for her future, in order to close the relationship as befitted an honourable man, he decided that he would henceforth pay her a monthly allowance out of what he earned. This was a fatal plan since it ensured that she would still be in his life, even if not living under the same roof, and a constant preoccupation to him as a recurring obligation which must always be settled immediately. She would also always know where to find him with her incessant demands for money. However, at that moment, he imagined that he would be able to be firm, and he swore to his mother that he would never see her again, and that she might go to Hell for all he cared.

'I've wasted ten years of my life in the struggle,' he added,[3] 'all the illusions of my youth are gone, and there is nothing left in me but bitterness which will perhaps endure for ever!'

Baudelaire left Jeanne Duval in April 1852, but the peace of mind which he had hoped and expected, did not descend on him. Temperamentally he was incapable of living without the society of women. He may have professed to despise them, but he could not do without them, and in the depths of his heart, though he would not admit it, he considered man as only a poor and coarse substitute. He found it necessary for his spiritual well-being to live amongst women. Merely by their presence they inspired him, and he felt it the highest form of happiness to be permitted to live in the shadow of the woman he loved, asking nothing in return, 'comme aux pieds d'une reine un chat voluptueux'.[4] It was delight for him to watch them as they sat combing their long hair, to see the graceful movements of their white arms as they moved backwards and forwards, in slow rhythm, and to smell the faint perfume of their powder and scent. He liked to gaze at their clothes set out ready for wear, to feel the soft texture of the silks and satins, and revel in the bright colours. He delighted in the billowy flimsy undergarments, as light as the foam of the sea. It was this feminine atmosphere that he needed more than physical possession. It may have been that each time he met a beautiful woman, who touched his imagination and senses, who was kind to him, he imagined that here was the woman amongst all others whom he could really love, and who would be to him all that he had dreamed. But, when he was in her presence, fear would seize hold of him once more, and the dread of failure, fear also that she might laugh at him and make a mock of him. Women, he thought, particularly young strong women, full of life and energy, were cruel and insatiable, '*quaerens quem devoret*' as he once wrote on a drawing he made of a beautiful, dark woman, probably Jeanne Duval. And so, to save himself humiliation, he pretended that all he wished was to be near them without asking anything further. With them he was witty and amusing, and because of that many clever society women were his close friends, and delighted in his company. He was a brilliant conversationalist, especially with women, and he charmed and stimulated them by his paradoxes. It is wiser, he used to say, never to possess happiness completely, since the regret for what might have been is sweeter than realization and success; or again, that desire for the unattainable keeps the heart eternally young. His woman friends would then clap their hands and smile, thinking how amusing Charles Baudelaire could be, and how there was never a dull moment if he were there, for he was unlike their husbands and lovers who could talk of nothing but the making of money, or politics.[5] They did not, however, guess the suffering that was hidden behind the witty speeches, nor the anguish that he often endured, when he was alone and felt the hunger and need for love and understanding. To hide his distress he built up amongst his friends the reputation of a man who hated love and despised women, who was sufficient to himself. This personality, which he deliberately forged for himself, became a steel armour riveted to his body, a mask clamped to his face, which he was now obliged to wear to the day of his death. He was solitary and alone, a shrinking figure inside his glorious shining armour. Since he was cut off from the kind of woman whom he could have loved, through the lie he was living, he turned to prostitutes for comfort, or else in human sympathy, to those who, for other reasons than his own, were also cut off from normal love. To these outcasts, he gave compassion and understanding.[6] His friends say that he was frequently to be seen amongst the whores in cafés and bars, that he used to drift amongst them, looking, as if in envy, at those whom he saw seated with them at the tables, laughing and happy together. He used to wander from bar to bar, late at night, unable to make up his mind to go home, and seeing others seemingly happy in their love as he contemplated his own loneliness, dark melancholy would settle on him. He himself rarely spoke to them, but they knew him well by sight, the man with the sinister expression who prowled about the cafés in the late hours, or sat alone at a table drinking; the man who haunted the *promenoir* at the Folies Bergère, watching the couples pass and thinking, as he saw each girl, that here was one whom he could love. Nadar says that Baudelaire often went with him and his friends there, or to the Casino Cadet, but that no one had ever seen him make a choice and go off with one of the women.[7] It was surely on such an evening that he conceived the poem, *A une Passante*.[8]

> *La rue assourdissante autour de moi hurlait.*
> *Longue, mince, en grand deuil, douleur majestueuse,*

Une femme passa, d'une main fastueuse
Soulevant, balançant le feston et l'ourlet;

Agile et noble, avec sa jambe de statue,
Moi je buvais, crispé comme un extravagant,
Dans son œil, ciel livide où germe l'ouragan,
La douceur qui fascine et le plaisir qui tue.

Un éclair . . . puis la nuit! – Fugitive beauté
Dont le regard m'a fait soudainement renaître,
Ne te verrai-je plus que dans l'éternité?

Ailleurs, bien loin d'ici! trop tard! jamais peut-être!
Car j'ignore où tu fuis, tu ne sais où je vais,
O toi que j'eusse aimée, ô toi qui le savais!

Seeking someone whom he could love, who would take
Jeanne Duval's place in his life, and on whom he could
lavish the overflow of his affection, who would make him
believe in himself, his choice fell on Marie Daubrun, and to
her he wrote the famous letter addressed to Madame Marie,
the recipient of which was for a long time a mystery. It is
not known where this letter remained hidden for so many
years, nor how it eventually came to light, and where it is
now. It was at first thought that she was an artist's model
in one of the studios which he visited, for he mentions in
the letter that she has been posing, though she may only
have been sitting for her portrait. Albert Feuillerat has,
however, now proved that the recipient of the letter was
Marie Daubrun, the actress, who some years later inspired
several of the poems from *Les Fleurs du Mal*, and for whom
he attempted to write plays.[9] The letter is undated and,
when it was first published in the poet's collected letters,
it was attributed to the year 1852. The edition has no notes
but the editor must have had some valid grounds for this
attribution. Feuillerat, however, believes that the letter was
written in 1847, and one of his main arguments is based on
the supposition that she may have been painted by Deroy,
who was Baudelaire's friend, and who died in 1848. The
poet, however, knew many painters and, since he had be-

come an art critic, visited many studios where he could have met her. Moreover, since she was a well-known actress, as well as beautiful, there were probably many artists who would have wished to paint her portrait. Crépet, the editor of the *Correspondance Générale* of Baudelaire, has accepted the arguments of Feuillerat, and has published the letter under the year 1847, after one dated 16 December. At the end of the letter in question Baudelaire has given his address as '15 Cité d'Orléans', and Feuillerat suggests that this may have been where he was living in 1847 since there is little information about him at that time.[10] But Baudelaire, who rarely gives his address in his correspondence, happens to tell his mother, when writing to her on 8 December 1847, that he is living at 36 rue de Babylone. There is no evidence that he was not still living there at the end of the month for, in later letters – 16 December 1847 and 2 January 1848 – he does not mention having moved, and he would undoubtedly have done so to his mother as they were not meeting then, and he thought it necessary to give her his address on 8 December. For 1852, on the contrary, after he left Jeanne Duval in April, we have no definite address for him until the one he gives in a letter dated 13 October, as 60 rue Pigalle.

When telling his mother, at the end of March 1852, that he was about to leave Jeanne Duval, he said that he was going to live, as a paying guest, with a doctor of his acquaintance – probably Doctor Pigeaire. If he did go to him he cannot have stayed very long, for in May he addressed a letter to Champfleury at the same address, which he would not have needed to do if he had also been living there. Between leaving his mistress in April 1852 and settling in the Rue Pigalle some time before October, he may well have been living in the Cité d'Orléans as we have no address for that period.

A further argument against attributing the letter to December 1847 is that it is signed 'Charles Baudelaire', whereas between the appointment of his *conseil judiciaire* in

1844 until some time in 1849, he always signed himself
'Charles Baudelaire Dufayis – or Defayis'.

For these reasons, there seem no adequate grounds for
doubting that the letter was written in 1852, as was formerly
believed. The most probable time for it to have been written
was either in May or September. Feuillerat shows that Marie
Daubrun was in Brussels between June and September
1852,[11] and it is known that, some time during the last few
months of the year, she became Banville's mistress.[12] A
previous mistress had just left him, and he turned for consolation to the actress. The first indication of this was in a
favourable review that he wrote on her performance as La
Duchesse de Chevreuse in a play entitled *Richelieu* by
Félix Peillon, which opened in October, and later, in December, he gave her the part of the 'Muse du Théâtre' in a
comedy called *Le Feuilleton d'Aristophane*, which he wrote
in conjunction with Philoxène Boyer.[13]

It is thought that it was in October that Banville and
Marie Daubrun became interested in each other. This may
explain the coldness which existed between him and Baudelaire in 1852, while their reconciliation in December[14]
may have been due to the fact that by then the latter had
become resigned to his lack of success with the actress, and
that he had turned his thoughts – perhaps on the rebound –
to Madame Sabatier, whom he addresses with the same
expressions which he had already used with so little effect
on Marie Daubrun.

In this letter, whenever it was written, Baudelaire expresses
a boyish worship which strikes a strange note when it is
remembered the kind of life he had been leading for five
or ten years. It was as if his spiritual crisis, and his separation from Jeanne Duval, had given him a new virginity,
and he was reacting against the sensual pleasures which he
had enjoyed with her. Now, like a boy, he begs the woman
whom he worships not to abandon him, promising to be
good henceforth, and not to importune her. It all breathes
innocence and purity, and it shows that those who are fun-

damentally pure of heart, cannot be corrupted by the life they lead, or even perhaps by their actions.

'Madame,' wrote Baudelaire,[15] 'Is it possible that I may not see you again? That is the vital question for me, as I've reached the point where your mere absence is a terrible deprivation for me. When I heard that you were giving up posing and that I was the unwitting cause of this, I felt strangely sad. I've wanted to write to you, although I'm not much in favour of letters; one regrets them nearly always. But I risk nothing since my mind is firmly made up to devote myself to you for ever.

'Do you know that our long conversation of last Thursday was very curious indeed? It's that conversation which has left me in a new frame of mind, and which is the reason of this letter. Wasn't that situation peculiar? – A man says "I love you!" and a woman answers "Me? Love you? Never! One man alone has my love, and woe betide the man who came after him, for he would receive only my indifference and my contempt."

'And that same man, merely to have the pleasure of gazing for a few moments into your eyes, allowed you to speak of another man, and of him alone, allowed you to grow passionate as you thought and talked of him. These confidences which we exchanged had a curious effect on me. You're no longer merely a woman whom one desires, but a woman whom one loves for her frankness, for her passion, for her youth, vitality and her wildnesss.

'I've lost a great deal through these explanations, since you were so positive and definite that I was obliged to submit immediately. But you, Madame, you've greatly gained since you've inspired in me deep esteem and respect. Remain for ever thus, and keep it safe, this passion which makes you so beautiful and so happy!

'But return to me, I implore you, and I'll become gentle and humble in all my desires. I deserved your contempt when I said that I'd be satisfied with your crumbs! I was however lying! Oh! if you only knew how beautiful you

were that evening! I didn't dare pay you any compliments –
all that is so commonplace! But oh! your eyes, your lips,
and now, as I close my eyes, I seem to see your person in
living flesh and blood before me. And oh! I feel that this
is final!

'But return to me, I implore you on my bended knees! I
don't say that you'll find me devoid of love; you'll never be
able to prevent my imagination from playing round your
arms, your beautiful hands and your eyes where all your
vitality is concentrated, nor round the whole of your adorable human personality – no you won't be able to prevent
that! But don't fear! You're for me an object of worship and
it would be impossible for me to defile you. Your whole
being is so gentle, so beautiful, the very air you breathe is
sweet!

'You symbolize for me life and movement, not so much
on account of your vivacity and mobility, or of the wild side
of your nature, as on account of your eyes which can inspire
only immortal love. How could I ever convey to you how
much I love your eyes and how much I appreciate your
beauty? It has in it two contradictory forms of grace, which,
however, don't clash in you – they are the grace of a child
and the grace of a woman. Oh! believe me when I tell you
from the bottom of my heart that you are a charming
creature and that I love you deeply. It is a pure feeling
which binds me for ever to you. In spite of your wish, you'll
be henceforth for me my talisman and my strength. I love
you, Marie! There is no doubt about that! But the love
which I feel for you is the love of a Christian for his God;
and don't ascribe so worldly a name, and so often associated
with shame, to the mysterious and immaterial worship, to
the chaste and sweet feeling which binds my soul to yours
against your will. That would indeed be sacrilege!

'I was dead and you gave me life once more! Oh! if you
only knew how much I owe to you! I've drawn from the
deep well of your pure eyes joys that I'd never even dreamt
of! Your eyes have taught me the happiness of the soul in

its most perfect and delicate form. You are henceforth my only queen, my passion and my beauty! You are that portion of my being which a spiritual essence has shaped!

'Through you, Marie, I'll be great and strong! Like Petrarch I'll immortalize my own Laura! Be my guardian angel, my muse and my Madonna, and lead me in the path towards beauty!

'Deign to answer me one single word, I implore you, one single word! There are, in the life of every human being, obscure and yet decisive days, when an expression of friendship, a glance, a few hastily scribbled words, may drive one towards madness or distraction! I swear to you that I've reached that point! One word from you will be the thing twice blest which one looks at incessantly, which one learns by heart! If you only knew how much you are beloved! See, I'm kneeling before you, say but one word. But you'll never say it!

'He is indeed happy, a thousand times happy, the man whom you've chosen amongst all others, you so full of wisdom and beauty, so full of many talents, wit and heart, so infinitely desirable! What woman could ever take your place? I don't dare crave a visit — you'd only refuse it! I prefer to wait! I'll wait for years, and when you'll see that you're loved so stubbornly, though with deep respect, and with the completest self-effacement, you'll remember then that you had begun by ill-treating me, and you'll admit that it wasn't kind! But I'm not free to refuse the blows which it shall please my idol to give me! You've been pleased to dismiss me, and I'm pleased to worship you! That point is settled!'

Perhaps this letter was written even as late in 1852 as October, and perhaps the man referred to is Banville.

Marie Daubrun did not understand, she did not return his love and she allowed him to depart. Perhaps she considered his letter unbalanced, hysterical, affected or insincere, and was afraid of friendship with a man so unlike those whom she usually met. Perhaps she found it difficult, with her temperament, to sustain the position of an idol, and, moreover, few women find attractive the position of a saint in a gilded shrine. Whatever may be the reason, she did not respond and he was left with his heart as empty of love as ever and craving for sympathy and understanding.

During all that time he was very lonely and unhappy. There was no one to whom he could talk, for he had separated from his mistress, and his mother was in Madrid. Her letters to him were no consolation for, instead of comfort, they were full of reproaches and inquiries about the progress of the works the publication of which he had several times announced to her. She had hoped that, after his separation from Jeanne Duval, to whom she had ascribed his failure during the previous years, he would show signs of reform, but there was no change that she could see. When her letters arrived he no longer opened them with joy and excitement, but sometimes carried them round for weeks unopened in his pocket – even months at times – not daring to read her reproaches. The sight of her writing was beginning to have the same paralysing effect on him as the writing of those creditors whose letters were full of threats, and demands for payment.[16]

Baudelaire now found that he could not shake off, in a night, the evil habits of idleness established during ten years. Months slipped by without his having any good news to announce to his mother, and so he did not write though, in imagination, he composed many letters which pride forbade him to commit to paper, for he had made a vow not to write again until he had something good to tell her.[17] Each day he hoped that he might be able to inform her that he was now out of the wood, but it was a vain hope. He would have liked her to be able to speak of him to her husband, without apologies, without being obliged to make allowances for him, but, in spite of hard work, he had not yet found a paper prepared to give him a contract. He made the unsuccessful attempts at independent journalism mentioned in the previous chapter, and he himself was to blame

– or his circumstances – for the failure of his book of translations to appear in January 1853.[18] His completed manuscript
of *Les Histoires Extraordinaires* was to have been handed
in by January 1853, but, already in the previous October,
he saw clearly that he would be unable to fulfil his contract,
and might run the risk of losing it completely through his
inability to keep his side of the bargain,[19] on account of the
disorder of his life. Shortly after his separation from Jeanne
Duval, in April 1852, he had taken lodgings somewhere –
perhaps at the Cité d'Orléans – but soon he took such a
violent dislike to his landlady that he felt that he could not
live another night under her roof, and one day he left the
house not to return. Unfortunately he omitted to inform
her of his decision, and to tell her not to keep the room for
him – he disliked encounters with people over money matters, and he had probably intended writing to her after he
left, but had forgotten, or postponed doing it. Weeks later
he sent for his books and papers which he now needed, but
the landlady would not relinquish them until he had paid
the rent for all the weeks since he had left, for she pretended
not to have known that he intended to vacate the room. As
usual he had no money to do this, but he needed his books
and papers urgently since his translations of Poe were
amongst them, and he could not finish the volume without
them. He tried to buy further books on credit, but some of
them could no longer be procured, and in desperation he
hurriedly bungled the translations which were due to appear, sent them in and received payment for the work. When
he saw it in proof he was seized with scruples, and his sense
of perfection was so horrified at the carelessness of the production that he scrapped the type, and was obliged to defray
the costs out of his own pocket. In the meantime, he had
spent the money he had received in payment, and was unable to reimburse his publisher. Besides losing his contract,
he had the added mortification and humiliation of realizing
that Lecou considered him unscrupulous.[20] He had, moreover, planned to send his stepfather a finely bound copy of

this, his first important publication, as an olive branch, and pledge of his esteem. Now the General would never know of his intention.

This was not the end of his misfortunes. He had also received two hundred francs from the *Revue de Paris* as an advance on an article dealing with the art of caricature, but the notes and illustrations for it also had remained in his lodgings with the rest of his papers, and he could not retrieve them. This closed the *Revue de Paris* to him as Maxime Du Camp, the editor, who at the best of times did not hold a good opinion of him, now considered that his conduct was only on a par with what he had previously heard of his reputation. Baudelaire fell once more into despair and pessimism, and began to think that he would perhaps never be able to breast the tide of misfortune, that his predicament was hopeless.

'What's going to happen to me?' he wrote to his mother. 'What on earth is going to happen to me? Sometimes I long to sleep for ever, but I can't sleep for I'm always thinking!'

He was still living in great poverty and, all that winter, he who always suffered very much from the cold could afford no fire and used to sit writing with his fingers cramped and frozen. His clothes also had become so threadbare that he was often afraid that they would fall to pieces if he moved. Then, one day, reading in the Court Circular the movements of ambassadors abroad, he saw a paragraph praising his mother's generosity to the poor in Madrid, saying that they would regret and miss her when she returned home. He could not restrain a momentary feeling of anger and jealousy as he read the praise, for he considered that he himself was one of the poor who needed her ministrations most strongly, and yet she allowed him to remain in destitution.

She, on her side, was not at all happy in her mind on his account, as she gave charity to others, for she could not efface from her memory the picture she had of him on her return to Paris the previous year, his look of poverty and suffering. Her heart had been wrung to see him looking so shabby, ill-fed and uncared-for – he had seemed to her a failure, a '*raté*'. She had remembered then all that she had read about the Bohemian artists and men of letters, of their tragic fates, and wondered whether her only child was perhaps to end like that. She was afraid that he might be deteriorating physically, becoming careless about his appearance, for his revolutionary friends in 1848 as she remembered them – and those of his student days – had seemed to her unkempt and unwashed. She could not unburden herself to her husband of these homely fears, and so could not resist mentioning them to her son when she wrote to him, but to him this was the greatest insult of all, that she should confuse him with the riff-raff of Bohemia, and imagine him capable of sinking so low. He asked her how she was not ashamed of even conceiving the idea of any degradation in his person – 'l'avilissement de ma personne' as he said. He was known amongst his friends for the meticulous care which he bestowed on his personal appearance, and he explained to her scornfully that no matter how strained were his financial means, and whether he was dressed in fine clothes or in rags, he spent, and would always spend, two whole hours each day at his toilet.

However, time was flying fast, and he was no nearer solving his problems.

The White Venus
1852 — 1854

DISAPPOINTED in his love for Marie Daubrun, Baudelaire remained as lonely as ever, still hungry for affection. It was then that he looked at Madame Sabatier with new eyes, and seemed to see her for the first time, thinking to find in her deliverance from his longings. He had known her now for many years, without being very intimate with her, since the days when he had first seen her at Fernand Boissard's rooms in the Hôtel Lauzun, after he himself had left the Île-Saint-Louis. Madame Sabatier had been the constant guest at the apartments of some one or other of the group of artists who had made their home there, since the day, now many years ago, when Roger de Beauvoir, with Musset, Arago, and the banker Mosselmann, had seen her from his balcony window, coming from the public baths, at the other side of the river, her brilliant hair shining in the sunlight. 'What a beautiful girl!' said Musset, leaning over the balcony, to see her better. 'Why not ask her up for a drink, she must be thirsty,' said Mosselmann, who was always practical as befitted a banker. 'A very good idea!' cried Roger de Beauvoir, who was the host, and ran down forthwith to catch her up before she went too far. The girl had beautiful copper-coloured hair, now hanging down over her shoulders, damp after her swim, and glinting in the sunlight. This was Apollonie Aglaé Sabatier whom Mosselmann was soon afterwards to make his mistress, and to install in a comfortable furnished flat in the Rue Frochot where, on Sundays, it was her custom to entertain her intimate friends – poets and artists – whom she had met at Boissard's parties.[1] This was the story. It has been alleged, however, that this romantic tale is fictitious,[2] and that she first met Alfred Mosselmann when she was singing at a charity concert, where he was one of the patrons. He was struck by her beauty, and determined to make her his mistress. Perhaps also he was moved by her singing, for she had a pleasant soprano voice, and used to sing Mozart and romances by Auber with much talent and grace, as Gautier said in a notice of her concert.[3]

Madame Sabatier was a year younger than Baudelaire, for she was born in April 1822, the daughter of a sempstress called Léa Marguerite Martin, whom the Préfet des Ardennes Harmand, seduced and made pregnant. He was made a viscount by Louis XVIII in 1822, then calling himself Harmand d'Abancourt, and did not want to burden himself with a woman with two illegitimate children; so, by means of a substantial dowry, he got her married off to a sergeant who had won the cross of *Chevalier de la Légion d'Honneur* on the battlefield in 1813. He recognized the paternity of Aglaé, and she was called Aglaé Josephine Savatier. Later she took the name of Apollonie, by which she was always known, and changed Savatier to Sabatier, on the grounds of euphonism.

Madame Sabatier – as she later called herself although she was not married – was a lovely woman, of beautiful proportions, with slender ankles and wrists, and her hair was like burnished copper, with golden glints wherever it caught the light, falling in soft curls and silken waves round her face. She had the fresh pink and white complexion which usually accompanies auburn hair, and her cheeks did not need rouge to enhance their brilliance, while her eyes always sparkled with a mischievous look, and her lips seemed unable to refrain from curling into a smile of roguish amusement. It was in praise of her that Gautier wrote *À une Robe Rose*, and *J'aime ton nom d'Apollonie*. Her friends used to say that nature had formed her for the express purpose of serving as a model for a sculptor or a painter, and she amply fulfilled her destiny, for most of the artists of her time left pictures or statues of her. The sculptor Clésinger had seen her once at a fancy-dress ball given by Roger de Beauvoir, in the more or less undraped state which an artists' ball permitted, and had asked for permission to make a bust of her. It was she who served as a model for his composition, *La Femme Piquée par un Serpent*, which created a sensation and a scandal when it was shown at the *Salon* in 1847. It was the most popular – or notorious – exhibit of that year, and crowds were always to be seen near it, for it gave rise to much discussion and controversy. Prudish critics and members of the public took exception to it on account of what they called its purely sensual appeal. They said that the name was only the pretext for pornography, since the serpent played only a supernumerary part in the composition, and that it was the effects not of poison, they claimed, which were seen in the expression of the woman, but the throes of an orgasm. Adverse criticism may have been due to the opposition of the 'forties and 'fifties to the new realism which was beginning to invade art, and certainly the woman in *La Femme Piquée par un Serpent* was far from resembling the conventional nude, for she was not a goddess, a nymph or a dryad, but a human woman of flesh and blood, obviously capable of the same passions as ordinary mortals.

Apollonie was also exhibited in the *Salon* of 1851, painted by Ricard and described by Gautier in his article in *La Presse* on 8 April 1851.

Madame Sabatier was one of the famous beauties of the Second Empire, and she was known by everyone in the artistic world. She was celebrated not only for her beauty but for the elegance of her clothes and for the kindness of her heart, and it was said that everywhere she went she brought happiness and joy. Certainly her personal charm made her apartment at the Rue Frochot the meeting-place of all the most interesting people in the literary and artistic world. She received at her Sunday parties, as well as Baudelaire and Gautier, Barbey d'Aurevilly, Du Camp, Clésinger, Meissonier, and the ubiquitous Ernest Feydeau. The women guests were in a minority. There were Adèle – called Bébé, her young sister, twelve years her junior – Sizina Neri, and Ernesta Grisi, Gautier's mistress, whom the other guests called his 'compagne morganatique'.

Madame Sabatier had many friends because, unlike most other beauties of the day, she did not demand constant attention for herself, nor did she expect all men to make love to her. They felt at ease with her since they could relax in her presence, and discuss serious problems without boring her, or fearing she might turn the conversation to trivial or personal matters. For an acknowledged and professional beauty she was singularly lacking in consciousness of self. Moreover she was not prudish, and permitted great freedom of language in her presence, and of subjects discussed, for she did not feel responsible for the morality and behaviour of her guests. Nor did she expect any particular kind of conversation or conduct as a necessary tribute to her feminine or personal dignity and modesty. Very often at her Sunday parties there was much coarse – and even lewd – talk, especially if Gautier were present, for the licence of his conversation was proverbial amongst his friends, if he felt at ease and was not afraid of shocking the susceptibilities of those present. The letters which he wrote to her, when he was absent from Paris, are so pornographic and bawdy that they are impossible to quote without becoming liable to prosecution for obscenity.[4] They form a striking contrast to those which Baudelaire wrote to her during the same period.

In everything written about her Madame Sabatier appears as a large-hearted woman who succeeded in making her friends at home by her warm sympathy and by her interest in their smallest concerns, and also because she did not feel it necessary to mould them, or to alter them in any way. She had courage, as well as charm, and she did not bewail her fate when her fortunes changed and she was left with little or nothing, but bore her poverty with fortitude, good humour and philosophic calm. In the season of her splendour she had been open-handed with her friends and had saved nothing for a rainy day, so that, for a time, she was as poor as when she had started. In middle age, when her beauty faded and she could no longer command the same attention – especially the same financial attention – she could not afford to lead a life of luxury, and she was obliged to sell her furniture and her works of art, and to dress more simply. She did not lose heart, but bore her reverses with unfailing good humour and, even in defeat, kept the proud and triumphant air which was her greatest charm when she was young.[5] With the few relics of her past luxury which she managed to save from the auction of her effects in 1864, she furnished a tiny flat and, in spite of straitened means, her new home kept an air of elegance and comfort. There she lived and entertained her friends with the same generosity as before. She, who had been accustomed to be served by others, now did her own housework, but with gaiety, and her friends used to hear her laugh and sing, as she stirred her pots and pans, or wielded her duster and broom. No one could guess whether she ever now thought of bygone days, or regretted the golden past.

The tide turned for her before long. Richard Wallace noticed her and, in 1866, he made her his mistress. In 1870, when he inherited his mother's fortune of over sixty million francs, with the palace of Bagatelle, which had been built for the Comte d'Artois, brother of Louis XVI, and later Charles X, he settled a large sum on her, and she was rich once more, living in an apartment in the Avénue de l'Impératrice. She tried to revive her Sunday parties, but all those who had come formerly were either dead or dispersed – Baudelaire died in 1867 and Gautier in 1872. She lived out her last years in a house in Neuilly, in the Boulevard Victor Hugo, and died in 1889 at the age of sixty-seven. To the end she seems to have remained 'la très chère, la très belle, la très bonne', to whom Baudelaire, in secret, had dedicated his spiritual love and worship.

It was towards the end of 1852 that he began to think of her with feelings deeper than those of mere friendship. It was nine months after he had parted from Jeanne Duval, and either six or seven months – or else a couple of months – after his disappointment in Marie Daubrun. It was a time of loneliness, depression and poverty.

As he sat on Sundays in Madame Sabatier's room, he thought that at last he had found intelligence, beauty and kindness all in one person, and her apartment, with its snowy table-linen, its silver and its flowers, became for him a haven of peace, a centre of delight, a contrast to the sordidness of his own lodgings, with creditors waiting for him on the doorstep, to catch him as he came in or out. He describes to his mother how he had once hidden in his 'cabinet de toilette' in order to evade them when they came into his room.[6] He was never absent from her parties and he could not help being touched by the kindness which she showered on all her guests, on old Dumas, on Gautier, Flaubert, and on many lesser lights, indiscriminately. She singled no one out for special attention, but Baudelaire, in his loneliness and depression, used to compare her kindness towards him with what he considered his mother's neglect, and could not help reading into it more than she perhaps intended to express.

It does not matter whether Madame Sabatier was all that Baudelaire imagined or not; all that matters is his attitude to her, the emotion which she kindled in him, and the new insight which we gain into his personality from his relationship with her. In this is revealed, as never before, the sensitiveness, the delicacy and the gentleness of his character. In the sordidness of his life, he needed someone in whom to believe in order to be able to realize that beauty and goodness still existed. All he asked of Madame Sabatier was to be able, through her, to preserve this faith, and he asked for nothing for himself, no attention or return, nothing except that she should continue to be gracious and good, and not disappoint him in his ideal. In his love he became a child once more, with the sensitivity of a boy, ready to be wounded by life, with the illusions and idealism of the very simple – or the very great. To believe in Madame Sabatier, as he believed in her, mere naïveté was not sufficient; it needed also spiritual qualities, a depth of nature and a delicacy of heart which few men possess.

Some people may smile ironically when they think of all the virtues which he saw in her, and they compare his letters with those of Gautier. How could the pure woman whom he worshipped tolerate the other's smutty correspondence, and must there not have been something in her which called for just this response? Was Baudelaire only an innocent fool to see in her his 'muse' and his 'madonna'? But the smile is turned against the scoffers. His whole nature was enriched whenever he contemplated, in imagination, her goodness and her beauty, for he wrote as one transfigured when he thought of her, and it was in her that he found his inspiration, because she was so much better and nobler than he could ever hope to be. She became not only his dream, but his superstition as well, and he thought of her unceasingly.[7] If he had not been able to dream of her he often felt that he would have lost his reason in the kind of life that he was leading. Whenever he did anything particularly foolish or wrong, he used to say to himself, 'What would she think of me if she knew this?'[8] Whenever he did anything of which he was proud, he used to feel that here was something which raised him up towards her in spirit. And whenever he discovered anything which moved him deeply, or gave him pleasure, he used to long to share his joy with her. It was in her honour that he composed his most beautiful and spiritual love poems, the cycle of the White Venus. When he sent her the volume of *Les Fleurs du Mal*, on its publication, he marked the poems which were hers, and they are nine in number: *Tout Entière, Que diras-tu ce Soir, Le Flambeau Vivant, À celle qui est trop gaie, Réversibilité, Confession, L'Aube Spirituelle, Harmonie du Soir, Le Flacon.* Seven of these he had sent to her but two – *Har-*

monie du Soir and *Le Flacon* – perhaps because they seemed to suggest that love was past – she saw only on publication. All these poems owe much to his new conception of poetry, and are amongst his most perfect compositions.

He composed this second cycle of love poems between the years 1852 and 1854, but he was not content with merely writing them and hiding them away until he could find the means of publication. Although he did not expect any return for his love, nor wish to reveal his identity, he longed for Madame Sabatier to know that someone felt this adoration for her, and worshipped her from afar. To bring his devoted homage to her notice, he used to send her letters in a disguised handwriting, an ugly, cramped backhand script, in which he enclosed the poems he had just composed. The first letter was sent on 9 December 1852.

'The person for whom these verses have been composed,' he wrote, 'is most humbly entreated not to show them to anyone else, whether they please her or disgust her, or whether they seem to her completely ridiculous. Deep feelings have their modesty which they can't bear to have violated. And isn't the absence of signature proof of this deep-rooted modesty? The man who wrote these lines in the state of meditation into which he is so often cast by the vision of the woman who is their inspiration, loves her deeply, without ever telling her of his passion, and will cherish for her always the most tender of affections.'

He enclosed in the letter a poem, *À celle qui est trop gaie*, one of the poems banned when the book appeared. One wonders why he sent it to her, and what she thought of it, for it expresses pique and anger rather than love or worship, and it contrasts with the feelings expressed in the letter which accompanied it. Feuillerat thinks that this poem was really inspired by Marie rather than by Madame Sabatier, that the 'ballet de fleurs' in it recalls a play in which she had once acted, *Les Fleurs Animées*, and that the physical description of the woman is more true of Marie than of

Madame Sabatier.[9] But the poet seems often to have thought that his Muse and Madonna laughed too easily – witness the poem certainly inspired by her, *Semper Eadem*, in which he says:

> *Taisez-vous, ignorante! âme toujours ravie!*
> *Bouche au rire enfantin!*

Also a letter in which he talks of her 'méchante figure oujours pleine de gaieté'.[10]

He may have conceived this poem one Sunday evening as he wondered with disgust how she could listen so calmly to the obscene conversation of Gautier, to his 'porqueries' as they have been called. Did the suspicion then cross his mind, and torture him, as he heard her silvery laugh break out at some particularly daring sally, that she was only vain and shallow after all, and coarse like all the rest? Did he perhaps then wonder whether his idol would ever be able to appreciate the poems which he was composing for her, or understand all that was in his heart, which he had never yet expressed? Perhaps it was only because she had not suffered, and had only danced on the surface of life, that she could thus laugh at nothing. He felt then a savage desire to make her suffer too, as he himself was suffering, to make her share the bitterness in his heart.

> *Ta tête, ton geste, ton air,*
> *Sont beaux comme un beau paysage;*
> *Le rire joue en ton visage*
> *Comme un vent frais dans un ciel clair.*
>
> *Le passant chagrin que tu frôles,*
> *Est ébloui par la santé*
> *Qui jaillit comme une clarté*
> *De tes bras et de tes épaules.*
>
> *Les retentissantes couleurs*
> *Dont tu parsèmes tes toilettes*
> *Jettent dans l'esprit des poètes*
> *L'image d'un ballet de fleurs.*

Ces robes folles sont l'emblème
De ton esprit bariolé;
Folle dont je suis affolé,
Je te hais autant que je t'aime!

Quelquefois dans un beau jardin
Où je traînais mon atonie,
J'ai senti comme une ironie,
Le soleil déchirer mon sein;

Et le printemps et la verdure
Ont tant humilié mon cœur,
Que j'ai puni sur une fleur
L'insolence de la Nature.

Ainsi je voudrais, une nuit,
Quand l'heure des voluptés sonne,
Vers les trésors de ta personne,
Comme un lâche ramper sans bruit,

Pour châtier ta chair joyeuse,
Pour meurtrir ton sein pardonné,
Et faire à ton flanc étonné
Une blessure large et creuse,

Et, vertigineuse douceur!
À travers ces lèvres nouvelles,
Plus éclatantes et plus belles,
T'infuser mon vénin, ma sœur!

This was, however, a rare and passing phase, for otherwise she inspired in him only gentle and spiritual feelings, and he asked her for nothing, but her prayers.

Mais de toi je n'implore, que tes prières,
Ange plein de bonheur, de joie, de lumières.[11]

It was when he was lonely, particularly, that he thought of her, when his life felt more than ever unendurable, and his thoughts always took the form of verse.

'Imagine if you will,' he wrote,[12] 'that sometimes, crushed beneath the weight of bitter grief, I can find relief only in composing verses for you, and that afterwards I'm obliged to yield to the innocent longing of showing them to you, and that I'm also, at the same time, obsessed by the hideous terror of displeasing you – that explains my cowardice.'

He thought of her then with a love which had in it an intensity resembling religious fervour, and this gave him courage when he felt himself sunk in a state of sin, as he says: 'Quand mon être est roulé dans le noir de sa méchanceté et de sa sottise, il rêve profondément de vous.'[13] And, another time, he tells her that, after a night of pleasure and desolation, his soul belonged to her.[14] This was in a letter in which *L'Aube Spirituelle* was enclosed.[15]

> *Quand chez les débauchés l'aube blanche et vermeille*
> *Entre en société de l'Idéal rongeur,*
> *Par l'opération d'un mystère vengeur*
> *Dans la brute assoupie un Ange se réveille.*
>
> *Des Cieux Spirituels l'inaccessible azur,*
> *Pour l'homme terrassé qui rêve encore et souffre,*
> *S'ouvre et s'enfonce avec l'attirance du gouffre.*
> *Ainsi chère Déesse, Être lucide et pur,*
>
> *Sur les débris fumeux des stupides orgies*
> *Ton souvenir plus clair, plus rose, plus charmant,*
> *À mes yeux agrandis voltige incessamment.*
>
> *Le soleil a noirci la flamme des bougies;*
> *Ainsi, toujours vainqueur, ton fantôme est pareil,*
> *Âme resplendissante, à l'immortel Soleil.*

In his letters to Madame Sabatier, Baudelaire carried on a conversation – one-sided, it is true – but having spoken to her himself, he felt that he knew her, that she was beginning to understand him as no one yet had ever understood him, and in imagination he used to hear her answer all that he longed to hear her say in person. He continued to conceal his identity, for he was afraid that she might find him ridiculous, that she might scorn his love, as Marie Daubrun had done, and he was afraid also of importuning her.

'I don't know,' he wrote,[16] 'what women think of the worship which they sometimes inspire. Some people say

that they must take it all as a matter of course, and others
that they only laugh at it. Do they then think that women
are only cynical and vain? As far as I'm concerned, it seems
to me that a noble disposition can only be proud and happy
at the thought of its beneficent influence! I don't know
whether I'll ever be granted the supreme bliss of talking to
you in person of the influence which you've acquired over
me, and of the perpetual glow which your image kindles
in my mind! I'm content, for the time being, to swear to
you once more that no love was ever more disinterested, so
ideal, so full of respect, as the one which I cherish secretly
for you, and which I'll hide for ever with the care which
this tender respect commands me.'

In this letter he enclosed *Le Flambeau Vivant*.[17]

> *Que diras-tu ce soir, pauvre âme solitaire,*
> *Que diras-tu mon cœur, cœur autrefois flétri,*
> *À la très-belle, à la très-bonne, à la très-chère,*
> *Dont le regard divin t'a soudain refleuri?*
>
> *— Nous mettrons notre orgueil à chanter ses louanges.*
> *Rien ne vaut la douceur de son autorité;*
> *Sa chair spirituelle a le parfum des Anges,*
> *Et son œil nous revêt d'un habit de clarté.*
>
> *Que ce soit dans la nuit et dans la solitude,*
> *Que ce soit dans la rue et dans la multitude,*
> *Son fantôme dans l'air danse comme un flambeau.*
>
> *Parfois il parle et dit: 'Je suis belle, et j'ordonne*
> *Que pour l'amour de moi vous n'aimiez que le Beau;*
> *Je suis l'Ange gardien, la Muse et la Madone.'*

Although he thought of her incessantly, and often followed her without her being aware of it, shyness always prevented him from talking to her directly. Often when out
walking his steps would carry him, unconsciously almost,
past her house, and he used to stand, like a lovelorn youth,
to gaze up at her window. One evening, as he stood thus
near her door, he saw a carriage waiting, and he thought to

himself: 'How strange and wonderful it would be if that car were waiting for her, and she should suddenly appear!' So deep in meditation was he, that he did not hear the steps approaching and he was startled suddenly to hear a well-known voice beside him, the beloved voice, the sound of which brought him joy, but joy filled with pain, and it said: 'Good evening, Monsieur!' It was she, his beloved, and in his dreaming he had not heard her come. All through the rest of the evening he seemed to hear the silvery tones of her voice ring out in his brain, and he repeated to himself, try-ing to imitate its inflections, 'Good evening, Monsieur!' [18]

The last letter which Baudelaire wrote to Madame Sabatier was on 8 May 1854, and the last poem which he sent her, enclosed in it, was the *Hymne* – one of the loveliest of the poems inspired by her – which, for some reason we cannot guess, he did not publish in the first edition of *Les Fleurs du Mal*. It is true that many poems were jettisoned through lack of space, but this is one which should have been preserved even if another had to be sacrificed. It ap-peared for the first time in *Le Présent* in November 1857. He intended to publish it in the second edition of *Les Fleurs du Mal* but told his editor that he could not find the manu-script. [19] It is, however, strange that he did not obtain the text from the review.

> À la très chère, à la très belle
> Qui remplit mon cœur de clarté,
> À l'ange, à l'idole immortelle,
> Salut en l'immortalité!
>
> Elle se répand dans ma vie
> Comme un air imprégné de sel,
> Et dans mon âme inassouvie
> Verse le goût de l'éternel!
>
> Sachet toujours frais qui parfume
> L'atmosphère d'un cher réduit,
> Encensoir oublié qui fume
> En secret à travers la nuit,

Comment, amour incorruptible,
T'exprimer avec vérité?
Grain de musc qui gis, invisible,
Au fond de mon éternité!

À la très bonne, à la très-belle
Qui fait ma joie et ma santé,
À l'ange, à l'idole immortelle,
Salut en l'immortalité![20]

Suddenly the letters and the poems ceased, and one wonders why. Had he grown tired of her light-heartedness and found her shallow? Was his silence due to disappointment? This is unlikely since the last poem is one of love, and since, moreover, he did not forget her. When he wrote to her next, more than three years later, to send her his volume of *Les Fleurs du Mal*, this time in his own undisguised handwriting, he told her that he had not forgotten her, and could never forget her. Perhaps it was that she had seen through his disguise, and he had realized that he was unmasked. It cannot have been very difficult to guess his identity, for there were few amongst her friends capable of writing such poems, and she may have fixed on him by a process of elimination. It is probable that she did not keep the vow of secrecy he had laid on her, and that he discovered – or guessed – that profane eyes had seen his expression of intimate feeling and had defiled it by curiosity. He may have feared – and in this he would have done her an injustice, for she was never less than kind – that she had made a mockery of his letters and poems before her assembled guests, when he was absent; before his *bête noire*, Ernest Feydeau, perhaps. He would not have been able to endure the thought of his most sacred feelings being the subject of jokes or witticisms. It is clear that when he wrote again he was conscious of having been unmasked, and this with a man of his temperament would have been enough to make him cease exposing himself any further to the risk of ridicule.

'You did get your own back on me, didn't you?' he wrote later.[21] 'Especially with your young sister. The little wretch froze me with horror one day when we met by going off into a burst of laughter, right in my face, and saying: "Are you still in love with my sister, and do you still write her beautiful letters?" I understood then that, while trying to hide myself, I was doing it very badly, and also that, beneath your charming face, you hid an uncharitable nature. A rake may be a lover, but poets can only be worshippers, and your little sister isn't calculated to understand eternal matters.'

There was also a further reason. In 1854 Baudelaire renewed his acquaintance with Marie Daubrun. Their relationship, which was passionate and not spiritual, took his mind away from other ties, and gave rise to a further cycle of love poems of a totally different inspiration.

[8]

The Green-Eyed Venus
1854—1856

IT had been known from the beginning that in the collection of *Les Fleurs du Mal* there are two cycles of love poems, the sensual cycle of the Black Venus, and the spiritual cycle of the White Venus. It is now believed that there is a further cycle which might be called the cycle of the Green-Eyed Venus, or of the Golden-Haired Venus, inspired by the actress Marie Daubrun.[1] This cycle would consist of nine poems, *Le Poison*, *Ciel Brouillé*, *Le Chat*, *Le Beau Navire*, *L'Invitation au Voyage*, *L'Irréparable*, *Causerie*, *Chant d'Automne* and finally *À une Madone*. These poems occur, in a group, in *Les Fleurs du Mal*, just after the Madame Sabatier cycle, and before the poems celebrating a heterogeneous group of other women. They are more passionate than the poems addressed to the White Venus, but less bitter than those addressed to the Black Venus.

Marie Daubrun was seven years younger than Baudelaire and was now, in 1854 at the age of twenty-six, at the height of her beauty. She started her stage career in 1846, at the age of eighteen, in the name part of a vaudeville entitled *Mademoiselle Langé*, at the Théâtre du Vaudeville. In July of the same year, and in the same theatre, she took the part of Harmance, the pansy in a vaudeville entitled *Les Fleurs Animées*, and, in September, the part of Claire in a further vaudeville called *La Nouvelle Héloïse*, after the novel by Rousseau. It was, however, in the title part of *La Belle aux Cheveux d'Or*, at the Théâtre de la Porte Saint Martin, in August 1847, that she reached fame,[2] and the name of Mademoiselle Georges, of the Comédie Française, was even mentioned in connection with her by the *Mercure des*

Théâtres.[3] One of the poems inspired by her, *L'Irréparable*, was entitled *La Belle aux Cheveux d'Or*, when it first appeared in *La Revue des Deux Mondes* in June 1855.

During a large part of 1853 Marie Daubrun was away on tour, but in June 1854 she was acting in a play at the Théâtre de la Gaîté in Paris,[4] which means that she must have been back before that for rehearsals. Her main part that year was that of Margue, in *Le Sanglier des Ardennes*, the following month, in the same theatre.

It is then that Baudelaire grew interested in her again, and began to haunt the theatre. In a letter of 21 July to his mother, he mentions going every night at 11 o'clock to the Théâtre de la Gaîté, presumably to call for Marie Daubrun, and to see her home. The following month, on 14 August, he asks her for a loan in order to buy flowers for Marie, whose name day was the following, the Feast of the Assumption. He was also busy trying to obtain for her better parts[5] and to persuade journalists to write favourable notices.[6] His efforts seem to have been unavailing. Perhaps it was because she was difficult to work with, for she upset the plans of theatre managers, was spiteful to her fellow-actors, and was said to have gone the round of all the theatres of Paris.[7] Now, at the end of 1854, she was in the midst of a quarrel with Hostein, the Director of the Gaîté, for she had broken her contract in the course of production of a play, and he threatened to sue any theatre which gave her a part.

At this time Baudelaire seriously considered writing for the theatre. As a young man he had toyed with the idea, as with many others, but had abandoned it. Now he was working on a play entitled *L'Ivrogne*, in which there was to be a part for Marie, and so far advanced was it that he offered it to the Director of La Gaîté in November 1854. In its unfinished form it seems dramatic, and to possess qualities which might make for success, though it is more in the taste of the twentieth century than of the Second Empire.

Baudelaire's last letter to Madame Sabatier was written in May 1854, and it was during 1854 and 1855 that he composed

the first seven of the nine poems inspired by Marie Daubrun.
In *Le Beau Navire* and in *Le Chat* he describes her physical
charms.

> *Je veux te raconter, ô molle enchanteresse!*
> *Les diverses beautés qui parent ta jeunesse;*
>   *Je veux te peindre ta beauté,*
> *Où l'enfance s'allie à la maturité.*
>
> *Quand tu vas balayant l'air de ta jupe large,*
> *Tu fais l'effet d'un beau vaisseau qui prend le large,*
>   *Chargé de toile, et va roulant*
> *Suivant un rhythme doux, et paresseux et lent,*
>
> *Sur ton cou large et rond, sur tes épaules grasses,*
> *Ta tête se pavane avec d'étranges grâces;*
>   *D'un air placide et triomphant*
> *Tu passes ton chemin, majestueuse enfant.*
>
>   .   .   .   .   .
>
> *Tes nobles jambes, sous les volants qu'elles chassent,*
> *Tourmentent les désirs obscurs et les agacent,*
>   *Comme deux sorcières qui font*
> *Tourner un philtre noir dans un vase profond.*
>
> *Tes bras, qui se joueraient des précoces hercules,*
> *Sont des boas luisants les solides émules*
>   *Faits pour serrer obstinément,*
> *Comme pour l'imprimer dans ton cœur, ton amant.*
>
> *Sur ton cou large et rond, sur tes épaules grasses,*
> *Ta tête se pavane avec d'étranges grâces;*
>   *D'un air placide et triomphant*
> *Tu passes ton chemin, majestueuse enfant.*[8]

This tallies with Banville's description of her in the poems
entitled *Inviolata* and *En Silence* from his collection *Les
Améthystes*, while, in *Vers Saphiques*, from the same book,
he describes her cruelty and harshness;

> *Il me faut bénir ta blonde toison,*
> *Tes beaux yeux armés pour la trahison,*

> *Et ton sein de neige, et le noir poison*
> *Qu'a versé ta main.*

He also says that if she finds a heart on her path she always
tramples it underfoot without a qualm. 'Mon cœur a saigné
sous tes doigts,' he complains in *Les Baisers*.[9] This recalls
Baudelaire's lines from *Ciel Brouillé*.[10]

> *O femme dangereuse, ô séduisants climats!*
> *Adorerai-je aussi la neige et vos frimas,*
> *Et saurai-je tirer de l'implacable hiver*
> *Des plaisirs plus aigus que la glace et le fer?*

Le Poison, however, does not leave any doubt as to the
passionate quality of Baudelaire's feelings for her.[11]

> *Tout cela ne vaut pas le poison qui découle*
> *   De tes yeux, de tes yeux verts,*
> *Lacs où mon âme tremble et se voit à l'envers . . .*
> *   Mes songes viennent en foule*
> *Pour se désaltérer à ces gouffres amers.*
>
> *Tout cela ne vaut pas le terrible prodige*
> *   De ta salive qui mord,*
> *Qui plonge dans l'oubli mon âme sans remords,*
> *   Et, charriant le vertige,*
> *La roule défaillante aux rives de la mort!*

Nevertheless, he was afraid that there might be nothing
left in his heart for anyone else, that Jeanne Duval had laid it
waste and bare. He laments in *Causerie*:[12]

> *Vous êtes un beau ciel d'automne, clair et rose!*
> *Mais la tristesse en moi monte comme la mer,*
> *Et laisse, en refluant, sur ma lèvre morose*
> *Le souvenir cuisant de son limon amer.*
>
> *– Ta main se glisse en vain sur mon sein qui se pâme;*
> *Ce qu'elle cherche, amie, est un lieu saccagé*
> *Par la griffe et la dent féroce de la femme.*
> *Ne cherchez plus mon cœur; les bêtes l'ont mangé.*

Mon cœur est un palais flétri par la cohue;
On s'y soûle, on s'y tue, on s'y prend aux cheveux!
– Un parfum nage autour de votre gorge nue! …

O Beauté, dur fléau des âmes, tu le veux!
Avec tes yeux de feu, brillants comme des fêtes,
Calcine ces lambeaux qu'ont épargnés les bêtes!

Baudelaire longed for more than mere passionate satisfaction with Marie Daubrun. He hoped also for a settled life of calm and perfect peace, and even luxury. It was then that he composed for her *L'Invitation au Voyage*, in which he describes his dream-land, like some fairy Holland, as a suitable setting for her Flemish beauty, some East Indian Holland in Java or Sumatra, exotic enough to assuage his love of the strange, a country where everything would be, like his beloved, serene and calm, where he would enjoy 'luxe, calme et volupté' in ordered peace.

Mon enfant, ma sœur,
Songe à la douceur
D'aller là-bas vivre ensemble!
Aimer à loisir,
Aimer et mourir
Au pays qui te ressemble!
Les soleils mouillés
De ces ciels brouillés
Pour mon esprit ont les charmes
Si mystérieux
De tes traîtres yeux,
Brillant à travers leurs larmes.

Là, tout n'est qu'ordre et beauté,
Luxe, calme et volupté.

Des meubles luisants
Polis par les ans,
Décoreraient notre chambre;
Les plus rares fleurs
Mêlant leurs odeurs
Aux vagues senteurs de l'ambre,

Les riches plafonds,
Les miroirs profonds,
La splendeur orientale,
Tout y parlerait
À l'âme en secret
Sa douce langue natale.

Là, tout n'est qu'ordre et beauté,
Luxe, calme et volupté.

Vois sur ces canaux
Dormir ces vaisseaux
Dont l'humeur est vagabonde;
C'est pour assouvir
Ton moindre désir
Qu'ils viennent du bout du monde.
– Les soleils couchants
Revêtent les champs,
Les canaux, la ville entière,
D'hyacinthe et d'or;
Le monde s'endort
Dans une chaude lumière.

Là, toute n'est qu'ordre et beauté,
Luxe, calme et volupté.[13]

As he dreamed of this new and ordered life, he contemplated the years behind him, so sadly squandered. One day he found, amongst his papers, a bundle of his mother's letters, and he paused to read them through; but they only saddened him, for they spoke of little else than debts unpaid, disappointments, and they symbolized for him the bygone years so badly spent. He could not continue his reading and put them away again.[14] It was at this time that he composed *L'Irréparable*, in which he poured out his regrets for the misspent years, and sorrow that nothing will ever now wipe out the past, and allow him to begin again, with new attachments.[15]

Pouvons-nous étouffer le vieux, le long Remords,
Qui vit, s'agite et se tortille,

Et se nourrit de nous comme le ver des morts,
   Comme du chêne la chenille?
Pouvons-nous étouffer l'implacable Remords?

Dans quel philtre, dans quel vin, dans quelle tisane,
   Noierons-nous ce vieil ennemi,
Destructeur et gourmand comme la courtisane,
   Patient comme la fourmi?
Dans quel philtre? – dans quel vin? – dans quelle tisane?

Dis-le, belle sorcière, oh! dis, si tu le sais,
   À cet esprit comblé d'angoisse
Et pareil au mourant qu'écrasent les blessés,
   Que le sabot du cheval froisse,
Dis-le, belle sorcière, oh! dis, si tu le sais,

À cet agonisant que le loup déjà flaire
   Et que surveille le corbeau,
À ce soldat brisé! s'il faut qu'il désespère
   D'avoir sa croix et son tombeau;
Ce pauvre agonisant que déjà le loup flaire!

Peut-on illuminer un ciel bourbeux et noir?
   Peut-on déchirer des ténèbres
Plus denses que la poix, sans matin et sans soir
   Sans astres, sans éclairs funèbres?
Peut-on illuminer un ciel bourbeux et noir?

L'Espérance qui brille aux carreaux de l'Auberge
   Est soufflée, est morte à jamais!
Sans lune et sans rayons, trouver où l'on héberge
   Les martyrs d'un chemin mauvais!
Le Diable a tout éteint aux carreaux de l'Auberge!

Adorable sorcière, aimes-tu les damnés?
   Dis, connais-tu l'irrémissible?
Connais-tu de Remords, aux traits empoisonnés,
   À qui notre cœur sert de cible?
Adorable sorcière, aimes-tu les damnés?

L'Irréparable ronge avec sa dent maudite
   Notre âme, piteux monument,

> *Et souvent il attaque, ainsi que le termite*
>   *Par la base le bâtiment.*
> *L'Irréparable ronge avec sa dent maudite!*

There can be little doubt that Baudelaire and Marie
Daubrun were lovers, though only for a short time, a few
months at most. At the end of 1854, unable to obtain any
work in Paris on account of her quarrel with Hostein, she
was obliged to accept an engagement in a company going on
tour to Italy, where she spent nine months until it finally
went bankrupt and she was forced to return to France in
August 1855. Baudelaire then tried to obtain a part for her
in a play by George Sand, *Maître Favilla*, which was to open
at the Théâtre de l'Odéon; for Hostein, who would have
sued a Boulevard theatre, would not have been able to do
so with one of the state subsidized establishments. He wrote
to the author on behalf of the actress, who promised to do all
that she could, but Marie Daubrun was not given the part.[16]

In the meantime Baudelaire had not abandoned his dream
of establishing himself in calm and ordered surroundings,
probably with Marie Daubrun when she returned to Paris.
He had not seen his mother for a year, for she had become
dismayed and disgusted at his continued failure to earn a
regular living. She had been back in Paris now for two
years, since her husband had been elected to the high office
of Senator, but her son did not even know her address.[17]
She refused to communicate with him, and returned his
letters, unopened, through Ancelle.[18] At last, however, he
determined to make one last effort to reach her, for he felt
that he must, at all costs, establish himself respectably. He
thought that the tide in his affairs was beginning to turn,
that he had proved that he could get his writings published,
for there were many now accepted by editors, and more
were promised. He felt that he could now with dignity beg
for an advance, in order to make a permanent home, for he
was tired of the mean furnished rooms in cheap hotels, which
had been his lot for the past ten years. He intended this to
be his final establishment, and never to have to move again,

to be free of sordid lodgings, and of the necessity for going out, hail, rain or shine, for every meal. He wanted a home of his own, where he could collect together his books and pictures. He chose an apartment in a quiet house in the Rue d'Angoulême where he could, he said, at last be housed like a gentleman. To do this he needed money for furniture and fittings. And so he wrote to his mother again to ask her permission to obtain from his capital, through Ancelle, a loan sufficient to start him in his new life. He wanted also to be reconciled with her and to make her promise that, as soon as he was settled in his own home, she would come to visit him twice a week. He wished to have her blessing on his new undertaking, and also to be able to present her with a copy of his first book, the translations of Poe, which, after its many vicissitudes, was at last due to appear in the New Year.

As usual he postponed writing. When at last he sent his letter, the matter was urgent, for he had already given up his old rooms, and he needed an immediate reply.

'It's tomorrow I must leave,' he wrote in the postscript,[19] 'I should really have left my quarters today! After all, on second thoughts, as I've rarely hidden from Monsieur Ancelle anything of my life, I thought it better to show him this letter before giving it to him to send on to you. I don't imagine you'll find anything to take offence at in such an action! He pointed out to me that the strong wish which I express to see you again was perhaps not accompanied by sufficient apologies. But all these regrets, these apologies, these can be guessed, they are obvious, and I'd already expressed them to you in two previous letters, which you didn't read! There are certain things which are thought visibly, so to speak! Can you believe that I was happy at having hurt you, and at having worsened the wrong opinion you have of me? – I beg you most earnestly once more, do be generous, and you'll be pleased with the result! Who is to prevent us, once I'm leading a regular life, from seeing one another, and meeting a couple of times a week? In that way I'll be able to keep you informed of my life, and then, thanks to this further concession I'm asking from Ancelle, there'll be no danger of further shocks!'

Madame Aupick did not write to her son, but only to Ancelle, to whom she said: [20]

'The state of Charles distresses me very much! You could, to set his mind at rest, write to him to inform him that I agree to this further sacrifice of fifteen hundred francs of capital. That's his main concern! Don't promise anything else! He has so bitterly hurt me, and his attitude is so far from being what it should be, that I don't feel at all disposed to renew our relations. I've never gone to see him that I didn't come back displeased with him. My advice only irritates him, and then he's insolent to me! As you can readily imagine, I can't possibly tolerate that! All the same, in spite of the coolness on my part, I'm very much perturbed by his state of neglect and distress, and there's nothing I wouldn't do to alleviate his condition. Unfortunately, what can I do? Save on my allowance, that's all! But it makes no difference whatsoever, nothing alters his horrible life! It's all very discouraging!'

Nevertheless she did sanction the further sale of capital.

It was not, however, Marie Daubrun who occupied the new apartment with him. When she returned to Paris at the end of 1855, she went not to Baudelaire but to Banville, and they set up house together. Perhaps she had found Baudelaire too difficult, and he had certainly not proved an influential protector. Moreover he was becoming notorious as a writer, and the selection from *Les Fleurs du Mal*, published by the *Revue des Deux Mondes* in June that year, had created a scandal, and had been violently attacked in an article in *Le Figaro* in November. Banville was ill and needed her – dependence and need often attach a lover more closely than passion – and she nursed him with great devotion. It was to him that she gave, and not to Baudelaire, 'luxe, calme et volupté'. His letters to Poulet Malassis give a charming picture of their domestic happiness, and he declared that his

Histoire d'une Comédienne had been written 'on the corner of the hospitable table of Mademoiselle Marie Daubrun'. [21]

Marie Daubrun did not then occupy the new apartment with Baudelaire, Jeanne Duval came instead.[22]

After he had parted from her in April 1852, he did not see her except once a month to give her the allowance he was paying her. Then she had fallen ill.[23] In spite of past unhappiness between them, in spite of the harm she had done him, he was deeply moved by the sight of her utter ruin, her poverty and abject humility. He remembered the years they had spent together which had not been all unhappiness. He recalled that she was not solely to blame for the state into which she had sunk, and he remembered the good in her in the past: how she had sold her jewels and furniture to help him; how he had beaten and often tortured her by his temper and his moods. With his better education, his clearer vision of beauty, he should have been able to set her an example of how a decent human being should live, and yet, instead of that, he had set her an example of nothing but idleness and debauch.

He set up house again with her at the end of December 1855, and when he sent her to Ancelle, to collect part of the advance which his mother had sanctioned to furnish the apartment, he said to him in a letter: [24]

'I beg you not to chaff Jeanne about our previous difficulties, or make any reference to her about them. That would be too cruel!'

There occurs in *Les Journaux Intimes* of Baudelaire a passage of deep psychological analysis, which appears without any commentary or date, but which could conceivably refer to this reconciliation: [25]

'Ému au contact de ces voluptés qui ressemblaient à des souvenirs, attendri par la pensée d'un passé mal rempli, de tant de fautes, de tant de querelles, de tant de choses à se cacher réciproquement, il se mit à pleurer; et ses larmes chaudes coulèrent dans les ténèbres sur l'épaule nue de sa chère et toujours attirante maîtresse. Elle tressaillit, elle se sentit, elle aussi attendrie et remuée. Les ténèbres rassuraient sa vanité et son dandysme de femme froide. Ces deux êtres déchus, mais souffrant encore de leur reste de noblesse, s'enlacèrent spontanément, confondant, dans la pluie de leurs larmes et de leurs baisers, les tristesses de leur passé avec leurs espérances bien incertaines d'avenir. Il est présumable que jamais, pour eux, la volupté ne fut si douce que dans cette nuit de mélancolie et de charité; – volupté saturée de douleur et de remords.

'À travers la noirceur de la nuit, il avait regardé derrière lui dans les années profondes, puis il s'était jeté dans les bras de sa coupable amie, pour y retrouver le pardon qu'il lui accordait.'

They started life together again and Baudelaire built fresh hopes on it for some happiness for both of them, in this new relationship based on their new-found understanding. It must have been at this time that, inspired by Jeanne Duval, he composed *Le Balcon*, in a vein of reminiscent sadness, as he recalled, with some hope for the future, the happy days of the past.[26] It ranks, at all events, amongst his loveliest achievements.

> *Mère des souvenirs, maîtresse des maîtresses,*
> *O toi, tous mes plaisirs! ô toi, tous mes devoirs!*
> *Tu te rappelleras la beauté des caresses,*
> *La douceur du foyer et le charme des soirs,*
> *Mère des souvenirs, maîtresse des maîtresses!*
>
> *Les soirs illuminés par l'ardeur du charbon,*
> *Et les soirs au balcon, voilés de vapeurs roses.*
> *Que ton sein m'était doux! que ton cœur m'était bon!*
> *Nous avons dit souvent d'impérissables choses*
> *Les soirs illuminés par l'ardeur du charbon.*
>
> *Que les soleils sont beaux dans les chaudes soirées!*
> *Que l'espace est profond! que le cœur est puissant!*
> *En me penchant vers toi, reine des adorées,*
> *Je croyais respirer le parfum de ton sang.*
> *Que les soleils sont beaux dans les chaudes soirées!*

La nuit s'épaississait ainsi qu'une cloison,
Et mes yeux dans le noir devinaient tes prunelles,
Et je buvais ton souffle, ô douceur! ô poison!
Et tes pieds s'endormaient dans mes mains fraternelles.
La nuit s'épaississait ainsi qu'une cloison.

Je sais l'art d'évoquer les minutes heureuses,
Et revis mon passé blotti dans tes genoux.
Car à quoi bon chercher tes beautés langoureuses
Ailleurs qu'en ton cher corps et qu'en ton cœur si doux?
Je sais l'art d'évoquer les minutes heureuses!

Ces serments, ces parfums, ces baisers infinis,
Renaîtront-ils d'un gouffre interdit à nos sondes,
Comme montent au ciel les soleils rajeunis
Après s'être lavés au fond des mers profondes?
– O serments! ô parfums! ô baisers infinis!

Notoriety
1855—1857

ALTHOUGH Baudelaire's writings were not yet well known to the general public, he was beginning nevertheless to be considered as a figure in the literary world of Paris. This was chiefly due to his art criticism and his translations of Poe which were appearing in various periodicals. He had been known now for almost ten years in the literary cafés for the originality of his aesthetic doctrine, and in certain quarters for the unpublished poems which he used to recite to all who would listen. He had a small following amongst certain young writers, mostly amongst the lesser stars such as Babou, who gave vent to their spite against the popular established authors by praising him and professing to see virtue in his inability to find a publisher. He was considered sufficiently prominent for Nadar to include him in his *Panthéon,* an immensely long caricature lithograph, published in 1854, which spread over the whole of the window space in the shop in which it was exhibited. On it straggled in procession all the well-known and notorious literary figures of the day, led by Victor Hugo, and followed by Lamartine, Musset, Vigny, and other writers of the Romantic movement; next came the journalists, such as Janin, Paul de Saint Victor and Thierry; also such politicians as Guizot and Thiers; and finally the younger aspirants to fame: Du Camp, Champfleury, De Cormenin and Baudelaire.[1]

The critic and journalist, Charles Monselet, who did not waste his time on insignificant personalities, also mentions Baudelaire in his *Lorgnette Littéraire, Dictionnaire des Grands et des Petits Auteurs de mon Temps.* He realized that the kind of fame and notoriety which the poet enjoyed made him many bitter enemies. There were those who temperamentally disliked his writings, and genuinely considered him a danger to the public. But there were, as well, those who felt that his idealistic and disinterested literary attitude was an unspoken – and often vocal – condemnation of their own self-seeking behaviour, and that his spiritual preoccupations were an unflattering contrast to their own materialistic interests. Monselet claimed that the antagonism which he aroused was due to the fact that he was alleged to be writing a book entitled *Conversations de Monsieur Charles Baudelaire avec les Anges*.[2] Now that he was becoming well known these enemies began to attack him from all sides.

It was at this time that Buloz, the editor of the *Revue des Deux Mondes*, the stronghold of orthodox and conservative Romanticism since its foundation in 1830, decided on risking the venture of publishing a selection of his poems. This was a signal honour since this periodical never condescended to print the works of those who had not arrived, and on whom the public had not placed the seal of success. Amongst the poems which Baudelaire submitted, he chose eighteen representative ones, chiefly those which struck a new or daring note.[3]

The selection appeared on 1 June 1855, but the editor, anxious over what his regular subscribers might think of his experiment, was careful through the pen of Émile de Montégut to disclaim any responsibility for the sentiments expressed.

'In publishing the poems which follow,' he declared, 'we believe that we are proving once again that we are prepared to welcome and encourage all kinds of new ventures and experiments, whatever their nature may be. What seems to us worthy of interest and note in these poems is their expression of a certain form of moral anguish which, even if we do not share it, we should learn to know, as it is one of the most typical phenomena of our age.'

If the arrangement of the poems, in their order of publication, indicates a plan, and is not merely, as is possible, the result of chance, then it is a pessimistic one. The largest number of the poems express the poet's tragic inspiration, such as *Un Voyage à Cythère*, *L'Irréparable*, *De Profundis Clamavi*, *Le Vampire*, and so forth, while those which give hope of release, like *Réversibilité* and *L'Aube Spirituelle* – both inspired by the White Venus – are followed immediately by others which contradict them, as, for instance *Le Tonneau de la Haine* and *La Destruction* – entitled here *La Volupté*. Moreover, the selection starts with *Au Lecteur* which suggests that all humanity is in the throes of Satan, who holds the strings which move us, and ends with *L'Amour et Le Crâne* which describes how love, that 'profane effronté', is seated on the head of humanity, blowing light bubbles into the air, but each of these bubbles is formed from the flesh and blood of the unfortunate victim.

> Car ce que ta bouche cruelle
> Éparpille en l'air
> Monstre assassin, c'est ma cervelle,
> Mon sang et ma chair!

June 1855 was not a time when poetry aroused great interest in the readers of *La Revue des Deux Mondes*, or in the general public, none of which paid much heed to the poems, and only one critic deigned to notice them, Louis Goudall, in a scathing review, published only five months later, in November, in *Le Figaro*. He declared that he had frequently heard Baudelaire read his poems in the cafés of the Latin Quarter, and had also heard him expound his theory of aesthetics, but it had always seemed to him an amazing mystery how the poet could manage to preserve his reputation for ten years while doing nothing more than publishing, on rare occasions and for a minute number of ignorant and chattering initiates, a few sensational articles. Unfortunately for him, Goudall went on, he could not resist the temptation of publishing his poems in *La Revue des Deux Mondes*, and, as a result, his reputation was now shattered to powder and dust. He then enumerated what he considered the poet's

defects and deficiencies – the paucity and puerility of his
ideas, the pretentiousness of his inspiration, the scrofulous
nature of his disgusting poetry, poetry of the slaughter- and
charnel-house. He concluded by prophesying that Baudelaire, as a poet, was exploded and would henceforth be only
one of the 'Dead Sea fruits' of modern poetry.[4]

It was a stupid and ignorant article, which infuriated
Baudelaire, and his friends and admirers. It was rumoured
that the publisher Michel Lévy, who had been toying with
the idea of bringing out an edition of the poet's verse, said
on reading it that it had clinched the matter and had decided
him on publication. It was a pity that this rumour was
false. He does not seem ever to have considered the matter
seriously, since he could have secured the offer of the book
any time that he wanted it. Baudelaire was desperately
anxious to obtain a contract for his poetry, and he had
already given Lévy the rights on his two volumes of translations from Poe.

1855 was, however, a good year for Baudelaire, and one
that rightly gave him hope and confidence in his future. He
had written, and had managed to publish, two important
articles on the *Exposition Universelle* in May and June; he
had placed two volumes of translations, and he had published a large number of *Les Fleurs du Mal* – he had the
whole book ready for press, if a publisher would take it; his
first two prose poems, *Le Crépuscule du Soir* and *La Solitude*,
had appeared in the volume entitled *Fontainebleau*; and his
play *L'Ivrogne*, which showed originality in conception and
psychology, would have required little work to complete it,
if he could have found a manager prepared to produce it.[5]

Yet, in spite of everything, he was financially no more
prosperous than before, and it was in December that year
that he had to resort to borrowing in order to establish himself in his new apartment.

Matters became still more difficult with the New Year.
Those who had been scandalized at the publication of his
poems in *La Revue des Deux Mondes*, found a focus for

their disapproval in Goudall's article, and it was rumoured that some of them had complained to Buloz, who had felt obliged to discontinue the publication of further poems.

Baudelaire's first real book to appear in print was the volume of his translations from Poe which, finally, came out in March 1856, after prolonged delays. It was an immediate success and, although it was reprinted before the end of the year, it did not bring him much gain financially. He had disposed of the rights on unfavourable terms. He also failed to secure strong literary support for it. He had sent it to Sainte-Beuve, hoping that he would review it, for his opinion carried much weight since he was the most influential writer in the Second Empire, and could have turned the tide in Baudelaire's favour, had the protection which he professed to give his young friend been more active than a mere expression of good will. The poet had expected, and hoped, much from his friendship and, when the time came to put it to the test, he ended his letter of request with the words: 'Thus I hand over to you my ever distressed soul!'[6]

Sainte-Beuve answered in a few days,[7] promising vaguely that he would do all that he could for him, and asked for particulars about the American author to help in his notice, which Baudelaire gave him by return of post, thanking him for his kindness. The article was never written.

Baudelaire tried next to obtain a review from Barbey d'Aurevilly whom he had met in 1854, when they were both working on *Le Pays*, who was a personal friend and who admired his writings.[8] Barbey d'Aurevilly was not popular, however, at that time with his editor and always had the greatest difficulty in obtaining the books he wanted for review. He wrote, in answer, one of his flamboyant letters, full of expressions of friendship, full also of his usual diatribes against the contemporary literary state of affairs.[9]

'Two words only, my dear Baudelaire,' he wrote. 'I've just returned from my circuit to my G.H.Q. and I find your letter and your book, which had arrived a few days before my return.

'No indeed! your letter didn't offend me. Offend me! Ye Gods! and why on earth should it? It was, on the contrary, very pleasurable to me, for it gave me valuable information; it expressed you so well, you, whose mind I admire and in whom I believe. For an old believer like me, faith is even more important than friendship. I didn't answer your letter at once, because, at the moment, I'm like a ball rebounding again and again, and I've no time to rest!

'Thank you for your book. No article of mine will appear in anything else before the one I write on it, that's if they grant me permission to do it. I've just written in this fierce and indomitable fist to Cohen, but I've drawn in my claws, and fawned on him to obtain it. Will they grant it to me? Everything is doubtful with such a man, who flutters about from one thing to another, and changes his mind each morning. Dutacq wrote to me that one had to bow and scrape before Cohen to obtain the books one wants to review. I hadn't known this in time, and had written a long article on the so-called posthumous works of Racine; but that article was pure and entire waste of time. Nisard had sent in his, and since he is a complete idiot, he walked in over my prostrate body. In the brute creation it is the strong who conquer the weak; in the intellectual and social world, it's the contrary that happens; the feeble trample the strong underfoot. What imbecility! But that's exactly what happens. Indeed a nice world!

'If you read *Le Pays*, you must have seen that everyone is writing literary articles, X. Y. and Z. They cough up the most lamentable rubbish, which can't be described in gentlemanly language! And, in putting them in his literary page, Cohen imagines that he is following in the footsteps of *Le Journal des Débats*. Isn't that funny enough to make one laugh until one cries ... tears of blood? My dear Baudelaire, if I'm permitted to write your review, you'll be pleased with it!'

Barbey d'Aurevilly did, in fact, review the book in *Le Pays* very favourably, saying that the translator was 'de première force'.[10]

When Baudelaire set up house again with Jeanne Duval at the end of 1855, he hoped very much from this reconciliation. But, in his strained financial situation, their relationship soon began to break down, and he was living in constant state of anger and rage. To relieve his tortured nerves, he used to take it out of his mistress, and to make her suffer for his disappointment, frustration and failure. He was not always responsible for his actions, but the wrangling between them became more bitter, since they were both ill and worn out by anxiety.

The crash came soon, this time from Jeanne Duval, who decided that she could not endure the situation any longer, and that she must break away and be free. It may have been that she was moved by the sight of the poverty and distress of her lover, for, in spite of what her detractors have always claimed, she seems at times to have felt some affection and consideration for him. Now she assured him that it was for his ultimate good that she was leaving him, and that he would one day be grateful to her for her action. Baudelaire, however, who had once parted from her of his own accord, and had lived for nearly four years without her, now seemed broken-hearted. He had built much on the hope of their new life together, and it seemed to him that he had failed with his mistress also, as well as in all the rest, since he had obviously not succeeded in making her happy. Three and a half years earlier, when he had left her, he had considered her an obstacle to his intellectual and spiritual development, a destructive influence to his happiness, but now he calls her his only companion and sole friend, the only person who, knowing his weaknesses, did not despise him. He had hoped, after their reconciliation, that everything would now go well between them, and had counted on it. Nevertheless she left him in September 1856, and it seemed to him the most shattering blow of his life.

'My dear Mother,' he wrote when the disaster happened,[11] 'I implore you not to answer me in a letter like the one you sent me last time. I've endured lately too much trouble, humiliation and even suffering, to need you to add your little quota....

'I didn't write to you, although I very much longed to do so, because the explanations I'd have to give you would have caused you joy, a kind of maternal joy which I couldn't have borne. The condition I was in must have been very noticeable, for Lévy, seeing me in such a pass, alternately depressed and alternately in a state of fury, didn't ask me any questions, but left me entirely alone, and didn't ask me to work.

'My relationship with Jeanne, my liaison of fourteen years is over! I did everything which was humanly possible to prevent the break occurring. The struggle and the parting lasted a fortnight. Jeanne kept on answering me imperturbably that I'd an obstinate character, and that, moreover, I'd be grateful to her one day for her decision. But I know well that, whatever pleasant adventure happens to me – money, joy or personal vanity – I'll always regret that woman! So that my grief, which you'll not understand, may not seem to you too childish, let me confess that, like a gambler, I'd put all my hopes on that one head, and this woman was my sole amusement, my only pleasure, my only companion, and, in spite of all the inward shocks of a stormy relationship, the thought of a permanent separation had never clearly entered my mind. And even now – although nevertheless I'm now quite calm – I find myself suddenly thinking, as I look at something beautiful – a lovely landscape, or something else pleasant – why isn't she with me to admire this, to buy this? You see, I don't hide my wounds! I took a long time, I assure you, to understand that perhaps work would bring me pleasure, and that, after all, I'd got duties to accomplish, but I heard, repeated in my mind constantly, "What's the good of all this?" – not to mention a thick haze in front of my eyes, and a buzzing in my ears. – That lasted a long time,

but it's over now! When at last I took in that it was hopeless, then I was seized with indescribable rage, and I remained ten days without sleeping, and violently sick, and
obliged to hide myself because I was crying all the time!
My obsession was a selfish one, for I saw before me an endless number of years, lonely years, without friend or lover,
years of solitude and risk, with no comfort for the heart! I
couldn't even draw consolation from my pride, for all this
has happened through my own fault, I've used her and
abused her! I've taken pleasure in torturing her, and now
I've been tortured myself!... But what's the point of going
on with this tale, which must only seem to you absurd? I
could never have believed that purely psychological suffering
could cause such physical torture, or that, a fortnight afterwards, one could become a different man and attend to one's
work. Here am I then, alone for ever, that's very likely,
for I can never again put my confidence in another
creature, any more than I do in myself! I've henceforth
nothing to do but to occupy myself with my financial
interest, and my fame, without any other pleasure but
literature.

'I send you my very best love!'

Baudelaire would have liked to have been able to give
Jeanne Duval a sum of money sufficient to assure her future,
for he was tortured by the fear that she might be in serious
want, and his heart grew heavy whenever he imagined her
destitute and weighed down by unpaid bills. He begged Ancelle for help to provide for her, but this was the kind of
request which the lawyer did not receive gladly.

After she left Baudelaire she seems at first to have lived by
her own efforts, for she refused to see him, saying that she
knew his character too well and wanted to have nothing further to do with him. He, on his side, was afraid to go to see
her, being afraid to reopen his wounds, but he sent her
what money he could rake together. During the early months,
after she had left him, she was constantly in his mind and he
could not forget her. He heard a rumour once that she was

about to leave Paris, to return to her native land, and this was in a certain measure a relief, for she would then be cared for by her own people. Nevertheless, he was sad to think that she was to live and die far away from him, she who had occupied so large a place in his life.

In his loneliness and depression, the only things which gave him hope and courage were desire and longing for personal fame. 'I've got a diabolical thirst for glory.' [12]

He was determined that he was going to succeed and he set to work with eagerness and energy.

He was, however, not permitted to work in peace. The attacks in the press began once more with renewed vigour, and this time he was the victim of scurrilous abuse when obscene and false details of his private and personal life were related. *Le Figaro* still had its knife in him and, in November 1856, it launched a fresh attack on him, exactly a year after Goudall's review, this time in an article by the novelist, Edmond Duranty, dealing with the newest personalities of modern French literature. He mentioned young men with skulls and crossbones, amongst whom, he said, the prime mover was Baudelaire, who made use of the foolish trappings of mystery and horror merely to shock and to astound the public. He was, declared Duranty, a literary bogeyman who was always on the point of emerging from the case in which he hid his books, the books which did not exist. For ten years he had done no more than this, and the only thing which had given him life was his volume of translations from Poe, to whom he clung like a barnacle in order to share his cloak.

Baudelaire was being humiliated in every way by his editors. Almost anyone was considered of more importance than he, and he had to make way for others. In December 1856 About's serial, *Germaine*, took the place of his work, and next it was the serial by some other writer, while in February, the following year, the *Letters of an Australian Miner* by Antoine Fauchery ousted his translations.[13] He was himself to blame for the delay in the publication of his second volume of translations from Poe, because he had so much difficulty in composing the preface for it, and this led to a coolness between himself and his publisher, Michel Lévy.[14]

In the meantime his mother was again growing anxious and impatient, seeing that his second book, which he had promised for so long, was not appearing, and she began to add her recriminations to those with which he was being bombarded from all sides. This he felt was more than he could endure, and he wrote her a bitter and cruel letter, for he was at the end of patience and courage.[15]

'My dear Mother,' he wrote, when she had refused to advance any money on either the translations of Poe which were to appear the following month and for which he would then be paid, or for the collection of poems, *Les Fleurs du Mal*, which he said he had already sent to the printer, 'I've just received your letter, at exactly three o'clock, and I answer you immediately.

'Firstly I expected a blunt refusal from you, to become involved in all this, and so I'm not too much upset. But God grant me an inspiration of how to find by tomorrow morning the five hundred francs I need today. It's useless to write to Ancelle, you know perfectly well that he's too stupid to do a reasonable thing by himself, and, in any case, I couldn't apply to him without your sanction. The miserable man has been my complete ruin, without knowing it, the ruin of my fortune, the ruin of my time. He'll never know or realize the enormous compensation he owes me.

'As for you, my dear mother, I must say that I didn't at all understand your letter, absolutely not at all. *I live in terrible solitude, and in constant anguish, and you send me abuse.* ... It's indeed too much! – It's enough to say "no" calmly, and then to change the subject. The funny thing is that I didn't expect the kind of help I begged you (I felt that you wouldn't understand it, and I bet you don't understand my letters any better than I understand yours!) but I did expect,

I say, at least a few compliments, or at least some praise, on my courage and my diligence, which are able to surmount so much humiliation, so much abuse, so much injustice, which have made of me the strangest martyr in the whole of Paris. I expected also a few words of affection and encouragement. But there was nothing of that, nothing at all. – Indeed, in short, I find it impossible, and have always found it impossible, to understand on what your mind feeds, in what kind of atmosphere you live. You show me sometimes such symptoms of pig-headedness in minor points, that, far from feeling anger, I feel on these occasions completely disarmed, and ready to forgive you everything.

'I realize how much I'll hurt you by these last lines; you'll not understand, and you'll feel an insult is intended. And yet, I swear to you, that I understand your affection, and I know your devotion, and I know well that I've an enormous debt of gratitude to discharge towards you. But, good Heavens! how dangerous and clumsy your affection can be sometimes.

'Truth, however, must burst out sometimes, and it's really too hard to receive a torrent of abuse (yes, it is abuse) in one's most difficult moments.

'And then, when one has had the misfortune to incur debts, they always increase, and all expenses increase also, without anything being able to stop this lamentable spiral. That is a platitude which all the poor wretches know, who have got into debt. And I know that, until they are completely settled, I'll be in Hell. It's you I owe that to, and yet I don't love you any the less.

'I beg you, if you find any bitterness in this letter, to do your best to forgive it; that won't be too difficult for you, if you remember all I've endured in the situation which has lasted such a long time.'

Les Nouvelles Histoires Extraordinaires appeared finally in March 1857, with the *Notes Nouvelles sur Poe* as an introduction, the article on which he had spent so much time and patience, and which contains some of his most interesting and original aesthetic theories, which will be discussed in the following chapter.

He sent the volume again to Sainte-Beuve, hoping that he might at last obtain some recognition from the foremost living critic, but previous disappointments had made him now less sanguine than formerly, and he only tentatively suggested his hopes of a notice. He pencilled on the copy he sent, 'À mon maître et ami, Souvenir?' hinting, doubtless, at a promise of an article, and he said in his letter:[16]

'You are too kind to take offence at the impertinent inter-rogation mark which I added to the word "*souvenir*" on the copy of the *Nouvelles Histoires Extraordinaires* which I left for you at the *Moniteur*. If you can see your way to be agree-able to me, I'll think it quite natural; — if you can't I'll think it natural also.'

Sainte-Beuve answered saying that he did remember, but he asked for a little time. The article was never written. The critic did not dare this time, any more than on the previous occasion, to express openly his opinion on so controversial a writer as Charles Baudelaire.

In April 1857 Baudelaire succeeded in publishing nine further *Fleurs du Mal* in *La Revue Française* and three more in *L'Artiste* in May. Those which came out in *La Revue Française* were *La Beauté*, *La Géante*, *Le Flambeau Vivant*, *Harmonie du Soir*, *Le Flacon*, *Le Poison*, *Tout Entière*, *Sonnet* (*Avec ses Vêtements ondoyants, etc.*) and *Sonnet* (*Je te donne ces Vers*). And those in *L'Artiste* were *L'Héautonti-morouménos*, *L'Irrémédiable*, and *Franciscae Maea Laudes*.

At the same time his entire collection of *Les Fleurs du Mal* was in the press, and almost ready, for it came out in June 1857.

Baudelaire had suffered so many disappointments, humi-liations and injustice, that he looked into the future with apprehension and terror, even though this event was the one he had hoped and longed for during so many years.

'I shan't bore you, or tire you with my private sorrows,' he wrote to his mother.[17] 'I'd however like you to know that not a single day passes without my gaze turning towards your little house. But oh! what emptiness round me! What darkness, what nocturnal moral gloom, and what terrors of the future!

'I send you my love and I love you dearly!'

[10]

Essays in Criticism
1852—1859

IN the eighteen-fifties, before he had published *Les Fleurs du Mal*, Baudelaire was known chiefly as an art critic, and his fame in this respect had been gradually developing since his second *Salon* of 1846 which Prarond had described as a 'catechism' of painting. His most interesting and original articles, however, were written in the period after his infatuation for the writings of Poe began, when he discovered many of his own ideas. This gave him confidence in his own aesthetic doctrine and the ambition to formulate it for publication. His richest period as a critic runs from 1852 to his departure for Belgium in the spring of 1864. During this time he was occupied in defining his aesthetic ideal, and in composing the poetry which would exemplify it. To appreciate his poetry, which is his main claim to immortality, it is necessary to understand his doctrine of art. His poetry was the crystallization – unconscious almost – of his vision, in a poem, while his criticism was a meditation on the nature of a work of art, and the principles which underlie it.[1] He reflected deeply on these problems and he believed that every great artist by the force of circumstances was bound eventually to become a critic. He was very much interested in the survival of his own criticism, and did not underrate its importance, since he valued it as highly as his poetic works. Towards the end of his life, when he was having difficulties in finding a publisher, he could have obtained a contract for his book of poems, but he did not wish to separate it from his other writings, which he considered made an organic whole, and one of his deep sorrows and regrets was the thought that he might die without seeing his criticism published in book form. 'It is hard to die,' he wrote to his mother,[2] 'without having at least published my critical work!' He was never to enjoy this pleasure, for it was published only after his death in his complete works, when it had been bought up, at the auction of his writings, at a bargain price.

Through his artistic training and the breadth of his reading and taste, he was well suited to the tasks of a critic, and few have written on the art of painting with more technical insight, and at the same time with more appreciation of its general aspect. Even if he had never composed his poems, he would still deserve fame as a critic. In aesthetic matters his ideas were more penetrating and sensitive than those of Sainte-Beuve, who is nevertheless acclaimed as the greatest French critic of the nineteenth century. Sainte-Beuve was a man who had read widely on a large range of subjects since his earliest boyhood, and the sureness of his touch with regard to the past, as well as his competence in dealing with many branches of learning, had been thereby developed. He was, however, more interested in personalities, in history, in ideas, than in aesthetic principles. The value of his criticism lay in his erudition and knowledge, in his psychological insight, rather than in his artistic perception, and he did not possess the intuitive feeling by which to gauge the value of contemporary art and literature. Here he was often mistaken in his judgements. Many of those amongst his contemporaries whom he praised have not stood the test of time. He supported Ernest Feydeau and not Flaubert; Béranger and not Baudelaire. But almost all the artists whom Baudelaire admired and singled out for praise have survived the destruction of time; and, still more significant, they are prized today, allowing for the difference in taste and conventions between his age and ours, for the same qualities which he found in them. He showed penetration in his judgement of Delacroix, at a moment when that artist was being abused by every critic, and praised him so heavily in 1855 that he lost his contract with *Le Pays*. Delacroix' exhibition of 1859 was called his Waterloo, and, after that

date, he ceased submitting any further pictures to the *Salon*.
It was to thank the poet for the sympathetic understanding
in his *Salon* of 1859 that he wrote to him: [3]

'How can I ever thank you sufficiently for this further
proof of your friendship? You come to my aid when I'm
abused, and torn to pieces by a large number of serious
critics – or who, at least, consider themselves as such! These
gentlemen seem to want things on the largest scale possible,
but I simply submitted what I'd ready, without waiting to
measure them to discover whether they corresponded with
the proportions which seem to be required in order to reach
posterity with decency and decorum. But, having had the
pleasure of pleasing you, I can now bear their complaints
with equanimity. You treat me as only the very illustrious
dead are treated! You make me blush, even though you
give me the greatest pleasure! Such is human frailty!

'Goodbye, and publish more often! You put something of
yourself into everything that you write, and the admirers of
your talent complain only of the rarity of your publications.'

At the height of his own financial distress, Baudelaire
spent much valuable time in trying to find subscribers for
a set of etchings by Meryon, against the opinion of his contemporaries, because he believed in his future as an artist.

Baudelaire is more assured as a critic of painting than of
any other art, for he had been trained in it from childhood.
In his *Journaux Intimes* he says of pictures, 'Ma grande,
mon unique, ma primitive passion'; [4] and, in his *Note Autobiographique*,[5] 'Goût permanent, depuis l'enfance, de toutes
les représentations plastiques.' His articles on the plastic arts
are appreciated by painters as well as by the lay mind. On
the other hand, when he writes on music, it is as an amateur
who knows little of the art from the technical point of view,
but who merely enjoys listening to certain forms of composition which affect his senses, and who is stimulated and
inspired by the visions and fancies which they awaken in
him. These are, however, individual and personal and would
be of little value to a musician. When we read what he wrote

about Wagner, we realize that, although he was emotionally transported by this music, he did not *listen* to it in the true sense, but allowed himself to be borne away by it, as by some mighty sea, which he could neither understand nor withstand.

The period of Baudelaire's most original work in criticism runs parallel with that of his highest creative writings, that is to say it belongs to seven or eight years between 1852 and 1859 or 1860. The most fertile years were those between 1855 and 1859. In May and June 1855 he published the series of articles dealing with different aspects of the *Exposition Universelle*. Next came the *Introduction* to his first volume of translations from Poe in 1856, which was vastly superior to his first articles of 1852; then, in 1857, came his *Notes Nouvelles sur Poe*, which served as an *Introduction* to the second volume of tales. After this, in 1859, there was his greatest *Salon*, which is far more than a mere notice on an exhibition, but is as well an essay on creative imagination. In that same year he wrote his pamphlet on Constantin Guys which could serve as an introduction to modern French painting, but which was published only in 1863. After 1859 he produced little that was new, and most of his articles after that date incorporate much of what he had previously written in other connections – as his study of Gautier borrows the most interesting passages from his *Notes Nouvelles sur Poe*, and, in his obituary for Delacroix in 1863, he quotes the most significant passages from his earlier article of 1855.

The critical writings of his maturity begin with his articles in the short-lived *Semaine Théâtrale*, mentioned in an earlier chapter. The first, in November 1851, is an outburst against the triviality of the common-sense school, the *École du Bon Sens*, with its false ideal of utility; and it demanded truth in literature, not merely realism. The second, in January 1852, is a violent attack against the current classical inspiration – obsession might be a more correct description – which was so widespread in the middle of the nineteenth century, as a reaction against the Gothic convention of

Romanticism. At that time many monstrosities had already been perpetrated in the name of Hellenic beauty, but the disease had not yet reached its most virulent stage, when the disciples of Louis Ménard were to preach a return to Greek polytheism, as the most satisfactory and complete expression of human wisdom. It was original in 1852 to oppose this influence, and Baudelaire said in his article, entitled *L'École Païenne*:[6]

'Depuis quelque temps j'ai tour l'Olympe à mes trousses, et j'en souffre beaucoup; je reçois des dieux sur la tête comme on reçoit des cheminées. Il me semble que je fais un mauvais rêve, que je roule à travers le vide et qu'une foule d'idoles de bois, de fer, d'or et d'argent, tombent avec moi, me poursuivent dans ma chute, me cognent et me brisent la tête et les reins.'

The insincerity of such art repelled him, just as he was irritated when he saw modern painters trying to reproduce the *naïveté* of Cimabue, and he considered it nothing better than a pastiche, a 'pastiche inutile et dégoûtant'. He concluded that it was intellectual suicide to disown Christian philosophy and religion, and added that he had suffered, long enough already, this foolish and childish make-belief.

'Je connais un bon nombre d'hommes de bonne foi qui sont, comme moi, las, attristés, navrés et brisés par cette comédie dangereuse. Il faut que la littérature aille retremper ses forces dans une atmosphère meilleure.'

He thought that the only way in which literature could renew itself was by seeking inspiration in its own age, in contemporary emotion, for, as he was to say when writing of Guys as the painter of modern life: 'Toute notre originalité vient de l'estampille que le temps imprime à nos sensations.' Only laziness induced an artist to declare that everything which was modern was ugly; it was simpler to believe that than to try to extract the core of beauty from ordinary sights of everyday life, which did not possess remoteness to lend them false charm. He believed that life gave unconsciously to everything in which it was sincerely manifested a mysterious core of beauty, a seed which could not fructify until an artist had breathed upon it. Thus all forms of modernity were capable and worthy of becoming classic, and if they did not do so the fault lay with the artist and not with the age. It was this appreciation of the beauty in modernity which he admired in Courbet.[7] 'Il faut rendre à Courbet cette justice qu'il n'a pas peu contribué à rétablir le goût de la simplicité et de la franchise, et l'amour dés- intéressé, absolu de la peinture.'

This sense of modernity must not be confused with the realism which was in vogue at the time, the material realism exemplified in the writings of Champfleury, Feydeau and Duranty, which aimed at being a faithful record of what the physical eye had perceived. He may have been drawn towards realism for a short time, between 1844 and 1848, but by 1852 he had completely abandoned it for more idealistic principles. Both he and Flaubert stand in a similar relationship to the Realist Movement, both disliking its manifestations, and both refusing to be classed amongst its exponents. Baudelaire called it 'une injure dégoûtante jetée à la face de tous les analystes, mot vague et élastique qui signifie pour le vulgaire, non pas une méthode nouvelle de création, mais une description minutieuse des accessoires.'[8]

When he became sure of his direction, he felt nothing but contempt for their ideal of art because it did not take into account spiritual reality, and did not see beyond the material facts which he himself found trivial and boring. In his *Salon* of 1859 he said:[9] 'Je trouve inutile de représenter ce qui est, parce que rien de ce qui est ne me satisfait.' He therefore expressed an almost twentieth-century dislike of that in- vention, new in his day, photography, and declared that those who asserted that they worshipped nature, and that the function of art was to be a faithful copy of nature, had found their prayers answered in an almost miraculous man- ner – but as if by some evil genius – by Daguerre. If faith- fulness to nature is the hallmark of art, then photography which, theoretically, is intended to be its most accurate representation, must be the most perfect of all the arts. The logical outcome of realism, as the new school understood it, was that photography should be prized as the essence of art. Baudelaire's artistic intuition recoiled from such a doctrine; for he had always claimed, even in his earliest articles, that art existed only by reason of what man added of his own substance, of his own soul, to the raw material of nature. He could not endure the Romantic idealization of nature, nor the Rousseau myth of the nobility of natural man, uncorrupted by civilization. He believed, on the contrary, that the only value in man consisted in his spiritual essence, which only self-discipline and self-culture could develop, and that this was of greater price than anything which could be discovered in nature. The Romantic poets had been obsessed by nature, whether they saw her cruel and relentless – as Vigny did, or friendly and consoling – as did Lamartine, but they were always self-conscious in their attitude towards her and were unable to treat her naturally. Baudelaire felt that such behaviour was an affectation, and he tried to put nature in her proper place, for he thought that man lost his pride and dignity by being too humble with her. The violence of his opinions is due to his reaction against sentimentality.[10]

'La nature fut prise dans ce temps-là comme base, source et type de tout bien et de tout beau possible. ... La nature n'enseigne rien, ou presque rien, c'est à dire qu'elle contraint l'homme à dormir, à boire, à manger, et à se garantir, tant bien que mal contre les hostilités de l'atmosphère. C'est elle qui pousse l'homme à tuer son semblable, à le manger, à le séquestrer, à le torturer. C'est cette infaillible nature qui a créé le parricide et l'anthropophagie, et mille autres abominations que la pudeur et la délicatesse nous empêchent de nommer. C'est la religion qui nous ordonne de nourrir des parents pauvres et infirmes. La nature (qui n'est autre chose que la voix de notre intérêt) nous commande de les assommer. Passez en revue, analysez tout ce qui est naturel, toutes les actions et les désirs de l'homme naturel, vous ne trou-

verez rien que d'affreux. Le crime est originellement naturel.
La vertu, au contraire, est artificielle, surnaturelle, puisqu'il
a fallu, dans tous les temps, et chez toutes les nations, des
dieux et des prophètes pour l'enseigner à l'humanité
animalisée.'

Nature, he claimed, had no imagination – how boring
were her endless green trees and meadows – and he would
have liked, for a change, the meadows to be painted red and
the trees bright blue. These are sentiments previously expressed by Petrus Borel in his *Champavert*.

To Baudelaire the exuberance of nature, when left in an
undisciplined state, seemed vulgar and pretentious. Writing to Desnoyers in 1855, who had asked him for poems on
nature for inclusion in an anthology which he wished to
publish, he said: [11]

'You ask me for verses for your little collection, verses
about nature, don't you? On the woods, the great oak-trees,
on greenery, insects and the sun, no doubt? But you well
know that I'm incapable of sentimentalizing over vegetables,
and that I'm opposed to this extraordinary new religion
which, by its nature, is bound to shock a spiritual being. I'll
never be able to believe that the soul of the gods resides in
plants, and even were it so, it wouldn't interest me in the
slightest, I'd still hold my own soul of higher price than
that of these sanctified vegetables. Indeed, I've always
thought that there was something distressing and almost
vulgar in the eternal reflowering and renewal of nature.'

He considered that the only part that nature could play
which was of any value was that of stimulus – an *incitamentum* he called it – for the artist, in bringing out what was
deep in himself, in a latent state. [12]

'La nature extérieure n'est qu'un amas incohérent de
matériaux que l'artiste est invité à associer et à mettre en
ordre, un "incitamentum", un réveil pour les facultés som-
meillantes. Pour parler exactement, il n'y a dans la nature
ni ligne ni couleur. C'est l'homme qui crée la ligne et la
couleur.'

In a desire to wipe out the convention of belief in the beauty of natural things, he was often led to write paradoxically in favour of artificiality, and even of artifice. Believing that the function of art was not to imitate nature, or to reform her, but to do better what she had often only hastily conceived, he devoted a whole chapter to the significance of make-up in women, not because it simulated the freshness of youth, but because it altered and improved what nature had roughly executed. Human skin, in its natural state, he thought, was often faulty and discoloured, but powder and paint brought the discordant tones together, harmonizing them and creating unity; just as silken tights drew the jarring elements of the body into a symmetry which resembled that of a statue.[13]

'Ainsi, si je suis bien compris, la peinture du visage ne doit pas être employée dans le but vulgaire, inavouable, d'imiter la belle nature et de rivaliser avec la jeunesse. Qui oserait assigner à l'art la fonction stérile d'imiter la nature? Le maquillage n'a pas à se cacher, à éviter de se laisser deviner; il peut, au contraire, s'étaler, sinon avec affectation, au moins avec une espèce de candeur.'

Many of the paradoxes by which he illustrated his theory have been repeated to his detriment, for instance the episode related by Maxime Rude. Baudelaire said to him one day, in great excitement:[14]

'"I've just seen the most delightful and charming girl at the Variétés. She has the most lovely brows imaginable, drawn with a pencil, eyes which owe their depth to the judicious use of mascara, a voluptuous mouth which would be non-existent were it not for her lipstick, and the most beautiful hair, which is a wig!"

'"She must be a monster!" answered Rude.

'"She is a great artist!" replied the poet.'

Search for beauty, aspiration towards beauty, was the main preoccupation of Baudelaire's mature life, and for him beauty was essentially a spiritual reality, of which the manifestations here on earth were only symbols, imperfect symbols. This attitude has already been mentioned in connection with his theory of *correspondances*.

It is in the articles where he tries to define his conception of beauty, the nature of inspiration, and the function of art, that Baudelaire owes most to Edgar Allan Poe, and borrows most from him. Evidently he had read and meditated on the ideas expressed in the *Marginalia* and especially in *The Poetic Principle*, which he uses extensively in several critical works, from the articles dealing with Poe himself to his *Salon* of 1859.

It must not be imagined that he is here guilty of sly plagiarism, as many critics have suggested. In the *Notes Nouvelles sur Poe* he mentions *The Poetic Principle*, acknowledging his indebtedness to it, even though he does not always place his borrowings between inverted commas. Sometimes he quotes directly from the text, and indicates that he is doing so; at others he summarizes what he is using, suggesting his proceeding; but elsewhere he restates the theories which he thinks valuable, in his own words and without acknowledgement, although Poe is used as an illustration.

It is not probable that he wished, deliberately, to take credit for what he had not conceived. Rather he had assimilated the ideas of the American, had made them part of his own substance, so that his own life-blood flowed through them and gave them new life. Moreover, he was passionately anxious to propagate in France certain aesthetic theories which seemed to him permanently true and vital, and not to claim priority of invention. He found in Poe's writings confirmation and formulation of his own poetic intuitions, and absorbed them in himself, later giving them back in a slightly different form, more succinctly, stripped of pedantry and clumsiness, and embellished with more elegance of phrase.

It was in Poe that he found the theory – or rather its formulation – that art was the greatest, and perhaps the

only, means of effecting beauty in this world, art inspired
by the mysterious and undying attraction for the ideal.[15]

'C'est à la fois par la poésie, et à travers la poésie, par et à
travers la musique, que l'âme entrevoit les splendeurs situées
derrière le tombeau; et quand un poème exquis amène les
larmes au bord des yeux, elles sont le témoignage d'une
nature exilée dans l'imparfait qui voudrait s'emparer im-
médiatement, sur cette terre même, d'un paradis révélé.'

Sometimes the opinions which Poe expresses are those
which were generally held by the Art for Art's Sake Movement, as when both Poe and Baudelaire claim that poetry
should have no other aim but itself.[16]

'Une foule de gens se figurent que le but de la poésie est un
enseignement quelconque, qu'elle doit tantôt fortifier la conscience, tantôt perfectionner les mœurs, tantôt enfin
démontrer quoi que ce soit d'utile. La poésie n'a pas d'autre
but qu'elle-même; elle ne peut en avoir d'autre, et aucun
poème ne sera si grand, si noble, si véritablement digne du
nom de poème que celui qui aura été écrit uniquement pour
le plaisir d'écrire un poème.'

On many occasions Baudelaire castigates the didactic
element in certain literature of his day, which he calls the
greatest heresy of modern times. He voiced his disgust of the
École du Bon Sens, of such works as *Le Fils Naturel*, by the
younger Dumas, in the preface to which the dramatist
stated: 'Toute littérature qui n'a pas en vue la perfectibilité;
la moralisation, l'utile en un mot, est une littérature
rachitique et malsaine.' The same disgust he found also in
Poe, though not the same illustration; but, he adds, what
he did not find in the American author, belief in the en-
nobling function of the highest art, the conviction that no
real work of art, which fulfilled the conditions of beauty,
could be pernicious art. He only maintained that for an artist
to impose his own view of morality and conduct was to follow a sanctimonious and self-satisfied aim, since moral
standards are prone to be variable and fallible. He firmly
believed, however, that all great art, by reason of its spiritual

inspiration, which was inseparable from it, could raise humanity up from the rut of vulgar interests and materialism.[17]

'Je ne veux pas dire que la poésie n'ennoblisse pas les mœurs – qu'on me comprenne bien – que son résultat final ne soit pas d'élever l'homme au-dessus du niveau des intérêts vulgaires; ce serait évidemment une absurdité.'

He expresses the same sentiments in a letter to Swinburne,[18] when he declares that a great poem must by its very nature suggest some kind of moral, but that it is for the reader to discover it, if he is ready to receive it. The lesson is, in fact, in himself rather than in the poem, which had only served the purpose of unlocking a portion of his being which he had not known, hitherto, existed.

His views here are interesting at a moment when there seemed otherwise, in France, no alternative to common-sense didacticism other than the arid theories of pure art which produced the poems of those who, like Banville, confined themselves to technical gymnastics.

Baudelaire, who was at heart a moralist, believed that it was only through self-discipline, through self-improvement, that a man could become an artist and be granted the spiritual experience of beholding ideal beauty. Only those who succeeded in eradicating impurities from themselves would be able to discover the most effective metaphors to symbolize their vision, would be able to decipher the symbolic book of nature. All great artists, he thought, experienced horror and recoil from a state of sin and imperfection, on account of its discord in the perfect harmony.[19]

'Ce qui exaspère l'homme de goût dans le spectacle du vice, c'est sa difformité, sa disproportion. Le vice porte atteinte au juste et au vrai; comme outrage à l'harmonie, comme dissonance, il blessera plus particulièrement certains esprits poétiques; et je ne crois pas qu'il soit scandalisant de considérer tout infraction à la morale, comme une espèce de faute contre le rhythme et la prosodie universels.'

Baudelaire attempts to formulate his definition of beauty,

and in this he follows no one, but is entirely original. For
him, unlike the other poets of the Art for Art's Sake Movement, beauty did not reside in the subject itself, but in what
each artist brought to it. Thus beauty could never be static
or immutable, but bore inevitably the hallmark of the individual artist, which he calls its 'dose de bizarrerie', that is
the personal idiosyncrasy of the artist, his own particular
escape from the conventional, his original way of conveying
his experience and suggestion. Beauty could never be banal
and commonplace.

   'Le beau est toujours bizarre. Je ne veux pas dire qu'il soit
volontairement, roidement bizarre, car dans ce cas il serait
un monstre sorti des rails de la vie. Je dis qu'il contient
toujours un peu de bizarrerie naïve, inconsciente, et que c'est
cette bizarrerie qui le fait particulièrement le Beau! Ren-
versez la proposition, et tâchez de concevoir un beau banal!
Or comment cette bizarrerie, nécessaire, incompressible,
variéc à l'infini, dépendante des milieux, des climats, des
mœurs, de la race, de la religion, et du tempérament de
l'artiste, pourra-t-elle jamais être gouvernée, amendée,
redressée, par les règles utopiques conçues dans un petit
temple scientifique quelconque de la planète, sans danger
de mort pour l'art lui-même? Cette dose de bizarrerie qui
constitue et définit l'individualité, sans laquelle il n'y a pas
de beau, joue dans l'art – que l'exactitude de cette comparaison en fasse pardonner la trivialité – le rôle du goût
ou de l'assaisonnement dans les mets, les mets ne différant
les uns des autres, abstraction faite de la quantité de substance nutritive qu'ils contiennent, que par l'idée qu'ils
révèlent à la langue.'[20]

   Beauty must also reflect the total destiny of man, and it
will then have sadness in it, for the fate of man is tragic. In
Fusées he declares that beauty 'a quelque-chose d'ardent et
de triste – des besoins spirituels, des ambitions ténébreuse-
ment refoulées.'[21] And beauty, since it represents the whole
of life, must have in it something of ugliness and sin, something of both Heaven and Hell, of both sunset and dawn.[22]

Beauty, however, always remains beyond the grasp of the artist, and mysterious, seizing hold of him against his will, and leaving him no further liberty.[23]

'Ah! faut-il éternellement souffrir ou fuir éternellement le beau? Nature, enchanteresse sans pitié, rivale toujours victorieuse, laisse-moi! Cesse de tenter mes désirs et mon orgueil! L'étude du beau est un duel où l'artiste crie de frayeur avant d'être vaincu.'

Baudelaire's spiritual view of art led him inescapably to belief in the unity of all art, of all the arts. Since art is the symbol of spiritual experience, then all the different arts are the concrete expression of the same experience. In an earlier chapter mention has been made of his doctrine of the total aspect of beauty, which each of the arts expresses in its own language. This is one of the most important of his aesthetic articles of faith, and he describes it as a self-evident fact which only blindness and lack of perception have prevented man from recognizing.[24]

'Ce qui serait vraiment surprenant, c'est que le son ne pût suggérer la couleur, que les couleurs ne pussent pas donner l'idée d'une mélodie, et que le son et la couleur fussent impropres à traduire les idées; les choses s'étant toujours exprimées par une analogie réciproque, depuis le jour où Dieu a proféré le monde comme une complexe et indivisible totalité.'

In his article on Delacroix, he describes the musical impression which one of his pictures left on him.[25]

'Ces admirables accords de sa couleur font souvent rêver d'harmonie et de mélodie, et l'impression qu'on emporte de ses tableaux est souvent quasi musicale.'

He evokes the same sensation in his poem, *Les Phares*:[26]

> *Delacroix, lac de sang, hanté des mauvais anges,*
> *Ombragé par un bois de sapins toujours vert,*
> *Où, sous un ciel chagrin, des fanfares étranges*
> *Passent comme un soupir étouffé de Weber.*

Baudelaire's spiritual view of beauty led him to the belief

that it could not be perceived through the aid of the senses alone, but only through imagination. Imagination then became for him the most precious of all the faculties, and by imagination he did not mean mere fantasy – in this he followed Poe – for he mistrusted romantic illusion. Imagination for him was a divine faculty, the queen of faculties, who puts order into what the eye has merely seen. He says in his *Salon* of 1859:[27]

'Tout l'univers visible n'est qu'un magasin d'images et de signes auxquels l'imagination donnera une place et une valeur relative; c'est une espèce de pâture que l'imagination doit digérer et transformer. Toutes les facultés de l'âme humaine doivent être subordonnées à l'imagination, qui les met en réquisition toutes à la fois.'

It is imagination which perceives the secret and hidden connection between things, the eternal 'analogies' which are the only substance of true art. Imagination teaches man to use metaphors,[28] since only a man gifted with the highest order of imagination can read the book of nature with enough insight to choose amongst the wealth of metaphors laid out for his choice those which are most expressive. Imagination can take to pieces the work of the Creator, and build it up again into something new. It would be rash to claim that the combination of trees, mountains, rivers, or lakes which we call a landscape, has any beauty in itself, since its only beauty lies in the vision which the artist has of it, and in his capacity to realize his vision.

The alliance between painting and poetry had been formed earlier in the century, when Gautier said that poets and painters worked with the same tools, in the same substance, for the same aims; but he had no true understanding of the connection which might exist between poetry and music, and was merely advocating that pictorial poetry should take the place of the sentimental outpourings of the Romantic poets concerning nature.

Baudelaire, however, dreamed of a total aspect of beauty, appealing to all his senses at once, 'fondus en un':[29]

> *O métamorphose mystique*
> *De tous mes sens fondus en un!*
> *Son haleine fait la musique,*
> *Comme sa voix fait le parfum.*

Like Poe he felt that music, more than any of the other arts, was capable of expressing spiritual beauty. This is the experience of most sensitive people. When they have heard Beethoven's *Missa Solemnis*, or the last quartets, or the Ninth Symphony, they are made aware that the composer has undergone an intense spiritual and mystical experience, which could thus find its adequate expression only in music, for music can evoke what cannot be rendered in logical words. Hoffmann said, in his *Kreisleriana*, that music was the common speech of nature, that, with its mysterious sounds, it can speak directly to us, but that when we try to express this message in other hieroglyphics we can only give the shadow of what we have perceived.

In *The Poetic Principle* Poe expresses similar sentiments:

'It is in music perhaps that the soul most nearly attains the great end for which, when inspired by the Poetic Sentiment, it struggles – the creation of supernal Beauty. It *may* be, indeed, that here this sublime end is, now and then, attained in fact. ... And thus there can be little doubt that in the union of Poetry with Music, we shall find the widest field for Poetic developments.'

Thus, in his poetry, Baudelaire tried to emulate music as nearly as possible, and often did succeed in expressing its most subtle emotions. Like Poe, he realized how poetry could be enriched from a union – even fusion – with music. In the rough draft of a preface to the second edition of *Les Fleurs du Mal*, which was never finished, he wrote:[30]

'La poésie touche à la musique par une prosodie dont les racines plongent plus avant dans l'âme humaine que ne l'indique aucune théorie classique.'

Although he knew little of it Baudelaire enjoyed listening to music which possessed evocative power, which aroused in him, as the Symbolists were to say, 'un état d'âme', and the music of Wagner was a revelation to him of almost the same order as that of the writings of Poe. He was much interested as well in Wagner's aesthetic doctrine, so like his own. Wagner believed also that painters, poets and musicians had an identical aim, enjoyed the same vision, which they made concrete in their own form of art to give a total impression of Beauty. He believed that none of the arts could henceforth exist alone, and conceived of a communal corporation of the arts – a kind of *United Arts Organization* – in which each art worked for the common weal. He imagined one single form of art, which would comprise them all, and for him this one glorified form was to be musical drama, which would become the focal point of all the arts – a synthesis. This was to be the final art, the perfect harmony, capable of expressing what each art could not achieve separately and alone. It meant a comradeship between all the arts, a fusion, in which each lost some of its sovereignty and individuality while working for the united cause.

Baudelaire's theory was more subtle. He did not wish art to add to the common fund what the others had been unable to bring, he did not envisage co-operation. On the contrary, since Beauty is indivisible, is one single reality, since seeing and hearing are only different manifestations of the same experience and sensation – different windows opening into the soul – he believed each art could separately achieve the same effect as the others; each could glide imperceptibly into the other, adopting its means of expression. In his case the practice was successful for he was a master in the art of suggestion, but the theory had its dangers in less experienced hands. Mallarmé also, who was as gifted as Baudelaire in the art of *correspondances* – perhaps even surpassing him – reached subtlety of evocation. His aim was to make his poems, like music, capable of a multiplicity of interpretations. Commentators do him a disservice, go counter to his deepest intentions, when they try to tie him down to one single and definitive meaning.

Later some of the poets of the Symbolist Movement, carrying Wagner's and Baudelaire's theories to their logical conclusion, may be blamed for many of the abuses and excesses of the School. They tried to make poetry express what it was incapable of expressing, and took over, often disastrously, the methods of music. Since their poetry, like a piece of music, was to be capable of many diverse interpretations, there was the risk that a joke and parody, like the *Déliquescences d'Adoré Floupette*, by Henri Beauclair and Gabriel Vicaire, might be taken seriously as true poetry. It was such a clever and subtle parody of the excesses of Symbolist verse, that many believed it was an original work, composed in all good faith, and the taste of the time was so strange that no one was surprised at its title, nor at the author's name, with the result that praise or blame was showered on it in the same proportion as on any new and daring work of art. The young poets were gifted and some of their efforts, such as the poem entitled *Suavitas*, did, in fact, like *Jabberwocky* in *Through the Looking-Glass*, attain the suggestivity of music:

> *L'Adorable Espoir de la Renoncule*
> *A nimbé mon cœur d'une Hermine d'Or.*
> *Pour le Rossignol qui sommeille encor,*
> *La candeur du Lys est un crépuscule.*
>
> *Feuilles d'ambre gris et jaune! Chemins*
> *Qu'enlace une valse à peine entendue,*
> *Horizons teintés de cire fondue,*
> *N'odorez-vous pas la tiédeur des mains.*
>
> *O Pleurs de la Nuit! Étoiles moroses!*
> *Votre aile mystique effleure nos fronts,*
> *La Vie agonise et nous expirons*
> *Dans la Mort suave et pâle des Roses.*

Closely linked with Baudelaire's worship of beauty was his appreciation of good craftsmanship, of work well done, and he realized the truism that it is only with perfection of form that a work of art can hope to reach immortality, and that, without technique flawless of its kind, no artist is worthy of the consideration of posterity. Oscar Wilde wrote, in *The Critic as an Artist*, that every century which produces great poetry is in that respect an artificial century, and that the work which seems to us to be the most natural and simple product of its time, is always the result of the most self-conscious effort. There is no art without self-consciousness, and self-consciousness and the critical spirit are one and the same thing. Baudelaire thus believed that the more gifted a poet was, the more he needed self-criticism and knowledge of his craft, and that no talent, however great, could excuse carelessness in this respect.

'Plus on possède d'imagination,' he wrote,[31] 'mieux il faut posséder le métier pour accompagner celle-ci dans ses aventures et surmonter les difficultés qu'elle recherche avidement.'

He expressed passionate revulsion against fluent writing based on mere inspiration, and never considered it a compliment when he was praised for his facility. To his mother he wrote:[32]

'I don't know how many times you've spoken to me of my facility. It's a very common expression, but which can apply only to superficial minds. Do you mean facility in conception or in expression? I've never possessed either, and it ought to be self-evident that the little amount of work I've produced has been the result of long and painful labour.'

It is this dislike of facile fluency which explains his very severe, and somewhat unjust, appraisal of Musset, about whom he once wrote to Armand Fraisse:[33]

'Except about the time of my First Communion, that is to say at an age when anything connected with whores and silken ladders seems a religious experience, I've never been able to endure that prince of fops, with his impudence of a spoilt child, calling heaven and earth to witness on account of his commonplace adventures, with his slimy torrent of mistakes of grammar and prosody, and his total incapacity to appreciate the labour by which a mere flash of inspiration can become a work of art.'

His letters to his publisher, whenever he was in the throes of bringing out a book, reveal his scrupulous self-criticism as an artist. Often he paid for the resetting of type, or the destruction of sheets, out of his own pocket, rather than allow a work to appear which did not come up to his high standard of achievement. When he was lying paralysed in Belgium and could not write himself, but was obliged to dictate to others what he wanted to say, his last conscious acts showed anxiety for the accuracy in the printing of the titles of his poems which were being published in a review, and concern about a punctuation mark which had been misplaced;[34] also, when thanking a friend for his collection of poems, he called his attention to a mistake in rhythm in one line.[35]

He did not value technique for the sake of technique, or originality, as did Banville, and he never discusses prosody in his critical articles. His efforts in composition were always aimed at reaching a clearer crystallization of his vision, and this was very different from the old-maidish precision of Hérédia.

Since each of his poems was intended to be the evocation of an experience based on intense emotion, at one given moment, he agreed with Poe in thinking that a long poem did not exist and was a contradiction in terms; that, as the American author says in *The Poetic Principle*, 'a poem deserves its title only in as much as it excites by elevating the soul. The value of a poem is in the ratio of this elevating excitement. That degree of excitement which would entitle a poem to be so called at all, cannot be sustained throughout a composition of any great length.' Baudelaire believed that long poems were written only by those who had not sufficient talent or powers of concentration to compose shorter works. He goes on to say, paraphrasing Poe's arguments, but acknowledging the source of his opinions:[36]

'Un poème ne mérite son titre qu'autant qu'il excite, qu'il enlève l'âme, et la valeur positive d'un poème est en raison de cette excitation, de cet enlèvement d'âme. Mais par nécessité psychologique toutes les excitations sont fugitives et transitoires, cet état singulier, dans lequel l'âme du lecteur a été, pour ainsi dire, tirée de force, ne durera certainement pas autant que la lecture de tel poème qui dépasse la ténacité d'enthousiasme dont la nature humaine est capable.'

Although his poems are generally short, Baudelaire needed a great deal of time to perfect them, to make them express the intensity of his spiritual experience, and he would never enslave his vision to the rules of technique. This is probably responsible for some weaknesses of expression in certain of his poems, for he seems to have sometimes preferred a weak line to a false note in his theme.

It is beyond the scope of this work to analyse the prosody of Baudelaire, since this has been often attempted, almost always unsympathetically. He has usually been weighed in the scales of the accepted standards of nineteenth-century verse, and condemned where he gives short measure. It is impossible to claim that there are no weak lines in his work, though it should be said that, like all great artists, he eventually found for himself in his noblest achievements the mould and the discipline best suited to his particular genius, and it is immaterial that this is not the mould of Victor Hugo or Leconte de Lisle. He did not, however, to any great extent, break away technically from the conventional rules and regulations, but accepted generally the prosody of his age, for he was no innovator in form, and does not seem to have desired to be one in essentials. Nevertheless, he was obviously often hampered, on account of his individual theory of poetry, by the rigidity of the French forms – or, if not exactly hampered, certainly delayed. In spite of this his most perfect achievements are those in the circumscribed form, when he was able, by infinite patience and labour, to discipline his inspiration, while sacrificing nothing of its intensity. His finest poems in verse surpass, as works of art, even his most beautiful poems in prose. It is, however, probable that he would have welcomed the innovation of *vers libre* if he had lived long enough to see it.

The noblest qualities in Baudelaire's poetry come from his spiritual view of art, his belief that God and Beauty mean one and the same thing, and for him technique was only the short cut to reach experience of that vision, but could never be an end in itself. It is this spiritual view which eventually altered his conception of the Dandy.

In his own day few listened to Baudelaire when he expounded his aesthetic doctrine, or else they thought him an eccentric madman.[37] It was only after 1865, when he had little time left to live, that some of the more original amongst the younger writers began to realize his importance. Then, in February 1865, Mallarmé published in *L'Artiste* a prose poem which is the evocation of the impression which *Les Fleurs du Mal* had made on him. And, in November of the same year, Verlaine brought out in *L'Art* the only discerning and sympathetic analysis of his writings which appeared during the poet's lifetime. This was the beginning of the first stage of the spread of his influence, and Sainte-Beuve, writing to him, said:[38] 'If you were here you'd be made, willy-nilly, an authority, an oracle, a consulting poet!'

This, however, was not until January 1866, and it was then too late as far as Baudelaire himself was concerned. Two months later he was paralysed, incapable of work, and incapable even of speech.

[11]

The Trial for Obscenity
1857

BAUDELAIRE's one collection of poems, *Les Fleurs du Mal*, long expected, appeared on 25 June 1857. It had suffered many changes and vicissitudes during the previous twelve or thirteen years. As we have seen, a large number of the poems had been composed by 1844, during his period of leisure and luxury at the Hôtel Lauzun. The first mention in print of such a collection was in 1846, when the poet announced its imminent publication under the title *Lesbiennes*, but it did not then appear. By 1848 he had abandoned his first title and was announcing a collection of poems to appear in 1848 entitled *Limbes*.[1] Jean Pommier suggests[2] that this new title may be due to the influence of Fourier who calls 'périodes lymbiques' the beginning of socialism and industrialism. This is certainly the interpretation which some of Baudelaire's contemporaries put on it, and one of them, writing in *La Presse* in 1848, surmised, solely from the title, that the book would be inspired by socialism. This meaning might correspond with the poet's preoccupations during his short revolutionary period, and with the inspiration of some of the poems which he composed at that time. If so it must have been short-lived for, by 1849, Baudelaire despised the ideas of Fourier. When publishing a number of the poems in *Le Messager de l'Assemblée* in 1851, and after mentioning that they are taken from a future collection entitled *Limbes*, he states that they are intended to evoke the spiritual crisis of modern youth.[3] This suggests that he was using the word roughly in its theological sense of *Limbo*, the region on the borders of Hell where dwell those who have been denied Heaven because they have not yet received

the grace of baptism. In 1852 when he sent a batch of poems
to Gautier hoping for publication in *La Revue de Paris*, the
title *Limbes* still held good. In that year, however, by a
strange coincidence, another volume of poems, by a man
called Véron, was published under that title – Baudelaire's
book would not have suffered by comparison since Véron's
only expressed the whimpering sentimentality of dying Romanticism [4] – but Véron was well known at that time, was
even admired by Gautier, and Baudelaire dropped his title
for *Les Fleurs du Mal*. This title, although it suggests only
one aspect of the work, has been generally considered to
suit the whole collection admirably, but its chief value was
that it was bound to startle and to arouse interest. It was not
even of Baudelaire's invention, for Asselineau says that he
heard the critic Hippolyte Babou suggest it to him one
evening at the Café Lemblin, when he was lamenting the
loss of his previous title. The company had cheered the suggestion and the poet had adopted it. He probably did not
intend that it should be interpreted in its usual meaning,
but in its medieval and symbolical sense, that is to say
that certain plants are the emblems of sins and vices. This
is borne out by his description of the frontispiece he
wished Bracquemond to draw for the second edition,[5] which
was to depict plants symbolizing the seven deadly sins stifling
the tree of knowledge and goodness. The plan was eventually
abandoned since the artist was unable to carry out what
Baudelaire wanted, but it was realized later in Brussels by
Rops, and it served as the frontispiece to *Les Épaves* published in Belgium in 1866.

For some unknown reason, Baudelaire again delayed publication and was silent for some years about his collection
of poems; but he was adding to it, and enriching it, for this
was his prolific period, after his mind had been fertilized
by the writings of Swedenborg and Poe. Nothing more was
heard until eighteen poems from it were published in *La
Revue des Deux Mondes* in June 1855, under the title *Les
Fleurs du Mal*.

After the poems had appeared in this review Baudelaire had tried to persuade Michel Lévy to bring out a volume of his poetry, as well as his translations from Poe, but the publisher, as has been described, held back – he may have been nervous since, at this time, Baudelaire was being fiercely attacked on all sides. At last the poet, to precipitate matters, told him that he was thinking of accepting an agreement which the printer Poulet Malassis was prepared to sign. Lévy may have smiled incredulously – his portraits show irony in the curl of the lips – for Poulet Malassis was not known as a publisher. Baudelaire's assertion was nevertheless partly true. The printer had become anxious to branch out into publishing since, five years before, he had inherited the press from his father. For the past few months he had been contemplating bringing out a collection of Baudelaire's poems which he admired, but he had delayed because he was doubtful whether his capital was sufficient for so hazardous a venture. He was only beginning, and his first venture, *Les Odes Funambulesques*, had not yet appeared, although it was in the press. Banville was, however, a successful author, who already had several books to his name. The notorious Baudelaire was a different proposition, and Poulet Malassis had very little capital to risk. His father had earned his living by printing the local newspaper and directory at Alençon, but he himself when he took over had occasionally, for his own pleasure and that of his friends, printed literary booklets, in limited editions on fine paper and beautifully produced. He had thus brought out some of Asselineau's articles – *L'Histoire du Sonnet* and *Les Albums et les Autographes*.[6] He had also published a reprint of an extract from Poe, translated by Baudelaire, *La Philosophie de l'Ameublement*, but unfortunately, through careless proof-reading, he had allowed the author's name to appear as 'Beaudelaire' and the poet had insisted on the whole edition of twenty-five copies being destroyed.

Now Baudelaire, having mentioned to Lévy the possibility of an agreement with Poulet Malassis, was afraid that the

latter might refuse to consider publication.[7] Finally, after
much discussion, the contract was signed in December 1856,
and the poet was to submit his completed manuscript in
January 1857. The edition was to be a thousand copies, sold
at two francs each, and the author was to receive twenty-five
centimes a copy – a royalty of about twelve and a half per
cent – which was a fair bargain for poetry.

As far as the business side was concerned, Baudelaire
could not have fallen into worse hands: Poulet Malassis was
as temperamental and as vague as any artist, and his imagination, his intellectual curiosity and his passion for learning,
place him among men of letters rather than amongst businessmen. A well-printed book, in a limited edition, and
bought only by connoisseurs, gave him more pleasure than
a popular and financial success. He ranks amongst the most
interesting literary figures in the middle of the nineteenth
century, and the books he published are now rarities eagerly
sought by bibliophiles who consider him an innovator in
typography. Asselineau says that in the early days of the
Second Empire, when printing had become vulgar and com-
mercialized, when books were sold at two or three pence, a
few pioneers tried to reintroduce good printing, and that
amongst these Poulet Malassis occupied an honourable place.[8]
For two or three shillings he brought out books printed on
excellent paper, in good type, and with artistic tail-pieces.
Later he added frontispieces by well-known engravers. His
danger was too soft a heart, and he often allowed himself
to be persuaded to publish at a loss the works of a friend.
Banville writes of him wittily:[9]

> *Le typographe Malassis*
> *Que, tout bas, invoque sans trêve,*
> *Le poète inédit qui rêve*
> *Triste et sur une malle assis.*

Baudelaire handed in his manuscript in February 1857,
and the disputes and recriminations began; for the book
took five months to produce, on account of his meticulous

proof-correcting. Poulet Malassis, who had known him intimately now for ten years, and had noticed the disorder and confusion of his private life, could never have believed that he would have been so scrupulous. He himself was inclined to be somewhat slap-dash for he did not consider that a few inaccuracies mattered if the production was otherwise good. But now, each day during the five months of printing, Baudelaire was bombarding him with letters about every sort of detail – sometimes doubts about spelling, sometimes about the use of capitals, sometimes objecting that the paper was too thin and that he disliked the shape of the inverted commas. He spared neither himself nor his publisher, and it was a miracle that the friendship survived for it was often stretched to breaking point. After Poulet Malassis died a note was found amongst his papers saying that there was in his library a copy of the proofs of *Les Fleurs du Mal* 'which bears testimony to its author's passion for perfection, but which also gives a good idea of the superhuman patience of his publisher'.[10] Once, when he was exasperated by Baudelaire's insistence on what he himself considered an unimportant trifle, he wrote on the proofs he was returning: 'I begin to suspect, my dear Baudelaire, that you're only pulling my leg and making a fool of me, which I certainly don't deserve!'[11]

Once, in exasperation, he complained to Asselineau, 'It's impossible to make any headway with Baudelaire, and I'm going to make up my mind to reimburse the firm for the cost of his manuscript. My reliance on him during all my dealings with him is a constant source of complaint from my brother-in-law, who – between ourselves – is justified, for we've had nothing yet, neither proofs of the collection of poems, nor a copy of the book of prose.'[12]

The poet was, however, always ready to see his publisher's point of view. When he had insisted on too many corrections after the type had been set up, he always paid the extra out of his own pocket – or, more likely, added it to his debts. All the changes took time, and the printing works were so encumbered with the set type that no new production could be undertaken until *Les Fleurs du Mal* was out of the way. By the first week in March the book was printed. Yet, two months later, Poulet Malassis was remonstrating with Baudelaire over the delay in publication. Baudelaire answered: [13]

'I'm still struggling with some thirty lines which aren't satisfactory. Don't imagine I've got the facility of Banville!'

Later, when his publisher again complained of the time the book had already taken, he answered: [14]

'I well know, I tell you, how unpopular one makes oneself with all this sort of plaguing, but I'm paying your firm the compliment of taking it seriously, and you once said yourself that you agreed that, in every kind of production, nothing less than perfection was worth while.'

Once Baudelaire almost brought their association to complete disaster by writing an insulting letter to the publisher's brother-in-law, de Broise, who was urging his partner to hasten publication and get the work off their hands. Luckily Poulet Malassis recognized the poet's writing and intercepted the letter. When he had recovered his temper, Baudelaire admitted that his friend had acted sensibly.[15]

'I come now to the second of your eternal complaints concerning "the proof-corrections of Monsieur Baudelaire",' he had written to de Broise. 'If you don't want any more corrections, then you shouldn't send me any more of the scandalous proofs you sent me while Malassis was away in Paris.... These justifications, and the terms in which I feel obliged to make them, are extremely painful to me, but I'd like to call your attention to the following considerations: If you'd been quicker, and less slovenly, you'd not have experienced the necessity – always easy to find – of making these eternal complaints!'

In the end Poulet Malassis imagined that the book would never appear; he began to grow slack and interested in other plans. There seemed no reason why the proof-correcting should ever end, with the poet becoming more meticulous with each new batch. A few days more or less would make no

difference when, after five months of incessant labour, there
was so little to show. It was the poet's turn now to grow exasperated and in June he wrote: [16]

'Why on earth, my dear fellow, don't you write to me?
Have you sworn to leave the proofs full of mistakes, and to
add fresh ones in the tenth sheet, especially in the *Table of
Contents*? What in Heaven's name prevents you from sending me decent proofs, after I've made the corrections, and
before printing? But it's completely impossible to obtain
anything regularly from you! Have you even received the
corrected *Table of Contents*?'

Poulet Malassis was himself too much of an artist to remain long annoyed with Baudelaire on such a score and it is
said that the friendship between the two men, if anything,
was strengthened by this painful experience.

It is alleged that Baudelaire, on the advice of his publisher,
shortened the book, and cut out certain poems which he had
intended to print.[17] He certainly did not publish *L'Albatros*
in this edition, although it had been composed some fourteen years previously, nor the lovely *Hymne*, inspired by
Madame Sabatier, and written several years before. Also, on
the advice of Gautier, he shortened his dedication, since 'a
dedication should not be a "profession de foi".' [18] In its first
proofs there is a mistake, strange for Baudelaire to make.
He had first written 'Au parfait magicien ès langue française'
which, when his error was pointed out to him, he altered to
'ès lettres françaises'.

Baudelaire prepared his publicity very carefully and arranged for copies to be sent to every important poet at home
and abroad. We know that in England, Tennyson, Brown-
ing and De Quincey received theirs; Hugo in Guernsey, and
Longfellow and Willis in the United States.[19]

Les Fleurs du Mal was on sale on 25 June 1857, and soon
afterwards a bombshell burst, in the form of a notice by
Bourdin in *Le Figaro* on 5 July – the paper had not forgotten
its old animosity and this was its third major attack. Bourdin began as Goudall had done two years previously, by

saying that for fifteen years Baudelaire had been hailed as a great poet by a small coterie of admirers who had the audacity to rank him higher even that Hugo, Musset or Béranger. Now that he had ventured to publish a collection of poems, Bourdin said, it was time to review his position and to investigate the grounds on which this phenomenal reputation was based. He had no authority to pass judgement and it was merely his personal and private opinion he was giving for what it was worth. 'Never,' he declared, 'have so many brilliant qualities been squandered! There are moments when one has doubts of the sanity of Monsieur Baudelaire, but there are others, on the contrary, when no doubt is possible! The poems are, for the most part, the monstrous repetition of the same words and ideas. Never, in the space of so few pages, have I seen so many breasts bitten – nay, even chewed! – never have I seen such a procession of devils, of fœtus, of demons, cats and vermin. The whole volume is an asylum full of the inanities of the human mind, of all the putrescence of the human heart. All this would be permissible if the object was to cure them, but they are incurable!' He added the titles of the poems which he considered most pernicious, and ended: 'One can say, indeed it is our duty to do so, that one might conceive of the imagination of a poet of twenty being inspired to treat such subjects, but nothing can justify a man of more than thirty uttering such monstrous monstrosities in a printed book!'[20]

According to Asselineau,[21] it was Billaut, the Minister of the Interior, who prompted the article in *Le Figaro*, furious that Flaubert had been acquitted at the trial of *Madame Bovary* earlier in the year, and determined that this time his victim should not escape.

The rumour soon sprang up amongst Baudelaire's friends that another prosecution for obscenity was impending. The poet himself did not believe that this was serious – no government which had elections on its hands, as was happening in France, would have time to bother about an obscure author.[22] A few days later he heard from Leconte de Lisle,

who had the news from a reliable source, that proceedings
were to be instituted after all, and the whole edition confiscated. Unfortunately Leconte de Lisle had allowed nearly
a week to elapse between hearing the news and informing
Baudelaire, who was now much annoyed with his publisher
for not putting a large number of copies of the book immediately on sale as soon as the rumour of the prosecution
started. Most of the edition was still in sheets, and only a
hundred copies had been bound. He wrote at once urging
Malassis to hide away the sheets before they could be
seized.[23]

'Quick! Quick! Hide away, and hide carefully, the whole
edition! You must have nine hundred copies in sheets!
There were a hundred at L.'s and they seemed very astonished when I said I wanted to save fifty of them. I've put
them in a safe place, and I've signed a receipt for them. That
leaves fifty to throw to the Cerberus of justice.

'That's what happens when one sends a copy to *Le
Figaro*!! That's what happens because you didn't properly
launch the book! If you'd done all that you should have done,
then at least we'd have had the consolation of having sold
out the whole edition in three weeks, and we'd only have
had the notoriety of the prosecution, and it's easy to get
out of that!... I'm sure that this misfortune has happened
as a result of the article in *Le Figaro* and the chatter of
foolish people. Don't gossip! Don't frighten your mother,
or de Broise, and come up to town quickly, so that we can
agree about everything! I'll write you an "official" letter,
which I'll ante-date, and you must destroy the envelope.'

The following day, 12 July, a further incriminatory article
appeared in *Le Figaro* – unsigned this time. On his copy
Baudelaire added that it had been written by a certain
Habans, a protégé of the Minister of the Interior,[24] and this
would support the view that it was Billaut who was the chief
mover.

It was soon apparent that Baudelaire was not going to
escape the clutches of the law. He tried then to whip up

support amongst influential friends, acquaintances and other men of letters. He counted on Mérimée, who had been approached on his behalf.[25] Mérimée said, however, that he would not lift a finger to save Baudelaire from being burnt at the stake – except to advise the Minister to burn others first. When asked to intervene he wrote:[26]

'I believe you mean a book entitled *Les Fleurs du Mal* – a very indifferent work, and not all that dangerous, which contains a few odd flashes of poetic talent – as indeed there may be in any poor devil who knows nothing about life, and who is tired of it merely because some girl of easy virtue has deceived him. I don't know the author, but I'd bet my bottom dollar that he's still a virgin and quite a decent fellow. That's why I'd be just as glad if he wasn't burnt!'

Baudelaire's most influential close friend was Sainte-Beuve. Surely he would at last take up the cudgels since he had praised the poems in manuscript! A favourable article from his pen in the official government paper, *Le Moniteur*, would have a very salutary effect. Sainte-Beuve, however, although prepared to praise the book in private, was afraid to voice the same opinions in his official capacity. Earlier in the year he had defended Flaubert, and had made it clear that he disapproved of the case against *Madame Bovary*, but he was given to understand that the Minister of the Interior took exception to a government paper supporting a work which he was prosecuting. An article had appeared in *L'Univers* deploring the acquittal of Flaubert, and suggesting that Sainte-Beuve should be dismissed for daring to defile an official organ with printing an article in favour of a work which was 'envahi par l'ordure'. Some years later, writing to Turgan, the editor of *Le Moniteur*, Sainte-Beuve mentions the 'raisons impérieuses' which had prevented him from reviewing *Les Fleurs du Mal*,[27] presumably the imperative need not to offend the Minister. His life had been a hard struggle to gain recognition and material security, and he was afraid of jeopardizing everything. After the revolution of 1848 he himself had suffered through misunderstanding, and had realized how small a thing is needed to shipwreck a stable career. All he wanted now from life was freedom from anxiety and a certain modicum of leisure to carry on, in peace and quiet, the intellectual pursuits which meant much to him.

He did, however, ask his colleague on *Le Moniteur*, Thierry – who in any case reviewed contemporary works – to write an article on *Les Fleurs du Mal*. This was to be the plank which would bear the poet to safety, and it was awaited by him and his friends with feverish excitement.

In those days of press censorship, when a touchy and nervous régime saw veiled attacks in everything, each article which appeared in print had first to obtain government approval, and this caused many hampering delays. When the type of Thierry's article was being set up, Baudelaire, accompanied by the faithful Asselineau, stood from evening until the early hours on the Quai Voltaire, opposite the offices of *Le Moniteur*, to wait for news of it. From time to time he used to go into the building to find out how it was progressing.[28] The first news which came was that the article was finished, and that Thierry was correcting the proofs before taking them to Turgan to pass. The editor's position was delicate as he was responsible to the government. The information came that he had approved it and that the edition of the paper was being put into proof. This was not the critical stage. Before it could be put on sale, it had to obtain the approval of the Minister of State, Fould, and this was the most dangerous stage.

At eleven o'clock, Baudelaire and Asselineau, standing on the pavement outside the offices, saw Turgan appear, and then drive off in a cab. They waited for over an hour, scarcely daring to speak, until at last they saw the editor's cab return. As soon as he had disappeared into the building, Baudelaire dashed in after him to find out the result. All was well! Approval had been granted, and the paper was being printed off.

The article appeared the following morning, and Bau-

delaire was very much pleased with it, hoping that it would
be a spanner in the works of the case for the prosecution.
Thierry had never met Baudelaire and did not know him,
but wrote in glowing terms of his talent and work. He compared him to Dante and said that the Florentine poet would
recognize himself in the French poet, adding that this was
indeed high praise. Baudelaire, he claimed, had not rejoiced
at the contemplation of vice and evil, but had looked them
straight in the face, as enemies whom he knew well, in order
to withstand them courageously. He had hidden nothing,
had forgotten nothing, and had remained true to himself
throughout. It was the kind of book, he added, that one
could write only once in a lifetime, a work of uncompromising realism composed in the noblest style. One would be
able to achieve such a result only once – provided one could
do it at all.[29]

The article created a good impression amongst those who
were already well-disposed, but it enraged the Minister of
the Interior, who then tried to find some other means of
repairing the harm done by what he called 'the terrible mistake of the government paper'.

The Minister of Justice, Abbatucci, was anxious to proceed with the case. He wanted to prove that censorship did
not act for political reasons alone, but that the aim of the
government was to safeguard public morality as well, and
to protect the youth of the country from pernicious influences. He also felt that Fould had slighted him by approving
Thierry's article without consulting him. Fould had acted
within his rights but Abbatucci, esteeming the case one of
grave importance, considered that his own views should have
been canvassed, and he now made common cause with
Billaut, pretending to think that Fould had been influenced
by his long-standing friendship with Madame Aupick.
Billaut, quite unconstitutionally, prohibited *Le Pays* from
publishing Barbey d'Aurevilly's article in praise of *Les
Fleurs du Mal*.[30] Barbey d'Aurevilly retaliated by showing
the script to Fould and sending a copy to Baudelaire, to

help him in preparing his defence. There now arose a conflict between the three ministers – of the Interior, Justice and State – and Fould was no longer able to support the poet against his colleagues, and against public opinion.

In the meantime the campaign against him in the press continued. The day after Thierry's article, there appeared in the *Journal de Bruxelles* an assault even fiercer than those in *Le Figaro*, and this may have precipitated matters.[31]

'I was recently discussing in these columns,' said the article, '*Madame Bovary*, that disgraceful "best seller", which is, at the same time, a literary outrage, a moral calamity, and a social symptom! However, this atrocious novel is a work of piety compared with the collection of poetry which has just appeared under the title *Les Fleurs du Mal*. Its author is a certain Monsieur Baudelaire, who has translated Poe, and who, for the past ten years, has been passing for a great man in one of these little coteries whence comes the putrescence of the Realist and Bohemian press. Nothing could possibly give you the faintest idea of the heap of filth and horror contained in this one book. Quotation is not even possible to a decent pen! It is because of this, and because of the deep feeling of disgust aroused, which is stronger than anything else, that Monsieur Baudelaire may succeed in escaping the chastisement of self-respecting people.'

The sheets of *Les Fleurs du Mal* were ordered to be seized, and they were confiscated at Alençon on 16 July. Even this did not depress Baudelaire. He thought that he would be acquitted, like Flaubert, and that the trial might even increase his sales.

'I beg you,' he wrote to his mother,[32] 'to consider this scandal, which is creating a sensation in Paris, only as the foundation of my fortune.'

He wrote then to Fould to make sure of his support.[33]

'The letter which I have the honour of writing to your excellency,' he said, 'has no other object than to thank you for all the good services which I have received from you. In doing this I am fulfilling no more than a duty, especially at a moment when an incomprehensible piece of bad luck has made me perhaps the unwitting cause of displeasure to you, which would be indeed a matter of real concern to me.

'*Le Moniteur* has published an excellent review of the second volume of the works of Poe, of whom I am the proud translator. Monsieur Turgan has drawn the attention of the public to the third volume, and finally *Le Moniteur* has printed a wonderful notice of one of my books which is at the moment in danger of prosecution, *Les Fleurs du Mal*. Monsieur Thierry, with praiseworthy caution, pointed out that the book was addressed to a small number of readers only, and he praised it for the literary qualities which he was kind enough to find in it. He ended by saying that the pessimism and despair of the book in question were sufficient proof of its morality.

'Yesterday I had the idea of sending a private request to the Minister of Justice, but then I thought that such a step might be taken as an admission of guilt, and I do not feel guilty. On the contrary, I am extremely proud of having produced a book which expresses horror and terror of vice. I have abandoned the idea of using this means of defence, and, if I have got to defend myself, I shall be able to do it with dignity.

'And so, Monsieur le Ministre, why should I not frankly admit that I am begging you for your patronage, in so far as it is possible to obtain it from you, from you who, by your intelligence more than by your office, are the natural protector of arts and letters? Unfortunately arts and letters never feel sufficiently protected. But please believe that, even if it were not possible for you to grant it to me, I should nevertheless still continue to consider myself under an obligation to you.

'I beg you therefore to believe in my feelings of deep respect and gratitude, and I remain, Monsieur le Ministre, the most humble and obedient servant of your excellency.'

Fould was not able to prevent the prosecution from taking its course, and the most that Baudelaire could now hope

was that his case should be put in the best light possible. The
Imperial Prosecutor, Pinard, was reputed to be broadminded, in spite of his office.[34] In a recent case, it was said
that, although obliged to prosecute, he had even demanded
the acquittal of the accused, on the grounds that those who
imagine that they represent public opinion often only represent in fact its caricature.

On the other hand, it was alleged that he had felt humiliated at losing his case against *Madame Bovary*, in which he
had been made to appear in a ridiculous light, and it was
not known whether since then he had learnt sense, or
whether he had only become obstinate.

Baudelaire went to call on him before his case came up,
and showed him the favourable notices which his book had
received, which he had had reprinted and bound together
as a booklet. Pinard seems to have received him genially,
and this might account for the fact that he appeared to
present the case for the prosecution in a half-hearted manner.

The poet's next task was to prepare his own defence. On
the advice of friends, he chose Chaix d'Est-Ange as his
lawyer, and then consulted with Sainte-Beuve on his best
line of argument, for Sainte-Beuve had a wide experience of
life, and should be able to recognize what evidence would
carry most weight. The critic prepared for him what he
called *Petits Moyens de Défense*.[35] But the document does
not do him credit for the line of defence is mean, opportunist
and undignified. He advised Baudelaire to plead 'extenuating circumstances', to say that everything had already been
used in the realms of poetry when he had come along; that
Lamartine had taken Heaven, Hugo the earth – indeed
even more than the earth – Laprade the forest, Musset passion; that Gautier had taken Spain, and others home and
rural life – meaning himself – What then was there left for
him, a latecomer, when he wished to be original? He had
been forced to choose, what he had in fact chosen, Hell and
evil.

Sainte-Beuve advised him to draw the attention of the

court to the case of Béranger – at the same time intimating
that he was moved by no desire to smirch the reputation of
a distinguished national poet whom the Emperor himself
had thought fit to honour recently by a public funeral. Many
of Béranger's poems were of a highly suggestive nature, but
no exception had been taken to them, because they had been
in a light vein. Sainte-Beuve also thought that *La Ballade à
la Lune* of Musset might be produced with effect, by quotation from its more salacious passages. Baudelaire dutifully
followed Sainte-Beuve's advice, and helped his lawyer to
collect the more suggestive passages from Béranger and
Musset.[36] This advice was ill-advised from beginning to end
because of its petty cleverness and desire to score small
points, and, worst of all, it went counter to the poet's most
profound intentions when composing the poems. He had
been inspired not by any ambition to be original, or to produce work in a style that other writers had not yet practised
– he would have cared little for such spurious originality.
His best defence would have been the expression of his first
instinctive reaction: disgust and horror at the accusation of
indecency and immorality. All he had wanted was to be
true to himself and to his vision of the world and the destiny
of mankind, to express his loathing of the sin and vice to
which man is prone, and his compassion for the misery of
his degradation, considering his aspiration for higher things.
How could all this be immorality? He claimed that the book
must be judged in its entirety, taking into account the plan
and the total intention of the collection, and that isolated
poems could not be detached from their context without
altering the meaning of the whole. 'The book must be
judged as a whole,' he said, 'and then there follows a terrifying morality!'[37] A powerful argument which might have
been used, but was not brought forward, was that if the
morality of his accusers could be enforced, it would mean
that only consoling books could be written, proving to man
that he is born good and that all mankind is happy – an
abominable piece of hypocrisy, Baudelaire added.[38] As for

the obscene passages in Béranger and Musset, it was perfectly true that these existed, but it was not a sound defence
since it was based on the grounds that others who were
guilty had escaped with impunity. The prosecution was
not slow to realize the point and answered it in anticipation.
It would have been wiser for Baudelaire to confine himself
to the nobler attitude which he himself would have adopted
naturally; it would have been wiser for him to instruct his
lawyer to underline the beauty and tragic element in his
writings, but this, although touched upon, was completely
swamped in the smaller issues.

On 20 August 1857 Baudelaire came up before the court
at the *Palais de Justice*, in what is called the *Sixième
Chambre Correctionnelle*. In this same court the Goncourt
brothers were to appear the following year, on the same
charge, for having printed a quotation from a certain writer
called Tahureau, alleged to be indelicate, but they were
acquitted when it was discovered that he was a Renaissance
poet studied by Sainte-Beuve in a work 'couronné' by the
French Academy, *Le Tableau de la Poésie Française au
Seizième Siècle*. The *Journal* of the Goncourt gives a vivid
picture of the dreary court, with its discoloured pea-green
paint, its long windows thickly coated in grime, its crucifix
staring down at the accused from the wall, and its clock
ticking inexorably.

The *Sixième Chambre Correctionnelle* was the court in
which cases of petty larceny, burglary and vagrancy were
tried. Baudelaire was obliged to wait his turn amongst
tramps, petty thieves and men accused of indecent assault.
It was the middle of August, and the court must have been
stifling and evil-smelling, especially where the multifarious
accused were congregated. They made a strange contrast:
Baudelaire glowering and proud, and de Broise, a poor,
terrified little rabbit of a man, afraid of everything, asking
for nothing but to be allowed to carry on his business in
peace, and most of all to remain respectable and solvent. He
had never approved of his brother-in-law's publishing mad-

ness, and had especially never approved of Baudelaire, but
here he was, through no fault of his own, sitting on the
accused bench, amongst a lot of vagrants, before the eyes of
everyone, while he would have wished to sink through the
floor with shame. Poulet Malassis had been unavoidably
detained at Alençon and had thus been obliged to send his
partner to represent him. He was always able to joke about
everything, and if he had been there he might have made
witty and spicy comments which would have made Baudelaire smile – certainly the hours would have been less
tedious. Instead there was only de Broise who, at the best
of times, got on his nerves.

It was vacation time, just after the most important annual
holiday, the Assumption, on 15 August, and the court was
crowded with students and holiday-makers; for this was a
free and exciting entertainment. There were many women
present, since there was the chance of its being a lurid case,
with lewd details and at least the possibility of obscene
quotations.

All Baudelaire's friends who were in Paris came. Suddenly
he saw to his horror old Ancelle elbowing his way through
into the front row.[39] The lawyer, with his snow-white hair
and his respectable pompous bearing, was a striking figure
amongst Baudelaire's bohemian friends. He was not content with sitting silently with them, but insisted on engaging
them in conversation; trying to find out how the case was
going and what the chances were of acquittal. Poor old man,
knowing all the tricks of the trade and painfully anxious
on his ward's behalf, he had come to glean the first news
and to see what could be done. Baudelaire, however, would
not give him credit for anything but idle and malicious
curiosity, and he suffered tortures at the idea that his
'guardian' might make him ridiculous, or that the court
might be unfavourably disposed towards him, if they discovered that he had a *conseil judiciaire*.

When the case began, Pinard, the public prosecutor, was
obviously ill at ease, and he spoke, it is said, half-heartedly.[40]

He opened by pointing out that to attack a work of literature
on the score of immorality was always a delicate matter; if
the action failed the author had immediately a large sale
for his work; if it succeeded, he became a public martyr.
Neither eventuality was desirable. He went on to say that
the action was all the more difficult and delicate with an
author like Baudelaire, well protected and warmly acclaimed
in some literary circles. The main thing for the court to
decide was whether, in their opinion, the accusations of the
prosecution were justified and proved. He pointed out to the
court that it was not a band of literary critics called upon
to settle the difference between two schools of thought, but
that it had been entrusted with a precise duty to perform
by the legislative body, which had laid it down that certain
things were an offence against public morality. The onus of
deciding whether, in this case, the boundary had been
crossed, lay with the court, and it was, as it were, a band of
sentinels whose duty it was to see that the limits were not
transgressed.

He proceeded then to quote certain passages from *Les
Fleurs du Mal* which he declared could only be called
lascivious and obscene. They came from *Les Bijoux*, *Le
Léthé*, *Les Femmes Damnées* and *À celle qui est trop gaie*.
The accusation against this last poem could be substantiated
only by an unjustifiably pornographic interpretation of the
final verse.

He next went on to demonstrate in what manner religious,
as well as moral, decency had been transgressed, and he
claimed to have proved that the poet had offended against
that noble Christian code which is the only solid foundation
of decent moral standards. He cited, in support of his accusation, *Le Reniement de Saint-Pierre*, *Abel et Caïn*, *Les
Litanies de Satan*, and *Le Vin de l'Assassin*. If he had been
capable of humour, it could be imagined that he must have
mentioned the last poem as a joke, for the alleged offence
occurs in the last two lines of the final verse, where a drunkard, who has just murdered his wife in a frenzy of inebria-

tion, says that he is now free, that he intends that night to be drunk to his heart's content, without fear or remorse, that he will lie on the ground and sleep like a dog, and that he will care about nothing, even if a heavy cart, laden with stones, should crush his guilty head, or cut him in two. He cries:

> *Je m'en moque comme de Dieu,*
> *Du diable, ou de la Table Sainte.*[41]

Pinard directed the court to censure strictly the modern tendency which permitted everything to be said and described, since he said that such outspokenness awakened in those who had no experience of life a curiosity about matters of which they were better ignorant. He had quoted enough, he said, to prove that there had been in effect an offence against public morality. Either a sense of decency did not exist, or else it had been violated by the poems in question. He answered in advance the objection that many other books with dangerous tendencies had escaped censure. If that argument were accepted, then the government would find its hands tied in the future. Sometimes it used its discretion, as it was unwilling to draw the attention of the public to a publication which otherwise would have escaped notice, but this could not be allowed to hamper the action of future governments. He summoned the court, before it was too late, to stop the dry-rot, the canker in the midst of their civilization, and ended with the peroration: 'Be merciful to Baudelaire the human being, who is a man of restless and unbalanced temperament, but, by banning certain poems of the book, give a warning to others which has become necessary.'

The poet must have writhed as he listened.

Next came the lawyer for the defence, Chaix d'Est-Ange. Most of Baudelaire's contemporaries are agreed in condemning his speech as inept. Yet to those who read it with modern unbiased eyes it seems an honest, if pedestrian, piece of work which amplifies the arguments which he had

been given, though allowing too much space to quotation
from Béranger, Musset and Gautier. This was not his fault
as he had been instructed to do precisely this. He was not a
literary man who would on his own have appreciated *Les
Fleurs du Mal*, and he may even have believed in his heart
that the case for the prosecution was proved, and so had
been interested chiefly in obtaining the most favourable
sentence possible. His contemporaries probably felt that a
more subtle and quick-witted lawyer would have been able
to modify his speech once the prosecution had anticipated
some of his more important arguments, but he continued
with them to the end just as if they had not been dealt with.

He demonstrated that Baudelaire was an honest artist;
that his book was a sincere work, in which he had tried to
plumb the dark depths of the human soul, but only to
awaken horror of sin and vice; and that description of evil
did not entail approval of evil. All dramatists, he declared,
painted human passions and weaknesses, and he showed
how, if they were translated into prose, many of Baudelaire's
poems became perfectly orthodox sermons. He emphasized
the argument that the book was to be judged in its entirety,
and accused the prosecution of being unfair when it lifted
passages out of their context to quote them.

The largest part of his speech, however, was taken up with
lengthy quotations from Musset and Béranger, and also a
particularly long passage from *Mademoiselle de Maupin* by
Gautier. This last work would most certainly have been
prosecuted and banned if it had been published in that
extremely touchy period of the Second Empire. He concluded by stating that there was nothing to be found in
Baudelaire's writings as daring as some of the things which
were printed with impunity every day.

When the speeches were over the judges filed out to deliberate, and were absent for a time which seemed intermin-
able to those who were waiting. At last they returned, and
the chairman read out the verdict.

They acquitted Baudelaire of blasphemy, and declared that, in this respect, the case had not been proven.

As for the offence against public morality, they decided that here there had been violation, and that any moral intention the poet might have had in writing the poems did not diminish the sordid realism of the pictures painted, which must undoubtedly lead to the unhealthy stimulation of the senses by their coarseness, which was 'offensant pour la pudeur'.

The penalties were to be a fine of three hundred francs on Baudelaire, for having written and published the poems, and a fine of a hundred francs on each of the partners – Poulet Malassis and de Broise – for having printed them. Six poems were to be banned and deleted from further copies sold, these being: *Les Bijoux, Le Léthe, À celle qui est trop gaie, Lesbos, Les Femmes Damnées*, and finally *Les Métamorphoses du Vampire*.

This ban lasted for almost a century. On 31 May 1949, after twenty-five years of sporadic attempts to get the judgement reversed, it was finally quashed, and Baudelaire vindicated and rehabilitated, so that the poems can now legally appear in *Les Fleurs du Mal*. In fact most editions had always printed them, either separately at the back, under the title *Pièces Condamnées*, or else in the collection called *Épaves* which was published in Brussels when the poet was in Belgium in 1866.[42]

When the crowd dispersed, Asselineau went up to Baudelaire to commiserate with him but, seeing his look of disappointment and rage, he asked him: 'And did you really think you'd be acquitted?' The poet almost shrieked in answer: 'I thought they'd make amends to me for the public affront of the case.'[43]

Baudelaire's anger was justified. For many years now his main preoccupation had been with religion and philosophy, and by philosophy he meant inquiry into the mystery of the destiny of man. He had intended his work to give a picture –

an evocation would be nearer to the truth – of the whole of
man, in his qualities and defects, in his dreams and failures,
and this evocation could not consist solely of smiling visions.
He himself was very conscious of the dual polarity of man,
his aspiration towards God, as well as towards Satan. 'Il y a
dans tout homme, à toute heure, deux postulations simultanées, l'une vers Dieu, l'autre vers Satan.' [44] *Les Fleurs du
Mal* was based on this clash, this contrast – *Spleen et Idéal*
he called it – and he saw the pull towards sin as stronger
than that towards virtue. He believed in sin as an entity, and
this was rare in the positivist era of the Second Empire,
when most thinkers followed Taine in declaring that vice
and virtue did not exist as moral factors, that they were only
two different substances like vitriol and sugar, and that no
one could claim that one was better than the other, but
only that they were dissimilar. In his poems Baudelaire
expressed hatred of sin, and terror and horror of its power,
and he could think of no other way of explaining it except
through the machinations of some being outside man,
through Satan. Thus he opens his collection with a poem
indicating the stranglehold that Satan has on man, and the
many wiles he uses to lead him astray. He can take many
shapes to delude him, the form of his virtues as well as of
his vices, and one of his most dangerous tricks is to make
man believe that he does not really exist. It is necessary,
therefore, for man to get to know him and himself. Baudelaire then undertakes a full examination of self, in the
person of the poet, and of all the various temptations which
beset him, which are more dangerous to him than to others,
because his tasks and obligations are of the noblest. The
snares for him are beauty of every kind, and love, whether
sensual, passionate, or spiritual. Love fails and is followed
by *spleen*, and nostalgic regret for the vanished fairylands
of the past. He tries to find forgetfulness in various forms of
vice, in revolt and blasphemy, in intoxication, but all end in
disillusionment and despair. There remains only the one

hope that, after death, all will be made good and all explained, that death will make the ideal flowers bloom, which on earth withered before they blossomed. This first version of *Les Fleurs du Mal* ended with *La Mort des Artistes*, which was its culmination.

The poem ends:[45]

> *Il en est qui jamais n'ont connu leur Idole,*
> *Et ces sculpteurs damnés et marqués d'un affront,*
> *Qui vont se martelant la poitrine et le front,*
>
> *N'ont qu'un espoir, étrange et sombre Capitole!*
> *C'est que la Mort, planant comme un soleil nouveau,*
> *Fera s'épanouir les fleurs de leur cerveau!*

This plan will alter somewhat in later editions of *Les Fleurs du Mal*, but will remain the same in essentials.[46]

The notoriety of *Les Fleurs du Mal* permitted Baudelaire to publish the first batch of his prose poems, which appeared in *Le Présent* on 24 August. They were: *L'Horloge, Un Hémisphère dans une Chevelure, L'Invitation au Voyage, Crépuscule du Soir, La Solitude* and *Les Projets*, and their collective title was *Poèmes Nocturnes*.[47]

Losing his case was, however, a bitter blow, a blow from which he never fully recovered. He received, it is true, much sympathy from well-known writers, though this was not always of a personal nature, but inspired by irritation against the government, its intolerance in religious matters and the puritanism of its moral principles in questions of art, and was not of much comfort to the poet himself as an artist. The liberal-minded Catholic writer, De Custine, wrote to Barbey d'Aurevilly:[48]

'I entirely share your opinion concerning the poet who has been condemned. Our black-robed puritans are doing their best to turn this world into a convent school devoted to the training of young girls. In such a place one might be able to remain ignorant of evil, but in our world as it is, one can only fear and hate it. If we exclude from our literature the depiction of vice, then we must abandon not only all art, but religion as well, beginning with the Bible itself, and delete from it half its chapters, starting with the *Song of Solomon* and many verses from the *Epistles of Saint Paul to the Romans*, where vice is described in a truly horrible manner, with a sincerity which would horrify the law courts if they found it in the works of a modern.'

Victor Hugo also wrote to him from exile in Guernsey, and his letter, very typical of him, was intended chiefly as an attack against the régime which he hated and which he was happy to see put itself so patently in the wrong.

'May I congratulate you?' he wrote.[49] 'One of the few decorations which the present régime can grant, it has bestowed on you! What it is pleased to call its justice has condemned you in the name of what it calls its morality. That is an added crown for you.'

These letters were small consolation to Baudelaire for the destruction of the entire edition of his poems, for the shipwreck of his hopes of fame, for the stigma attached to him of a pornographic poet, and for the reputation of a terrifying monster. One of Gautier's friends relates that he was once on a botanic excursion with a legal acquaintance at Montmorency, and the acquaintance for some reason embarked on a long indictment of Baudelaire, declaiming it as if in a court of law. At one moment he paused, and exclaimed, pointing to a man who was passing: 'Why, there he is, the wretch!' Gautier's friend stopped in his tracks as if he had been told 'beware, there's a rattlesnake on the ground beside you!' But, when he caught sight of the poet, he found it impossible to believe that this sad and gentle creature could possibly be the same man whom the lawyer had just been vituperating. This was the beginning of his own conversion to the works of Baudelaire.[50]

[12]

The End of a Dream
1857

EVEN in the midst of his worry over his trial, Baudelaire had not forgotten Madame Sabatier, and when *Les Fleurs du Mal* appeared he set aside one of the special copies printed on fine paper. He sent this to her as soon as he had a moment of respite in his consultations with his legal adviser, two days before the case was due, enclosing a letter written for the first time in his own handwriting.[1]

'You didn't think,' he wrote, 'for a moment, did you, that I could have forgotten you? As soon as the book was published I set aside a copy for you, printed on fine paper, and, if it is not clothed in a garment more worthy of you, the fault isn't mine, but that of my bookbinder, from whom I ordered something much more original. . . .

'This is the first time that I write to you in my own handwriting, and, if I weren't so weighed down by business and the necessity of writing letters, I'd seize this opportunity of begging your forgiveness for so much past foolishness and childishness. . . .

'Permit me then, at the risk of causing you amusement also, to renew the protestations of admiration which so amused your little sister! Imagine a combination of fancy, sympathy and respect, mingled with a childlike innocence and gravity, then you'll have a faint conception of that very sincere element, which I'm incapable of defining better. It wouldn't be possible for me to forget you! There've been, they say, poets who have lived for the whole of their lives with their eyes fixed on a beloved image. I'm convinced – but perhaps I'm biased in this – that fidelity is one of the signs of genius. You're to me more than a cherished image

conjured up in a dream, you're my superstition! Whenever
I do something particularly foolish I say to myself: "Goodness! if she were to find that out!" Whenever I do something
good I say to myself: "Here's something which raises me
up, in spirit, towards her." ...

'Remember that there's someone who thinks of you incessantly, and that there's nothing mean in his thoughts, but
that he's sometimes a little hurt by your mischievous gaiety.
I entreat you most earnestly to keep henceforth for yourself
alone anything I may confide in you. You're my constant
companion, my secret! And it's the fact of that intimacy, in
which, for so long now, I answer myself in your name, which
gives me the boldness of this familiar tone. Farewell, dear
Madame. I kiss your hands with profound devotion.'

Madame Sabatier was deeply moved by his gentle and
respectful tone. In the rough-and-tumble life which she led
she had learnt to take things as they came without worrying
and not to expect too much from men – indeed, in her
opinion, there was cause for gratitude if they were merely
generous, and not too inconsiderate in their demands. She
was unaccustomed to respect and worship, and this was a
novel and strange experience which gave her a new pride
and confidence. She was inured to the coarse jests of men
like Gautier, who thought it necessary, whenever they talked
or joked with her, to make some reference – veiled or overt –
to her physical attractions, and to their desire for her. She
had never yet been treated as a Madonna, nor worshipped
and loved for five years without being asked for any return.
All the men whom her experience had taught her to know
had expected return, with interest, for whatever they bestowed on her of either sentimental, or more materialistic,
attention. She found Baudelaire's childlike and unclaimful
giving of love strangely moving and flattering. She did not,
however, understand him any better than anyone else with
whom he ever came into contact. She realized his shyness
and diffidence, and divined his sensitiveness, but she
imagined that he was asking nothing only because he did

not dare to make demands. She would never have dreamt it possible that he could think of her without the desire and hope of physical possession, for she could not understand passionate love which did not expect consummation – and his love had been passionate in its expression. Since she was not proud and rarely considered her own personal dignity, and since she was generous and warm-hearted, she took the first step herself, thinking the simplest way of showing her appreciation was to offer herself to him – the gift of the body had always seemed to her a simple and natural thing. The day after she received his letter she invited him to come alone to her apartment and thought that matters would take the usual course. But events with Baudelaire were never normal. When she saw him sitting shyly and silently before her, with love, happiness and worship shining from his eyes, she was swept off her feet by a sensation she had never yet experienced, and thought that she had never seen him clearly during all the five years when he had sat in her drawing-room. She fell deeply in love with him herself, on the spot, and ceased to be mistress of the situation. After he left her, having treated her with his accustomed respect, she wrote, out of the fulness of her heart, a pathetically naïve and girlish letter, coming strangely from a woman of her age and experience, to find an outlet and expression for her new emotion.[2]

'Today I'm more calm, and I can feel more clearly the impression of our Tuesday evening together. I can tell you, without the danger of your thinking I'm exaggerating, that I'm the happiest woman on the face of the earth, that I've never felt more truly that I love you, and that I've never seen you look more beautiful, more adorable, my divine friend! You can preen yourself with pride, if you like, but it's no use your trying to look at yourself in a glass, for whatever you do, you'll never be able to assume the expression which I caught sight of, for one fleeting moment! And now, whatever happens, I'll always see you in this way, for that's the Charles I love! You may purse your lips and scowl as much as you like, I'll not worry, but I'll merely close my eyes and see the other Charles.'

Baudelaire began to take fright. He had not counted on matters going as far as this, but had imagined in his ignorance of women that when he was granted the privilege of intimacy with her, Madame Sabatier would just allow him the supreme happiness of describing his devotion to her and would become the vessel into which he poured the divine feelings and dreams which she had awakened in him. He had imagined that their intimacy would merely be an extension of his relationship with her during the previous five years – his vision miraculously come to life. He had longed for this pleasure for many years, and now there was the danger of everything being spoilt by the gross ardours of a woman. He had been right, he then thought, to be afraid of women – woman ever seeking whom she may devour. He was aware of his inadequacy in front of them, and there had also always been an element of doubt and suspicion at the back of his mind about her. Her mischievous eyes and mouth were not there for nothing, and she was too ready to laugh on every occasion. She was perhaps laughing at him now, for had she not shown to her little sister the letters in which he had poured his soul, letters which were intended for her alone, and which he had entreated her to keep a secret? Perhaps she had even read them to her assembled friends, to Houssaye, Gautier, and the hateful Feydeau? Were all these men now discussing his most intimate feelings, and encroaching on his spiritual privacy? His sensitive imagination could visualize the scene, and he felt he could not endure the degradation of what it saw. He was seized with panic when he thought of the situation which he had now created and all the problems and knots so hard afterwards to unravel.[3] To assume lack of faith was easier and safer, and he may perhaps even have believed the things he said, as he wrote them – they may have been merely a subconscious protection for his physical inadequacy with a woman whom he loved and respected. He professed contempt for women for desiring men, for being desired by them, he pretended to despise them in their capacity of 'répugnante utilité' and of 'triste nécessité'. Suddenly, beset by difficult and emotional turmoil, he felt his passion grow cool, saw himself driven into a corner, and obliged to fight with his back to the wall. He began to put her off with all manner of excuses, he tried all sorts of arguments with her, but she was becoming more passionate and exasperated by his continued 'timidity', and tried to force him to take her. In the last stages of consternation, he could only save himself by flight, and driven to desperate action he composed the famous and much discussed letter of 31 August 1857.

Most critics hold the view that this controversial letter was written after Baudelaire and Madame Sabatier had become lovers for one night, and it was inspired by disillusion. This does not seem possible. It was not like him to express to anyone, and to a woman least of all, his disappointment in her. The letter seems, on the contrary, to have been written by a man in a panic, who is trying to extricate himself, with some shred of decency, from an impossible situation. When he exclaims that from having been a goddess she has become, in a few days, a mere woman, it does not follow that they have been lovers, but rather that he finds himself faced with difficulties and entanglements, which have taken the bloom from their relationship. There was no other escape open to him, except through insolence, and he wrote, giving vent to his doubts and contempt of women. That probably had been his intention as he started his letter, but he was again moved by tenderness and love before its close:[4]

'I've destroyed the torrent of puerilities heaped up on my table because I didn't consider them serious enough for you, my dearest beloved! I take up your two letters again and I'll answer them once more! In order to do this I'll need all my resolution for my nerves are so frayed I could scream, and I awoke this morning with the same unaccountable feeling of psychological distress with which I left you yesterday evening.'

He went on to answer her letters, point by point:

'"Complete absence of modesty!" But it's precisely for that reason that you're so dear to me! "It seems to me that I've been yours since the first day I saw you! Do what you like with me, for I'm yours, body, mind and soul!" I advise you strongly to hide away that letter! – Do you know what you're saying? There are people prepared to imprison those who don't pay their bills, but no one is ready to chastise the repudiation of protestations of love and friendship. And so I said to you yesterday "You'll forget me and betray me! The man who now interests you will only end by boring you!" And today I add to that that he alone will suffer who, like a fool, places trust in matters of the heart. – You see, my dear, that I've got horrible prejudices against women. – In short I lack faith! You've a beautiful nature, but it's a woman's nature!

'You see how, in a few days, our relationship has been completely transformed! In the first place, we're both worried by the fear of hurting a good man who's still in love with you.⁵ And then we're also afraid of our own passion, because we know – or at least I do – that there are knots difficult later to untie! And then finally, finally. – A few days ago you were a divinity, which is a beautiful and undefiled state, but now you're a woman – and supposing, unfortunately, I ever had the right to be jealous? – What a torture even to think of it! But, with someone like you, whose eyes are full of smiles and attentions for everyone, one would suffer the tortures of the damned!

'The seal on your second letter has a motto the gravity of which would please me if I thought you understood it: *"Never meet or never part"*. That means that it's better never to have met, but that once one has met one should never part. On a letter of farewell such a seal has its irony and humour!

'However, come what may, I'm a fatalist! But what I realize fully is that I loathe passion – because I know it too well, with all its degradation.

'But now, all of a sudden, the beloved image, which stands high above all the circumstances of my life, becomes too attractive!

'I don't dare reread this letter, as I'd then probably feel obliged to alter it, for I'm afraid of having hurt you. It seems to me that I must have uncovered aspects of the bad side of my nature.

'I think it's impossible to bring you to that foul Rue Jean-Jacques Rousseau.[6] But I've many things to say to you, and you must write and tell me how I can do that.

'Farewell, dearest beloved! I'm angry with you, only for being too charming. When I take away with me the perfume of your arms, and your hair, I take away also the longing to return to them once more. But then, what an unbearable obsession!

'On second thoughts I'll take this letter round myself to the Rue Jean-Jacques Rousseau in case you happen to go there today. It will get there quicker that way.'

In the last page of the letter Baudelaire allows his real feelings to appear, and especially his sadness and regret because he knows that this will mean the end of everything between them, the end of his dream. It reveals how much he had suffered at the dragging down of his love into the quagmire of material life. He could not bear the thought of his Muse and his Madonna coming to meet him in one of the low hotels which shelter couples for an hour or two in their casual and sordid fornication.

Madame Sabatier did not yet understand, for she was too simple to have any conception of what he meant. How could he talk of love, and yet express contempt for the object of his devotion! Was it only that he was timid and shy? Or had she, perhaps, without knowing it, wounded his susceptibility – she realized that she had never known a man as sensitive as he? Had he perhaps – and this suspicion tortured her most of all – grown tired of her, and ceased to love her? Or was he still obsessed by Jeanne Duval? She could not refrain from a feeling of jealousy as she contemplated this possibility. It remained to the end a mystery to her, how the poet could feel love for the mulatto woman, with her haggard and dissolute face. She once found a picture of her, which she kept always with her, and on it she had written the naïve and revealing remark, expressing her amazement. 'His ideal!'

She wrote again, in answer to his cruel and pitiable letter, and there are no reproaches in what she says, only bewilderment and desolate sadness.[7]

'My dear! Would you like me to tell you what I really think, the cruel suspicion which hurts me very much, that is that you don't love me! Hence your terrors, your hesitations at forming a relationship which, in these conditions, would naturally become the source of weariness to you, and to me an endless torture. Haven't I the proof in one sentence of your letter, which is so definite that it chills me to the very marrow? "I've not got faith!" You've no faith! But then you can't be in love. Isn't that as clear as daylight? Oh God! How this thought makes me suffer, and how much I long to weep on your breast! It seems to me that this might bring me peace! But, however we stand, I'll not put off our meeting tomorrow, for I want to see you, if only to practise my part as a mere friend! Oh! why did you try to see me again?

'Your most unhappy friend.'

Baudelaire did not keep the appointment, for he was terrified of meeting her, of having a verbal explanation. He felt himself driven into a corner, and he sent her a letter of excuse. She, for her part, felt humiliated in her deepest feminine instincts, since she had sunk her pride in her love, and had offered herself shamelessly to him. He had spurned her gift and made her feel a brazen hussy. She had imagined that he had desired her, and she had only been trying to make things easier for him, but now she felt soiled and diminished in her own eyes. But she wrote again because she could not face, what her natural intelligence told her was true, that love between them was in fact over, and her letter, pathetic in its sincerity, gains sympathy for her from all who read it.[8]

'What comedy, or rather what tragedy, are we enacting? For I don't know what to conjecture, and I must confess that I'm most anxious and disturbed. Your behaviour has been so mysterious for the past few days that I'm completely at sea. It's all too subtle for a simple clodhopper like me. Please enlighten me, my dear, for I ask only to understand! What chill and deadly wind has blown on the beautiful flame? Or is it merely the result of further reflection? If that's so, it comes a little late, my dear! Alas! has it all happened through my fault, through my most grievous fault? I ought to have been more grave and firm when you came to me first. But what can you expect? When one's heart beats fast and one's lips quiver, all sensible thoughts fly out of the window....

'Your letter has just arrived, and I needn't tell you that I was expecting what it says. And so we're not to have the pleasure of seeing you for a few moments? They tell me you're terrified of meeting me *tête-à-tête*, and yet that seems necessary. But you can do what you like. When you've got over this whim of yours, write to me, or come to see me. I'm kind and I'll forgive you for having hurt me!

'I can't resist the temptation of saying a few words about our misunderstanding, and yet I'd fully determined on a conduct full of dignity! But before a single day had passed, my heart had already softened, and yet, Charles, my anger was justified! What can I believe when I see you fleeing more and more from my embraces, if it isn't that you're still thinking of that other woman, whose black face and soul have come between us? In short, I feel humiliated and diminished, and if it weren't for my self-respect I'd abuse you! I'd love to see you suffer, for jealousy devours me, and no reasonable thought is possible on such occasions! Oh! my dear, I wish you the good luck of never having to endure this! What a night I spent, and how I cursed this cruel love!

'I waited for you all today! In case the fancy should take

you to come here tomorrow, I must tell you that I'll only be at home from one o'clock until three o'clock, and, in the evening from eight o'clock until midnight!

'Farewell, my Charles! And how fares what is left of your heart? Mine is more calm now! I'm subduing it in order not to bore you with its weakness! You'll see, I'll be able to make its temperature sink to the level that you want. It will, naturally, cause me pain, but, to please you, I'll resign myself to bearing all possible suffering!'

Baudelaire did not return to her, and he ceased for a time even to attend her Sunday evening parties, at which he had been, for years, her most faithful guest. He pretended that it was largely on account of pressure of work, and once because he did not want to feel obliged to congratulate Feydeau on his recent novel. Each time that he sent her a letter of excuse it was almost cold and distant in its impersonality. All he could find to say was that he was dismayed and distressed at her suffering, and at everything which caused her pain. Soon he was ending his letters with the conventional formulas used by any polite and well-brought-up Frenchman when addressing a lady whom he scarcely knows. He was signing himself 'Votre bien dévoué ami et serviteur' or was sending her 'mille amitiés'.

After a period of disappointment and suffering Madame Sabatier seems to have made up her mind to accept defeat, realizing that nothing more would be of any avail – not prayers, humiliation, passion or serenity. She accepted defeat, understanding the obstacle which separated them, and she showed the greatness of her heart in not bearing him a grudge, nor avenging herself on him for her humiliation. She remained a close friend but it was not true to say, as many biographers have done, that ten years later when he was paralysed and incapable of speech she used to go to play Wagner to him in the nursing-home in Paris where he lay dying, and that she was one of his untiring visitors to the end, when he could only show appreciation with his eyes. That was, as it happens, the period when she was the mistress of Richard Wallace, and was in Italy with him. She heard of Baudelaire's death only when she returned to France, long after he was gone.

By the end of September 1857 Baudelaire and Madame Sabatier were on a new footing of calm friendship, when love was no longer mentioned between them. The following year he wrote to her saying: [9]

'I embrace you like a very old comrade whom I'll always love! Indeed the word "comrade" is a misrepresentation, since it is too coarse and trivial an expression, and not tender enough!'

After much inner turmoil and conflict, she accepted finally the part he offered her, of an old and trusted friend, and she kept a permanent place for him in her affections, often advising him for his good. She was to write to him later: [10]

'Are you now more cheerful, and is the play shaping well? I very much fear, my dear, that you do very little work! Which is unfortunate for the public, and disastrous for yourself, because it seemed to me that I detected in the plan which you developed before me, the possibility of success! I'm convinced that, in less than a fortnight, with regular work, you'd finish it. But to achieve this you'd have to give up opium, and all the wild fancies which float through your mind, to the detriment of your work, at every step. However, I'm only wasting my time and trouble preaching to you. But, since after all, you'll do exactly as you like, I don't repent too much my little sermon! Having said all this, I want you to know that when the fancy takes you to see me, you can come and look me up!'

Baudelaire, for his part, kept to the end of his life a tender and compassionate feeling towards Madame Sabatier – perhaps because he felt remorse. What she could never have understood, or guessed, was the sadness that he must have felt when the bright bubble of his idealized worship of her suddenly burst. There is no doubt that the events of August and September 1857 damaged the relationship between them, as far as he was concerned. The harsh wind of reality ravaged the fairylands of his dream, and he was never again able to evoke it with his Madonna as queen. For ever afterwards he would remember her as a woman with features distorted by passion and desire, with tears of human suffering on her cheeks, which he had caused to flow; he would remember for ever the sorry and undignified part he had been forced to play, and especially the humility which had placed his Madonna beneath his feet.

She may have thought that all would be healed between them when she had granted him the platonic friendship which he had seemed to want, but she would not have been able to realize his grief at the loss of his ideal, his suffering at knowing that henceforth he would remain alone in his inviolable solitude. He wrote no more love poems and love letters to her, for this was the end of that chapter. The poem *Semper Eadem* expresses the last phase – there can be little doubt that it refers to her, for the epithets are those which he usually applied to her, when describing her beauty. It expresses also failure to find any human soul ready to understand him.[11]

> *D'où vous vient, disiez-vous, cette tristesse étrange,*
> *Montant comme la mer sur le roc noir et nu?*
> *– Quand notre cœur a fait une fois sa vendange,*
> *Vivre est un mal. C'est un secret de tous connu.*
>
> *Une douleur très simple et non mystérieuse,*
> *Et, comme votre joie, éclatante pour tous.*
> *Cessez donc de chercher, ô belle curieuse!*
> *Et, bien que votre voix soit douce, taisez-vous!*
>
> *Taisez-vous, ignorante! âme toujours ravie!*
> *Bouche au rire enfantin! Plus encor que la vie,*
> *La mort nous tient souvent par des liens subtils.*
>
> *Laissez, laissez mon cœur s'enivrer d'un mensonge,*
> *Plonger dans vos beaux yeux comme dans un beau songe,*
> *Et sommeiller longtemps à l'ombre de vos cils!*

The events of August 1857 – his trial and his discomfiture

with Madame Sabatier – left Baudelaire a discouraged, disillusioned and ageing man. His book of poems, on which
he had centred his high hopes, was banned and had to be
rewritten to be republished, and he himself was more than
ever open to scurrilous attacks; and, finally, the ideal relationship which he had hoped to enjoy lay in fragments at
his feet. Hitherto, in spite of suffering, disappointments and
reverses, he had remained fundamentally an optimist, with
hopes in his future. In the remaining years of his life his
chief characteristic was to be dark pessimism, disgust with
the world, and doubt even of his ultimate success. Soon he
would lose the desire – or perhaps only the hope – of personal
glory, and his sole longing would then be to pay his debts
and to reach honourable and self-respecting peace.

PART THREE

Je te hais, Océan, tes bonds et tes tumultes,
Mon esprit les retrouve en lui! Ce rire amer
De l'homme vaincu, plein de sanglots et d'insultes,
Je l'entends dans le rire énorme de la mer.

[1]

The Widow's Son
1857—1859

BAUDELAIRE'S first reaction to the banning of the poems, on which he had expended so much love and labour, was refusal to submit, a feeling of bravado, and determination to sell his book in spite of the law. From this attitude he drew a kind of desperate courage which, for a time, prevented him from sinking into pessimism. He was irritated to find that his publisher did not follow him in this; for Poulet Malassis, who always managed to make the best of everything, was now selling off copies of *Les Fleurs du Mal* in a mutilated form, with blank sheets inserted to take the place of the poems which had been banned, or even with stumps of pages left where they had been cut away. The poet considered this a deception on the public, as well as a crime against serious publishing. He wanted the book either sold in its original form – even if clandestinely – regardless of the consequences, or else scrapped to make way for a new edition. He had often been shocked by the levity, and occasional lapses of good taste, on the part of his friend, in spite of his passion for well-produced books.

'If you could only understand,' he wrote to him,[1] 'the harm you're doing yourself with your absurd surgical operation. Complaints have hung fire for a time, but now they've broken out. Naturally, as was within my rights, I put all the blame on Malassis. All I beg you most earnestly, for the moment – and it is a prayer, but what effective words could I use with a temperament of such levity as yours? – not to do anything about the new pages, until we've agreed, both of us, about the best way of doing them. It may be necessary to compensate one or two of the hundred fools who fell into the trap, by giving them a decent copy!'

Baudelaire was finally persuaded by his better judgement to submit to the verdict of the court. He went to see Pinard, the prosecutor, had a long conversation with him, and found him well disposed – it may indeed have been Pinard who advised him to write directly to the Empress Eugénie to ask for the remission of his fine.

'Madame,' he wrote,[2] 'It needs great presumption on the part of a poet to dare occupy the attention of Your Majesty with so trifling a matter as mine. I have had the misfortune to be sentenced by the court for a collection of poems entitled *Les Fleurs du Mal*. I had imagined that I had produced a work of great beauty, and moreover a work the intention of which was clear. It has been misunderstood and misinterpreted, so that I have been condemned to republish the book, and delete some of the poems – six per cent. I must add that I have been treated by the court with perfect courtesy, and that the very terms of the verdict imply recognition of my pure and lofty intentions. However, the fine, increased by a total of costs completely unintelligible to me, is beyond the proverbially poor means of a poet, but, encouraged by the proofs of high esteem which I have received from friends in high places, and at the same time, confident as I am that the heart of the Empress is always open to compassion for spiritual and mundane troubles, after ten days of indecision and timidity, I have conceived the plan of soliciting the gracious kindness of Your Majesty, and of begging you to intervene on my behalf with the Minister of Justice.

'I have the honour of remaining the most devoted and obedient servant and subject of Your Majesty.'

The result was that his fine was reduced from three hundred to fifty francs.

Now that he had humbled his arrogant pride, he determined to retrieve his failure in another way. Writing to Poulet Malassis, he said:[3]

'I've decided, as you know, to submit entirely to the verdict, and to compose six new poems far more beautiful than those which have been banned!'

With submission and resignation courage seemed to abandon him, and he sank into depression, into a lethargic state of mind which left him incapable of work. The proofs of his new book – the translation of *Gordon Pym* – remained on his table for several months uncorrected, since he did not seem able to summon up enough strength of purpose to work on them. There seemed to be nothing ahead of him but desolation and sterility.

The verdict against *Les Fleurs du Mal* not only damaged Baudelaire with the general public, but was responsible also for strained relations between his mother and himself, at a time when they both needed each other.

Madame Aupick was now a widow. The husband whom she had loved passionately for more than thirty years died in April 1857. In the midst of her grief she must often have felt relieved that he had not known of the disgrace of her son of whose manner of life he had so often disapproved – particularly because it caused her distress. The passage in his will which refers to her is a warm tribute to the position which she had occupied in his life, even though it is couched in the pompous language which was natural to him, and which his stepson had always found so irritating.[4]

'I entrust to the care of my friends my beloved wife, whom for thirty years I found at my side always tender and devoted, and who contributed so much to the easy fulfilment of the exercise of my duties – especially abroad – where the grace of her lively mind, and the courtesy of her manner gave her drawing-room a charm which everyone was pleased to recognize. I give her my last thought as I seek refuge in the bosom of my Maker.'

The change in her circumstances was now great. She had been left in straitened means on account of her husband's principles, and all she had now was the small pension of a General's widow, the little capital which her first husband had left her, and the proceeds from the sale of Aupick's

effects. On this she decided to live in the little country villa
which he had bought for her as a holiday resort at Honfleur,
in which they could forget together in peace and seclusion
their life of pomp and dignity. There she thought she would
be able to recall him more easily than in a new small apartment in Paris, which was all she could now afford and which
bore no trace of him.[5]

This little house in Honfleur once stood in a street which
was subsequently renamed Rue Charles Beaudelaire – it is
ironical that after his death, he should be commemorated
with his name spelt in a way he could not tolerate during
his lifetime. The house was eventually absorbed in an asylum
later built on the spot, and the part where the poet once
stayed was to become the ward for inmates suffering from
contagious diseases – a posthumous symbol of the views of
those who had protested against the dangerous influence of
Les Fleurs du Mal![6]

The '*maison joujou*' as Baudelaire used to call it, which
had been enlarged and improved by General Aupick, had
beautiful views of the sea from all its windows, and it was
while occupying two of its upstairs rooms that the poet
composed his loveliest nature poems – amongst them *Le
Voyage*. The General, describing the house to a friend,
wrote:[7]

'My wife is as happy as a child with the new house, the
chief beauty of which is provided by nature, since from her
drawing-room, from her dressing-room, as well as from
her garden, she has a marvellous view, which is not to be
despised even if one has lived for three years on the Bos-
phorus. As for me I just laze away the time, reclining in a
green and shady bower at the edge of the cliff, with a few
books open beside me in case I need them, and I dream to
the murmur, or crash, of the waves – as the case may be –
on the shingle below, to which charm a new one is added in
the song of the warblers which I protect in my function of
king and master of the place.'

After General Aupick died, all his furniture and effects

were sold, the carriages and the horses, but his wife did not regret them, now that the husband with whom she had enjoyed them was no longer with her. All she asked, she said, was to be allowed to finish her days in peace in the little house he had loved so well. His friends gathered round her, to make her forget her inconsolable grief – particularly Emon, a retired gunner, who also lived at Honfleur, and he and his wife were constant visitors at her villa.

This peace she longed for was not to be. Suddenly, in the quiet of her retreat at Honfleur, there burst the bombshell of her son's trial in August, when her husband had been dead barely five months. She was obliged to go about the conventional little provincial town, in her widow's weeds, knowing that neighbours came out on to their doorsteps and whispered as they watched her pass, the mother of the man who had been convicted of obscenity. She had moreover been obliged to write to influential friends of her husband to beg for their support in favour of the stepson whose conduct had always scandalized him, and whose present predicament he would have deplored. So horrified had she been by what she had read of her son's book in the newspapers, and at what she heard of it by rumour, that she refused the copy he wished to send her, and would not read it for herself to form her own opinion of it.[8] He was very much hurt by her harshness and lack of sympathy.

'You've thought fit,' he complained,[9] 'to add your reproaches to the insults with which I was being bombarded from all sides.'

Later he was to say to her,[10] 'You're always ready to stone me with the crowd!'

Yet Baudelaire had felt drawn very close to his mother in her great grief, closer than he had been for many years, so that even she had noticed the difference in his behaviour towards her.[11] He had felt tender and protective, knowing that she had no one else but him now to count on, and realizing also that he was henceforth responsible for more than just himself. He had hoped that they would once more live happily together, as they had once done, thirty years before, during her first widowhood.

The General's friends, who had rallied round to see that she was not exploited by her wastrel son, did their utmost to prevent her from living with him, and he was too proud to plead for himself. She herself, as she listened to their arguments – such reasonable arguments – was bewildered and frightened, and they persuaded her at length that, if they lived together, he would only bring her to ruin. Since her childhood, poisoned by poverty and envy, the spectre of ultimate destitution had haunted her, and even the life of an ambassadress had not been able to lay it. She remembered also that her son was now thirty-five, middle-aged, and that he was not yet earning a regular living. She recalled his incessant demands for loans and advances during recent years, his ever-plausible excuses – for such they seemed to her, and had seemed to her husband. She remembered her own weakness, and how the only way she could harden her heart to refusal was by severing all connection with him. She could not forget how once he had begged her to write to Ancelle for an advance of a hundred and fifty francs. In the letter she had sent him to give to the lawyer, she had stipulated for fifty only. He, thinking – or pretending to think – that she had made a mistake, had added a one in front of her fifty, making the sum what he had originally demanded.[12] True, he had written at once to tell her what he had done, and true, the money was his, even if it was tied up, but the fact remained that he was capable of an action which her husband would have called unscrupulous. She was afraid of what he might do if they were living under the same roof, and she told him, before he had thought of suggesting it, that she would never live with him.[13] Although she was his mother, she did not realize the delicacy of his feelings towards her: that, now she was poor, he would not try to obtain money from her, and that he would never bring disgrace on the house which she lived. She did not know that, as long as her husband was alive, he considered that she had had enough, and more than enough, and that what he borrowed then would not be greatly missed in her life of luxury. It would only mean at most for her a difficult moment of explanation with her husband. Writing to her a couple of months after the death of her husband, he said:[14]

'I would like, briefly, to explain to you the reasons for my behaviour to you and for my feelings, since the death of my stepfather. You'll find in this the explanation of my attitude towards this great misfortune, and, at the same time, of my future conduct. This event was for me a solemn thing, as it were, a call to order. I've often been very harsh and unfair to you, poor mother, but I could consider that somebody else had charge of your happiness – and the first idea that struck me, at the time of the death, was that, henceforth, it was I who had charge of it, that everything which I had formerly indulged in – idleness, selfishness, insolence, which always exist in solitude and in a disordered life – all this was henceforth forbidden to me. Everything which is humanly possible to do to create for you a new and special happiness, will be done.'

She remained full of doubts. Prompted by her husband's friends, she had omitted to include her son's name in the announcement of his death – as if this was no concern of his – and, when she had seen him at the funeral, amongst the General's colleagues, she had been forcibly struck by his shabby appearance, his air of failure, and his lack of an established position. She remembered then all that her husband had hoped for him, in the early days of their marriage, and she felt more than ever disappointed and disillusioned.

The Emons, particularly, were driving her against him, deliberately and maliciously, in a way her husband would never have attempted, for, though stern, he had been a just man. At his funeral Baudelaire had stood awkwardly, in self-conscious misery, as an outsider, not represented in the 'lettre de faire part', while his stepfather's friends had treated him distantly and coldly, as if he had been an intruder. And when, after the ceremony in the church was over, he had stood in line amongst the other relatives, to receive the condolences of those who had come to pay their respects to the deceased General, Ambassador and Senator, he had been humiliated by the way they had taken his hand with undisguised ill-will and disapproval. Only Monsieur Jacquotot, his own father's friend and a member of his *conseil de famille*, who had not seen him for twenty years, had realized his grief, and had spoken to him with sympathy and kindness. He had touched him by a remark which showed that he fully understood the part which he must now play in his mother's life. 'You'll now make your home with your mother, won't you?' [15]

The Emons were determined that this should never happen, and his mother was afraid to stand up to them, reluctant to defend her own son before them. As long as they were at Honfleur, she did not invite him to come, even for a short visit. Shortly after the funeral, writing to the wife of her stepson, Alphonse Baudelaire, she said:

'Tell Alphonse that I'm well pleased with his brother – at least in respect to his feelings. As far as order and method are concerned, I don't know whether he'll ever change, but I greatly fear not. However, when the Emons are away on a visit to their daughter, I'll take advantage of their absence, when I'm alone, to invite Charles to come and pay me a visit.' [16]

Things had indeed come to a sad pass when Baudelaire had to wait until the conventional friends of his dead stepfather were absent, not from his mother's house, but only from the town where she now lived, in order to visit her. And, when at last her invitation arrived, her letter was so harsh, and so full of warnings of what he was not to do, with so many strict injunctions that he was on no account to run up bills at Honfleur – a thing he would not have contemplated doing – that his wounded pride and affection prevented him from accepting the invitation, although he was longing to see her.[17]

In the meantime he had sunk once more into a state of deep depression, when he felt, as he says, 'Un immense découragement', and a sensation of spiritual isolation. He used to say to himself each morning as he started work, 'What's the use of all this!'[18]

When Christmas came, he was still alone and far from his mother, and he decided that he could not allow the day to go by without a word from him, for she must be lonely too, on her first Christmas as a widow, without her beloved husband.

'My dearest Mother,' he wrote,[19] 'I'm going this evening – or rather this night – if alas! I've got the time to do so – to write you a long letter, and send you a little packet which has been ready for you this long time. I say "if I've got the time" for I've been sunk for many months now in a great state of inertia which has prevented all work. Since the beginning of the month my table has been cluttered up with proofs which I've not had the energy to touch. But a time comes when one must, even if with great pain, drag oneself out of these depths of inertia. These cursed holidays have the gift of reminding one, in a cruel way, of the flight of time, how ill-spent it has been, and how full of sorrow. I'll try to explain to you tonight how I've been driven, after having resolved to look after you for ever, to shut myself away from all confidences – even if you don't understand all that I'm saying, you'll perhaps admit I had, to a certain extent, some excuses. . . .

'The packet which I've been keeping for you is composed, firstly of articles which I've written myself and which appeared during the second half of the year; and secondly of articles written about *Les Fleurs du Mal* – from the few I enclose – and there were so many that, at last, sickened quite as much by the praise as by the stupid abuse, I gave up reading them – you'll be able to judge the disastrous stir created by the book into which I've poured some of the causes of my fury and despair. And finally the book itself which you refused, so strangely, to accept when you thought fit to add your reproaches to the insults with which I've been overwhelmed on all sides.

'I'd have liked, for Christmas, to be able to send you the third volume of Poe, but I've admitted above that the proofs have been lying on my table for over a month, without my being able to shake off my lamentable sloth.

'This copy of *Les Fleurs* is my own private one. I owe it to you since I gave yours to Monsieur Fould. These were the last two printed on hand-made paper. I'll be able to procure an ordinary copy for myself. I tremble with sloth at the thought that, before the book can be legally sold, I'll have to reprint it, and compose six poems, to replace those which are banned.

'I'll send you a more detailed letter with the packet this evening, or tomorrow morning at latest!

'I send you my very fondest love, and I beg you henceforth to be full of kindness towards me, for I swear that I need it badly! If ever a man was ill without its concerning medicine, then it's me!'

It was not until New Year's Eve that he wrote the further promised letter, and then he told her the reasons to explain his silence since the previous August – his pride, his sensitivity, and his grief at finding that she listened to what the Emons said against him. He ended his letter, saying: [20]

'I don't believe, dear Mother, that you've ever realized my unbearable sensitivity. We're at present very weak and alone. Why shouldn't we try, once and for all, to be happy through each other?'

At last his mother ventured to read his book and, almost against her will, she was deeply moved, in spite of her prejudices, and was able to recognize his talent. She was also excited, when she read the notices which had appeared, and admitted that she had been mistaken, and had judged him on the opinion of others. Her letters were then so full of unwonted praise that her son was even embarrassed, so unused was he to her approval. [21] She even wrote to her stepson Alphonse Baudelaire to express her delighted surprise. [22]

'Would you believe it, your brother is moving towards a fine and great reputation! *Les Fleurs du Mal*, which created such a stir in the literary world, contains, alongside horrible and offensive descriptions, some marvellous poems of great purity of language and simplicity of form, which produce a wonderfully poetic effect. He possesses, to a great degree, the gift of writing. Charles, in spite of his eccentricity, has undoubted talent. If *Les Fleurs* had been an indifferent work, it would have passed unnoticed like many another, you may be sure. And is it not better to have too much ardour and inspiration than sterility of ideas, and commonplace expressions?

'As for his translations of Poe, as a work of style, they are very remarkable, even astonishing! They are as fine as an original composition! I'd not realized that he knew English so well.

'At last I feel full of hope for the future of your brother, and, when I think of the past, I'm grateful to see this passion for work, even extreme love of work, coupled with the resolve to pay his debts with his own earnings.... I count on his visit here, in the midst of the beauties of nature, and through association with me, to see him return to a more gentle inspiration.

'I've allowed myself to talk to you at great length about Charles, because I'm sure that you'll rejoice with me in his success, and I know he'll have many more!

'I send you both my love.'

She was now planning to have her son, not only on a visit to Honfleur, but to live with her permanently, in spite of the objections of the Emons. She wrote then, as usual, to Ancelle for advice: [23]

'Monsieur Emon is trying his best to prevent me from having Charles to live with me, and he speaks of him, not only severely, but very harshly as well – about his selfishness and his thriftlessness. But all this can't alter my determination. Since Charles is lonely and wishes us to live together, then I must agree to his request.'

She next wrote, asking him to come and live with her, and he was very much touched, for this was the kindest and most friendly letter he had received from her for many years.

'My dearest mother,' he said,[24] 'You wrote me a charming letter three weeks ago, the only one of that sort for many years now – and I've not yet answered it. You must have been unpleasantly surprised! I want to tell you that when I read that letter, I understood that I was still loved, more than I'd known, and that many things could still be altered for the better, and that happiness might yet be granted to us.

'In all the different ways in which, most probably, you've tried to explain my silence, you've perhaps been unjust. The truth is that your kind and maternal letter almost hurt me. I suffered when I realized how sincerely you wished to have me with you, when I realized that I'd have to grieve you since I wasn't yet ready to leave. Firstly, I don't dare to leave Paris at the moment with a book in process of printing.[25] You know the horrible and meticulous care I take of everything. I'd be most anxious, and rightly so.

'And then, imagine for a moment the horrible life I'm leading, which leaves me so little time for work and for the infinite number of things which I must settle before I leave. At the beginning of the month I had to waste almost a week, in hiding, to avoid arrest, and I'd left all my manuscripts unfinished at home. This is only one of the thousand vicissitudes of my life.

'It's awful to have happiness almost within one's grasp and not to be able to seize it. And to realize that not only is one going to be happy oneself, but going to bring happiness also to someone to whom one owes it. And then add to all that suffering, the one which perhaps you'll not understand. When the nerves of a man are strained by an infinite amount of anxiety and suffering, the devil, in spite of all his good resolutions, slips every morning into his brain in the shape of this thought: "Why not rest one day more in oblivion of all these things? Tonight, at one fell swoop, I'll accomplish all the necessary things." And then night comes, and the mind reels at the thought of the amount of things left undone, overwhelming sadness induces sterility, and next day the same old comedy begins again, with the same resolution, the same honesty, and the same confidence.

'But I'm sincerely longing to get away from this cursed town where I've suffered so much, and where I've wasted so much time. Who knows whether at Honfleur my brain mayn't grow young once more in happiness and peace? I've in my mind a score of novels and two plays. I don't dream of a worthy, commonplace fame! I want to overwhelm people, and astound them, like Byron, Balzac or Chateaubriand! But, is there still time left for that? Oh! if only I'd known, when I was young, the value of time, health and money! And these cursed *Fleurs* that I've got to do again. I need peace for that! To become, artificially, and by will-power, a poet once more, and to return to a path that one had thought finally traced and finished, to treat once more a subject one had thought exhausted, and that merely to obey the dictates of three magistrates! Seriously, without exaggeration, I believe that, at Honfleur, through hard work, I'll be able to settle my debts in two years, that is to say, earn three times as much as here. What a misfortune that you didn't offer me this arrangement nearly a year ago, when I wasn't yet sunk so deeply in terrible difficulties.

'And now to return to the relation of my plans of happiness. I'll be able to read and read again! Without hindering my output! All my days will be spent in rejuvenating my mind! For I must confess, mother dear, that my miserable education has been sadly and cruelly interrupted by my folly and tribulations. And youth is flying fast, and I think sometimes with terror of the flight of the years. They are, however, only made up of hours and minutes, but, when one is wasting time, one thinks only of the fraction of time and not of the sum total.

'Here indeed are good plans, and I don't think that they

are impossible to realize, since, at Honfleur, I'll have no excuse for not fulfilling them.

'When you read my letter I don't want you to imagine that it is selfishness alone which prompts me. The greatest part of my thought is this: "My mother doesn't yet know me, she has scarcely seen me, we've not had time to live together, but we must nevertheless find a few years of happiness together." Goodbye! It's half past four. In imagination I kiss you with all my heart. This letter is disgracefully scribbled, but I've scrawled it in large characters because I thought it would tire your eyes less.'

Baudelaire was going through one of his habitual periods of financial difficulty, or rather his distress had been steadily growing because he had been able to do nothing to alleviate it. He was earning very little, for many periodicals and newspapers were afraid to employ him since the unsavoury law case. He did not want to settle at Honfleur with many pressing debts, for he did not wish to run the risk of being arrested in his mother's house, or of his creditors coming to wait for him on her doorstep. This, he knew, would almost kill her with shame.

He considered then a way out of his difficulties. He thought that the time had at last come to reconsider his financial situation with a view to seeing what arrangements could be made in the matter of his debts, and what was the best use to which his remaining capital could be put. But his legal disabilities made it impossible for him to do anything himself without his mother's consent, and without the help of a lawyer. Ancelle would have been the most natural person to approach, but he had become an obsession with him, and was growing more irritating to him. Confronted by Ancelle in person he felt inhibited, as if he could not speak, and he used to imagine that he could read in the lawyer's face the unfavourable things he must be thinking about him. Whenever possible he used to write to him, but Ancelle, for many years now, had adopted the plan of taking no notice of his letters, of making him wait for his money, in the hope that the pressing need might pass. And he had heard too often, during the past fourteen years, of his ward's desperate need and distress, to be impressed now and to believe in his future thrift. He was besides, at this moment, absent from Paris. Baudelaire then thought of Jacquotot, who was also a lawyer and who had been the only person to show him sympathy at the funeral of his stepfather the previous year. He would not be likely to be ill-disposed from the beginning since he had not seen him for twenty years. The day after he wrote to his mother, to expound his plans for the future, he wrote also to Jacquotot, at great length, to put his financial situation before him and to explain what he would like done on his behalf.[26] What is remarkable in this document is its moderation. He would have liked to ask for more, but he did not wish to appear grasping, and only someone of his incurable optimism could have believed that what he asked could bring anything but a very temporary alleviation to his difficulties. The sum he asked would have paid only the most pressing of his debts, and would have given him peace for very few months. He proposed to Jacquotot that, since he would be living free of cost in his mother's house, he would leave with Ancelle all his income for the following year, on the condition that this amount was now advanced to him, either as a loan or through the selling out of capital, to pay some of his most pressing debts, which hindered him from settling at Honfleur. He well knew that Ancelle would not believe in his promise not to ask for any income during the coming year, but he begged Jacquotot to make the matter clear to his mother, so that she should inform Ancelle of her wishes, and not ask his advice, as was her unfailing habit.

When Jacquotot heard the account of Baudelaire's life since his majority, he was surprised, as anyone would have been, that the debts had not been entirely paid at the time of the nomination of the *conseil judiciaire*. He considered that it had been cruel to leave the young man for almost fifteen years with a burden of debt crushing him.[27] Jacquotot interviewed Baudelaire five or six times, and thought his projects reasonable. He then wrote to Madame Aupick to put them before her, but with judicial caution did not express any personal opinion on the advisability of acceding to his request, merely saying that she would be able to decide herself whether she could agree to his demands.[28]

She herself then wrote to her son to say that she agreed to the arrangements suggested, and he began, full of hope, to make plans for leaving Paris immediately and for the dispatching of his books and pictures. He even contemplated buying bookshelves to bring with him. The three thousand francs which he was to obtain would, he said, satisfy the appetite of the ravenous sharks – the old creditors being merely tigers, who awoke once or twice a year only. He was planning a long stay, and he asked whether he would be able to get a glimpse of the sea from his window.[29]

Then the blow fell! Nothing could be done without the help of Ancelle, and Madame Aupick omitted to tell her son that she had not, as he had requested, merely written to the lawyer to acquaint him with her wishes. He was an old friend, and she had written to him for advice, telling him what her son had suggested. Baudelaire received her letter on the Saturday morning, just after he had posted a note to her, and he realized at once that, now Ancelle was involved, there would be endless delays, and that perhaps everything would be changed. Moreover he had promised his most pressing creditors immediate settlement, and they would show him no mercy. All his dreams had been in vain and his plans were all shattered.

'I've had three days of joy,' he wrote to his mother,[30] 'that's always something, for joy is rare! So, in spite of everything, I thank you for it very sincerely! But it was only a dream! I haven't abandoned all hope of going to Honfleur – my longing for that grows every day – but I'll now go with my own money, when I've been able to extricate myself, by my own efforts, from my difficulties.

'I entreat you, mother, don't be angry with me. I'll cer-

tainly go, but when? I don't yet know but, I'll do my utmost
to bring it about. I received this morning your fatal letter,
and so the letter I sent you yesterday, with all the detailed
explanations, is cancelled.

'I'll be obliged to deal quickly with all the difficulties into
which I'll now be plunged, for I'd convened several people
for the coming week. It's enough to make one mad! But
however awful all that is, it isn't the worst! Ancelle, to
whom, no doubt, you've written, will come and bother the
life out of me with his help. He'll weary me with his hateful
conversation, and I need peace so badly! He'll force his way
into my room; he'll worm his way into my affairs, and try to
drag the story of my need from me! At the mere thought
of his visit, my suffering turns to rage. And when he sees
how obstinate I am in refusing everything he'll try to do me
as much harm as possible on the pretext of helping me. I
can't even flee from Paris to avoid him, for the cure would
be worse than the ill. He's going to force his way into my
business, as he did at my trial, when he engaged all my
friends in conversation, whom he didn't know at all, because he's always mad keen to get to know everything and
everyone, and to have his finger in every pie. All my friends
used to ask me who was the tall man who seemed to know
me so well, and I had my eyes anxiously glued on him, because I was afraid that he might compromise me, or make
me ridiculous.

'And so I beg and implore you, if you've not already written to him, not to write anything to him; or, if you've written
to him, write to him again and tell him that your agreement
and our plans are all off. I want to live! I don't want this
plague of an Ancelle to come and rob me of my time and
peace – my peace!

'I beg you not to be offended if I prefer my hell to that
help which has always been my curse. I trust I may count
on you so that Ancelle doesn't come to meddle ... I've never
had a really serious quarrel with him, and I've never yet
insulted him. But that might easily happen! I'd be ashamed

and grieved, but the harm would be done! One of my great
joys in going to Honfleur was to escape from him completely.

'I send you my love.'

In the meantime the harm had been done! One afternoon, while Baudelaire was out, Ancelle descended on the
hotel where he was living, and, not finding his ward at home,
tried in his clumsy way to discover for himself what it was
that he owed. His indebtedness to the hotel had been mentioned as one of his most pressing needs. It is probable that
Ancelle wished to investigate this account with a legal eye,
since Baudelaire, even at the age of thirty-five, was still
being fleeced by tradespeople. It is also very likely that the
landlord did not enjoy this scrutiny and made it seem, when
he reported the lawyer's visit to Baudelaire, as if Ancelle
had come to spy on him. It is improbable that a man like
Ancelle would ask the questions which the landlord divulged,
with a show of unwillingness, saying that he had begged him
not to mention them to Baudelaire. 'Does Monsieur Baudelaire come in late?' 'Does he receive women in his room?'
Ancelle certainly denied the accusations later when he
learned of them.[31] It is probable that he was speaking the
truth; for he was a blunt and honourable man. True, he
had rooted objections to selling out capital to pay debts and
probably did not accept on trust the figures which Baudelaire
had given to Jacquotot, which he wanted to investigate for
himself. And, since he was not very sensitive himself, he
could not understand how someone who, for fifteen years
now, had been in the lamentable financial situation in which
Baudelaire found himself, could at the same time be sensitive about these debts. Before settling the business he probably wished to discuss it thoroughly with him from all
angles. When Baudelaire heard of the visit himself in the
garbled account of the landlord, he was beside himself with
fury at the thought that he was being spied upon – his nerves
had already been upset that morning by his mother's letter –
and he flew into one of the rages for which he had been
notorious in his youth, but which, latterly, had become more

rare. On that Saturday afternoon he wrote seven letters to his mother – almost hourly – dashing them off whenever a fresh monstrosity occurred to him of which he could accuse Ancelle, and he poured out the pent-up irritation and annoyance of fifteen years. It was only with the utmost difficulty that he was prevented from going, on the spot, to Ancelle's house to strike him, and to provoke him to a duel. The whole situation was one of those which seem so comic to the onlooker, but so tragic to those engaged in them. The first letter, written at two o'clock in the afternoon, ends: [32]

'Ancelle is a scoundrel whose ears I'm going to box in front of his wife and children! I'll go and box his ears at four o'clock – it's now half past two – and if he isn't at home I'll wait for him. I swear that this will have an end, a terrible end!'

By four o'clock the landlord, somewhat terrified at the storm which he had aroused, had managed to dissuade him from going out to Neuilly to find Ancelle. Instead he wrote once more to his mother:

'I shan't go out to Neuilly today! I agree to wait for my revenge! Did you order him to come and libel and insult your son? Monsieur Charles Baudelaire, whose name is pure and unsullied!

'I insist on apologies! I insist on profound apologies! I insist that he's severely reprimanded!

'To what scoundrel have you delivered me, without my knowledge, without warning me? I'm distressed at the worry I'm causing you, but I must have my revenge! If striking amends aren't made to me, I'll hit Ancelle, and I'll hit his son! It'll be a fine thing to see a *conseil judiciaire* summoning Monsieur Charles Baudelaire for battery and assault.'

At five o'clock he wrote again:

'I'll cost you a lot of postage tomorrow as I've no money today! But you must, mother, realize my situation. And when I think that I'd absolutely no inkling of what was happening! Honestly did you hire that gibbering idiot as a private detective – it was the day before yesterday but I've only just found out – to inquire into my manner of living, to come and question the servants, making himself perfectly ridiculous, to backbite me, me who am thirty-seven years old! I'm really distressed at the grief I'm causing you. I've work to do, and now I must find seconds in case there's a definite quarrel between Ancelle and myself, or his son and me. The little fellow is old enough for that! I insist on definite apologies, and a thorough expression of regret, and I insist on all this happening before two or three witnesses chosen by myself. If it doesn't happen I'll go on brutally until the bitter end! And what kind of seconds shall I need? They would have to be discreet and faithful friends, to whom I can admit that, through my mother's unconscious action, I've been insulted by my *conseil judiciaire*. And when I remember that most of my friends are married, and have children, and may refuse such a dangerous service. But I've decided to drive matters to their bitter conclusion, as in one of these rages which luckily occur only once every ten years or so. It must all end!

'I insist on apologies! I've tears of rage in my eyes! And don't you feel insulted yourself? Where on earth was he dragged up? Am I destined all my life to be insulted? I insist on apologies, and I'll drag them out of him by force, if necessary!'

And so the letter continued all through the day. At last he said:

'I've consulted several people on what I ought to do. I know it's a nasty thing to strike an old man in front of his children. Yet I must have amends! What am I to do if I don't receive amends? I must at least go and tell him in front of his wife and children what I think of him. And supposing I'm insulted once more! What then? What shall I do? Heavens above! Into what embarrassments have you cast me! And I need rest! I ask for nothing else! What on earth have I done to be deprived of what the meanest person on earth has a right to? I repeat again I'm sorry for all the trouble I'm going to cause you with all these letters. But truly what have I done to that scoundrel, what have I done to you, that you should set him on me thus?

'He's a man completely devoid of honesty and delicacy, without honour, he's destroyed my life, and it's in him you choose to confide your maternal fears, and it's him you ask to help me in an affair which needs discretion, in a matter concerning which I'd put myself unreservedly in your hands, and trusted you entirely!'

After the emotional disturbance of this Saturday, Baudelaire was ill for several days. At last he felt better, but he still refused to meet Ancelle on friendly terms, and then Madame Aupick in desperation sent Jacquotot whom he finally allowed to take charge of his affairs for the time being. Jacquotot made him see the impropriety and discourtesy of his conduct towards a man of Ancelle's age and position who was, at the same time, one of his mother's most trusted friends.[33] Ancelle, for his part, remained as usual unperturbed by Baudelaire's tantrums and vagaries, which he had known since his infancy, and wrote to his ward as if nothing had occurred to make relations strained between them, meeting him on the same footing as before.

The sad result was that, even when the paltry three thousand francs were finally paid, Baudelaire had lost so much time and energy in the emotional upheaval, that he was obliged to remain in Paris to finish the work which should long since have been published. The business of selling the shares, and getting the proceeds handed to his creditors, had dragged on into the second week in March, and by that time he was in difficulties with the proofs of the volume of Poe, *Gordon Pym*, which Michel Lévy was publishing. Lévy was beginning to grow impatient, as the book should have appeared before Christmas, but had been delayed on account of the poet's lethargical state at the time. He had moreover lost, or mislaid, the proofs, and was obliged to go to the press itself, at Corbeil, to correct them on the spot, while the operatives waited to proceed with the printing. In the middle of May he was still in Paris, and by then it had become once more impossible for him to move, for he was in fresh entanglements and difficulties. He was trying to negotiate a contract for his *Mangeur d'Opium* with *Le Moniteur*, which finally refused it. *La Revue Contemporaine* was clamouring for his *Haschisch*, on which he had already been paid in advance. All this, coupled with his usual financial embarrassments, made it impossible for him to be away from the capital.[34]

The third volume of Baudelaire's translation from Poe appeared in May 1858, but, during the six years since he had first tried to introduce the American author into France, the taste of the public had somewhat changed. They had at first hailed him with great enthusiasm, but now readers were beginning to grow weary of the macabre style, and were turning to realism or frivolity. Even Barbey d'Aurevilly, who had been one of Poe's most fervent admirers, now praised him with many reservations, and his article on *The Adventures of Gordon Pym*, in May 1858 in *Le Réveil*, described its author as a drunken and anti-social poet, the king of La Bohème. This saddened Baudelaire and caused a coolness between him and his former friend. It was not until 1883, when taste had once more veered towards Poe, that Barbey d'Aurevilly repented his harshness and admitted that he had been misinformed by calumnies inspired by hatred.[35] By this time, however, Baudelaire had been dead for over fifteen years.

The poet was still being violently attacked in the press from all sides. Even his former school-friend, Louis Ménard, who had not the generosity to forget the wound his pride had received eleven years before, when Baudelaire reviewed his *Prométhée Délivré* harshly, wrote one of the most spiteful notices which *Les Fleurs du Mal* received.[36] He declared that Baudelaire's ambition was to pass for a wicked devil with a cloven hoof, but that when one read his book one imagined him as something quite different, a clumsy youth in a long frock coat, with sallow complexion, short-sighted eyes and the hair-cut of a seminarist. Although he babbled interminably of vice, in reality it was easy to see that he had only the salacious imagination of those who have spent their life in seclusion. The disease he complained of was not the one he suffered from, and, noting his passion for decay, no doctor would falter in his diagnosis. His real disease consisted in having lived too long in an imaginary world, peopled with unhealthy phantoms, who would vanish at the contact of reality. Until that happened he would remain a schoolboy suffering from arrested development.

His old enemy, *Le Figaro*, in an article published in June 1858, was not content with merely abusing him personally – this he might have endured with contemptuous pride – but was as well so unjust about his attitude to his elders in the poetic world, that he was goaded into answering, a thing he had never done before. His letter to the editor is a dignified reply which does him credit, but the injured are always in the wrong, and it would have been wiser if he had observed his usual silence, for *Le Figaro* printed his letter the following week, with a spiteful commentary.[37]

The article, by a certain Jean Rousseau, is a clever and witty attack, but it is easy to be amusing at the expense of others. His theme was that Baudelaire did not really exist as a person, but was only the incarnation of a character, Daniel Jovard, from the collection of stories by Gautier, entitled *Les Jeunes-France* and published in 1833. He said that Gautier had been satirizing a literary coterie of his youth, 'les écrivains échevelés', who had died a natural death as a result of their excesses. Unfortunately, added Rousseau, he had recently become unpleasantly aware that these monstrosities of 1830 had not been exterminated, and that Daniel Jovard had broken loose once more, to appear this time under the name of Baudelaire. The comparison between Jovard and Baudelaire, using the poet's writings as illustration, was wittily contrived, and must have amused the readers of *Le Figaro*. The reporter libellously hinted at personal knowledge of depravities in the poet's private life, and he claimed that there were no extenuating circum-

stances in favour of Jovard, alias Baudelaire, because he had
learnt nothing since his escape from romanticism – not
even any new vices – for he still practised the same forms
as twenty-five years before, the same epileptic style, in order
to give the impression of depth of ideas. Rousseau ended by
saying that his literary misdeeds, so boldly and brazenly
committed, had for a long time wearied many people, who
now considered that the moment had come for justice to
intervene with repressive measures, and to imprison Baudelaire, alias Jovard, the escaped convict, in the place from
which he ought never to have been allowed to escape, namely
Gautier's work.

All this Baudelaire could have endured with contempt,
but what was more than he could stand was that the critic
claimed that but for Gautier he would never have existed
and nevertheless he was ungrateful to him and abused him
whenever possible.

The same week as this article appeared, Baudelaire read
as well a review from the pen of Sainte-Beuve, in praise of
Ernest Feydeau's *Fanny*, and he could not restrain a feeling
of envy, when he reflected that the famous critic had never
yet published a single line on him, and yet deigned to notice
a 'pot-boiler' such as *Fanny*. After *Le Figaro* had exercised
its wit at his expense, he wrote once again to Sainte-Beuve,
in the hope of persuading him to review his latest volume
of Poe.

'I've just read your article on *Fanny*,' he wrote,[38] 'and I
needn't tell you how charming I found it!... But with you
it's no use beating about the bush, as you're too clever not to
see through it. Well! that article inspired me with a horrible
jealousy. They've spoken so much of Loève-Weimars,[39]
and of the services which he rendered to French literature.
When shall I ever find a decent fellow to do as much for
me?

'By what cajoling and coaxing could I ever obtain such a
service from you, my so influential friend? And didn't you
almost offer to do that for me, right at the beginning? And

aren't *The Adventures of Gordon Pym* an excellent pretext for a general survey of my work in this respect?

'These last few days I've been literally dragged through the mud, and – pity me, it's the first time I've ever forgotten my pride and dignity – I was weak enough to reply. I know well how busy you are, and how concerned for all your lectures, for all your duties, etc., etc. But if one didn't occasionally overdo kindness a little, how would one ever be the hero of goodwill? If one didn't sometimes say too much good about decent people, how would one ever compensate them for the abuse of those who try to say all the harm they can about them?

'Well! be it as it may! I'll say to you, as I always do, your will be done, and I'll think it all right.'

Once more the article was not written.

At the same time Baudelaire was doing his utmost to get away from Paris to settle with his mother at Honfleur. He had already dispatched the greater part of his books, pictures, and other belongings, but the only thing which was now delaying him was the insoluble problem of settling his most pressing debts.

'I'm ill with sadness and distress,' he wrote to Poulet Malassis.[40] 'And to think that a charming house is waiting for me and that, merely on account of a few miserable debts, this promised land is closed to me!'

His mother also was anxiously awaiting his arrival, not only because she anticipated pleasure for herself from his company, but because she was hoping to exercise a reformative influence on him. Writing to her stepson, Alphonse Baudelaire, she said:[41]

'You're quite right to hope that the life together which I'm about to take up with Charles will be beneficial to him. Heaven only knows how much I hope for that myself! But what tireless and ceaseless efforts I'll have to make to succeed in influencing that strange and remarkable character!'

In December 1858 Baudelaire spent a fortnight at Alençon, trying to persuade Poulet Malassis to lend him, on the security of his future works, a sum of money sufficiently large to keep his creditors at bay for a few months. At last the publisher, who had never been able to resist for long the appeals of a friend in need, advanced him what was necessary to appease the ravening wolves for a period of six months. This loan was to be repaid out of the anticipated profits from the second edition of *Les Fleurs du Mal* and from *Les Paradis Artificiels*. At the end of 1858, these were not very valuable pledges since neither book was ready yet, and *Les Paradis Artificiels* was not to appear until 1860, while the second edition of *Les Fleurs du Mal* was published only in 1861.

With the money advanced by his publisher, Baudelaire was enabled to leave Paris, and he spent the first six months of 1859 with his mother in Honfleur, the last happy and peaceful period of his life.[42]

She prepared a bedroom, and also a study for him, on the second floor, looking over the sea, and furnished them with the best pieces that she possessed, for she had good taste and knew what would please him. At Honfleur, beside the sea, in the quiet and comfort of his mother's house, the years seemed to fall away from him, and he felt almost young again and full of hope. 'How happy I could be here,' he said to her,[43] 'if only I had no debts!' He became interested in the parish gossip, and told Asselineau, with the biting humour and irony of his youth, the scandalous story of the wife of one of the local celebrities, who had been discovered in compromising circumstances with her lover, by the parish priest, in one of the confessionals.[44] Since when the church had been kept locked, except during the actual hours of the services and sacraments. The terrors and obsession of the unknown, which had tortured him for so many years, now left him, and he was able to sleep once more, without the nightmare sensation of falling into a pit, from which he was unable to rise again. As he worked, he looked out over the ever-changing face of the sea, and the different transformations of nature.[45] There, freed from immediate anxiety, he felt that life could still be good, and inspiration returned to him, so that he composed in these months, a large number of poems, many of them amongst his greatest, such as *Le Voyage*.

It was only the peace and respite of a short dream which could not last, and he was back in the maelstrom of Paris in June 1859. The cause was that Poulet Malassis was now in as grave financial difficulties as he himself, and required a portion, at least, of his debt repaid. *The Opium Eater* was not yet finished, and the poet had nothing ready for publication, and he had no regular work on any paper, nothing on which he could raise an advance. He was therefore obliged to return to Paris, to see how he could secure somehow a sum of money to extricate his publisher from his present predicament. They had evolved a complicated system between themselves, by ingenious borrowing and re-borrowing from one another, to avoid the danger and misfortune of two bills falling due the same day for either of them.

'How wonderful it'll be,' said Baudelaire to Poulet Malassis,[46] 'when we'll no longer be obliged to play this eternal game of battledore and shuttlecock!'

Baudelaire's power of returning the missile was, however, considerably weakened through his lack of remunerated work, while he was at Honfleur.

Another preoccupation also kept Baudelaire in Paris during the summer and autumn of 1859. Marie Daubrun, who had been absent from the capital between 1857 and 1859, returned there to play in *Les Pirates de la Savane* at the Théâtre de la Gaîté, and he renewed his relationship with her. Perhaps it was she herself who sought him out this time, for she was in need of help. Banville was in hospital, very seriously ill, and she therefore required support in her career from another quarter. We know by the reply of Ponson du Terrail, who was a friend of the dramatic author, Anicet-Bourgeois, that the poet wrote to him in November to seek his good services in obtaining a part for her.[47] It may

have been only tender and brotherly affection that he felt
for her this time – at first at all events – and perhaps she had
wounded him too deeply when she had left him, at their
last encounter, but it was inspired by her that in the autumn
of that year he composed *Chant d'Automne*.[48]

> *Bientôt nous plongerons dans les froides ténèbres;*
> *Adieu, vive clarté de nos étés trop courts!*
> *J'entends déjà tomber avec des chocs funèbres*
> *Le bois retentissant sur le pavé des cours.*
>
> *J'écoute en frémissant chaque bûche qui tombe;*
> *L'échafaud qu'on bâtit n'a pas d'écho plus sourd.*
> *Mon esprit est pareil à la tour qui succombe*
> *Sous les coups du bélier infatigable et lourd.*
>
> *Il me semble, bercé par ce choc monotone,*
> *Qu'on cloue en grande hâte un cercueil quelque part.*
> *Pour qui? – C'était hier l'été; voici l'automne!*
> *Ce bruit mystérieux sonne comme un départ.*
>
> *J'aime de vos longs yeux la lumière verdâtre,*
> *Douce beauté, mais tout aujourd'hui m'est amer,*
> *Et rien, ni votre amour, ni le boudoir, ni l'âtre,*
> *Ne me vaut le soleil rayonnant sur la mer.*
>
> *Et pourtant aimez-moi, tendre cœur! soyez mère,*
> *Même pour un ingrat, même pour un méchant;*
> *Amante ou sœur, soyez la douceur éphémère*
> *D'un glorieux automne ou d'un soleil couchant.*
>
> *Courte tâche! La tombe attend; elle est avide!*
> *Ah! laissez-moi, mon front posé sur vos genoux,*
> *Goûter, en regrettant l'été blanc et torride,*
> *De l'arrière-saison le rayon jaune et doux!*

One feels this time not passion but an autumn chill in
his feelings for her, the last diluted rays of the setting sun,
as he must often have felt them, on the northern sea at Honfleur. The 'bruit mystérieux' which 'sonne comme un départ'
indeed soon rang out for him. A few days after the poem
appeared, on the last day of November 1859, in *La Revue*

Contemporaine, when Banville came out of the nursing-home where he had been having treatment, she left with him for the south of France where he was to recuperate. They seemed to have lived openly and happily together in Nice, and the following year he dedicated his *Mer de Nice* to her.[49]

For Baudelaire, however, even if his love was now calmer, this further blow from her was shattering. In profound bitterness, distress and rage, he composed *À une Madone* in December 1859, just after she had left.

In this poem he identifies his own Marie with the Virgin of the Seven Sorrows, and says that he will build her an altar 'au fond de ma détresse'. With his glittering verses he will carve a crown for her head, embroider a cloak for her with his bitter tears, and her gown will be his burning desire. Her foot will rest on the serpent which is devouring his entrails, and his flaming thoughts will burn like tapers before her shrine. He will pierce her heart with seven daggers, not the conventional daggers of the seven sorrows, but the daggers of the seven deadly sins. Marie is no longer the divine inspirer, the Muse, the Madonna; she is Mary, the earthly inspirer of vice and sin.

> *Enfin, pour compléter ton rôle de Marie,*
> *Et pour mêler l'amour avec la barbarie,*
> *Volupté noire! des sept Péchés capitaux,*
> *Bourreau plein de remords, je ferai sept Couteaux*
> *Bien affilés, et, comme un jongleur insensible,*
> *Prenant le plus profond de ton amour pour cible,*
> *Je les planterai tous dans ton Cœur pantelant,*
> *Dans ton Cœur sanglotant, dans ton Cœur Ruisselant!* [50]

It is a powerful and terrible poem which gains added poignancy from the circumstances of its composition. It is difficult to decide which is uppermost and strongest in the heart of the poet – love or hatred. This poem closes the Cycle of Marie Daubrun, the green-eyed Venus.

Baudelaire did not, however, forget her immediately and he may have been thinking of her when he wrote, a couple

of months later, to Madame Sabatier, to excuse himself for
having seemed to neglect her.[51]

'And if I tell you that I'm suffering great grief, that I've
never known such turmoil, and that I need solitude, you
won't believe me! But if I tell you that my nose is swollen
and red like an apple, and that, in such cases, I don't even
go to see men, perhaps you'll believe me!'

He was eventually able to regard Marie Daubrun with
contempt and remember only her beauty which in retrospect he still adored, as he reveals in the last poem she inspired, *L'Amour du Mensonge*, which he sent to Poulet
Malassis in March 1860. The accompanying note said:
'Here's another *Fleur du Mal*! You'll doubtless recognize
the heroine of this flower!' His contempt is mingled with
bitterness.

> *Es-tu le fruit d'automne aux saveurs souveraines?*
> *Es-tu vase funèbre attendant quelques pleurs,*
> *Parfum qui fait rêver aux oasis lointaines,*
> *Oreiller caressant, ou corbeille de fleurs?*
>
> *Je sais qu'il est des yeux, des plus mélancoliques,*
> *Qui ne récèlent point de secrets précieux;*
> *Beaux écrins sans joyaux, médaillons sans reliques,*
> *Plus vides, plus profonds que vous-mêmes, ô Cieux!*
>
> *Mais ne suffit-il pas que tu sois l'apparence,*
> *Pour réjouir un cœur qui fuit la vérité?*
> *Qu'importe ta bêtise ou ton indifférence?*
>   *Masque ou décor, salut! J'adore ta beauté!* [52]

Baudelaire's passion for Marie Daubrun, with that for
Jeanne Duval, were the strongest emotions of his life. He
never fully recovered from the shock of her last betrayal,
and to her must go some of the blame for the bitterness and
pessimism of his declining years.

[2]

The Artificial Paradises
1860

ON New Year's Eve 1859, as he looked back on the year drawing to its close, Baudelaire considered that, in spite of unhappiness, it had been a year less ill-spent than many others, for he had now five volumes, either published or almost ready for publication. His *Salon* of 1859, one of his greatest critical works, had appeared in June; his booklet on Gautier in November; his *Paradis Artificiels* was all but ready; a volume of critical essays needed only a little more work, and his second version of *Les Fleurs du Mal* was nearly completed. He was full of hope for the future and, writing to his mother for the New Year, he said: 'Here's a year less badly employed than the others, but it's only a quarter of what I intend to achieve during the coming year.'

He was not yet at the end of his tribulations however. When he got back to Paris the previous June, he had found Poulet Malassis unable to meet his obligations. He had started publishing scarcely two years before, with little capital and he had been dogged by ill-luck ever since. The fault was to some extent his – he seemed incapable of realizing where his financial interests lay – but the loss of the whole edition of *Les Fleurs du Mal* and the fine had been a piece of bad luck which no one could have foreseen. In 1858 he was again in difficulties, this time on account of his reprint of *Les Mémoires de Lauzun*.[1] It was a scholarly production, well edited by Louis Lacour, which richly deserved its success. Like *Les Fleurs du Mal* it was indicted for obscenity, but the case was dismissed, and the whole edition was soon sold out. The second edition was published early in 1859 but, following a personal quarrel between Lacour and the President of *La Société des Gens de Lettres*, proceedings were again instituted on the score of the new preface entitled *The Tribulations of an Editor*. As a result of circumstances into which it is unnecessary to digress, the editor and publisher lost their case – the editor was fined one hundred francs and given three months' imprisonment, while each of the publishers was sentenced to one month's imprisonment and a fine of a hundred francs. Poulet Malassis treated the prison sentence as a joke, but the fine was a more serious matter. De Broise could not see that either penalty was a subject for levity. As for their friends, the news that timid little de Broise was once more sentenced for publishing obscene literature seemed the best joke imaginable, for the unfortunate man was always an object of fun and the butt of witticisms.

'Is de Broise still in prison?' wrote Jean Wallon to Poulet Malassis.[2] 'The temporary loss of his liberty may perhaps inspire him to be henceforth more tolerant of literary lapses. Tell him from me that I greet him, like a swallow, through the iron bars of his black dungeon, and tell him also from me, to practise the classic sympathy of prisoners for spiders!'

After he was released Poulet Malassis continued publishing with the same undeserved lack of success, but he did not alter his methods to please popular demand. His fine production of the unpublished works of Piron, in November 1859, was one which could have appealed to a very small section only of even the cultivated public.

As for Baudelaire's works, de Broise was unwilling to risk further money on them. He had no confidence in their market value, present or future, and it was he who had tried to insist on the printing of only a limited edition of Baudelaire's study of Gautier.[3] This had angered the poet who considered it an insult to Gautier as well as to himself. His pride was wounded at the implied suggestion that Poulet Malassis was publishing his works merely as an act of friendship, and not as a business proposition. After much arguing, and many protestations of undying friendship on both sides, followed by further delays to obtain a preface from Victor Hugo, the pamphlet finally appeared in November 1859. It was put on sale at the low price of one franc, but even at that was not sold out when Poulet Malassis went bankrupt in 1862 – so perhaps de Broise was a more acute businessman than his partner.

Baudelaire had regained courage and energy during his visit of six months to Honfleur, and was now ready to embark on the publication of the several volumes which Poulet Malassis was prepared to print if he could persuade his partner to take the risk. He wished the first of these to be his *Paradis Artificiels*, after the two parts which it comprised had first appeared serially in *La Revue Contemporaine*. In the spring of 1858, when the project had first occurred to him, he had hoped to publish the two parts, one shortly after the other, under the comprehensive title, *L'Idéal Artificiel*. The first, *Haschisch*, came out in September that year, but he was still engaged on *Opium* and, until it had been serialized, the collection was held up.

He had been able to complete the *Haschisch* in a few months – an unusual occurrence with him – because in 1851 he had published an article on that subject, and was now able to use the previously assembled material in a revised form, even though his attitude to drugs had undergone a complete transformation. The second part he found very much more difficult because he was using, not his own experiences, but those of De Quincey as described in the *Confessions*, and he was forced to make a selection amongst a mass of material, retaining certain passages from the original while summarizing the rest in his own words. From the outset he had not found it easy to achieve satisfactory results with this method, and when he first handed in the finished result to Calonne, the editor of *La Revue Contemporaine*, he was much dissatisfied with it.

'My *Opium* is causing me a great deal of trouble,' he wrote to his mother,[4] 'and I feel I've produced something rather nasty!'

This was evidently also the opinion of his editor, who returned him his manuscript to be rewritten, in December 1858. Several months elapsed and, in March 1859, Calonne wrote to him impatiently:[5]

'You persist in sending me poems! That's all very well, and I thank you very much for them! But send me some prose! Your *Haschisch* will be completely forgotten by the time your *Opium* appears!'

When the manuscript was eventually finished, there ensued Baudelaire's usual torment at the hands of the editors. Calonne, who fancied himself as a literary critic, tried to insist on alterations and cuts while the poet, on his side, attempted to save his work from mutilation, and to plead for the retention of quotations from the English, the beauty of which he was trying to impress on the recalcitrant editor. Final agreement was reached only at the end of almost a year of constant disputes. Then it was Baudelaire's turn to hold up publication, so that the contribution began to appear only in the second half of January 1860. The fifteen months of bickering with Calonne inoculated him against any desire to remain a regular contributor to *La Revue Contemporaine*. When the last section of his *Opium* had appeared, he wrote to his mother,[6] 'I'm leaving *La Revue Contemporaine* for I've suffered too much with them on the score of my *Opium*.'

Baudelaire had certainly found it extremely difficult to adapt De Quincey in French, and now that the task was finished and about to appear in book form, he was not at all certain that he had produced something which could be called a work of art.

'I'd have been glad,' he wrote to Poulet Malassis,[7] 'if you'd told me what you thought of the general appearance of the book, and of *Opium* in particular. De Quincey is a terribly conversational and digressive writer, and it was not an easy matter to bring order to the summary and to give it a vivid form. Moreover I had to blend my own personal feelings with the opinions of the original author, so as to form a mixture in which the separate ingredients were not apparent. Have I succeeded? That question isn't the result of childish vanity, but arises from the solitude in which I now live, since I've reached the pitch of sensitivity when the conversation of almost everyone is intolerable to me. On the other hand, I confess that I'm always anxious to know whether these works which progress so slowly – sometimes on account of circumstances, and sometimes through my own fault – are of a serious enough nature to be offered to the public.'

Now that the manuscript was at last ready for the printers, it was Poulet Malassis himself who delayed, because de Broise was doing his utmost to dissuade him from publication. Baudelaire, whose procrastination had driven most editors to the verge of insanity, was incapable of enduring a similar failing in others. 'What?' he wrote to his publisher.[8] Are the *Paradis* not yet being printed?'

Again, a week later, he complained that Poulet Malassis was bringing out a mass of rubbish, and did not take advantage of the fact that the public had begun to express an interest in his *Paradis Artificiels*.[9]

It was not until March 1860 that printing began, but this time the work progressed quickly, taking little more than a month, and the book was published in the first week of May 1860. Baudelaire was a long time in deciding on a title, and as late as December 1859 he had not yet found one that pleased him. He considered first *L'Idéal Artificiel*, next *Le Paradis Artificiel*, and it was only in the final proofs that he fixed on *Les Paradis Artificiels*. The book was dedicated to the mysterious J.G.F. to whom *L'Héautontimorouménos* in the second *Les Fleurs du Mal* was also inscribed. Most critics believe, without any valid grounds, that they represent Jeanne Duval, who had taken many different names in the course of her life to evade her creditors, but this does not seem psychologically true when taken in conjunction with the terms of the dedication. Both Crépet and Pommier propose the theory that they stand for 'Jeanne Généreuse Femme' or 'Grande' or 'Glorieuse Femme'! Porché, in *Baudelaire, Histoire d'une Âme*,[10] gives another interpretation which possesses more verisimilitude. He believes that they stand for 'Juliette Gex-Fagon', a lady who moved in artistic circles in the middle of the nineteenth century and who was known to be on friendly terms with Baudelaire, with whom she used to share the pleasures of the artificial paradises.

Baudelaire was very nervous about the success of this book, since he had received very little encouragement hitherto, and since not only his own future, but that of his friend and publisher, depended on its reception. When sending a copy to his mother he said:[11] 'I'm horribly afraid of having a fiasco with my book. And just think, I'll have to publish four more in the course of this year!'

From the very beginning, the book did not have a fair chance, for its publisher had not sufficient capital to advertise it properly. Baudelaire had wished copies to be sent to the main English papers because of De Quincey,[12] but he had been unable to persuade the firm, while he himself had not received enough copies to present to all the people who might review it – and its success would depend on the kind of press it received.[13] This time he did not try to approach Sainte-Beuve directly himself since, after years of bitter experience, he had learnt the uselessness of such an attempt. He wrote to Dalloz, the editor of *Le Moniteur*, whose literary critic Sainte-Beuve was, asking that his book might be reviewed. The editor replied that it was worthy of Sainte-Beuve, and advised him to go and see him. It is the custom in France for the author to approach the critic directly himself, with his book, to obtain a notice. He wrote once more to Sainte-Beuve, this time apologetically:[14]

'I'm writing before calling because I've got a sort of feeling that I'll not have the pleasure of finding you at home.

'I've just written Monsieur Dalloz somewhat on these lines: "Will you get *Les Paradis* reviewed? I know so-and-so on *Le Moniteur*." And Dalloz replied: "The book is worthy of Sainte-Beuve" – it's not I who say this – "Go and see him on the matter!" I'd not have dared to think of it myself. Many reasons, which I can easily guess, might perhaps prevent you from reviewing it, and also the book mightn't please you. However! I need support more desperately than ever, and it was only right that I should admit my need to you! Be kind to me for I'm going through a great crisis!'

Sainte-Beuve did not answer this appeal any more than any of the others, and was not moved to break his usual silence.

Les Paradis Artificiels received some favourable notices – a kind review by Glatigny in *L'Orphéon* in June; praise in *La Gazette de France* in July; a favourable article with some reservations in August in *Le Pays* by Barbey d'Aurevilly, who did not consider that it was sufficiently Catholic in its outlook. But, as Baudelaire said to Poulet Malassis, there was nothing really important.[15]

There was also the kind of imbecility to which Baudelaire had become inured for almost ten years. *La Revue Européenne* declared that in spite of his moral protestations in his recent work, the intellectual health of Monsieur Baudelaire had not improved, and that it was doubtful whether it ever would.[16] Some critics alleged that he was only once again trying to 'épater le bourgeois', and others mention in connection with him Black Masses and Satanism. One of them wrote:[17]

'The poet of *Les Fleurs du Mal* appears once more in *Les Paradis Artificiels*. For Monsieur Baudelaire opium and hashish are first and foremost diabolical substances of modern invention. There is no doubt about that! For him to swallow a pellet of hashish is the same as to swallow Satan; to drink a spoonful of opium is the same as to drink Satan! Here is the bread; here is the wine; the sacred host and the chalice! The devil's table is the counterpart of the communion table! I've already mentioned the Black Mass!'

Even the Goncourt brothers describe those degenerates

who, on the model of Baudelaire, read Poe and indulge in hashish.[18]

Only a favourable article from the pen of Sainte-Beuve might have silenced this unjust and senseless criticism, but he did not deign to write one.

Since Baudelaire linked together his article on hashish and his adaptation of the *Confessions* of De Quincey as *Paradis Artificiels*, the two articles must be considered as one work. It was planned between 1858 and 1860 and it is clear that he did not obtain the idea from Musset who, at the age of eighteen, to earn some pocket-money, had translated De Quincey in 1828. Baudelaire did not know of his predecessor at this time. Poulet Malassis, writing to Spoelberch de Lovenjoul, says that at work on his *Paradis Artificiels*, Baudelaire once found on the quays in Paris a copy of Musset's translation, which was signed 'A.d.M.' but did not associate it with him and, seeing how carelessly the work had been done, did not buy the book.[19] He probably discovered the *Confessions* through *Les Hallucinations* by Brierre de Boismont, which he knew well and which mentions it frequently.

In composing *Les Paradis Artificiels* Baudelaire's intention had not been to set forth the relative merits of hashish and opium as drugs to procure sensuous pleasures. The title he finally chose is significant and should be taken into account, for it indicates that, in spite of its great joys, he wanted to condemn the machine-made heaven, the fool's paradise, which can be reached by means of drugs. It follows, therefore, that it matters little whether the drug be opium or hashish.

Like most of his literary contemporaries, Baudelaire started taking drugs of some sort at an early age, at the latest soon after his return from the East. It may well have been earlier since, in the collection of poems by d'Argonne, Levavasseur and Prarond, mentioned in an earlier chapter, there occurs a poem dated 1842, in which reference is made to his drug-taking habits.[20] There is little doubt that he was a member of the *Club des Haschischins* which used to meet in Fernand Boissard's rooms at the Hôtel Lauzun.[21] On the other hand, Théo Varlet asserts, basing his judgement on his own experience of drugs, that Baudelaire had little experience of the effects of hashish, and that he probably discontinued the practice very soon, before 1845.[22] This may be true yet, to the uninitiated, his description of the effects of hashish rings true. Even if he did not continue taking hashish, he certainly indulged in opium, and that often to excess. Adrien Marx says that he frequently saw him swallow enough to kill five people,[23] and Baudelaire himself often mentions in his letters between 1844 and 1850[24] that he is in the habit of taking large doses of opium. It is possible that he later gave up the habit, and returned to it only when he was in constant pain, after 1858 – there are frequent references to his taking the drug in the letters of that year.[25] At some later date he probably discontinued the practice, since, after 1865, when he was in Belgium, he talks of the habit in the past tense, and expresses the utmost horror of opium.[26]

All this can only be surmise, but what is certain is that, whatever may have been his practice earlier, when he was composing *Les Paradis Artificiels* he disapproved of the use of drugs and deplored their effects – especially spiritually. To Armand Fraisse, who wrote to congratulate him on the publication of the book and to ask for information concerning opium and hashish, he answered: [27]

'Beware of all drugs! I've now a horror of all drugs on account of their tendency to amplify time and to exaggerate everything! It's impossible to remain not merely a businessman, but even a man of letters, after such a continual spiritual orgy!'

Baudelaire was one of the few writers of his time to realize the danger of degradation for the human personality in the continual absorption of drugs, especially spiritual degradation through the weakening of the will. These were the effects which he had found so disastrous in himself. *Les*

Paradis Artificiels is very significant for understanding his
spiritual development at this stage; and it is more important
to realize what views he had reached about drugs in general,
and especially those which enable man to avoid suffering, to
hide from himself the misery and degradation of his state,
than to discover to which drug he was most addicted. His
attitude was not one of delight that these substances had
been granted to man to gain escape, but rather horror at the
fundamental immorality of trying to obtain something for
nothing, of trying to reach Heaven by a gratuity pressed into
the hand of the keeper of the heavenly gate. The interest in
Les Paradis Artificiels does not reside in discovering to what
extent, if any, he added to the sum of knowledge of the sensations of drug-addicts. Varlet proves that Baudelaire did
not get the sensations from hashish which he himself had
experienced; while Clapton shows[28] that he brings nothing
new in his experiences as an opium-smoker, nothing which
was not already to be found in De Quincey, and claims that
in this respect Baudelaire is disappointing since he had
promised to describe his personal sensations as well.

But clearly Baudelaire had not intended to increase our
understanding of an opium-smoker's psychology and experiences. The *Poème du Haschisch*, he claimed, in the opening remarks of the lecture he gave in Brussels in 1864 on *Les
Paradis Artificiels*, is entirely his own.[29] But *Le Mangeur
d'Opium* he confesses, in the same connection, is an adaptation of the *Confessions* of De Quincey, and the intention
was to reveal the English author to the public as an opium-
smoker, and not himself. While he admits, however, that he
no longer knows to what extent he has identified himself
with his author's personality,[30] his intention was certainly
not to give a picture of his own dreams. True, he said to
Vigny that he had introduced a few ideas of his own, but
with great humility;[31] and told Poulet Malassis that it was
a matter of blending his own sensations with those of his
author.[32] Yet this does not justify the assumption that he
meant to describe his own experience while under the in-

fluence of opium. We should rather infer that he was merely giving his personal reactions after reading the *Confessions* of another, his reactions to their author. Naturally he could not fail to see the parallel between his own spiritual experience and that of De Quincey. In the preface to the first article, on hashish, he states clearly what he intends to do when the time comes to treat opium.[33] The effects of opium, he says, have already been treated in a striking manner and he would not dare to add anything of his own. He will therefore content himself with giving a summary of that fine book, *The Confessions of an Opium-Eater*, and he declares that the part which he himself found most dramatic was where the author describes the superhuman efforts he had to exercise in order to escape the fate to which he had so recklessly condemned himself.

Clapton claims that Baudelaire's method was to give as his own De Quincey's words without quotation marks, sometimes altering them to suit his own case, and that this is his only original contribution to the work.[34] This assertion might lead to misconception, since it seems to suggest that Baudelaire was trying to attribute to himself the words written by another author, a foreigner, in circumstances where there would be little danger of detection. This would be doing Baudelaire a grave injustice, for he himself explains that he is only retelling in a shortened form the tale told by De Quincey. Naturally, whenever possible, he would use his author's own words. Thus his process was not exactly quotation – it allowed latitude for free rendering. What he wanted was to put the *Confessions* in a form acceptable to French readers. All this would sufficiently account for what Clapton remarks on, the fact that Baudelaire's additions to De Quincey are slight. But even though he does not give his own dreams under the influence of opium it does not follow, as Clapton seems to believe, that he was incapable of the visions of a De Quincey. His emphasis is on another aspect of the problem. One is left with no doubt when reading the magnificent prose poem in the section on hashish, en-

titled *L'Homme Dieu*, how vivid was his experience under
at least one drug.[35]

'Le haschisch s'étend alors sur toute la vie comme un
vernis magique; il la colore en solennité et en éclaire toute
la profondeur. Paysages dentelés, horizons fuyants, per-
spectives de villes blanchies par la lividité cadavéreuse de
l'orage ou illuminées par les ardeurs de l'espace, allégorie
de la profondeur du temps – la danse, le geste, ou la déclama-
tion des comédiens, si vous vous êtes jeté dans un théâtre –
la première phrase venue si vos yeux tombent sur un livre –
tout enfin, l'universalité des êtres se dresse devant vous avec
une gloire nouvelle non soupçonnée jusqu'alors. ... La
musique, autre langue chère aux paresseux ou aux esprits
profonds qui cherchent le délassement dans la variété du
travail, vous parle de vous-même et vous raconte le poème
de votre vie; elle s'incorpore à vous, et vous vous fondez en
elle. Elle parle votre passion, non pas d'une manière vague
et indéfinie, comme elle fait dans vos soirées nonchalantes,
un jour d'opéra, mais d'une manière circonstancée, positive,
chaque mouvement du rhythme marquant un mouvement
connu de votre âme, chaque note se transformant en mot, et
le poème entrant dans votre cerveau comme un dictionnaire
doué de vie.'

Baudelaire saw in De Quincey a further and terrible proof
of his conviction that drugs were one of the greatest dangers
to the ultimate salvation of man, that they were one of the
most powerful and enticing temptations of the devil. He
had been struck, while reading the *Confessions*, to find in
De Quincey the same incapacity, the same lack of energetic
purpose, which he had discovered in himself, and which was
causing him so much distress. This is the explanation of the
fact which Clapton deplores, that his contribution to the
work of De Quincey is a purely moral one. His strongest
sentiment was one of remorse at the tragic waste, and also
conviction that the tawdry artificial Heaven was bought at
too high a price in degradation and remorse, and this wiped
out for him all memory of pleasure.

His attitude was different from that of Cocteau who, thirty-five years ago in his *Opium*, compared life to an express train moving swiftly and inexorably towards its inevitable goal, death, and said that a man who smokes opium is enabled to jump down from the train – whether he permanently disables himself is not stated – and occupy himself in the green meadows along the track with other things than contemplation of inevitable death. When they tried to cure him he complained that opium gave him the only really happy hours of his life, and he considered that the mood induced in him was far more pleasant than his new state of health. He was not proud of his cure, but, on the contrary, was ashamed of having been banished from the fairyland, in comparison with which the world he came to inhabit seemed to him to resemble those dull topical films which depict a Cabinet Minister unveiling a public monument.

Baudelaire would not have been capable of such self-delusion. He would have realized that, however much he enjoyed himself on the bank amongst the flowers and forgot the train, it would be waiting for him at the next station and he would be taken, struggling perhaps in an undignified fashion, into one of its carriages, before it departed once more on its inexorable way.

Who shall say that Baudelaire's contribution of agony and remorse is a smaller one than if he had described only the tawdry and tinsel joys of the Artificial Paradises? Whether we approve or not of this moral attitude, it is the one most typical of him at this stage and one must understand it if one is to realize his struggles with himself and his agony of helpless remorse. Though he was no puritan and had a leaning towards pleasure, he never indulged himself without a struggle. Even when most conscious of the joys of the Artificial Paradises, he was fully aware of the resulting deterioration in himself, and never deceived himself. The moral intention is clear from the beginning of the preface to *Le Poème du Haschisch*, where he says: [36]

'Parmi les drogues les plus propres à créer ce que je nomme

"l'Idéal Artificiel", les deux plus énergiques substances sont le haschisch et l'opium. L'analyse des effets mystérieux et des jouissances morbides que peuvent engendrer ces drogues, des châtiments inévitables qui résultent de leur usage prolongé, et enfin de l'immoralité impliquée dans cette pursuite d'un faux idéal, constitue le sujet de cette étude.'

He repeated this moral still more clearly in his lecture in Brussels, in May 1864 : [37]

'Dans tout cela il y a beaucoup de choses qui regardent les médecins; or je veux faire un livre non de pure physiologie, mais surtout de morale. Je veux prouver que les chercheurs de paradis font leur enfer, le préparent, le creusent avec un succès dont la prévision les épouvanterait peut-être.'

It is perfectly clear from this what Baudelaire's intention was, and whether it is what his readers hoped for, or imagined they would receive, is of little account. If they seek in his work undiluted sensual pleasure, then they will only be disappointed. They will never find with him pleasure and self-indulgence without their inevitable accompaniment – the bitter dregs of remorse.

It is impossible to gauge to what extent the poet's genius was enriched from his use of drugs, since we cannot know what he would have been without them. What one might be tempted to ascribe to the effects of opium or hashish, might merely be the result of his sensitive nervous system and unusual imagination. It is probable that he did not even know himself. It may be that the poems in which the connection seems most obvious – as, for instance, in *Le Poison* and *Rêve Parisien* – are not those in which are found its most fundamental traces. *Rêve Parisien* is precisely the kind of poem which the uninitiated would expect a poet to compose under the influence of drugs, and this might have been artificially contrived. It somewhat resembles a picture in the abstract style of painting, or a theosophist representation of an aura.

Since drugs have the faculty of releasing material buried in the subconscious, of freeing the mind from the self-consciousness and difficulties of expression, since they tend to transmit an extraordinary vividness of perception to every sensation, so that each little insignificant detail is magnified and illuminated, and since, moreover, this acute awareness of an infinite number of vibrations is one of the distinguishing qualities of Baudelaire's art, it may be that his aesthetic perceptivity was in part derived from the use of drugs. If this were so, then such poems as *La Vie Antérieure*, *Parfum Exotique*, or even *L'Invitation au Voyage* – and others like them – might conceivably have been written, if not exactly under the influence of drugs, at least with the memory of the exquisite state of sensibility engendered by their use. They would thus owe more to opiates than *Rêve Parisien*.

The dreams of opium and hashish are not everlasting, for there comes the awakening, the hideous awakening, when the world, which so short a time before was like a fairyland, resembles the dance hall when the party is over and the rubbish has not yet been cleared away. Then the only way of finding peace is to escape once more into the land of magic, but the price is higher this time, and the dose must be increased to take one the whole of the way. Varlet even, a champion of the 'paradise of hashish', has to admit, when he says that it is difficult to recapture the joys of the major and minor paradises, that with repetition the magic life becomes, at length, as narrow and as boring as real life itself.[38] Baudelaire clearly realized the slavery which this craving for the other life could become:[39]

'Chaînes, en effet, auprès desquelles toutes les autres, chaînes du devoir, de l'amour illégitime, ne sont que des trames de gaze et des tissus d'araignée! Épouvantable mariage de l'homme avec lui-même!'

Baudelaire contemplated with horror the ravages in the human personality caused by prolonged indulgence in drugs, and especially the weakening of the will by the draining away of energy. This was the tragedy which he saw in De Quincey's life, the sad fact that his mind was teeming

with ideas and projects, but that he had not the determination to give them shape on paper. It is clear in describing
the case of De Quincey he is thinking of himself as well.
He relates how that author, all aflame with enthusiasm, decided to write a commentary on Ricardo, how the work got
so far that he made arrangements with a local printer,
stipulating that extra hands should be taken on to expedite
matters, how the book was almost ready and was twice advertised, for there was only the preface left to compose, but
this De Quincey could not bring himself to write.[40] As
Baudelaire says:[41] 'L'impuissance se dressa, terrible, in-
franchissable, comme les glaces du pôle.' All the arrangements had to be cancelled and the hands dismissed, for the
preface was never written. Baudelaire saw this as a terrible
chastisement: to have one's imagination overflowing with
visions, and yet be unable to grasp them; to have lost none
of one's faculties for admiration of noble conceptions, and
yet to be paralysed in one's power to give form to these
conceptions. This was for him confirmation of what he had
declared in an early poem: 'Et votre châtiment naîtra de
vos plaisirs!'[42]

The undermining of the will was not the only danger;
more serious was the state of self-delusion drugs induced.
The addict loses none of his worship of beauty and love of
virtue – in fact these seem to be strengthened – and it seems
to him that a voice is whispering in his ear, assuring him
that, since he perceives what other human beings are incapable of imagining, he is superior to all other men; that
since he admires virtue, he must of necessity be virtuous;
then, like Rousseau, he will cry: 'I am the most virtuous of
men!'[43]

Baudelaire came eventually to consider indulgence in
drugs as a kind of moral suicide, destroying man in his
highest faculties – in dignity and honour – and persuading
him to sell his soul for a worthless heaven in order to escape
the law of life – work and suffering. 'En effet,' he says, 'tout
homme qui n'accepte pas les conditions de la vie vend son

âme!' [44] Henceforth he will describe 'la fertilisante douleur' and 'l'indispensable douleur', since it is through suffering alone that the seeds of greatness in man can be fertilized and bear fruit. On spiritual grounds, he declared that he was inclined to deprecate the discovery of soporifics, in spite of the services which they had rendered to mankind, because they tended to undermine human liberty, in its deepest sense, and to counteract 'l'indispensable douleur'. [45]

Baudelaire believed, what many thinkers have felt since the Renaissance, since the liberation of man, that there was something spiritually unsatisfactory and barren in laying so much emphasis on the pursuit of happiness, on the inherent right of man to happiness, and on the value of such happiness could it even be obtained. But, since the nineteenth century with its phenomenal development of material comfort, bringing standardized 'happiness' within the reach of all and making it the sole aim of life, his words have for mankind a deep and ominous significance. He says: [46]

'Ces infortunés, qui n'ont ni jeûné, ni prié, et qui ont refusé la rédemption par le travail, demandent à la noire magie les moyens de s'élever, d'un seul coup, à l'existence surnaturelle. La magie les dupe et allume pour eux un faux bonheur et une fausse lumière: tandis que nous, poètes et philosophes, nous avons régénéré notre âme par le travail successif et la contemplation; par l'exercice assidu de la volonté et la noblesse permanente de l'intention, nous avons créé à notre usage un jardin de vraie beauté. Confiants dans la parole qui dit que la foi transporte les montagnes, nous avons accompli le seul miracle dont Dieu nous ait octroyé la licence.'

This moral aspect of *Les Paradis Artificiels* pleased critics of the Second Empire no more than it does many today. Even Flaubert, who otherwise appreciated the work wholeheartedly, considered it a weakness in an otherwise noble production for the author to have taken sides, and come down against drugs. In his opinion this attitude was prejudiced and unscientific. The arguments should merely have been produced, and the reader allowed to make up his mind for himself.

'You are very kind, my dear Baudelaire,' he wrote,[47] 'to have sent me such a book! Everything in it delights me – its aim, its style, and even its paper. I've read it very carefully, and I must thank you most warmly for having made me acquainted with such a charming man as De Quincey. How easy it is to like him!

'But here is my criticism – to clear the objections away first. It seems to me that in a subject treated from such a lofty height, in a work which is really the beginning of a natural science, in a work of observation and induction, you have – and several times at that – insisted too much on the Evil One. One scents, as it were, a kind of Catholic leaven here and there. I would have thought it better if you hadn't blamed opium and hashish, but only excess. And, anyway, how do you know what will be the outcome of it all later? But please note that this is merely my personal opinion, and that I don't insist on it in any way! I've never considered it the privilege of a critic to substitute his own ideas for those of the author. Also, what I'm cavilling at in your book is perhaps what constitutes its chief originality and greatness. To be unlike anyone else, that is the most important thing!

'And now, having admitted my only grievance, I'd be unable to tell you adequately how excellent I found your book from start to finish, for it is written in a noble and virile style, in one of deliberate artistry. You've succeeded in being classic, while, at the same time, remaining the supreme Romantic whom we all love....

'These drugs have always aroused great longing in me, and I've even got some excellent hashish made up for me by Gastinel, the chemist. But it terrifies me! I blame myself bitterly for this! ...

'I'm awaiting with impatience your further *Fleurs du Mal*. My objections would, of course, not apply there! A poet has a perfect right to think what he likes – but a scientist? Perhaps I'm only talking nonsense, but I think I know what I'm trying to say, and we'll discuss it all another time! How much work you get done, and what good work!'

'I thank you most sincerely for your kind letter!' Baudelaire answered.[48] 'I was much struck by your criticism, but, having gone as thoroughly and as deeply as I could into the memory of my dreams, I've come to the conclusion that I've always been obsessed by my incapacity to account for certain spontaneous actions and thoughts of man, without the hypothesis of the intervention of an evil force outside himself. And the whole of the nineteenth century massed against me will not make me blush for this significant admission. Please note that I'm not giving up the pleasure of changing my mind or contradicting myself....

'You tell me that I get through a lot of work! Is this a cruel jest? Many people, not counting myself, think that I'm not doing much! To work truly, that means to work all the time, and to have no time for the pleasures of the senses, or for day-dreaming! It means becoming the quintessence of determination, always in action. Perhaps one day I'll reach that point!'

Les Paradis Artificiels, coming as it does at a critical stage in Baudelaire's career, casts a bright light on many aspects of his personality, for it reveals how far he has progressed spiritually since 1852, when the mature poet began to appear for the first time, fortified by the support which he found in the works of Poe and Swedenborg. It reveals also how changed his outlook has become since the pleasure-loving days at the Hôtel Lauzun, and since the days of *spleen* in the years preceding the revolution of 1848. It can be seen as opening the last phase of his life when, in the midst of defeat – defeat in the worldly sense – admitted and acknowledged, he accepted his humiliations and tribulations, with pious resignation. Forgetfulness of self, and absence of desire for self-glorification, are his main characteristics in his last phase, until death finally closed the struggle. The last words of *Le Mangeur d'Opium* might indeed have been written for himself: [49]

'Mais la Mort, que nous ne consultons pas sur nos projets et à qui nous ne pouvons pas demander son acquiescement, la Mort qui nous laisse rêver de bonheur et de renommée, et qui ne dit ni oui ni non, sort brusquement de son embuscade, et balaye d'un coup d'aile nos plans, nos rêves, et les architectures idéales où nous abritions en pensée la gloire de nos derniers jours.'

[3]

The Ghost of the Dead Years
1859—1861

IN spite of Baudelaire's high hopes on New Year's Eve, 1860 opened as badly as possible for him. Early in January he experienced a strange seizure – probably the first symptoms of the tertiary stage of the disease from which he was to die a few years later.

'The day before yesterday,' he wrote to his mother,[1] 'I experienced a most peculiar seizure. I was absent from home, and hadn't broken my fast for some time. I believe it was something in the nature of a cerebral congestion. An old woman revived me by some strange methods. However, when I came to my senses, another seizure occurred. I experienced great weakness and giddiness, and frightful nausea, so that I could hardly go upstairs without feeling as if I was going to faint. At the end of a few hours it was all over; I came home yesterday evening, and I'm perfectly well now, but exhausted as if after a long journey. A curious detail of my unfortunate adventure is that never for an instant did I completely lose consciousness, and I was terrified that someone might imagine that I was drunk!'

His state of health was not improved by his financial situation. He was finding it impossible to keep on good terms with any paper, or to obtain contracts from any new periodical. Since the beginning of the year he had been in the throes of a quarrel with *La Revue Internationale* of Geneva, where his translation of *Eureka* by Poe had been appearing since the previous October. As a result of his dispute, he withdrew his manuscript before publication was completed, and he did not even receive payment for the extracts which had already appeared.[2] He was also on very bad terms with

Calonne at *La Revue Contemporaine*, where his *Mangeur
d'Opium* was in process of publication. Eugène Crépet, who
was editing an anthology of modern French poetry, had invited him to compose certain of the commentaries on the
poets, and had paid him an advance of six hundred francs,
but he insisted on certain changes which the poet refused
to accept, preferring to pay back the money, although he
had already spent it, which would entail further borrowing.[3] He was also trying to obtain a contract from *Le Constitutionnel*, but had been unable to come to terms with the
editor, Grandgouillet, and the agreement was never signed.[4]

As a result of these various misfortunes he was in great
financial distress. In the meantime the years were swiftly
flying by, and he had not yet been able to bring his mother
the peace and contentment for which she had hoped. The
two years which, in 1858, he had assured her would be ample
to pay his debts, were almost over, and he was no nearer to
his goal. Her husband had been dead now for three years,
but she had only enjoyed six months of her son's company,
and she was often lonely, and especially apprehensive about
the future. 'Although I know well you're good and kind,'
she wrote to him,[5] 'and that you're able to earn money, I'm
often terrified that you'll ruin me one day!' She was thinking
especially of the bills which often arrived at Honfleur, in
spite of her prohibition, and which she frequently paid for
fear of local scandal. These arrived at her house because
the creditors realized that there was more chance of their
being settled by her than by Baudelaire himself.

'I beg you most earnestly,' he wrote to her,[6] 'be kind to me,
and remember that I'm in great distress and that my mind
isn't in a normal state. Don't send me one of your torrents
of reproach which hurt me so much, although you think I
haven't any feelings. Then I don't want to cause you sleep-
less nights, or any physical upset. You can't imagine the
anxiety you cause me when you tell me things like that.
Then I begin to tremble, and sometimes, on account of your
reproaches, and sometimes through fear of hearing distress-

ing news concerning your health, I'm afraid to open your letters. Faced by a letter from you, I lose all courage.

'If you only knew what thoughts occupy my mind! The fear of dying before I've accomplished what I've got to do. The fear of your death before I've been able to make you happy, the only human being with whom I can be happy, without lies or deception. The horror of my *conseil judiciaire* – I must say it – which tortures me night and day. And finally, saddest of all, my terror of not being able to cure myself of my vices. These are my habitual thoughts. To awake each morning, to face all these tragic facts – my reputation, my poverty, etc.!'

What he could never do, however, even in his periods of greatest poverty, was be economical and spend less. After his death it was discovered that he owed more than eighty pounds to one restaurant alone, La Tour d'Argent, and there were many others. Sometimes, when he had managed to obtain the money to settle a pressing account – as when his mother allowed him to sell a valuable shawl for what it would fetch – he spent the money on a new suit made to measure.[7] He would not descend to wearing ready-made clothes, and he describes humorously and ironically an expedition with Ancelle to the department store where the lawyer bought his own suits off the peg, and where he hoped now to encourage his ward to become a customer. To pacify him, Baudelaire bought a cheap ready-made suit, but never wore it. In spite of poverty, he had lost none of his instinct for elegance;[8] he remained a dandy whose mistress was still richly dressed.[9]

In August 1860, he committed what was to him a criminal action. Poulet Malassis had entrusted him with a sum of money belonging to the firm, and he had borrowed it without permission to pay some pressing bills, hoping to return it before it was needed. No money was coming in. When his friend asked for repayment he had not the means to meet his obligations, and he was terrified of being thought a thief. He knew that the only way of obtaining money quickly

was through his mother, who would instruct Ancelle to
advance it, or to sell capital. Realizing how his mother would
look on his behaviour, and afraid to tell her himself, he
begged her confessor, Father Cardinne, to break the news
to her.[10] He himself wrote to her only some days later, explaining that he was imperatively obliged to be in possession
of fifteen hundred francs by 9 August, and imploring her to
see Ancelle did not procrastinate in his usual manner.[11] If
by the 10th the money was not paid, there would be a scandal, and he might even be put in jail

Ancelle, however, was not to be put out by a trifle like
that, and he perhaps thought that it would be a good thing
if his incorrigible ward was properly frightened this time.
He did not send the money by special messenger, as requested, nor go to see Baudelaire immediately on receipt
of Madame Aupick's letter. He was a busy man, being Mayor
of Neuilly as well as a practising lawyer, and he had other
things to worry about besides his ward's eternal and sordid
money difficulties. He did not approve of selling out capital.
The three thousand francs which had been provided in 1858
had served no good purpose, and there was no reason to hope
that this time matters would be any better. Baudelaire
waited at home all day, but Ancelle did not come. He then
called on him at Neuilly but did not find him in. He waited
until late at night in the avenue outside his house, hoping
to catch him as he came in, but there was no sign of him.
When he reached home he found that no message had yet
arrived. At last, at eleven o'clock, almost beside himself with
anxiety, he wrote once more to his mother:

'Since, by seven o'clock this evening, I'd not yet received
any news from Monsieur Ancelle, not even a note, I rushed
out to Neuilly, but he'd gone out after dinner, and I stood in
the Avenue until half past ten to catch him when he came
in. After that I returned to Paris. Tomorrow morning at
seven o'clock I'll go back again and I anticipate with weariness that I'll have to argue with him, resist the assault of
his curiosity, drag him away almost by force and take him

in a cab. And supposing that isn't possible, what will happen then? What will become of me? On the tenth it won't yet be too late. But for that the business ought to have been done on the eighth. And, even supposing it can be done, I'll have the fag of keeping an eye on him until he's deposited the money where it should have been long ago. I know very well that since I got myself into this serious mess, I've no right – with you at all events – to complain. Nevertheless I can't help feeling, firstly, that, since I've proved that I'm sometimes capable of good, I deserve a little generosity; and secondly that both he and I received your letters yesterday morning, yet two whole days have elapsed since then. My whole life always hangs on the whims of that irresponsible fool. How heartily sick I am, for many years now, of living twenty-four hours each day. When shall I ever live with pleasure? I send you my love and I thank you very much for all you've done for me. But what on earth am I to do? Does he know the exact amount? Does he know that the date is the ninth?'

Ancelle, as usual, yielded in the end, the money was paid and Baudelaire was temporarily saved, but it was only a short respite. He emerged from the affair ashamed of himself and doubtful whether he would ever be able to redeem himself, and make something of his life.

'I'll die,' he wrote a few days later,[12] 'without having done anything with my life! I used to owe twenty thousand francs, and now I owe forty thousand. If I've the misfortune of living a long time, that debt can easily be doubled again.'

> *En vain j'ai voulu de l'espace*
> *Trouver la fin et le milieu;*
> *Sous je ne sais quel œil de feu*
> *Je sens mon aile qui se casse.*
>
> *Et brûlé par l'amour du beau,*
> *Je n'aurai pas l'honneur sublime*
> *De donner mon nom à l'abîme*
> *Qui me servira de tombeau.*[13]

In his utter loneliness, in his torturing doubt of himself – his greatest suffering – Baudelaire would have liked to be able to pray for help and comfort, but he had not yet sloughed his egoism, he was not yet sufficiently humble, and the words would not come to him, nor the simplicity of faith. He begged his mother to pray for him, since he could not pray for himself.

'I'm horribly unhappy!' he wrote to her.[14] 'I'm too weary to explain anything! I'm horribly unhappy, but if you think that a prayer of yours can have any effect – I'm not sneering – pray for me as hard as you can, for I need it badly. When I don't write to you it is that everything is going badly. But when you don't write to me, I imagine all sorts of dreadful things – illness, or anger, etc. If only, within the next two or three days, the play, for which I've got a new plan, could be accepted, then I'd be saved.

'Good-bye! I send you my love full of sadness.'

In his weariness, and despair of ever achieving anything, he was troubled again, as he had been once in his youth, by the temptation of suicide. Death would be an easy escape, and he longed for rest from anxiety, for peace and endless sleep. What restrained him was reluctance to depart leaving his affairs in confusion and his debts unpaid. It is indeed touching that, after all the years of scheming, borrowing and repayment, to keep himself from foundering completely, he should still care about the honour of his name, and wish to leave the world unencumbered by debt. He remembered, too, his mother, her lonely old age, and also Jeanne Duval, for whom no one else would care when he was gone. She had not left Paris after all, when they had separated, but was still in his life, and one of his most constant preoccupations. Just as in his youth his last thought, when he contemplated suicide, had been for her, so now, in October 1860, not knowing whether he would have the courage to go on, he wrote to his mother and begged her to look after his mistress if he were suddenly to die. His mother had just written to him to complain that, far from his debts being paid off, as he had said they would be in the space of two years, they seemed to be increasing.

'Alas! I've only one thing to answer,' he wrote to her.[15] 'My debts have doubled through the inevitable tendency of all debts to double themselves after a certain length of time, as all those who have studied the question have noticed. I used to owe ten thousand francs to Arondel [16] but, for the last few years, I owe him fifteen thousand. I borrow to pay him, and, to give you an example, all the money derived from the proceeds of my books during the past sixteen months goes entirely to pay the interest on a debt of three thousand francs incurred to go and settle at Honfleur. Moreover, the total sum is increased through the difficulty of working in the midst of such tortures, while expenses run on all the time. You're always racking your brains to try to understand, instead of simply saying: the *conseil judiciaire*. That ghastly error which has ruined my life, which has poisoned all my days, and colours all my thoughts with hatred and despair! But you'll never understand!

'And now I'm going to speak to you very seriously, without exaggeration, of many sad thoughts. I may die before you, in spite of the superhuman courage which, hitherto, has sustained me. What has been restraining me during the past year and a half, is the thought of Jeanne. How would she live after my death since you'd have to pay my debts out of what I might leave! And a further reason. How could I leave you alone? And also how could I leave you the horrible difficulty of unravelling this mess which I alone understand? The mere thought of the preliminary spadework I'd have to do so that someone could understand my affairs, is sufficient to make me postpone the carrying out of a plan which I'd consider the most sensible of my life. I must also add that pride sustains me, and a savage hatred of all men. I trust I'll always be able to control myself so that I can have revenge one day, and be able to say what I like, without fear of consequences – and all sorts of other foolishness.

'Although I don't wish to frighten you, or grieve you, or give you any cause for remorse, I've grounds for believing that one day a fit of madness might seize hold of me, because I'm very weary, and have never known joy or security. After your death, it's sure and certain, since the fear of hurting you while you're alive can still restrain me, but after your death nothing could hinder me. And so to explain everything clearly, it's two charitable preoccupations which now prevent me – you and Jeanne. You certainly can't say that I live for my own pleasure. I come now to the point. Whatever may be the fate which overtakes me, if, after making a complete list of my debts, I were to die, you must, if you're still alive, do something for that former beauty, now a poor cripple. All my literary contracts are in order, and I'm convinced that a day will come when everything that I've written will sell well. Conventional decency obliges me to make you my heir. I repeat, if through illness, accident, or despair, I found myself relieved of the weary burden of life, you must, after the reasonable and sordid settling of my debts, devote whatever is left over to the relief of that unfortunate woman, and give her also the proceeds, however small, from the sale of my poetry, translations, and prose works. One of her brothers has suddenly turned up; I've seen him, and spoken with him, and he'd probably also come to her aid. He has no money, but he's earning something. I've just reread what I've written and frankly I think that, considering the state of your health, it is abominable of me to send it to you. It will serve at least to show the habitual tenor of my thoughts.'

In October 1860 he went to Honfleur again to see whether he could obtain any alleviation of his lot, to see whether there was any hope of quashing his *conseil judiciaire*, so that he could control his capital and use it to settle his debts, or at least to secure some loan. He hoped for three thousand francs when he set out for Honfleur, but obtained only four hundred francs, which was useless for his purpose, and so he merely squandered the sum.[17] He found his mother in some financial embarrassment herself, as she had to face unforeseen expenses in connection with her house, to shore up the soil against a landslide. 'I came here,' he wrote to Grandgouillet,[18] 'to obtain some money, but found none, and on Sunday I return to the inferno of Paris.'

Suffering made Baudelaire think of Jeanne Duval again, and with more tenderness, for he felt bound to her by a past life of now twenty years. Her need of him, moreover, drew him closer. She depended on him as not even his mother did. His mother at least had an income of her own whereas Jeanne had nothing except what he gave her, and she was now ill, prematurely aged and infirm, paralysed on one side. He knew what it was to feel deserted, and he could not forget their years together, nor that he alone could undertake responsibility for her, when she was herself incapable. 'I'm forced to play the part of father and guardian,' he said,[19] 'and it's no longer merely a question of spending for I've also got to think for a person whose mind has become deranged.'

He understood Jeanne fully, how she had brought most of her suffering on herself through her own intemperance and folly – it had been very much the same with himself. He had committed actions like hers, only she was stupid and less conscious than he of degradation and shame. They might neither of them be very good but perhaps together they might be able to make something of their lives. Besides, she was to him the ghost of the happy past, and he could see in her the memories of the far-off days at the Hôtel Lauzun in the distant haze of a dream.

Her hair, her heavy black hair, which in his eyes age and illness had not yet touched, her hair could still make him dream and lift him out of his sordid life, just as opium might, awakening in him memories which had lain sleeping for so long that he had thought them dead, memories of the days of youth, when he still believed in hope. He evokes such feelings in *La Chevelure*.[20]

J'irai là-bas où l'arbre et l'homme, pleins de sève,
Se pâment longuement sous l'ardeur des climats;
Fortes tresses, soyez la houle qui m'enlève!
Tu contiens, mer d'ébène, un éblouissant rêve
De voiles, de rameurs, de flammes et de mâts:

Un port retentissant où mon âme peut boire
À grands flots le parfum, le son et la couleur;
Où les vaisseaux, glissant dans l'or et dans la moire,
Ouvrent leurs vastes bras pour embrasser la gloire
D'un ciel pur où frémit l'éternelle chaleur.

Je plongerai ma tête amoureuse d'ivresse
Dans ce noir océan où l'autre est enfermé;
Là mon esprit subtil que le roulis caresse
Saura vous retrouver, ô féconde paresse,
Infinis bercements du loisir embaumé!

Cheveux bleus, pavillon de ténèbres tendues,
Vous me rendez l'azur du ciel immense et rond;
Sur les bords duvetés de vos mêches tordues
Je m'enivre ardemment des senteurs confondues
De l'huile de coco, du musc et du goudron.

Longtemps! toujours! ma main dans ta crinière lourde
Sèmera le rubis, la perle et le saphir,
Afin qu'à mon désir tu ne sois jamais sourde!
N'es-tu pas l'oasis où je rêve, et la gourde
Où je hume à longs traits le vin du souvenir!

It was at this time also that he composed *Le Cheval de Race* quoted in an earlier chapter.[21]

Jeanne Duval, however, was incapable of treating him well. Money was now the only thing she valued and she tried to obtain it from him in every possible way. Her greed was not wholly wickedness or perversity, but was chiefly due to her craving for drugs and drink. Once, during his stay at Honfleur, when he had placed her in a nursing-home, in the hope of curing her of dipsomania, he had been unable to go in person to pay the money for her fees. He asked Poulet Malassis to do this for him, to pay one hundred and twenty francs for her board, and thirty francs to Jeanne herself for her nurse, to save her pride, so that the woman should not despise her. Two or three times in the letter, he implored his friend not to fail him, fearing that they might not keep Jeanne Duval at the nursing-home if he was not in Paris to look after her himself.

'Even if this is a burden and a bore to you,' he wrote,[22] 'I rely on your friendship. I don't want them to turn my poor old paralytic out into the streets, out of the home. She might herself be pleased about it, but I want them to keep her until all methods of cure have been tried.'

By the same post he wrote to Jeanne Duval herself, telling her what he had done, and begging her to let him know immediately if she failed to receive the money. Thinking that perhaps she could obtain the same sum twice, she told him it had not been paid. Baudelaire, who could never take things calmly, was immediately thrown into a state of grave anxiety, terrified of what might become of the unfortunate woman if her bills were not settled. He tried to get the money advanced by his mother, and there was a painful scene between them because she accused him of seeking to obtain it under false pretences. His nerves frayed through apprehension, he answered her harshly. As a result they were both ill for several days. Then he wrote to Poulet Malassis, accusing him of negligence,[23] but learned the truth, and was obliged to write in abject apology.[24]

'I apologize most humbly and deeply for my stupid complaint. I was taken in by a letter from the miserable woman – not, as a matter of fact, written by herself, for she is no longer able to write – telling me that she had received nothing. In her unhappy mind, stupefied by illness, she had conceived the ingenious plan of trying to get the money twice over, without pausing to reflect how easy the whole business would be to check. My mother, from whom I tried to borrow the amount until your money turned up, made a terrible scene, and I retaliated. My mother fell ill, and I myself have been in bed since the fourth, with my inside upset, and neuralgia, which shoots about according to the change of wind, and its darting pains are so sharp that I can't sleep! Such are the results of anger and anxiety. However, it must all have an end, since work, time and money are one and the same thing. Again all my apologies.'

In his letter there was no word of reproach against his mistress, and he did not bear her a grudge for the mean part she had played. He understood and forgave her, determined to make her few remaining years as happy as he could. The only letter from him addressed to her which has come down to us is affectionate and kindly, written when he was away at Honfleur, apologizing because he could not do more for her just then, and trusting that she was not too lonely in his absence.

'My dear child,' he wrote to her,[25] 'you mustn't be too angry with me for having left Paris so suddenly without having taken you out to enjoy yourself. You realize how worn out with anxiety I've been, and my mother, who knew perfectly well that out of the five thousand francs which now fall due, two thousand have to be repaid at Honfleur, was bothering me about them. Besides, she's lonely. However, everything turned out all right in the end. But just imagine, the very day before, I was sixteen hundred francs short. Calonne acted very generously and got me out of the hole! I promise you that I'll come back in a few days. I've got to meet Malassis, and besides I've left all my portfolios at the hotel. Henceforth I'm no longer going to make these prolonged stays in Paris which cost so much, and it would be much better to come frequently and to remain only a few days. In the meantime, since I may be absent for a week, and I don't wish you, in your present state, to be short of money even for a day, go and see Ancelle. I know I've overdrawn a bit on next year, but you know that, in spite of his reluctance to advance anything, he's fairly generous. This small sum should enable you to await my arrival, and the New Year will surely bring me money.... I've found my room quite changed, for my mother, who can't ever rest, has beautified everything – or thinks she has. I'll come back soon, and if, as I believe and hope, I have some money I'll take you out to enjoy yourself.

'While the roads are so slippery don't go out alone!'

At the end of 1860 when he was so unhappy, Baudelaire once more wondered whether he and Jeanne Duval could again try to live together, and weld the pieces of their two shattered lives into a whole. She, as well as he, was lonely and unhappy, and, moreover, was not getting the special care which her paralysed condition needed. In December he rented a small apartment in Neuilly, which in those days was a country village on the outskirts of Paris and where she would be away from the noise of the streets, while he himself would not have so far to go to wait on Ancelle. They moved into their new home for Christmas, but this attempt at life together was no more successful than all previous efforts. Early in the New Year he was convinced that their plan had failed. He was desperately unhappy again, and was already contemplating abandoning the new home, leaving her in sole possession, and returning to what he most hated and had never become accustomed to, the furnished room of a cheap hotel. In his own home he had been put in a false and humiliating position, and his pride did not permit him to remain.[26]

After he had settled in Neuilly with Jeanne Duval her brother turned up, not as he had hoped, to provide for his sister, but to live on her. He used to spend the whole day in the apartment, from eight o'clock in the morning until nearly midnight, sitting in her room, so that Baudelaire was never able to talk to her in private. The brother's presence infuriated him. As he said to his mother,[27] 'when one has lived for nineteen years with and for a woman, one always has something to say to her.' For almost a month he controlled himself, not wanting to upset her since she was weak and ill, but at last, when he could endure the situation no longer, one night after the brother had gone out of the house, he went to her room to discuss the situation. Very

gently he explained that he had rented the apartment because he wanted to live with her once more, and had imagined that this was what she too desired. He added that he
did not expect her to dismiss her guest, since she had a perfect right to entertain whom she wished in her own home,
especially her own brother. But he could not continue to
live like this, under the same roof with her, and never seeing
her alone. Since she now had her own family to look after
her, he said, he would return to his mother, who needed
him and was old and lonely. Since he was living all day with
her, her brother should help to support her, because he himself was in grave financial difficulties.

Jeanne Duval reported to her brother what Baudelaire
had said. He answered brutally that he had no intention
of doing anything either in the present or the future, and
he had the insolence to suggest that Baudelaire should by
now have become inured to his state of penury, and that no
man should burden himself with a mistress unless he had
sufficient means to provide for her.[28]

When this conversation was repeated to him, Baudelaire
was beside himself with rage and declared that if it had
been said to him personally, he would have struck the man
in the face. She, frightened by his anger, promised that
she would ask her brother to leave, but said that she did not
think that he would listen to her. Baudelaire, suspecting
that there were other reasons, that perhaps she was in some
ways in his clutches, tried to find out from her whether she
had ever borrowed money from him – that was what probably would have happened in his own case. The contrary
was the truth. He discovered that her brother had been
living at her expense for more than a year, even before the
apartment at Neuilly was taken, and was unwilling to lose
his free board. It was no wonder, Baudelaire said, that she
was so badly dressed and never had any money to pay her
doctor's and chemist's bills. In spite of his anger, however,
he was moved by sorrow when he saw her distress.

'At the sight of all those tears on that aged face, at the

sight of so much weakness in the poor feeble creature, I
was touched and my anger fell, but I'm in a constant state
of irritation which my other worries have not tended to
diminish.' [29]

The weeks went by but still the brother did not leave, and
Baudelaire knew no peace, living between a scoundrel and
a weak-willed invalid. The suspicion also tortured him that
he was not in fact her brother, but a former lover, or a
pimp, living on the money she obtained from his successor.
Finally, after a quarrel more bitter than the rest, he left the
house and never again lived with Jeanne Duval. He did not
see her for almost three months, and in the meantime his
own affairs went from bad to worse. At last, one day at the
end of March 1861, he saw her once more. She had dragged
herself along to him for help, on leaving the workhouse
hospital, where she had to go after he left her, for she had
no money. He had imagined that her brother was bound
to look after her when there was no one else. The contrary
had, however, happened and the brother had allowed her to
go to the public ward, selling in her absence the furniture
from the apartment, and making off with the proceeds. [30]
This was January 1861, and it was now the end of March.

Thus Baudelaire did not escape. Although he never again
lived with her, Jeanne Duval was back once more in his
life, the same burden as ever. There was nothing more to
hope from her. Drugs and drink, illness and paralysis, had
wrought destruction on her mind and body, and she cared
little to what baseness she sank in order to obtain money
to gratify her vices. She felt a certain warmth towards Baudelaire, and a pricking of conscience, when he was near,
but drugs and drink play such havoc even with the best
feelings that she forgot all decency when she needed money.
She borrowed money, in his name, from his friends, knowing that he would not repudiate the debt. She sold presents
from him, even to his best friends like Poulet Malassis, because she realized that this would humiliate him more than
anything, and imagined, in her hazy, muddled brain, that if

she hurt his vanity she might get more money. She even begged for help from his mother, alleging that he was leaving her to starve. Madame Aupick, always mistrustful of her son's conduct, and suspecting that he was trying in this way to force her to provide for his mistress, wrote to reprimand him. Deeply hurt, as he always was at his mother's doubt of him, he answered her bitterly:[31]

'I don't require your hints on integrity,' he wrote, 'nor do I need to defend my conduct. I generally hide my life, my thoughts and my fears, even from you. I can't and won't tell you all my grievances. Firstly, it would take at least fifty pages, fifty pages of suffering for me. All I need say is this: When you think of my character – which you partly know – sensitive, violent, extravagant, and placing pride before everything else, is it at all likely, I ask you, that I'd commit such an inhuman action through meanness? Meanness indeed! But what have I done for seventeen years, if not forgive? – I admit that the woman was once beautiful and that so my patience might seem interested. But, when illness and old age struck her down, what have I done for more than three years? I've done what the egoism of men doesn't always do. And I even added the eagerness of pride to my charity.'

He went on to relate all Jeanne Duval's cruelty, mentioning some action which he says that he has not dared to confide in anyone.[32]

'In January there occurred something so monstrous that it made me very ill – I've not mentioned it to anyone! – I can't describe it to you now! – the mere telling of it would rasp and fray my throat!'

The only way he could save himself from her was by pretending not to provide for her himself, but sending her the money in a disguised way, so that she did not know whence it came. If ever he yielded to her, she always attributed his leniency to weakness but not to generosity or pity, and it encouraged her to further exorbitant demands. He continued to provide for her as long as he lived, and his last thoughts before his final breakdown were full of concern for her, apprehension of what would become of her in the event of his death. When he died his mother did not carry out his last wishes. Although she knew very well that his mistress was the chief of his preoccupations, she blamed her too much for the tragedy and suffering of his life ever to forgive her. She never sought to discover the whereabouts of the unfortunate woman to relieve her distress, with what money Baudelaire left – and he died still owning some capital which he had wanted used for this purpose. Jeanne Duval disappeared completely after his death, no one ever knew where. Nadar is said to have been the last person to see her, in the distance in 1870, dragging herself painfully along on a pair of crutches. At that time the poet had been dead for three years.

Many harsh things have been said of Jeanne Duval, yet no one is justified in judging her, since Baudelaire was able to understand and to forgive her. It is best to think of her as she had been in the days of her flaming youth, at the Hôtel Lauzun, when she had kindled the passion in him which is responsible for the magnificent cycle of sensual love poems; or else as he saw her at the end, during their last attempt at life together, when he composed in her honour *Un Fantôme*, describing her as the ghost of the girl she had once been, now a poor paralysed old woman, in whom there lingers still, like the faint trace of some rare perfume in a bottle which has been cast aside, the memory of her former beauty. That was his final vision of her and although, with uncompromising clarity, he could see what she had become, this did not efface the memory of what she had been formerly, nor diminish his gratitude for what she had once given him in the olden days, when she had the power to grant favours.

The poem is divided into four parts. In the first, *Les Ténèbres*, he describes himself as banished alone in the 'caveaux d'insondable tristesse' where there comes to visit him a ghost. He does not at first recognize her, but finally realizes that it is she, the woman who had once been his joy. The second part, *Le Parfum*, is the image which her perfume evokes before his eyes, so that he can see her once more as she was in the days of her glory and of her great beauty:

> Lecteur, as-tu quelquefois respiré
> Avec ivresse et lente gourmandise
> Ce grain d'encens qui remplit une église,
> Ou d'un sachet le musc invétéré?
>
> Charme profond, magique, dont nous grise
> Dans le présent le passé restauré!
> Ainsi l'amant sur un corps adoré
> Du souvenir cueille la fleur exquise.
>
> De ses cheveux élastiques et lourds,
> Vivant sachet, encensoir de l'alcôve,
> Une senteur montait, sauvage et fauve,
>
> Et des habits, mousseline ou velours,
> Tout imprégnés de sa jeunesse pure,
> Se dégageait un parfum de fourrure.[33]

The third part, *Le Cadre*, is the frame for her beauty – the clothes she wore, when 'tout semblait lui servir de bordure', the rich furniture, the jewels, when her very body seemed unconsciously in love with all this wealth and luxury.

Then, last of all, in the fourth part, *Le Portrait*, comes the picture in its golden frame. Time has faded it and made it almost unrecognizable. Yet, when he looks at it more closely, he sees, beneath the faint colours which the years have almost rubbed away, the face he had loved so long ago:[34]

> La Maladie et la Mort font des cendres
> De tout le feu qui pour nous flamboya.
> De ces grands yeux si fervents et si tendres,
> De cette bouche où mon cœur se noya,
>
> De ces baisers puissants comme un dictame,
> De ces transports plus vifs que des rayons,

Que reste-t-il? C'est affreux, ô mon âme!
Rien qu'un dessin fort pâle, aux trois crayons,

Qui, comme moi, meurt dans la solitude,
Et que le temps, injurieux vieillard,
Chaque jour frotte avec son aile rude.

Noir assassin de la Vie et de l'Art,
Tu ne tueras jamais dans ma mémoire
Celle qui fut mon plaisir et ma gloire.

This is the last picture which Baudelaire wished to preserve of Jeanne Duval, and for it he was willing to forget the
suffering and the tribulations, the quarrels and the bicker-
ings, the angry words and the deceit. Which of them was
most to blame mattered little in the end, and the poet at
least considered the suffering worth while, for she had been
the most vivid and most permanent emotion in his life.
With Madame Sabatier he had been transported into a
rarefied atmosphere where he could not breathe for long;
with Marie Daubrun he had known no security; but with
Jeanne Duval he had lived an intensely human life – even
if it had been at times the lowest form of life. With her he
had experienced almost a family life, with all the friction,
the quarrels, the humiliation, the state where nothing is
hidden, which is possible only amongst those whom a family
tie unites. Jeanne Duval had seen him as no one else had
ever seen him with all his defences lowered; for they had
known such shame together, that she could never despise
him, and with her he could unbend and rest. With others
he felt obliged, by self-respect and dignity, to hide his
wounds, but with her he could doff his pride, and rest from
the weariness of constant strife and struggle with himself
to attain perfection.

In the meantime the second edition of *Les Fleurs du Mal*
had appeared in January 1861, with thirty-five new poems to
take the place of the six which had been banned from the
first edition. For the first time in his life, the poet expressed

satisfaction with one of his works. Writing to his mother,
for New Year's Day 1861, he said:

'*Les Fleurs du Mal* is ready – there's only the cover left
to do and the frontispiece. There are thirty-five new poems
in it, and the old ones have been completely revised. For
the first time in my life I'm almost satisfied. The book is
almost good! It will remain as a proof and pledge of my
disgust and hatred of everything!'

He had first contemplated composing a preface in which
he would set forth his literary theories and aesthetic ideals,
in which he would answer the criticism to which he had been
subjected for so many years, and we can see from his correspondence and several drafts of the plan that have come
down to us, that he had, at first, attached a great deal of importance to the drawing-up of this manifesto. At the last
moment, however, discouraged and weary – and also afraid
of making himself ridiculous – he dropped the project.[35]

'Faced with the devastating vanity and uselessness of
explaining anything to anyone,' he said, 'I stopped short.
Those who know me well will guess what I mean, and for
those who can't or won't understand me, I'd only be piling
up explanations in vain.'

Amongst the new there are two early poems – *L'Albatros*
and *Le Rêve d'un Curieux* – which, for some reason, he did
not publish in the first edition; there are further additions
to the three cycles of love poems – such as *Duellum, Le
Fantôme, Semper Eadem, Chant d'Automne and À une
Madone* – but the majority are poems of *spleen* and pessimism, which were composed in the years of struggle and
depression since his trial, and which express weariness of
life, horror of the swift flight of time, and the sensation
of being carried away to destruction by a force stronger
than himself – poems such as *La Fin de la Journée, Obsession, L'Horloge, Le Goût du Néant*, and many others. This
was now the habitual colour of his mind. He says in one of
them, *Le Goût du Néant*:[36]

Morne esprit, autrefois amoureux de la lutte,
L'Espoir dont l'éperon attisait ton ardeur,
Ne veut plus t'enfourcher! Couche-toi sans pudeur,
Vieux cheval dont le pied à chaque obstacle bute.

Résigne-toi, mon cœur, dors ton sommeil de brute!

Esprit vaincu, fourbu! Pour toi, vieux maraudeur,
L'amour n'a plus de goût, non plus que la dispute,
Adieu donc, chants du cuivre et soupirs de flûte!
Plaisirs ne tentez plus un cœur sombre et boudeur!

Le Printemps adorable a perdu son odeur!

Et le temps m'engloutit minute par minute,
Comme la neige immense un corps pris de roideur,
Je contemple d'en haut le globe en sa rondeur,
Et je n'y cherche plus l'abri d'une cahute.

Avalanche, veux-tu m'emporter dans ta chute?

With the sensation of the void around him, his terror of darkness grew, and even of sleep – although he longed for rest and peace. It seemed to him that all night long he kept falling into a bottomless pit, on the sides of which God was painting, without respite, a mysterious nightmare.[37] He once said to Nadar, 'I see such terrible things in my dreams that I long sometimes not to sleep at all – if only I wasn't afraid of being too tired.'[38]

Even in his waking hours he enjoyed no respite – he could feel time, almost as if it were a living entity, mocking him, and taunting him for his incapacity. Sometimes his obsession with the swift flight of time and the sensation of being crushed beneath the appalling weight of the misspent years made him incapable of work. One of his friends relates that he had removed the hands from his clock and written on its dial, 'It is later than you think!'[39] He was obsessed by any symbol of the passage of time. He says in *L'Hor-loge*:[40]

Souviens-toi que le Temps est un joueur avide
Qui gagne sans tricher, à tout coup! c'est la loi.
Le jour décroît; la nuit augmente; souviens-toi!
Le gouffre a toujours soif; la clepsydre se vide.

Tantôt sonnera l'heure où le divin Hasard,
Où l'auguste Vertu, ton épouse encor vierge,
Où le Repentir même (oh! la dernière auberge!)
Où tout te dira: Meurs, vieux lâche! il est trop tard!

As he looked around the world he saw universal failure – his
own and that of humanity in general. Everywhere, even in
nature, he heard the bitter, sardonic laugh of vanquished
man! He says in *Obsession*: [41]

Grands bois, vous m'effrayez comme des cathédrales;
Vous hurlez comme l'orgue; et dans nos cœurs maudits,
Chambres d'éternel deuil où vibrent de vieux râles,
Répondent les échos de vos De Profundis.

Je te hais, Océan! tes bonds et tes tumultes,
Mon esprit les retrouve en lui; ce rire amer
De l'homme vaincu, plein de sanglots et d'insultes,
Je l'entends dans le rire énorme de la mer,

Comme tu me plairais, ô nuit! sans ces étoiles
Dont la lumière parle un langage connu!
Car je cherche le vide, et le noir, et le nu!

Mais les ténèbres sont elles-mêmes des toiles
Où vivent, jaillissent de mon œil par milliers,
Des êtres disparus aux regards familiers.

The plan, the architecture, which existed already in the
first edition, is broadly the same in this new version. There
is the old fundamental contrast and division into *Spleen*
and *Idéal*, except that the tragic aspect of the conflict has
been further emphasized by the addition of the new pessimistic poems, far more despairing than those written fifteen
years before, after the appointment of his *conseil judiciaire*.
The most significant change is in the addition of a new

section entitled *Tableaux Parisiens*. This contains eighteen
poems, eight of them taken from the section *Spleen et Idéal*
in the first version, and ten of them new. They are poems
expressing his compassionate humanity, deeper in feeling
than those of the same vein written in the period leading
up to the revolution of 1848 – new poems like *Les Sept Vieillards*, *Les Petites Vieilles*, and *Les Aveugles* – and poems of
nostalgia for the past more intense than the earlier *Je n'ai pas
oublié voisine de la Ville* or *La Servante au grand cœur dont
vous étiez jalouse* – new poems like the superb and symbolical *Le Cygne*, which opens: [42]

> *Andromaque, je pense à vous! Ce petit fleuve,*
> *Pauvre et triste miroir où jadis resplendit*
> *L'immense majesté de vos douleurs de veuve,*
> *Ce Simoïs menteur qui par vos pleurs grandit,*
>
> *A fécondé soudain ma mémoire fertile,*
> *Comme je traversais le nouveau Carrousel.*
> *Le vieux Paris n'est plus (la forme d'une ville*
> *Change plus vite hélas! que le cœur d'un mortel).*

And which ends:

> *Paris change! mais rien dans ma mélancolie*
> *N'a bougé! palais neufs, échafaudages, blocs,*
> *Vieux faubourgs, tout pour moi devient allégorie,*
> *Et mes chers souvenirs sont plus lourds que des rocs.*
>
> *Aussi devant ce Louvre une image m'opprime:*
> *Je pense à mon grand cygne, avec ses gestes fous,*
> *Comme les exilés, ridicule et sublime,*
> *Et rongé d'un désir sans trève! et puis à vous,*
>
> *Andromaque, des bras d'un époux tombée,*
> *Vil bétail, sous la main du superbe Pyrrhus,*
> *Auprès d'un tombeau vide en extase courbée;*
> *Veuve d'Hector, hélas! et femme d'Hélénus!*
>
> *Je pense à la négresse, amaigrie et phtisique,*
> *Piétinant dans la boue, et cherchant, l'œil hagard,*
> *Les cocotiers absents de la superbe Afrique*
> *Derrière la muraille immense du brouillard;*

> *À quiconque a perdu ce qui ne se retrouve*
> *Jamais, jamais! à ceux qui s'abreuvent de pleurs*
> *Et tettent la Douleur comme une bonne louve!*
> *Aux maigres orphelins séchant comme des fleurs!*
>
> *Ainsi dans la forêt où mon esprit s'exile*
> *Un vieux Souvenir sonne à plein souffle du cor!*
> *Je pense aux matelots oubliés dans une île,*
> *Aux captifs, aux vaincus! . . . à bien d'autres encor!*

The section entitled *La Mort* has been enriched with three
further poems. Amongst them is the sublime *Le Voyage*, a
more noble coping-stone to the edifice of *Les Fleurs du Mal*
than that of the first version, *La Mort des Artistes*. Now
Baudelaire sees death not merely as the fulfilment of earthly
dreams, death which 'fera s'épanouir les fleurs de leur
cerveau', but as the final voyage of discovery of a land which
will bring satisfaction to a heart longing for perfection.
The poem ends: [43]

> *Ô Mort, vieux capitaine, il est temps! levons l'ancre!*
> *Ce pays nous ennuie, ô Mort! Appareillons!*
> *Si le ciel et la mer sont noirs comme de l'encre,*
> *Nos cœurs que tu connais sont remplis de rayons!*
>
> *Verse-nous ton poison pour qu'il nous réconforte!*
> *Nous voulons, tant ce feu nous brûle le cerveau,*
> *Plonger au fond du gouffre, Enfer ou Ciel qu'importe?*
> *Au fond de l'Inconnu pour trouver du nouveau!*

Baudelaire was justified in his satisfaction with the second
version of *Les Fleurs du Mal* for it is, in every way, a nobler
and more profound achievement, both in thought and in
expression, than his first conception.

[4]

De Profundis
1861

AFTER Baudelaire had left Jeanne Duval at the end of January 1861, he was alone once more. He could never become inured to these quarrels and bitter partings, and, each time, they left him ill and incapable of work. He was worried also on his mother's account and she, as usual when such events occurred, was shaken in her confidence in him. She had been disgusted when, in spite of previous disappointments, he had set up house once more with Jeanne Duval, and her letter held nothing but recriminations and complaints, with few expressions of affection.

'Your letters,' her son wrote to her,[1] 'are full of errors, craziness of all sorts and the most absurd suppositions! I've not seen Jeanne again! Moreover, I repeat, all your letters are insane! You send me only torrents of vile abuse, and I can't ever get used to it!'

Nevertheless there was no one else to whom he could go for comfort and relief from the load of misery which was weighing him down, and he used often to write to her, although he did not always post the letters.

'Alas! my dearest Mother,' he wrote to her once,[2] 'is there still any time left for us to be happy together? I hardly dare believe it any more! I'm forty years old, I've got a *conseil judiciaire*, terrible debts, and, worst of all, my will-power is perhaps destroyed! Who knows but what my mind itself mayn't be affected too! I don't know myself! I can't know since I've lost even the power of making any effort!

'First of all I want to tell you something which I don't tell you often enough, and which you don't probably know, especially if you judge me solely by appearances, and that is that my love for you goes on increasing. It's disgraceful to have to confess that even this very love doesn't give me the courage to raise myself. I gaze back at the old past years, I spend my time thinking of the shortness of life – nothing more – and my will-power grows rustier and rustier! If ever a man knew *spleen* and hypochondria while young, it's certainly me. And nevertheless I long to live, and I'd like to know, even for a short time, security, fame and satisfaction with myself. But something full of dread in me whispers: "Never more!" Yet something else says to me: 'Try again!" Of all the plans and projects piled up in two or three portfolios, which I daren't open any more, how many shall I ever finish now? Perhaps none of them!'

This letter, written some time in February or March, was not posted immediately, and then many things happened. He learned from his mother that l'Abbé Cardinne had burnt in disgust the copy of *Les Fleurs du Mal* which she had insisted on his sending to the priest, against his better judgement. Baudelaire had been unable to obtain enough copies from his publisher for all his own friends, and he was infuriated that a priest should have destroyed the one he had secured for himself with so much difficulty.

He was once more anxious about Jeanne Duval who came out of hospital destitute at about this time, when he had imagined that she was being cared for by her brother.

Then his mother had written to him a further letter of accusation and complaint, telling him that he was killing her, and that she was longing for death to release her from her misery.

All this was more than he could endure in the despair which had afflicted him now for many months, bringing him once more to the brink of suicide. He began to pray for help, he who had been unable to pray since his youth. He wrote to his mother again, this time in bitterness, taking up the letter he had begun in February.[3]

'The previous page was written a month ago – six weeks

perhaps, or even two months. I can't remember any more when it was! I've fallen into a sort of perpetual nervous terror, with frightful sleep, and still more frightful waking, entailing the utter inability to work. The copies of my book have remained for a month on my table, and I haven't had the energy to wrap them up and dispatch them. I've not written to Jeanne, I've not seen her for nearly three months, and naturally, since it was impossible, I haven't sent her a penny. She came to see me yesterday, after she had just come out of hospital, since the brother, who I imagined was supporting her, had sold up part of her furniture during her absence. In this horrible state of mind – incapacity and hypochondria – the temptation of suicide obsessed me again. I can confess it now since it has passed. At every hour of the day the obsession was torturing me for I saw in it perfect escape, escape from everything! At the same time, for three months, and through a strange contradiction, but only apparent, I prayed all the time – to whom, to what definite being? I don't at all know! – to obtain two things: for myself the strength to go on living, and for you many long years. Let me add, by the way, that your longing to die is cruel and absurd, for your death would be the last blow for me and would mean the impossibility for ever for me of finding happiness.

'The obsession has at last disappeared, conquered by violent, and inescapable, work – an article on Wagner finished in three days, working at the press itself, but without the spur of immediate printing I'd never have had the energy to finish it. Since then I've been ill again, with weakness and fear. I've been a couple of times fairly bad, and something which is particularly distressing is that when I'm falling asleep – and even in my sleep – I hear voices distinctly, and even whole sentences, but quite commonplace and trivial, and having no bearing whatsoever on my work.

'Then your letters came, and they weren't of a nature to cheer me. You're always armed to stone me with the crowd!

That's been the case since my childhood as you well know! How is it that you're always for your son the opposite of a friend – except in money matters?

'I'd been careful to mark in the Table of Contents all the new poems, and it was easy for you to see that they were all composed to fit the plan. It's a book on which I've been working for twenty years and I'm no longer free not to publish it.

'As for Father Cardinne, that's a serious matter, and not in the way you think! In the midst of all my troubles, I'll not have a priest come and fight against me in the mind of my old mother, and I'll see that it doesn't happen again, if I can, and if I've got the strength. The conduct of that man is monstrous and inexplicable! As for burning books, that's no longer done, except by lunatics who like to see paper blaze! And I'd stupidly deprived myself of a precious copy to please him, and to give him something he'd been asking me to give him for three years! And now I've no copies left for my friends! But you've always found it necessary to humiliate me before someone or other. At one time it used to be Monsieur Emon – don't you remember? And now it's before a priest who hasn't even the decency to disguise his opinion from you, which might hurt you. And, moreover, he didn't understand that the book is based on Catholic inspiration. But that's quite another matter!'

Two considerations alone had restrained him from committing suicide, he explained: one, that he thought it was his duty to leave full explanations of how his debts should be paid, and that he had not yet left a full account of them; and the other that he did not want to die without, at least, publishing his works of criticism.

He was still trying to work, but it seemed to no purpose, for the money slipped through his fingers, into the hands of his creditors, before it had even reached his pockets. Once again, in dire necessity, he used money which was not his to use, but belonged to Poulet Malassis, hoping to be able to replace it with what was due to him from another quarter.

Unfortunately, his own debtor did not repay him. This time he did not try to obtain the money through his mother or Ancelle, but – as he himself admits – he had the desperate courage to write to his friend to confess, hoping that, out of consideration for their long-standing friendship, he would wait for repayment.[4] The meeting which he had dreaded took place, but Poulet Malassis was so kind and forgiving that Baudelaire felt even more humiliated than if he had been angry and merciless.[5] Nevertheless, the publisher himself was in sore need of money, and Baudelaire had to find some means of repaying him with the shortest possible delay.

Next, in addition to his other worries, he fell ill again, very seriously this time, not merely from the nervous attacks from which he had been suffering for the past few years and to which he had almost grown accustomed, but from symptoms the gravity of which he recognized immediately. Syphilis had broken out again, for the third time, when he had thought himself permanently cured after the second attack ten years before. This time it took a more serious form than on either of the previous attacks, and he was suddenly overcome with terror and dismay, as he saw himself an incurable invalid, ruined by ill-health, incapable of work at this serious juncture of his life, when his affairs were in such grave disorder.

To save himself from complete shipwreck, the first essential thing for him, who had frittered away so many idle hours, was to learn to work, and to acquire a taste for it. 'The more one works, the better one works, and the more one wishes to work,' he says in his private journals.[6] And later: 'At each moment we are crushed by the thought and the sensation of time. There are two ways only of escaping from this nightmare and of forgetting it. Pleasure and work. Pleasure wears us out, but work strengthens us! Choose then!'[7]

Deliberately he tries to galvanize himself to action, and his journals abound in advice to himself, and in expressions of despair and frenzy when he has failed. 'Work from six in the morning, fasting, until midday, work blindly, madly and without aim, and we'll see what the result will be!' He works at anything, it does not matter what, to keep himself forcibly occupied, and not to allow himself to drift into daydreaming. He copies out his notes, draws up time-tables for future work, calculating how much he will be able to earn if he can only sustain this pace. 'Go over and classify all my letters – two days – and all my debts – two days. There are four categories – notes of hand, big debts, little debts, friends. Classify my notes – two days.' [8]

When he has worked in this way for some time, hope springs up once more in his heart, and he wonders whether all may not yet be saved. 'Everything can still be repaired! There is still time! Who knows but whether new joys. Fame. The payment of my debts. The prosperity of Jeanne and of my mother!' [9]

He reflects then how often he has failed in the past, and adds sadly: [10] 'I've never yet known the joy of a plan fully carried out!'

He realizes that the danger with him has always been that he has allowed himself to postpone until the morrow many things which should have been done that day, and that no more time may be left to him. He remembers with terror his illness and that he may die soon, or else become incapable of work. Then in a panic he cries: 'Too late perhaps! – My mother and Jeanne! – For pity's sake, my health! – Illness of Jeanne! – Infirmity and loneliness of my mother!' [11]

He prays then that through him, through his illness or death, no suffering may come to his mother.

'Don't chastise me through my mother, Lord, and don't chastise my mother on account of me! Give me the strength to perform my duty every day, and thus become a hero and a saint.' [12]

It is necessary here to make some mention of the two

books which make up *Les Journaux Intimes* – *Fusées* and
Mon. Cœur mis à nu – from which the above quotations
have been taken. These passages, until some years ago, were
thought to belong to the second, *Mon Cœur mis à nu*, and
attributed to a later period, when Baudelaire was in Belgium.[13] Crépet, after a close study of the manuscripts, concluded that the passages in question came not from *Mon
Cœur mis à nu* but from *Fusées*; that the two works were
not, as had been hitherto believed, volume one and two of
the journals; that there was overlapping and no sequence
in their composition.[14] *Fusées*, he believes, was composed between 1855 and 1862, not begun in 1851 as was formerly
thought; *Mon Cœur mis à nu* was written between 1859
and 1864 – this would mean that some of it still belongs to
the Belgium period where Baudelaire went in 1864. Crépet
considers that *Fusées* should contain the passages which are
most finished and ready for publication. It does not matter
for interpretative – or aesthetic – purposes whether the passages are ascribed to *Fusées* or to *Mon Cœur mis à nu* so long
as they are attributed to the correct period. In mood they
would seem to belong to the most desperate moment of the
poet's life, when he was faced with the temptation to suicide,
in 1861 when he had not yet climbed out of the trough of
despair. They are very like in tone the letters which he wrote
to his mother that year between February and June.

In 1861 came the lowest ebb of Baudelaire's spirits, full
of forebodings of disaster. It began in February and is reflected in the letters to his mother which have been called
by a critic, with singular insensitiveness, self-pitying.

Baudelaire, as we know, began his despairing letter in
February, but did not finish it then. He had reached a state
of complete panic when he cried: 'I must get to Honfleur
as soon as possible, before I sink any lower! How many pre-
sentiments have already been sent by God that it's time to
act!'[15]

He thought then of his mother and that she alone could

save him. He took up his letter again in despair, becoming
once more a child beseeching her for help and comfort. He
confessed to her his obsession with suicide, assuring her that
it was now past, but he needed help from outside in order
to recover.

This long letter is the one which so many critics have
misunderstood, seeing in it merely the expression of a
Freudian Œdipus complex. It can be interpreted in a less
complicated manner. It was natural that at a moment when
he saw death near, Baudelaire should return in imagination
to the happy days of childhood, and that, after the tragedy
of his later years and the panic of the present, he should
look back to them and see them as the only happy years
of his life and to his mother as the only person who had
ever given him comfort and peace.[16]

'My dearest Mother, if you've really got maternal genius,
and if you're not too weary, will you please come to Paris?
Will you come and see me, and even take me away? On
account of a thousand desperate reasons I can't myself go to
Honfleur at present to get what I long for so much, a little
courage and affection. At the end of March I wrote to you
"Shall we ever see each other again?" I was in the midst
of one of these crises when one catches sight of truth stark
naked! I'd give anything to spend a few days with you, the
only person to whom I'm really attached – a week, three
days, even a few hours! You don't read my letters carefully
enough! You imagine I'm lying, or at least exaggerating,
when I speak of my despair, of my health, and of my horror
of life! I tell you I want to see you and that I can't go to
Honfleur!

'Every time I take up my pen to explain my situation to
you, I'm terrified; afraid of killing you, of destroying your
weak body! And, without your knowing it, I'm constantly
on the brink of suicide! I do believe that you love me passionately, even blindly, for your character is so noble! I
too loved you passionately in my childhood. Later,
under the weight of your unfairness, I've sometimes been

lacking in respect towards you – as if maternal injustice could ever excuse filial disrespect – I've often had remorse for it, although, as is my habit, I've never said anything to you about it. I'm no longer the self-willed, ungrateful child I once was! Deep reflection on my life and on your character, has helped me to understand my faults, and all your generosity. Nevertheless the harm was already done by your rashness and by my fault. We were certainly intended to love each other, and to end our lives as peaceably and respectably as possible. Nevertheless, in the appalling circumstances in which I find myself, I'm convinced that one or other of us will cause the death of the other, and that we'll end by mutually killing each other. After my death it's certain you wouldn't live any longer, for I'm the only thing which keeps you alive. After your death, and especially if you died through a shock caused by me, I'd most certainly kill myself! Your death, by the way, of which you speak so glibly and with so much resignation, wouldn't alter anything, for the *conseil judiciaire* would still remain, nothing would be paid and I'd have on top of it all the horrible feeling of total isolation. As for me committing suicide, it's absurd isn't it? You'll say "Are you going to leave your poor old mother alone?" Indeed I believe that, although I haven't strictly the right to do that, the amount of suffering I've had to endure for almost thirty years might be enough to excuse me. "And what about God?" you'll ask! I certainly wish with all my heart – and how sincerely I say this nobody but myself could possibly know – to believe that an invisible being is concerned about my fate, but what does one do to believe? The thought of God reminds me of that cursed parish priest! Even in the grief which my letter will surely cause you, I don't want you to discuss the matter with him. That priest is my enemy – perhaps only through utter stupidity. ...

'A very rash step was taken by you in my youth, and your rashness, coupled with my past mistakes, overwhelms me. My situation is desperate! There are people who bow and scrape before me, and there may even be some who envy me! My literary situation is more than good. I can do what I want and everything will one day be printed. But since I possess an unpopular kind of talent, I'll earn very little money, but I'll leave great fame, I know that well, provided I've got the courage to live! My spiritual health? Rotten! Ruined perhaps! And yet I'm full of plans! *My Heart laid bare*, several novels, two plays – one of them for the Théâtre Français. Will all that ever be finished? I can't any longer believe it! My situation with regard to my credit is appalling – that's the serious matter. Never any rest, insults, abuse, gibes and contumely, of which you can't have any conception! But which paralyses my imagination and undermines it! I earn some money, it's true, and, if I hadn't any debts, and hadn't any more income left, I'd be rich! Consider this very carefully! I'd be able to give you some money, I'd be able, without risk, to be charitable to Jeanne. I'll speak about her later on. It's you yourself who have demanded all these explanations. But all this money melts away in an extravagant and unhealthy life – for I live very badly – and in the paying – or rather the partial redemption of old debts, in fees for renewal, etc. Later on I'll come to positive details, for I need to be saved, and you alone can save me. I want to tell you everything today. I'm alone, without friends, without mistress, without even a cat or dog. To whom can I go for comfort? I've got only the portrait of my father and it remains silent!

'My physical health which I need so badly for you, for all my duties, that's another question; I must speak of it to you, although you pay little heed to it. I don't mean these nervous attacks which weaken me every day, and destroy my courage – insomnia, nightmares, weakness – I've mentioned them too often already. I need have no false shame with you, need I? You know that when I was very young, I contracted a venereal disease, which I thought later was completely cured. It broke out again in Dijon after 1848, and it was once more checked! Now it has returned in a new form – discoloration of the skin and weariness in all the joints. You can believe me for I know what I'm talking about! But perhaps, in the despair and depression into which I've fallen, my terror exaggerates the harm. However, I need serious treatment and it's not in the kind of life I'm leading now that I could ever get it!

'I'll leave all that aside for the moment, as I want to return to my day-dreaming before I come to the plan I wish to put before you. I take pleasure in this dreaming. Who knows whether I'll ever again be able to open my heart to you, which you've never really known or appreciated? There was in my childhood a period of passionate love for you! Listen, and read without fear. I've never said so much to you before. I remember a drive in a cab with you, when you'd just come out of a nursing-home, and you showed me, to prove that you'd been thinking of your son, pen drawings which you'd done for me. Don't you think I've got a cruel memory. Later on I remember the Place-Saint-André des Arts and Neuilly – long walks and endless affection. I remember the quays that were so melancholy at evening time. Oh! these were for me the good old days of my mother's tender affection. Please forgive me for calling these the good old days which were probably unhappy for you! But I was still living in you, and you were mine alone. You were at the same time my idol and my friend. You'll perhaps be astonished that I'm able to speak with such warmth of so distant a time. I'm amazed at it myself! It's perhaps because I've felt once more the longing for death, that the things of long ago rise up so clearly in my mind.

'You know what a frightful education your husband chose to give me later on. I'm forty and I never think of schools and of the fear that my stepfather inspired in me, without a stab of pain. And yet I loved him, and nowadays I've learnt enough wisdom to be able to be fair to him. But nevertheless he was obstinately clumsy with me. But I'll pass over all that quickly, for I see tears in your eyes.

'Later on I escaped from home, and, from that moment,

I was completely done for. I was carried away solely by love
of pleasure and of perpetual excitement – travelling, beautiful furniture, pictures, etc. Today I'm dearly paying for all
that! As for the *conseil judiciaire*, I've only one thing to say.
I realize today the tremendous importance of money, and
I understand the seriousness of everything that appertains
to money. I can quite well believe that you imagined that
you were wise and were working for my good. But there's
a question which has always worried me. How does it happen that the following idea never occurred to you? "It's
possible that my son may never acquire, to the same extent
as I, an aptitude for practical conduct, but it's possible also
that he might become, in other respects, a remarkable man.
In that case what shall I do? Shall I condemn him to a dual
and contradictory existence? On the one hand an honoured
life, on the other a life which he hates, and in which he is
despised? Shall I condemn him to bear right into his old
age a shameful sign, a sign which does him untold harm,
and which induces incapacity and depression?" It's of course
evident that if the *conseil judiciaire* hadn't taken place
everything would have been squandered, and I'd have been
obliged to acquire a taste for work. The *conseil judiciaire*
has, in fact, taken place, everything is, in fact, squandered,
and I'd old and unhappy!

'Is recovery still possible? That's the vital question! All
this dwelling on the past was solely to show you that I'd a
few excuses in my favour, if not exactly justification. And,
if you feel any reproaches in what I've written, you must
know that, at least, this in no way alters my admiration for
your warm heart and my gratitude for all your devotion.
You've always sacrificed yourself – you've got a genius for
sacrifice! Now, however, I beg for more than that, I crave, at
the same time, advice, support, complete understanding
between you and me, and help. I implore you to come to
Paris! Come, come, for I'm at the end of strength, of courage and of all hope! I see long stretches of horror ahead of
me! I see my literary career cut short for ever, I fear a

catastrophe! You can easily ask some of your friends for hospitality for a week – Ancelle, for instance. I'd give anything in the world to see you, to kiss you! I'm terrified of a catastrophe, and I can't go home at the moment!'

He went on then to tell her what he would like to suggest. He had, he admitted, often considered summoning the *conseil de famille* and putting his case before them, pointing out how he had produced eight books in appalling conditions, and had been constantly held back, at every turn, by the overwhelming debts incurred in his youth. He had never taken this step, he declared, out of consideration for her feelings, but now he wanted her to persuade Ancelle to consent to sell out a substantial portion of his capital to settle, finally, the greatest part of his old debts – not merely to reach a temporary alleviation, as in 1858, but to reach a state which would give him freedom from anxiety for several years. This would permit him to take his health in hand, to rest and to follow the treatment necessary for recovery, as well as to compose the books which he knew he could write. With the income from his remaining capital, he would like to provide for Jeanne Duval in some home, where she would be well cared for, and not feel too lonely.

'I implore you,' he wrote to his mother,[17] 'give me peace and rest, and the opportunity for work and a little affection. ... Be discreet in your confidences to Ancelle. He is kind, but narrow-minded, and he is incapable of believing that the wastrel whom he has had so often to take to task, can, at the same time, be an important man. He'll allow me to die through pig-headedness! Instead of thinking solely of money, think a little of my fame, of my peace and rest, of my life in general.'

His mother was naturally much frightened and upset on the receipt of his letter, and immediately dispatched an order for five hundred francs to him, before making her preparations for coming to Paris. Next she wrote to Ancelle to explain to him Baudelaire's plan. The lawyer, never easy to persuade in such matters, was less so now than ever.

Although he realized perfectly well what awaited him in an interview with his ward, he would not consent to embark on any business without thoroughly discussing the matter with him. On receipt of Madame Aupick's letter, he set out one evening to call on Baudelaire at dinner-time. They dined together in a restaurant but, before the meal was even over, he had got on the poet's nerves by his implied assumption that this was merely an evening of pleasure together, by his matiness and chattiness with everyone – even sending for the proprietor to ask him whether he was English or German, whether he had been established in his present place for long, and whether business was good. Having thoroughly irritated Baudelaire by his off-hand manner, as if he was about to deal with a matter of minor importance, he deigned to talk business.[18] In all kinds of subtle – and the poet considered underhand – ways, he tried to obtain from him the names of the people with whom he was implicated in financial transactions. Baudelaire had always withheld this information, being very conscious of his position before the law, and had always insisted on paying his creditors himself in person. This may have been one of the reasons why Ancelle was always so reluctant to make a complete settlement – he did not trust him to hand over a large sum of money to his creditors – and he may also have mistrusted the honesty of those creditors themselves. Apparently Ancelle made it clear that he would not sell out the amount needed to yield the twenty thousand francs asked for. He had seen capital to the amount of four thousand francs sacrificed scarcely three years before to help Baudelaire to settle at Honfleur, and this loss of income had not produced, as far as he could see, any tangible result. Moreover, nine months ago, in August, further shares had been given up, with a further loss of two thousand francs of capital, to get him out of a scrape into which he ought never to have fallen. It was madness even to contemplate entrusting so large a sum to a man who possessed no sense of reality, and never knew to what use money should be put. He brought himself to consent to a further sacrifice of four thousand francs, but this was only a drop in the ocean of Baudelaire's debts and useless as a settlement. It merely gave him the few months' freedom from acute anxiety which the similar arrangement had given him after his stepfather's death. Nevertheless, such were his recuperative powers, even at this stage, that he thought he was saved, and he began to make plans once more for the future. He even sent his mother, as a token of gratitude, two little Chinese coffee trays, purchased with some of the money destined to pay his debts.[19] She was naturally not as grateful as he expected her to be, for she would have preferred to see him develop a more serious and responsible attitude towards money. When he sensed her disappointment, he thought it was because the little trays had failed to please her, and as compensation, he sent her a quantity of China tea – in those days no mean gift.[20]

It was in a spirit of deep submission and spiritual peace that Baudelaire composed *Recueillement* in the autumn of 1861, a poem which expresses the sadness and resignation of the final Baudelaire. It marks the beginning of the last phase of his development when, in the midst of ruin, he was still able to find cause for hope. It is also one of his most musical and harmonious poems.[21]

> *Sois sage, ô ma Douleur, et tiens-toi plus tranquille!*
> *Tu réclamais le Soir; il descend; le voici:*
> *Une atmosphère obscure enveloppe la ville,*
> *Aux uns portant la paix, aux autres le souci.*
>
> *Pendant que des mortels la multitude vile,*
> *Sous le fouet du Plaisir, ce bourreau sans merci,*
> *Va cueillir des remords dans la fête servile,*
> *Ma Douleur, donne-moi la main; viens par ici,*
>
> *Loin d'eux. Vois se pencher les défuntes Années,*
> *Sur les balcons du ciel, en robes surannées;*
> *Surgir du fond des eaux le Regret souriant:*

Le Soleil moribond s'endormir sous une arche,
Et, comme un long linceul traînant à l'Orient,
Entends, ma chère, entends la douce Nuit qui marche.

The Candidate for the
French Academy
1861 — 1862

IT would not be right to see Baudelaire at this time as merely
sunk in depression and despair, bereft of all interest in
intellectual and artistic concerns. This was the time when
he discovered the music of Wagner which was to be the last
great passion of his life, and when he became the friend of
Manet. It was also now that, forgetful of his own preoccupations and worries, he tried to find a publisher for Meryon's
etchings, when he could obtain none for himself. In the early
months of 1860 he worked hard to persuade Poulet Malassis
to bring out an album of views of Paris, with a descriptive
letterpress. At this time the artist was mad, and unable to
look after his own interests.[1] Baudelaire's first idea had been
that it should consist of a dozen etchings depicting the old
Paris which was fast disappearing before the new one of
Baron Haussmann, and that he himself should use some of
the poems from *Tableaux Parisiens* in *Les Fleurs du Mal*
to match the etchings. Meryon, unable to take in this plan,
was possessed by the madman's obsession that, somehow, he
was being cheated, and he refused to have anything to do
with it. Then Baudelaire suggested that he should compose
passages of poetic prose to describe the subject of the etchings but this, likewise, was turned down by Meryon, who
would accept only a letterpress which was chosen by himself and which reads like pages from a guide-book. Baudelaire, who usually controlled himself with difficulty,
accepted this project, though he would not sign such a
monstrosity. All this he did for nothing, wasting months of
his time in an effort to meet the wishes of a madman, be-

cause he had compassion on his condition, and thought highly of him as an artist.

In the same way, although he could not find such employment for himself, he tried to get work for Daumier, who had been dismissed in the middle of the month from *Charivari*.[2] Later he wasted eight months of his leisure in preparing for publication Léon Cladel's manuscripts – who had not yet learnt to write – because he thought he had discovered undeveloped talent in him, and wanted to teach him his trade.[3]

Most of these acts he performed through pity and artistic integrity, but with Wagner it was a case of possession, similar to what he had experienced with Poe. Hitherto, although he had enjoyed music in a sensuous and amateurish way, he had never given it serious consideration as a noble art. However, he now found in the music of Wagner, and in his aesthetic doctrine, many similarities to his own ideals, and his excitement was very like that which had seized him, more than ten years before, when he had discovered the writings of Edgar Allan Poe.

In the same way now he wearied his friends with his talk of the musician, and expressed the same horror of those who did not know his compositions as he had once of those who were ignorant of Poe. He even insisted on dragging reluctant friends – like long-suffering Asselineau – to orchestral concerts, to hear the new music.

'I daren't speak any more of Wagner,' he wrote to Poulet Malassis,[4] 'everyone has made too much fun of me. But that music has been one of the really great joys of my life, and it is certainly fifteen years since I've felt so carried away by anything.'

The concert at which he became acquainted with Wagner's music was the famous one at the Théâtre des Italiens on 25 January 1860, when the general public received its first experience of what had been announced as the music of the future. Wagner had hoped that this concert would retrieve for him the humiliations he had endured on his previous visit to Paris, between 1839 and 1842, but the result was not what he anticipated. He had announced beforehand that his music was going to revolutionize the art from top to bottom, and the whole of musical Paris flocked to listen. There were the older musicians, Auber and Berlioz, secretly hostile, but too intelligent and sensitive not to be aware of what the music meant. Berlioz sat all the evening in the box most in view of the audience with a disdainful expression on his face, and was evidently jealous of this newcomer who was soon to outstrip him. In his Memoirs he does not mention the concert although it was one of the sensations of the year.

Before the concert had even begun, the critics had separated into two antagonistic camps. The official musical paper, *La Gazette Musicale*, had been hostile to Wagner for years, and had declared from the outset that he was devoid of talent and ideas. The musician came to conduct in person and, although there was no show of real enthusiasm, the audience was intent on being courteous. At the first interval there was some uncertain applause and intermittent cries of 'Bravo!', but the result was not the sweeping success which Wagner had anticipated, and had even announced. In the foyer the critics, who collected to discuss the evening's entertainment, mostly complained of the length and boredom of the selections chosen. The most favourable comment was that it was all 'du pur Meyerbeer' or else 'du Weber travesti'. In the press the following morning those critics who were not actually hostile were condescending and smug.

For Baudelaire, on the contrary, the whole evening had been one of revelation. After the first bars of the *Prelude* to *Lohengrin* he felt, as he says,[5] 'délivré des liens de la pesanteur, et je retrouvai par le souvenir l'extraordinaire volupté qui circule dans les lieux hauts. ... Alors je conçus pleinement l'idée d'une âme se mouvant dans un milieu lumineux, d'une extase faite de volupté et de connaissance, et planant au-dessus et bien loin du monde naturel. ... À partir de ce

moment je fus possédé du désir d'entrer plus avant dans
l'intelligence de ces œuvres singulières. J'avais subi (du
moins cela m'apparaissait ainsi) une opération spirituelle,
une révélation. Ma volupté avait été si forte et si terrible,
que je ne pouvais m'empêcher d'y vouloir retourner sans
cesse.'

When he saw the indifference with which most of the
critics treated the concert he could not refrain, although
he did not know Wagner personally, from writing to him
to express his own pleasure, at least, and his sense of revelation: [6]

'I've always imagined that however accustomed to fame a
great artist may be, he'll not be indifferent to sincere compliments, especially when these are, as it were, a cry of
gratitude, and that these compliments may have some special
value coming from a Frenchman, that is to say from a man
little prone to enthusiasm, and born in a country where
music, no more than poetry and painting, is understood.
First of all I want to tell you that I owe you the greatest
musical joy that I've ever experienced in my life. I've reached
an age when one no longer enjoys writing to famous men,
and I'd have hesitated a long time to express my admiration
to you by letter, if I didn't see every day shameful and
ridiculous articles in which every effort is made to discredit
your genius! You're not the first man for whom I've found
it necessary to blush for my country. Finally, indignation
has persuaded me to express my gratitude to you, and I
said to myself: "I wish to separate myself from the rest of
these fools!"

'The first time that I went to the Théâtre des Italiens to
hear your music, I wasn't favourably disposed towards you,
and I'll admit it, I was full of prejudices, for I've so often
been taken in by so much of the music of pretentious quacks
that I've heard! But by you I was immediately conquered!
What I felt can scarcely be described, and if you'll deign not
to laugh, I'll try to express it to you. First of all, it seemed
to me that I already knew that music; then, when I'd re-

flected on it later, I discovered whence came this illusion, for it seemed to me that the music was my own, and that I was recognizing it, as one recognizes the things one is destined to love. To anyone, except to a sensible man, this might seem perfectly ridiculous – especially coming from someone who, like me, doesn't know music, and whose whole musical education consists in having heard, with great pleasure it's true, some wonderful music by Weber and Beethoven.

'Next, the characteristic which most struck me was the large scale. I've found in your works the solemn majesty of the great aspects of nature, the great passions of man. One feels immediately carried away and conquered ... I felt all the majesty of a life larger than our own! And another thing, moreover, a feeling of a strange nature, the pride and the joy of understanding, of allowing myself to be penetrated and overcome, a joy almost sensual, like the feeling of rising into the air, or of floating on the sea! And, at the same time, the music expressed the pride of life. And finally I felt – and I beg you not to laugh – sensations which probably come from the nature of my mind, and of my frequent preoccupations. There seemed to me something uplifting and uplifted, something aspiring to rise higher, something sublime ... the final utterance of the human soul which has reached the paroxysm of ecstasy.

'I began to compose a few thoughts on the selections from *Tannhaüser* and *Lohengrin* which we'd heard, but then I felt the impossibility of saying anything adequate!

'I could continue this letter indefinitely. If you've been able to read me so far, I thank you. I've only now a few words to add. Since the day when I first heard your music, I say to myself continuously, especially in my moments of despair, "If I could only hear some Wagner tonight!" There are doubtless other men like me, so why wouldn't you give us further concerts, adding new pieces? You've given us a foretaste of new joys, have you then the right to deprive us of the rest? Once more, Monsieur, I thank you! You've brought me back to myself, and to the contemplation of greatness at a difficult and tragic time for me.

'I don't enclose my address, because you might then think that I've a favour to ask you.'

Wagner did not have very much difficulty in discovering who Baudelaire was, and the poet soon became a frequent guest at his Wednesday evening musical parties. Wagner seems to have been flattered by what seemed to him the youthful enthusiastic worship of Baudelaire. He does not seem to have realized that he was dealing with one of the greatest poets of his age, and he made no great efforts to get to know him further, but was satisfied with his homage.

Baudelaire worked intermittently for over a year on his article on Wagner, and at last finished it in haste in a few days at the printers, while they were waiting for his copy.[7] It appeared on 1 April 1861 in *La Revue Européenne,* and was subsequently published, as a pamphlet, with the addition of *Encore quelques Mots* by Dentu, in May the same year. The booklet did not arouse much interest, did not sell well and, five years later, was remaindered at half-price.[8]

Richard Wagner et Tannhaüser à Paris is not as intellectually satisfying, or as professionally competent, as Baudelaire's art criticism. He knew little of the technique and craft of music, far less than he did of painting. Here he contents himself with expressing lyrically the feelings awakened in him as he listened to the music. This kind of subjective criticism – subjective impressionism would be a more apt description – would not have been possible with classical music, but it was very suitable as a *correspondance* in literature of the music of Wagner, which indeed owed much to literary conceptions.

Baudelaire's article appeared shortly after the fiasco of *Tannhaüser* at the Opéra. Early in 1861 Wagner had returned to France, determined not to content himself this time with mere symphonic concerts, but to produce one of his own operas. Before the work could be put on at the Opéra innumerable difficulties had to be surmounted: an order had to be obtained from the Emperor, who cared little for music, and to whom it was a matter of indifference whether Wagner was heard or not. This difficulty was got over through the help of Madame Metternich who persuaded Napoleon to grant the required authorization. The news of this intervention created from the outset an unfavourable state of mind in the public, for here was a foreign work, produced under the sponsorship of a foreigner, a hereditary enemy.

The next difficulty concerned the expenses of production. Wagner was as impossible as Baudelaire to deal with on account of his insistence on the smallest detail, and also because of the extravagance of his ideas of production. He tried to insist on having twenty-four horn players, when it was doubtful whether that number of efficient horn players could have been found in the whole of France. He wanted also, as local colour, huntsmen and large packs of hounds cavorting on the stage.

He was not alone in making difficulties. It was next the turn of the artists themselves to complain. They said that they were being overworked, and that the music was so barbarously written for the human voice that their vocal cords would be permanently strained. Worst of all, the conductor, furious that a foreigner should try to tell him how music should be played – even his own – and thinking that he knew better than Wagner how his opera should be performed, refused to follow his instructions. In desperation, the composer was obliged to take the baton himself, and this did not make matters any less strained.

The first performance, on thirteenth March, was undoubtedly a success, though violently contested. Yet in order to obtain permission to perform on subsequent nights, Wagner had to make concessions to the regular patrons of the Opéra, and to accept substantial cuts in his work, so that the usual ballet could have its place in the evening's entertainment. With magnificent arrogance, he agreed, saying that, since his fame was established the whole world over, the reputation of his work could look after itself, and that he was ready to let the management treat it like the composition of any dead musician – that is to say, introduce any changes which they considered necessary to ensure its acceptance by the French public.[9] His concessions were unavailing, and opposition grew to such an extent that, after 25 March, he decided to withdraw the opera.

Immediately on the publication of his article, Baudelaire sent a copy of it to Wagner, who replied with a cordial letter:[10]

'I have on several occasions been to your house, without finding you in. You can imagine how anxious I am to tell you the tremendous pleasure you have given me by your article, which honours and encourages me more than anything that has ever been said about my poor talent. Will it be possible for me to tell you soon, in person, how transported I felt as I read those beautiful pages which explain to me, just as the finest poem might, the impressions which I am proud to have awakened in so highly sensitive a temperament as yours?

'A thousand thanks for all your good favours to me, and believe me I am proud to be able to count you among my friends.'

Baudelaire's attitude to Manet was not one of such hero-worship. Their friendship was the result of intimate understanding between two very similar personalities with similar aspirations, and Manet does in fact stand in relation to the painting of his age very much in the same way as Baudelaire does to the literature. Manet, like Baudelaire, was, in the same facile way, described at first as a realist, and he resented the label with the same vehemence as the poet. He also used to declare that the artist must be of his own time, and paint exactly what he saw with his own eyes, but with him, as with Baudelaire, this did not entail triviality and squalor. It meant only the discovery of beauty and splendour in ordinary things where others had not dreamt of seeking them, and it meant, above all, the sublimation of the commonplace. Many of Manet's pictures could easily be the subject of poems from *Les Fleurs du Mal* – *Le Déjeuner sur l'Herbe*, or *Olympia* – while the girl in the picture entitled *Le Bar des Folies Bergère* expresses all the sadness and the weariness of a Baudelaire character as she gazes out at 'le spectacle ennuyeux de l'immortel péché.' [11]

Even their contemporaries realized the affinities between the two – Monselet, in an article entitled *Le Salon des Refusés*, published in 1863, called Manet 'the pupil of Goya and of Charles Baudelaire.' [12]

Baudelaire and Manet met at a time when the painter had not yet developed his individual style, and many paths seemed open to him. He was still under the influence of Romanticism. But, after his *Buveur d'Absinthe*, which was refused at the *Salon* of 1859, he began to rouse in his public the same kind of horror which Baudelaire also awakened, and each of his subsequent pictures shocked in the same way as each new book by the poet. Manet, no more than Baudelaire, desired this scandalous notoriety, and all he asked was to be allowed to carry on his work in peace. He suffered quite as much as did the poet, from being continually misunderstood, and was no more indifferent than he to ordinary rewards and honours.

In 1862 there occurred an event of significance for the future of Manet's painting – the visit of a troup of Spanish dancers to the Hippodrome in Paris. He and Baudelaire went every evening to see the star, Lola de Valence, perform. As they watched the wild, almost exotic, dancing the poet must have dreamt of Mauritius; while the painter may have thought of Rio, where he had been dispatched in a merchant ship, as a young man, to distract his mind from his passion for painting. Lola de Valence was the subject of several of his pictures, amongst them the beautiful portrait which now hangs in the Louvre. Baudelaire composed a quatrain for it which, although it evokes the picture to perfection, cannot rank amongst the highest achievements of his poetry. For Manet the encounter was more significant artistically;

for it was the beginning of his interest in Spain, which was to be one of the most fruitful influences on his art.

Baudelaire has often been adversely criticized for never having written an article on Manet's work, when there were several of his good pictures that were painted before he died. He knew *Le Buveur d'Absinthe* and could have mentioned it in his *Salon* of 1859 – except that he made a practice of not discussing works which had been refused – as *Le Buveur d'Absinthe* had been. In 1863 he published an article on Constantin Guys as 'the painter of Modern Life'. Why not then on Manet as 'The Painter of the Future'? That was the year of *Le Déjeuner sur l'Herbe*, and Baudelaire also knew *Le Gamin aux Cerises*, *Le Chanteur Espagnol*, *Lola de Valence* – for which he wrote the quatrain – and *Le Guitariste*. He mentions this last picture in his article entitled *Peintres et Aqua-Fortistes* in 1862 – the few words of praise in this article are, in fact, all that he ever wrote publicly about the painter. He did, however, support him in private! He flew to his aid when he thought he was being unfairly treated by the critics,[13] and wrote long letters of encouragement to him when he was discouraged, letters which Manet greatly valued.[14] He inspired him to persevere in the vein best suited to his genius, and gave him what he himself had received from Poe, in a similar critical moment of his own career, confidence in his powers and in his aspirations.

The discovery of Wagner and friendship with Manet distracted Baudelaire for a time from his dark thoughts of failure, suicide and death. They gave him the courage to continue in his own ambitious plans for furthering his fortunes, the most important of which was his attempt at election to the French Academy.

In the meantime the affairs of Poulet Malassis had been going from bad to worse. There had been the unfortunate case of his *Mémoires de Lauzun* in 1859. Neither the *Balzac* by Gautier, nor the *Gautier* by Baudelaire, had sold well, nor the fine complete edition of the works of Piron. *Les*

Paradis Artificiels on which both he and Baudelaire had counted had been no more successful. By the middle of 1860 de Broise was going round with a long face, making it perfectly clear to everyone that he thought the business was on the verge of collapse. From the very first he had disliked his partner's publishing venture, especially because of the ruffians with whom it now entailed consorting. All he had ever asked, and what he had expected when he had married the daughter of old Poulet Malassis, was to be permitted to go on living quietly in Alençon, printing the local paper and the directory, as the firm had done since time immemorial. He was now constantly urging his partner to insist on Baudelaire repaying the sum he had owed since 1859; but, in 1860, the poet was incapable of repaying anything.

Poulet Malassis had enjoyed one piece of good fortune in buying outright for a couple of hundred francs the novel of Edmond Duranty entitled *Le Malheur d'Henriette Gérard* – not entirely by luck for he had realized its possibilities when he had read it in manuscript.[15] But this novel, which proved a great success, was initially published in an edition of only twelve hundred copies, and this was not enough to keep the business from foundering, much less put it on its feet again.

In desperation Poulet Malassis and de Broise began to think of other plans. One of these was to produce, in competition with big publishers like Lévy and Bourdillat, shoddy cheap little books, sold for a shilling. Baudelaire was very much opposed to this plan,[16] because he considered that the firm had made a name for itself with well-printed books, sold at five or six shillings, and that it would now ruin its reputation with no corresponding financial gain.

Hitherto Baudelaire and Poulet Malassis had succeeded in avoiding having to pay instalments on debts both the same day. By judicious borrowing from each other, and counter-borrowing, they had so far managed to keep bankruptcy at bay, but it was the poet who chiefly profited from the arrangement, for he was deeply in his friend's debt.

The scheme was becoming increasingly difficult to work by reason of the pressing nature of the debts, and the shortness of money on both sides. With de Broise at his back, nagging and complaining, Poulet Malassis himself began to regret his association with Baudelaire, and to imagine that without him he might be saved – in this he was unjust, for he was scarcely more businesslike himself and had, in a very short time, ruined a prosperous concern. Baudelaire, on his side, was frequently hurt when his publisher used to write to him complaining about his improvidence, and the confusion of his financial situation,[17] suggesting that they should part company, so that he could succeed in getting his works published elsewhere, and then repay what he had borrowed. 'We'll founder and sink together,' he kept on repeating in panic.[18]

'I've only hurriedly read your letter,' Baudelaire wrote,[19] 'and I believe – until I have time to go into the matter thoroughly – that it contains a dream full of rashness. We must consider everything very carefully! I wouldn't refuse, for anything in the world, to take any step which might be of service to you. But, honestly, have we come to that? You must consider what it would cost me to part from you! We've got far more than mere money transactions binding us together – numerous though these are, as I know only too well! There's a charm in our relationship which I'd never find anywhere else. I'm not saying this to flatter you, or to pay you compliments! You well know that you sell more slowly than other publishers, and so you can't be suspicious of the feeling of friendship which prompts what I'm saying to you! In any case, unfortunately, if Hetzel wants anything of mine, it certainly isn't my critical works, the value of which he doesn't even guess.... I'll try to come round to see you tomorrow, or the day after.'

As he considered ways and means of retrieving his tottering fortunes, Poulet Malassis, at the instigation of Baudelaire, conceived the mad and romantic plan of opening a bookshop to save the middleman's profit, where the beautifully printed books published by the firm could be displayed and seen to advantage. Hitherto he had found the greatest difficulty in persuading booksellers to give his productions sufficient prominence in their windows, and he had only a Paris office where the books were stored and ordered as needed by the firms. Had he been businesslike, and if he had possessed capital at his back, the venture might have prospered. There is no doubt that his work ranks amongst the most interesting publishing ventures of nineteenth-century France. With enough backing to go on losing money for a few years more, he might in the long run have reached success and prosperity. As it was, it was only when his business had disappeared that the public realized how original he had been. In his short six years as a publisher he had brought out the first edition of *Les Odes Funambulesques* of Banville, and his complete works as well; *Les Poèmes Barbares* and *Les Poésies Complètes* of Leconte de Lisle; two editions of *Les Fleurs du Mal, Les Paradis Artificiels* and *Gautier* by Baudelaire; *Émaux et Camées* and *Balzac* by Gautier; the poetry of Sainte-Beuve; *Portraits du dix-huitième Siècle* by Monselet; *Lettres Satyriques* by Babou; *Essais sur l'Époque Actuelle* by Montégut; *Esquisses Parisiennes* by Banville; several novels by Champfleury; memoirs and documents on the French Revolution; a history of the press in eight volumes; and the unpublished works of Piron. He would have been rich if he had possessed the sums which these works published by him were eventually to fetch.

At the end of 1860 Poulet Malassis rented a ground floor in the Passage Mirès, at the corner of the Rue de Richelieu, near the Bourse, an ideal and central situation. A large sum of money was expended on decorating the shop, which opened in January 1861, in time for the publication of the second edition of *Les Fleurs du Mal*.[20] Everything was solid as well as elegant in style. The bookshelves were of massive oak, and above them were hung medallions representing the writers published by the firm – Hugo, Gautier, Banville, Babou, Leconte de Lisle, Baudelaire, Asselineau and Monselet – and some of these were the work of Lafond and Legros. At the back of the main counter, fixed into the woodwork, was the trademark of the firm, representing on a scroll encrusted with enamel, a chicken flapping its wings, and slipping off its perch – a pun on the publisher's name – and the same design was carried out in several colours on the china stove designed by Bracquemond.

Poulet Malassis did not, however, take his shop seriously. For him it was only a new and fascinating toy, a *salon* where he entertained his friends, who came more for the pleasure of his witty conversation than to make purchases. It was a pity that he did not appoint a stern manager to run the business side; someone with more character and energy than timid and crotchety little de Broise. He might have become one of the most famous and picturesque figures in the publishing world in Paris. He certainly possessed all the necessary qualities – culture, taste, wit, generosity and charm. And it was indeed his generosity and kindheartedness which were largely responsible for his ruin, since he soon became the prey of impecunious Bohemians like Monselet and Babou, who were professional *tapeurs*, notorious cadgers and spongers. They were always to be seen hanging round the shop at lunch-time, hoping for a free meal, and their hopes were rarely disappointed. Poulet Malassis never failed to invite them either to one of the near-by restaurants, or else to his own flat, since he was famous for his luncheons and dinners.

There was more conversation than business carried on in the Passage Mirès, where Poulet Malassis expounded his magnificent plans for the future of the firm – a beautiful edition of the *Iliad* and the *Odyssey* translated by Leconte de Lisle, a third and more luxurious edition of *Les Fleurs du Mal*. He was also contemplating having a stall at the international exhibition which was about to open in London.

De Broise, however, was growing progressively more anxious. He was a married man with a family, unwilling to be implicated in the bankruptcy which he saw imminent, and he wanted, in his mean and cautious way, to escape while the going was good, to separate from his brother-in-law before the crash occurred. He therefore suggested that the time had come to divide the activities of the business. He himself would keep, as his share, the printing works at Alençon, with the contract for the local paper; while his partner took the shop and the publishing activities. He knew perfectly well that the printing works and the contract had been, for years now, the only source of income and that the publishing business and the shop had to spend money with profits which were dubious and to be made only in the very dim future. Poulet Malassis does not seem to have realized that his share was very much of a Barmecide portion and so agreed.

It was the steady reputation of de Broise which had for some time been keeping the business together. So, when it became known that he had separated from his brother-in-law, the banks began to grow suspicious and refused credit. Next it was the turn of the firms with whom he did business to clamour for repayment and to refuse further supplies.

'You're entirely mistaken,' Baudelaire wrote to him,[21] 'in your explanations to account for the refusals. When I have the pleasure of seeing you again, I'll explain everything to you fully. Here, briefly, is the gist of the matter. The clerk stated that you hadn't settled your account within the agreed time, and another clerk, who had obviously been to the bank, declared that the business had been worth more in the days of de Broise and that his departure explained the refusal of the bank at Alençon. You can see that I haven't made all that up. You've tried in your letter to make me feel your annoyance with me, which as a matter of fact I recognized is fully justified. But it's no use! I'm suffering enough myself from what has happened, and I've received

too many good services from you to be able to think of anything else!'

Poulet Malassis was still clamouring for repayment of his
loan – or at least part of it – but it was a time when the poet
was totally without funds. The second edition of *Les Fleurs
du Mal* was not doing well. He had hoped that its success
might make up to him for the failure of *Les Paradis Artificiels* in the previous year, from which he had also hoped
so much. There was, however, little advertisement for it,
and there had not even been enough review copies. There
were only three important notices. Two had been unfavourable – one by Alphonse Duchesne in *Le Figaro* and one by
Pontmartin in *La Revue des Deux Mondes* – and one favourable by Leconte de Lisle, in *La Revue Européenne*, which
had appeared only a year later. Even this was not inspired
by genuine admiration and liking for Baudelaire and his
writings – de Lisle made his review the pretext for discussing poetry in general, the latitude which should be the right
of every artist, and the deplorable contemporary taste in
literature in France. It was, in fact, a veiled reply to the
criticism to which he himself had been subjected, and contains not one word of intelligent appreciation of *Les Fleurs
du Mal.* The two unfavourable notices were more flattering to
Baudelaire as a poet; both reviewers obviously hated his work
and would gladly have seen it destroyed, but both, realizing
that he was someone who must now be taken into account,
forced themselves to consider it seriously – this in itself was a
victory for the poet – and both admitted that he possessed
great talent, although he had scandalously abused it. Duchesne
even declared that he was one of the three greatest poets of
the age, far below Gautier, but a little above Banville. This
was a significant admission when one remembers that Vigny
was still alive, Hugo also, though in exile, and Leconte de
Lisle at the height of his powers. The critic would not admit,
however, that Baudelaire had any philosophy of life, only a
masterly technique which he had used for unfortunate ends.
Having in this way tried to be objective and fair, he allowed

his spite full rein, and painted a very unpleasant picture of the poet, using passages from *Les Fleurs du Mal* as evidence. Pontmartin also allowed him great talent, but said that he had a diseased and unhealthy nature, and regretted that he should have wasted so much time in corrupt investigation because he did not know how to enjoy beauty. Both of them took him for granted as a great poet who, unfortunately, 's'est trompé de route'.

By the middle of 1861 it was obvious to everyone that the months of the firm of Poulet Malassis were numbered and that, when it disappeared, Baudelaire would be dragged to ruin in its wake, that his books would be sold off cheaply, almost as waste paper, and that other publishers would hold their hand, waiting to see whether they could get him on their own terms, when his situation had become desperate. Realizing this he had to consider how best to save himself. It was the lowest ebb of his spirits and fortunes.

Baudelaire never saw things simply and realistically, but always through a mist of rosy romanticism, and the plan he now conceived for rehabilitating his fortunes was the wildest of his schemes, which had never erred through moderation. Now, encouraged by friends as much lacking in a sense of reality as he – they may, of course, have urged him on as a joke, or have imagined that he himself was playing a trick on the public – he decided to go up for election to the French Academy. In July 1861 he began to consider the project seriously, and to approach his friends for support. Many of them were profoundly shocked when they learned of his proposal. The poet realized that his talent was not popular, that he irritated many people, and that most misjudged him as a pornographic poet, but he was incapable of seeing himself clearly with the eyes of others, or of realizing the full extent of the horror he awakened in most of his readers – and the astonishment he caused even in moderate men. It would never have occurred to him that cultured opinion could mistake his meaning, or that the Academicians themselves might regard his presumption at offering him-

self for election as an outrage, the attempt of an 'untouch-
able' to force his way into their temple.

It was the same as when he foolishly imagined that the
government would decorate him in compensation for the
indignity it had put on him in his trial in 1857. When the
Feast of the Assumption passed in August 1863, and the list
of new honours was published without his name, he was
bitterly disappointed – especially as Murger and Sandeau
figured in it.[22]

Sainte-Beuve, a practical man, who always realized clearly
what other people were thinking – in this manner he had
been able to turn his insight to his own advantage – was
surprised that a man who otherwise had an acute critical
faculty, should be so lacking in social intuition; and that a
man of forty, who had mixed for twenty years with men of
letters of the capital, should not be able to gauge the result
of his action on the most conventional and reactionary section of the literary world.

Baudelaire's attempt to secure election to the French
Academy has usually been misunderstood. Most people, not
realizing that he could be so simple as to imagine it a feasible
project, have thought that he was merely trying to play one
of the tricks for which he was famous, and they considered
this the best trick of all. One modern critic has even
asserted[23] that he was only indulging his masochistic tendencies in order to find occasion for suffering in his failure
– as if Baudelaire needed extra cause for suffering at the end
of 1861! He was, on the contrary, in deep earnest, although
he may have pretended later, when he saw his mistake, that
he had merely been offering himself as a scapegoat for the
rest of his fellow-poets. In 1861 he was serious but he miscalculated the strength and nature of his unpopularity. In
spite of his deep-ingrained and instinctive confidence in his
own talent, there was in him as well a feeling of insufficiency
and doubt, fear that his belief in himself might after all
be only self-delusion. This inferiority complex had been
one of his tortures since childhood, and it would have made

a difference to him to receive public recognition, the recognition of a cultured body of opinion, for this would have helped him to bear with courage his lack of popular success. Recognition would also have given peace and contentment to his mother who appreciated tangible results and honours, and she would no longer be able to taunt him with his failure, if he were a member of the Academy. The title of Academician would have enabled him to sell his books, and it would have silenced public opinion, especially those who were jealous of him and were taking advantage of his lack of popularity to attack him cruelly and unjustly. There were as well small emoluments attached to membership of the Academy, and facilities for making money with the prestige of the title. Baudelaire was at this time anxious above all else to be able to command a paying public for his writings.

'I'm quite willing to accept your compliments,' he wrote to Poulet Malassis,[24] 'which, by the way, don't at all console me, on the aristocratic nature of my works, but I want the public to pay me, and I don't care whether it understands me or not.'

It is clear from his letters to his mother, between July 1861 and February 1862, in which he refers to his candidature, that he was quite serious in his attempt and did not consider it ridiculous. When he first began to consider the possibility of election, he said to his mother: 'Membership of the Academy seems to me the only honour which a man of letters can solicit without shame.'[25]

Later, when he had suffered humiliation from a host of Academicians, he told her that he was offering himself for election chiefly to please her.

'Believe me, if you like,' he wrote to her,[26] 'but I'm going through with this mad scheme, chiefly for your sake. As far as I'm concerned, the only thing that interests me is the amount of the miserable little emoluments attached to the honour. For you must know that I don't need the approbation of all these old fools – I'm only using the expression which some of them use about the others – but I said to myself that you attached great importance to public honours and that if, by a miracle – for that is the only way to describe it – I should be successful you'd be overjoyed. It's true that I also thought: "If by the most extraordinary piece of luck I was to succeed, my mother would understand at least that I can't remain any longer in the ignominious position in which I now find myself."'

These letters do not show that he really considered his project hopeless, even though it was hazardous.

There were two places vacant – that of Scribe and that of Lacordaire. Baudelaire intended to offer himself for election to the latter's seat, since he had always greatly admired his spiritual work, not only on account of Lacordaire's ideas, but also on account of the language in which they were expressed.[27] As he considered himself primarily a poet with a spiritual aim, he saw nothing incongruous in the fact of applying for Lacordaire's chair. But all those who heard of his choice, even those friends who professed to admire him, thought it an added piece of impudence on the part of the author of *Les Fleurs du Mal* to presume to follow in the footsteps of the author of *Les Confessions*. Even Sainte-Beuve treated the matter as a joke and, when Baudelaire went to inform him of his plans, he burst out laughing and said to him: 'This is tremendous! Your attempt doesn't at all surprise me, and I bet, to put the finishing touches to your audacity, you're going to compete for Lacordaire's chair!'[28]

Baudelaire was deeply hurt to discover that, even after *Les Paradis Artificiels*, an old friend like Sainte-Beuve should not have realized that his chief preoccupation had been, for years, spiritual and moral.

Shortly before Christmas 1861 Baudelaire began his visits, the humiliating ordeal which all candidates for election to the Academy must undergo, of calling on all Academicians, even on those whose support they have no hope of obtaining, and whose opposition and ill-will are well known beforehand. Many of them refused to receive him as they considered his candidature an outrage. For a man so sensitive and so thin-skinned, the whole proceeding was a constant torture, and he frequently complains to his mother of his humiliations. Some of those who consented to receive him did so expressly to insult him, as did Villemain.[29] Then, weary of the indignity, he tried to find out which of them would not receive him badly, in order to call on the others when he would be sure not to find them at home.

'Try and find out for me,' he wrote to Asselineau,[30] 'not whether I can win Augier over to my side – I imagine that's impossible – but if I can safely call on him without demeaning myself, and without being humiliated.'

He was doubtful of what Augier's attitude to him might be, on account of his unfavourable comments on the *École du Bon Sens,* of which the dramatist was the most important member.

Baudelaire seems to have remained under the delusion that Mérimée was favourably inclined, as he had been at the time of his trial in 1857, and he refers to him several times in his correspondence. It is strange that he should ever have received this impression. The only time Mérimée ever supported him was at the end, when he was paralysed, and that was to obtain a small pension for him from the Imperial government. In one of his letters, Mérimée refers to him in a way which is far from flattering:[31]

'As I scarcely go out nowadays,' he wrote, 'I read a great deal. They've just sent me Baudelaire's complete works, which have maddened me! He was insane and died in a public ward, after writing some poems which earned the praise of Victor Hugo, but which have no claim to fame beyond the fact that they were banned for obscenity. But now they are trying to turn him into a misunderstood genius!'

Baudelaire had the added humiliation of being obliged to make his calls on the successful and prosperous Academicians shabbily dressed and on foot, when everyone of importance in Paris possessed his own carriage. Lamartine, an

old man now, and forgotten since 1848, received him charm-
ingly, in a style worthy of the son of a former ambassadress
of France, and, with the courtly manners of a former diplo-
mat himself, made him feel at ease, but he tried to dissuade
him from a project in which he saw nothing but disappointment for him.[32]

One of the few benefits which Baudelaire gained from his
ill-starred candidature, was belated friendship with Vigny.
The pity was that this sympathetic understanding came so
late. Vigny was even then dying of cancer – his death
occurred the following year – and he was in constant pain,
so that he could receive few visitors, and only for very short
periods. He was one of the few eminent writers of the age
whom Baudelaire felt that he could respect and admire,
and he had wanted to meet him for a long time, although
he had not dared previously to bring himself to his notice.
Unwilling to make a purely formal call, and perhaps be
turned away if Vigny were too ill, he wrote and begged to be
told when his visit would not be inconvenient. Vigny, in
spite of his delicate health, received him and kept him for
three hours; Baudelaire went away dazzled by his charm and
kindness, and, since Vigny was a sincere and honest man,
his advice was valuable.[33] So overcome was Baudelaire by
the unexpected sympathy of a man of sixty-five, a generation
older than himself and thus unprepared by instinct to feel
in harmony with his inspiration, that he wrote to him immediately on his return home, and sent him all his published
writings, in a desire to be appreciated and understood by
him.

'I got back home yesterday quite dazzled by your kindness,' he wrote to him,[34] 'and since I desire most earnestly
to be understood by you, I'm sending you something more
than you asked for. In the two pamphlets I enclose – *Wagner*
and *Gautier* – you may find passages that will please you.
Here are also *Les Paradis Artificiels*, to which I'm weak
enough to attribute some importance. The first part is entirely by me. The second is the analysis of the book by De

Quincey to which I've added, here and there, but very humbly, a few personal ideas. Here too are the *Fleurs* – the last copy I've got, on decent paper. The truth is that I'd intended it for you this long time. All the old poems have been revised, and all the new ones are indicated by a pencil mark in the *Table of Contents*.

'The only praise which I crave for this book is recognition that it isn't a mere collection of poems, but that it has got a beginning and an end. All the new poems were deliberately composed to fit into the strange plan which I'd already conceived....

'I thank you, Monsieur, once again, for the charming manner in which you received me. I wasn't at all expecting it, in spite of the picture I'd already formed in my mind of you. You're for me a further proof of my conviction that great kindness and perfect charity always accompany great talent.'

Vigny read, if not everything which Baudelaire sent him, at least the poems, and was deeply moved by them. He was one of the few people who discovered in him what he would have liked others to see in him.

'Since the end of December,' Vigny wrote to him,[35] 'I've been very ill and almost the whole time in bed. But there I read your words and reread them. I must tell you that these *Fleurs du Mal* are, on the contrary, *Fleurs du Bien* for me; how much they charm me and how unjust I think you are towards this nosegay so deliciously fragrant with the perfume of spring, to have given it this title so unworthy of it. But, how much I regret, at times, that the air is poisoned with a stench, as if from Hamlet's graveyard.

'If your own health permits you to come and see how I manage to disguise the wounds of mine, come on Wednesday at four o'clock in the afternoon, and you'll learn, you'll read, you'll feel, how I've read you. But one thing you won't know and that is with what pleasure I've also read to others, to other poets, the real beauties of your poems, too little appreciated as yet, and hitherto too superficially judged.

'You had told me, at first, that your official letter to the Academy had already been dispatched. In my opinion that was an error, and I told you so, but a mistake which could no longer be undone, and I resigned myself to seeing you flounder in that quagmire. But now that you tell me it was only a project, I advise you frankly not to persist along that tortuous path which I know so well, and not to send in a line suggesting your name as a candidate for any of the vacant chairs. When I see you, I'll have time to put before you my very serious objections, and I'm sure you'll understand them.

'*Venite ad me!*'

Vigny well knew, from bitter personal experience – he had made six vain attempts himself at election and had been successful only on the seventh – that there was nothing in store for Baudelaire but senseless humiliation, since the Academy would never elect him. But Baudelaire was not yet prepared to listen to wise advice.

At this point Sainte-Beuve at last had to break the silence he had preserved hitherto on Baudelaire's writings. In his official capacity, he was obliged to discuss the candidates. It was all the more impossible for him to remain silent, after the commotion that had occurred three years before, as a result of one of Hippolyte Babou's unfortunate articles. In February 1859, Babou, thinking he was doing Baudelaire a service – or perhaps merely wishing to attack the natural enemy of all other critics, the successful Sainte-Beuve – published an article in *La Revue Française* in which he pointed out how curious it was that a famous critic should notice favourably a book such as the *Fanny* of Ernest Feydeau, and yet remain silent about *Les Fleurs du Mal*. He mentioned no names, but it was clear to everyone which critic was intended. He ended his article by saying that although this critic, seated in his meteorological observation post, was on the look-out for the literary currents of the future, so far from dragging a remarkable work out of obscurity and revealing it to the public, a work which was destined to reach posterity but which might remain unknown unless some authority drew attention to it, so far from risking quixotically his reputation and popularity in a foolish act of honour and justice, this critic had lauded *Fanny* to the skies, but had remained silent about *Les Fleurs du Mal*.

The effect was even more spectacular than Babou can ever have hoped, for there was sufficient truth in it to wound Sainte-Beuve bitterly. But what Babou had certainly not expected, was to rouse Baudelaire's annoyance. Baudelaire had no desire to be championed by the like of Babou, and particularly not in this way. He was, moreover, afraid that Sainte-Beuve might imagine that he himself had inspired the attack, especially as the same review of *Fanny* had been the occasion of his own reproach to the critic, but on behalf of the *Madame Bovary* of Flaubert. To write privately, however, was a very different matter from voicing a grievance in the public press, and he would never have sunk to that. In spite of disappointment, he was genuinely attached to Sainte-Beuve – he understood him and found much in him to admire, and it was one of his characteristics not to be attached to people by reason of the good they did him. It is probable that he understood perfectly well the reason why the critic did not champion him openly. It was only after a bitter struggle that Sainte-Beuve had reached his present eminence. He was a member of the Academy, a guest at Court, and his ambition was now to become a Senator. After more than thirty-five years of incessant toil, he was tired and only desired peace, and that nothing should endanger the refuge he had built for himself. Baudelaire understood all this and did not bear him any ill-will for being reluctant to jeopardize his security. He wrote immediately to him to explain that he had had nothing to do with Babou's article and had not even known that it was being written. Sainte-Beuve in his answer pours out the vials of his wrath and bitterness, and shows himself for what he was, a thin-skinned and spiteful man. Very cleverly he tries to make Baudelaire feel that he has been offended as well, and advises him never to publish anything in a paper which has insulted them both. He went on to say that for the past twelve years he had been aware of Babou's spite and jealousy, and had kept a record of everything. 'Nowadays,' he added,[36] 'envy has no serpents round its head; its skin is mottled, its smile is no more than an ugly grimace, and, although it tries to be amiable, it has the kind of face that cannot possibly arouse sympathy in anyone. Today, envy's name is Babou!' He ended by advising Baudelaire not to worry whether he had succeeded in proving to others that he was worthy of note, assuring him that he had sufficient talent to dispense with approbation. This advice strikes an ironical note when one reflects how badly in need of support Baudelaire was at this time.

Now, in January 1862, Sainte-Beuve, who himself never forgot a grudge, must have remembered the Babou affair, and realized that many of Baudelaire's friends would be waiting to see what he would do. This time he could not avoid writing of him, but he was careful to do so in such a manner as not to cause offence in high places, or give the impression of any intimacy with so dubious a poet. He did not give himself away before the respectable readers of *Le Constitutionnel* by acclaiming unreservedly the man who created such a scandal in his age, and who had been so un-justly condemned. His article as support for Baudelaire was less than useless. In the superior tones of one performing a duty, and with a seeming air of generosity, as if to an un-known writer whom, out of the kindness of his heart, he did not put in his place in spite of his presumption, he gently relegated him to his rank amongst the minor poets of his age. Yet Baudelaire's name is the only one of the candidates of that time which has reached fame. Octave Feuillet may still be remembered as a second-rate novelist, but the rest – Jules Lacroix, Cuvillier Fleury, Camille Doucet – are all long-forgotten celebrities.

Talking of Baudelaire Sainte-Beuve said:[37]

'At first one wondered whether Monsieur Baudelaire, in

putting in for election, was not trying to play a trick on the Academy, trying to personify, as it were, an epigram, and suggesting to its members thereby that it was high time that they thought of adding to their number a man of letters, and a poet, to wit Théophile Gautier, his master. Many a member of the Academy, completely ignorant of his existence, had to be shown how to spell Monsieur Baudelaire's name.'

Sainte-Beuve could not have suggested more subtly that the poet was totally unknown.

'It is not as easy as one might imagine to prove to a body of Academicians who are statesmen and politicians that there are in *Les Fleurs du Mal* some poems very remarkable for their talent and artistry; or to show them that in *Les Petits Poèmes en Prose, Le Vieux Saltimbanque* and *Les Veuves* are two gems, and that, in short, Monsieur Baudelaire has succeeded in building for himself, far away, at the extreme point of a promontory hitherto considered uninhabitable, at the extreme borders of the known regions of Romanticism, a strange little pavilion of his own, highly ornamented and artificial, but, at the same time, mysterious and elegant, where Poe is read, and exquisite sonnets are recited, where narcotics are indulged in for the purpose of writing of them afterwards, and where a thousand poisonous drugs are drunk in the finest porcelain cups.'

This detail was not calculated to advance the poet's candidature with the Academicians.

'This strange little pavilion made of marquetry, with its highly ornamented and complicated originality, which for some time now has been attracting attention, at the extreme point of the Kamtschatka of Romanticism, I call Baudelaire's *folly*.'

Many critics have here misunderstood Sainte-Beuve's meaning, thinking he was referring to what he called the poet's madness, whereas what he was wanting to suggest is the '*folie*', the little country house, usually of curious architecture and decoration, very sophisticated, where people went to enjoy themselves, without restraint and away from prying eyes.

'The poet is pleased to have constructed something which was thought impossible, in a place where no one ever imagined that anyone could go.

'Does this suggest, after one has explained everything to the best of one's ability to respectable, and somewhat startled, colleagues, that these highly-spiced refinements and curiosities should seem to them sufficient qualifications for membership of the Academy, and that the author himself can seriously have thought so?'

Sainte-Beuve does not answer his question – suggesting that it is through a desire not to be too hard on his presumptuous young friend – but he adds the only argument which occurs to him to give in support.

'What is certain is that Monsieur Baudelaire gains from being seen in person, and, that where one expected to meet a strange and eccentric man, one sees a polite, exemplary and respectful candidate, a well-bred young man, refined in his speech and, in every respect, a gentleman in the accepted meaning of the word, "tout à fait classique dans les formes".'

It was as if Sainte-Beuve were trying to give the impression to his readers that he had met Baudelaire for the first time when he had come to pay his official call and that, contrary to what he, in common with most other people, had expected, he had been gratified to find a gentleman where he had imagined a slovenly and disreputable Bohemian. It must be admitted that it is somewhat inadequate to say of one of the greatest poets of the age that he is presentable and that his manners will not disgrace him. How vastly different is this article from Vigny's generous letter! Sainte-Beuve, like Vigny, did, however, try to dissuade him from persisting, and said:[38]

'I told you, from the outset, that, in my opinion, the task was hopeless! Leave the Academy what it is now, more surprised than shocked, and don't outrage it by returning to the attack, especially not for the chair of such a man as Lacordaire. You're a man of moderation, and you yourself must realize that.'

At last, seeing that he was receiving little support, even from his friends, Baudelaire allowed himself to be persuaded to withdraw, and Sainte-Beuve wrote to describe to him the impression which his letter of resignation had made upon the assembly.

'And when they came to your last phrase of thanks,' he said,[39] 'couched in terms so modest and so polite, they all said aloud: "Very good indeed!" And so you left behind you a very favourable impression. Isn't that something?'

Nevertheless, although in his heart he had never expected to be successful, Baudelaire was disappointed at the result of his mad project. He had hoped, at least, to be acclaimed by certain people whose opinion he valued, to have his talent spoken of with words of praise, and to be described as perhaps one of the literary martyrs of his age. But, except for Vigny's letter, which was obviously sincere, and a few fulsome compliments by Lamartine which were only so much froth, he had experienced nothing but humiliation. It was a severe blow to discover what others really thought of him, and to realize that even those who most admired him did so only apologetically and never in public.

This attempt at retrieving his fortunes, like all previous ones, proved unsuccessful, and he did not know which way to turn for help.

[6]

Implacable Life
1862 — 1864

RESPITE for Baudelaire was always of short duration, and 1862 was a disastrous year. It opened tragically with another seizure, which took a new and more terrifying form, and he mentioned it to no one, but merely referred to it in his *Journaux Intimes*, when he thought that he might be losing his mind. He lived for the remaining years of his life with this torturing fear.[1]

'Today, twenty-third January 1862, I received an ominous warning. I suddenly felt the cold wind from the wings of madness!'

The year began with his disappointment in connection with the Academy, and ended with the bankruptcy of his publisher, when his works were sold up for little more than the paper on which they were printed.

At the beginning of 1862 he had no regular work on any paper.[2] *La Revue Fantaisiste*, on which he had counted, had gone bankrupt. It had been edited by a scatterbrained youth of nineteen, Catulle Mendès, and its life lasted only nine months, from the middle of February 1861 until the middle of November. *La Revue Européenne* had also crashed, and he had published in it, between April and November 1861, five poems as well as his article on Wagner.[3] It was alleged at the time that the Government had sacrificed this review to *La Revue Contemporaine*, and whether this is true or not, Baudelaire certainly believed it.[4] After its failure he was unable to return to the *Contemporaine* on account of his quarrels with its editor earlier in the year, when he had even threatened to challenge him to a duel because of the changes the editor had made in his poems without obtaining his consent. It had seemed at one time as if he had found a permanent berth there, for Calonne, after reading *Les Fleurs du Mal*, had been anxious to secure him as a regular contributor. Between 1858 and 1861 he had published in the review, as well as his *Les Paradis Artificiels*, thirteen poems. But relations had never been anything but strained, and the editor, who fancied himself as a stylist, used to take it upon himself to 'improve' Baudelaire's poems. This ended in a quarrel fiercer than the rest, when Calonne accused him of being conceited and self-sufficient, and the poet then paid him all he owed him in order to be able to sever his connection with the paper.

Finding himself with no work at the end of 1861, Baudelaire tried to obtain a grant from the Government – there was a special fund for the purpose of helping and encouraging writers who were in difficulties. As long as his stepfather had been alive, pride had prevented him from applying, but, after his death, he made use of the fund in June 1857 for the first time, and for several years after that obtained small grants on divers occasions. In 1860 he was allotted several sums amounting to a total of thirteen hundred francs.[5] The authorities seem to have considered this sufficient for he received only a small grant the following year. Now, at the end of 1861, he judged that his situation warranted substantial help from the literary fund, and he therefore applied to Pelletier, one of its administrators, who had been a close friend of his stepfather and had been responsible for obtaining a grant for him in 1857.

He wrote first on 13 December, giving as chief grounds the failure of *La Revue Fantaisiste* and *La Revue Européenne* and mentioning that the disappearance of the latter had been due partly to government intervention in favour of *La Revue Contemporaine*, and to which it was now impossible for him to return because he had left it on the invitation of the *Européenne*. His letter was a personal appeal to a friend on whom he counted for help in his need, and he asked for a substantial grant, a thousand francs, to keep him from

anxiety for some months, to enable him to finish the books
on which he was working, and also to find a publisher for
those already completed.[6] Pelletier does not seem to have
been able to come to his rescue, for three weeks later, not yet
having received an answer, Baudelaire wrote once more to
ask for an interview in order to put his case in person, and
he ended:[7]

'Imagine, Monsieur, the plight of a man who asks for a
favour, and then may remain for a month without knowing
whether it can be granted, without even knowing whether
the request has even been received.'

Pelletier answered this time, expressing his good-will and
sympathy, but promising nothing, and when no results were
yet produced, the poet wrote once more on 12 February,
explaining further his situation, with arguments to support
his application. He appealed again on 19 March – this time
somewhat coldly – asking for an interview with the Minister
himself, in the hopes of obtaining a definite reply, instead
of being put off with promises and excuses, and asking to be
allowed to state in person 'why I consider my application
justified!'

Following these requests he was granted on 2 April the
paltry sum of three hundred francs instead of the thousand
which he had counted on, and from which he had intended
to pay six hundred to Poulet Malassis.[8] Now he had nothing
to offer him, and little prospect of anything for he had
found no firm willing to risk publication of his aesthetic
articles. Poulet Malassis was in too low water to risk any
further money on these unprofitable ventures, and now, in
an attempt to save himself at the eleventh hour, was publishing works of a kind bound to bring him into a clash with
the authorities and hasten his downfall – pornographic and
obscene books and, because he was still the revolutionary of
1848, politically dangerous pamphlets. In December 1861 he
was, in fact, fined for his subversive booklet, *L'Empereur
et le Roi Guillaume.*[9]

Finally, at the request of one of his creditors, a printer

probably jealous of him, Poulet Malassis was imprisoned for debt in November 1862.[10]

He was treated with extreme severity and not even permitted to see friends. A month after his arrest, they had not yet been able to visit him.[11] In the meantime he was declared bankrupt, and Baudelaire was left without a publisher, with all his works on his hands, while other firms waited to see whether they could obtain them cheaply, for they could afford delay and he could not.

Even though beset by difficulties, Baudelaire's behaviour did not tend to make his own situation any easier. He was still in constant dispute with editors, one after the other, and he could not remain on good terms with anyone for whom he worked. The fault was not entirely his since everything he wrote was, from the first, suspect, and editors scrutinized his copy more carefully than that of any other contributor. This in itself, with someone as touchy as Baudelaire, was sufficient to fire off an explosion. To one of his editors, Louis Martinet, who had ventured to suggest certain changes in his text, he answered : [12]

'I'm very much grieved to hear that a piece of criticism which was inspired by a profound admiration for Daumier, does not please you in its entirety, for I've made a prolonged study of caricature and comic art. Since you believe – as far as I can gather from your note – that my article can't be published under the régime of Napoleon the Third, you must then simply delete it. Please believe in my sincere attachment to you, but I can't submit to circumstances, for, since my childhood, I've formed the habit of believing myself to be infallible. I realize, however, that I must yield to you in all cases where you think the contrary would harm you, but, in this case your belief is false and merely the result of foolish timidity, and I'm convinced that the article could appear with pleasure to everyone and no danger to yourself. Nevertheless let's delete it !'

It is true that in his case, in terror of the law, editors went beyond their prerogatives and changed, not merely what might be dangerous to themselves, but also actually what they did not like in his text. It must also be admitted, in their defence, that they found it difficult to make the public accept his work and, with the best will in the world, they were not often able to employ him, since subscribers used to complain and threaten to terminate their subscriptions. There are many references in Baudelaire's correspondence to the tortures he was experiencing at the hands of his editors. When he became a contributor to *La Presse*, after the failure of *La Revue Fantaisiste* and *La Revue Européenne*, he described to his mother what he was enduring:[13]

'I'm writing to you today from the offices of *La Presse*, where I imagined I had found a safe berth, and now I'm enduring the tortures of the damned, real tortures. I may have to abandon the idea of publishing my prose poems here, and they would have meant fifteen numbers. How on earth am I ever to make up that money?'

Later there occurred his epic dispute with Charpentier, the editor of *La Revue Nationale*, where he was then publishing his prose poems, after his final quarrel with Houssaye, the editor of *La Presse*. Charpentier had altered his text without consulting him, after the proofs had been corrected and the poet had passed them for printing. When at last he saw his work in the finished form, he wrote in fury to the editor:[14]

'I've just seen the two extracts published in *La Revue Nationale*, and I've found some inexplicable changes in them since I saw the proofs and passed them. That is the reason, Sir, why I've fled from so many papers and reviews. I said to you: "Cross out the whole passage if a comma displeases you, but don't cross out the comma for it is meant to be where it is." I've spent the whole of my life learning how to construct a sentence and I can say, without boasting, that what I send to the printers is complete down to the smallest detail. And do you really and sincerely believe that "les formes de son corps" is the equivalent of "son dos creux et sa gorge pointue", especially when it refers to the black races of East Africa? I want to thank you very much for having given me the hospitality of your columns, but I know what I'm writing about, and I describe only what I've seen personally. If you had only warned me in time, I could have deleted the whole passage.'

With these endless quarrels, entailing endless delays, Baudelaire was without money and his life was truly distressing. He was seen wandering about in his shabby clothes amongst the down-and-out who were the only people he could now bear to see. He suffered tortures at the end of each month when money had to be collected somehow to pay innumerable creditors, and this was becoming increasingly difficult since he had drained all sources of supply. He had then to set out on these weary expeditions on foot, to distant quarters of Paris, to try to obtain loans from friends, mortgages on his future and past works, even pawning articles which he, or his mother, did not immediately need. He used to return home exhausted and fling himself on his bed, incapable of doing anything. Every time that the bell rang, a spasm of terror would seize him, for he always imagined that it must be another creditor coming for repayment, someone who had managed to track him down. To avoid being discovered and imprisoned for debt, he was obliged to sleep in a different place almost every night, and he wandered from La Place de la République to La Rue Pigalle, from L'Hôtel de Folkestone to L'Hôtel de Dieppe, from Paris to Neuilly, and he found peace nowhere. He did not dare go to his mother's house for rest, since he realized that he would immediately be found there and thus bring disgrace on her home. What could he say to her now, since, for years, he had used up all expressions of hope, and for years he had assured her, with perfect sincerity, that it would soon get better? Now he scarcely dared hope for better things, since one cannot continue indefinitely to borrow on the future.

Sometimes, when he returned to his mean lodgings, to the sordid attic in the cheap hotel where he could often not afford either light or heat, he, who had loved beauty, and had dreamt of living surrounded by it, would gaze with horror at the broken furniture, the grey-white curtains which hung before the window-panes where the raindrops left blackened furrows in the coating of grime, thence to the calendar, where the fateful days for repayment were marked in red, and finally to the heaps of uncorrected manuscript lying piled up on his table. He would then long for escape, and, closing his eyes, would dream of wonderful fairylands, of magnificent palaces with marble staircases, pools and fountains, with softly falling water, like cascades of jewels, loggias where the loveliest of women sat gazing at their reflection in the limpid pools as they combed their flowing hair. There were flowers everywhere, scents, and music coming out of the distance, from amongst the trees; there was everything to delight and charm the senses, and make the mind forget. It was the land described in *La Vie Antérieure*: [15]

> *J'ai longtemps habité sous de vastes portiques*
> *Que les soleils marins teignaient de mille feux,*
> *Et que leurs grands piliers, droits et majestueux,*
> *Rendaient pareils, le soir, aux grottes basaltiques.*
>
> *Les houles, en roulant les images des cieux,*
> *Mêlaient d'une façon solennelle et mystique*
> *Les tout-puissants accords de leur riche musique*
> *Aux couleurs du couchant reflété par mes yeux.*
>
> *C'est là que j'ai vécu dans les voluptés calmes,*
> *Au milieu de l'azur, des vagues, des splendeurs,*
> *Et des esclaves nus, tout imprégnés d'odeurs,*
>
> *Qui me rafraîchissaient le front avec des palmes,*
> *Et dont l'unique soin était d'approfondir*
> *Le secret douloureux qui me faisait languir.*

Then, suddenly, a knock came upon the door, like the blow of a pole-axe on his head, and the vision dissolved as swiftly as a fade-out on the screen:

En rouvrant mes yeux pleins de flamme
J'ai vu l'horreur de mon taudis,
Et senti, rentrant dans mon âme,
La pointe des soucis maudits;

La pendule, aux accents funèbres,
Sonnait brutalement midi,
Et le ciel versait des ténèbres
Sur le triste monde engourdi.[16]

He was back again in his sordid room, where the clock upon the chimney-piece, with its mournful ticking, seemed to shriek in his ear, with jarring voice: 'Je suis la vie, l'insupportable vie, l'implacable vie.'[17] Life had seized hold of him once more, driving him like a dumb beast to the inevitable slaughter-house.

During these months his misanthropy grew, and he hated all his fellow-men, for there was little on account of which he could be grateful. All he asked now was to be able, as he said, to flee from the horror of the human face,[18] and he imagined that everything had changed, that it was no longer the delightful Paris which he had known in his youth. Sainte-Beuve's secretary, Troubat, once said to Crépet, that he often used to meet Baudelaire at the Casino in La Rue Cadet, wandering amongst the people on the Promenoir, terrifying the women by fixing his eyes upon them but appearing not to see them. They said that he gave them the creeps and they thought him mad.[19] Sometimes he used to sit alone at a table in a café, with a glass of beer before him which he did not touch. It was the gayest moment of the Second Empire, the time of the waltzes of Métra and the light music of Offenbach, the period of *La Vie Parisienne* and *La Belle Hélène*. In the café, where he sat alone, men were coming and going, with girls on their arms, and all were happy and carefree, but he alone was grim and silent.

'What are you doing there?' asked fat and jovial little Monselet, coming up to his table one day, and trying to rouse him from his despondency. Baudelaire only glanced

up at him, with a dark and sinister gaze, as he answered:
'I'm watching an endless procession of death's heads!'[20]

Another time Audebrand said:[21]

'The author of *Les Fleurs du Mal* used to appear fairly
often, in the evening at the Café Robespierre. He was no
longer the Charles Baudelaire whom I had known formerly,
in 1845, in the offices of the *Corsaire-Satan*, but aged and
faded, and, although still slight, somewhat heavier than
formerly. He was eccentric-looking with his white hair and
his clean-shaven face, and less like a poet of bitter and
voluptuous pleasures than a priest from Saint Sulpice. Not
having lost his taste for misanthropy he used to sit alone at
his table, having asked for a pot of beer and a pipe which he
filled with tobacco, lit and smoked without uttering a single
word the whole evening. But, as he had many new friends
and admirers amongst the young men of the Passage
Choiseul, it often happened that one of these neophytes used
to go up to him to pay him court, with great ceremony, or
else to read him his poems. Sometimes one of them, imagining that he would give him pleasure, showed him a paper
in which he was mentioned. "Monsieur," Baudelaire used to
answer, with signs of deep disdain, "who gave you that rag?
Let me tell you that I never look at such filth – *ces
cochonneries-là*." And he went on smoking again.'

This is one of the last impressions left of the poet.

He became increasingly solitary and, although he had
once been a brilliant conversationalist, was happy now only
when he was alone. Many of his prose poems reflect this
search for solitude, as for instance *À une Heure du
Matin*.[22]

'Enfin seul! On n'entend plus que le roulement de quelques fiacres attardés et éreintés. Pendant quelques heures,
nous posséderons le silence, sinon le repos. Enfin! la tyrannie
de la face humaine a disparu, et je ne souffrirai plus que par
moi-même.

'Enfin! Il m'est donc permis de me délasser dans un bain
de ténèbres! D'abord, un double tour à la serrure. Il me

semble que ce tour de clef augmentera ma solitude et forti-
fiera les barricades qui me séparent actuellement du monde.

'Horrible vie! Horrible ville!'

He looked back on his day, and found that he had spent it
without profit; he thought of all the detestable people he
had met, the meaningless things he had said, and he hoped
now that night might bring him strength and help him to
recover pride and dignity, allow him to believe once more in
himself. The poem ends with a passage in which the autobiographical intention is clear:

'Mécontent de tous et mécontent de moi, je voudrais bien
me racheter et m'enorgueillir un peu dans le silence et la
solitude de la nuit. Âmes de ceux que j'ai aimés, âmes de
ceux que j'ai chantés, fortifiez-moi, soutenez-moi, éloignez
de moi le mensonge et les vapeurs corruptrices du monde; et
vous, Seigneur mon Dieu! accordez-moi la grâce de produire
quelques beaux vers qui me prouvent à moi-même que je ne
suis pas le dernier des hommes, que je ne suis pas inférieur
à ceux que je méprise!'

Peace did not, however, come to him immediately. Alone
in his room, in the small hours of the morning, it was the
past, the squandered past, that he saw revolving before him:
all the years for which he had so little to show. Was it all his
own fault, he wondered, or was it ill-luck, 'le guignon', against
which he had so often railed? He could not be anything but
mercilessly sincere with himself, and he did not feel that he
could, with honesty, attribute all the wastage to fate. As he
wrote to his mother then: [23]

'There are, I believe, few examples of a life so lamentably
frittered away as mine has been. I don't mean to tell you –
and moreover I shouldn't have the time to do so – the terrible
struggles with myself, and all the despair.'

He remembered then all the failures he had seen, and
wondered whether he too was one of these, a member of the
large horde of those who would never succeed. He could not
bear to think any more about the past. Sleep and darkness,
he decided, were the better part.

> *– Vite, soufflons la lampe, afin*
> *De nous cacher dans les ténèbres.*[24]

But perhaps some escape could yet be found and life might
perhaps be made bearable if one despised it, if one disguised
it, and found a way of not seeing it, if one could always be
in a state of intoxication – with art, with music, with poetry,
with love or even drugs or drink. Later Renan was to say:

'What indeed is it that saves us? It is merely the reason
which each one of us has found for living! And the means
of salvation are not the same for each. For one man it is
virtue, for another it is the passion for truth; for yet another
love of art; for others again, ambition, travelling, women
and, at the lowest degree of the scale, drugs and drink.'

Baudelaire writes in his prose poem, *Enivrez-Vous*:[25]

'Il faut être toujours ivre. Tout est là; c'est l'unique question. Pour ne pas sentir l'horrible fardeau du Temps qui brise
vos épaules et vous penche vers la terre, il faut vous enivrer
sans trêve.

'Mais de quoi? De vin, de poésie ou de vertu, à votre guise.
Mais enivrez-vous.

'Et si quelquefois, sur les marches d'un palais, sur l'herbe
verte d'un fossé, dans la solitude morne de votre chambre,
vous vous réveillez, l'ivresse déjà diminuée ou dispersée,
demandez au vent, à la vague, à l'étoile, à l'oiseau, à l'horloge,
à tout ce qui fuit, à tout ce qui gémit, à tout ce qui roule, à
tout ce qui parle, demandez quelle heure il est; et le vent, la
vague, l'étoile, l'oiseau, l'horloge, vous répondront: "Il est
l'heure de s'enivrer! Pour n'être pas les esclaves martyrisés
du Temps, enivrez-vous sans cesse! De vin, de poésie ou de
vertu, à votre guise!"'

Nevertheless the poet could see no possible salvation in
this world. Life, he says, is the ward of a public hospital,
where each man is obsessed with the longing to move,
imagining that he would surely be cured if only he could
change his bed. But no place on earth has power any longer
to tempt the poet's desires, and he begs to be transported

anywhere, anywhere provided it is out of this world.[26]

In his solitude and distress Baudelaire turned his thoughts increasingly towards the contemplation of eternity. When at night he could not sleep, and gazed out at the expanse of the sky, he used to wonder whether there was anything beyond that heavy black roof which hung, as it were, over a dungeon where captive humanity was chained. Was the sky perhaps nothing more than the painted drop-scene of an ill-composed melodrama, in which poor mortals play the parts assigned to them, in an action full of senseless 'blood and thunder'? Or was it merely the pall of smoke over an immense witch's cauldron, in which humanity boiled incessantly, to be brewed into some infernal charm?

The poems which are the result of this state of mind were published later under the title *Nouvelles Fleurs du Mal* in *Le Parnasse Contemporain* in 1866. They are such poems as *Épigraphe pour un Livre Condamné, Le Gouffre, L'Examen de Minuit, Le Couvercle*, and *Les Plaintes d'un Icare*. Of them a reviewer wrote:[27]

'In the fifteen poems by Charles Baudelaire, which *Le Parnasse Contemporain* has just published, there are no longer to be found that clever combination of immoral and horrific elements which were to be found in 1857 in *Les Fleurs du Mal* and which earned for it a conviction in the law court. Instead of this deliberate and revolting realism, of which *Une Charogne* is a typical example, there is a sorrowful nostalgia for idealism. Realism is often only the expression of disappointed idealism. This seems to be the case with Monsieur Baudelaire, to judge from his poem *Les Plaintes d'un Icare*.'

This review is a small sign of change of mind in the public, faint awareness of the true quality of Baudelaire's art. The poem mentioned ends:[28]

> *En vain j'ai voulu de l'espace*
> *Trouver la fin et le milieu;*
> *Sous je ne sais quel œil de feu*
> *Je sens mon aile qui se casse;*

Et brûlé par l'amour du beau,
Je n'aurai pas l'honneur sublime
De donner mon nom à l'abîme
Qui me servira de tombeau.

The answer perhaps lay somewhere, and perhaps God knew the meaning of the riddle, the wherefore and the why, the reason for all the suffering of the world. Baudelaire himself had seen so much helplessness, disease and pain, during his wanderings through the city, and in the underworld of sin and ugliness, so much suffering in dumb creatures who did not understand what they did nor why they were in the world, but there was perhaps a plan somewhere, in which misery and despair had a meaning, in which all the victims fitted: [29]

'Quelles bizarreries ne trouve-t-on pas dans une grande ville, quand on sait se promener et regarder? La vie fourmille de monstres innocents. – Seigneur, mon Dieu! vous le Créateur, vous le Maître; vous qui avez fait la Loi et la Liberté; vous le souverain qui laissez faire, vous le juge qui pardonnez; vous qui êtes plein de motives et de causes, et qui avez peut-être mis dans mon esprit le goût de l'horreur pour convertir mon cœur, comme la guérison au bout d'une lame; Seigneur, ayez pitié des fous et des folles! O Créateur! peut-il exister des monstres aux yeux de Celui-là seul qui sait pourquoi ils existent, comment ils se sont faits et comment ils auraient pu ne pas se faire?'

At this time Baudelaire was anxiously in search of God for himself, and was even contemplating going for a retreat to the Benedictine abbey of Solesmes. When a friend of his told one of the monks of his project, the latter is alleged to have replied 'Indeed! if he comes we shall receive him!' [30]

To reach God, it was necessary to develop humility and complete forgetfulness of self. It was then that Baudelaire discarded his ambition for worldly fame or personal glory, and thought only of becoming a saint. There now arose in his mind a new conception of the Dandy, no longer endowed solely with external characteristics but with spiritual qualities added. He was aiming now at an ideal no longer merely literary or artistic, but largely spiritual. It was no longer perfection of art he strove to attain, but perfection of soul. His *Journaux Intimes* show him trying to rid himself of his faults, and to build something out of the ruins. The phrase returns again and again: 'Before all else one must aim at being a great man, and a saint *for oneself alone*. That is the only important thing in life!' [31] And again: 'I must work incessantly, even without hope of gain, do away with all kinds of pleasures, and become what one might call a model of greatness!' [32]

He was now able to pray. 'Grant me the strength,' he wrote,[33] 'to do my duty immediately and every day, and thus become a hero and a saint.' With prayer he felt a sensation of security and peace, and was then able to write: 'The man who says his evening prayers is like a captain who places sentinels on duty. He can sleep.' [34] In the heart which had been harrowed by sin and suffering, and watered by bitter tears, there now sprang up a new spiritual flower, unknown to him hitherto; trust in God's mercy and forgiveness, in him who had been guilty of the sin of despair, believing in the irreparableness of the past which nothing could efface. Now he could hope for redemption and absolution. In 1863, having accepted his sufferings and tribulations in a spirit of Christian humility, he was able to bow down before the Almighty and even give thanks for having been sorely tried. 'My humiliations have perhaps been benefits from God,' he said.[35] In his humility he turned to the only source of comfort that he knew, to God Whom he calls the friend whom we seek in vain, 'l'ami qui manque toujours',[36] 'God is the eternal confidant in that tragedy in which each of us is the hero.' [37] And having thus reached complete renunciation of self, having resolved to do his duty every day and to trust to God for the rest, he asks himself whether his 'phase of egoism is over for ever!' [38] When he had reached the stage of accepting his suffering and tribulations in a spirit of Christian humility, he composed *L'Imprévu* which marks a further

step in his spiritual pilgrimage. This poem, with its beautiful
Biblical line, 'Mon âme dans tes mains n'est pas un vain
jouet', might indeed have altered the plan, the architecture,
of the third version of *Les Fleurs du Mal* which he did not
live to finish. The poem ends: [39]

> — *Cependant, tout en haut de l'univers juché,*
>   *Un ange sonne la victoire*
>
> *De ceux dont le cœur dit: 'Que béni soit ton fouet,*
> *Seigneur! que la douleur, ô Père, soit bénie!*
> *Mon âme dans tes mains n'est pas un vain jouet,*
>   *Et ta prudence est infinie.'*
>
> *Le son de la trompette est si délicieux,*
> *Dans ces soirs solennels de célestes vendanges,*
> *Qu'il s'infiltre comme une extase dans tous ceux*
>   *Dont elle chante les louanges.*

When he published this poem, the poet appended a note
to it which said: 'The author of *Les Fleurs du Mal* is here
turning his thoughts towards eternal life. It was bound to
come to that.'

On the publication of *Les Fleurs du Mal*, Barbey d'Aurevilly had said that there were only two courses open to its
author, either to blow his brains out, or to become converted,
and Baudelaire had now chosen the second course. But,
with his habitual irony, he had added: 'Note, however, that,
like all the newly converted, he is very strict and very fanati-
cal!' After this he wrote with peace: [40]

'I swear to myself to take henceforth the following rules
as everlasting rules for my life: To say every morning my
prayers to God, the fount of all strength, of all justice, to
Mariette and to Poe, to beg them to intercede for me, to pray,
then, to grant me the necessary strength to accomplish my
duties, and to my mother a long enough life to enjoy my
transformation. To work all day, or at least as long as my
strength permits me. To beg Him to grant me life and
strength for my mother and for me. To divide everything I
earn into four equal parts — one for daily life, one for my

creditors, one for my friends, and one for my mother. To follow the principles of the strictest sobriety, the first of which is total abstinence from all intoxicants of whatever kind they may be.'

After he had accepted his fate with humility and resignation, his faculty for work returned, and he felt, what he had not experienced for many months past, full of energy and hope. He had not written to his mother for six months, having nothing good to tell her, but now he was able to write without shame, for he felt that he had won a victory over himself.[41]

'You must have been racking your brains,' he wrote to her, 'trying to discover why I'd ceased writing to you! The true and only reason was the disgust I felt with myself – but perhaps you guessed it. I'd promised myself only to write to you when I'd shaken off the weight of lethargy which had been oppressing me for so many long months. How did it happen that I sank so low, to such a depth that I myself thought I'd never be able to rise again; and how was I able, by the most excessive hard work to cauterize my illness, so that I didn't even feel fatigue? I don't at all know. I only know that I'm completely cured, and that I'm a miserable creature full of sloth and violence, and that habit alone can counteract the vices of my temperament. My idleness had become such terrible suffering, the insane obsession with my literary incapacity had so terrified me, that I flung myself headlong into work, and then discovered that I'd lost none of my powers. But there is grave danger in allowing oneself to lie fallow.'

It has frequently been said that Baudelaire turned to religion only when his health was ruined, and his mind weakened through disease. These sceptics should read the *Journal* of Maine de Biran, who had embarked on his philosophic writings, at the end of the eighteenth century, a convinced atheist, and had finally reached, through the exercise of his intellectual faculties alone, complete faith in God. More than anyone else in the nineteenth century, he contributed to bring religious thought back into philosophy. During the last years of his life he realized that, with his pride of intellect, he had relied too much on himself alone, and he discovered, after he grew old, that he had only played with the shadow of things, and had never reached reality. Finding in himself that he had built only on shifting sands, that there was no stability in him, he turned, little by little towards God, and, a few months before he died, he begged for the final revelation: 'Lord, unseal Thou my eyes, lest I fall asleep in death, in the death of the spirit.' [42]

These words were written shortly before he died. Five years earlier, he had entered in his diary the fine passage where he says that it was not weakness, nor failing health, nor old age, nor fear of death, which had finally driven him into the arms of God.

'They say,' he wrote, [43] 'that if men become pious and devout as they advance in years, it is because they are afraid of death, and what awaits them in the life hereafter. But from my own experience, I am convinced that without any such terrors or imaginings, religious sentiment may develop as one advances in years, because then the passions having become stilled, imagination and sensibility are less excited or excitable, and reason therefore less troubled in its workings, less obscured by the images or affections which once absorbed it. Then God, God Almighty, emerges as it were from behind a cloud; our soul feels Him, sees Him, and turns towards Him, the source of all light, because now that the world of sensation begins to fail us, now that phenomenal existence is no longer bolstered up by external and interior impressions, we feel the need to lean on something which abides for ever and will not play us false, on reality, on an absolute and everlasting truth, and because, finally, this religious sentiment, so pure in its essence, so delightful to experience, can make up to us for all our other losses. The fear of death or of hell has nothing in common with this feeling; on the contrary it is diametrically the opposite.'

It is possible to believe that Baudelaire found at last in

religious peace the 'renonciation totale et douce' of which Pascal wrote on the night of his great spiritual experience.

The work on which Baudelaire had been engaged, and to which he now returned with new zest, was his *Spleen de Paris*, his collection of prose poems, which give a vivid impression of his life and thoughts during this period, for many of them are autobiographical in character. The subject matter is very similar to that of the poems in verse of this period – they are written in a pessimistic mood and reflect the ageing and saddened Baudelaire. But they express as well his change of heart and his spiritual ambitions. They are further *Tableaux Parisiens*, like those in *Les Fleurs du Mal*, expressing even more poignantly his compassion for outcasts and failures.

Spleen de Paris was a work of which Baudelaire was most fond and he had been working on it for many years – was indeed still working on it – in Belgium at the time of his final collapse. Ill-luck had, however, dogged it from the very beginning and he was never to see it published, save for a few odd fragments in reviews.

The idea of writing such a work had come to him after he had read the *Gaspard de la Nuit* of Aloysius Bertrand, who had died in hospital in 1842, and, in his preface, he explains his intention: [44]

'It is while turning over the leaves, for at least the twentieth time, of the famous *Gaspard de la Nuit* of Aloysius Bertrand, that the idea came to me to try to achieve something similar, and to apply to the more abstract modern world, or rather to a world which is more modern and more abstract, the same method which he used for the life of olden days which is so strangely picturesque. Who amongst us has not dreamt, in his ambitious moments, of poetical prose which was at the same time musical, but without rhyme or rhythm, yet supple and distinct enough to adapt itself to the movements of the soul, to the meanderings of reverie, and to the prickings of conscience?'

Baudelaire began writing prose poems as early as 1855,

when two appeared in the *Hommage à C. G. Denecourt,
Fontainebleau*, entitled *Crépuscule du Soir* and *Solitude*.
Six more appeared in *Le Présent* in August 1857, under the
title *Poèmes Nocturnes*, with an accompanying note which
said that they would be continued in the next issue, but no
more were published. The reasons for the discontinuation
are not known – Baudelaire may have quarrelled with his
editor or perhaps the public was not interested, especially
as it was that month that the trial of *Les Fleurs du Mal* took
place. In 1859 a selection of them was accepted by *La Revue
Française*, but like almost every periodical with which he,
Baudelaire, was connected, the review went bankrupt before
the poems appeared. Next some were published in *La Revue
Fantaisiste* in 1861, whose hold on life was also weak, for it
lived for only a few months. By the end of 1861 the poet had
a large batch of prose poems ready and he approached many
editors so that they could be serialized before they came out
in book form. He thought of Arsène Houssaye, whom he had
known when he was editing *L'Artiste*, who had printed some
of his work in that review and who was now directing *La
Presse*. He began negotiations in December 1861, but they
were very protracted. The poems began to appear only at the
end of the following August, and Houssaye was finally
persuaded to publish them, on the insistence of Hetzel, who
wanted to bring out an illustrated edition but was held up
because they had not yet all been serialized.

'Read this carefully,' Hetzel wrote:[45] 'for I wish I could
write it in letters of fire. You've got the opening section of the
prose poems of Baudelaire, and before I can publish them,
they must first appear in a paper. Baudelaire is an old friend
– what matter! for we've got many friends – but he's without doubt the most original prose writer and the most individual poet of our age – and no paper has the right to
withhold such a classic, a compound of compositions which
are not classic – publish it then quickly – immediately –
and give me the opportunity of reading it. Really original
people are rare!'

This decided Houssaye, and a large selection of prose poems was published in *La Presse* in August and September 1862. Houssaye was, however, a vain and dictatorial editor who made his staff feel who was master, and Baudelaire soon began to endure his usual ordeal while his work was being butchered and mutilated, and these were the 'véritables tortures' of which he wrote to his mother in his letter of 22 September. The third instalment was being printed and relations between editor and contributor were strained almost to snapping point. There was worse to come. After the poems had begun to appear, one of Baudelaire's enemies pointed out to Houssaye that in the second and third instalments three poems were included which had already been published elsewhere, and thus were no longer exclusive to *La Presse*. True, they had been revised and altered but this on the top of all the previous irritation with Baudelaire, infuriated Houssaye; he threatened to take the matter to law, and broke the contract, refusing to publish any further instalments. Baudelaire was very much upset, not only at the loss of fees, but especially at the implied accusation of sharp practice. He did not feel that he had done anything reprehensible. He had wanted the whole collection to appear together in *La Presse*, so as to give the total impression before it was published in book form. He did not consider that appearance in the *Revue Fantaisiste* could count as previous publication, since it was defunct and copies were unobtainable. And, even while it existed, it had no more than about a hundred readers. He had taken advice from friends beforehand and they had assured him that there was nothing unscrupulous in his action. He had also revised, and almost rewritten most of the poems. He begged for an interview with Houssaye so that he could explain everything to him in person.[46] The meeting – if indeed Houssaye ever granted it – came to nothing. Baudelaire was never able to be humble and obsequious, and Houssaye had always been jealous of his own personal dignity, and anxious to make everyone conscious of his power.

Between the end of September 1862, when he parted
from *La Presse*, and June 1863, when he published two prose
poems in *Le Boulevard* and two more in *La Revue Nationale*,
he did not succeed in publishing any further instalments
of his prose poems. And it was in June 1863 that he quarrelled with Charpentier, the editor of *La Revue Nationale*,
on account of the changes which he had made, without
consulting its author, in *La Belle Dorothée*. The result was
that Baudelaire ceased for several months being a contributor to the paper, and never became a regular member of the
staff. He published there odd isolated prose poems in the
last quarter of 1863, then no more until those which appeared
in *Le Figaro* in February 1864.

The modern city as a source of inspiration, used sym-
bolically, had been increasing in significance for Baudelaire,
and in his prose poems he wanted to do for contemporary
Paris what Aloysius Bertrand had achieved for his native
Dijon, when he evoked the Middle Ages. There is, however,
a marked difference between the two poets. Bertrand's are
more purely descriptive, while those of Baudelaire show
more outstanding spiritual and moral qualities. Bertrand's
poems may be narrative or descriptive, or sometimes a combination of both, but the most successful artistically are the
short descriptive pieces – *Ma Chaumière*, *Chèvremorte*, *Le
Soir sur l'Eau* or *Le Gibet*. His prose poem usually consists
of a short lyrical passage, containing a single theme, and
creating an impression of unity. Many are the subject matter
of a painting transposed into poetical prose. In this he differs
markedly from Baudelaire whose style is nearer to verse
and to the evocative power of music, and fulfils the conception that poetry is not merely writing in verse, but consists
of what the *Symbolistes* were to call 'un état d'âme', the
communication and suggestion of emotion.

Baudelaire wrote three types of prose poem. The anecdotal,
the descriptive or evocative, and a mixture of the two. Many
are indeed narrative, autobiographically narrative, but he is
most successful and original in those where the narrative

aspect is least present, in those which are suggestive and evocative. Such prose poems as *Le Cheval de Race*, *Les Fenêtres* or *Le Port* are amongst his most effective. To quote only *Le Port* : [47]

'Un port est un séjour charmant pour une âme fatiguée des luttes de la vie. L'ampleur du ciel, l'architecture mobile des nuages, les colorations changeantes de la mer, le scintillement des phares, sont un prisme merveilleusement propre à amuser les yeux sans jamais les lasser. Les formes élancées des navires, au gréement compliqué, auxquels la houle imprime des oscillations harmonieuses, servent à entretenir dans l'âme le goût du rhythme et de la beauté. Et puis, surtout, il y a une sorte de plaisir mystérieux et aristocratique pour celui qui n'a plus ni curiosité ni ambition, à contempler, couché dans le belvédère ou accoudé sur le môle, tous ces mouvements de ceux qui partent et de ceux qui reviennent, de ceux qui ont encore la force de vouloir, le désir de voyager ou de s'enrichir.'

Much of the substance of *Spleen de Paris* is the same as that of *Les Fleurs du Mal*, but, as it was composed over a much shorter period of time, during the last phase of the poet's creative life, it is more homogeneous in quality. On the whole, it is more mature in conception – or more consistently so – containing less turmoil and strife, more peace and serenity, and also more harmony in the contrast between *Spleen* and *Idéal*, between the flesh and the spirit. There is a closer alliance between the aesthetic ideal of the artist, and the spiritual ideal of the moralist, and we reach, perhaps, a fuller awareness of the final Baudelaire, when the Dandy-Artist had become the Dandy-Saint. The collection depicts man's spiritual ascent from materialism to spirituality, and the moral import of *Spleen de Paris* cannot be separated from its aesthetic beauty.

In *Spleen de Paris* the prose poem, as a literary form, comes of age, capable of standing alongside the verse poem as a vehicle of expression. Before Baudelaire it was little more than lyric prose but, with him, it reached moral,

aesthetic and spiritual status. Banville, discussing the rare
treat which the poet was offering to the readers of *La Presse*
in his *Spleen de Paris*, said that its publication was a literary
event of the most significant order.[48] Banville and Hetzel,
however, were exceptional in their day, and most readers
did not realize the artistry of Baudelaire's new venture.
The danger was, as the poet himself realized,[49] that the prose
poems might be taken for plans of poems which were
later to be written in verse. That was indeed what Catulle
Mendès declared,[50] and Leconte de Lisle was of the same
opinion.

Nowadays, enthusiasts discovering the poems in prose
for the first time are tempted to rate them even higher than
those in verse, but this is a distorted view. There have been
many magnificent French prose artists, but few French
poets in whom the essentially poetic quality has been so
marked as in Baudelaire, and his highest achievements lie
in the circumscribed form of verse, on the occasions when he
has succeeded in disciplining his inspiration, without at the
same time losing originality and power. The same themes
treated in both forms – *La Chevelure*, *L'Invitation au
Voyage*, *Crépuscule du Soir* – reach nobler heights when
translated into verse than into prose.

In July 1863 Baudelaire, once more without any source
of income, conceived a new plan. His faculty for devising
new money-making schemes, in spite of constant failure, is
a source of amazement. Poulet Malassis had been talking
for many months of settling in Brussels, to escape from the
creditors whom he could not pay and to bring out the
obscene little books which had always been published abroad
during the seventeenth and eighteenth centuries, and
thence smuggled into France. He was not averse from making money out of the vices of others, and thought that in
this manner he might yet retrieve his fortunes. Baudelaire
was very much opposed to this[51] and even on financial
grounds did not consider it a lucrative proposition. Although
he was far from being a puritan, he said that he had never

felt the faintest desire to possess one of these futile little books, even one with rare illustrations.[52]

He was, however, fired with the desire to accompany Poulet Malassis to Belgium, to try his luck in a new venture, in a country where he was not yet known. He was obsessed by the terror of dying in poverty, and he felt that he must do something to relieve the burden of his debts. The previous year he had said to his mother,[53] 'I despise people who care only for money, but I've a hideous terror of servitude and destitution in old age.' His plan was to make a tour of the main towns of Belgium, giving lectures on literary subjects. Belgium was in those days very much what the United States were for Europe in the nineteen-twenties, a gold-mine on a small scale. Asselineau says that Baudelaire's idea was to make a tour very similar to those made by Thackeray and Dickens round England and the United States, when they had earned substantial sums of money with comparative ease. There was, moreover, in Brussels a large circle of French refugees who had lived there since they had fled from France after the *coup d'état* of December 1851, and who were always ready to welcome any writer from the capital. To them, Paris was still the capital, and Brussels merely a provincial town in which their business forced them to reside.

In spite of everything which has been said to the contrary, this lecture tour was only a subsidiary consideration with Baudelaire. This can be clearly seen in the letters to his mother [54] where he discusses with her his reasons for leaving France. He was still vainly looking for a publisher for his works, now that Poulet Malassis was bankrupt, and he was hoping that in Brussels he could personally interest the important firm of Lacroix and Verboeckhoven which had published *Les Misérables* of Hugo, and had paid handsomely for it. This firm had a large capital and could afford to advertise extensively, as it sold all over the world. He would be certain of success, if they would consent to take over his work.

In August 1863, when he was planning to set out on his
travels to be in Brussels before the winter season began, he
found himself without ready money. He then conceived the
brilliant idea of obtaining a subsidy from the government,
in his quality of well-known art critic – this claim to fame
had never been in dispute – and he applied for a grant to go
and study art in Belgium. The prospect was not entirely mad
since subsidies were frequently given from the literary fund
for similar purposes – though not to men of such notoriety
as Baudelaire enjoyed.

Notwithstanding his inward qualms, Baudelaire always
approached those in high places with pride and dignity, and
never in the cringing spirit of one asking for patronage or
bounty. His letters of application were now couched in the
terms of one who believed that those in authority must
realize his importance and worth.[55] He wrote first on 3
August and imagined he would receive a favourable reply
by return of post. The letter was addressed to Marshal Vail-
lant, who, as Minister of the Emperor's Household, had
control also of the Ministry of Fine Arts. He did not ask in a
spirit of humility, but merely stated, after giving a list of his
qualifications and publications:[56]

'I am on the point of leaving France for some time, and I
await, from your kindness, the wherewithal to leave.'

Four days later, on 7 August, since no answer had yet
come, he wrote again, this time more coldly, though with no
greater humility or obsequiousness, but as if demanding
very politely his rights, the right to be subsidized, in his
quality of art critic, in order to produce a study of the art
galleries of Belgium. Scrawled across the letter can be seen,
signed by a certain Bellaguer, a note which states: 'I am
opposed to it on principle!'

Even then he did not lose hope. The following day, 8
August, he told Poulet Malassis that he could not oblige him
on a certain matter since he had to do his packing, and pay
all his last moment visits before leaving for Brussels in a
few days.[57]

A fortnight again elapsed, and then finally he received an answer, a flat refusal:[58]

'In answer to your letter dated 7 August,' the reply said, 'in which you expressed the desire to obtain, from the funds in my department, a grant to enable you to make a trip to Belgium, which was to become the subject of the book which you intend to publish in the future, I much regret to have to inform you that the state of the funds does not permit me to give a favourable answer to your request.'

The poet was furious, although it cannot be said that he had serious grounds for complaint, since three weeks is not an excessively long time for a Government department to take to answer a request for financial aid. He replied in one of his black rages:

'Monsieur le Ministre,' he wrote,[59] 'I have received today the letter in which you inform me that the funds do not permit you to comply with my request for a grant to enable me to make a trip to Belgium the object of which is purely artistic. If the refusal of Your Excellency had reached me a fortnight ago, it would have spared me much worry. As it is, I shall be happy if the complaint which I am here voicing may, in the future, draw your attention to these uncivilized and malapert delays towards a writer of my rank. I am convinced that many writers of greater fame have frequently felt the necessity of making similar painful complaints.'

This answer must have created a sensation in the Government department, for the phrase 'uncivilized and malapert delays' has been heavily underlined with a red pencil. Baudelaire never grew hardened to disappointment, and each successive one was always the cause of the same heartburning. Writing to his mother a few days later, he said: 'For the last few months all my plans, even those which seemed best founded, have crumbled away, one after the other.'[60]

It has been usually said that it was the poet's lack of resolution which postponed his trip to Belgium for nine months, and that he could not make up his mind to leave. The truth is that it would have availed him nothing to be resolute since he did not possess the means to carry out whatever plans he might make.

In the end it was Poulet Malassis who left first, on 15 September 1863,[61] and Baudelaire wrote to beg him to do his utmost to obtain a contract for him to lecture in Brussels in November.[62] The publisher was not successful in obtaining this contract and he did not yet leave Paris. Perhaps Poulet Malassis was too deeply involved in publishing his *Parnasse Satyrique du dix-neuvième Siècle* on which he set to work immediately on his arrival and which was advertised to appear early in November.

Baudelaire was still hoping to find in France a publisher who would take his complete works – his *Fleurs du Mal*, *Spleen de Paris*, *Les Paradis Artificiels*, and especially his critical articles, in which no one had yet expressed any interest. He did not wish to separate his poems from the rest of his writings, which he could have done, since they were his easiest work to place. He was afraid of being forgotten, because he had published nothing since the second version of *Les Fleurs du Mal* almost three years before, and people were always saying to him, 'Aren't you doing any work? When are you going to publish another book?'[63]

He asked for nothing better than to bring out a book, if he could only find a publisher. It was lack of popularity, rather than incapacity for work, which was hindering his production.

Finally, in desperate need of money, he was obliged to divide his writings, sold to Hetzel the rights on *Les Fleurs du Mal* and on *Spleen de Paris* for five years, and received an advance on the purchase price, the balance to be paid when he handed in the completed *Spleen de Paris*. Hetzel, who wished to produce an illustrated edition of both these works, was uninterested in the rest of his writings. He was, however, a fair and compassionate man, who released the poet later from his contract, subject to the repayment of the advance, so that he could try once more to place his complete works together, which had lost more than half their value by the absence of these two volumes.

At the same time Baudelaire was obliged in order to raise some money to sell his rights on his translations of Poe, since he had earned nothing for months, except the pitiable fees paid by *La Revue Nationale* for two prose poems in October 1863. The translations of Poe had been for years his sole regular source of income, and they had brought him in, for the most part, four or five hundred francs a year. He had expected to obtain between twenty and forty thousand francs for the rights, but Lévy would only offer the miserable sum of two thousand francs, and for that price obtained possession of five volumes of translations. The poet was not even able to enjoy the results of the sale, since the money was paid directly to his creditors, without ever passing through his hands.

In the autumn of 1863 Baudelaire wrote the last of his great aesthetic articles, the one inspired by the death of Delacroix on 13 August. It appeared in *L'Opinion Nationale* in September and November. The most interesting parts of this obituary are those in which he returns to aesthetic ideas already treated in earlier essays in criticism.

In November a piece of luck came his way which made him believe once more that fortune was at last going to smile on him. His old enemy, *Le Figaro*, which had torn him to pieces regularly for years, suddenly decided to publish his article on Guys, composed four years before, for which he had never been able to find an outlet, and which had lain for the past two years at the offices of *Le Pays*, the editor of which was much annoyed when he subsequently discovered that its author had dared to allow it to be printed elsewhere, before he had definitely refused it.

The article was preceded by a laudatory paragraph from the pen of Bourdin, whose review of *Les Fleurs du Mal* had been responsible in 1857 for drawing the attention of the authorities to the alleged obscenity of the book. Now Baudelaire began to wonder whether the tide had finally turned for him, and he might at last become a permanent contributor to 'la grande presse' and not be at the mercy of periodicals which had so precarious a hold on life.

This article, one of the most interesting and suggestive that Baudelaire ever wrote, could even nowadays, after nearly a century, serve as an illuminating introduction to the impressionist school of painting in France. It was composed during the same period as his *Salon* of 1859 and his essay on Gautier, but it possesses even more spontaneity, freshness and conviction. It sets forth clearly, moreover, his fundamental conception of beauty, what he considered its dual aspect – the eternal elements closely linked with those which were transient and fugitive. He found in the drawings of Guys the perfect answer to his plea in his *Salons* of 1845 and 1846, for the expression in art of 'la beauté moderne', and the title of the article – *Le Peintre de la Vie Moderne* – is significant. What he appreciated in the painter was his truth in rendering modernity, the elements which he himself had incorporated in his poetry, the passing elements which set their seal on an age, and without which no truth was possible. He realized that Guys' works could become precious archives of the civilized life of his time.

'M.G. garde un mérite profond qui est bien à lui: il a rempli volontairement une fonction que d'autres artistes dédaignent et qu'il appartenait surtout à un homme du monde de remplir. Il a cherché partout la beauté passagère, fugace, de la vie présente, le caractère de ce que le lecteur nous a permis d'appeler la *modernité*. Souvent bizarre, violent, excessif, mais toujours poétique, il a su concentrer dans ses dessins la saveur amère ou capiteuse du vin de la vie.'[64]

Having finally succeeded in publishing what he knew to be one of his major critical essays gave Baudelaire confidence and hope. *Le Figaro*, moreover, announced that it was to print, in the near future, several instalments of his poems in prose. Writing to his mother for New Year's Day 1864, he assured her of a radical improvement in his fortunes, and implored her patience and forbearance for only a few months more, when all would certainly be well. In January he was also offered the chance of contributing to *La Nouvelle Revue de Paris*, but there ensued his customary difficulties with all those who published him. The editor of the magazine, Le Barbier, asked him to delete the word 'imbécile' from his script, but he refused with acrimony and, after calling him a priggish usher – he had been at l'École Normale – removed his copy. Le Barbier, trying to defend what he called 'les coupures indispensables', said to Taine that Baudelaire was eaten up with inordinate vanity, and always tried to insist on every single word that he wrote being accepted without comment.[65]

Baudelaire still had *Le Figaro* on which to count. In February 1864, it printed a selection of his poems in prose, with a further complimentary foreword by Bourdin, announcing that they 'would be continued in our next'. They were not continued, and this was one of the most cruel and bitter disappointments of the poet's life. There was no opportunity for misconception, for the editor wrote personally to inform him that publication had been discontinued because the readers had been bored with the poems.[66] Anxious lest his mother should imagine that the blame for this might be his, he wrote to tell her the truth.[67] There is no word of complaint or anger in his letter, but only the extreme weariness which is beyond the relief of words.

'I must really write to you,' he said, 'or else you'll only imagine some mystery, for you've got the wildest imagination. The explanation is, however, very much simpler. It is merely because my poems bored everyone – so the editor told me – that they have been discontinued.

'I've fallen into the most horrible state of lethargy. Not only have I books and articles of all sorts in arrears – promised and even paid for – but I'm overwhelmed with a great deal of urgent business, some of it in Belgium. On the other hand, I suffer too much from never seeing you, and so I'm going to try to pull myself together, do the most urgent things, and try to obtain some money from two or three sources, so as to come and spend a few days with you. Then I move on to Brussels where perhaps fresh disappointments are in store for me, but perhaps also a great deal of money.

'I send you my very best love, and beg and implore you not to go and imagine foolish things, I've sufficient real causes for despair in my life, without adding to them any imaginary ones.

'If I could only stay at Honfleur until the tenth or fifteenth, it would do me a lot of good.'

PART FOUR

J'écoute en frémissant chaque bûche qui tombe;
L'échafaud qu'on bâtit n'a pas d'écho plus sourd.
Mon esprit est pareil à la tour qui succombe
Sous les coups du bélier infatigable et lourd.

[1]

The Lecture Tour
1864

BAUDELAIRE finally left for Belgium in April 1864. Perhaps he had grown tired of waiting for a contract, or perhaps Poulet Malassis, no longer preoccupied with his *Parnasse Satyrique du dix-neuvième Siècle*, now had the time to give his undivided attention to his friend's business, and had succeeded in obtaining for him the promise of a series of lectures for April. The latter is more likely; it does not seem possible that, a few days after his arrival in a town where he was unknown, Baudelaire would have been able to arrange matters for himself.

When Baudelaire left for Brussels he was within a few days of his forty-third birthday, but looked many years older, and he is described as an aged and white-haired man. From the photographs taken at the time a tragic face looks out, with a desperate hunted look in the dark eyes. There is courage still in the noble brows, though only deep disgust in the bitter mouth which drags down at the corners to form deep furrows that seem to cut into his face, running from nose to chin.

In 1864 Brussels was only a provincial town, still very self-conscious and unsure of itself. Belgium had existed, as an independent nation, for barely thirty years – it had become a kingdom in 1830, after being the cockpit of Europe since time immemorial. It possessed as yet no vigorous and independent literary or artistic life – this was not to happen until after 1883 – and the half century between 1830 and 1880 was a period of material consolidation which left little time or energy for artistic movements. The local writers followed the French Romantic movement, copying it in all its defects, when its influence was already waning in France, and showed little originality or feeling for style. When Taine visited Belgium in 1868, a few years after Baudelaire, he declared that Belgian literature was non-existent, and that the country was content to leave to other nations the part which Mary had played at the feet of Jesus, being satisfied for itself with that of Martha.

Nevertheless Brussels had four artistic clubs which played an important part in its social life: La Grande Harmonie, almost exclusively devoted to music, which organized concerts during the winter season; Le Cercle des Nobles, a conservative club the aims of which were social rather than cultural; Le Cercle du Commerce, which collected the big businessmen; and there was Le Cercle des Arts, alleged to be run solely by and for the benefit of the French refugees, which was culturally the most important club in Belgium.

When Baudelaire arrived he stayed at a hotel half way up an old street, which ran from the Grand Place in the direction of the Bourse. The hotel, though unpretentious, was far from being the cheapest he could have found. He continued to stay there, even when his financial state deteriorated, because he had become so much indebted to the landlady that it was impossible for him to leave.

His lectures were organized under the auspices of Le Cercle des Arts which met in a gothic palace opposite L'Hôtel de Ville. The first lecture was to deal with Delacroix and was first billed for 30 April, then for 1 May, and then for 2 May. It was well attended, because many wanted to see the notorious French poet whose name was a byword. The lecture was praised by the most eminent Belgian critic, Frédérix, who reported it very favourably in *L'Indépendance Belge*.[1] His friends alleged that Baudelaire was much encouraged by his reception, and that he had good hopes for the future. Reading between the lines of the letter to his mother, however, one wonders whether he really believed that even the first lecture had been an unqualified success. To his mother he said:[2]

'Here's a report of my first lecture – Frédérix – and they say it was a phenomenal success. But, between ourselves, I believe that everything is going badly. I've arrived too late, and there's terrific avarice and unparalleled slowness in everything, as well as a lot of empty heads! In short, the people are even more stupid than the French.'

He went on to say that, as the winter funds of the Cercle des Arts were almost exhausted, and the real object of his visit was to meet the publisher Lacroix, who was unfortunately away in Paris for the moment, he had consented to accept a reduced fee of fifty francs for the lecture he had given and for the one he was about to give, and had asked permission to give three further lectures free, after Lacroix had come back. Out of his lecture tour – in the capital at all events – he would thus gain the sum of one hundred francs.[3] This statement about the reduction of his fee is important in view of what he was to assert later.

The second lecture, given on 11 May, was devoted to Théophile Gautier. Remembering his reception at his previous lecture, Baudelaire was full of confidence as he stepped on to the platform, especially as he had recently written a study of the poet with which he had been well pleased, and he knew that he could now speak with feeling of a man whose talent he admired as much as Gautier's.

The fame of his first lecture had gone abroad and it was probably rumoured that he was not all that his reputation claimed, that the most innocent girl could listen to him without having cause to blush, for this second lecture was attended by a great crowd of women and girls. Brussels, then as now, had a large number of finishing schools where the daughters of the upper middle class and aristocracy were sent to put the crowning touches on the unsound fabric of their education. The teachers, to whose care they were entrusted, must have thought that here was a good opportunity to allow them to hear French straight from Paris, the pure language with no trace of a local accent.

Baudelaire was received with applause and he felt con-

fident. Then a most unfortunate event occurred! All through
his life some demon prompted him to strange actions which
he always afterwards bitterly regretted when he found
himself ostracized. He began by thanking his audience for
their kind reception at his first lecture, saying that he was
particularly touched since it had been the first time he had
ever spoken in public. 'I am all the more touched by the
kind reception you have given me,' he said,[4] 'since it is with
you I lost my virginity as a speaker – "ma virginité d'orateur"
– virginity which is no more to be regretted than the other –
"virginité qui n'est d'ailleurs pas plus regrettable que
l'autre".'

The effect was instantaneous! There were suppressed
giggles in the ranks of serried schoolgirls. The outraged
mistresses rose in a body, and marshalled their charges out
of the hall which was left almost empty. Into this almost
empty auditorium Camille Lemonnier crept shortly afterwards. He was a youth of twenty, who, as a schoolboy, had
read *Les Fleurs du Mal* with passionate eagerness. Having
heard of the first lecture, he decided to attend the second
and see the poet who had aroused such enthusiasm in him.
He was to become twenty years later the leader of the literary
renaissance in Belgium, but in May 1864 he was nobody,
only a nervous youth, frightened because he was late and
anxious lest the hall should be so overcrowded that he might
not get in. He found the stairs leading to the amphitheatre
empty, a janitor slid back the heavy silent doors, then the
loveliest voice he had ever heard, almost like a woman's
low-pitched voice, fell upon his ears, and the voice was saying
in beautifully modulated tones, enunciating clearly each
syllable, 'Gautier, the master and my master!'

Camille Lemonnier slipped into the hall, and, even when
writing *La Vie Belge* almost thirty years later, he still recalled his feeling of amazement as he saw the empty benches
in the vast theatre, and Baudelaire speaking to a handful of
people the words that a gathering of kings should have
heard.

There was a little table in the centre of the platform, and he was standing beside it in the light of a lamp, his beautiful slender hands accompanying, with rhythmic gestures, the modulations of his voice.

After an hour the small audience had still further diminished, and soon there were only two rows left, but Baudelaire did not seem to notice. He went on speaking, as he gazed into the distance, addressing the silent walls – and perhaps they seemed to him a more receptive audience than the one seated before him.[5]

Finally there was no one left but the spellbound youth who never forgot that day as long as he lived. Baudelaire at last finished, in a mounting crescendo, ending in the final cadence : 'I salute in Théophile Gautier my master, the great poet of the century.' Then, bending his slim figure from the waist, he gave three stiff little bows as if to a real audience, and, stepping between the curtains at the back of the stage, disappeared from view. Lemonnier was left alone, silent and moved almost to tears. The janitor came to remove the lamp, and he crept downstairs.

At the third lecture, which dealt with *Les Paradis Artificiels*, Baudelaire, recalling his experience at the previous lecture, completely lost his nerve. When he came on to the platform, he was shivering as if with fever, and stammered so badly that no one could understand what he was saying. Realizing that he was not holding his audience, he finished his lecture with his head buried in his notes, having seemingly lost interest, and merely reading. It is not known what occurred at the last two lectures, nor even if he ever delivered them, for there is no record of them.

Baudelaire was not the draw that was expected and many people were disappointed at not seeing someone more in accordance with the legend, someone eccentric, who looked as if he had just returned from a witches' sabbath, after a Black Mass. 'How strange,' a woman said to him.[6] 'You're quite respectable looking, and I'd imagined that you were always drunk, that you didn't wash, and that you stank!'

In Brussels they came to the conclusion that since he was polite and well-mannered he could not possibly have written *Les Fleurs du Mal*, and must be an imposter.[7]

When Baudelaire, as usual short of money, wrote to the club to claim his fees, the secretary sent the janitor with a note enclosing one hundred francs, saying that this was the fee for the two lectures, and that the others had been delivered free. By then Baudelaire had forgotten that he had accepted this arrangement after his first lecture, but only remembered that, in the first instance, a fee of a hundred francs for each lecture had been mentioned. He now thought he was being cheated because he had signed no agreement, that the Belgians were taking advantage of the fact that he was a helpless foreigner to deprive him of his due.[8] The Belgians have always been much pained at this accusation of sharp practice and have maintained that there must have been some mistake. A reading of Baudelaire's letters to his mother would have solved the mystery in a moment.

Baudelaire could not admit his failure to his mother. She had so much wanted him to succeed, and he had promised again and again that, at last, things would go well. He did not write to her for several weeks, and when he finally did write in the middle of June, he made pathetic efforts to make his defeat seem less complete – not because he was vainglorious, but because he wished to give her what little comfort he could. 'No one remembers lectures ever having been such a success as mine,' he said.[9]

He had not yet lost heart. He still hoped to wipe out all his arrears of debt with the contract which he felt sure he would sign with Lacroix and Verboeckhoven for the three books he had to offer – *Les Paradis Artificiels* and two volumes of criticism – unfortunately *Les Fleurs du Mal* and *Spleen de Paris* had been disposed of to Hetzel the previous year, and he did not know whether he would be able to get out of this contract. He was, however, finding obstacles in the way of meeting the directors of Lacroix and Verboeckhoven, who obviously did not want to see him. Yet he had

planned the five lectures especially to impress Lacroix, the
senior partner of the firm, who had received an invitation to
each but had not attended any, and had not even thought of
replying. In the end it was one of the shareholders of the
firm who, having heard Baudelaire lecture, became interested
in him, and arranged an interview. This interview was only
with the junior partner who said that he could do nothing
without Lacroix, and that he would give him an answer
when Lacroix returned.[10] Baudelaire believed that someone
had been working against him with the firm, and that some
of Victor Hugo's followers had spread slanderous gossip
about him in Brussels. This suspicion seems to have been
well founded. A rumour was certainly circulated that he
was a spy sent by the Imperial Government to investigate
the activities of refugees in Belgium. Baudelaire believed
that this action had been taken as a revenge for the anonymous letter which he had published in *Le Figaro* in April,
just before he left for Belgium, to protest against the manner
in which the banquet, arranged to celebrate the anniversary
of Shakespeare's birth, had been organized. The originators
of this celebration were for the most part followers of Hugo
still living in France, and their unacknowledged object was
really to advertise the work on the English dramatist which
Hugo was about to publish. Many people in France had
protested against this particular form of advertisement, in
private, but Baudelaire alone had had the rash daring to do
so publicly.[11] After saying, amongst other things, that the
whole world would naturally wish to join together for the
purpose of celebrating the birthday of the immortal play-
wright, he ventured to ask whether the organizers of the
banquet had really been moved by a disinterested feeling of
admiration, or whether they had been actuated by a desire
not solely to commemorate the name of Shakespeare. He
had, he added, been grieved to notice that none of those
who held even the smallest appointment under the Imperial
Government – such as Émile Deschamps, the well-known
translator of *Romeo and Juliet* – had been invited.

He went on to speak of what he called the monstrous 'adulterous union' between the Romantic Movement of 1830 and the democratic movement after 1849, since when *Olympio* – the name by which Hugo had designated himself for the past twenty years – his entire family and all his disciples discovered evidence to prove their philanthropic and democratic theories, so that even Shakespeare had become for them the true example of the socialist. 'Finally,' he declared, 'the little kowtowing coterie of this poet in whom God, in his inscrutable mystery, has been pleased to mingle foolishness and genius, considered the moment opportune to use the anniversary of Shakespeare's birth as a pretext to announce and advertise the forthcoming book by Hugo on the English dramatist, which, like all his works, will contain many examples of great beauty, and also stupidity which will distress his most fervent admirers.'

All this may have been true, but it was not wise for Baudelaire, at a moment when he still needed support, to attack the most important man of letters of his age, and he should have realized that a man as vain as Hugo would never forgive so bitter an attack, and would certainly discover who had perpetrated it. Since the publication of his *Contemplations*, he had come to consider himself the prophet of a new religion, the equal of Christ – indeed superior, for he came after Him and could correct the mistakes He had made. On his 'rocher de proscrit', in the middle of the raging seas, he saw himself as calling destruction down upon the modern cities of debauch and vice. His passionate interest in spiritualism had increased his confidence in his mission, ever since the evening when Death, by means of the planchette, had summoned him to compose a book and to entitle it *Conseils à Dieu*, and told him that he was to leave injunctions that, after his death, this work was to be published, in sections at different intervals. So that, even dead, he would still be able to help the living. 'Jesus had only one Resurrection, but you will be able to fill your tomb with resurrections!'[12] There even exists a photograph of Hugo, taken in a pensive mood, under which he had written 'Victor Hugo speaking with God'.

In the matter of Shakespeare Hugo also felt qualified to speak; for the dramatist had spoken to him several times, through the planchette.

The account of these *séances* as related by Gustave Simon [13] shows them to have been astonishing examples of unconscious hypnotic suggestion by the poet to his son Charles, the only successful medium in the household. When in a cataleptic state Charles was able to turn out fluent Victor Hugo verse and he, who normally could not write at all, could produce verse at an even greater speed than his father. The son, given the right conditions, could do this even if his father was out of the room, and Hugo did not realize the true cause.

During the *séances* when Shakespeare appeared, Hugo was not always present but it seemed to make little difference to the result. When the dramatist had first been materialized, it had struck a sceptical onlooker as strange that he should deliver his messages in French – neither Hugo nor his son knew English at that time – but, when asked for the reason of this odd behaviour, the spirit had explained that this was on account of the superiority of the French language. Apparently, with corporeal flesh, spirits slough off racial prejudices and national pride as well. The message in verse which came to Hugo said that, when one of his works blossomed on earth, Shakespeare took it in his hands and all the other authors sat round to listen. Cervantes, with raised finger, silenced Molière, and all of them exclaimed: 'Let's see what it's about!' They all listened with fixed attention and Shakespeare said that he had often seen Dante weep when Hugo had shown how love can exist even in the soul of the ugliest creature, while Aeschylus, the God of awe, used to tremble at the tremendous emotions which Hugo roused. 'Your voice is sacred!' cried Shakespeare to Hugo. 'Carry on the good work! After *Hamlet* and *Don Juan* your plays are the second wave that beats against our heavenly shores. The work of art of the world lives, and it reigns. It is man's key of love to open Heaven! Let us then heap work of art upon work of art! I, Shakespeare, today, and you, Hugo, tomorrow!'

Baudelaire's conduct must have seemed to Hugo and his clique little short of blasphemy and sacrilege. His action was especially foolish since he was counting on Hugo's support to persuade Lacroix and Verboeckhoven to print his works.[14] It is, indeed, probable that Hugo, or one of his friends, queered his pitch with the firm, who were eager to secure further works from the Sage of Guernsey since the success of *Les Misérables*.

Baudelaire had not yet abandoned hope of a contract, and he decided on a new plan – one of the strangest ever devised to attract hard-headed businessmen. He made up his mind to give a party at which he would read a selection from his writings. This would surely make them realize his value. He decided to borrow the rooms of a new friend, a stockbroker called Crabbe, who was, at the same time, an art connoisseur and a cultivated man. He intended also to invite official people whose presence, he hoped, would dispel the rumours which had been circulating about him.[15]

On the evening of the party the three large rooms, opening one into the other, were bright with flowers and candles in the crystal chandeliers, while at the end of the furthest room were tables set with a profusion of cakes and sandwiches, wines and liqueurs. Thirty guests had been invited – fifteen by Baudelaire, and fifteen by Crabbe – but it was hoped that many more would come. Of Baudelaire's guests only five came – two had written to refuse but the other eight had treated the invitation with contempt and had not even bothered to reply. Five of Crabbe's guests also came – ten people in the three vast rooms where their voices echoed strangely, with refreshments for a large reception.

Baudelaire, as was usual with him in these moments of crisis when things were going badly, was horribly nervous but was trying to keep up his spirits and to pretend that, if everything was not going well, he at least was unaware of it. He wandered amongst his guests, talking to them, and a journalist who admired him – probably Frédérix, certainly someone perspicacious – said to him : 'There is in your works a Christian quality which has not been sufficiently noticed – il y a dans vos œuvres quelquechose de chrétien qu'on n'a pas assez remarqué.' The words seemed to reverberate through the empty space, and an old man, at the end of the room, in the corner where the stockbroking friends of Crabbe had congregated to discuss their own affairs, not quite catching what was said, muttered to his friends in an audible whisper, 'He says we're a lot of cretins – il dit que nous sommes des crétins.'[16]

Baudelaire thought that there was no point in waiting for further guests who would certainly not now come – the evening was a failure already – and he began to read his works, but he soon saw the few guests fidget and grow uneasy, as they tried clumsily and in vain to stifle their yawns. Suddenly he stopped in the middle of a poem and, turning his back on his guests, he went over to the table and helped himself to food and drink. His own friends were dismayed and mortified, but he himself only rocked with silent, mirthless laughter. With a baldness more tragic and effective than detailed description he himself gave a stark and ruthless account of the party to his mother.

Lacroix had not come to the lectures, neither did he come to the party, or answer the invitation. Baudelaire was to meet him a few days later for his final answer. This time again he saw only the junior partner, Verboeckhoven, who informed him that an agreement was out of the question.[17]

Everything for which Baudelaire had come to Brussels had now failed, but he did not despair. He decided that Belgium was a country now much in the news, and that he would write a book about it, and thus retrieve his fortunes.

He was expected back every day in France, but still he did not arrive.

'How I long to be home,' he wrote to his mother,[18] 'and to see my notes and all my pictures! Sometimes I'm depressed because I imagine that I'll never see Honfleur again. But don't go and think that this is a presentiment. It's only one of my fancies on my bad days.'

His delayed return has been misinterpreted. It was not due to irresolution as his friends in France imagined when they wondered why he did not come home from Belgium since he hated it so much. It is clear from his letters, if they are carefully read, that he was waiting for good news from Paris in order to be able to go home in safety, for he had left heavy debts behind him still unpaid. He mentions on several occasions in his letters that he cannot go back to Paris without enough money to pay substantial instalments on these debts, so as to be able to spend some time at Honfleur free from the danger of arrest.[19] He was waiting especially to hear whether he had yet secured a publisher, and also for news of various articles and poems which he had sent to reviews in France – *L'Opinion Nationale*, *La Vie Parisienne* and *Le Monde Illustré* had articles of his, but none of them had replied.[20] *La Revue de Paris* had prose poems which they had said they would publish in December 1864, but they were in such low water that they could not pay him anything before February of the following year, and even then were unable to settle with him in full.[21] His pride could not contemplate returning empty-handed, in a worse plight than when he had left with bright hopes for the future. He determined that he would remain in what he called punishment in Belgium until he had retrieved his failure, and would come home only when he had signed the contract which would assure his future.[22]

At Christmas, when he had not yet received any news, he could endure his exile no longer, and he planned to go home after all; but, at the last moment, he decided that he could not face the ordeal and he sent messages to explain his change of plans. To Ancelle who had written in complaint, he answered:[23]

'Do you want to know the explanation of the mystery,

why I cut our appointment? At the last moment, in spite of my longing to see my mother, terror seized me at the thought of enduring my Gehenna again, of passing through Paris without being certain of having a substantial sum of money to distribute to my creditors, which would assure for me real rest at Honfleur. And so I wrote to the reviews and to my friends, and to the person who is looking after my affairs – that is to say the business of the disposal of the four volumes which I had come confidently to offer to that wretch Lacroix.'

He added that, every day, he was expecting important news from Paris. When Ancelle wrote again, expressing surprise at his scruples, he replied:[24]

'There's no other reason but my anxiety. I wish to come back only when I can do so with pride, with certain duties accomplished.'

He hoped, with a confidence which never diminished, that all would be well. Everything must be well, he thought, in the new fresh year that was about to open, for he always had a touching belief in the good resolutions of New Year's Day.

'I don't need the solemnity of this day,' he wrote to his mother for the first of January 1865,[25] 'the saddest of all days in the year, to remember you and all the commitments I've accumulated for so many years. My principal duty – perhaps my sole duty – should be to make you happy. I think of it endlessly. Will this ever be granted to me? I think sometimes, with a shudder of terror, that God may suddenly rob me once and for all of the possibility of ever achieving it. Firstly I promise you that this year you'll not have to suffer any further demands for financial help on my part. I blush to think of all the privations I've already made you endure. Perhaps this year I'll be able to repay part of the money. I promise you that not a single day of the year will pass without work. Reward must surely then come!

'My mind is full of dark obsessions. How difficult it is to do one's duty every day without flinching. How difficult it is, not to think out a book, but to write it without flagging – to have courage every single day! I've calculated that everything I've got in my head would have cost me only fifteen months of work if I'd worked hard. How often I've said to myself: "In spite of my nerves, in spite of my terrors, in spite of my solitude, come, courage! Good results will perhaps then come!" How often has God granted me a reprieve of fifteen months! But I've always interrupted hitherto the fulfilling of my plans. Shall I ever have the time now – even supposing I've the courage to do so – to make good all that I've got to accomplish yet? If I were only sure of having five or six years ahead of me! But who can count on that? Death is now an obsession with me, not on account of any foolish terrors – I've suffered so much already, and I've been so often chastised already that I believe that many things can be forgiven to me – but nevertheless death is abhorrent to me because it would annihilate all my plans, and because I've not yet accomplished one third of what I've got to accomplish in this world. . . .

'I am, however, in good hope! I've entrusted my literary business to someone in Paris. I think that I'll soon have news for you. I think I'm being attended to.

'I send you my tenderest love with all the emotion of a child who loves only his mother.'

[2]

The Notary Turns Literary Agent
1864 — 1866

IT has been the invariable custom, even amongst Baudelaire's most fervent admirers, to deplore the idleness and mental incapacity of his years in Belgium. It is impossible to claim that he was working strenuously during his stay in Brussels, or that he produced any writings of outstanding literary value. As a writer his career undoubtedly ended when he left Paris in April 1864, and the books on which he was working in Brussels – the book on Belgium and *Mon Cœur mis à nu* – exist only in fragmentary form, and could be omitted from a study of his writings. Nevertheless, in fairness, it should be recognized that he had no inducement to work and to produce more, since no one seemed to want what he had already written. Constant failure is bound to have a discouraging effect on production, even with a man in good health – and he was slowly dying by then. He himself declared that he would not finish his book on Belgium until he was certain of having an offer for it – he said this only after he had suffered repeated refusals from publishers to whom he had submitted the scheme. As soon as he had said this he was bitterly ashamed of his mercenary attitude towards his writing, for at this time he was striving to foster and develop in himself disinterested love of work without any thought of reward or personal fame. But, in the precarious state of his health, his will was often weak and he frequently allowed himself to drift into idleness and apathy. Yet he was harder on himself than anyone else could ever have been, and it is because he wrote so frequently of his indolence and mental incapacity that others have adopted the same attitude towards him. It is very doubtful whether anyone else

would have worked more strenuously in the conditions in
which he found himself in Belgium. The ideal of conduct
which he set himself, however, was so high that he suffered
tortures whenever he fell short of it.

There must have been many articles in an unfinished state,
the notes of which got lost after his death, articles mentioned to his mother,[1] for instance, *Chateaubriand et le
Dandysme Littéraire*, *La Peinture Didactique*, *Les Fleurs du
Mal jugées par l'Auteur lui-même*, and an answer to two
articles entitled *Henri Heine et la Jeunesse des Poètes*, and
La Préface de la Vie de Jules César par Napoléon III.

He had several articles lying in the offices of reviews which
did not print them, and did not even return his manuscripts.
In February 1865 *Le Figaro* sent him back his translation of
Poe's *Marie Roget*, alleging that it was too intellectual and
too profound for its readers. *La Revue de Paris* had accepted
poems, but could not afford to pay him for what it had used,
much less give him a promise of future employment. Besides
all this, after he died, eleven prose poems were discovered
in the offices of *L'Opinion Nationale*, the existence of which
the editor had completely forgotten until news of the poet's
death gave his name temporary value as publicity.[2] Since
Poulet Malassis' bankruptcy Baudelaire had not succeeded
in finding anyone interested in his unpublished critical
articles nor in *Les Paradis Artificiels*, which could rank as
unpublished since it had been so scantily advertised and
reviewed when it appeared. He was seriously ill, and without any money except for the small advances which Ancelle
sent him, and what his mother lent him out of her small
income. He used then to spend hours each day duplicating
his writings by hand himself since he could no longer afford
a copyist, and writing long letters of advice and admonition
to those who were engaged in finding him a publisher – not
to mention the letters to his mother and to Ancelle. It was
no wonder that he did not possess the time or energy or
peace of mind for original composition.

Then, to add to his discouragement, he learned that

Lacroix and Verboeckhoven had commissioned someone else to produce a translation which he had suggested as a good commercial proposition, offering to do it himself – the *Melmoth* of Maturin.[3]

Anyone would have been discouraged with less, and he began to wonder whether anything of his would ever sell again.

'Could it possibly be, perhaps,' he wrote to his mother,[4] 'that my name had no more commercial value, and that these three volumes of articles are unsaleable? No! this can't possibly be true! But I'm sometimes so discouraged that I tend to believe it.'

The terror of irremediable failure grew on him, and there is little doubt that this discouragement affected his production, for he was able to rouse himself at the slightest sign that matters were improving. Writing later to his literary agent, Lemer, who had not got in touch with him for many months, he said, when at last he heard from him:[5]

'To give you an idea of the weakness of my character, I must tell you that, when I didn't hear from you, I imagined that henceforth no book of mine would ever sell again, and consequently there wasn't any point in finishing the *Spleen* or *La Belgique*. As you see, I was in the most utter state of discouragement! But your letter did me an immense good, and I've begun work again on the *Spleen*, which will be finished without fail at the end of the month.'

He certainly could have finished his book on Belgium with very little work if he could have found a publisher. But the publishers were worried because of its bitter tone, afraid that it might make difficulties between them and Belgium which was France's best customer for printed books. We can judge from his letters, and also from the plan of the work,[6] how far it had already advanced. From this scheme, it is not easy to tell what it would have been in its completed form since with him frequent rewriting during gestation was of vital importance. But the book was fully sketched out and needed only to be written, to be filled

in, though, with him, this would not have been swift.
Whether it would ever have ranked amongst his greatest
works is difficult to say. Probably it would not have done
so – it would have been a book inspired by bitterness and
rancour, and would thus have contained some element of
didacticism, being written, not merely for artistic purpose,
but to prove a thesis, to attack, as forcibly as possible, what
he calls 'cette canaille bourgeoise', a money-grubbing commercial society antagonistic to all forms of art. His prejudices
would probably have distorted his vision, and so would his
obsession with the villainy of the Belgian character, which
had become an 'idée fixe' with him. His disappointment
might have gained the upper hand and his disillusionment
at his personal lack of success in Brussels. His highest
achievements have always been in those works in which he
had no thesis to defend or to prove.

His thoughts were now all centred in finding shelter and
a final resting-place in a sound and reputable firm, one which
would bring out editions at regular intervals of those books
which he considered had a permanent interest – his *Fleurs
du Mal* for instance – a firm that would accept further books
from him, so that he could eventually have a score or so
bringing him in a regular income, as the translations from
Poe had done until he had had to sell them. He now longed
passionately for some stability in his life, for respectability,
and to be able to feel that no one could any longer look
askance at him.

'I no longer dream of making a fortune,' he wrote to his
mother,[7] 'but only of paying my debts, and of being able to
produce a score of books which will assure me a steady
income.'

He did not consider pleasure any longer, for he said that
all pleasure as such merely bored him, and that his only
real joy was in the perfecting of his mind.[8]

Since his own efforts at securing publication had been
in vain, as well as those of friends like Commandant
Lejosne, whom he could no longer expect to go on hawking

his manuscripts round Paris, he decided to do what he should have done many years earlier: put his entire production in the hands of a literary agent. But he had an unfortunate failing, that of surrounding himself with untrustworthy associates, and now his choice was not a wise one. He chose Lemer, a man who had once been a publisher in a small way, and who hoped one day to return to that; who was not an honest man and who did not further his client's interests. Whether even an honest agent could have achieved anything is doubtful! All publishers by now knew of Baudelaire's plight and were giving him a wide berth. They hoped later to acquire rights over his books if they did not act precipitately at first – as Lévy had done in the case of the translations from Poe. Baudelaire himself was well aware of what Lévy would do if given the chance,[9] and he often described his avarice.[10]

Lemer was not merely useless, but harmful. At first Baudelaire had been doubtful about him, but had finally chosen him because he thought that since he was also in low water, he would be more likely to be energetic in order to rise with his client.[11] Later it transpired that Lemer realized that Baudelaire would one day be a good investment and did not want now to tie him up with any publisher; hoping, when he himself went back into business, to be able to secure his works at a bargain price.

In February 1863 Baudelaire approached Lemer with the offer of a share in the proceeds if he could secure him an agreement.

'For many years now,' wrote Baudelaire,[12] 'I've been contemplating finding a man who would take the entire charge of my literary affairs – if he were, at the same time, a personal friend it would be perfect. I've learnt through bitter experience that I'm myself totally incompetent in such matters. I don't at all know why it is that I haven't the intelligence for such business, but I've made a fool of myself so often on that score, that I've decided henceforth not to meddle in it any more. Firstly, will you be the person for whom I've been looking? I ought to have come to this decision years ago, but nevertheless it's never too late to mend! Secondly, I must ask you how much you'd expect for your services, that's to say, what percentage on the contracts you would negotiate for me. Although we've known each other for many years, I'm obliged to ask you this stupid question. But I've always heard that, in business, false shame was foolish! I needn't tell you that whatever you decide will be right for me. Only I hope to find a zealous ally.

'I must now explain to you how my business stands. I hope that next year – or perhaps even in a few months, if I can get a little rest – I'll have more to offer you. I want, at the moment, to dispose of four books the summaries of which I enclose – *Les Paradis Artificiels* which was so unfortunately published a few years ago that it can virtually be considered as unpublished. I consider the book satisfactory as it stands and I'll neither add nor retrench anything. Next, *Réflexions sur quelques-uns de mes Contemporains* divided into two parts, or two volumes. This is not, as you might be tempted to imagine, merely a collection of newspaper articles. Although they have appeared at widely separated intervals and are unknown for the most part, they are linked together by a single, systematic and coherent line of argument. I'm very anxious to show what I've done in the field of aesthetic criticism. Then there's a fourth book, *La Pauvre Belgique*, but this isn't yet quite finished. I've been able to turn to profit my nine months' stay here, but I want to add a few chapters on the provinces, on some old towns, but the weather has been so bad that I haven't been able to move around.'

March and April slipped by, and Baudelaire still remained in Belgium waiting for news from Lemer. May and June likewise went by without news. Then, like the man in the fairy story by Grimm, Baudelaire sent a friend to find out what had become of Lemer, then a second friend to discover what had become of the other friend, and finally a third to find out what had become of all of them. Even then he received no report. His mother also was beginning to grow anxious, for he had now been abroad for almost eighteen months, was earning no money, and had nothing to live on save what she and Ancelle sent him. And every time he wrote to her he said that he was just about to sign an agreement which would solve all his difficulties. The only person in whom she could confide her fears was Ancelle, who knew her son's weakness and yet had never lost his affection for him.

'I ought, by now, to have grown accustomed to the curious life he leads,' she wrote,[13] 'so far outside all accepted ideas, and resign myself. But I can't, for I cling foolishly, madly, to the thought that I must, before I die, get some satisfaction and contentment through him. But now the matter is becoming urgent, for I'm growing very old, and fairly feeble. He's got little time left to give me this satisfaction towards which I aspire. I shan't ever get it now. I might have found consolation and comfort in distinguished literary successes – for Charles has the stuff for that in him. But here once more cruel disappointments awaited me, since Charles has chosen a strange style of writing as absurd as himself, which brings him few admirers. It's true he has got his originality on his side – and that is something – he'll never produce anything commonplace, and he'll never borrow from others, for he's got so much in himself.

'I might add – but this is strictly between ourselves – that he'd often like to see you attach more importance to his literary affairs. He claims that, although they're moving slowly, they're nevertheless moving!'

Ancelle had always tried, to the best of his unliterary ability, to take an interest in Baudelaire's life and affairs, to try to understand what were his aims, but, on account of the sensitive and morbid self-consciousness of his ward, his efforts had met only with scorn, and even at times with hostility. In spite of all this, Ancelle had remained devoted to him. Now, although he was an old man, he tried to educate himself in modern trends in literature, and to read so that he could discuss intelligently with Baudelaire. And, although the poet made fun of his new interest in poetry, and said that he knew as much about literature as an elephant about dancing the cakewalk, he was nevertheless touched, and a better understanding began to develop between them, so that almost all the letters which he wrote from Belgium were written to him.

Ancelle was not content with studying modern authors themselves, but he needs must read reviews as well, and attend lectures, and he was always filled with pride when a lecturer devoted a whole hour to the works of Baudelaire. He wrote once to him, to give him an account of such a lecture, thinking it would encourage him to know that he was not being forgotten. It also gave him a feeling of importance to say that he himself concurred with the lecturer's remarks. Here again he met with no success.

'Whoever heard of going to a lecture by Deschanel?' Baudelaire wrote to him.[14] 'Do you really mean to say that you were idiotic enough to go and listen to that fool, a lecturer fit only for a girls' school?'

Ancelle never allowed himself to be ruffled by his ward, but went on quietly studying modern literature and sending him cuttings from the papers in which he was mentioned.

To Baudelaire, anxiously waiting for news, was added in July 1865 the scare of the Pincebourde stranglehold. In 1862, when Poulet Malassis had asked Baudelaire to repay the money he had advanced, the poet had been unable to do so and had given him a mortgage of five thousand francs on his published works – *Les Fleurs du Mal, Spleen de Paris*, and *Les Paradis Artificiels*. Now, in 1865, Poulet Malassis was in difficulties again and trying to collect, wherever he could, any money due to him; and Baudelaire was no more able then than in 1862 to repay him.

Then Pincebourde, who had once been a clerk in the firm, and was now setting up on his own, came forward to offer two thousand francs for the mortgage, that is for the rights on three volumes of Baudelaire's works. In 1862 the poet, without realizing what he was letting himself in for, had signed an agreement which stipulated that, if the loan was not repaid by July 1865, Poulet Malassis was free to dispose of the rights. Pincebourde, realizing that Baudelaire's stock might rise in the not too distant future, was anxious, while he was in financial difficulties, to secure the property of his writings. He had gone to Brussels to try to make the poet sign a contract for a future book, but Baudelaire had no confidence in the man whom he called 'that Auvergnat of the publishing trade.' [15] Pincebourde had left him uttering the threat that he would find a way of forcing him to agree,[16] and he had gone immediately to make his offer to Poulet Malassis. If Baudelaire was unable to find forthwith the sum Pincebourde was offering, he would fall completely helpless into his clutches, with his most saleable work alienated, and this would mean total ruin.

Baudelaire was always reluctant to trouble people with his own business, but it was now imperative for him to write again to Lemer, to tell him that the matter which had been urgent in February was now desperate,[17] and he could no longer afford to wait indefinitely for an answer, since by 10 July it would be too late. He decided to go in person to Paris, to discuss the matter, and to try to discover how near he was to obtaining a contract for him from some publisher. He set out suddenly, one afternoon, without any luggage, and arrived in Paris late at night. It must have been then, as he was coming out of the Gare du Nord, that Catulle Mendès met him.

He describes Baudelaire as coming down the steps of the station, unkempt and without any luggage, looking, what he had never looked before, somewhat ashamed of himself.[18] Catulle Mendès, at the time in his early twenties, astonishingly good-looking and drunk with success, suspected that the poet had no money in his pockets, for his financial difficulties were by now public property. He invited him to spend the night with him and sleep on the couch in his sitting-room. As they sat together that evening Baudelaire was preoccupied, and busy making calculations on a slip of paper. When Mendès asked him what he was doing, he answered that he was reckoning all that he had made from his writings in the odd twenty years since he had begun to write. 'And do you know how much I've made in the whole of my life,' he asked bitterly, 'from the whole of my works – my poems, my prose compositions and my translations?' He paused and then answered his own question, 'Fifteen thousand eight hundred and ninety-two francs and sixty centimes – and don't forget the sixty centimes, the price of a whiff!' Mendès was horrified when he reflected on the fortunes which some writers had gained, on the immense income on which Victor Hugo could count.

Later Baudelaire told him that if he could ever again become strong, he would write a long poem about India, in which he would express all the 'mélancolie lumineuse du soleil', and that he now dreamed only of the sun, of heat and peace. Then he unrolled before him all his visions, describing them in his richly modulated voice, which always mysteriously moved all those who heard it. Later in the night, long after he had fallen asleep, Mendès awoke and he heard Baudelaire, in the next room, weeping in the dark, and vainly trying to stifle his sobs, weeping when he thought that all the rest of the world was asleep. Mendès felt too young and inexperienced to go and bring him comfort, for this despair was something which he had not yet encountered in his happy and carefree life. Next morning, when he awoke, he found that Baudelaire had already slipped away while he had been asleep, leaving a note which merely said, 'Good-bye!'

Baudelaire saw his agent that day but Lemer merely put him off with evasive answers, saying that he could have disposed more easily of the works if he still had *Les Fleurs du Mal* and *Spleen de Paris* to offer as well, and he suggested that Hetzel might no longer be anxious to publish them when there was this Pincebourde 'sword of Damocles'. This was true, and when the poet went to see him, he liberated him from his contract, subject naturally to the repayment of the advance he had already received.[19]

Lemer was now discussing the possibility of obtaining a contract from the Garnier Brothers. For now, with *Les Fleurs du Mal* and *Spleen de Paris* perhaps available, the proposition he had to offer was more interesting. But it was very doubtful whether the deal could be pushed through in a few days, and no contract could save Baudelaire unless it was signed before 10 July – it was by then 5 July.

The following day he went to see Ancelle to discover whether there was, by any chance, any loophole in the agreement with Poulet Malassis, but Ancelle could detect no flaw. His only hope – a poor one – was that Lemer should secure an immediate agreement with Garnier.

In deep depression and dejection Baudelaire went to see his mother at Honfleur to spend with her the last fateful days of waiting. He had not intended to tell her of his troubles – he had borrowed so much from her during the past year and a half in Brussels – but she, noticing that he was even more preoccupied than usual, did not rest until she had extracted the story of his distress from him.[20] This was something which she could imagine and understand, the danger of the complete loss of his capital, even if it was only literary, and she insisted on borrowing the sum to release him from immediate danger. Thus, in a few moments, the problem was solved, which had been causing anxiety and despair.

The sensation of release from overpowering anxiety was so strong that, in an instant, he seemed to grow almost young again. He spent the following evening with his old friends – Banville and Asselineau – they were surprised to find him in good heart and spirits, describing wittily his life in Brussels, when they had heard rumours that he was very ill. This was the last time, says Asselineau, that Baudelaire's friends possessed him entire and whole.[21]

Next day he returned to Brussels, to his debts there, be-

cause he did not wish to pass for a thief with people who
had trusted him. All that was left for him to do now was to
await news from Lemer. In July Lemer had assured him
that everything was on the point of being settled, and yet
a month went by without news. In August he heard that
negotiations were still proceeding, but that the elder brother
was reluctant to sign the contract although the younger
brother, Hippolyte, was prepared to do so. On 9 August,
Lemer informed him that he expected to sign the agreement
on the twelfth of the month.[22] When August slipped by
without news, Baudelaire, in desperation, wrote to Sainte-
Beuve to ask him to say a word on his behalf to Garnier.[23]
It is not known whether Sainte-Beuve was able to do anything, but both September and October went by without
any further progress. Lemer said it was because Hippolyte
Garnier, the brains of the firm, had been away on holiday
since August,[24] but, in November, the agent informed Baudelaire that the brothers were still deliberating.

   In the meantime Baudelaire's situation in Belgium was
growing desperate, and he was afraid that the sum he
might obtain from Garnier would disappear in settling his
debts in Brussels, leaving his state in France as involved as
ever.[25] Ancelle, moreover, was now growing anxious lest his
ward should once more insist on the sale of capital to pay
his debts.[26] He advised Baudelaire to leave Belgium surrep-
titiously, abandoning his luggage at the hotel, and not to
settle his account. The poet was horrified at such a piece of
advice coming from a man of probity like Ancelle, and he
refused it emphatically.

   He waited until the end of the year for news, and every
day used to see on show in the bookshops the rubbish which
was being printed in France. Everything seemed to succeed
in getting published, everything, save his own works.[27]

   Anxiety was destroying him and making him more than
ever incapable of work, and he could not refrain from feeling
that Fate was indeed against him, and that Chance had
cast her evil eye on him.

'As for my ill-luck,' he wrote to his mother for Christmas 1865,[28] 'my *guignon*, of which I'm for ever complaining, I'm not of the same opinion as you. I realize my faults, my idleness, as well as you do – indeed I willingly exaggerate the sum of my misdeeds – but nevertheless I maintain that Paris has never been just to me and hasn't paid me, in esteem any more than in money, what is due to me. And the best proof of the bad luck which pursues me is in the fact that my own mother even, on many occasions, has turned against me. In three and a half months' time I'll be forty-five. It's too late, I know, to make even a small fortune – especially with my unpopular talent – and it may even be too late to pay my debts, and to safeguard a free and honoured old age. But if ever I retrieve the energy and freedom of speech I once enjoyed, I'll relieve my anger in awe-inspiring books. I'd like to put the whole human race against me. I believe I'd find in that a joy which would make up to me for everything.'

At last, when even Christmas Day went by without bringing any news, he wrote to Ancelle, as the only person who would not resent the trouble put on him, to beg him to try to unravel the Garnier mystery, to discover whether Lemer had lost interest in his business, and to point out to him, tactfully, how desperate was his situation.[29] Baudelaire was now himself beginning to have doubts, if not of the honesty of Lemer, at least of his energy, but he still did not wish anything done which might offend him.

'We mustn't insult Lemer,' he wrote,[30] 'who is guilty perhaps only of apathy, or seem to be setting him aside in a business which he himself has started.'

Ancelle went to see Lemer, and, with his lawyer's knowledge of human nature, summed him up as a poor and shifty customer, who was not dealing fairly with Baudelaire's work. It came out later that Ancelle had been right and that Lemer had presented the proposal as badly as possible to Garnier, so that it was bound to fail, in order to force Baudelaire to publish with him.[31] It also transpired that he had not even been to see Hippolyte Garnier, without whom nothing could have been effected.[32]

In January 1866 Baudelaire was anxious that Lemer should not imagine that he had sent his lawyer to spy on him.

'We must be careful,' he wrote to Ancelle,[33] 'not to offend him, and, moreover, even if I adopt the plan you suggest, we can't throw Lemer aside without convicting him of incapacity. We mustn't ever be underhand.'

In the meantime Lemer was preserving his usual silence and then, in a last desperate resort, the poet handed his business over to Ancelle to see whether he would succeed where others had failed in securing him a contract. In the lonely years in Belgium he had grown to appreciate the wholeheartedness of his lawyer's friendship.

'Remember,' he wrote to him,[34] 'that, in spite of what my mother says, I recognize and appreciate the depth of your friendship.'

Thus Ancelle, the suburban lawyer and Mayor of Neuilly, became a literary agent. With his habitual pomposity he took his duties very seriously, and considered that he had now sufficient acquaintance with literature to be a judge of what was suitable. He even permitted himself to alter his client's manuscripts where he thought that their tone might hinder their sale, but this, strangely enough, evoked only a mild rebuke from the poet – he would not have let an editor off so lightly. Baudelaire merely requested him to submit his work in the form in which he had sent it to him.[35]

'I place all my trust in you,' he wrote to him when he handed over his business to him,[36] 'but I do beseech you to be prudent! Out of affection for me you'll now become my literary agent, and you'll try to dispose of the five volumes in the course of the month of February.'

[3]

My Heart Laid Bare
1864 – 1866

DURING the weary months of waiting Baudelaire's life in
Brussels became tragic. He suffered many humiliations
which must have been grievous to a sensitive and independent man. He was earning no money at all and was obliged
to depend on the small sums which Ancelle, or his mother,
sent him from time to time. Although he was over forty, he
had to render an account to his guardian for every penny
that he spent. He suffered the humiliation of having no
money for all the trifles which he needed personally –
stamps, tobacco, stationery and medicines – and the longing
to procure these things became an obsession with him.[1] He
was obliged, to his great shame, to call the attention of his
mother and friends to the fact that their correspondence
addressed to him was insufficiently franked, and he said
that every time a letter came for him he dreaded that they
would say to him at the hotel office: 'Another thirty centimes to pay, Monsieur Baudelaire.'[2] He could not afford
to have his shoes repaired, or his hair cut, and soon he was
ashamed to go out; he thought that people in the streets
were looking at him in astonishment, because his hair was
hanging in locks over his collar at the back.[3]

By March 1865 he had paid nothing to his landlady since
the previous October, and she was beginning to look coldly
at him, and even to remonstrate with him, when he passed
the office door to go out. Every time a letter came for him
from abroad, she used to go up to his room to find out
whether it contained money from home, and he then
thought of the plan of having his correspondence addressed

to him *poste restante*, and fetched it himself as long as his health permitted him to go out.

Day after day, he awaited news from France. He was concentrating on the hours of the arrival of the post from abroad, so that he could go and find out whether anyone had written to him, see whether his contract was yet signed, and he was saved, discover whether his friends were remembering him actively, and if any periodical had sent any money. Nothing of interest ever came for him, however, and as the days went by with nothing, he began to think that he was being forgotten and that he might as well be dead, or on a desert island. The constant waiting was wearing him down. He could think of nothing else, and he had no energy for work, no courage to write the books which no one wanted to read. It was then that he discovered Shelley's *Stanzas written in Dejection, near Naples*, and saw the application of the sentiments expressed, to himself.

> *Alas! I have nor hope nor health,*
> *   Nor peace within nor calm around,*
> *Nor that content surpassing wealth*
> *   The sage in meditation found,*
> *And walked with inward glory crowned –*
> *Nor fame, nor power, nor love, nor leisure.*
>
> *Some might lament that I were cold,*
> *   As I, when this sweet day is gone,*
> *Which my lost heart, too soon grown old,*
> *   Insults with this untimely moan;*
> *They might lament – for I am one*
> *   Whom men love not – and yet regret,*
> *Unlike this day, which, when the sun*
> *   Shall on its stainless glory set,*
> *Will linger, though enjoyed, like joy in memory yet.*

He was desperately homesick for France, to hear French spoken by French and not by Belgian people, and he longed to drink with anyone, provided it was not a Belgian. Whenever he saw anyone leaving the hotel, and the luggage being hoisted on to the cab, he used to say to himself, 'He's a lucky man, for he can travel, he can leave when he wants to.'[4] He felt constantly nostalgic longing for Paris, where he had lived for the whole of his life, for the boulevards, and the cafés bright with lights – the Belgians did not know what real café life meant – for the hum of the streets, for the beautiful gardens. Sometimes, at the end of hope, he used to think that all would be well if only he could see his native land again, and could get back to Paris.

Then he used to dream about his room in his mother's little house at Honfleur, with his books and his pictures, and it became for him his Paradise Lost. He used to think of his mother more and more, and wonder whether it would ever be possible for him now to pay his debts and be for her the son she wanted to have, to make her few remaining years happy and contented. He felt very much ashamed as he reflected what he was doing to her, for he was now living almost entirely at her expense, and she was feeling the financial strain so much that she was even talking of selling her house and dismissing her maid.[5] When he thought of this he was overcome with remorse and humiliation, for there seemed nothing that he personally could do. She had been far from well recently, and he was afraid that she might be beginning to break up – she was now past seventy-two, and seemed to be growing very feeble, also to experience difficulty even in writing. His letters to Ancelle in 1865 are full of concern for her health.

As he sat in his hotel room, anxiously waiting for news, he used to dream once more of the long-ago past, when they had been happy together, and it seemed to him at times as if he had difficulty in recalling her features, so dim and blurred in his mind her image seemed to have become, and he longed for a photograph which he could have always with him, to look at whenever he wished to see her.

'I'm horribly lonely and bored,' he wrote to her for Christmas 1865, the last Christmas for which he was ever to send her wishes, 'and my only pleasure is to think of you. My thoughts turn incessantly towards you, and I can see you in your bedroom, in your drawing-room, working, coming and going, always on the move, grumbling and scolding me from a distance. And then I see you once more in imagination, in my childhood with you in the Rue Hautefeuille, and later in the Rue Saint-André-des-Arts. But I awake suddenly from time to time from my dreaming, and I say to myself in terror: "The only important thing is to form the habit of work, and to make of this horrible companion my one and only joy, for a time will come when I'll have no other." It tires you, doesn't it, to write to me? It seems to me that I gathered that from your last letter. Just send me a line from time to time, to tell that you're well, but only of course if it's true.

'I'd love to have a photograph of you. It's a longing that has suddenly taken hold of me, but I fear it isn't possible now. I'd have to be there, for you don't know anything about such matters. There is, I know, an excellent photographer at Le Havre, but all photographers, even the best, have stupid prejudices, and they consider a good likeness one in which every wart, every wrinkle, and every blemish in the face is clearly visible, or even exaggerated. The harder and clearer the image is the better pleased they are. It's only in Paris that they'd be able to do what I want – that's to say, a true picture, but with the soft outline of a drawing. But we'll think of it later, shan't we?'

He had grown to hate most of those whom he met in Belgium so much that he ceased to visit anyone except the painter, Félicien Rops, and Poulet Malassis. The latter had settled, seemingly permanently, in Brussels. He had rented an apartment, had engaged servants to look after him, and his house became the meeting-place of many strange people – actors, poets, writers of all sorts, and even advanced socialists. The respectable neighbours used to be suspicious of the comings and goings, of the noise and laughter, and the sounds of merrymaking until the small hours. They suspected subversive plots. Poulet Malassis, with his funny little pointed beard and mocking eyes inspired no confidence; nor did Baudelaire, who was a frequent visitor, and who had the reputation of practising every sort of evil.[6] Poulet Malassis remained to the end the eternal *gamin* of the Latin Quarter who took nothing seriously. Baudelaire had often in the past complained of this levity and lack of deep outlook on life; but in Belgium, when everything else was black, it was this faculty of seeing the funny side of everything and of making a long nose even at Fate, which sometimes brought a smile to his bitter face. Under a photograph of himself which he presented to Poulet Malassis he wrote: 'To the only being whose laughter has brightened my melancholy in Belgium.' The publisher did not even take his own misfortunes seriously, how then could he take to heart those of others? Of his own death he joked in the manner of Scarron, and it is said that, on his last outing, before he took to his bed never to rise again – he was by then back in France – he said to a friend, as they were passing near the Morgue: 'Don't let's go in, they'd only keep me there!'[7]

At this time, Baudelaire got to know Victor Hugo and his family, who spent most of 1865 in Brussels. At first he was irritated by them for there was only one person who counted in the household and that was *Olympio*. When he spoke both sons obeyed, listening to their father's slightest word as if they were still little boys. He soon grew very fond of Madame Hugo, and she was very kind to him; perhaps he found in her the same quality which Sainte-Beuve had discovered thirty-five years before, when she had sat apart, silent and neglected, in her drawing-room in the Rue Notre-Dame des Champs, at the time of the Bataille d'Hernani. Baudelaire talked to her of Paris and of Sainte-Beuve. Perhaps he knew of the stormy episode when Sainte-Beuve had loved her and had even refused a university appointment to remain near her – it was said that she had returned his love and become his mistress. Perhaps Baudelaire knew all that and wished to show his understanding. It was all many years ago and she was now white-haired with only a short time left to live, while Sainte-Beuve was an ageing Senator, also not far from the grave.

Madame Hugo seems to have grown fond of Baudelaire, and there was always a place laid for him at her table whenever he pleased to come.[8] She even sent her own doctor to him when she saw how ill he was in the winter of 1865.

Baudelaire was always liked by middle-aged women and he had many close friends among them – witness the letters Madame Meurice wrote to him when he was in Belgium, which suggest also the quality of his compassionate understanding. At first Madame Meurice had thought him affected, but she became later one of his most devoted friends. For her part she realized the wound that lay behind the mocking words in which he described the fiasco of his trip to Belgium and his disappointments.

'I'm writing in answer to your letter,' she said,[9] 'and I do so without any feeling of constraint, for it isn't my mind that presumes to answer you, but my bluntness and directness. As soon as I recognized your writing on the outside of your letter, I felt real joy, though the Belgian stamp saddened me a little. You're still too far from us! However, you think of me sometimes, and you felt the need to let me know of it today – that's not enough for me but it will help me to be patient for a little longer.

'I smiled at first as I read of your adventures, but as I reread them, I felt a kind of pity – now don't be offended, this pity has nothing in it that need wound you, on the contrary. It seemed to me that you were suffering and would gladly have confided in me, but your pride and your mistrust restrained you. But there's no need of that with me! You know me well enough by now to realize that I'm not always laughing, and that I'm your old friend!

'Come! What are you doing in Brussels? Nothing, I dare wager! You're bored stiff, and here everyone is waiting for you with impatience. What string is tying you by the wing to that Belgian cage? Tell us quite simply and frankly. Your little group of friends here misses you badly, and asks for nothing better than to come and cut the string. What's needed? Is it an appointment? We'll get one for you. Or must we have you fetched by the police or the armed forces? Once again, come back; we miss you so much! Manet is so discouraged that he tears up his best sketches. Bracquemond doesn't even argue any more, and I wear out my old piano in the hopes that its sounds may reach you and draw you back. We've music every week at my house. Your absence is the only shadow at these gatherings. They were planned at a moment when the rumour went about that you were expected. We believed it, and we gathered together to wait for you. From time to time, like sentinels crying out in the night, we call "Baudelaire doesn't come!" But there's only black silence! You're also falling down, you know, in your devotion to Wagner. What can I add so that you should understand how essential it is that you come back? Oughtn't it to be enough when I say: "Come! my grateful friendship for all that you've been to me when my heart was over-flowing with pain and bitterness, my calm and serene friendship of today, call out to you in welcome!" Write to me at once and tell me what's keeping you. Or, better still, take the train and come. If you were kind you'd ring at my door on Saturday. We dine at seven. It's the evening for our music. You'd be there to receive all our friends, who would be astounded and happy to see you. Leave those rascally Belgians there whom I despise so much that no scruple on earth would make me stay another day with them. In spite of everything I'll expect you on Saturday. Astonish me, astonish us all by coming.'

He did not, however, arrive, and it was Madame Meurice who was later to come to him, when he returned to France, paralysed and incapable of speech, and played Wagner to him in the nursing-home, where he lay waiting for death, so as to fill his long and empty hours with music.

Sometimes rumours came to him from the outside world that he was beginning to be noticed favourably. There was a letter from Swinburne, news also that Mallarmé had spoken of him with approbation in England as early as 1862; recently rhapsodies of praise from young Verlaine, in a new review entitled *L'Art* in December 1864 and January 1865, the most intelligent and sympathetic notice his works were to receive during his lifetime; and, finally, an evocation in poetic prose of his writings by Mallarmé published in *L'Artiste* in February 1865, which showed true appreciation of *Les Fleurs du Mal*. It was becoming increasingly clear that the Baudelaire School was beginning to exist.

The poet was secretly flattered, though a little frightened, by these young imitators,[10] but he was pleased to be able to send his mother the cuttings of the articles in which he was mentioned, and to prove to her that, in spite of appearances, he was someone who would one day count. Even the absurd lecture by Deschanel, of which he had made such fun when he had heard that Ancelle had attended it, was flattering, for Deschanel never bothered to deal with anything or anyone who was not of topical or significant interest.

Sometimes encouraged by favourable notices from abroad he used to try to write, but it was mostly when horror and shame of his idleness suddenly seized hold of him, that he began to work feverishly, doing anything so long as he was occupied. He used then to copy out poems to dispatch to reviews, make schemes of the articles and books which he intended to write when he had peace and freedom from the demoralizing torture of waiting, and he made endless time-tables of work, of all he intended to achieve. The book on which he was working at this time was *Le Spleen de Paris*, though he only composed one poem for it in Belgium, *Les Bons Chiens*, published in *L'Indépendance Belge* in June 1865, and it is the only one of his compositions in which he has spoken favourably of dogs. Thereby hangs an amusing tale. Stevens, the famous Belgian painter of animals, with whom he was friendly, appeared one day in a magnificent red waistcoat which Baudelaire immediately coveted. Every time he saw it he used to remark on its beauty, until at last one day, in a café, Stevens said to him, 'Well! since you admire it so much, would you like to have it?' The poet, overjoyed, accepted with alacrity, and the painter immediately divested himself of the waistcoat, in the café crowded with people, to the amazement and interest of some English tourists who happened to be present and who, seeing him strip, were hoping to witness a fight. It was afterwards, in gratitude for this gift, that Baudelaire composed *Les Bons Chiens*, a prose poem which expresses his growing gentleness of mood and compassion.[11]

All those who knew him at this time speak of his kindness and sympathy to others. Although in desperate financial straits himself, he was constantly worried about the plight of Jeanne Duval, who, he had heard, was threatened with blindness in addition to her other afflictions.[12] It was then that he made the drawing which is usually taken for a likeness of her, but which is, in reality, an expression of his nostalgia for the past, in the midst of present loneliness. It was also at this time that he was beginning to show more understanding and appreciation of Ancelle's devotion to him, and gratitude for it.

From all the accounts written by those who knew him in Belgium, it can be seen that religion was a growing interest in him, and that, for the first time perhaps, he showed sympathy for the personality of Christ. 'L'éternel crucifié. Mon attendrissement', he wrote in notes for his book on Belgium.[13] We have, moreover, the account of how he behaved one year at the procession for the feast of Corpus Christi.[14] As he was watching it pass, he noticed a very old man tottering on his feet and walking with difficulty. Seeing him the crowd began to snigger and to make remarks about his unsteady gait and his candle guttering from his stumbling. Baudelaire, infuriated by this boorishness, suddenly left his friends, dashed into the religious cortège and, seizing the candle from the old man, offered him his arm. After that he followed the procession round the town, until it ended at the Church of Sainte-Gudule, with the old man leaning on his arm.

Scoffers, like Poulet Malassis, declared that they now found him very much changed, that he had become 'très calotin'.[15] Nadar, too, who was often in Belgium at this time, used to complain of the puritanism of his ideas and behaviour.[16] Nadar's secretary, Georges Barral, relates an episode which occurred when he, Baudelaire, his master, and some other friends, had spent an evening together, at the end of which, as usual, they had repaired to a well-known brothel.[17] As the older men disappeared, each with his woman, Baudelaire laid a restraining hand on the young man's arm, and held him back. Then, while they sat alone together, he talked seriously to him about life, advising him to follow Lacordaire's example, and said: 'Bad examples are only too frequent and dangerous, but they are not necessarily contagious, if the character is resolute and well-tempered. Life is long and offers many opportunities for corruption, so one must arm oneself against it from the very outset. It is only a question of forming the habit.' He drew his young companion's attention to the *Conférences* by Lacordaire, and, in a grave voice, pronouncing each syllable very clearly, he quoted the passage which ends: 'Do not dishonour in yourself the good which makes you a man' as if he were delivering a sermon on chastity. Then their noisy friends came back again. There followed loud bursts of laughter and shouts of joy, while champagne flowed, and Nadar cried, 'Let's drink and drink! Wine and women, there's nothing else in the world!'

Barral says that Baudelaire then seized him by the arm and dragged him out of the brothel. He had put on his flowing black cloak and, with his grey hair falling in locks over his shoulders, he seemed to the young man to grow in stature and to become a veritable prophet. He never forgot that evening and, forty years later, it was still vivid in his mind.

At this time Baudelaire was working on *Mon Cœur mis à nu* which, although it cannot rank amongst his greatest works, bears witness to his ultimate development as a spiritual being, and this final vision explains much in retrospect which, otherwise, would not have been made clear from the purely literary works, whilst these literary works themselves take on a new significance and a deeper meaning, when seen in the light of this last phase. It is easier then to apprehend what he was aiming at during his years of maturity. *Mon Cœur mis à nu* is the 'examen de conscience' of an upright man who never deluded himself into thinking that he was better than he was. Never perhaps was the poet so worthy of admiration and pity as now, in defeat. A new Baudelaire is here seen who was not apparent in his greatest works, a man broken and defeated in a worldly sense, striving against great odds, yet keeping in his suffering nobility and pride. As Pascal says in his *Pensées*: 'Toutes ces misères-là mêmes prouvent sa grandeur. Ce sont des misères de grand seigneur, misères d'un roi dépossédé.'

He never abandoned the fight, and never completely lost courage and hope, for he wrote then,[18] 'As long as I've not got definite proof that in the real battle, the battle with time, I'm beaten, I'll not consent to say that my life has been wasted! And even then!'

As 1865 rolled on Baudelaire's health grew worse, making it impossible for him to work, even when he had the strength of mind to bring himself to do so. 'It's this drowsy condition which makes me doubt all my faculties,' he wrote.[19] 'At the end of three or four hours of work I'm fit for nothing.'

In December and January he was very ill indeed. His doctor does not seem to have understood his case, and thought his illness was merely nervous. Medical science had not yet realized the connection between venereal disease and paralysis. It is only at this time, moreover, that he ever mentions being in the care of a doctor. He seems, on other occasions, to have been content with his own amateur diagnosis, or that of his friends, and to have relied on the kind of prescriptions which are to be found in daily papers, and which were probably as efficacious as water.

He suffered greatly when his attacks came on. He used to wake up in the early hours shivering with fever, and remain in this state until late in the morning, when he would fall asleep for a few hours, only to awaken later, worn out and incapable of work. All his energies were spent in nerving himself to endure the pain, so that, when the crisis was past, he was exhausted.[20]

Even when he was not suffering from such an attack, his nerves remained strained. When he was walking in the street the impression that someone was walking behind him gave him the feeling that he was about to faint, and, as soon as he fixed his attention on anything, even on a picture in a gallery, the sensation returned, accompanied by violent migraine, and he often imagined he was going mad. This fear of madness was his greatest terror, and he contemplated consulting a mental specialist when he next went to Paris. This was, however, only a month before his final collapse.[21]

Sometimes the seizure took the form of falling wherever he might be, so that he could not even sit upright in a chair, but was safe only when lying on his back, and he used often to remain thus, prostrated in a state of coma for some hours. In January 1866 he stayed in bed for several weeks, unable to get up for fear of falling. Lying on his back and incapable of work, he used to turn over in his mind all his worries – his debt, his increasing incapacity, the Garnier affair about which he had no news, his mother's health and growing feebleness. All this revolved and twisted in his mind, almost driving him mad.[22] He used to try to face the situation with courage and fortitude, and he used then to say to himself: 'Now supposing this is the beginning of apoplexy, what shall I do then, and how shall I put my affairs in order?'[23] Several times he thought he was cured, and started to work again, but the attacks returned. Poulet Malassis, who saw him frequently, began to be much disturbed at the changes he noticed in him at each meeting. Now, for the first time in his life, the poet began to drink to excess, because brandy gave him a temporary sensation of security and well-being. Poulet Malassis wrote to Troubat, Sainte-Beuve's secretary, that when Baudelaire came to see him he used to put away the brandy decanter, because he would drink glass after glass, which was bad for him in his precarious state of health.[24]

He once sent a brief account of his attacks to his mother so that she could consult her own doctor on his behalf, since he was dissatisfied with his medical adviser in Brussels. She became seriously alarmed when she read the note intended for the doctor. She imagined that he must be very ill indeed – which was true – and she wanted him to return home immediately, so that she could look after him herself. She was even prepared to ask Ancelle to raise the money in any possible way, or to borrow it herself, so that he could leave Belgium. He emphatically refused this offer and wrote assuring her that he was much better, and that he had written to her only when he was cured. He would take nothing from her, he said, except perhaps a loan, and then only when his contract was finally signed, and he thus was certain of being able to repay the money.[25]

'I won't have you write to Ancelle,' he said. 'You mustn't worry him. He knows that I've been ill several times, and he knows very well, moreover, that I'm longing to come home and to pay what I owe here. . . .

'I absolutely refuse your help. I won't take any more money from you. And I refuse to give particulars of what I owe here. At the utmost I might accept help if my contracts were signed, for there would then be a chance of my being able to repay the money. I've full confidence in Ancelle. He only needs directing. But I've the most horrible fear of your wild imagination, and I don't want you to get false ideas into your head. You mustn't write to Ancelle, promise me you won't! The unfortunate man has enough as it is to worry about, trying to find his way about this kind of business which is quite new to him. You mustn't be angry with me for refusing. I'm too much ashamed of all the money

I've already taken from you. I thank you very much all the same, and I send you my fondest love.'

Then the final blow fell. Ancelle had not been a success as a literary agent, for he had only made confusion worse. Lécrivain, on his return to Brussels from Paris, told Baudelaire that his incessant visits to the Garniers had merely irritated the firm, as well as his attitude of mistrust towards everyone. He, moreover, gave the impression that the poet was desperately anxious to secure an agreement quickly, and this only made the publishers more keen on keeping him waiting. Lécrivain also opined that they would not do business except with Baudelaire himself, probably because they thought that he would be more easily browbeaten than a lawyer.[26]

Finally, the sole result of Ancelle's intervention was to make Garnier at length refuse categorically to publish anything at all by Baudelaire. Thus the prize, which, for a year, had seemed to be dangling within his reach, was, at last, wrenched out of his grasp. He had never contemplated that the deal could possibly fail, and had always thought that the only difficulty was agreement on terms, that the haggling on the part of the firm had been for the purpose of securing the rights more cheaply.

Baudelaire received Ancelle's letter on Sunday, 18 February. Although it was a crushing blow, he did not give way to despair, but immediately began to write to the lawyer to advise him concerning other publishers to whom the works could be offered – skinflint Lévy, Amyot, Dentu, Faure, and even the respectable school-text firm of Hachette. Ancelle, on his side, was now beginning to grow flustered. Being a literary agent was not as easy as he had imagined, and he did not understand the psychology of publishers. He set about the business in a clumsy manner, taking everyone into his confidence and explaining to all and sundry the disappointment they had just suffered at the hands of the Garnier brothers. Baudelaire was terrified that the news would spread right through the whole of Paris,[27] in which the publishing world was like a small village where all gossip was soon known by everybody, and that Ancelle might close to him all the firms in France; for they would all learn, what, as a matter of fact, they knew already, that he was in great financial distress, and desperately anxious to find a publisher.[28]

He decided that the only thing for him to do was to leave all his things temporarily in Brussels and to return to Paris to see what he could do himself on the spot. He had now spent two years in Belgium to no purpose. He was in a much more serious condition than when he had arrived, since, as well as his debts in France which had not diminished, he now had those he had incurred in Brussels. His mother, in her anxiety, only rubbed salt into his wounds.

'You write very wild things to me,' he said to her,[29] 'and your reproaches on my rashness aren't likely to comfort me. I was deceived by Belgium. I was deceived by Lemer. Now I must extricate myself from my difficulties alone, and, by my own efforts, repair the harm done. You might, at least, leave me to my fate, without adding your reproaches to the rest!'

[4]

The Wheel is Come Full Circle

1866—1867

BAUDELAIRE was expected back in Paris on 15 March, but the day passed and he did not arrive, for he was now more seriously ill than ever, and unable to move. The failure to obtain a contract from Garnier had been a bitter blow and seems to have crushed him. There was no immediate hope of an agreement anywhere else, there was no reason why other firms should be more easily persuaded.

Before he returned to France he wished to say farewell to Rops at Namur, and to see, for the last time, the Jesuit church of Saint-Loup in that town, which he loved so well, and which, in his notes on Belgium he calls – so aptly for himself as it turned out – 'ce terrible et délicieux catafalque'.

It must have been shortly after 5 March that he went to Namur. On that date, he wrote to his mother and to Troubat, telling both of them he was soon returning to France, and making appointments with them. There are no further letters for a fortnight, until 20 March, when he wrote again to his mother to tell her he was unfortunately obliged to postpone his departure for Paris, that he wrote with difficulty, and would explain the reason later. He did not tell her how ill he was, but merely said that he was neither ill nor well, and that he had difficulty in working.

Baudelaire and Poulet Malassis were to spend the night with Rops and his father-in-law at Namur. They went together to visit the church, when suddenly, as the poet was extolling to his friends the beauty of the carving on the confessionals, he seemed to stumble or stagger, and fell to the ground. His friends helped him to his feet again, and he pretended that it was nothing, that he had only slipped on the shining marble pavement. Yet, in his heart, he must have realized that something serious was amiss, for it was this that he had been dreading for so many months. Poulet Malassis, who had been noticing for some time how ill he had been looking, was far from reassured, and the following morning went to his room to see how he was before they set out for Brussels. Baudelaire was standing irresolutely by his washstand, holding a toothbrush in his hand as if he were wondering what he had intended to do with it, and then, seeing his friend look at it, quickly slipped it into his pocket, wet as it was, like something which he wanted to hide. Poulet Malassis was more anxious than ever, but he managed to disguise his feelings. Afterwards, in the train, Baudelaire, who was shivering with cold or perhaps fever, asked to have the window opened when it was the contrary he had intended to say. He was immediately aware of his mistake, and pretended that it had only been a slip of the tongue.

Back in Brussels Baudelaire remained far from well, complaining of being very stiff, of finding difficulty in moving, and even in writing. He hoped that this was only rheumatism and that it would soon pass off. It was then he wrote to his mother to tell her that he was obliged to postpone his return for a few days. It was a short and apparently cheerful letter, chaffing her about her faulty spelling, and giving her the impression that it was only his business trips in Belgium, to collect material for future articles, which were delaying him. This was the last letter he ever wrote in his own hand.

It must have been now, after his return from Namur and before 22 March, when he became paralysed, that his encounter with the photographer Neyt occurred, although the latter declared later that it was on 29 March.[1] By that date he could no longer have gone out alone. Neyt said that Baudelaire came to fetch him in the evening to go out to dinner. The photographer had not heard that he was ill and at first noticed nothing amiss. As they sat over their dinner

they talked about Namur, but Neyt noticed that his friend
was eating very little and that, as the evening wore on, he
grew more silent and abstracted – his mind was obviously
elsewhere. Suddenly he would stop, with his glass in his hand
uplifted, as if making an effort to remember what it was he
had intended to do with it, wrinkling his brows with the
exertion of thought. There was an expression of terror in
his eyes, and he looked as if he were living some nightmare,
as if he felt himself falling down into some bottomless pit.
Then, suddenly, having taken hold of himself, he seemed to
remember where he was and what he was doing. He had
the courage to go on as if nothing was wrong, and he said
nothing of what he was feeling.

Neyt, in order to cheer him, showed him the photographs
which he had taken of him some time previously, and
offered him copies, but Baudelaire handed them back, saying
that he hated the sight of his own face, and that it disgusted
him. He was drinking many glasses of brandy, and there
were long periods of silence, when his friend tried to make
him talk, but often he did not seem even to hear what was
being said to him. He was shivering, and seemed to be keeping a strong hold on himself to prevent himself from trembling in all his limbs. With a shaking hand, he was trying to
find the handle of his coffee-cup, and, when he had found
it, he clung to it as though afraid to let go, as though it was
the only stable thing in his world. Shortly afterwards he
roused himself from his abstraction, and, taking his hat from
the peg, began to leave the restaurant with unsteady steps,
as if drunk, while saying to Neyt: 'I'll see you this evening!'
although it was then late at night.

Neyt, strange to relate, allowed him to depart alone and
it was only much later, after reflecting on the strangeness
of the poet's behaviour, and overcome with compunction,
and anxiety, that he set out to look for him. He went to his
hotel, but heard that he had not yet returned, and then,
really frightened, he went round to all the possible cafés to
try to find him. He discovered him at last, at one o'clock in

the morning, in a bar, sitting alone on one of the high-backed benches, with a glass of brandy before him, and he wondered what he had been doing since he had left him at ten o'clock. He now looked dazed and weary, and Neyt had no difficulty in persuading him to leave with him and to go home. As they walked along together Baudelaire leaned heavily on him and his movements became increasingly laboured, until finally, when they reached the hotel, he was unable to walk upstairs, and his friend was obliged to carry him up on his back. He laid him on his bed, but when he began to undress him to make him more comfortable, Baudelaire kept shouting at the top of his voice, 'Go away! Do go away!' Neyt left him finally because he was afraid of rousing the whole hotel.

Next morning, still feeling anxious, he returned to the hotel, and found the poet just as he had left him the previous night, lying fully dressed on his bed. The lamp on the table was still burning, but it was dying down through lack of oil, and the flame looked tiny and strangely red in the full daylight. The poet himself had once described such a moment in his *Crépuscule du Matin.*[2]

> *Où, comme un œil sanglant qui palpite et qui bouge,*
> *La lampe sur le jour fait une tache rouge.*

Neyt touched his shoulder, thinking he was asleep, and Baudelaire opened his eyes, looked at him, but he could not say a word. Neyt then fetched a doctor who diagnosed hemiplegia with resulting loss of speech.

This must have occurred between 20 and 23 March, for it is confirmed by Baudelaire in the letter to his mother which he dictated to his doctor and in which he said that, as a result of a further seizure, he was now incapable of movement.

In the meantime, after his return from Namur, Poulet Malassis had not been able to shake off a feeling of uneasiness, and he had written to friends in Paris, saying how very ill Baudelaire seemed. They wrote offering to find the money for him to return, if he would accept it, but he refused, hoping that, in a few days, he would have recovered and would be able to go through his own efforts.[3]

Then occurred the stroke which left him paralysed on one side though he recovered his speech. He was still living in his hotel, without any money, and the landlady, thinking that he was about to die, was becoming unpleasant. At his dictation the doctor wrote to his mother, begging her to obtain money from Ancelle by whatever means, so that he could settle his account and leave the hotel. He did not wish to alarm her about the state of his health and so it was difficult to make her understand how pressing was his need.

'It's a long time, a very long time,' he wrote to her, 'since Ancelle has written to me. I'd meant to postpone my return to Paris until I'd finished the work on which I'm engaged, and until I'd received money to pay something on account to the hotel here, but, since my last letter, three days ago, I've had a new seizure, and now I can't move. Write, if you can, to Ancelle to send some money *immediately* to Madame Lepage, the landlady of my hotel – whatever he can or will send – tell him especially not to gossip or be officious, impress that well upon him. The doctor who is kind enough to write under my dictation, tells me to assure you you need not worry, and that, in a few days, I'll be ready for work again.'

His mother was so much upset by this letter – she had been uneasy concerning his health for several months – that she wanted to dispatch Ancelle to Brussels immediately and to make arrangements for her son to return to France. She was prepared to sell out capital, or borrow herself, to procure a thousand francs to free him from debt at the hotel. She wrote immediately to her son for further news of his health, and also the name of his doctor, so that she could get from him a true account of his illness.

'I'm writing to you at once,' he said,[4] 'since you insist on an immediate answer. I don't believe that Ancelle will send a thousand francs to Madame L. I won't have him come to fetch me. Two days before I fell ill one of my friends in Paris offered me money on behalf of my friends, in case I was ill and wanted to return suddenly to France. But I refused as I thought I could go through my own resources.

'The doctors, and all my friends, are of the opinion that I should give up all literary work for six months and live in the country.

'Doctor Léon Marcq.[10] place de l'Industrie.

'How are you? I send you my love.'

Soon, as a result of Poulet Malassis' letters to his friends in France, the rumour spread that Baudelaire was dying in the public ward of a hospital in Brussels, and the report even reached the daily papers. Rops, when he read the story, felt that it was an insult to the poet's devoted friends, among whose number he was proud to count himself, and unfair to Baudelaire himself, since the rumour would do him professionally incalculable harm. He wrote to a friend in Paris, asking him to contradict the gossip.[5]

'You'll please oblige me by informing Monsieur Pierre Véron,' he wrote, 'that he's vainly and falsely announcing that our friend Charles Baudelaire is dying in a public hospital. Firstly he isn't dying, and secondly, Charles Baudelaire has made enough devoted friends in Belgium, amongst whose number I've the honour to be, who wouldn't have allowed him to be taken to a public ward as long as they had the smallest hole in which to receive him. What I'm asking you is very important, and you'd greatly oblige me if you'd say all this on my behalf to Monsieur Pierre Véron – you can, if you like, show him this note.'

Although Baudelaire could not write himself, he still took an interest in literary matters, and kept his ideal of perfection in production. He was receiving the proofs of the poems which were to appear in *Le Parnasse Contemporain*, and he was dictating through a friend the most minute recommendations for their publication – anxiety over the absence of a dash, a title misspelt, and the kind of type

used. At the same time his old friend Prarond, with whom
he had lost touch, sent him his recent collection of poems,
and Baudelaire took the trouble to dictate an appreciation
of it, and also to call his attention to a line the rhythm of
which was faulty.

The last two letters which Baudelaire dictated are dated
30 March 1866, one to his mother and the other to Ancelle.
To his mother he said:

'The answer that I sent on Monday must have reached you
on Tuesday evening. Wednesday, Thursday and today
Friday, you might have sent me news of yourself, and if you
haven't done so, it is because you imagine that I'm only
thinking of myself. You must send me news of yourself. I've
received a letter from A. who says he's coming here soon.
There's no need for that, at least, it's premature. 1. Because
I can't move. 2. Because I've got debts. 3. Because I've six
towns to visit, say a fortnight, and I don't want to waste the
fruit of all my work. I feel that his main reason is to please
you and to obey you and that's why I'm writing to you about
it, though, as a matter of fact, I'm prepared to come back as
soon as possible. Write me a long and full letter about yourself. I send you my fondest love.'

To Ancelle, he said:

'I thank you very much for your kind letter, and I appreciate very much the feelings which prompted it. But, on the
one hand, I see that you are in too great a hurry, and on the
other, that you're doing it to please my mother. 1. I can't
move. 2. I've got debts. 3. I need, to finish my work, to visit
five or six towns. We can come to an agreement by correspondence on most of the points. Don't forget the woman at
the hotel. I don't want you to begin all over again the Dentu
business, but you know my intentions, and leave the plan
with him only if he seems keen to come to an agreement.
Tell him, if you like, that I'm ill, but don't tell him the
truth about my condition. Write to me soon. My mother
was prepared to give a thousand francs to the cursed woman.
Obey her.

'Please forgive my laconic style, but someone else is writing for me.'

In these letters Baudelaire was being optimistic about his chances of recovery. Immediately after he had composed them, illness struck again, and this time he was left without power of speech. When his condition became alarmingly worse Poulet Malassis wrote to Ancelle to tell him how serious it was. The lawyer left Paris immediately, arriving in Brussels the following day, and he made arrangements for Baudelaire to enter a nursing home since he could not receive proper care at the hotel. He was taken to an establishment run by nuns, L'Institut de Saint-Jean et de Sainte-Élisabeth, in the Rue des Cendres – an appropriate name, 'the street of the ashes' – on 3 April. His mother, who at that time was far from well herself, was not told of the gravity of his condition, and the newspapers were requested not to publish any news of him.[6] Indeed she seemed more concerned over the state of his spiritual than over that of his physical health. Writing to Ancelle, she said:

'Think of his soul, I entreat you most earnestly, and find a priest for him who is kind and sympathetic. I've always wanted to see a good priest in touch with my son, to inspire him with resignation and patience in his sad state.'

Baudelaire recovered the use of his limbs to a certain extent, but his speech grew very quickly worse. Soon the only two words he could remember were 'sacré nom' which were always interpreted as an oath. With these two words, he who had loved and practised the art of conversation was obliged to express the whole gamut of his feelings and thoughts – joy, sorrow, anger and impatience – and he used sometimes to fly into a rage at his inability to make his meaning clear, and to answer those who spoke to him. Gautier used to say that paralysis had merely severed the thread which linked his mind and his speech together, that thought still lived in him, as could be divined from the expression in his eyes, but that it was imprisoned in its dungeon of flesh, and without means of communication with the outside world.[7]

Ancelle was a busy man who could not stay away indefinitely from his work, and he was obliged to return soon to Paris, where he felt it his duty to tell Madame Aupick the truth about her son's condition. Old and infirm as she was, she started off with her maid for Brussels, determined, if possible, to take him home with her to Honfleur.[8] She was, at first, horrified by the sight of his disablement but, after she had grown accustomed to it, she was able to help him by occupying his attention, by talking to him most of the day, sitting near him and encouraging him by her mere presence. She was much moved to find all her letters to him, tied with a ribbon, on the table beside his bed, and she spoke to him of the past, relating to him many episodes of his youth which she had rarely mentioned to him since their dream of living together had never materialized. She dwelt especially on the time when they had been alone together, when life had been happy for him. He listened with obvious pleasure, smiling at times, except when he wanted to ask some question and then his face was tortured with the vain effort of trying to find the words to express his meaning.

His mother realized that he was not happy in the nursing-home, and that what irritated him especially was the curtailment of his liberty, being under restrictions and ordered by others to do things. Sometimes, like an obstinate child, to show his independence, he used to do the contrary of what he had been told to do, for his one idea was that he would not allow anyone to domineer over him. To his mother, however, he had become a child once more, and she wished to take him back to Honfleur to look after him and cherish him. She seemed almost to derive comfort from the thought of his dependence on her. Nevertheless she understood that it was inhuman and cruel to curtail his liberty of movement since he was now able to walk again, leaning on a stick, and she planned to remove him from the nursing-home. The nuns were kind and good according to their lights, but they were, mostly, simple and uneducated women, with little experience of life, and none of literature. They thought that he used the only two words he could say because he wanted to swear, and imagined that he must be possessed by the devil, for they had heard rumours that he was a Satanist. They used to cross themselves in terror when he went by, and kneel to pray for help, when they heard the dread words 'sacré nom!' fall from his lips. Yet he was gentle and patient most of the time, except when his inability to express what he wanted to say drove him wild, and then he would shout the unmentionable words, frightening the other patients who were beginning to feel the strain of having, as they thought, a monster living amongst them. The Mother Superior complained to Madame Aupick that it was not pleasant to have a patient who had no religion, and that he was no longer a welcome inmate. Baudelaire's mother retaliated that she, for her part, was much displeased with the harshness and lack of sympathy of the nuns towards their patient, when she had imagined that those who had taken religious vows were always kind and gentle. 'It's too late to educate them at this late stage,' she added coldly, 'but the food could be improved.'[9] Since she got no satisfaction from the Superior, she decided to remove her son, who had spent a fortnight in the nursing-home, and was now well enough to resume his normal life, with certain precautions and care.

When he had left the convent, and the heavy doors had closed behind him, the nuns threw themselves on their knees on the threshold and, with clasped hands, begged for God's blessing. Then the priest came and sprinkled holy water in the entrance hall to exorcize the evil spirit which had dwelt for a time amongst them.[10]

Baudelaire returned to the Hôtel du Grand Miroir and stayed there for nearly three months, living a quiet, and seemingly happy life, sitting in the sun or walking in the parks – it was then summer. A newspaper report said that he was much better physically and that, although he could not express his thoughts through lack of speech, his mind

was still intact.[11] But an unpublished letter addressed to
Léon Domartin, the Director-General at the Ministry of
Science and Art, gives a different picture; it is from a friend
of Baudelaire's doctor and says that the poet was in a sorry
condition, with only intermittent flashes of lucidity – this
does not seem true, and at least must be exaggerated, since
he was living alone at the hotel. The letter added that
his infirmity, for an artist in words, was worse than
death.[12]

His friends did not neglect him and Stevens and Malassis
used to take him out to dinner, or to spend a day in the
country. One such outing is described by Malassis in a letter
to Asselineau, and says that Baudelaire expressed nothing
but serenity and happiness, as he gazed upwards with a
resigned look, whenever he had tried in vain to speak.[13]

At last his friends subscribed to hire a private carriage in
the train so that he could return home safe from the prying
eyes of inquisitive strangers. He arrived back in Paris on
2 July 1866, after two and a half years of exile.

There was a crowd of friends at the station, waiting for
him at the barrier, as he stepped down from the train.
Amongst them was Asselineau, the closest of his friends, who
had known him now for twenty years, and who had loved
and understood him better than all the others. It was to him
that he used to confide the personal details of his health
when he began to feel anxious about it.[14] Asselineau alone
saw the homely side which he hid from others, and was the
only one of his friends ever to have been intimate with him.
Now, when Asselineau saw him alighting from the carriage,
supported on the right by Stevens, and leaning heavily with
his left hand on his stick, looking like an old man, he could
not restrain himself and he burst into tears. Baudelaire
could say nothing to comfort him, for he had no word at his
command, and his only audible means of expression was
laughter. So now he laughed to reassure his friends, but it
was a mockery and a parody of mirth.

Baudelaire could not yet live with his mother at Honfleur. He needed care and special treatment. He became therefore a patient in a nursing-home in the Rue du Dôme, not far from L'Avenue d'Eylau, where he occupied a ground-floor room, looking on to a pleasant and quiet garden. Here he was able to hang some of his own pictures and to have his books with him. It is said that his health rapidly improved. He could receive his friends, which he did with seeming pleasure, delighting to hear them talk, although he could say nothing himself, and he seemed happy and contented. The specialists who were attending him gave reasonable hopes for his complete recovery.

His mother was making plans for giving up her little house at the sea, in order to come to Paris to settle near him, but her presence seemed to have a harmful effect on him, so the doctors advised her to return home and only to come to see him on periodic visits. Her detractors interpret this as a sign that Baudelaire hated her and was only now showing his real feelings. It is probable that his attitude was due to anxiety on her behalf, for he knew that she was happy only in her own home, with the memories of her husband, and he also realized that she was now too old and infirm for the bustle of life in a capital city. Earlier he had forbidden her to go out alone when she came to Paris to visit him.[15] He must also have recalled in her presence all he had intended to do for her, which he would now never be able to do, and smarted to think that he would never be able to bring her the satisfaction and content, which she had mentioned to Ancelle and longed to receive from him.

After she had installed him in his new and final home, she returned alone to Honfleur.

A petition was organized by some of his friends, the most active being Banville and Champfleury, and signed by a number of eminent men of letters, for a government grant to help Baudelaire in his present financial distress. Victor Duruy was the Minister of Education then, and had the disposal of funds destined to encourage science and literature. He was not an admirer of Baudelaire's work, and this

may account for the meanness of the grant which was
eventually allotted.[16]

Baudelaire's friends based their claim chiefly on his translations, and on his having been an occasional contributor
to important papers and periodicals – *Le Moniteur*, *La Revue
Contemporaine* and *La Revue des Deux Mondes*. They did
not emphasize his position as a poet, feeling perhaps that this
would not have carried weight, and that it was wiser not to
awaken the memory of the unfortunate trial of *Les Fleurs
du Mal*. Banville and Champfleury succeeded in persuading
several writers to add personal notes of recommendation to
the petition – Sainte-Beuve, Sandeau and Mérimée. Mérimée was probably invited to sponsor the application on
account of his friendship with the Empress Eugénie. Sainte-
Beuve, who had always managed to obtain support for himself in high places, drew particular attention to the fact that
Baudelaire was the son of a former ambassadress.

'I wish to support very strongly,' he wrote, 'the application
of my fellow-signatories. Monsieur Baudelaire is one of the
most subtle and distinguished men of letters whom the past
fifteen years have produced. I should also like to mention
that he is the son, by a first marriage, of Madame la Générale
Aupick. His mother, who loves him dearly, lives on the
pension granted to her by the Emperor as the widow of an
ambassador. At the present moment half of this income
goes on the support and treatment of her beloved son. Will
you, Monsieur le Ministre, in the kindness of your heart,
take into consideration this concourse of circumstances
worthy of your attention?'

While Sandeau had written:

'With all my heart I add my name to those of my friends
to bring to the sympathetic attention of Your Excellency the
present situation of Charles Baudelaire. Monsieur Baudelaire is a poet, a real poet. He is also in great distress. This
is sufficient to touch the generous heart of Monsieur Duruy.'

And Mérimée added:[17]

'After the testimony of Sainte-Beuve and Sandeau con-

cerning the works of Charles Baudelaire, it is unnecessary
for me to express the admiration I feel for his writings and
talent. I need only add that I have always appreciated the
goodness and simplicity of his nature. Never has a man of
letters suffered so much misfortune, and I do not know anyone who deserves, to such a degree, the kindness of the
Minister of Education.'

In October 1866 the sum of five hundred francs was voted
for the use of Baudelaire, not a pension but one solitary
grant – hardly enough to provide for him for two months,
while he was doomed to die slowly for over a year. The
doctors did not then know the inexorable progress of general
paralysis, nor that the disease was incurable. At first he grew
better, and even reached the stage of writing on a slate the
things which he wanted, but it was slow work, when he was
obliged to hold his right hand steady with his left. The
doctor, noting his improvement, started teaching him to
speak, beginning, as if he had become a child once more, by
making him repeat little phrases such as 'Bonjour, Monsieur!' and 'the moon is pretty!'

Then Madame Aupick wrote, on his behalf, to Hetzel,
the kindest of his publishers, of whom she had heard but
whom she did not know herself.[18]

'Without having the pleasure of knowing you personally,
Monsieur, I'm addressing this request to you, and that is to
go and see my poor son, Charles Baudelaire, who is in Dr
Duval's nursing-home, where he was placed after two attacks
of apoplexy, as a result of which he has remained aphasic –
that is to say, deprived of the power of speech. When it was
recently suggested to him that some of his friends should
be invited to visit him, he greeted the mention of your
name with the *greatest pleasure*, because he has for you
deep friendship. This is my reason and excuse for importuning you, as well as my profound grief. Charles, without
being able to speak himself, will be able to hear and understand everything you say to him. Although he is not in
complete possession of his intellectual powers – that wonder-

ful outstanding intellect he once enjoyed – he hasn't entirely lost their use. Besides, who can estimate to what extent these faculties have deteriorated since he is unable to express ideas?

'In the hope that you may accede to my request, Monsieur, I send you, in anticipation, my grateful thanks and my respects.'

Baudelaire was never without friends in the nursing-home. Nadar, Asselineau and Banville used to visit him every day, and also some of his women friends, like the Comtesse de Molènes, and Madame Meurice who played Wagner to him. Sometimes when he was feeling better he was able to go out for country walks and to lunch at the houses of friends. Nadar relates that, when they had reached his flat, Baudelaire used to indicate by signs that at the nursing-home they were not keeping his hands as scrupulously clean as he liked. He would not rest until his friend had washed them and trimmed his nails, and then he would look at them with admiration, holding them up to the light and smiling at them.[19]

Those who met him then say that his mind was still intact, and that he continued to show an interest in the things which had been a pleasure to him before he fell ill – the works of Poe, the music of Wagner, the painting of Delacroix and Manet, and the poetry of Sainte-Beuve. Nadar describes how the poet once silently 'discussed' with him the subject of immortality. In this passage of his book he achieves a certain nobility of tone, which serves to retrieve from triviality and vulgarity an otherwise shallow work, and it rings true when it is placed beside what we have learnt from other sources of the poet's preoccupations during the last phase of his life.

'Nous discutions de l'immortalité de l'âme,' wrote Nadar.[20] 'Je dis *nous*, parce que je lisais dans ses yeux aussi nettement que s'il eût pu parler. "Voyons! comment peux-tu croire à Dieu?" répétai-je. Baudelaire s'écarta de la barre d'appui où nous étions accoudés et me montra le ciel. Devant nous, au-dessus de nous, c'était, embrassant toute la vue, cernant d'or et de feu la silhouette puissante de L'Arc de Triomphe, la pourpre splendide du soleil couchant. "Sacré nom! Oh! sacré nom!" protestait-il encore, me ripostait-il indigné, à grands coups de poing vers le ciel. Les deux seuls mots qui pussent sortir des lèvres d'où avaient jailli des plaintes immortelles.'

All through the winter of 1866–7 his doctors believed that he would get better, and he himself was certain of it. In his own mind he had settled on the last day of March 1867 for the termination of his illness – perhaps because with April spring would have begun – and he had marked the date with heavy black underlining on the calendar. Asselineau says that Lévy came to see him before that to persuade him to sign an agreement, but he only pointed to the calendar to indicate that he would do no business until April, when he would be able himself to discuss everything with him.

In March Madame Aupick was told by the authorities at the nursing-home that he had expressed the wish to visit her at Honfleur. She was overjoyed and began to make preparations for his arrival, but she was nervous in case he should grow bored there since he spent most of the day indoors. In April his visit was postponed, as all his previous visits had been – it was just like the old days before his illness.

Then it began to be noticed that all he had learnt with so much labour was beginning to slip from him once more. When documents were brought to him to sign, he was unable to remember his name, and would remain, his pen uplifted, with a puzzled look on his face, until one of his own works was brought to him and he would then copy the name from its cover with slow deliberation.

Sometimes he improved visibly, but sometimes there was again a setback, and then he would gaze at his friends with dumb suffering in the dark eyes where was concentrated the last flicker of his life.

When March went by and April came and he was no
better, he seemed to lose all hope of getting well, or even the
desire to live. There was no more gaiety, and he made no
further efforts to write or speak.

It was Asselineau who used to keep Madame Aupick
informed of all the changes in her son's condition, and his
sympathetic understanding did much to make the last
agonizing year more bearable for her. He used to write to
her daily, after he came away from the nursing-home, and,
in his kindness, he understood exactly what it was that a
mother would like to know – the little homely details. He
used to make Baudelaire send her messages and tell her he
was asking for her. It was always to Asselineau that she
wrote, never to Banville, or to Gautier, or Sainte-Beuve.
With them she did not feel at ease and guessed their hidden
hostility towards her, so she was always afraid of troubling
them. They never made her feel, as did Asselineau, that
they really loved her son. With him she could be natural,
and it was to him that she sent inquiries about the material
details of the invalid's life – whether his room was sufficiently heated, since he suffered greatly from the cold, and
whether he needed any special medicines.[21] She came to
treat him like another son, and she was soon signing her
letters to him 'your affectionate old friend and mother'. After
Baudelaire's death Asselineau used to go and stay with her
at Honfleur to cheer her loneliness. Since she was then partially paralysed, the visits cannot have been exciting for him.
He used to occupy her son's room looking out over the sea,
which no one else was allowed to use, and she would talk to
him of 'le cher disparu' and weep before him with no feeling
of constraint or shame.[22] Later she remembered him generously in her will.[23]

On 21 May, made anxious by the sad tone of Asselineau's
letters, Madame Aupick, in spite of her infirmities, set off
for Paris to discover for herself why her son's promised visit
did not take place. She found him so much worse than when
she had last seen him that she decided to settle in a neigh-

bouring hotel so as to be able to spend all day beside him in the nursing-home, until late at night.

He now refused to get up, except occasionally, and even then would not stir from his room, but sat by the window without moving, his chalk-white hands folded on his lap, and his burning eyes staring out of his face the colour of ashes, no trace of emotion on his shrunken features. Sometimes he seemed to make a desperate effort to rouse himself, to fix his attention on what was being said to him and to answer his friends, but then once more he used to slip back into vacancy.[24] He would allow no one to shave him or to brush his hair, and he looked like a dishevelled vagabond – or a mad prophet for there were still the remains of spiritual distinction in the ravaged face with the noble brow. Once Madame de Molènes persuaded him to allow her to comb his long hair and beard. Then she brought him a mirror so that he could admire the change in his appearance. He did not recognize the strange face with the white hair and beard which looked out at him from the glass – he had not seen himself for some months – and he bowed to himself as to a stranger.[25]

After June 1867 he never stirred from his bed again. At the beginning of July it looked as if the end was near, but he lingered on through that month, and the next as well.[26] Through most of August he lay motionless as in a coma, showing only by occasional changes of expression in his eyes that he sometimes realized his friends were near. He could no longer grasp Asselineau's hand when his friend raised his from the bed where it lay as something that was no longer his – a dead branch still hanging to a tree.

His mother did not leave his side during his last week. For two days before he died he lay unconscious, his eyes wide open, seeing nothing. Before the end, however, he is said to have recovered complete consciousness and to have asked for – or to have let it be known that he wanted to receive – the last sacraments. It is always a delicate matter to decide

how much importance to attribute to the alleged behaviour
of the dying – especially in the case of a man paralysed and
known to be incapable of speech. His mother certainly believed in the completeness and sincerity of his orthodox
religious conversion at the end – witness her letters to his
friends after his death – and most of the reports emanate
from her. One of these said: 'Before dying, Charles Baudelaire, who had recovered his reason, asked to receive the
sacraments and confessed to the parish priest. The author of
Les Fleurs du Mal died a Christian.' [27] Charles Bual, who
paid his last visit to Baudelaire immediately after this,
describes how the poet made the sign of the Cross several
times, with an expression of utmost joy, though all he could
say repeatedly was 'Sacré nom! Ah! Sacré nom!' [28] The
original meaning of the expression was, after all, 'Sacred
Name of Christ!' Such behaviour would not lack verisimilitude if the development and curve of his life are taken
into consideration. Baudelaire had at last found his resting-
place, and respite from struggle and strife, and he was now
ripe for everlasting peace. As in classical tragedy, he had
worked out his salvation, had been granted his vision, and
was ready to depart. He could then utter the cry of Othello:
'If after every tempest come such calms, may the winds blow
until they have wakened death!'

Baudelaire died peacefully on the last day of August 1867
in his mother's arms. At the end she had him once more for
herself alone, as when he was a child before the battle of
life began and now, bending over him to catch his last
breath, she crooned to him as she had done when he was a
baby. Her maid Aimée said to her: 'See how he looks at
you, Madame! He can surely hear you. He's smiling at
you!' [29]

He did, in fact, die smiling, and this smile, transfiguring
his ravaged face, lingered on it even after death, like the last
rays of the setting sun, so that his mother was never able to
forget it. It seemed to her that all the discord between them
melted away under its radiance, that he understood at long

last her deep love and appreciated it, that he was her grateful and submissive child once more.

The morning after Baudelaire died Nadar wrote to de Villemessant, the editor of *Le Figaro*, to ask to be allowed to write the poet's obituary.

'Baudelaire was dying yesterday evening,' he wrote,[30] 'and he must indeed be dead this morning! In any case, it seems to me impossible that he should still be alive tomorrow. I'll let you know as soon as I hear definite news. Many stupid things will now be said about this greatly gifted and honourable man, which will bitterly hurt and anger those who loved and respected him. If you want the *truth* about him in your paper, I'm prepared to give it to you. Asselineau, who'd have performed this task in every way far better than I, is holding back, waiting for the most suitable occasion, and I didn't feel that I should try to overrule him, when I understood the reasons for his decision. Give me an immediate answer – but don't publicize my offer – and I'll hand you in the notice this morning, or on Monday at latest.'

Written on the letter, in another hand, appear the words: 'I accept with much pleasure. H. de V.'

Even the day following Baudelaire's funeral the kind of stupidities which Nadar had contemplated did in fact appear, as in *La Presse* on 3 September.

'Today they are burying Baudelaire,' wrote the columnist, 'who has just died after a distressing period of degeneration. Baudelaire was not essentially a man of letters; he was born and remained all his life a man of the world, who did not consider writing as a profession but rather as an aristocratic pastime. His youth was spendthrift. He made a journey to the Far East whence he brought back a passion for tropical eccentricity, with Negro ideals in his blood, and the wildness and bitter tang of the sea! His mother's second husband was General Aupick, and she spent most of her life at Honfleur. Baudelaire often went there, when he was discouraged or depressed, or when he wanted a safe retreat; thus, in order to be within easy reach of this haven, he chose to live in the rue d'Amsterdam, at the Hôtel de Dieppe, where he occupied a small room. From there he used to escape at the slightest whim, and jump into a train to Honfleur, to enjoy material comforts, and the books, works of art, curios, drawings and souvenirs he had collected in his travels, which he kept there. A small allowance was paid to him by his *conseil judiciaire* every month, not to him directly but to his landlord to settle his expenses at the hotel, and even his cabs and cigars. His writings paid for his amusements. He did not produce much, but his articles and poems were eagerly sought after by papers and reviews. He polished his style with voluptuous and meticulous care, adding endless touches to it, as he bent over a Chinese desk, inlaid with mother-of-pearl, which embellished his hotel room, and he only consented to relinquish his proofs with the utmost regret. He went out only when his mood and his financial situation were favourable. He took great pains with his clothes, and always wore shoes of fine patent leather, full black trousers; he aroused attention by his nonchalant and disdainful attitude, and by the strong perfume which emanated from him.'

Baudelaire's ill-luck – his 'guignon' – held out to the bitter end. It was difficult to collect people for his funeral since he had died on a Saturday – and a Saturday in August – when most people were away on holiday in the country. The summonses to the funeral were sent out on the Sunday and many people did not hear of it until late on the Monday, when everything was over.

The funeral service was held in the Église Saint Honoré in Passy, and there were barely a hundred people present. Scarcely half that number followed the procession to the cemetery of Montparnasse, where the poet lies buried in the same grave as his stepfather.

Asselineau had wished Baudelaire to be vindicated at his funeral, granted recognition in death if not in life, and to be given a burial worthy of him.[31] He therefore sought to persuade Sainte-Beuve to give the funeral oration at the graveside. But Sainte-Beuve here failed Baudelaire as usual. He declined on the score of his failing health. True, he had undergone a major operation a couple of years previously, from which he never fully recovered, and as a result of which he was to die in 1869.

Asselineau is alleged to have approached Gautier next, whom Baudelaire had admired and to whom he had dedicated his *Fleurs du Mal* – Gautier was now the most famous living French poet, with Vigny and Musset dead, Lamartine silent, and Hugo in exile. It is claimed that he, too, declined the honour.

The absence of both Sainte-Beuve and Gautier from Baudelaire's funeral was unfavourably noticed by young Verlaine, with the uncompromising ruthlessness of youth.

'It was a pity,' he wrote,[32] 'that the absence of a famous person was noticed and described as discourteous; it was a greater pity still that this opinion was justified. Comments also were made on the absence from this sad ceremony of Théophile Gautier whom the Master had loved so well.'

Baudelaire had now become for his young followers 'the Master'.

Disapproval was also expressed by his disciples because *La Société des Gens de Lettres* sent no representative to the funeral.

It must be said in Gautier's defence, if not exoneration, that we now know, from two separate sources, that he was in Geneva at the time. The first source is his letter, written from Geneva to his daughter Estelle, to thank her for sending good wishes for his birthday which occurred on the day Baudelaire died.[33] The second source is the diary of his mistress, Eugénie Fort, in which it is recorded that he left for Geneva on 26 August, and that, on 2 September, he had not yet returned to Paris.[34]

But Gautier need not have left France at a moment when it was well known that Baudelaire was dying, especially as it was not a business trip, but only a holiday visit to Carlotta Grisi; or he might have returned to Paris for the funeral.

His letter to his daughter does not express regret or grief for
the loss of his friend, but merely mentions, at the end, that
he must now set to work on his 'undertaker's' job of composing Baudelaire's obituary. It is on the whole a gay letter.
Gautier was, however, said to have such a horror of death
that he made it a rule never to attend funerals, or to mention
dying at all. He once offended Ernest Feydeau deeply by
not expressing sympathy over the decease of his wife.[35]

Monday, 2 September 1867 was a sultry day, and the
oppressive heat prevented the older men from following the
procession to the graveside. A heavy clap of thunder, just
as the hearse was entering the cemetery gates, seemed to
thin out the ranks still further.

Théodore de Banville gave one of the funeral orations. He
was the oldest of Baudelaire's friends, having known him
since the luxurious days at the Hôtel Lauzun, and he was,
as Baudelaire described him, the best friend for happy,
youthful and carefree days. Now, Banville was so much
moved with grief, and anger at the conduct of his fellow
men of letters, that his words were scarcely audible.[36]

'This man whom Death has now felled,' he began, 'bears
away with him so large a part of my heart that I cannot
gaze at his coffin without my eyes overflowing with tears.'

Then, with an effort, he pulled himself together, and paid
a tribute to the man of letters in Baudelaire. He mentioned
the difficulties he had encountered in receiving recognition,
but declared that there had been signs in recent years that
this was coming to an end and that the poet, if he had lived
only a few years longer, would have found himself honoured
and respected. He said the near future would claim in no
uncertain terms that he was not merely a poet of talent but
a poet of genius, and that it would become progressively
clear how large a place his work occupies in the literature of
the nineteenth century. His work was essentially French,
essentially original and essentially modern. Baudelaire was
one of the few poets who had not experienced the sway of
Victor Hugo and who had not imitated him, or Musset, or

Lamartine. He did not strive, as other contemporary poets did, to improve men, to turn art into a sacred mission, but accepted modern man in his entirety, with his weaknesses, his aspirations and his despair. He had thus been able to give beauty to sights which did not possess beauty in themselves, not by making them romantically picturesque, but by bringing to light the portion of the human soul hidden in them, and he had thus revealed to literature the sad and often tragic heart of the modern town. That was why he haunted, and would always haunt, the minds of modern men, and move them when other artists left them cold.

'Farewell, Baudelaire!' he ended. 'Your friends will never cease from mourning you, you who have been their example and their pride. Farewell! Great friend, great artist, and great poet! Farewell!'

The rain had begun to fall before he had finished speaking, and the people standing at the graveside were more concerned for their clothes – their black broadcloth and their expensive silk hats – than anxious to hear further speeches. They scarcely listened to Asselineau, who was almost speechless with grief and rage. He did not talk so much of the artist as of the man, and it was the man especially whom he sought to vindicate. He remembered, as he spoke, how empty life would now seem with Baudelaire gone, with whom he had never known a moment of boredom, without whom he felt that his life was shattered, and that nothing would ever be the same for him again. So stricken by grief was he that he even contemplated leaving Paris, and burying himself somewhere in the provinces where nothing would remind him of his loss.[37] He was filled with disgust as he thought of all the stupid and cruel things which had been said about Baudelaire, and he tried before his apathetic audience to destroy the Baudelaire legend, saying that only those who had not known him disliked him, and that he had possessed at the same time a great mind and a warm and generous heart.

Then he noticed that everyone was in a hurry to leave,

for the rain was now falling in torrents. He was himself too much overcome by grief to speak coherently as he saw that no one was paying any attention to what he was saying, and the shame of it overcame him so that he brought his remarks to a close.

The rest of the sad rites were hurried through. The damp earth was quickly shovelled on to the coffin, and the pit closed in.

Then those who had endured the ceremony to the bitter end broke away and dashed for shelter.

CONCLUSION

Nous devrions pourtant lui porter quelques fleurs.
Les morts, les pauvres morts, ont de grandes douleurs,
Et quand Octobre souffle, émondeur des vieux arbres,
Son vent mélancolique à l'entour de leurs marbres,
Certe, ils doivent trouver les vivants bien ingrats.

Conclusion

AFTER her son's death Madame Aupick had no desire to live any longer, but she was determined not to die until she had seen his debts paid, his books published, and his name vindicated. She divided up his personal belongings – his books and his pictures – amongst his close friends. She did not realize their worth, but some of them eventually proved valuable to those who received them, for Baudelaire had a sure taste and instinct for what would last, and, although he never had large sums of money to dispose of he managed to assemble a fine collection of drawings especially – works by Legros, Meryon, Guys, Delacroix, Devéria, Whistler, Jongkind, Rethel and so forth.

Now that the poet was dead, and in danger of being forgotten, Banville and Asselineau wished to bring out, as soon as possible, a complete edition of his collected works. In their search for a publisher – the task was easier for them than it had been for the author himself – their choice finally fell on Michel Lévy, chiefly because he possessed the rights in the translations of Poe, and thus Baudelaire's works could be brought out in a uniform edition. Lévy, of whose avarice the poet had so often complained, would offer no more than two thousand francs for the rights on all his works – *Les Fleurs du Mal*, *Spleen de Paris*, *Les Paradis Artificiels* and two volumes of criticism – but Madame Aupick, for the pleasure of seeing her son's works published together as a whole, was prepared, in the end, to accept this mean offer. Money was no longer an object to her, as she had enough to last the few remaining years of her life, and there was no one to whom she wanted to leave it.[1] Lévy, however, eventually secured the rights for an even smaller sum. Baudelaire had died intestate. A distant relative on his father's side came forward to claim his share of the inheritance, and so the works – the author's only possession – were put up for auction in November 1867. The bidding started at one thousand francs, but was eventually forced up to seventeen hundred and fifty, and for that sum – about seventy pounds – Lévy secured the rights on all Baudelaire's writings in five volumes for fifty years, until the copyright expired.[2] There was no one at the sale prepared to risk more than seventy pounds and thus they fell under the auctioneer's hammer for less than fifteen pounds apiece. This was exactly ninety years ago. During that time a new opinion of Baudelaire has gradually formed so, since the copyright expired in 1917, scarcely a year has passed without some new edition of his works appearing. He has been translated into almost every European language. His greatest admirers claim that he revolutionized the manner of thinking, writing and feeling of western Europe, and that his aesthetic criticism marks a date of paramount importance, not only in the history of poetry, but also of art in general.

Lévy's complete edition began to appear in 1868, with a preface by Théophile Gautier. As soon as the first volume was published Madame Aupick wrote to him, in that ecstatic style which her son used affectionately to deride.

'Monsieur, I heard from Monsieur Asselineau,' she said,[3] 'that you had written for the new edition of *Les Fleurs du Mal* an Introduction which is a veritable masterpiece. This news brought me immense joy in the midst of my sorrow, in the sad life to which I am now condemned, a joy such as I did not expect ever to feel again. If I hadn't feared to importune you, I would have written to you immediately, but I thought then that I'd wait until it had appeared, and I silenced my heart which was crying out to you incessantly "thank you!" I have just received the beautiful article, and, without waiting any longer for the joys which are further promised, I come to tell you of my happiness, you, the tender and devoted friend of my son, that I am penetrated with gratitude for all that you have done for his memory. And he, too, you must believe it, is smiling at you from above, for he is hovering near you, looking after your happiness – at least it pleases me to believe this – and he loves you still as he loved you for so many years.

'Please receive, Monsieur, the assurance of my sympathy and of my sincere wishes.'

The reasons for Baudelaire's universal popularity today are not difficult to explain. To appreciate him well it is not necessary to adopt an academic and historical attitude or to study him in relation to his own age and the literary movements of the nineteenth century. Textual commentaries can largely be dispensed with; there are few obscure references which depend for their effect on the knowledge of some other literary text, and it matters little for the pure enjoyment of his poems where he obtained his inspiration, whether he borrowed it from others. Each poem stands complete in itself, with its own message for those who can receive it. He can be read today at the distance of a century as if he had written for the present generation, with a knowledge of its problems and interests. His appeal is still vital because he was not fettered by the fashionable opinions and evanescent whims of his own age, and he made no concessions to the spirit of his own time in order to gain popularity. All his life he fought against the false reasoning and false taste of his contemporaries, against the futile enthusiasms which have dated, and he had the courage to proclaim the shortcomings of those who enjoyed established reputations.

It is not easy to place him in any definite category of nineteenth-century poetry. In his dates he belongs to the Art for Art's Sake Movement; but, although he has many affinities with it, he has as many dissimilarities. He shared its dislike of the Romantics, of the poetry of Lamartine and Musset – particularly of the latter on whom his judgement was especially harsh, since he could not understand how one could give the name of poet to a man who had not the faintest idea of how a mere reverie could be turned into a

work of art, and he poured contempt on what he called his
'confidences de table d'hôte'. He shared the reluctance of
his fellow-poets to use literature as a 'déversoir' for personal feelings; their dislike for the romantic idealization of
love in all its manifestations and for seeing in it the justification of everything. But whereas the others excluded it from
their poetry, except in its most platonic expression, he clearly
differentiated between its various forms, between love and
lust, the former symbolized by the Cycle of the White Venus,
and the latter by the Cycle of the Black Venus.

Like the other poets of his time Baudelaire reacted against
the pathetic fallacy of the Romantics, which saw nature as
a friend and comforter of man. Where the others saw her as
beautiful and indifferent, and tried to reproduce objectively
and accurately that beauty in their poems, he saw her only
as the source of raw material for the artist to assemble according to his fancy, and he realized that if the faithful
reproduction of a landscape is the ideal, then this will inevitably lead to the idealization of photography as the
height of art. Contrary to his contemporaries he did not
consider that there existed any beauty in nature until the
artist had put it there by seeing its significance. This did
not mean, as has frequently been suggested, that he was
indifferent to nature – his *Salon* of 1846 is sufficient proof to
the contrary – but only that he considered that she should
be put in her place, one lower than the work of art which
was the outcome of her inspiration.

Like the others Baudelaire turned away from the romantic
interest in medieval subject matter and local colour. But he
did not adopt their Hellenic revival, which he considered a
'pastiche inutile et dégoûtant', and his escape from medieval-
ism was into the modern world. He believed that no poet
could achieve greatness unless his own age had set its seal
upon him.

All the poets of the Art for Art's Sake Movement worshipped beauty, but Baudelaire saw it in a different way
from his contemporaries. For them beauty was in the sub-

ject itself and part of its essence, and it was the poet's aim and duty to reproduce it in his works. Baudelaire, on the contrary, saw it in the quality which the artist himself brought to it; it consisted in his own vision of it. Beauty was the flame of the fire, the radiance of the energy, generated by the spiritual shock which the artist received when he was moved, and this spiritual shock could come from objects hitherto considered ugly. He did not see – as many critics have claimed – beauty in ugliness, but he only said that out of ugliness he could distil beauty. 'Tu m'as donné ta boue,' he said, addressing the modern town, 'et j'en ai fait de l'or.'

Baudelaire shared his contemporaries' admiration for work well done, for perfection of technique, but here, too, his attitude was different. With them perfection of technique meant practised craftsmanship, and Art for Art's Sake tended to become Art for Craft's or Technique's Sake. For him there could be no perfection of technique without a high degree of spiritual development. He was the only poet of his age who was not inspired by the rationalist and positivist ideals of the time, and who was preoccupied with spiritual values. During the years of his maturity he was more concerned with this search for a spiritual ideal than with any other interest, and his art, even in its form, is closely linked with it.

Baudelaire died unrecognized, with all his works out of print and many of his writings still unpublished, but the situation has greatly altered in the ninety years since his death. Nowadays critics in every country place him amongst the greatest European poets. Should this seem exaggerated it can certainly be said, without fear of contradiction, that he ranks amongst the two or three great French poets of the nineteenth century. He was more profound and sincere than Victor Hugo, and, at his best, more deeply moving, though his work may not possess the same variety of note. Vigny and Musset are not worthy of being placed in the same category with him, and he is more human than Leconte de

Lisle. He may not be as original a genius as Rimbaud, but he is a profounder and more balanced artist. He was more capable of emotion and thought than Verlaine, more of a conscious artist. Verlaine's poetry possessed a purely lyrical and personal appeal which has rarely been surpassed in French verse; and his inspiration was thistledown blown hither and thither by the wind so that his poems sprang up, almost without his volition, in whatever soil the light seeds found rest. He wrote, as the spirit moved him, in a veil of plaintive melancholy.

> *Écoutez la chanson bien douce*
> *Qui ne pleure que pour vous plaire.*[4]

He would not, however, have been capable of the spiritual aspirations and intellectual preoccupations of Baudelaire, and could not have analysed himself sincerely. When we think of Verlaine small songs rise up in our mind:

> *Il pleure dans mon cœur*
> *Comme il pleut sur la ville.*[5]

Or again:

> *Qu'as-tu fait, ô toi que voilà*
> *Pleurant sans cesse,*
> *Dis, qu'as-tu fait, toi que voilà,*
> *De ta jeunesse.*[6]

Or else:

> *Tout suffocant*
> *Et blême, quand*
> *Sonne l'heure,*
> *Je me souviens*
> *Des jours anciens*
> *Et je pleure;*
>
> *Et je m'en vais*
> *Au vent mauvais*
> *Qui m'emporte*
> *De ça, de là,*
> *Pareil à la*
> *Feuille morte.*[7]

Baudelaire would not have been content to weep in gentle melancholy over the days that were no more, or over his own failure and deficiencies. Like a surgeon bending over the operating table and cutting into the flesh to find the root of some tumour, he probed into the depths of his being to discover the cause of moral disease. He did not shrink from inspecting closely the evidence of sin and evil which he found in himself. Most of what we know in his disfavour he himself told us, leaving nothing for anyone else to say, and no one could have been harder on him, nor have judged him more severely, than he did himself. He wrote of himself just as he saw himself, concealing nothing, and keeping no shred of vanity beneath which to hide his shame. As a result he has been maligned and misunderstood.

With full knowledge and understanding of his life, the Baudelaire of the legend vanishes, the Byronic and satanic figure, and he appears as he truly was, a man composed of weakness and strength, and especially a man of great vulnerability. Few have been as hypersensitive as he – as if his nerves had no outer covering of flesh between them and the cold air – and so he suffered from circumstances which others would scarcely have noticed. This sensitive shyness was hidden beneath a sophisticated and polished manner and few people guessed its existence. He suffered tortures of nervous apprehension whenever he had to face the public gaze, even in such a trivial matter as presenting a ticket to the scrutiny of that board of top-hatted officials sitting at the 'contrôle' of any French theatre. 'For a timid nature,' he wrote in his *Journal*,[8] 'the "contrôle" of a theatre strongly resembles the judgement seat in the infernal regions.'

This sensitive diffidence must be given its important place in his psychological composition, for it colours his relations with his public, his editors, with his friends, and especially with women. Many examples of it are to be found in his life – his terror of failing, of being found ridiculous, his misgivings at every new undertaking.

'Would you believe it,' he wrote to his mother,[9] 'that now

I feel nervous – nervous of what? Of not being successful! That's the explanation of the indecision which has hampered me so often.'

He envied his self-confident and more obtuse friends, like Nadar and Champfleury, and to the latter he wrote:[10]

'It's quite evident that you're a happy man, happy through yourself! But I'm far from being in that state, for I'm always dissatisfied with myself.'

He possessed great pride, and his pride increased with his misfortunes, when it was the only luxury which he could afford. 'The lower I sink in poverty and misery,' he wrote to his mother,[11] 'the prouder I become!' But, on the other hand, he had no vanity or conceit. He saw clearly the insincerity and false thinking of others, feeling and dreaming that he could do better himself. Then he suddenly remembered all that others had said of him, and he would analyse himself, wondering whether it was only vanity after all which led him to believe that he could do better than those whom he despised. Doubt would lay its heavy hand on him, and the suspicion torture him that he did not, after all, possess the talent or power to achieve what he had dreamt of achieving, that perhaps they had been right, all those who had found him wanting. This morbid terror increased as he grew older, when it seemed as if his dreams were not now to be realized. 'Grant me the grace, Lord God Almighty,' he wrote,[12] 'to compose a few beautiful verses which will prove to me that I'm not the least of all men, that I'm not inferior to those whom I despise.'

With this sensitive shyness there was sent, as its natural accompaniment, extreme fastidiousness – fastidiousness in his person, in his habits, in his dealings with others and in his methods of composition. His dandyism was merely a further expression of this fastidiousness of mind and body. In this he was a contrast to Verlaine, who never suffered unduly from the degradation into which he had sunk through excess in drink. Verlaine felt himself to be a sinner, and he used to weep tears of repentance, but he does not seem to have grown distasteful to himself. Baudelaire, on the contrary, though he never lost his sense of human dignity, expressed disgust of what he had become. It is easy to imagine what he suffered when he discovered, at an early age, that he had contracted syphilis. This explains much of the bitterness of his work.

> *Dans ton île, ô Vénus! je n'ai trouvé debout*
> *Qu'un gibet symbolique où pendait mon image. . . .*
> *– Ah! Seigneur! donnez-moi la force et le courage*
> *De contempler mon cœur et mon corps sans dégoût.*[13]

Asselineau declared, in his speech at the graveside, that only those who did not know Baudelaire disliked him. In all that we know of him he certainly appears as a devoted and sympathetic friend, and there are many examples of his disinterested friendship. In 1860, at the height of his own financial distress, he wore himself out tramping the streets of Paris to find subscribers for a set of etchings by Meryon. He wasted days and weeks of his precious time preparing Léon Cladel's manuscript for the press. His behaviour to Jeanne Duval gives proof of his human sympathy and sense of obligation. For twenty-five years he gave her the greater part of what he earned, and his constant anxiety at the end was that she should not be left in want, or that he might die suddenly, leaving her without resources.

This tenderness and sympathy were, however, accompanied by weakness of will and irresolution, and his aspirations were often beyond his powers of realization. 'How difficult it is,' he wrote to his mother,[14] 'not just to conceive a book, but to write it without flagging!' His imagination used to fly on ahead leaving his power of realization far behind it. At the beginning he could see his plan sketched out in all its ramifications. He got the creative 'kick' out of this dreaming, and felt as if he had achieved everything, but the thought that he must now clothe these bare bones with flesh filled him with weariness, and his friends all show how he would do anything at all to postpone the critical moment of starting to work. He would say that he was waiting until the new hour began, he would do the same for the days, then for the weeks, for the months and finally even for the years. He was for ever making plans of what he would do during the coming week, beginning early on the Monday morning, or on the first day of the new month, or again on the first day of the year. He had a childish and touching confidence in New Year's resolutions, but nothing could cure him of his habit of day-dreaming.

'The devil, in spite of all my good resolutions,' he wrote,[15] 'slinks every morning into my mind in the shape of this thought: "Why not rest for the moment in forgetfulness of all these things? This evening, at one fell swoop, I'll accomplish all the most urgent business." Then evening comes, and my mind reels at the sight of the multitude of things left undone; overwhelming depression induces incapacity, and then, the following day, the same old comedy starts off once more, with the same hopes and the same illusions.'

Later, as a result of his lack of popularity, there came a sense of the futility of all effort. It was as if he said to himself: 'What is the use of all this labour since no one cares to read the work in its completed form?'

He himself realized only too clearly this failing, and his *Journal* abounds in timetables of work, where the days and the weeks are divided into portions with each having its ascribed task. He calculated all that he would accomplish in the given time, and all the money he would earn. Unfortunately the plans exist only on paper, for most of the tasks were never performed. The tragedy was that there was so much that he dreamed of doing, but never finished, so many masterpieces that existed merely in his imagination, and of which only the titles have come down to us.

In spite of his human sympathy – or perhaps because of the nature of that sympathy – Baudelaire remained a solitary spirit whom no one really understood, despised and criticized by lesser writers because, in the trivial round of life, he had fallen short of what they themselves had achieved. They could not understand how it came to pass that he was unable to harness the talent which they grudgingly granted him, to his own advancement. Ever since childhood he had experienced a sense of solitude, even in the midst of close friends. 'Sentiment de solitude dès mon enfance. Malgré la famille, et au milieu des camarades, surtout – sentiment de destinée éternellement solitaire.'[16]

None of his friends fully understood him, and to few of them he opened up his heart. Banville admired him but, as the poet himself admitted, he was a friend for happy days. Gautier was never a close friend, no more than Sainte-Beuve. With Asselineau he joked and talked of homely matters, but there were depths in him which Asselineau could not have appreciated. Baudelaire did not easily give himself to others, and as he grew older his solitude became complete. When he had accepted it, it became his greatest source of spiritual wealth.

Baudelaire was not merely a poet of talent; he was also, in the same way as Pascal had been, a moral investigator. His early religious upbringing, his Jansenist background, had given him the habit of self-examination – of examining his conscience for confession – and he persevered in this even when he had ceased being a practising Catholic. He tried to see clearly into himself, not to shrink from what he brought to light, and to set down what he had found, in order to draw general conclusions from his discoveries. So much afraid was he of ascribing good to himself which did not in reality exist, that he was harder on himself than he need have been. Medical students always find in themselves symptoms of whatever disease they may be studying, and, in the same way, Baudelaire discovered in himself all the evil which he was investigating. This scientific research into the human heart interested him even as a young man, and it is himself whom he describes in *La Fanfarlo*.[17]

'Nous nous sommes tellement appliqués à sophistiquer notre cœur, nous avons tant abusé du microscope pour

étudier les hideuses excroissances et les honteuses verrues
dont il est couvert, et que nous grossissons à plaisir, qu'il est
impossible que nous parlions le langage des autres hommes.
Ils vivent pour vivre, et nous hélas! nous vivons pour savoir.'

The result was that he vivisected himself in the process
of investigation into the hidden workings of the human
heart, and became a martyr to his work of discovery. It was
not, however, as a psychoanalyst has suggested,[18] because he
was a masochist, and a worshipper of his own failure. From
contemplation of the sordid workings of the human heart,
he grew to hate himself as well as others, and became his
own tormentor, his own inquisitor, as he said himself:[19]

> *Je suis la plaie et le couteau!*
> *Je suis le soufflet et la joue!*
> *Je suis les membres et la roue,*
> *Et la victime et le bourreau!*
> *Je suis de mon cœur le vampire,*
> *– Un de ces grands abandonnés,*
> *Au rire éternel condamnés,*
> *Et qui ne peuvent plus sourire!*

The common run of men consider immoral those artists
who show us our shame, and destroy the lie on which man's
self-respect and pride are based. This would explain the
criticism of those who, for so long, accused Baudelaire of
obscenity and immorality. He brings men up, with a shock,
in front of their real selves, making them realize, with horrible clear-sightedness, what are their real motives, showing
them the canker in their heart, and that is why so many
have feared him and, as a result, disliked him. He exempts
none from his criticism, since all have the same seed of evil
in their hearts, and he addresses his reader, as linked together with him in the same fellowship of sin, 'Hypocrite
lecteur, mon semblable, mon frère.'[20]

The hypocritical and superficial attitude towards art, which
accused works such as his own of immorality, was one

which Baudelaire refused to tolerate. When preparing his defence in 1857, he wrote in the notes for his lawyer:[21]

'Such a morality would mean that henceforth only comforting books should be written, with the purpose of proving that man is born good, and that all men are happy. What abominable hypocrisy!'

The most intense emotion expressed in Baudelaire's writings is disgust of sin, disgust of human weakness and vice. He did not claim that all the flowers which he gathered were beautiful. Yet they form part of the essence of beauty, because it can only arise out of the expression of the whole of life in which sin has its place, and because they are grown from the suffering and recoil of a sensitive nature in front of ugliness which contrasted violently with the ideal perfection of which he dreamed and towards which he aspired. Baudelaire could not agree with Taine's cynical statement[22] that vice and virtue do not exist as moral concepts, that they are merely two physical products like vitriol and sugar, which are different, but not superior or inferior one to the other. The more he studied his own heart, the more convinced he became that there was no other way of explaining man's aptitude for sin, except through the intervention of some power of evil outside him. 'There is in man,' he said,[23] 'a mysterious force which modern philosophy will not take into account, and nevertheless without this force a quantity of human actions remain unexplained, and unexplainable.' This conviction of the power of the devil disgusted the liberal-minded thinkers of the nineteenth century, but he remained unrepentant in front of their positivist beliefs. He recognized in himself a passionate admiration for virtue, and, at the same time, an unwilling attraction towards vice, what he calls 'two simultaneous and contradictory attractions – one towards God and one towards Satan'.[24]

It is true that he painted vice and sin in pleasing colours, even when recoiling from them. But sin and vice are pleasing, horribly and treacherously so! How could they otherwise have the power to lure man from what he knows is highest?

'Le vice est séduisant,' says Baudelaire,[25] 'il faut le peindre séduisant; mais il traîne avec lui des maladies et des douleurs morales singulières; il faut les décrire. Étudiez toutes les plaies comme un médecin qui fait son service dans un hôpital.'

It is Baudelaire's painting of the pleasures and resulting horrors of vice which so scandalized the critics. Yet he was a moralist in the Christian tradition, who expresses revolt against the lure of the flesh, and horror of the pleasures which leave a bitter taste of ashes in the mouth. He demonstrated clearly, without didactic aim, the fundamental truth that retribution inevitably follows excess and vice, that every action bears in itself the seed of its own punishment or reward. As Swinburne said of him:[26]

> *And with each face thou sawest the shadow on each,*
> *Seeing as men sow, men reap.*

Baudelaire himself expressed it clearly in *Les Femmes Damnées*:[27]

> *Descendez, descendez, lamentables victimes,*
> *Descendez le chemin de l'enfer éternel!*
> *Plongez au plus profond du gouffre, où tous les crimes,*
> *Flagellés par un vent qui ne vient pas du ciel,*
>
> *Bouillonnent pêle-mêle avec un bruit d'orage.*
> *Ombres folles, courez au but de vos désirs;*
> *Jamais vous ne pourrez assouvir votre rage,*
> *Et votre châtiment naîtra de vos plaisirs.*

Many of his poems, even amongst those which aroused most hostility, make perfectly orthodox sermons in the tradition of the Church, in the tradition of Bossuet or Bourdaloue. All through the ages the Church has made man ponder on his latter end, and on the vanity of attachment to the pleasures of the flesh and the joys of mortal life, for this world will fade away, and the body crumble in the earth. That is the note of a large part of Baudelaire's work, the pathetic vanity, the hopeless vanity and emptiness of earthly pleasure, the vanity of all which is not eternal. In the Cluny Museum in Paris many examples of *memento mori* are exhibited, bronze or marble objects made to sit on a writing-table, perhaps to serve as paper-weights. In shape they are half skull and half head; and on one side the countenance is fair as it is in life, with smiling features and rounded contours, while on the other the bones appear as the face has been eaten away, and maggots and worms can be seen crawling in and out through the shreds of flesh. These were pious objects, created and intended to lead man's wandering thoughts back from joy in the pleasures of the world to contemplation of eternity. They are the same in spirit as the poem *Une Charogne* quoted in an earlier chapter.

Baudelaire was very much opposed to the sentimental romantic view of the noble criminal, whom we see in Hugo's *Les Misérables*. Nor did he believe, as his contemporaries did, in Rousseau's theory that man was born good and was corrupted only by society. On the contrary he thought that nature left to herself and untamed was monstrous, that it was only through discipline and education that man could learn to slough his evil tendencies. He knew, from experience, that good behaviour needed constant effort from man, and that true progress could not come from gas or electricity, but only from the diminution of original sin, from an improvement of the evil nature with which man was born.

The keynote of Baudelaire's inspiration is the feeling of remorse, which is very different from the arrogant Byronic consciousness of sin. Paul Claudel wrote: 'Baudelaire a chanté la seule passion que le dix-neuvième siècle pût éprouver avec sincérité, le remords.' [28] But here he differs from Christianity, for it is not possible to be truly Christian and not to take into account the Redemption. Up to the last phase of his life, he was guilty of the sin of despair, and did not believe that remorse could wipe away guilt – it would have seemed to him too easy to trust in mere repentance to efface the results of sin.

> *Nos péchés sont têtus, nos repentirs sont lâches;*
> *Nous nous faisons payer grassement nos aveux,*
> *Et nous rentrons gaîment dans le chemin bourbeux,*
> *Croyant par de vils pleurs laver toutes nos taches.*[29]

He was tortured by the sensation of the irreparableness of the past, by the knowledge that what was done could never now be undone, that his actions were graven deep in stone which nothing would ever erase. Remorse would not give him back the wasted past, nor heal his diseased body. He was haunted by the memory of opportunities lost for ever, as the ghost of all the squandered years rose up to taunt him, and he could not rid himself of the obsession of his sinfully misspent life.

'I gaze back at all the dead years,' he wrote,[30] 'the horrible dead years. ... I think that there are few examples of a life so frittered away as mine has been. I can't tell you all the struggles with myself, nor all the despair.'

He writes in *L'Irréparable* :[31]

> *Pouvons-nous étouffer le vieux, le long Remords*
> *Qui vit, s'agite et se tortille,*
> *Et se nourrit de nous comme le ver des morts,*
> *Comme du chêne la chenille?*
> *Pouvons-nous étouffer l'implacable Remords? ...*

> *L'Irréparable ronge avec sa dent maudite*
> *Notre âme, piteux monument,*
> *Et souvent il attaque, ainsi que le termite,*
> *Par la base le bâtiment.*
> *L'Irréparable ronge avec sa dent maudite.*

He did not believe that repentance and remorse gave man the right to the remission of sins, the right to forgiveness, though, in the last phase of his life, he came to allow himself to hope in God's mercy and grace. It was not the power of repentance, he thought, which gave dignity to man, but his power of suffering, and, by suffering, he meant a spiritual emotion – suffering for him was man's sensitivity to his own degradation, and regret for it. That man should still be able to feel ashamed and to suffer from his state of sin was, in his eyes, the greatest proof of his dignity.

> *Car c'est vraiment, Seigneur, le meilleur témoignage*
> *Que nous puissions donner de notre dignité*
> *Que cet ardent sanglot qui roule d'âge en âge*
> *Et vient mourir au bord de votre éternité.*[32]

Suffering is the tribute which man pays to virtue and to goodness. This belief was not the result of masochism.[33] Many religious thinkers have held the same belief, and, rather than a sign of weakness, the acceptance of suffering as the essence of life seems, on the contrary, to bring energy and a sense of purpose, and to be a more solid foundation on which to build a moral system than on the futility of a quest for happiness.

Certain critics, interested in the spiritual aspect of Baudelaire's work – Charles du Bos and Stanislas Fumet, for instance – have tried to demonstrate that he was an orthodox Catholic, and have sometimes misread the texts in their attempt to prove their point, as did du Bos when he read *De Profundis Clamavi* as an appeal to God:[34]

> *J'implore ta pitié, Toi, l'unique que j'aime,*
> *Du fond du gouffre obscur où mon cœur est tombé.*

These lines, quoted apart from their context, might give rise to this interpretation, but a study of the variants, and also the position which the poem occupies in *Les Fleurs du Mal*, indicate that it was once entitled *La Béatrix*, and that it was addressed to his mistress, Jeanne Duval. As far as is known, Baudelaire was never, after he reached adult years, a practising Catholic – too much importance should not be attributed to the reported sentiments of a paralysed and dying man, incapable of speech. If ever he reached faith, in the Catholic sense, it could only be in his last phase,

when he attained the humility which is the preliminary for
grace. For many years he dabbled in various mystical philo-
sophies, taking something from each, but not subscribing
fully to any. As a man does not lose his racial characteristics
by taking out nationalization papers in another country,
however, he was unable to shake off the imprint he had
received from his early faith; he found, what Rimbaud was
to discover later, that 'on est esclave de son baptême'.[35] He
remained a psychologist formed by Catholicism, and his
manner of considering moral problems was Catholic.

Except in the days of his rebellious youth, the most constant of Baudelaire's preoccupations was a quest for spiritual
values, a hunger and thirst for spiritual food. He used to
say that he was bored in France because everyone there was
like Voltaire.[36] In his younger days he had tasted the
pleasures of the senses – the highest and the lowest – in
search of what Pascal calls 'le divertissement', something
which will make one lose consciousness of self and of the
years slipping by without meaning. All these pleasures had
proved vain! He had only found everywhere 'le spectacle
ennuyeux de l'immortel péché',[37] and he had come to the
conclusion that there was nothing worthy of the attention
of an intelligent and spiritual being, except religious thought
in some form. Art for him, at least his own art, was an expression of this belief. He was convinced that to have a great
artistic purpose was the surest way of freeing the human soul
from its fetters. His work shows, stage by stage, how he
reached the certainty of the vanity of all the 'divertisse-
ments' which make men forget impending doom, by blind-
ing their eyes, or rushing them along so fast that they can no
longer see whither they are going, the vanity of all the
artificial paradises.

Like Saint Bernard, Pascal and Maine de Biran, seeking
everywhere the perfect 'divertissement', and discovering
nothing except the frailty of man and his incapacity for
finding happiness, serenity or peace, through his own efforts
alone, without the intervention of some exterior spiritual

aid – God's grace, or whatever we care to call it – Baudelaire saw in humanity's age-long quest for spiritual food proof of God speaking through man, God's charity flowing, like the circulation of the blood, from God to man, and returning again to God. God spoke, it seems, similar words to those which Pascal heard in the dark watches of a night of struggle with doubt and despair, 'Tu ne me chercherais pas si tu ne m'avais trouvé; ne t'inquiètes donc pas!'[38]

Baudelaire finally reached, though by a different route, the same solution as Pascal and Saint Bernard, not by closing his eyes or ignoring the problems of this world, but through an intimate study of himself. His progress towards final harmony is the same as the development of his aesthetic theory. His mysticism is also seen in the importance which he assigns to art, in his worship of beauty, in his high ideal of poetry.

'Literature must come before everything else,' he wrote,[39] 'before food and pleasure, before even my mother.'

He was incapable of producing superficial work to make money. Even when he was in the direst straits and most of his contemporaries were doing it, even then he did not pander to public taste. His private life may have been squalid, but with a pride which was the only luxury he could afford, he kept his art away from triviality. However disorganized his private life became, with the recklessness of a rich king, he lavished on his work infinite and loving care. In his humility he considered himself a wasted piece of machinery which nothing could ever now improve, for there was no clean page left for him, yet he was conscious that, worn-out tool though he might be, he could yet produce a work of beauty which could endure for ever.[40]

> Quand on m'aura jeté, vieux flacon désolé,
> Décrépit, poudreux, sale, abject, visqueux, fêlé.

Art and beauty were greater than he, so it mattered little if he were lost and wasted, provided the work endured. The conviction that he was a poet, and that, in the scheme of things, the status of a poet was the highest possible, gave him the courage to bear the misery and squalor of his life.

No one was more surprised than Baudelaire himself at being accused of immorality when his collection of poems was published. He had intended, taking his own experience as the text, to depict the tragic struggle of mankind. Valéry's opinion that, in his desire for originality, he sought to discover the beauty in sin and ugliness, is not in accordance with the facts.[41] He is contradicted by the poet's own words, who said to Ancelle, in a moment of frankness:[42]

'Must I say it to you, who haven't guessed the truth any more than anyone else, that in that terrible book I've put my whole heart, my most tender feelings, all my religion – in a disguised form – and all my hatred? Even were I to write the contrary, and swear by all the gods, that it was only a composition of pure art, of artistic jugglery with words, a work of imitation – I know not what else – I'd only be lying like a trooper.'

Through a study of his own heart, Baudelaire reached not only knowledge of self, but also of contemporary man, of the being whom Banville, in his speech from the graveside, called modern man, that complex creature with its subtle, varied and sophisticated emotions. Man, as Baudelaire saw him, is the product, good or bad, of modern civilization, the product of an old and over-intellectualized civilization, with his *blasé* tastes and his feverish search for something new and exciting. What interested the poet chiefly was to depict the inner conflict in this neurotic creature, between instinct and spirituality, a conflict which has always existed but to which the despair and the doubt of modern times have added a more tragic quality. He believed that one could not withdraw from life without mutilation, that man must live in his own time, and discover what sublimity he could in it. He did not try, as did most of his contemporaries, to escape from the problems of modern life into a classical past. It would have seemed to him a betrayal of his birthright to isolate himself in an ivory tower, because the conditions of life did not please him, and because his contemporaries did not appreciate him. He realized the danger of becoming a detached observer. 'Tout homme qui n'accepte pas les conditions de la vie vend son âme,' he said.[43] That was why he deplored the use of drugs, even though he derived pleasure from their use – the artificial paradises – because he saw in them an attempt to escape the law of life, work and suffering. 'Elles suppriment le travail du temps,' he said,[44] 'et veulent rendre superflues les conditions de poète et de philosophe.'

Thus it is in the teeming city that Baudelaire found the material for his study of the heart of modern man, and became the greatest of the city poets. Except for his one journey to the East when he was twenty, and the disastrous trip to Belgium in 1864, he never left Paris except for short visits and then did not stray far from the capital. To the depths of his nature he loved the city in which he had been born, even when realizing the vice which it contained:

> *Je t'aime, ô capitale infâme! Courtisanes*
> *Et bandits, tels souvent vous offrez des plaisirs*
> *Que ne comprennent pas les vulgaires profanes.*[45]

This love inspired him to give expression to the complex soul of Paris whose power all those who have ever lived within her walls have felt – sometimes to their benefit, but at other times to their detriment. Paris is a beautiful and mysterious, though often heartless, mistress, who gives her lover's ecstasy and subtle joys undreamt of elsewhere, holding them for ever enslaved to her poignant loveliness. Then, when she has bewitched them for her own ends, she drains them of will-power, disintegrating them, and leaving them henceforth unable to tear themselves away from her embrace.

The images left in Baudelaire's mind as a child, from which he was later to fashion his poems, were images of city scenes. Where a child born in the country dreams of mountains, rivers, lakes and the sandy shores of the sea, he saw long meandering streets crammed with houses rising

sheer and pointing their roofs and chimneys at the skyline,
instead of towering cliffs; public squares and gardens instead
of fields and meadows. It was not the song of the birds which
filled his waking hours, but the droning murmur of the
crowds in the narrow thoroughfares below, which he heard
at evening, leaning out of his window, when it often seemed
to him that he was on a high mountain listening to the
harmony which night made of the discordant sounds in the
streets beneath him.[46] It was not nymphs and shepherdesses
who peopled his dreams, but typical Paris characters – the
working people, gigolos and pimps, weary prostitutes, shop-
girls coming from their work, beggars in the gutters. Ordinary city life was teeming with all the things which he
needed for his art, the mystery and the beauty which others
failed to find there. The Romantics had been so much obsessed by nature, the Parnassians by the glamour of the
East, that they did not think of looking at the town with
sympathetic eyes. Baudelaire saw beauty in poor colourless
lives, the sublime in the humble, not in the people themselves, but in the intention of the Creator. He saw God's
writing in the lowly clay, even if it was somewhat effaced.
The pathetic and sugary sympathy which Coppée was to
feel could be appreciated by anyone, and this was the secret
of the phenomenal success of his poetry of humble life, but
the poverty which he described was sentimental, courageous
and clean poverty. Baudelaire, however, saw it stark and
raw, stripped of all sentimentality. He felt the common
humanity in everyone, and he did not need to make an
effort to get near to the poor and disreputable. He was very
different from the humanitarians, who were public-spirited
and altruistic, somewhat like district visitors, desiring to
help, because they felt it wrong that others should live in
such squalor, but carefully lifting their skirts, in case they
brushed against the dirt. There was no conscious effort on
Baudelaire's part to feel the pathos and dreariness of the
life of the underworld – the weariness of the worker, the
dreams of the drunkard, of the old beggar-woman whose

day was over. He used to wander into the secret and hidden depths of the town, follow all sorts of strange people, and observe the furtive individual lives which they attempted to protect against encroaching collectivity. He wanted to understand them all, with their personal idiosyncrasies. In *Spleen de Paris* he writes: [47]

'Quelles bizarreries ne trouve-t-on pas dans une grande ville quand on sait se promener et regarder? La vie fourmille de monstres innocents. – Seigneur, mon Dieu! vous le Créateur, vous le Maître; vous qui avez fait la loi et la liberté; vous le souverain qui laissez faire, vous le juge qui pardonnez; vous qui êtes plein de motifs et de causes, et qui avez peut-être mis dans mon esprit le goût de l'horreur pour convertir mon cœur, comme la guérison au bout d'une lame; Seigneur, ayez pitié, ayez pitié des fous et des folles! O Créateur! peut-il exister des monstres aux yeux de Celui-là seul qui sait pourquoi ils existent, comment ils se sont faits, et comment ils auraient pu ne pas se faire?'

It was original at this time to believe and to assert that the poet need not necessarily be public-spirited or have a social conscience, or use his art and talent for the betterment of the masses. After his short period of interest in revolutionary politics, Baudelaire came to believe that the only salvation lay in the full development of the individual, in the full exercise of all his powers, in his own efforts to find himself and his own harmony. He expressed contempt for those who imagined that they could make humanity happy in twenty-four hours. He poured scorn on those whom he calls 'the contractors of public happiness' – 'les entrepreneurs du bonheur public' – who try to persuade every unfortunate man that he is a king who has been unlawfully deprived of his kingdom. He believed that he alone is the equal of another man who is able to prove it; and he alone is worthy of enjoying liberty who is able to conquer it for himself. In *Assommons les Pauvres* [48] he describes how, by violence, and not by pity, a whining beggar was given back 'l'orgueil et la vie'.

There was one thing that he believed should be the right of everyone, liberty for the individual, liberty to protect his spiritual privacy, of whatever kind it might be, against all those who would encroach on it on the plea of improving him or of making him happy; the liberty, if it was his pleasure, to go to Hell his own way. The humanitarians, he thought, were mistaken in thinking that suffering lay alone in lack of material goods. He saw that the greatest source of misery in man was in himself, in his own inefficiency, and in his own sense of failure, and he told him this unpalatable truth. Nevertheless he had infinite sympathy for those who had failed in the battle of life – whether through the greed or avarice of others, or through their own weakness. He knew that there would always be the failures, whatever the form of government, that there would always be those who dropped out of the race, not only through force of circumstances and ill luck – 'le guignon' – but through their own sinfulness and human folly. He knew that he himself was considered a failure according to worldly standards – and even also according to his own. Cocteau says in *Opium*: 'The aesthetic of failure is the only one which lasts; he who does not know failure is lost.' Or as Baudelaire himself wrote:[49]

> *Ces yeux sont des puits faits d'un million de larmes,*
> *Des creusets qu'un métal refroidi pailleta.*
> *Ces yeux mystérieux ont d'invincibles charmes*
> *Pour celui que l'austère Infortune allaita.*

Baudelaire's work remains the monument of his existence and it forms a harmonious whole. What that harmony is can be seen in particular in the architecture of *Les Fleurs du Mal*, but his other writings – *Spleen de Paris*, *Les Paradis Artificiels* and his aesthetic criticism – form part of the same unity and enrich it. The poet always claimed that *Les Fleurs du Mal* was not a haphazard collection of poems, that it had a central idea and plan, and he even went so far as to say that it had a spiritual and Christian purpose. The same could be said about the totality of his writings taken as a single unit, and the harmony and symmetry which he was never able to achieve in his life he reached in his literary work, which he was able to round off, resolving all the discords in the final cadence. Yet, although it was in creative work that he reached this harmony, literary composition was not for him, as it was for the other members of the Art for Art's Sake School, an end in itself, but a tool which he used to perfect his personality – his immortal soul he might have said – and he never lost hope in the possibility of reaching perfection, in spite of his sense of failure. After he had abandoned the vain and foolish ambitions of youth, and had reached maturity, art was for him the 'correspondance' of something divine, the symbol of eternal beauty.

The fact that he composed the poems at different periods in his life, according to the inspiration of the moment, and not with the previous intention of fitting them into a pre-arranged plan, does not in any way detract from the importance of this plan – in any case, the poems he composed for the second edition of *Les Fleurs du Mal* were, in fact, deliberately written, according to his own testimony, to fit into such a plan.[50] Most of the poems were composed to give expression to certain emotions, and it was only afterwards that he saw what use could be made of them to illustrate the conception he had reached about life on earth, when he was able to examine his struggles from the outside.

The central idea of all Baudelaire's work is the investigation and depiction of the conflict between man and his destiny, between his idealistic aspirations on the one hand, and base reality on the other, which constantly threatens to annihilate them; between his inclination towards God and also towards Satan, between *Spleen* and *Idéal*. The struggle exists for all mankind, but, for the poet, it assumes a more tragic quality than for other men. He says in *L'Albatros*:[51]

> *Le poète est semblable au prince des nuées*
> *Qui hante la tempête et se rit de l'archer;*
> *Exilé sur le sol au milieu des huées,*
> *Ses ailes de géant l'empêchent de marcher.*

In the first portion of the section of *Les Fleurs du Mal* entitled *Spleen et Idéal* is shown the contrast between ideal beauty on the one hand, and harsh reality on the other, and there is expressed a horror and a hatred of life:

> *Elle pleure, insensée, parce qu'elle a vécu!*
> *Et parce qu'elle vit! Mais ce qu'elle déplore*
> *Surtout, ce qui la fait frémir jusqu'aux genoux,*
> *C'est que demain, hélas! il faudra vivre encore!*
> *Demain, après-demain et toujours! — comme nous!* [52]

Man has always sought forgetfulness of the harshness of life in love, but love, whether sensual, spiritual, or passionate, ends in failure and disappointment, and he is left finally with nothing but the dregs of bitter memory, and nostalgia for the fairyland of innocent childhood, when he did not know what life held for him.

> *Comme vous êtes loin, paradis parfumé,*
> *Où sous un clair azur tout n'est qu'amour et joie,*
> *Où tout ce que l'on aime est digne d'être aimé,*
> *Où dans la volupté pure le cœur se noie!*
> *Comme vous êtes loin, paradis parfumé!*
>
> *Mais le vert paradis des amours enfantines,*
> *Les courses, les chansons, les baisers, les bouquets,*
> *Les violons vibrant derrière les collines,*
> *Avec les brocs de vin, le soir, dans les bosquets,*
> *— Mais le vert paradis des amours enfantines,*
>
> *L'innocent paradis plein de plaisirs furtifs,*
> *Est-il déjà plus loin que l'Inde et que la Chine?*
> *Peut-on le rappeler avec des cris plaintifs,*
> *Et l'animer encor d'une voix argentine,*
> *L'innocent paradis plein de plaisirs furtifs?* [53]

But the past can never be recaptured and man is left with

depression and pessimism, with 'spleen'. At first it is the sadness which is an added ornament to youth, but it becomes, as life progresses, dark despair, when man contemplates the squandered past and realizes impending doom, while the clock, 'dieu sinistre, effrayant, impassible', cries 'meurs vieux lâche! il est trop tard!'[54]

There is, however, eventually as compensation, the belief in something higher than mere worldly success, a quest for moral victory. Then the poet sang of 'la fertilisante douleur' and finally reached the resignation of *Recueillement*, where he found a haven he had never expected to find, and came to believe in what he had never believed in before: the redemption and the forgiveness of sin, the power of God's mercy and grace. This was only right at the end of his life, and we do not know how far it would have altered the plan of the third version of *Les Fleurs du Mal* which he was preparing for publication when disease struck him down.

This was the individual problem as set forth in the section of his book entitled *Spleen et Idéal*. The setting and background for this conflict in modern man lie in the modern city, in the scenes described in *Tableaux Parisiens*. In the town are found a beauty which comes from sadness and pathos, enduring poverty and unrewarded labour, but also nostalgia for higher things.

All the exiles, the captives, the vanquished, in the city seek forgetfulness in the artificial paradises of drugs and drink, but all have the same effect, leading to an identical and horrible 'lendemain'.

Similar, too, in their results, are lechery and debauch. Lesbos with its monstrous passions can offer no joy to a heart longing for beauty, there can be no satisfaction there since 'les femmes damnées' are sinning against the law of life and have denied God in themselves. Excessive indulgence in physical pleasure leads only to the island of Cythera, where the mutilated corpse hanging on the gibbet symbolizes sinning man. Carnal passion ends in nausea and disgust.

> *Quand elle eut de mes os sucé toute la moelle,*
> *Et que languissamment je me tournai vers elle*
> *Pour lui rendre un baiser d'amour, je ne vis plus*
> *Qu'une outre aux flancs gluants, toute pleine de pus!*
> *Je fermai les deux yeux, dans ma froide épouvante.*[55]

This was all that was left of the beautiful woman for whom even the angels of Heaven were prepared to suffer damnation.

In disgust man breaks out into revolt against the power which has allowed such misery and suffering, in blasphemy against God who is lulled to sleep to the sound of mankind's weeping and wailing, and he applauds the action of Saint Peter:

> *Saint Pierre a renié Jésus . . . il a bien fait!*[56]

Revolt, however, is of short respite, for death eventually comes whether man blasphemes or not, death the dear sister of debauch, who may perhaps offer even sweeter joys.

> *Et la bière et l'alcôve en blasphèmes fécondes*
> *Nous offrent tour à tour, comme deux bonnes sœurs,*
> *De terribles plaisirs et d'affreuses douceurs.*
>
> *Quand veux-tu m'enterrer, Débauche aux bras immondes?*
> *O Mort, quand viendras-tu, sa rivale en attraits,*
> *Sur des myrtes infects entre tes noirs cyprès?*[57]

Man longs for rest from suffering, for night and the longer night which is death, for death which is 'le portique ouvert sur les cieux inconnus,' the consoler for everything.

> *C'est la Mort qui console, hélas! et qui fait vivre;*
> *C'est le but de la vie, et c'est le seul espoir*
> *Qui, comme un elixir, nous monte et nous enivre,*
> *Et nous donne le cœur de marcher jusqu'au soir.*[58]

Death will be the last journey, the greatest journey of all, the final voyage of discovery, and, in 1859, Baudelaire composed his magnificent poem *Le Voyage* to be the coping-stone of his work.

How limitless the world seemed when, young and full of hope, man started out on the adventure of life, but how small it seemed when he looked back to contemplate the countries through which he had passed! He had set out, as dawn began to break, his heart afire, and full of infinite desire. Each island that is sighted seems to him to be a new Eldorado sent by Heaven especially for him, but, as he draws near, he finds only brown rocks rising up into the cold morning light. All through the world, on his journeys, he finds only the same wearisome things which he had known elsewhere, and especially 'le spectacle ennuyeux de l'immortel péché', everywhere he sees only the same things in other colours:

> *Amer savoir, celui qu'on tire du voyage!*
> *Le monde, monotone et petit, aujourd'hui,*
> *Hier, demain, toujours, nous fait voir notre image:*
> *Une oasis d'horreur dans un désert d'ennui.*[59]

When the moment comes for the last fateful journey, whence there is no return, man will set sail on the seas of darkness with a heart as light and as full of hope as when he set out on the adventure of life, and on this last fateful journey he may perhaps reach a land where he will discover something new which will bring peace and satisfaction to his heart, and ease the longing which the world was never able to assuage:

> *O Mort! vieux capitaine, il est temps! levons l'ancre!*
> *Ce pays nous ennuie, ô Mort! Appareillons!*
> *Si le ciel et la mer sont noirs comme de l'encre,*
> *Nos cœurs que tu connais sont remplis de rayons!*
>
> *Verse-nous ton poison pour qu'il nous réconforte!*
> *Nous voulons, tant ce feu nous brûle le cerveau,*
> *Plonger au fond du gouffre, Enfer ou Ciel, qu'importe?*
> *Au fond de l'Inconnu pour trouver du nouveau.*

That ends the second edition of *Les Fleurs du Mal*, and it probably would have closed the third version of the collec-

tion. It is also a fitting Epilogue, a fitting climax to his work
as a whole. Although it is not the last in chronological order
of his writings, it crowns appropriately the enduring monument of his creative achievement. It expresses his ardent
longing to discover something which will give contentment
to his soul, and this aspiration is more typical of him fundamentally than the peace which he reached for so short
a time before the end.

Asselineau said that Baudelaire was a touchstone and
that only the stupid misunderstood him or disliked his work.
This is, however, too harsh a statement. He is a poet not
appreciated by the very young and inexperienced, even
when they are not stupid. They do not wish to hear of ship-
wrecked hopes as long as they can believe that happiness
may be obtained for the pursuing, and have not yet experienced man's chief source of despair, the suffering which
comes from realization of his own weakness. The very young
are frequently so much hurt and offended by what they
think is Baudelaire's cynicism and coarseness, that they fail
to perceive the quality of his idealism which often took the
form of torturing himself with contemplation of the things
which hurt and repelled him most. It requires the maturing
discipline of life and the depth of heart which comes from
experience which has not turned sour to appreciate his
greatest poems and the soil in which they grew. Youth sees
in Baudelaire chiefly what was there only by accident, what
was the fashion of his time, what was not the essential
Baudelaire.

His writings appeal especially to those who have reached
mature years, who have learnt all that life has power to grant
of hopes and disappointments, of joys and sorrows. It is for
them that he has written of the poignancy of departing
youth, not merely of the fading of outward beauty, but of
the withering of dreams and illusions, which drop away,
some to perish when the seeds are sterile, but some to blossom again. It is the poetry of experience, of saddened experience, which still finds cause for hope and faith.

Today his revulsions are our own. His disgust with senti-mentality and cant, his refusal to accept his ideals ordered ready-made, by number, from a factory. He could not en-dure the infectious nature of clap-trap idealism, for to him the easy-flowing milk of human kindness was often merely the result of indolence of mind, or the egoistic desire to feel morally solvent. This made critics say that he was a cynic who believed in nothing. But in this they misjudged him. In his *Journaux Intimes* he writes: [60]

'I have no beliefs as the people of my century understand them. Nevertheless I do possess some beliefs in a higher sense, which cannot be understood by the people of my time.'

He believed that ideals and standards were valuable only when we had formulated them ourselves from our own inner conviction and compulsion, that each of us must work out his own salvation, and find his own harmony. Many of his paradoxes were intended only to shake his readers out of complacency and security, to startle them into reflecting on what they had previously accepted on trust. He was not afraid to show, although this was one of the greatest causes of his unpopularity, that every kind of accepted principle – whether aesthetic, political or moral – might be hollow, and based merely on lazy reasoning or on false and worn-out assumptions.

In a materialistic age which believed in comfort and prosperity, he refused to be satisfied with such ideals, and he did not think that happiness could come from an abund-ance of goods and gadgets, or that their lack spelt unhap-piness. Today he would not believe that a car, a wireless or a television set, a bathroom or a refrigerator, would bring real improvement in the life of man. In his own age he did not see progress in steam, electricity or gas, and today he would not see it in atomic power. He saw progress only in the diminution of the innate evil in man – original sin he called it. He understood that this would come only when man's moral development kept pace with his technical achievement. The same problem is with us still today, in a more poignant form, when man's intellect has mastered many more fields than Baudelaire could ever have dreamt of, but when his moral advance has ceased, or even receded.

Many of those in whom Baudelaire today finds an echo, see, in his passionate longing 'pour trouver du nouveau', their own aspiration towards something beyond themselves and the pitiable quest for material comfort and happiness, something in which to lose themselves, a return to a spiritual philosophy of life, to a difficult religion which will make demands on man for effort and sacrifice, and will not play him false.

Appendix One

Articles possibly written by him

1. In *Le Socialiste de la Côte d'Or*, 26 July 1850, signed 'Un Passant'.

'Pourriez-vous me dire, chers Dijonnais, où je pourrais rencontrer un artiste à Dijon? on m'avait dit que, dans votre ville, tout le monde était artiste; que les pavés des rues eux-mêmes chantaient en chœur, et que les girouettes, la nuit, donnaient des sérénades; que les fontaines, en roulant dans les rigoles, récitaient de fraîches et pures élégies, et que les académiciens ne faisaient jamais d'alexandrins. Depuis que je suis dans votre excellente ville, je n'ai vu que des tours de force, chevaux et jockies, acrobates, clowns, maquignons; j'ai vu d'immenses affiches où l'on parlait du Bosphore, du Czar, du grand-turc, du sultan, et de mille autres carnivores; mais d'art et d'artistes, il n'en était pas plus question qu'à l'Académie. En arrivant à Dijon je croyais descendre dans un Eldorado, et, en vérité, je me suis fait présenter le budget municipal, et j'y ai vu figurer une somme assez forte destinée à plusieurs artistes, ainsi qu'à l'entretien d'écoles de musique vocale et instrumentale; je ne puis m'expliquer encore quelles sont les écoles ainsi entretenues aux dépens des citoyens de Dijon, et quels sont les artistes éminents qui reçoivent à titre d'encouragement et de récompense un morceau de ce gâteau de roi pétri à l'aide des sueurs du peuple et qu'on nomme l'impôt. J'ai également consulté les prolétaires et ils m'ont dit que jamais ils n'avaient vu d'artistes, et qu'ils n'en connaissaient point à Dijon; qu'ils avaient cependant tou-jours payé pour en avoir, mais que, jusqu'à présent, ils n'avaient assisté à d'autres concerts qu'à ceux que donnent, dans les belles soirées d'été, les grenouilles, les crapauds et les salamandres au fond des fossés marécageux qui entourent la ville.

'Ils m'ont dit aussi que, tous les mois, ils voyaient rouler des équipages aristocratiques du côté d'un grand bâtiment situé sur la Place d'Armes; que souvent ils avaient suivi ces équipages; qu'ils avaient vu alors le bâtiment éblouissant de lumières, et que, les pieds dans la boue, ils avaient écouté attentivement ce qui s'y passait; qu'ils avaient entendu des roulements de tonnerre, des éclats de rire diabolique, des conversations incompréhensibles, des rires fantastiques d'oiseaux inconnus, des hurlements et des bravos qui les faisaient pâlir – que cela durait des heures, que les équipages engloutissaient cette foule invisible, et que le bâtiment redevenait sombre et silencieux comme un grand tombeau.

'Et les prolétaires ajoutaient: "C'est probablement cela qu'on appelle les arts; mais nous n'avons jamais goûté quoique nous ayions (*sic*) toujours payé pour l'entretien et l'éducation des artistes."

'Allons, dis-je, voilà des malheureux qui ont fait de mauvais rêves et qui ont le cerveau troublé; ils me racontent des choses impossibles, je ne puis m'en tenir là.

'Et je me mis encore à chercher des artistes à Dijon et dans les environs.

'Je rôdais pendant trois jours et trois nuits; et je n'entendais le soir que le croassement des grenouilles, et la journée que le chant intermittent du grillon et de la cigale. Ces animaux sont intéressants; on les a souvent diffamés. Lafontaine, pour son compte, a blâmé particulièrement la conduite de la cigale, en lui attribuant un défaut qu'elle n'a pas; celle de parasite et d'emprunteuse; il a supposé que puisqu'elle chantait tout l'été, elle ne se donnait pas la peine d'amasser pour l'hiver, et qu'elle se trouvait obligée alors de recourir honteusement aux épargnes de la fourmi. Il ne me serait pas difficile de faire tomber cette insinuation en prouvant que la cigale n'a jamais été à charge de personne, et que, tout en chantant et faisant des pastorales au milieu des buissons, elle sait travailler pour vivre.

'Par exemple, si je prenais à tâche de réhabiliter la cigale, je ne ferais pas ce qu'a fait Lachambaudie; je ne dirais pas qu'il est juste que la fourmi nourrisse la cigale, ce serait prêcher le rétablissement des castes de l'humanité. Je ne crois pas qu'il soit dans la destinée de quelques êtres de supporter seuls les souffrances du travail au profit d'autres êtres qui n'auraient pour fonction ici-bas que l'insouciance et le plaisir.

'Chaque être dans la création porte en lui l'instinct sacré des arts. Ce qui lui manque, c'est la faculté de développer cet instinct sublime toujours refoulé par l'orgueil, car ce sont généralement les meilleures organisations qui ont le plus à souffrir de la perturbation actuelle. Il n'est pas un être aujourd'hui qui ne soit horriblement mutilé par la compression sociale, forcé qu'il est de faire abnégation de son âme et de son intelligence pour gagner chaque jour, à la sueur de son front, un maigre picotin pour lui et de fortes rentes à celui qui l'occupe.

'Ainsi Lachambaudie n'a nullement réhabilité la cigale; il n'a fait que sanctionner l'erreur de Lafontaine. Le poète des temps modernes n'est pas encore de ce monde.

'D'ailleurs, il y a sur terre des bipèdes qui prennent le titre de cigales, et qui ne chantent pas souvent, même en été; il y en a même qui ne sont que de méchantes sauterelles propres à dévaster les récoltes de tout un canton.

'Voilà ce que je pensais en cherchant des artistes, et je n'en trouvais toujours point. Tout à coup, sous de noirs cyprès, à l'ombre de pampres funèbres, je vis une foule de spectres tournoyer et opérer des évolutions étranges; cela formait comme un nuage épais se déroulant en volutes semblables à la fumée d'une pipe. Je m'approchais et chacun des spectres se détacha et roula dans la bière ouverte sous ses pas. Un seul resta debout, je le pris par la main et l'emmenai sous les rayons de la lune, je reconnus en lui un artiste, je fus ravi; sous son suaire, il tenait un violon dont il joua en dansant

de folles sarabandes. Le diable n'inventerait pas de pareilles
fantaisies, les notes sortaient de son violon comme des
étincelles électriques, puis s'éparpillaient dans tous les sens,
se confondaient aux étoiles et redescendaient du zénith au
nadir en traçant sur le ciel de mystérieuses arabesques; je
n'ai jamais vu feu d'artifice plus éblouissant. Arrêtez,
arrêtez, m'écriai-je, trompé par l'illusion et croyant parler
à un vivant, vous paraissez jongler avec les étoiles, vous faites
de la fantasmagorie, ce n'est pas le but de l'art. Il y a autour
de vous des gens qui souffrent et qui demandent des con-
solations; vous pouvez, vous et vos amis, être les médecins de
ces âmes souffrantes. Vous faites danser les morts et vous
oubliez les vivants; le peuple est là qui vous convie et qui se
lasse de pourvoir à tout et de ne jouir de rien. Il vous faudra
travailler un peu plus, cela est vrai, mais votre talent et votre
bourse ne feront qu'y gagner. Le prolétaire est un sol vierge
sur lequel les arts doivent prendre un nouvel et prodigieux
accroissement; le devoir des artistes est de marcher vaillamment à la conquête de ce nouveau monde. – Alors il s'écria:
Ce sont tous des huîtres, des mollusques, des polypes, des
bélîtres; ils ne vous comprendraient pas; ils sont faits pour
vous, mais nous ne sommes pas faits pour eux; et d'ailleurs
il y a un empêchement formel; nous nous compromettrions;
les princes des morts ne souffriraient jamais que nous allas-
sions mettre notre talent au service de la vile multitude; ce
serait fait de notre réputation et nous ne pourrions plus nous
présenter en bonne compagnie. Puis, me regardant de travers,
il ajouta entre ses dents: Je vois bien ce que vous voulez,
vous êtes Utopiste, un Albigeois, un hérétique, un Mani-
chéen, je vais vous dénoncer au saint-office; est-ce qu'il nous
est possible de mettre vos folies en pratique; mais où serait
la religion, la famille et la propriété? Des concerts populaires,
mais où donc, dans une grange? Nous n'avons pas de salle,
ordonnez-donc aux éléments d'en élever de cette place, beau
magicien.

'Je lui montrai alors du doigt un vaste cirque abandonné
et vide, et je lui fis lire les mots inscrits au fronton:

Fête équestre,
Donnée au profit des pauvres,
Par les amateurs de Dijon.

Eh! bien, lui dis-je, vous vous êtes laissé devancer par les chevaux, hâtez-vous de remplacer les deux premiers mots de cette inscription par ceux-ci: "Grand Concert Populaire!"

'Faites sentir au conseil municipal la nécessité d'acquérir ce cirque, d'en construire un plus vaste encore, aussi indispensable aujourd'hui aux réunions électorales qu'aux réunions littéraires et artistiques; démontrez à ce conseil la preuve que cette construction, loin de coûter quelque-chose à la ville, serait au contraire, une source de bénéfices aux époques où les troupes équestres viennent en province donner des représentations. Mais prenez l'initiative, organisez un premier concert, soit gratuit, soit au profit des pauvres, soit au vôtre, pourvu que le prix d'entrée en soit assez modique pour que le peuple, qui ne va plus s'ennuyer à la grand'messe, puisse au moins se réjouir au grand concert.

'J'allais continuer mon exhortation, mais un immense éclat de rire me coupa la parole, je me retournai, et vis la foule du cimetière qui nous avait suivis. L'artiste que je menais sous le bras me dit alors: "Mon cher, vous valez votre pesant d'or, nous laissons aux chevaux la gloire d'être philanthropes, et nous n'en sommes point jaloux." L'immense éclat de rire recommença, et cette foule insensée roula, comme une vaine poussière, dans la direction des cyprès. Il n'y a rien à attendre de ces morts vivants! Qui donc les arrachera de la bière où ils croupissent.

'Quand je fus revenu de mon étonnement, je crus avoir rêvé et je le crois encore; je me frottai les yeux et me trouvai en face du seigneur Polichinelle, dont le théâtre est adossé au cirque. Polichinelle avait tout tué autour de lui, et dansait en chantant sur les cadavres des matassins; le diable survint, la lutte s'engagea entre eux, lutte terrible, comme celle d'Achille et d'Hector; Polichinelle asséna sur la tête de son adversaire un coup qui lui cassa deux cornes; le Diable tomba foudroyé, aux grands applaudissements d'un cercle

de petits enfants, aux yeux émerveillés et brillants comme
des escarboucles.

'On ne peut s'imaginer combien il y a d'esprit et d'élo-
quence dans les coups de bâton de ce Polichinelle, combien
il y a de grâce dans ses poses et de malice sur son visage
sceptique. Au moins ce seigneur raisonne son égoisme, il en
démontre, nettement les conséquences; chacun de ses bons
mots est appuyé par un bon coup. À la bonne heure voilà un
gaillard qui se débarrasse hardiment du trop plein social et
qui est plus logique et plus franc dans ses arguments que
bien des malthusiens dont il est l'image, et qui, comme lui,
ne connaissent d'autres raisons que la raison du plus
fort.'

2. In *Le Représentant de l'Indre*, 5 February 1850, unsigned.
'*Le Travailleur* dit : "Nous avons le pouvoir à l'aide du
suffrage universel !" Posée sur cette base, la question est une
ridicule menace, rien de plus ! Il fallait dire : "Quand nous
aurons le pouvoir à l'aide du suffrage universel, voilà ce que
nous en ferons !" Car celui-là qui aspire au pouvoir sans
savoir ce qu'il en fera, celui-là est, à nos yeux, un des plus
grands coupables que puisse atteindre la justice.

'*Le Travailleur* adresse en outre ce petit compliment au
parti de l'Ordre :

'"Ces hommes qui n'ont d'autre souci que de chercher à
tuer l'ennui de leur vie fastueuse et indolente !"

'*Risam teneatis !* Ne dirait-on pas que le parti de l'ordre
est la cour de Sardanaple; qu'Alcibiade y fait l'amour; que
Néron y joue de la flûte; et que les Borgia y distillent leurs
poisons ! !

'Brave bourgeoisie de France, qui travaillez environ
quatorze heures sur vingt-quatre pour élever ta famille,
labourer ton champ, faire marcher ton usine, gérer la fortune que tu as acquise, ou travailler à celle que tu espères
... te voilà bien notée.

                    Fastueuse et indolente !

'Mais, si le désire notre très judicieux confrère, nous

pouvons lui donner un tout petit renseignement puisé dans les annales de ses amis et des nôtres.

'Tel bourgeois du parti de l'ordre a passé cinquante ans à étudier gravement l'histoire des hommes, sans jamais jeter un atome de fiel sur un principe ou sur une doctrine. Il a écrit dix volumes de philosophie historique qui porteront aux siècles les plus reculés le nom d'un grand citoyen.

Fastueux et indolent!

'Ce bourgeois de sa parole sévère a tenu en haleine tout ce que la France compte de fort et d'intelligent.

Fastueux et indolent!

'Ce bourgeois a gouverné son pays pendant douze années avec un immense labeur; il a tenu à la fois la tribune et le cabinet, l'opinion et les conseils du roi.

'Ce Sardanaple en habit noir, ce Néron de bibliothèques, sur la vertu de ses ouvrages qui ont enrichi vingt libraires, a prélevé quelquechose comme cinq on six mille livres de rentes, qui sont toute sa fortune personnelle et la paix de ses vieux jours.

Fastueux et indolent!

'Abstraction faite de toute personnalité politique que nous ne voudrions mettre en cause ni pour la louer, ni pour la combattre, tel bourgeois recevait des ambassadeurs étrangers, vêtu d'un gilet de tricot de laine. Il était l'incarnation vivante de la foi religieuse et des vertus de famille.

Fastueux et indolent!

'Maintenant voyons un peu le bilan méritoire du grand citoyen Armand Marrast, par exemple, ce pur, ce frère, ce socialiste, cet émérite!

Homme austère et vertueux!

'Il a couché ses enfants dans le lit d'un prince exilé; il a déchiré son bonnet rouge afin d'effacer à ses talons la roture de son origine.

'Dégoûté des gloires d'ici-bas, inconsolable de son divorce avec l'Assemblée Nationale, désespéré de maigrir et de ne plus avoir à châtier ses maroufles de laquais, M. Marrast a épousé la veuve d'un restaurateur; il dîne quatre fois par

jour, donne des bourrades à ses gâte-sauces, et endort sa
mélancolie dans les douceurs du pâté de foie et dans l'enivre-
ment de la truffe au vin de Champagne.

Homme austère et vertueux!

'Contradiction sur contradiction, confusion sur fausseté,
perpétuelles hallucinations de raisonnement que l'on présente au peuple en guise de vérités ... le socialisme est là
tout entier!

'Nous ne faisons point aux rédacteurs du *Travailleur*
l'injure de croire qu'ils préfèrent la *vertu* de certains social-
istes au *faste* de certains conservateurs; mais nous les mettons
en garde contre les pétulances d'opinion, et nous les en-
gageons à contempler de plus près *l'austérité* de ceux-ci et la
fastueuse indolence de ceux-là.'

3. In *Le Représentant de l'Indre*, 12 February 1850, unsigned.

'Sait-on comment *Le Travailleur de l'Indre* définit le
socialisme: "La réforme de quelques bien, uns des abus si
nombreux aujourd'hui." Ah! voilà qui est touchant, raison-
nable et fraternel! Soulignez chaque mot, chaque lettre, s'il
vous plaît, de cette incroyable phraséologie anodine que Basile,
Escobar et Tartuffe eussent enviée aux hommes noirs de la
République rouge. "La réforme de quelques uns des abus
si nombreux aujourd'hui." Eh! bien, dira le brave ouvrier, le
paysan simple, le bourgeois timide, ces gens là ne sont pas si
diables qu'ils sont rouges, puisqu'ils se bornent à demander
la réforme de quelques-uns des abus si nombreux aujourd'hui. Braves gens, qui pouvez ne pas le savoir, nous
allons vous dire en deux mots ce que la République rouge
appelle réforme des abus:

– La suppression de l'État (Voir P. J. Proudhon);
– L'Organisation par l'État de toutes les forces sociales
  (Voir Louis Blanc);
– Celui-ci veut que l'État ne soit plus. L'autre que
  l'État soit tout;
– La suppression du capital (Voir P. J. Proudhon);
– Le droit au crédit (Voir le citoyen Pelletier);

- Celui-ci ne veut plus de capital; l'autre en veut pour
  tout le monde; et par des moyens que la politesse de
  notre polémique nous permet seulement de taxer de
  coercitifs;
- La suppression de la propriété, ou plutôt des pro-
  priétaires; la plantation d'une myriade de peupliers
  symboliques sur toute la surface de la France. (Voir
  Pierre Leroux).

'Un cône tronqué surmonté d'une sphère dans le grand
sceau de la République. Il y a toujours quelque-chose de
tronqué dans la législation de ces messieurs.

'Quoi encore? Les choux au jasmin de M. Considérant, la
mer de limonade, l'anti-lion, l'anti-punaise, les géniteurs,
les jouvencelles, et les armées de petits pâtés dans les plaines
de Babylone, sans rien due des arômes planétaires et la
couronne boréale.

'Telles sont – nous en passons et des meilleures – les
monstruosités contradictoires, les sauvages absurdités, les
furies de colère et d'illuminisme que le parti socialiste garde
en serre-chaude sous ses douceresses et hypocrites insinua-
tions.

'Est-il possible que de grands garçons, sévrés sans nul
doute, ayant au menton poil rouge et peut-être gris, se donnent la mission de dissimuler la vérité de leurs documents
sous d'aussi plates menteries. Eh! messieurs, de grâce, ôtez
votre masque et relevez les basques de votre habit, on verra
sur votre nez les bésicles bleues du Dieu Proudhon, à votre
dos la queue PRENANTE du Dieu Fourier, vous ferez
rire le peuple à coup sûr; mais vous ne le tromperez
pas.

' "La réforme de quelques-uns des abus!"

'En vérité les diablotins ne valent pas le Diable; car celui-
là montre hardiment sa corne et son pied fourchu, tandis
que les autres se mettent sur la nuque une calotte d'enfant de
chœur. La réforme des abus! Qui donc y tient plus que nous?
Qui donc touchera les abus d'une main plus ferme, quand
nous pourrons empêcher la folie furieuse de passer par la

porte ouverte aux réformes? Que le vrai, que le bon peuple
ait donc confiance! Les abus seront supprimés, mais, avant
d'attaquer les petits, il y a bien de courir aux grands; car,
n'en déplaise *Le Travailleur de l'Indre*, l'anarchisme est un
forfait et le socialisme un abus.'

Appendix Two

THE RE-TRIAL OF *LES FLEURS DU MAL*

THE ANNULMENT OF THE SENTENCE
PRONOUNCED AGAINST *LES FLEURS DU MAL*
OF BAUDELAIRE ON 20 AUGUST 1857

Not only has the ban against the *Pièces Condamnées* from *Les Fleurs du Mal* of Baudelaire now been raised, but the verdict, the trial itself, has been quashed and rendered null and void, as if it had never occurred.

As a result of the trial for obscenity in August 1857, a certain number of poems from the collection *Les Fleurs du Mal* were banned, and its sale prohibited without their deletion.

The second edition, supervised by the poet himself and published in 1861, did not contain them, though he printed them in a collection entitled *Épaves*, which was published in Belgium in 1866, but this was banned in France.

The third edition, the posthumous one of 1868, did not contain them either, although the copies sold in Belgium possessed an added supplement which included them. However, most subsequent editions, even those sold in France, printed them in an Appendix, and usually did so with impunity, but the danger always existed that the Cerberus of justice might suddenly awake and take action. This occasionally occurred, as in 1924 for example, when an intact copy of the first edition was withdrawn from a public auction at the Hôtel Drouot by order of the *Parquet de la Seine*, the public prosecutor. Some years later a campaign to clear Baudelaire's name was initiated. The President of *La Société Baudelaire* – Victor-Émile Michelet – supported by Madame Renaud de Broise, the granddaughter of the de Broise who

was the partner of Poulet Malassis, Baudelaire's publisher,
approached the government with a request for a review and
revision of the verdict and sentence of 1857. This was eventually turned down on the grounds that it would no longer be
possible, so long after the event and in the absence of the
accused, to establish his innocence. *Le Garde des Sceaux*
declared that he did not consider that he had valid grounds
for referring the matter to the Supreme Court of Appeal,
and that he felt obliged to refuse the request. 'Il ne pouvait
en droit saisir valablement La Cour Suprême, et il se vit
contraint de rejeter la requête.'

Next the literary politician, Louis Barthou, took up the
matter and set himself the task of finding a legal loophole
for evading the difficulties, and, on 22 October 1929, submitted a bill to the Senate to enable a writer to lodge an
appeal against a sentence passed on a book on the grounds
that it was morally offensive. The projected law empowering
a claimant – or, in the event of his death, his next of kin –
through the offices of *La Société des Gens de Lettres* to
lodge such an appeal, was intended to go up to the *Chambre
Criminelle de la Cour de Cassation* – the Supreme Appeal
Court. The *Sénateur du Gard, Jean Bosc*, a member of the
Nîmes Bar, presented the case for the change in the law. He
said that great works of literature were not often immediately
understood or appreciated, and he pointed out that public
opinion, in certain periods, tolerated, without demur, great
licence in speech, thought and writing. The converse, he
added, was also true, and works of art were often considered
morally offensive in a way which their authors had never
contemplated. This was sufficient to demonstrate, he declared, that the law should not be invested with too much
power and authority when the evaluation of works of literature was in question. Judicial decisions, he said, when they
imply – deliberately or not – literary judgements, have to
reckon with posterity which, in its turn, often judges them
severely and condemns them. Bosc suggested that, although
it often did good, the law made frequent mistakes, and he

cited, as an example, *Manon Lescaut* which, during the Second Empire, had been placed on a list of morally dangerous works, and its sale prohibited in the provinces. He next mentioned Baudelaire, declaring that, in his case also, there existed a state of affairs which needed remedying. He held that, in certain exceptional instances, it should be possible to reverse the verdict of justice, and to recognize that an error had been committed which should be re-dressed: 'Dans certains cas exceptionnels il est nécessaire que l'on puisse revenir sur la décision de la justice, et que l'erreur reconnue soit moralement et matériellement recon-nue.' He suggested that twenty years should be allowed to elapse after sentence, and also that the review should oper-ate only in the case of works of outstanding merit, which had stood the test of time and literature. 'Le bénéfice de la révision serait réservé aux seuls ouvrages d'une inspiration probe et d'un mérite certain, déjà réhabilités par l'opinion publique et par le jugement des lettres.' Bosc's bill was unanimously adopted by *La Commission de Législation* and it was tabled for debate by the Senate, when political events occurred which postponed the matter. The inter-national scene was then much disturbed by the rise to power of Hitler in 1933, and by the death of Barthou, in October 1934, at the hands of a political assassin at Marseilles where he had gone to meet King Alexander of Jugoslavia, in his capacity of Minister for Foreign Affairs. After this public opinion became increasingly preoccupied by war, and the matter was indefinitely shelved.

After the end of the war, in September 1946, the bill was revived and presented again, by Georges Cogniot this time, and it was passed without a division by *L'Assemblée Con-stituante*. This did not, however, satisfy the supporters of Baudelaire who were not content with the mere raising of the ban against the *Pièces Condamnées*, but insisted, as well, that the verdict and sentence should be quashed and ren-dered null and void, and that it should be publicly recog-nized and admitted that the trial should never have taken place. 'Une réparation morale, fût-elle consacrée par l'unanimité de l'opinion, ne constitue pas la réparation qu'il peut convenir d'accorder à l'écrivain injustement frappé, à sa mémoire, à ses héritiers.'

They insisted on putting back the clock, and on bringing in a decree, 'un arrêt de justice' which should 'réduire à néant l'injuste condamnation'.

The new law, empowering the *Société des Gens de Lettres* to appeal for a review of a sentence, was promulgated on 22 October 1946, and then the Committee, using its new powers, decided, with only one dissenting voice, to demand the review of the trial of *Les Fleurs du Mal*, which had been injurious to Baudelaire's memory, damaging to his heirs, and the provisions of which, in some future period of intolerance, might again be used against them. At the beginning of 1947 the *Haut Chancelier* submitted the request and, on 3 November 1947, demanded that the *Procureur Général près la Cour de Cassation* should introduce a bill to quash the sentence of 20 August 1857. Falco, the *Haut Chancelier*, declared, in his speech, that it should be loudly proclaimed that all the poems of the collection *Les Fleurs du Mal* had never transgressed the limits permitted to a poet of genius, and that, on the contrary, far from being morally offensive, they were the fruit of the noblest inspiration, that they had become immortal and had found their rightful place amongst the finest examples of French literature, and amongst the permanent works of art of all times.

The *Gazette du Palais*, in its issue for the second semester of 1949, published the *Arrêt de la Cour de Cassation* – the verdict of the Court of Appeal – and the ruling of the Minister. The Court pronounced its decision on 31 May 1949, declaring that the poems which had been committed for trial did not contain one single obscene term, that they did not go beyond what was allowed to an artist, and that if the first judges had considered them indecent and immoral, it was only because they had not seen beyond the realistic external details to their profound symbolical beauty. Their verdict had been ratified neither by public nor literary opinion. The Court considered that the accusation of moral offensiveness had not been proved against the book, and that it was thus the duty and obligation of the Court to clear the memory of Charles Baudelaire, of Poulet Malassis and of de Broise of the injurious sentence. So, on 31 May 1949, the verdict and sentence of 20 August 1857 pronounced by the *Tribunal Correctionnel de la Seine*, were quashed and rendered null and void, and the poet was vindicated.

The material for this account has been obtained from the inaugural address by Léon Depaule, *Substitut du Procureur Général*, that is to say, Deputy Public Prosecutor, at the *Audience Solennelle de Rentrée de la Cour d'Appel* at Nîmes on 2 October 1951. He chose as the subject of his address at the opening session of the Court of Appeal, the final annulment of the verdict and sentence against the *Pièces Condamnées* from *Les Fleurs du Mal*, and the vindication of their author.

Appendix Three

THE ARCHITECTURE OF
LES FLEURS DU MAL

BAUDELAIRE always claimed that there was a coherent plan, an architecture, in *Les Fleurs du Mal*, even in its first version, that the book should not be judged as a mere collection of isolated poems, but as a unit. When preparing his *Notes et Documents pour mon Avocat* (*Les Fleurs du Mal*, Conard edition, p. 326) he wrote: 'Le livre doit être jugé dans son ensemble, et alors il en ressort une terrible moralité.' Barbey d'Aurevilly, reviewing the first version in *Le Pays* on 24 July 1857, said: 'Les artistes qui voient les lignes sous le luxe et l'efflorescence de la couleur percevront très bien qu'il y a ici une *architecture secrète*, un plan calculé par le poète, méditatif et volontaire. *Les Fleurs du Mal* ne sont pas à la suite les unes des autres comme tant de morceaux lyriques dispersés par l'inspiration et ramassés dans un recueil sans d'autre raison que de les réunir. Elles sont moins des poésies qu'une œuvre poétique de la plus forte unité. Au point de vue de l'art et de la sensation esthétique, elles perdraient donc beaucoup à n'être pas lues dans l'ordre où le poète, qui sait ce qu'il fait, les a rangées. Mais elles perdraient bien davantage au point de vue de l'effet moral.'

Of the second version of 1861, in which the unity is more pronounced, Baudelaire wrote to Vigny on sending him the book, 'Le seul éloge que je sollicite pour ce livre est qu'on reconnaisse qu'il n'est pas un pur album et qu'il a un commencement et une fin. Tous les poèmes nouveaux ont été faits pour être adaptés à un cadre singulier que j'avais choisi.'

The plan does not naturally follow the chronological order

of composition of the individual poems, but is based on the poet's view of man's life and destiny, at the moment when he was preparing his book for publication.

He himself declared that the central idea of the collection was a Christian one, and, writing to his mother on 1 April 1861, to protest against the action of her confessor in burning a copy he had sent him, he said: 'Et il n'a même pas compris que le livre partait d'une idée catholique.'

The plan is based on belief in the dual nature of man, in the contrast between his aspiration towards virtue and his inclination towards vice. This is indicated by the division of a large section of the book under the title *Spleen et Idéal*, the struggle between God and Satan. He says in *Mon Cœur mis à nu* (*Œuvres Complètes*, p. 1203): 'Il y a dans tout homme, à toute heure, deux postulations simultanées, l'une vers Dieu, l'autre vers Satan. L'invocation à Dieu, ou spiritualité, est un désir de monter en grade : celle de Satan ou animalité, est joie de descendre.'

His book expresses the struggle between both inclinations, the struggle against sin. He expresses horror at the power of Satan and the wiles he uses to ensnare man, his loathing of sin and vice. He saw man as inevitably sunk in vice. 'Mais je ne veux, pour le présent, tenir compte que de la grande vérité oubliée – la perversité primordiale de l'homme'; and further : 'Nous sommes tous nés marqués par le mal'. (Preface to *Nouvelles Histoires Extraordinaires*, p. ix, Conard edition.)

This is far from the Rousseau belief, favoured by the Romantics, that man was born good and that society corrupted him; or the later theory, followed by the positivists, that vice and virtue do not exist as moral factors, but are only two dissimilar products, such as vitriol and sugar. (Taine : *Introduction* to *L'Histoire de la Littérature Anglaise*.)

The title which Baudelaire had first contemplated for his collection, before he discovered that it had already been adopted by someone else, *Limbes*, is important and signi-

ficant. *Les Fleurs du Mal* was adopted only on the advice of
a friend and for want of a better one, but it suits only one
part of the book.

Les Limbes, Limbo, is the place, between Heaven and
Hell, inhabited by the souls of those who have not yet been
saved, and the collection of poems depicts their human
destiny.

The plan in the first edition of *Les Fleurs du Mal* seems
to be much more simple and less well co-ordinated than in
the second. The poems may have been inspired by personal
experience and thus subjective, but the plan is a philosophical one, based on the poet's intellectual idea at the
moment of publication.

The first edition opens with the bitter preface, addressed
to the reader, 'Hypocrite lecteur', and establishes the power
of Satan, the will of Satan, directed towards the destruction
of man, and describes the wiles he uses to achieve this end.

The book itself sets down these wiles and man's efforts to
circumvent them.

One of the major temptations which Satan offers man is
that of beauty, artistic beauty, and the first poems deal with
the artist, his tasks, his tribulations and his ambitions. They
are such poems as *Bénédiction*, *Élévation*, *Correspondances*,
Les Phares. From this the poet proceeds to self-examination
and a study of his own problem. This is reflected in such
poems as *La Muse Malade*, *La Muse Vénale*, *Le Guignon*,
Le Châtiment de l'Orgueil, and so forth.

Man is left with a longing for beauty – *La Beauté*, *l'Idéal*
and *La Géante* – and we are shown the various ways in which
he pursues it, the most important being through love. First
through sensual love, and we have the cycle of the Black
Venus, *Les Bijoux*, *Parfum Exotique*, *De Profundis Clamavi*,
Sed non Satiata, and others, through the bitterness of *Le
Vampire* and *Le Léthé*, to the destruction of *Une Charogne*,
but reaching the gentler haven of *Le Balcon* and ending
with 'Je te donne ces vers', which explains that although
others may judge her bitterly, she has remained enshrined

in his verse. Next follows spiritual love, beginning with
Tout entière, through *Harmonie du Soir*, which says that
her memory shines in him 'comme un ostensoir', and ending with *Le Flacon*, which describes how, after he has been
cast away, like a broken flask, there will still linger in him, as
a rare perfume, the memory of her whom he had idolized.
After this comes passionate love, and the desire to turn this
into companionate love, *Le Poison*, *L'Invitation au Voyage*,
but he is tortured by the conviction of the irreparableness
of the past, and the suspicion that life has destroyed his
heart:

> *Ta main se glisse en vain sur mon sein qui se pâme;*
> *Ce qu'elle cherche, amie, est un lieu saccagé*
> *Par la griffe et la dent féroce de la femme.*
> *Ne cherchez plus mon cœur; les bêtes l'ont mangé.*

Serious love ends in the self-torture of *L'Héautontimorouménos*, and the consolation of the lesser loves, *Franciscae
meae Laudes*, *À une Dame Créole* and *Moesta et Errabunda*.

Love, however, only ends in disillusionment; then follow
the series of *spleen* poems – *La Cloche Fêlée*, the various
evocations entitled *Spleen*, *Brumes et Pluies*, and ending in
L'Irrémédiable, of the certainty of being permanently sunk
in evil, as a ship frozen in an iceberg, and 'La conscience
dans le Mal'.

Then comes what one might call a nostalgic and escapist
division, with poems such as *Je n'ai pas oublié, voisine de la
Ville*, or *La Servante au grand Cœur*, with corresponding
hatred of the present.

After this we come to the section entitled *Fleurs du Mal*,
flowers symbolizing vices, such poems as *La Destruction*,
Femmes Damnées, *La Béatrice*, *Le Vampire*, and so forth.
This leads to blasphemy and revolt – *Les Litanies de Satan*
and *Le Reniement de Saint-Pierre*, followed by a section
praising escape in wine, which is not well placed in this
version of the poems, and finally the section dealing with

inevitable death. In death there will be the consolation of disappointed hopes, the final fulfilment of those who had never 'connu leur idole' here below, in a land where everything will be explained, and all that they tried to accomplish will be made good. This is *La Mort des Artistes*, the end of the first version of *Les Fleurs du Mal*.

The architecture of the second edition follows roughly the same plan as the first, but it has been enriched and made deeper with some additions. It opens with the same Preface addressed to the 'hypocrite Lecteur'. Then the section dealing with the destiny of the poet has *L'Albatros* added, showing that the artist, by reason of his wings, made for soaring to the ideal, is prevented from walking here below. There is also a new poem celebrating beauty, *Hymne à la Beauté*. Beauty, being composed of the sum total of life, must incorporate evil as well as good.

The cycle of the Black Venus, of the sensual love poems, now opens with a new poem, *La Chevelure*, for *Les Bijoux*, of the first edition, was banned. It has the addition of some poems in the bitter vein, *Duellum* and *Le Possédé*, but it possesses, as well, *Un Fantôme*, indicating what is finally left after the destruction of sensual love. The cycle of the spiritual poems opens with the somewhat disillusioned *Semper Eadem*, expressing realization that this love is only a 'mensonge' but accepting the deception, for the sake of the illusion. The third love cycle has the addition of the sad *Chant d'Automne* and ends now with the terrible and bitter *À une Madone*.

The *Spleen* section has been much enlarged with the addition of the poems written after the publication and failure of the first *Fleurs du Mal*, with such poems as *Obsession* and *Goût du Néant*, while *L'Héautontimorouménos* has been moved, more appropriately, into this section, and a new poem *L'Horloge* ends it, showing the swift flight of time, and the clock cries to him: 'Meurs, vieux lâche, il est trop tard!'

The nostalgic and escapist section has now become *Tableaux Parisiens*, and it has been much enlarged and enriched, with poems expressing compassion for failures, for those who have lost. Such poems as *Les Petites Vieilles, Les Aveugles, Les Sept Vieillards*. It also contains the magnificent nostalgic poem of *Le Cygne*, with its longing to return to the paradise lost. 'Tout poète lyrique', says Baudelaire in the article on Banville (*Œuvres Complètes*, p. 1105) 'en vertu de sa nature, opère fatalement un retour vers l'Éden perdu.'

This section is followed, more correctly I think than in the first edition, by the section celebrating the escape in wine, after which comes the section dealing with sin and vice, but with the absence of the banned poems – *Lesbos, Les Femmes Damnées* and *Les Métamorphoses du Vampire*. Then comes *Revolt*, which remains the same, and finally *Death* which now contains six poems instead of three, one of which is *Le Voyage*, which makes a nobler ending to the work than the *Mort des Artistes* of the first version.

We know that Baudelaire was preparing a third version of his book, when he was struck down by his final illness, and that he had many new poems to include in it composed since the publication of the second edition, and printed in *Le Parnasse Contemporain* in 1886 under the title *Nouvelles Fleurs du Mal* – poems such as *Le Couvercle, Le Gouffre, Plaintes d'un Icare* – which would have fitted in with the *Spleen* poems. There is also the poem *L'Imprévu*, expressing hope in God's mercy, which one would like to imagine would have come after *L'Horloge*, and have taken from the final pessimism of that section as expressed in that poem in the second edition. The poem of resignation, *Recueillement*, would probably have found its place in the nostalgic section of *Tableaux Parisiens*. I feel that *Le Voyage* would still have been the culmination, the coping-stone, of the third version of *Les Fleurs du Mal*, though Chérix believes that *L'Imprévu* would have occupied that position. (*Commentaire des Fleurs du Mal*.)

However, the editors of the third and posthumous edition of *Les Fleurs du Mal* have placed all the poems composed since the publication of the second edition, as well as any other poems of Baudelaire's pen which they could find, after his death, higgledy-piggledy, without any thought of plan, mostly in the section entitled *Spleen et Idéal*, putting the trifle *Lola de Valence* and *La Lune Offensée* amongst the *Tableaux Parisiens*, and *Épigraphe pour un Livre Condamnée* in the section dealing with evil and vice.

The third edition, although it contains all Baudelaire's poetry, is the least satisfactory of the version of *Les Fleurs du Mal*, for the architecture of the work has disappeared.

Bibliography

1

BAUDELAIRE'S WORKS

The fullest, and most complete, critical edition of Baudelaire's works is the one edited by Jacques Crépet and published by Conard. This is now complete, since the last volume, prepared by its editor, appeared posthumously in 1953. The first volume, *Les Fleurs du Mal*, appeared in 1922 and the edition thus took thirty years to complete. In the course of publication Crépet regretted having chosen for inclusion the posthumous edition of the poems, which Baudelaire had not revised, and later, in 1942, he published separately, with José Corti, and in collaboration with Georges Blin, a further critical edition of *Les Fleurs du Mal* based on the 1861 version, which is preferable to the first volume of the Conard edition. The Conard edition includes the whole of Baudelaire's correspondence, but it does not contain the *Vers Latins* of the poet, which were published by the *Mercure de France* in 1933, edited by Jules Mouquet.

The best edition of Baudelaire's works for the ordinary reader is the one edited by Yves le Dantec for the *Éditions de la Pléiade*, in which the complete works of the poet are now printed in one volume, with a further volume for the translations from Poe. It does not include the correspondence. This edition, entitled *Œuvres Complètes*, is the one referred to throughout this study, except where otherwise stated. The letters are quoted from the *Correspondance Générale* (Conard) in six volumes.

There are other works the authorship of which is doubtful: *Vers Retrouvés*, published by Émile-Paul in 1929, a large portion of which are attributed, on not very sound evidence, by their editor, Jules Mouquet, to Baudelaire. *Œuvres en Collaboration*, published by the *Mercure de France* in 1932, part of which was undoubtedly written by Baudelaire. *Mystères Galans des Théâtres de Paris*, published by Gallimard in 1938, and attributed by its editor, Jacques Crépet, in large part to Baudelaire.

II

WORKS DEALING WITH BAUDELAIRE

There is a very large bibliography of works dealing with Baudelaire, a large number of which are not of great interest. This list does not aim at being exhaustive, but only at giving the most important works, or those which have some special interest. The most complete and up-to-date bibliography of the works on the poet is that by Henri Peyre in *Connaissance de Baudelaire*, Paris 1951, which contains 337 names.

Aressy (L.), *Les Dernières Années de Baudelaire*, Paris 1947.

Asselineau (Ch.), *Baudelaire, sa Vie et son Œuvre*, Paris 1869.

Austin (Ll. J.), *L'Univers Poétique de Baudelaire*, Paris 1956.

Bandy (W. T.), *Baudelaire judged by his Contemporaries*, New York 1933.

Bandy (W. T.) and Mouquet (J.), *Baudelaire en 1848*, Paris 1946.

Banville (Th. de), *Mes Souvenirs*, Paris 1882.

Barthou (L.), *Autour de Baudelaire*, Paris 1917.

Bertaut (J.), and Séché (A.), *Baudelaire*.

Billy (A.), *La Présidente et ses Amis*, Paris 1945.

Blin (G.), *Baudelaire*, Paris 1939.
   Le Sadisme de Baudelaire, Paris 1948.

Cabanès (Dr), *Grands Névropathes*, Paris 1930.

Cassagne (A.), *La Versification de Baudelaire*, Paris 1906.

Champfleury (J.), *Souvenirs et Portraits de Jeunesse*, Paris 1872.

Charavay (E.), *Charles Baudelaire et Alfred de Vigny Candidats à l'Académie*, Paris 1879.

Charpentier (J.), *Baudelaire*, Paris 1937.
   L'Évolution de la Poésie Lyrique de Joseph Delorme à Paul Claudel, Paris 1931.

Cherix (R.), *Commentaire des Fleurs du Mal*, Paris 1949.

Clapton (G. T.), *Baudelaire et de Quincey*, Paris 1931.
   Baudelaire the Tragic Sophist, London 1934.

Coleno (A.), *Les Portes d'Ivoire*, Paris 1948.

Cousin (Ch.), *Baudelaire, Souvenirs et Correspondance*, Paris 1872.
   Voyage dans un Grenier, Paris 1878.

Crépet (J. and E.), *Baudelaire*, Paris 1907.

Crépet (J.) and Pichois (Cl.), *Baudelaire et Asselineau*, Paris 1953.

Du Bos (Ch.), *Approximations*, Paris, 1ère Série 1922 and 5ième Série 1932.

Du Camp (M.), *Souvenirs Littéraires*, Paris 1882.

Dufay (P.), *Autour de Baudelaire*, Paris 1931.

Ferran (A.), *L'Esthétique de Baudelaire*, Paris 1933.

Feuillerat (A.), *Baudelaire et la Belle aux Cheveux d'Or*, New Haven, U.S.A. 1941.
   Baudelaire et sa Mère, Paris 1944.
Flottes (P.), *Baudelaire*, Paris 1922.
Fondane (B.), *Baudelaire et l'Expérience du Gouffre*, Paris 1947.
Fumet (St.), *Notre Baudelaire*, Paris 1926.
Gautier (F.), *Baudelaire*, Brussels 1904.
Gautier (J.), *Le Collier des Jours*.
   Le Second Rang du Collier.
Gautier (Th.), *Portraits Contemporains*, Paris 1874.
   Portraits et Souvenirs Littéraires, Paris without date.
Gide (A.), *Prétextes*, Paris 1919.
Gilman (M.), *Baudelaire the Critic*, New York 1943.
Gourmont (R. de), *Promenades Littéraires*, Paris 1904.
Guex (A.), *Art Baudelairien*, Lausanne 1934.
Jouve (P. J.), *Tombeau de Baudelaire*, Neûchatel 1942.
Kahn (G.), *Baudelaire*, 1925.
   Silhouettes Littéraires, Paris 1925.
Kunel (M.), *Baudelaire en Belgique*, revised edition, Liège 1944.
Laforgue (R.), *L'Échec de Baudelaire*, Paris 1931.
Lemonnier (L.), *Les Traducteurs de Poe en France*, Paris 1928.
   Enquètes sur Baudelaire, Paris 1929.
Mansell-Jones (P.), *The Background of Modern French Poetry*, Cambridge 1951.
   Baudelaire, Cambridge 1952.
Massin (J.), *Baudelaire entre Dieu et Satan*, Paris 1945.
Mauclair (C.), *Baudelaire, sa Vie et son Œuvre*, Paris 1927.
   Le Génie de Baudelaire, Poète, Penseur, Esthéticien, Paris 1933.
Messaien (P.), *Sentiment Chrétien et Poésie Française*, Paris 1947.
Michaud (G.), *Message Poétique du Symbolisme*, 1947.
Nadar (G.), *Baudelaire Intime*, Paris 1911.
Peyre (H.), *Connaissance de Baudelaire*, Paris 1951.
   Les Générations Littéraires, Paris 1948.
Pichois (Cl.), *Le Vrai Visage du Général Aupick*, Paris 1956.
Pommier (J.), *La Mystique de Baudelaire*, Paris 1932.
   Dans les Chemins de Baudelaire, Paris 1945.
Porché (F.), *La Vie Douloureuse de Baudelaire*, Paris 1926.
   Baudelaire et la Présidente, Geneva 1941.
   Baudelaire, Histoire d'une Âme, Paris 1944.
Prarond (E.), *De Quelques Écrivains Nouveaux*, Paris 1852.
Prévost (J.), *Baudelaire*, Paris 1953.
Quennell (P.), *Baudelaire and the Symbolists*, revised edition, London 1955.
Raynaud (E.), *Baudelaire et la Religion du Dandysme*, Paris 1918.
   Baudelaire, Paris 1922.

Reynold (G. de), *Baudelaire*, Paris 1920.

Rhodes (S. A.), *The Cult of Beauty in Baudelaire*, New York 1929.

Rivière (J.), *Études*, Paris 1911.

Ruff (M.), *Baudelaire, l'Homme et l'Œuvre*, Paris 1955.
  L'Esprit du Mal et l'Esthétique Baudelairienne, Paris 1955.

Sartre (J. P.), *Baudelaire, Introduction* to *Écrits Intimes*, Paris 1946.

Séché (A.), *La Vie des Fleurs du Mal*, Paris 1928.

Seillère (E.), *Baudelaire*, Paris 1931.

Shanks (P.), *Baudelaire*, London 1920.

Soupault (P.), *Baudelaire*, Paris 1931.

Starkie (E.), *Petrus Borel, the Lycanthrope*, London 1954.

Suarez (A.), *Trois Grands Vivants*, Paris 1938.

Symons (A.), *Baudelaire*, London 1920.

Tabarant (A.), *La Vie Artistique au Temps de Baudelaire*, Paris 1942.

Thibaudet (A.), *Intérieurs*, Paris 1924.

Thomas (L.), *Curiosités sur Baudelaire*, Paris 1912.

Trial (Dr) *La Maladie de Baudelaire*, Thèse de Médecine, Paris 1926.

Turnell (M.), *Baudelaire*, London 1953.

Turquet-Milnes (G.), *The Influence of Baudelaire in France and England*, London 1913.

Valéry (P.), *Situation de Baudelaire*, Paris 1926.

Vandérem (F.), *Baudelaire et Sainte-Beuve*, Paris 1917.

Varlet (Th.), *Au Paradis du Haschisch*, Paris 1930.

Vivier (R.), *L'Originalité de Baudelaire*, revised edition, Brussels 1952.

Wyzewa (Th. de), *Nos Maîtres*, Paris 1895.

III

DOCUMENTS PUBLISHED IN REVIEWS, OF INTEREST FOR THE BIOGRAPHY OF BAUDELAIRE

Letters of Madame Aupick, published in the *Mercure de France*, 16 September 1912.

Letters of Madame Aupick, published in the *Mercure de France*, 1 September 1917.

Letters of Madame Aupick, published in the *Nouvelle Revue Française*, November 1932.

Letters from Asselineau to Poulet Malassis published in the *Bulletin du Bibliophile*, 1925.

Documents sur Baudelaire, published in the *Mercure de France* 1905, Vol. liii.

Nouveaux Documents sur Baudelaire, published in the *Mercure de France* 1906, Vol. lx.

Correspondence between General Aupick and Alphonse Baudelaire, published in the *Mercure de France*, 15 March 1937.

Documents dealing with the appointment of Baudelaire's *conseil judiciaire*, published in the *Mercure de France*, 15 March 1937.

Letters from Alphonse Baudelaire to General Aupick, published in the *Bulletin du Bibliographe*, Aug.–Sept. 1937.

IV

ARTICLES FROM REVIEWS, OF INTEREST FOR THE STUDY OF BAUDELAIRE

Bandy (W. T.), *La Vérité sur le Jeune Enchanteur*, *Mercure de France*, 1 February 1950.
　New Light on Baudelaire and Poe, *Yale French Studies*, 1953, No. 10.

Banville (Th. de), *Souvenirs*, published in *La Revue Littéraire et Artistique*, Vol. i, 1872.

Barrès (M.), *Méditations Spirituelles sur Baudelaire*, *L'Aube*, June 1896.

Cabanès (Dr), *Le Sadisme de Baudelaire*, *La Chronique Médicale*, 15 December 1902.

Cabanès (Dr), *La Maladie et la Mort de Baudelaire*, *La Chronique Médicale*, 1 December 1907.

Gautier (Th.), *Le Club des Haschichins*, *Revue des Deux Mondes*, 1 February 1846.

Gide (A.), *Baudelaire*, *Nouvelle Revue Française*, 1 November 1910.

Gilman (M.) and Schenk (E.), *On L'Albatros* of Baudelaire, *Romantic Review*, October 1938.

Glatigny, *La Maladie de Baudelaire*, *Intermédiaire des Chercheurs et des Curieux*, 1913, Vol. lxvii.

d'Hévassi (Ch.), *Le Voyage de Baudelaire aux Indes*, *Mercure de France*, October 1956.

Hignard (H.), *Baudelaire, Sa Vie, ses Œuvres*, *Revue du Lyonnais*, June 1892.

Kahn (G.), *Baudelaire*, *Mercure de France*, 1 April 1921.
　Baudelaire et son Influence, *Le Monde Nouveau*, May 1921.

Laforgue (J.), *Notes sur Baudelaire, Entretiens Politiques et Littéraires*, 1892.

Leakey (F.), *Baudelaire et Kendall*, *Revue de Littérature Comparée*, January–March 1956.

Lemonnier (L.), *Baudelaire au Lycée Louis le Grand*, *La Grande Revue*, September 1921.

Proust (M.), *À Propos de Baudelaire*, Nouvelle Revue Française, 1
    June 1921.
Séché (A.), *La Présidente*, Mercure de France, 1920, Vol. lxviii.
Suarès (A.), *Essai sur Baudelaire*, La Grande Revue, December 1911.
Thibaudet (A.), *Baudelaire*, Revue de Paris, 15 April 1921.

Notes

PART ONE

Chapter 1 – The Early Years 1821–1839

1. *L'Esprit du Mal et l'Esthétique Baudelairienne*, pp. 143–5.
2. Mouquet: *Baudelaire, Vers Latins*, p. 15, note 1.
3. Letter to Asselineau, printed in Appendix of *Baudelaire* by Crépet.
4. Not 1803 as has been hitherto stated. Vide Ruff *op. cit.*, p. 419, note 21.
5. *Op. cit.*, p. 418, note 22.
6. *Les Fleurs du Mal*, *Œuvres Complètes*, p. 169.
7. *Mon Cœur mis à nu* (*Journaux Intimes*), *Œuvres Complètes*, p. 1219.
8. *Les Fleurs du Mal*, xcix, *Œuvres Complètes*, p. 169.
9. Vide *La Morale du Joujou*, *Œuvres Complètes*, p. 673.
10. Letter quoted in Appendix of *Baudelaire* by Crépet.
11. *Le Vrai Visage du Général Aupick*.
12. *Mon Cœur mis à nu* (*Journaux Intimes*), *Œuvres Complètes*, p. 1201.
13. Letter to his mother, 1839.
14. Hignard in *Revue du Lyonnais*, June 1892, and in his own letter to his half-brother's young wife, 22 November 1833.
15. *Mon Cœur mis à nu* (*Journaux Intimes*), *Œuvres Complètes*, p. 1205.
16. Hignard, *op. cit.*
17. Ditto.
18. The young brother of his sister-in-law. She was a pretty young woman with whom Baudelaire, as a young man, was a little in love.
19. Letter, 22 November 1833. It is deliberately given in French, to give an example of the poet's prose style, at this early age.
20. *Crépuscule du Matin*, *Œuvres Complètes*, p. 173.
21. *Vers Latins*, p. 138.
22. Madame Aupick, letter to Asselineau, published in *Baudelaire* by Crépet, p. 258.
23. *Mon Cœur mis à nu* (*Journaux Intimes*), *Œuvres Complètes*, p. 1202.
24. Hignard, *op. cit.*
25. *Œuvres Complètes*, p. 1223.
26. *À Anthony Bruno*, *Œuvres Posthumes* (Conard), Vol. I, pp. 11–12.

27. *À Sainte-Beuve*, *Œuvres Complètes*, p. 70.
28. Ditto.
29. Léon Lemonnier, *Baudelaire au Lycée Louis-le-Grand*, *La Grande Revue*, September 1921.
30. *Journal des Débats*, 15 October 1864.
31. *Œuvres Complètes*, p. 41.
32. Mouquet, *Vers Latins*, p. 90. Letter from Prévot-Deseilligny to General Aupick, 18 April 1839.
33. Léon Lemonnier, *op. cit.*
34. Letter to his mother, 16 July 1839.
35. *Lettres de l'École Normale*, published in *Vers Latins* by Baudelaire, p. 24.
36. Letter to his stepfather, 16 July 1839.
37. Letter, undated, to Gautier from Asselineau, in Spoelberch de Lovenjoul collection at Chantilly.

Chapter 2 – The Latin Quarter 1839–1842

1. Letter to Asselineau, 1868, quoted in *Baudelaire* by Crépet, p. 254.
2. *Œuvres Posthumes*.
3. *Op. cit.*, p. 424, note 34.
4. *Op cit.*, p. 165.
5. *Vide* Starkie, *Petrus Borel, the Lycanthrope*, pp. 139–42.
6. *Vide* Poem XXIV, *Œuvres Complètes*, p. 56.
7. *Vers 1843*, published in *Juvenilia, etc.* (Conard) Vol. 1, p. 380.
8. *Œuvres Complètes*, p. 49.
9. Letter published by Féli Gautier in *Mercure de France*, January 1905.
10. Letter published in *Mercure de France*, 15 March 1937.
11. Paul Pérignon was a member of the *conseil de famille*, and Labie was a notary at Neuilly.
12. In France, in extreme cases like this, the family can, by appealing to the law, get a *conseil judiciaire* appointed to administer the money and prevent it from being squandered. The term *conseil judiciaire* applies to the man appointed to administer the inheritance.
13. Letter, 4 May 1841, published in *Le Figaro*, 5 March 1922.
14. Obituary by X. in *La Chronique de Paris*, 15 September 1867.
15. Letter published in *Mercure de France*, January 1905.
16. Poem quoted from the letter itself, to give it in the original version.
17. Letter, 20 October 1841.
18. Asselineau letter to Gautier, undated, but, after the death of Baudelaire, it was put in the Spoelberch de Lovenjoul Collection at Chantilly.
19. Letter to Gautier, above, in Spoelberch de Lovenjoul Collection at Chantilly.

20. *Op. cit.*, p. 171, and Appendix VIII.
21. Letter to mother, 25 October 1842.
22. Letter from Alphonse Baudelaire to General Aupick, January 1842, published in the *Bulletin du Bibliophile et du Bibliothécaire*, August–September 1939. Ruff claims that this letter should really be dated July 1842.
23. Letter quoted above.
24. *Mercure de France*, October 1956.

Chapter 3 – The Dandy 1842–1844

1. This is the date usually accepted, and given by his mother.
2. Hervé, *How to enjoy Paris*, 1842.
3. Letter to his mother, undated, p. 30, Vol. I, *Correspondance Générale*.
4. Letter to his mother, June 1843.
5. Roger de Beauvoir, article in *Le Quotidien*, 2 December 1845.
6. Delacroix, *Journal*, 1846.
7. *Préface* to 1868 edition of *Les Fleurs du Mal*.
8. Those wishing to know more about him could consult Starkie, *Petrus Borel*.
9. *Renaissance Littéraire et Artistique*, Vol. I, 1872, p. 3.
10. Asselineau, *Charles Baudelaire*, p. 41.
11. *Op. cit.*
12. It now hangs in the museum at Versailles.
13. Hignard, *op. cit.*
14. Nadar, *Baudelaire Intime*, p. 37.
15. Thomas, *Curiosités sur Baudelaire*, p. 31.
16. Letters from Boissard to Gautier, unpublished, Spoelberch de Lovenjoul Collection at Chantilly.
17. *La Presse*, July 1843, and *Revue des Deux Mondes*, 1 February 1846.
18. Banville, *Souvenirs*.
19. Asselineau, *op. cit.*
20. Letter to Ancelle, 18 October 1864.
21. Banville, *Souvenirs*.
22. Ditto.
23. The attribution of Privat d'Anglemont's poems to Baudelaire will be discussed in a later chapter, *The Fruits of the Tree*.
24. Article by Ange Bénigne – Madame de Molènes – in *Le Gaulois*, 27 September 1886.
25. Thomas, *op. cit.*, p. 29.
26. Ph. Audebrand, *Les Derniers Jours de la Bohème*, p. 145.
27. *Le Gaulois*, 27 September 1886.
28. F. Berthelot, *Louis Ménard et son Œuvre*.
29. Pierre Quinone, *Le Figaro*, 15 August 1880.
30. *Vide* Starkie, *Petrus Borel, the Lycanthrope*, pp. 89–96.

Chapter 4 – The Black Venus 1842–1844

1. Letter to his mother, undated, Autumn 1843.
2. Schanne, *Souvenirs de Schaunard*, p. 155.
3. Séché, *La Vie des Fleurs du Mal*, p. 45.
4. *À une Malabaraise, Œuvres Complètes*, p. 230.
5. Letter to his mother, 11 September 1856.
6. Nadar, *op cit.*
7. *Mon Cœur mis à nu (Journaux Intimes), Œuvres Complètes*, p. 1211.
8. *Les Fenêtres, Spleen de Paris, Œuvres Complètes*, p. 332.
9. It is now in the museum at Budapest.
10. *Le Serpent qui danse, Œuvres Complètes*, p. 102.
11. *Les Bijoux, Œuvres Complètes*, p. 215.
12. Banville, *Souvenirs.*
13. *Fusées, Œuvres Complètes*, p. 1190.
14. Nadar, *op. cit.*
15. *Mon Cœur mis à nu (Journaux Intimes), Œuvres Complètes*, p. 1199.
16. Ditto, p. 1216.
17. Ditto, p. 1213.
18. Letter printed in Appendix of *Baudelaire* by Crépet.
19. Hignard, *op. cit.*
20. *Œuvres Complètes*, p. 57.
21. Nadar, *op. cit.*
22. *Vide* Starkie, letter in *The Times Literary Supplement*, 11 October 1941.
23. *Œuvres Complètes*, p. 101.
24. *Fusées (Journaux Intimes), Œuvres Complètes*, p. 1182.
25. *La Fanfarlo, Œuvres Complètes*, p. 394.
26. *Fusées (Journaux Intimes), Œuvres Complètes*, p. 1183.
27. *Fleurs du Mal, Œuvres Complètes*, p. 106.
28. *Fleurs du Mal, Œuvres Complètes*, p. 100.
29. *Œuvres Complètes*, p. 217.
30. *Une Nuit que j'étais auprès d'une Affreuse Juive, Œuvres Complètes*, p. 106.
31. *La Fanfarlo, Œuvres Complètes*, p. 395.
32. *Le Vampire, Œuvres Complètes*, p. 105.
33. *Vide* letter 23 December 1848.
34. *Le Cheval de Race, Œuvres Complètes*, p. 335.

Chapter 5 – The Fruits of the Tree 1842–1844

1. *Mon Cœur mis à nu (Journaux Intimes), Œuvres Complètes*, p. 1216.

2. *Note Autobiographique, Œuvres Complètes*, p. 1230.

3. *Vers Retrouvés*, p. 145.

4. *Chronologie des Fleurs du Mal*, published in *L'Ermitage*, December 1906.

5. Hignard, *op. cit.*

6. *Baudelaire*, p. 311, by Crépet.

7. *The Romantic Review*, article by M. Gilman and E. Schenk, October 1938.

8. Hignard, *op. cit.*

9. Letter, 13 February 1843.

10. *La Rime (Poésies Fugitives)* by Levavasseur, quoted in *Vers Retrouvés*, p. 199.

11. *Baudelaire*, p. 39, by Crépet.

12. *Vers Retrouvés*, p. 199.

13. The arguments are fully discussed in view of the fact that these poems, attributed to Baudelaire, now appear in certain editions of his works.

14. *Vers Retrouvés*, p. 28.

15. *La Fanfarlo, Œuvres Complètes*, p. 390.

16. *Vers Retrouvés*, p. 57.

17. *La Fanfarlo, Œuvres Complètes*, p. 390.

18. *Vide* Starkie, *op. cit.*, pp. 89–96.

19. In his Introduction to Privat d'Anglemont's *Paris Inconnu*.

20. Also *À une Jeune Saltimbanque*, published in *La Silhouette* in September 1849. *Vide* note 23 in Chapter 4.

21. XIV, *Œuvres Complètes*, p. 50.

22. Spoelberch de Lovenjoul, *Les Lundis d'un Chercheur*, p. 288.

23. *Le Gaulois*, 5 October 1892.

24. *Vers Retrouvés*, p. 12.

25. Ditto, p. 13.

26. Ditto, p. 17.

27. On account of what he calls Prarond's 'mistake' over *Les Yeux de Berthe* Caussy refuses to accept his testimony that this poem is prior to 1843, since it was first published in 1861. There is, however, no valid reason to doubt its being an early composition.

28. *La Lune Offensée, Œuvres Complètes*, p. 251.

29. Letter, 23 December 1848.

30. *Vide* Starkie, *op. cit.*, p. 49 *et seq.*

31. Jules Bois, *Le Satanisme et la Magie*, p. 233.

32. *Les Hallucinations* (1845), p. 325.

33. *Les Litanies de Satan, Œuvres Complètes*, p. 190. 1845 is just outside the period under review, but it is impossible to place all the works in watertight compartments, for there is bound to be overlapping and the same vein continued, sometimes, at the beginning of the next period. 1845 is, moreover, near enough

not to alter the view we hold as to the stages of Baudelaire's development. It occurs moreover before he reaches the age of twenty-five.

34. Petrus Borel, *Champavert* (*Éditions de la Force Française*), p. 70.
35. *Vers Retrouvés*, p. 17.
36. *Rêve d'un Curieux, Œuvres Complètes*, p. 196.
37. *Le Rebelle, Œuvres Complètes*, p. 241.
38. Letter to Asselineau in *Baudelaire* by Crépet, p. 268.
39. *Revue de Paris*, October 1852.
40. *Œuvres Complètes*, p. 1396, note on the poem.
41. *Le Reniement de Saint-Pierre, Œuvres Complètes*, pp. 188–9.
42. *Champavert* was published in 1833, and the poems of Vigny and Nerval in 1844.
43. *Le Crépuscule du Matin, Œuvres Complètes*, p. 173.
44. *Les Deux Bonnes Sœurs, Œuvres Complètes*, p. 182.
45. *Une Charogne, Œuvres Complètes*, pp. 104–5.
46. By Mouquet in *Vers Retrouvés*, p. 33 *et seq.*, by Pommier in *La Revue d'Histoire Littéraire de la France*, April–June 1933, and in *Revue des Cours et des Conférences*, 30 April 1930, by Crépet in *Œuvres Posthumes*, Vol. I (Conard), pp. 443–9.
47. Prarond's Note, written in 1887 and published in *Œuvres Posthumes*, 1887.
48. *Un Café de Journalistes sous le Second Empire.*
49. Letter to mother, 16 November 1843.
50. Letter to mother, without date. *Correspondance Générale*, Vol. I, p. 34.
51. *Correspondance Générale*, Vol. I, p. 34 note.
52. *Les Mystères Galans des Théâtres de Paris* (N.R.F.) 1938, *Introduction.*
53. *Les Mystères Galans des Théâtres de Paris*, p. 8.
54. Ditto, pp. viii–ix.
55. Letter, 4 March 1844.
56. *Les Mystères Galans des Théâtres de Paris*, pp. 121–2.
57. Ditto, pp. 123–5.
58. Ditto, *Introduction.*
59. *Œuvres Posthumes*, Vol. I (Conard), pp. 48 and 55.
60. Letter.

Chapter 6 – The Day of Reckoning 1844

1. *Vide* letters to his mother in 1843 and 1844.
2. Letter to Nadar, 18 December 1844, also letter to *La Société des Gens de Lettres, Correspondance Générale*, Vol. I, p. 86. (No date given.)
3. Letter, 3 March 1844.
4. Letter, without date, pp. 68–9, *Correspondance Générale*, Vol. I.

5. *Mercure de France*, 15 March 1937.
6. *Vide* Chapter 2, note 12.
7. Letter, without date, *Correspondance Générale*, Vol. I, p. 42.
8. Ditto, p. 41.
9. Letter, 10 June 1850.
10. 20 November 1867 (*Bulletin du Bibliophile*, 1925).
11. Letter to his mother.
12. Ditto, 26 February 1866.
13. Asselineau to Poulet Malassis (*Bulletin du Bibliophile*, 1925).
14. Letter from Madame Aupick to Asselineau (*Mercure de France*, 16 September 1912).
15. Letter to Ancelle, 2 September 1864.
16. *Correspondance Générale*, Vol. III, p. 285 note.
17. Letter to his mother, 6 June 1862.

PART TWO

Chapter 1 – The Apprentice to Literature 1845–1847

1. *Vide* Starkie, *op. cit.*
2. *Spleen*, *Œuvres Complètes*, p. 144. N.B. – The period now under review runs from 1845 to 1851, and it is impossible to ascribe a definite date to each individual poem composed during the time. Some of the *Spleen* poems were published in reviews in 1851. They seem to express the mood of the beginning of the period, rather than the end.
3. It was at this time that Baudelaire joined his mother's maiden name to his own.
4. Letter, without date, *Correspondance Générale*, Vol. I, pp. 47–8.
5. *Mon Cœur mis à nu* (*Journaux Intimes*), *Œuvres Complètes*, p. 1219.
6. *Op. cit.*
7. *Œuvres Complètes*, p. 588.
8. Ditto, p. 88.
9. She used many different aliases – Lemer, Duval, etc. – to escape from her creditors.
10. Letter, 30 June 1845.
11. Letter, without date, *Correspondance Générale*, Vol. I, p. 75.
12. Ditto, p. 76.
13. *Vide Le Manuscrit Autographe* 1930.
14. This appeared here, without signature, and was discovered by W. T. Bandy, who published it in *Bulletin du Bibliophile*, February 1930. Baudelaire republished the article in *L'Écho des Théâtres*, 23 August 1846, signing it, so that this is generally considered its first appearance.
15. Cousin, *Voyage dans un Grenier*, p. 17.

16. Ditto, p. 16.
17. W. T. Bandy, *Vérité sur le Jeune Enchanteur, Mercure de France,* February 1950.
18. Published in facsimile by Mouquet in *Œuvres en Collaboration.*
19. pp. 1–2.
20. *Œuvres Complètes,* p. 1259.
21. *Correspondance Générale,* Vol. VI.
22. Baudelaire uses the legal phraseology as his brother was a lawyer.
23. Although announced, this was never published, and perhaps never written.
24. The hero of the romantic play of that name by Alexandre Dumas.
25. Parny was a late eighteenth-century poet much discredited during the Romantic Movement.
26. *Œuvres Complètes,* p. 934.
27. Proved by the records at the École des Chartes.
28. Letter, without date, *Correspondance Générale,* Vol. I, pp. 80–1.
29. Pommier, *Dans les Chemins de Baudelaire,* p. 290. Also Gilman, *Baudelaire the Critic,* pp. 46–52. This is the best book dealing with Baudelaire's critical writings.
30. *Salon de 1846, Œuvres Complètes,* pp. 604–5.
31. Ditto, pp. 671–2.
32. *Vide Curiosités Esthétiques* (Conard), p. 474.
33. *Œuvres en Collaboration,* p. 122.
34. *Œuvres Posthumes* (Conard), Vol. I, pp. 494–528.
35. Published in *Le Bulletin des Gens de Lettres.*
36. *La Cloche Fêlée, Œuvres Complètes,* p. 142.
37. Letter, 4 December 1847.
38. Letter, without date, *Correspondance Générale,* Vol. I, p. 79.
39. *Mercure de France,* 1905.
40. Letter, 4 December 1847.
41. Letter, 5 December 1847.
42. Letter to his mother, 16 December 1847.

Chapter 2 – The Revolutionary 1847–1848

1. Maillard, *Les Derniers Jours de la Bohème,* p. 85.
2. *Souvenirs et Portraits de Jeunesse,* p. 121.
3. Schanne, *Souvenirs de Schaunard,* p. 201.
4. Maynial, *Le Réalisme,* p. 29.
5. Quoted by Boisson in *Les Compagnons de la Vie de Bohème,* p. 106.
6. Letter to Champfleury, May 1845.
7. Dornier in *Revue de France,* March 1925.
8. *Portraits de Jeunesse,* p. 135.
9. *L'Artiste,* January 1868, *Le Monde Parisien.*
10. Letter to Sainte-Beuve, 2 January 1866.
11. *Œuvres Complètes,* p. 956.

12. *Crépuscule du Soir, Œuvres Complètes*, p. 164.
13. *La Mort des Pauvres, Œuvres Complètes*, p. 193.
14. *Baudelaire*, p. 10.
15. 16 February 1860.
16. Delvau, *Les Cafés de Paris*, p. 188.
17. *Souvenirs*, p. 289.
18. *Vide* letter from Madame Aupick to Asselineau, 11 June 1871, published in the *Mercure de France*, September 1912.
19. Dufay, *Autour de Baudelaire*, p. 21.
20. Ditto, *op. cit.*, p. 21.
21. *Note Autobiographique, Œuvres Complètes*, p. 1230.
22. Letter, 23 December 1848, generally said to have been written to General Aupick, but Ruff has suggested, *op. cit.*, p. 437, No. 67, that it is, on the contrary, written to his mother. This is indeed very likely for, by this time, he would not have written thus to his stepfather, and, during this time of estrangement from his mother, he might have written in such a distant manner.
23. Toubin, *Souvenirs d'un Septuagénaire*, published by Ch. Dornier in *La Revue de France*, March 1925 and October 1926.
24. Ditto.
25. Ditto.
26. *Œuvres Posthumes* (Conard), Vol. I, p. 350.
27. The two issues have been republished in *Œuvres Posthumes* (Conard), Vol. I.
28. Dornier, *op. cit.*
29. The best account for this period is contained in *Baudelaire en 1848* by Bandy and Mouquet, who have republished all the articles of the time.
30. *Op. cit.* The issues of the paper are published here.
31. Crépet, *Baudelaire*, p. 82.
32. Pichois, *Le Vrai Visage du Général Aupick*, p. 18.
33. Letter, 5 March 1852.
34. Letter to Ancelle, Idem.

Chapter 3 – The Slough of Despond 1848–1852

1. René Johannot in *Les Lettres*, January 1927, also in *Baudelaire, Histoire d'une Âme* by Porché, and in *Baudelaire en 1848* by Bandy and Mouquet. The source is, however, the same.
2. *Baudelaire* by Asselineau.
3. Letter to Ancelle, December 1849.
4. Letter to Ancelle, 10 January 1850.
5. This article appeared on 27 July 1850, after Baudelaire had left Dijon, but he might have submitted it before he left, for he was, at this time, sending many articles to various papers.
6. Letter to Ancelle, 10 January 1850.

7. *Op. cit.*
8. Letter to his mother, 8 December 1848.
9. Letter, 10 January 1850.
10. Letter to his mother, 6 May 1861.
11. He sent the poem to Gautier in 1852.
12. *Voyage à Cythère, Œuvres Complètes*, p. 185.
13. Letter to Gérard de Nerval, where he gives his address as La Rue Pigalle.
14. Simon Brugal, article in *Le Figaro*, January 1887.
15. *Les Lettres*, January 1927.
16. *Baudelaire en 1848.*
17. Given in Appendix I.
18. Simon Brugal, *op. cit.*
19. Letter to his mother, December 1850.
20. Maxime Du Camp, *Souvenirs*, Vol. II, p. 78.
21. Letters to Asselineau, 24 March 1868, published in Appendix of *Baudelaire* by Crépet.
22. *Souvenirs*, Vol. II, p. 87.
23. *Vide* Part II, Chapter II.
24. Published in *Baudelaire* by Crépet, pp. 281–302.
25. *Notes d'Asselineau sur Baudelaire*, published in *Baudelaire et Asselineau*, pp. 174–5.
26. *Œuvres Complètes*, p. 422.
27. *La Mort des Amants, Œuvres Complètes*, p. 193.
28. *Le Figaro*, 7 February 1925, article by Paul Fuchs.
29. *Œuvres Complètes*, p. 1092.

Chapter 4 – The Revelation of Poe 1852–1854

1. Letter to Poulet Malassis, 20 March 1852.
2. Letter to Ancelle, 5 March 1852, letter to his mother, 27 March 1852, and letter to Watripon, 10 May 1852.
3. *Notes sur Baudelaire*, p 175.
4. Unpublished letter to Jules Mouquet, 17 August 1949.
5. Letter, 27 March 1852.
6. *Vie de Baudelaire*, pp. 41–2.
7. Ditto, p. 42.
8. Ditto, p. 50.
9. Champfleury, quoted by Crépet in his *Baudelaire*, p. 453, letter from Wallon to Baudelaire.
10. Letter to Du Camp, 16 September 1852.
11. *Yale French Studies*, 1953, No. 10.
12. Some of the poems alleged to have been influenced by Poe, are early poems before he knew his work: *Une Charogne, Le Vin de l'Assassin, Les Litanies de Satan, Je t'adore à l'égal de la voûte nocturne*, etc.

13. Letter to Théophile Thoré, 20 January 1864.
14. Letter to Armand Fraisse, 18 February 1860. This letter, until recently in fragmentary form, has hitherto been incorrectly dated December 1858. It is in its correct place in the *Correspondance Générale*.
15. Letter to Poulet Malassis, 20 March 1852.
16. Letter to Armand Baschet, 3 February 1852.
17. *Œuvres Complètes*, p. 975.
18. *Vide* letter to Poulet Malassis, 20 March 1852.
19. Letter to Ancelle, 10 January 1850.
20. Letter to his mother, 30 August 1851.
21. *Quelques Poètes Nouveaux, Introduction.*
22. *Salon de 1846.*
23. Du Camp, *Souvenirs Littéraires.*
24. Published by Crès.
25. Undated letter, 1852.
26. *Souvenirs Littéraires*, Vol. II, p. 83.
27. Letter to Poulet Malassis, 20 March 1854.
28. Ditto, 15 December 1859.
29. Letter to *Ministre de l'État*, 11 July 1857.
30. Letter to Sainte-Beuve, 26 March 1856.

Chapter 5 – Towards a New Aesthetic 1852–1854

1. *Mon Cœur mis à nu (Journaux Intimes), Œuvres Complètes*, p. 1215.
2. Letter, 20 March 1852.
3. The best work dealing with the influence of Swedenborg in France at this time is that by P. Mansell-Jones: *The Background of Modern French Poetry*, in the chapter treating this subject.
4. Article on Gautier, *Œuvres Complètes*, p. 1029.
5. *La Mystique de Baudelaire*, p. 3.
6. *L'Ennemi, Œuvres Complètes*, p. 89.
7. *Notes Nouvelles sur Poe*, Introduction to *Nouvelles Histoires Extraordinaires* (Conard), p. xxi.
8. *L'Art Romantique, Œuvres Complètes*, p. 1078.
9. These theories are discussed in a later Chapter.
10. Article on Pierre Dupont, *Œuvres Complètes*, p. 952.
11. *Les Phares, Œuvres Complètes*, p. 86.
12. Ditto.
13. *Bénédiction, Œuvres Complètes*, p. 81.
14. *Les Phares, Œuvres Complètes*, p. 86.
15. *Traité du Narcisse.*
16. Quoted by Miss Dillingham in *The Creative Imagination of Théophile Gautier* (Princeton Psychological Review Co.).
17. As reported in the *Sunday Express*, 23 November 1952.

18. Quoted by Miss Dillingham, *op. cit.*
19. *Correspondances, Œuvres Complètes*, p. 85.
20. *Harmonie du Soir, Œuvres Complètes*, p. 119.
21. *Les Cahiers de Sainte-Beuve*, p. 36.

Chapter 6 – Solitude 1852

 1. Letter to his mother, 27 March 1852. It is from this letter that the
    material for this chapter has been largely obtained.
 2. Letter, 27 March 1852.
 3. Ditto.
 4. *La Géante, Œuvres Complètes*, p. 95.
 5. Letter to Madame Marie.
 6. This is, naturally, a personal interpretation.
 7. *Baudelaire Intime*, p. 130.
 8. *À une Passante, Œuvres Complètes*, p. 162.
 9. *Baudelaire et la Belle aux Cheveux d'Or.*
10. Ditto, p. 13.
11. Ditto, p. 87.
12. Crépet, *Baudelaire*, p. 313 note.
13. *Baudelaire et la Belle aux Cheveux d'Or*, p. 88.
14. Crépet, *op. cit.*, p. 313 note.
15. *Correspondance Générale*, Vol. I, p. 99.
16. Letter to his mother, 16 December 1853.
17. Letter to his mother, 26 March 1853.
18. Ditto.
19. Letter to Véron, 19 October 1852. Also letter to his mother, March
    1853.
20. Letter to his mother, 26 March 1853.

Chapter 7 – The White Venus 1852–1854

 1. André Billy, *La Présidente et ses Amis*, Chapters III and IV.
 2. Ditto, p. 47.
 3. *La Presse*, 3 June 1850.
 4. Gautier, *Œuvres Érotiques* (Paris Arcanes 1953).
 5. Judith Gautier, *Le Collier des Jours.*
 6. Letter, 28 July 1854.
 7. Letter, 8 May 1854.
 8. Letter, 18 August 1857.
 9. *Baudelaire et la Belle aux Cheveux d'Or*, p. 28.
10. Letter to Madame Sabatier, 8 May 1854.
11. *Réversibilité, Œuvres Complètes*, p. 116.
12. Letter, 7 February 1853.
13. Letter, 8 May 1854.
14. Undated letter, *Correspondance Générale*, Vol. I, p. 262.
15. *L'Aube Spirituelle, Œuvres Complètes*, p. 118.

16. Letter, 16 February 1854.
17. *Le Flambeau Vivant, Œuvres Complètes*, p. 115.
18. Letter, 18 August 1857.
19. Letter to Poulet Malassis, 30 August 1861.
20. *Hymne, Œuvres Complètes*, p. 220.
21. Letter, August 1857.

Chapter 8 – The Green-Eyed Venus 1854–1856

1. *Baudelaire et la Belle aux Cheveux d'Or.*
2. Ditto, pp. 82–3.
3. 19 August 1847, quoted by Feuillerat, *op. cit.*, p. 83.
4. Feuillerat, *op. cit.*, pp. 88–9.
5. Letter to his mother, 22 August 1854.
6. Letter to Paul de Saint Victor, 14 October 1854.
7. Feuillerat, *op. cit.*, p. 42.
8. *Œuvres Complètes*, p. 123.
9. From the collection entitled *Les Améthystes.*
10. *Œuvres Complètes*, p. 121.
11. Ditto, pp. 120–21.
12. Ditto, p. 128.
13. Ditto, p. 125.
14. Letter to his mother, 4 October 1855.
15. *Œuvres Complètes*, pp. 126–7.
16. Letter to his mother, 5 April 1855.
17. Letters to his mother, 19 March and 5 April 1856.
18. Letter, 20 December 1855.
19. *Correspondance Générale*, Vol. I, p. 357, note 1.
20. Feuillerat, *op. cit.*, p. 95 note 78, and p. 66.
21. Baudelaire's letter to Ancelle, 24 December 1855.
22. Letter to his mother, 4 December 1854.
23. Letter to Ancelle, 24 December 1855.
24. *Œuvres Complètes*, p. 1194.
25. Ditto.
26. *Le Balcon, Œuvres Complètes*, p. 108.

Chapter 9 – Notoriety 1855–1857

1. Advertisement in *La Presse*, 21 March 1854.
2. *Op. cit.*, pp. 20–21.
3. These poems included: *Au Lecteur, Confession, L'Amour et le Crâne, Un Voyage à Cythère, L'Aube Spirituelle, La Vie Antérieure, La Cloche Fêlée, Spleen, L'Irréparable* and nine other poems.
4. Article by Goudall quoted in Notes to *Les Fleurs du Mal* (Conard), p. 305.
5. Letter to his mother, 4 October 1855.

6. Letter, 19 March 1856.
7. Letter, 24 March 1856.
8. Letter, 26 March 1856.
9. Letter to his mother, 11 September 1856.
10. Barbey d'Aurevilly's article published in *Le Pays*, 10 June 1856.
11. Letter, 11 September 1856.
12. Letter to his mother, 4 November 1856.
13. Letter to his mother, 8 February 1857.
14. *Vide* letter to Poulet Malassis, 4 December 1856.
15. Letter, 9 February 1857.
16. Letter, 9 March 1857.
17. Letter undated. In the *Correspondance Générale* it is placed amongst the letters of 1855, yet in tone and mood, it would seem to have been written after the death of his stepfather. He would hardly have told her, during his life, that his heart was with her in her little house at Honfleur, which she shared with her husband, if he was alive and there. Also he mentions being alone, and it was in the early part of 1857 that he was separated from his mistress, Jeanne Duval.

Chapter 10 – Essays in Criticism 1852–1859

1. The best and fullest book on Baudelaire as a critic is the one by M. Gilman.
2. Letter, 1 April 1861.
3. Letter from Delacroix, quoted in notes of *Curiosités Esthétiques* (Conard), p. 493.
4. *Mon Cœur mis à nu (Journaux Intimes)*, *Œuvres Complètes*, p. 1219.
5. *Note Autobiographique*, *Œuvres Complètes*, p. 1230.
6. *L'École Païenne*, *Œuvres Complètes*, pp. 969–73.
7. Letter, 4 October 1855.
8. Letter, 19 March 1856.
9. *Salon de 1859*, *Œuvres Complètes*, p. 764.
10. Letter published in *Le Manuscrit Autographe*, 1927.
11. Letter to Desnoyers, 1855.
12. Letter, 4 November 1856.
13. Notes to *Les Fleurs du Mal* (Conard), p. 307.
14. Letter to his mother, 27 December 1856.
15. *Notes Nouvelles sur Poe*, *Nouvelles Histoires Extraordinaires* (Conard), pp. xx–xxi.
16. Ditto, p. xix.
17. Ditto, p. xx.
18. Letter to Swinburne, 10 October 1863.
19. *Notes Nouvelles sur Poe*, *Nouvelles Histoires Extraordinaires* (Conard), p. xx.

20. *Exposition de 1855, Œuvres Complètes*, p. 683.
21. *Fusées (Journaux Intimes), Œuvres Complètes*, p. 1187.
22. *Hymne à la Beauté, Œuvres Complètes*, p. 97.
23. *Le Confiteor de l'Artiste, Spleen de Paris, Œuvres Complètes*, p. 276.
24. *Richard Wagner et Tannhaüser à Paris, Œuvres Complètes*, p. 1043.
25. *Exposition Universelle, Œuvres Complètes*, p. 699.
26. *Les Phares, Œuvres Complètes*, p. 86.
27. *Salon de 1859, Œuvres Complètes*, p. 771.
28. Ditto, pp. 764–8.
29. *Tout Entière, Œuvres Complètes*, p. 114.
30. *Les Fleurs du Mal* (Conard), p. 376.
31. *Salon de 1859, Œuvres Complètes*, p. 757.
32. Letter, 11 February 1865.
33. Letter to Armand Fraisse, 19 February 1860.
34. Letter to Catulle Mendès, 29 March 1866.
35. Letter to Prarond, 29 March 1866.
36. *Notes Nouvelles sur Poe, Nouvelles Histoires Extraordinaires* (Conard), p. xviii.
37. Letter to Toussenel, 1856.
38. Letter to Sainte-Beuve, January 1866.

Chapter 11 – The Trial for Obscenity 1857

1. Announced in *L'Écho des Marchands de Vin*, in November 1848.
2. *La Mystique de Baudelaire*, p. 56.
3. Ditto.
4. *Vide* Notes to *Les Fleurs du Mal* (Conard), p. 302.
5. *Vide* Ditto, p. 371.
6. Dufay, *op. cit.*, p. 30.
7. Letter from Baudelaire to Poulet Malassis, 9 December 1856.
8. *Baudelairiana*, published in *Baudelaire* by Crépet.
9. Quoted by Dufay, *op. cit.*, p. 54.
10. Crépet, *op. cit.*, p. 103 notes.
11. *Vide* Notes to *Les Fleurs du Mal* (Conard), p. 313.
12. Jouasne, *Baudelaire et Poulet Malassis*, p. 28.
13. Letter, 14 May 1857.
14. Letter, 4 April 1857.
15. Letter, 15 March 1857.
16. Letter, 6 June 1857.
17. Letter to Poulet Malassis, 16 February 1857.
18. Letter to Ditto, 9 March 1857.
19. *Correspondance Générale*, Vol. II, pp. 59–61.
20. *Vide* Notes to *Les Fleurs du Mal* (Conard), p. 216.
21. *Baudelairiana*, in *Baudelaire* by Crépet.
22. Letter to his mother, 9 July 1857.

23. Letter, 11 July 1857.
24. *Vide* Notes to *Les Fleurs du Mal* (Conard), p. 317.
25. Letter to his mother, 27 July 1857.
26. *Correspondance Générale*, Vol. II, p. 80, note 3.
27. Letter, 20 February 1860.
28. *Baudelairiana*, in *Baudelaire* by Crépet.
29. Thierry's article is published in *Les Fleurs du Mal* (Calmann-Lévy) in Appendix.
30. Letter to his mother, 27 July 1857.
31. *Vide* Notes to *Les Fleurs du Mal* (Conard), p. 319.
32. Letter, 27 July 1857.
33. Letter, 20 July 1857.
34. Notes to *Les Fleurs du Mal* (Conard), p. 324.
35. Published in Crépet, *op. cit.*
36. Letter to Chaix-d'Est-Ange, July 1857.
37. *Notes et Documents pour mon Avocat*, published in *Baudelaire* by Crépet, Appendix I.
38. Idem.
39. Letter to his mother, 27 February 1858.
40. The speeches by the Public Prosecutor and by Baudelaire's lawyer are printed *in extenso* in *Les Fleurs du Mal* (Conard), p. 330 *et seq.*
41. *Le Vin de l'Assassin*, *Œuvres Complètes*, p. 176.
42. *Vide* Appendix II for the account of the annulment of the verdict of 1857.
43. Asselineau, *Baudelaire*, p. 63.
44. *Mon Cœur mis à nu (Journaux Intimes)*, *Œuvres Complètes*, p. 1203.
45. *La Mort des Artistes*, *Œuvres Complètes*, p. 194.
46. The architecture of the three versions of *Les Fleurs du Mal* is discussed in Appendix III.
47. *Crépuscule du Soir* and *Solitude* had already appeared in 1855 in the volume entitled *Fontainebleau*.
48. Crépet, *op. cit.*, p. 112 note.
49. Ditto, p. 113.
50. Unpublished letter from S. Jourdan to Gautier, 22 March 1868, thanking him for his article on Baudelaire published in *L'Univers Illustré*, and mentioning a glimpse he once had of the poet. Spoelberch de Lovenjoul collection at Chantilly.

Chapter 12 – The End of a Dream 1857

1. Letter to Madame Sabatier, 18 August 1857.
2. Letter from Madame Sabatier to Baudelaire, published in Crépet, *op. cit.*, p. 120.
3. Letter to Madame Sabatier, 31 August 1857.

4. Letter to Madame Sabatier, 18 August 1857. It is a pity that the person who owns the letters of Madame Sabatier has not published them, for the interpretation of this letter would be made easier if we could read the two letters of Madame Sabatier to which it is an answer. All the remarks concerning this letter are inspired by a purely personal interpretation of the material available.
5. The banker Mosselmann, who was keeping her.
6. The *Poste Restante* office was in the Rue Jean-Jacques Rousseau.
7. Letter published by Crépet, *op. cit.*, p. 124.
8. Letter quoted by Crépet, *op. cit.*, p. 125.
9. Letter, 2 May 1858.
10. Letter quoted by Crépet, *op. cit.*, p. 126.
11. *Semper Eadem, Œuvres Complètes*, p. 113.

PART THREE

Chapter 1 – The Widow's Son 1857–1859

1. Letter, 9 October 1857.
2. Letter, 6 October 1857.
3. Letter to Poulet Malassis, 30 December 1857.
4. Published in *Nouveaux Documents sur Baudelaire*, in *Mercure de France*, January 1905.
5. Letter to Alphonse Baudelaire, published in *Le Manuscrit Autographe*, 1927.
6. Article by Pichois in *Le Figaro Littéraire*, 12 April 1952.
7. Ditto.
8. Letter to his mother, 25 December 1857.
9. Ditto.
10. Letter to his mother, 1 April 1861.
11. Letter to his mother, 3 June 1857.
12. Letter to his mother, 31 December 1863.
13. Letter to his mother, 30 December 1857.
14. Letter to his mother, 3 June 1857.
15. Letter to his mother, 20 February 1858.
16. Letter to Madame Alphonse Baudelaire, published in *Le Manuscrit Autographe*.
17. Letter to his mother, 30 December 1857.
18. Ditto.
19. Letter to his mother, 25 December 1857.
20. Letter to his mother, 30 December 1857.
21. Letter, 19 February 1858.
22. Letter published in *Le Manuscrit Autographe*.
23. Letter to Ancelle, published in *Mercure de France*, January 1905.
24. Letter to his mother, 19 February 1858.

B.–30

25. The translation of *The Adventures of Gordon Pym*.
26. Letter, 20 February 1858.
27. Letter to his mother, 7 March 1858.
28. Letter from Jacquotot to Madame Aupick, *Correspondance Générale*, Vol. II, p. 141 note.
29. Letter, 26 February 1858.
30. Letter to his mother, 27 February 1858.
31. Letter to his mother, 29 March 1858.
32. Letter, 27 February 1857.
33. Letter from Jacquotot to Madame Aupick, 3 March 1858, *Correspondance Générale*, Vol. II, p. 166 note.
34. Letter to his mother, 13 May 1858.
35. *Le Constitutionnel*, 19 March 1883.
36. *Revue Philosophique et Religieuse*, September 1857.
37. Letter to *Le Figaro*, 10 June 1858.
38. Letter, 14 June 1858.
39. Loève-Weimars, the French translator of Hoffmann.
40. Letter to Poulet Malassis, 10 December 1858.
41. *Correspondance Générale*, Vol. II, p. 188, note 2.
42. Letter to his mother, 31 December 1858.
43. Madame Aupick, in a letter to Ancelle, published in *Baudelaire* by Crépet, p. 134.
44. Letter to Asselineau, 20 February 1859.
45. *Vide L'Étranger, Le Port, La Soupe aux. Nuages*, etc., in *Spleen de Paris*.
46. Letter to Poulet Malassis, 13 June 1859.
47. Crépet, *op. cit.*, p. 416.
48. *Chant d'Automne, Œuvres Complètes*, p. 128.
49. Feuillerat, *op. cit.*, p. 78.
50. *À une Madone, Œuvres Complètes*, p. 129.
51. Letter, 4 March 1860.
52. *L'Amour du Mensonge, Œuvres Complètes*, p. 168.

Chapter 2 – The Artificial Paradises 1860

1. Dufay, *op. cit.*, p. 57.
2. Ditto, p. 63.
3. Letter to Poulet Malassis, March 1859.
4. Letter to his mother, 11 December 1858.
5. Letter published in Notes to *Les Paradis Artificiels* (Conard), p. 297.
6. Letter to his mother, end February 1860.
7. Letter to Poulet Malassis, 16 February 1860.
8. Letter to Poulet Malassis, 4 February 1860.
9. Notes to *Les Paradis Artificiels* (Conard), pp. 325–6.

10. Porché, *Baudelaire, Histoire d'une Âme*, p. 255.
11. Letter to his mother, 10 May 1860.
12. Letters to Poulet Malassis, 22 and 27 April 1860.
13. Letter to Poulet Malassis, 18 May 1860.
14. Letter to Sainte-Beuve, 1860.
15. Letter, 18 August 1860.
16. Letter from Baudelaire to Poulet Malassis, 12 July 1860.
17. Alcide Dusolier, *Nos Gens de Lettres, Paradis Artificiels* (Conard), p. 316.
18. Gautier, *Preface* to 1868 edition of *Les Fleurs du Mal* (Michel Lévy).
19. Letter from Poulet Malassis to Spoelberch de Lovenjoul, 13 November 1864, published in *Le Goéland*, April–June 1952.
20. *Vers Retrouvés*, p. 15.
21. Gautier, *Preface* to *Les Fleurs du Mal*.
22. *Au Paradis du Haschisch*, p. 23.
23. *Indiscrétions Parisiennes*.
24. Letter to his mother, 4 December 1847, and to Ancelle, 10 January 1850.
25. Letter to his mother, 11 January 1858, to Madame Sabatier, 11 January 1858, to Poulet Malassis, 16 February 1859, and letter from Madame Sabatier to Baudelaire, quoted in Crépet, *op. cit.*, p. 126.
26. Letters to his mother, 22 December 1865 and 17 February 1866.
27. Letter published in Crépet, *op. cit.*, p. 193, note.
28. *Baudelaire et De Quincey*.
29. Article by Henriot in *Le Temps*, 27 February 1923.
30. Idem.
31. Letter to Vigny, 1861.
32. Letter, 16 February 1860.
33. *Les Paradis Artificiels* (Conard), p. 8.
34. Clapton, *op. cit.*, pp. 39–44.
35. *L'Homme Dieu, Les Paradis Artificiels, Œuvres Complètes*, pp. 454–65.
36. *Les Paradis Artificiels* (Conard), p. 7.
37. Ditto, p. 319.
38. *Op. cit.*, p. 169.
39. *Les Paradis Artificiels* (Conard), p. 46.
40. Ditto, p. 132.
41. Ditto, p. 133.
42. *Les Femmes Damnées, Œuvres Complètes*, p. 210.
43. *Les Paradis Artificiels* (Conard), p. 59.
44. Ditto, p. 64.
45. Ditto, p. 65.
46. Ditto, p. 69.

47. Letter from Flaubert to Baudelaire, *Les Paradis Artificiels* (Conard), p. 309.
48. Letter, 26 June 1860.
49. *Les Paradis Artificiels* (Conard), p. 196.

Chapter 3 – The Ghost of the Dead Years 1859–1861

1. Letter to his mother, 15 January 1860.
2. Letter to his mother, 14 April 1860.
3. Ditto.
4. Letter to his mother, 4 April 1860.
5. Letter, 26 March 1860.
6. Ditto.
7. Ditto.
8. Letter to his mother, 31 May 1862.
9. Witness the Manet portrait.
10. Referred to in his letter to his mother, 4 August 1860.
11. Letter to his mother, 7 August 1860.
12. Letter, 21 August 1860.
13. *Les Plaintes d'un Icare*, *Œuvres Complétes*, p. 242.
14. Letter, 8 October 1860.
15. Letter, 11 October 1860.
16. It is with Arondel that Baudelaire incurred the debt for the furniture which he bought while at the Hôtel Lauzun. After the death of her son, Madame Aupick managed to get the sum reduced by law.
17. Letter to Poulet Malassis, 18 October 1860.
18. Letter to Grandgouillet, 18 October 1860.
19. Letter to his mother, October 1859.
20. *La Chevelure*, *Œuvres Complètes*, p. 99.
21. *Le Cheval de Race*, quoted in Chapter 4, Part One.
22. Letter to Poulet Malassis, 29 April 1859.
23. Letter to Poulet Malassis, 4 May 1859.
24. Letter to Poulet Malassis, 8 May 1859.
25. Letter to Jeanne Duval, 17 December 1859.
26. Letter to Poulet Malassis, 16 January 1861, and to his mother, January 1861.
27. Letter to his mother, January 1861.
28. Ditto.
29. Letter to his mother, 5 January 1861.
30. Letter to his mother, April 1861.
31. Ditto, 17 March 1862.
32. Idem.
33. *Un Fantôme* II, *Œuvres Complètes*, p. 111.
34. Ditto, III, ditto p. 112.
35. Notes of a plan for a preface, *Fleurs du Mal* (Conard), pp. 372–7.

36. *Le Goût du Néant, Œuvres Complètes*, p. 146.
37. *Le Gouffre, Œuvres Complètes*, p. 242.
38. *Baudelaire Intime.*
39. *Intermédiaire des Chercheurs et des Curieux*, 30 September 1905.
40. *L'Horloge, Œuvres Complètes*, p. 150.
41. *Obsession, Œuvres Complètes*, p. 45.
42. *Le Cygne, Œuvres Complètes*, p. 155.
43. *Le Voyage, Œuvres Complètes*, p. 196.

Chapter 4 – De Profundis 1861

1. Letter to his mother, October 1859.
2. *La Chevelure, Œuvres Complètes*, p. 99.
3. Letter to Poulet Malassis, 29 April 1859.
4. Letter to Poulet Malassis, 4 May 1859.
5. Letter to Poulet Malassis, 8 May 1859.
6. *Mon Cœur mis à nu (Journaux Intimes), Œuvres Complètes*, p. 1225.
7. Ditto, p. 1226.
8. Ditto, p. 1228.
9. Ditto, ditto.
10. Ditto, ditto.
11. Ditto, p. 1227.
12. Ditto, p. 1220.
13. The *Édition de la Pléiade* still keeps them in *Mon Cœur mis à nu.*
14. *Journaux Intimes* edition edited by Crépet and Blin (José Corti).
15. *Mon Cœur mis à nu (Journaux Intimes), Œuvres Complètes*, p. 1225.
16. Letter, 6 May 1861.
17. Ditto.
18. Letter to his mother, 21 May 1861.
19. Letter to his mother, 27 May 1861.
20. Ditto, 30 May 1861.
21. *Recueillement, Œuvres Complètes*, p. 241.

Chapter 5 – The Candidate for the French Academy 1861–1862

1. Letters to Poulet Malassis, 8 January, 16 February, 9 March and April 1880.
2. Letter to Poulet Malassis, April 1860.
3. *Manuscrit Autographe.*
4. Letter, 1 February 1860.
5. *L'Art Romantique* (Conard), p. 207.
6. Letter quoted in *L'Art Romantique* (Conard), p. 509.
7. Letter to his mother, 1 April 1861.
8. *La Petite Revue*, 14 March 1866.

9. Letter of Wagner, quoted by Combarieu in *Histoire de la Musique*, Vol. III, p. 361.

10. Letter quoted in *L'Art Romantique* (Conard), p. 511.

11. *Le Voyage*, *Œuvres Complètes*, p. 196.

12. Quoted by Ph. Rebeyrol in *Baudelaire et Manet*, published in *Les Temps Modernes*, October 1949.

13. Letter to Thoré *circa* 20 June 1864.

14. Letters to Manet, 11 May 1865 and 28 October 1865.

15. Dufay, *op. cit.*, p. 72.

16. Letter to Poulet Malassis, 8 September 1860.

17. Letter, 27 September 1860.

18. Letter, December 1860.

19. Letter, 5 December 1860.

20. *Revue Anecdotique*, January 1861.

21. Letter 1862.

22. Letter to his mother, 22 August 1858.

23. René Laforgue, *L'Échec de Baudelaire*.

24. Letter, 14 July 1860.

25. Letter to his mother, 25 July 1861.

26. Letter to his mother, 25 December 1861. He is referring to his *conseil judiciaire*.

27. Letter to Vigny, 26 January 1862.

28. Ditto.

29. Letter to his mother, 25 December 1861.

30. Letter, end of 1861.

31. *Lettres à une Inconnue*, 29 June 1869.

32. Letter to his mother, 25 December 1861.

33. Ditto.

34. Letter, end of December 1861.

35. Letter quoted by Crépet, *op. cit.*, p. 441.

36. Letter, 23 February 1859.

37. *Nouveaux Lundis*, Vol. I, p. 400 *et seq.*

38. Letter of Sainte-Beuve, 9 February 1862, *Correspondance*, Tome I, p. 283.

39. Letter of Sainte-Beuve, 15 February 1862, *Correspondance*, Tome I, p. 285.

Chapter 6 – Implacable Life 1862–1864

1. *Mon Cœur mis à nu*, *Œuvres Complètes*, p. 1225.

2. Letter to his mother, 25 December 1861.

3. *Intermédiaire des Chercheurs et des Curieux*, 20–30 April 1930 (paragraph by Armands Lods).

4. Letter to his mother, 25 December 1861.

5. These records, No. F.17, 3115 (*Archives Nationales*), were dis-

covered by one of the librarians, Monsieur Monicat, through whose kindness I was enabled to consult them. Baudelaire's own letters have since been published, first by Ferran in *L'Archer* in December 1931, and later in the *Correspondance Générale*.

6. *Chef de Division* at the *Ministère de l'État. Vide L'Archer*, December 1931.
7. Letter, 19 January 1861.
8. Letter to Poulet Malassis, January 1862.
9. Dufay, *op. cit.*, p. 83.
10. Ditto, p. 85.
11. Letters to Poulet Malassis, 18 November and 18 December 1862.
12. Letter, December 1860.
13. Letter to his mother, 22 September 1862.
14. Letter published in *Petits Poèmes en Prose* (Conard), p. 235.
15. *La Vie Antérieure, Œuvres Complètes*, p. 91.
16. *Rêve Parisien, Œuvres Complètes*, p. 170.
17. *La Chambre Double* (*Spleen de Paris*), *Œuvres Complètes*, p. 277.
18. Letter to his mother, 11 August 1862.
19. Crépet, *op. cit.*, p. 154.
20. Ditto, p. 155, note 1.
21. *Un Café de Journalistes sous Napoléon III*, p. 295.
22. *À une Heure du Matin* (*Spleen de Paris*), *Œuvres Complètes*, p. 284.
23. Letter to his mother, 11 August 1862.
24. *L'Examen de Minuit, Œuvres Complètes*, p. 347.
25. *Enivrez-vous* (*Spleen de Paris*), *Œuvres Complètes*, p. 347.
26. *Anywhere out of the World* (*Spleen de Paris*), *Œuvres Complètes*, p. 347.
27. *L'Année Littéraire et Dramatique en 1867*.
28. *Les Plaintes d'un Icare, Œuvres Complètes*, p. 243.
29. *Mademoiselle Bistouri* (*Spleen de Paris*), *Œuvres Complètes*, p. 344.
30. Letter to Commandant Le Josne, 1 January 1863.
31. *Mon Cœur mis à nu, Œuvres Coumplètes*, p. 1212.
32. Letter to his mother, 11 August 1862.
33. *Mon Cœur mis à nu, Œuvres Complètes*, p. 1228.
34. Ditto, p. 1228.
35. Ditto, p. 1227.
36. Ditto, p. 1222.
37. Ditto, ditto.
38. Ditto, p. 1227.
39. *L'Imprévu, Œuvres Complètes*, p. 229.
40. *Mon Cœur mis à nu, Œuvres Complètes*, p. 1229.
41. Letter, 3 June 1863.
42. Maine de Biran, *Journal*, 6 June 1818.

43. Maine de Biran, *Journal*, 20 December 1823.
44. Preface to *Spleen de Paris*.
45. Letter to Arsène Houssaye, Christmas Day 1861.
46. Letter published in *Le Bulletin du Bibliophile*, 1 March 1926.
47. *Le Port (Spleen de Paris)*, *Œuvres Complètes*, p. 336.
48. In *L'Artiste*, October 1862.
49. Letter to Houssaye, Christmas Day 1861.
50. *Le Boulevard* 1862.
51. Letter to Sainte-Beuve, 4 May 1865.
52. Ditto.
53. Letter to his mother, 11 August 1862.
54. Letters to his mother, 25 November and 31 December 1863.
55. Documents in the *Archives Nationales*.
56. Letter, 3 August 1863.
57. Letter to Poulet Malassis, 8 August 1863.
58. Unpublished letter, existing only in a much scored-out rough draft in the documents at the *Archives Nationales*.
59. Letter, 26 August 1863.
60. Letter to his mother, 31 August 1863.
61. *Vide* notes in *Modern Languages Review*, July 1933.
62. Letter to Poulet Malassis, 15 September 1863.
63. Letter to his mother, 3 June 1863.
64. *Le Peintre de la Vie Moderne*, *Œuvres Complètes*, p. 912.
65. Letter to Taine, 19 January 1864, quoted in *Petits Poèmes en Prose* (Conard), p. 234.
66. Letter to his mother, 3 March 1864.
67. Ditto.

PART FOUR

Chapter 1 – The Lecture Tour 1864

1. *Vide* letter to Frédérix, 4 May 1864.
2. Letter to his mother, 6 May 1864.
3. Ditto.
4. Thomas, *Curiosités sur Baudelaire*, p. 53. Poulet Malassis also gives an account of this lecture in *La Petite Revue*, 21 January 1865; he signed his article with his mother's initials E.R.
5. In his letter to his mother, 11 June, Baudelaire says that he has been much fatigued since his lectures have always been twice the usual length.
6. Letter to Sainte-Beuve, January 1862.
7. Letter to Ancelle, 30 October 1864.
8. Letter to his mother, 11 June 1864, and letter to Ancelle, 27 May 1864.
9. Letter to his mother, 11 June 1864.

10. Letter to his mother, 17 June 1864.
11. The text of this letter is in *Œuvres Complètes*, p. 1162.
12. Simon, *Les Tables Tournantes à Jersey*, pp. 322–6.
13. Ditto, pp. 142–51.
14. Letter to his mother, 31 December 1863.
15. Letter to his mother, 11 June 1864.
16. Letter to his mother, 17 June 1864.
17. Letter to his mother, 31 July 1864.
18. Letter to his mother, 8 August 1864.
19. Letter to his mother, 11 June 1864, and letter to Ancelle, 18 December 1864.
20. Letter to his mother, 31 July 1864.
21. *Vide* letters of the editor to Baudelaire, Crépet, *op. cit.*, pp. 387–90.
22. Letter to his mother, 3 February 1865.
23. Letter, 18 December 1864.
24. Letter, 2 January 1865.
25. Letter to his mother, 1 January 1865.

Chapter 2 – *The Notary Turns Literary Agent 1864–1866*

1. Letter, 9 March 1865.
2. *Intermédiaire des Chercheurs et des Curieux*, Vol. XCIII, No. 1793 (paragraph by Armand Lods).
3. Letter to his mother, 9 March 1865.
4. Letter to his mother, 31 July 1864.
5. Letter to Lemer, 9 August 1865.
6. *Œuvres Complètes*, pp. 1279–98.
7. Letter to his mother, 11 February 1865.
8. Letter to his mother, 4 May 1865.
9. Letter to Ancelle, 18 February 1866.
10. Ditto, further letter, the same day.
11. Letter to his mother, 11 February 1865.
12. Letter, 23 February 1865.
13. Letter to Ancelle.
14. Letter to Ancelle, 18 February 1866, also letters to his mother, 17 and 21 February 1866.
15. Letter to Ancelle, 8 July 1865.
16. Ditto.
17. Letter to Lemer, 4 July 1865.
18. *Le Figaro*, 2 November 1902.
19. Letter to Lemer, 2 November 1865.
20. Letter to Ancelle, 8 July 1865.
21. *Vie de Baudelaire*, pp. 90–92.
22. Letter to his mother, 3 September 1865.
23. Letter to Sainte-Beuve, 4 September 1865.
24. Letters to his mother, 3 and 13 November 1865.

25. Letter to his mother, 13 November 1865.
26. Letter to Ancelle, 26 October 1865.
27. Letter to his mother, 13 November 1865.
28. Letter, 23 December 1865.
29. Letter to Ancelle, 26 December 1865.
30. Letter to his mother, 12 January 1866.
31. Remarks by Lécrivain, reported by Baudelaire to his mother, in letter of 21 February 1866.
32. Letter from Baudelaire to Troubat, 19 February 1866.
33. Letter, 18 January 1866.
34. Letter, 12 January 1866.
35. Letter to Ancelle, 18 February 1866.
36. Ditto, and letter of 22 January 1866.

Chapter 3 – *My Heart Laid Bare 1864–1866*

1. Letter to Ancelle, 8 February 1865.
2. Ditto.
3. Letter to Ancelle, 21 December 1865.
4. Letter to his mother, 4 May 1865.
5. Letter to his mother, 17 February 1866.
6. *Rops* by Lemonnier, quoted by Dufay in *Mercure de France*, 15 November 1928.
7. Dufay, *op. cit.*, p. 164.
8. *Vide* letter in Crépet, *op. cit.*, p. 380.
9. Letter 1865, quoted in Crépet, *op. cit.*, p. 408.
10. *Vide* letter to his mother, 8 March 1866.
11. Story told by Poulet Malassis in *La Petite Revue*, 27 October 1866.
12. Letter to Ancelle, 10 May 1864.
13. *Pauvre Belgique, Œuvres Complètes*, p. 1292.
14. Alphonse de Haulleville, in *Le Vingtième Siècle*, 31 July 1934, quoted by Léopold Levaux in *Les Masques de Baudelaire*, p. 51.
15. Porché, *Baudelaire, Histoire d'une Âme*, p. 419.
16. *Baudelaire Intime.*
17. *Souvenirs sur Baudelaire, Le Petit Bleu*, October 1907, quoted by Levaux, *op. cit.*, p. 48.
18. *Les Années de Bruxelles* (Édition de la Grenade).
19. Letter to Ancelle, 26 October 1865.
20. Letters, to Ancelle 8 February 1865, and to Asselineau 5 February 1866.
21. Letter to his mother, 17 February 1866.
22. Letter to his mother, 6 February 1866.
23. Letter to his mother, 12 February 1866.
24. Letter from Poulet Malassis to Troubat, quoted in Crépet, *op. cit.*, p. 190.

25. Letter, 10 February 1866.
26. *Mon Cœur mis à nu*, *Œuvres Complètes*, p. 1229.
27. Letter to Ancelle, 16 February 1866.
28. Letter to his mother, 21 February 1866, and also letter to Ancelle, the same day.
29. Letter to his mother, 26 February 1866.

Chapter 4 – The Wheel is Come Full Circle 1866–1867

1. Kunel, *Baudelaire en Belgique*, pp. 158–9.
2. *Crépuscule du Matin*, *Œuvres Complètes*, p. 173.
3. Letter to his mother, 26 March 1866.
4. Ditto.
5. Letter quoted in Crépet, *op. cit.*, p. 188, note 3.
6. Letter from Poulet Malassis to Troubat, quoted in ditto, p. 190.
7. *Mercure de France*, February 1905.
8. *Vide* letter from Madame Aupick to Ancelle, quoted in Crépet, *op. cit.*, p. 197.
9. *Nouvelle Revue Française*, 1932.
10. Spoelberch de Lovenjoul's remarks, quoted by Kunel in *Baudelaire en Belgique*, p. 102.
11. *La Petite Revue*, 7 April 1866, p. 200.
12. No. 5622 in the Bibliothèque Royale in Brussels, communicated to me by my pupil, W. H. Halls.
13. Letter from Poulet Malassis to Asselineau, 7 June 1866.
14. *Vide* letter, 5 February 1866.
15. *Les Années de Bruxelles* (Édition de la Grenade).
16. This petition is one of the documents, No. F.17, 3115, in the *Archives Nationales*.
17. The tone of this note is very different from Mérimée's real opinion of Baudelaire as expressed in the letter of 29 June 1869, quoted earlier.
18. Letter, 16 July 1866, published in Aressy, *Les Dernières Années de Baudelaire*, p. 197.
19. *Baudelaire Intime*.
20. Ditto, p. 139. This passage is worthy of being quoted in the original.
21. Letters from Madame Aupick to Asselineau, *Mercure de France*, September 1912.
22. *Vide* letter in Appendix of Crépet, *op. cit.*
23. Crépet, *op. cit.*, p. 272.
24. Du Camp, *Souvenirs*.
25. *Le Gaulois*, 27 September 1886, article by Ange Bénigne (Madame de Molènes.)
26. The material for describing these last days has been obtained

chiefly from Asselineau's letters to Poulet Malassis, to keep
him informed of Baudelaire's state of health, published in
Bulletin du Bibliophile, 1925.

27. Article in *La Presse*, 4 September 1867.
28. Article in *Durandol*, July 1894, quoted by Levaux, *op. cit.*, pp.
54–5.
29. Letter from Madame Aupick to Poulet Malassis, 18 September
1867, *Bulletin du Bibliophile*, 1925.
30. Unpublished letter, in the Nadar collection at the Bibliothèque
Nationale in Paris.
31. Letter from Asselineau to Poulet Malassis, 6 September 1867, published in Crépet, *op. cit.*, p. 273 *et seq.*
32. Verlaine, *Œuvres Posthumes*, Vol. II (Messein), p. 179.
33. Gautier's letter to his daughter Estelle, *Mercure de France*, 15 May
1929.
34. Eugénie Fort's unpublished diaries, 1857–1872 – she was Gautier's
mistress – communicated to me by my pupil, Joanna Richardson.
35. Billy, *La Présidente et ses Amis*, pp. 206–7.
36. From *L'Étendard*, 4 September 1867.
37. Asselineau's letter to Poulet Malassis, 6 September 1867, from
which this account of the funeral is chiefly derived.

CONCLUSION

1. Letters from Asselineau to Poulet Malassis, *Bulletin du Bibliophile*,
1925.
2. *Les Fleurs du Mal* (Conard), p. 397.
3. Unpublished letter in Spoelberch de Lovenjoul collection at
Chantilly.
4. Verlaine, *Sagesse* XVI.
5. *Romances sans Paroles*, III.
6. *Sagesse*, III, 6.
7. *Paysages Tristes*, V (*Poèmes Saturniens*).
8. *Fusées*, *Œuvres Complètes*, p. 1185.
9. Letter, 13 June 1865.
10. Letter, 6 March 1863.
11. Letter, 11 October 1860.
12. *À une Heure du Matin* (*Spleen de Paris*), *Œuvres Complètes*, p.
284.
13. *Un Voyage à Cythère*, *Œuvres Complètes*, p. 185.
14. Letter, 1 January 1865.
15. Letter, 19 February 1858.
16. *Mon Cœur mis à nu*, *Œuvres Complètes*, p. 1202.
17. *La Fanfarlo*, *Œuvres Complètes*, p. 375.
18. R. Laforgue, *L'Échec de Baudelaire*.

19. *L'Héautontimorouménos, Œuvres Complètes,* p. 148.

20. *Au Lecteur, Œuvres Complètes,* p. 80.

21. Crépet, *op. cit.,* p. 234.

22. Introduction to *L'Histoire de la Littérature Anglaise.*

23. *Notes Nouvelles sur Poe, Nouvelles Histoires Extraordinaires* (Conard), p. ix.

24. *Mon Cœur mis à nu, Œuvres Complètes,* p. 1203.

25. *Les Drames et les Romans Honnêtes, Œuvres Complètes,* p. 965.

26. Swinburne, *Ave atque Vale* (poem in memory of Baudelaire).

27. *Les Femmes Damnées, Œuvres Complètes,* p. 210.

28. Quoted by Rivière in *Études,* p. 24 note.

29. *Au Lecteur, Œuvres Complètes,* p. 79.

30. Letter to his mother, 11 August 1862.

31. *L'Irréparable, Œuvres Complètes,* p. 126.

32. *Les Phares, Œuvres Complètes,* p. 88.

33. R. Laforgue, *op. cit.*

34. *De Profundis Clamavi, Œuvres Complètes,* p. 105.

35. *Une Saison en Enfer, Œuvres Complètes (Édition de la Pléiade),* p. 212.

36. *Mon Cœur mis à nu, Œuvres Complètes,* p. 1207.

37. *Le Voyage, Œuvres Complètes,* p. 201.

38. *Pensées.*

39. Letter to Ancelle, 3 October 1864.

40. *Le Flacon, Œuvres Complètes,* p. 119.

41. *Variété,* II.

42. Letter, 18 February 1866.

43. *Le Poème du Haschisch, Œuvres Complètes,* p. 466.

44. Ditto, p. 469.

45. *Épilogue, Œuvres Complètes,* p. 354.

46. *Crépuscule du Soir, Œuvres Complètes,* p. 164.

47. *Mademoiselle Bistouri (Spleen de Paris), Œuvres Complètes,* p. 347.

48. *Assommons les Pauvres (Spleen de Paris), Œuvres Complètes,* p. 350.

49. *Les Petites Vieilles, Œuvres Complètes,* p. 159.

50. Letter to Vigny 1861, undated. *Correspondance Générale,* Vol. IV, p. 9.

51. *L'Albatros, Œuvres Complètes,* p. 83.

52. *Le Masque, Œuvres Complètes,* p. 97.

53. *Moesta et Errabunda, Œuvres Complètes,* p. 135.

54. *L'Horloge, Œuvres Complètes,* p. 150.

55. *Les Métamorphoses du Vampire, Œuvres Complètes,* p. 217.

56. *Le Reniement de Saint-Pierre, Œuvres Complètes,* p. 189.

57. *Les Deux Bonnes Sœurs, Œuvres Complètes,* p. 183.

58. *La Mort des Pauvres, Œuvres Complètes,* p. 193.

59. *Le Voyage, Œuvres Complètes,* pp. 196–201.

60. *Mon Cœur mis à nu, Œuvres Complètes,* p. 1201.

Indexes

INDEX OF NAMES

WORKS BY BAUDELAIRE QUOTED OR REFERRED TO IN THE TEXT

ORIGINAL WORKS